The Psychological Benefits of Exercise and Physical Activity

Jennifer L. Etnier, PhD
University of North Carolina Greensboro

Library of Congress Cataloging-in-Publication Data

Names: Etnier, Jennifer L., author.
Title: The psychological benefits of exercise and physical activity / Jennifer L. Etnier, PhD, University of North Carolina Greensboro.
Description: Champaign, IL : Human Kinetics, [2025] | Includes bibliographical references and index.
Identifiers: LCCN 2023003982 (print) | LCCN 2023003983 (ebook) | ISBN 9781718203624 (paperback) | ISBN 9781718203631 (epub) | ISBN 9781718203648 (pdf)
Subjects: LCSH: Exercise--Psychological aspects. | Physical fitness--Psychological aspects. | Mind and body.
Classification: LCC GV481.2 .E86 2025 (print) | LCC GV481.2 (ebook) | DDC 613.7/1019--dc23/eng/20230214
LC record available at https://lccn.loc.gov/2023003982
LC ebook record available at https://lccn.loc.gov/2023003983

ISBN: 978-1-7182-0362-4 (print)

Copyright © 2025 by Jennifer L. Etnier

Human Kinetics supports copyright. Copyright fuels scientific and artistic endeavor, encourages authors to create new works, and promotes free speech. Thank you for buying an authorized edition of this work and for complying with copyright laws by not reproducing, scanning, or distributing any part of it in any form without written permission from the publisher. You are supporting authors and allowing Human Kinetics to continue to publish works that increase the knowledge, enhance the performance, and improve the lives of people all over the world.

To report suspected copyright infringement of content published by Human Kinetics, contact us at **permissions@hkusa.com**. To request permission to legally reuse content published by Human Kinetics, please refer to the information at **https://US.Human Kinetics.com/pages/permissions-information**.

The web addresses cited in this text were current as of March 2023, unless otherwise noted.

Acquisitions Editor: Diana Vincer; **Developmental Editor:** Melissa Feld; **Managing Editor:** Melissa J. Zavala; **Copyeditor:** Marissa Wold Uhrina; **Proofreader:** Julia DeGraf; **Indexer:** Nan N. Badgett; **Permissions Manager:** Laurel Mitchell; **Graphic Designer:** Dawn Sills; **Cover Designer:** Keri Evans; **Cover Design Specialist:** Susan Rothermel Allen; **Photograph (cover):** SolStock/E+/Getty Images; **Photographs (interior):** © Human Kinetics, unless otherwise noted; **Photo Asset Manager:** Laura Fitch; **Photo Production Manager:** Jason Allen; **Senior Art Manager:** Kelly Hendren; **Illustrations:** © Human Kinetics, unless otherwise noted; **Printer:** Versa Press

Printed in the United States of America   10 9 8 7 6 5 4 3 2 1

The paper in this book is certified under a sustainable forestry program.

Human Kinetics
1607 N. Market Street
Champaign, IL 61820
USA

United States and International
Website: **US.HumanKinetics.com**
Email: info@hkusa.com
Phone: 1-800-747-4457

Canada
Website: **Canada.HumanKinetics.com**
Email: info@hkcanada.com

E8305

I dedicate this textbook to my spouse, Paige Wagner, with whom I am sharing life's journey. It is through our partnership that I have been able to reach my professional goals while maintaining an appropriate work–life balance and raising our three wonderful children together. Nothing I have accomplished would be possible or worthwhile without Paige by my side.

Brief Contents

Preface xv

Acknowledgments xix

1	Introduction	1
2	Answering Research Questions	17
3	Methods and Measurement for Exercise Psychology	35
4	Exercise and Stress	53
5	Exercise and Anxiety	71
6	Exercise and Depression	87
7	Exercise and Affect, Mood, and Emotions	103
8	Exercise and Pain	119
9	Exercise and Cognitive Performance	135
10	Exercise and Brain Health	155
11	Exercise and Self-Esteem	171
12	Exercise and Body Image	185
13	Exercise and Sleep	199
14	Exercise and Quality of Life	217

References 231

Index 251

About the Author 259

Contents

Preface xv

Acknowledgments xix

1 Introduction   1

History of Kinesiology   2
Why Study Human Movement?   3
A Historical View of Physical Activity Behaviors   4
The History of Physical Education   6
The History of Sport and Exercise Psychology   9
    Historical Figures in Psychology   9
    Connection Between Physical Education and Psychology   10
    Early Examples of Sport and Exercise Psychology   11
    The Formative Years of Sport Psychology   12
    Women in Sport Psychology   14
Sport and Exercise Psychology Today   14
Summary   16
Discussion Questions   16

2 Answering Research Questions   17

Research Terms   18
    Empirical   18
    Independent and Dependent Variables   19
    Confounding Variables or Covariates   19
    Psychometric Properties   19
    Statistical Significance   21
Research Designs   21
    Correlational Studies   21
    Cross-Sectional Studies   21
    Prospective Studies   22
    True Experimental Studies   22
Participant Assignment to Groups   22
    Within-Subjects Design   23
    Between-Subjects Design   23
    Mixed Design   24
Methods of Reviews of Empirical Studies   24
    Narrative Review   24
    Systematic Review   25

Meta-Analytic Review   25

Summary on Reviews   26

Mediators, Mechanisms, and Moderators   26

Mediators   27

Mechanisms   27

Moderators   28

Moderated Mediation   29

Limitations in the Study of Mediators and Mechanisms in Exercise Psychology Research   29

Mechanisms, Mediators, Theories, and Hypotheses in the Exercise Psychology Literature   30

Psychological Mediators   30

Physiological Mechanisms   30

Cognitive Theories   31

Biologically Based Theories   31

Other Biological Mechanisms   32

Summary   33

Discussion Questions   34

3 Methods and Measurement for Exercise Psychology   35

Definitions   36

Physical Activity   36

Exercise   37

Sport   37

Aerobic and Anaerobic Activities   38

Resistance Activities   39

Sedentary Behavior   39

Changes in Response to Physically Active or Sedentary Behaviors   39

Exercise Prescription   41

Exercise Paradigms   42

Acute Exercise   42

Chronic Exercise   42

Dose Response   42

Measurement in Exercise Psychology   43

Measurement of Physical Activity   43

Direct Measures of Physical Activity   44

Indirect Measures of Physical Activity   45

Physical Activity Recommendations   46

Measurement of Psychological Outcomes   48

Self-Report Measures   48

Behavioral Measures   49

Wearable Technology Measures   49

Biological Measures 49
Neuroimaging Measures 49
Summary 51
Discussion Questions 51

4 Exercise and Stress 53

What Is Stress? 54
Physical and Psychological Stressors 57
Prevalence and Costs of Stress 57
Mechanisms of Stress 58
Is Stress Good or Bad? 60
Exercise and Stress-Reduction Theories 61
    Physiological Toughness Hypothesis 61
    Cross-Stressor Adaptation Hypothesis 62
    Time-Out or Distraction Hypothesis 62
    Sense of Control Hypothesis 62
Measurement of Stress 62
    Psychological Measures 63
    Physiological Measures 64
    Stress Induction 65
    Patterns of Stress Responses 65
Evidence Relative to the Effects of Exercise on Stress 66
    Empirical Evidence 66
    Meta-Analytic Evidence 67
Summary 68
Discussion Questions 69

5 Exercise and Anxiety 71

What Is Anxiety? 72
What Are Anxiety Disorders? 73
    Generalized Anxiety Disorder 73
    Panic Disorder 74
    Phobias 74
    Obsessive-Compulsive Disorder 74
    PTSD 74
Prevalence and Costs of Anxiety 75
Treatment of Clinical Anxiety 77
Mechanisms of Anxiety 77
Theories and Mechanisms of Exercise and Anxiety 78
    Physiological Mechanisms 78
    Psychological Mediators 79

Measurement of Anxiety 80
    Somatic Activation 80
    Anxiety-Related Behaviors 80
    Self-Report Measures 81
Evidence Relative to the Effects of Exercise on Anxiety 82
    Historically Important Research 82
    Reducing Anxiety Symptoms in Nonanxious Samples 82
    Reducing Anxiety Symptoms in Clinically Anxious Samples 83
Summary 84
Discussion Questions 85

6 Exercise and Depression   87

What Is Depression? 88
Prevalence and Costs 89
Mechanisms and Mediators of the Effects of Exercise on Depression 91
    Physiological Mechanisms 91
    Psychological Mediators 94
Treatment of Clinical Depression 94
    Pharmacological Treatment 94
    Psychotherapy 95
    Electroconvulsive Therapy 95
    Treatment Selection 95
Measurement 96
Evidence on the Benefits of Exercise for Depression 96
    Empirical Evidence 97
    Meta-Analytic Evidence 99
Bidirectional Relationship 101
Specific Populations 101
Summary 102
Discussion Questions 102

7 Exercise and Affect, Mood, and Emotions   103

What Are Affect, Mood, and Emotion? 105
Theories and Mechanisms of Mood and of the Effects of Exercise on Mood 106
    The Dual Mode Theory 109
    Biological Mechanisms 110
Measurement of Affect, Mood, and Emotion 111
Empirical and Meta-Analytic Evidence on the Effects of Exercise on Mood 114
    Acute Exercise and Mood 114
    Chronic Exercise and Mood 115

Summary 117
Discussion Questions 117

8 Exercise and Pain — 119

Defining Pain 120
Prevalence and Costs 121
Theories and Mechanisms of the Experience of Pain 122
Mechanisms and Theories Explaining How Exercise Reduces Pain 124
Treatment 124
Measurement 126
Empirical and Meta-Analytic Evidence for Exercise and Pain 127
    Acute Exercise and Acute Pain: Evidence From Healthy Adults 127
    Chronic Exercise and Acute Pain: Evidence From Healthy Adults 128
    Chronic Exercise and Chronic Pain: Evidence From Adults Living With Chronic Pain 130
Summary 132
Discussion Questions 133

9 Exercise and Cognitive Performance — 135

What Is Cognitive Performance? 136
Prevalence and Costs 137
Theories, Mechanisms, and Mediators 137
    Theories for Acute Exercise 138
    Theories for Chronic Exercise 139
    Brain Structure and Function 141
The Measurement of Cognition 141
    General Cognition and Cognitive Domains 142
    Measurement in Three Cognitive Domains 142
Evidence Relative to the Effects of Exercise on Cognitive Performance 144
    Acute Exercise 146
    Chronic Exercise 150
Summary 153
Discussion Questions 154

10 Exercise and Brain Health — 155

What Is Brain Health? 156
Prevalence and Costs 158
Mechanisms Explaining the Potential Effects of Exercise on Brain Health 158
Measurement 160

Evidence Relative to the Effects of Exercise on Brain Health 162
　　Acute Exercise 162
　　Chronic Exercise 163
　　Exercise, TBI, and Stroke 166
Summary 170
Discussion Questions 170

11 Exercise and Self-Esteem — 171

Defining Self-Esteem and Self-Concept 172
Prevalence and Self-Esteem 176
Models, Theories, and Mediators of Self-Esteem 176
　　Self-Esteem Models Specific to Exercise 177
　　Psychological Mediators 178
Measurement 179
Evidence for Exercise and Self-Esteem 180
　　Empirical Evidence 180
　　Meta-Analytic Reviews 182
Summary 183
Discussion Questions 183

12 Exercise and Body Image — 185

Terms and Definitions 186
The Importance of Body Image 187
Prevalence 188
Links Between Body Image and Clinical Disorders 190
　　Muscle Dysmorphia 190
　　Clinical Eating Disorders and Disordered Eating 190
Mechanisms and Mediators 192
Measurement 192
　　Body Perception and Dissatisfaction 192
　　Affective Component 193
　　Body-Related Behaviors 193
　　Related Measures 193
Evidence Relative to Exercise and Body Image 193
　　Meta-Analytic Findings 194
　　Evidence Specific to the Anticipated Effects of Exercise on Disordered Eating 195
Summary 197
Discussion Questions 197

13 Exercise and Sleep — 199

Definitions of Sleep and Its Attributes 200
A Brief History of Sleep 201

How Much Sleep Do We Need? 203
Prevalence and Costs of Sleep Disorders and Sleep Deprivation 203
Theories and Mechanisms of Sleep 206
　Energy Conservation Theory 206
　Restorative Hypothesis 206
　Specific Restorative Processes in the Brain 206
　Two-Process Model of Sleep Regulation 208
Mechanisms for Exercise Affecting Sleep 209
Treatment for Sleep Disorders 209
Measurement 209
　Polysomnography 209
　Wearable Devices 210
　Behavioral Measures 211
　Self-Report Measures 211
　Measurement Limitations 211
Evidence on the Benefits of Exercise for Sleep 212
　An Empirical Study With Poor Sleepers 212
　Benefits of Exercise for Good Sleepers 213
　Benefits of Exercise for Insomnia 215
　Benefits of Exercise for Cancer Patients 215
Summary 216
Discussion Questions 216

Exercise and Quality of Life 217

Defining Quality of Life 219
Prevalence and Costs 221
Mechanisms and Mediators 222
　Physical Fitness 222
　Functional Fitness 223
　Psychological Mediators 224
Measurement 224
　Global Measures 225
　Specific Disease States 226
Evidence Relative to the Effects of Exercise on Quality of Life 226
　Empirical Evidence 227
　Meta-Analytic and Systematic Reviews 228
Summary 230
Discussion Questions 230

References 231
Index 251
About the Author 259

Preface

The Psychological Benefits of Exercise and Physical Activity is a textbook written for upper-level undergraduate students and for graduate students in kinesiology, exercise science, physical education, community and therapeutic recreation, social work, psychology, or other disciplines who are taking a course focused on exercise psychology. I have taught an exercise psychology course at undergraduate and graduate levels for many years. In teaching this course, I have typically spent slightly more than half of the semester focusing on the psychological theory and techniques that can be used to promote the adoption and maintenance of physical activity, with the remainder of the semester spent on the psychological benefits of physical activity. As a result, I have used textbooks that cover these two aspects of exercise psychology with approximately equal weight. The shortcoming of this approach is that because more than half of the course has been focused on behavioral change, I have had to limit the consideration of psychological benefits of exercise to cover the material within a single semester. Before the start of every semester, I would send an email to my students asking them to identify, from a list of 11 choices, the top 5 to 7 psychological outcomes they would like to cover in the course. Because I had less than half of the semester available for these topics, we would only consider the top 5 that were identified by the majority of the students. This meant that every semester, the topics that were not selected simply were not covered, leaving my students with a lack of familiarity with many psychological benefits that can accrue in response to exercise. Thus, the primary purpose of this textbook is to provide students with comprehensive coverage of most of the psychological benefits of exercise that can be delivered in a semester-long course.

Like this textbook, a few other exercise psychology textbooks focus exclusively or almost exclusively on the psychological benefits of exercise. But the challenge with these other textbooks is that many are too heavily weighted toward an explanation of research studies and physiological or neurological mechanisms, making them challenging reads even for advanced graduate students. Or, by contrast, they do not consider these important aspects of the literature at all, leaving both undergraduate and graduate students wanting for more information to complete their understanding of the topic and of the evidence supporting our understanding. This book is designed to be the Goldilocks of exercise psychology textbooks, with an appropriate and balanced consideration of research and mechanisms for a college-level class. Thus, a second purpose of this textbook is to provide comprehensive coverage of the psychological benefits of exercise with an ideal level of coverage of research and mechanisms that is appropriately delivered in a semester-long course.

I would guess that, as a college student, you have probably had at least some past experience with playing sports, participating in exercise (structured physical activity with the purpose of improving fitness), or simply being physically active (performing any behavior that results in energy expenditure significantly above rest). Assuming this is true, then you likely have had both positive and negative experiences in response to those activities. You might have felt the elation of a successful sport experience, the joy of a good run on a cool autumn morning, the pleasure of biking to a park, or the sense of accomplishment from learning a new sport skill. You also might have felt muscle soreness after exercise; fatigue from a physically exhausting, laborious day; or anxiety about performing in front of others. These varied experiences might have made you ask questions such as the following: Is there really such a thing as a feel-good phenomenon after exercise? Can you become addicted to exercise? Does exercise help you do better in school? Does exercise help or hurt when it comes to anxiety? These are all questions that can be answered through research conducted in sport and exercise psychology and are topics we will address in this textbook.

As a student taking an exercise psychology class, it is also likely that you intend to work with others in the future to promote physical activity. You might intend to be a personal trainer, a group exercise leader, a strength and conditioning coach, a mobility specialist, a physical therapist, a physician, an athletic trainer, a sport psychologist, a counselor, a social worker, a community or therapeutic recreation instructor, or a youth sport coach. In any of these career paths and many others, having a working knowledge of the psychological benefits of physical activity will serve you well. Although some people are motivated to exercise because of the physical health benefits that will accrue, many others need that extra motivation from knowing that physical activity will provide beneficial psychological outcomes that are important to them. This might include stress or anxiety management, cognitive performance, sleep, body image, or any other outcome that might benefit from physical activity. Your knowledge about these benefits will help you to motivate your clients to initiate and maintain a program of regular exercise.

Organization

The organization of this textbook is designed to facilitate teaching and learning. The textbook is arranged such that the initial chapters provide foundational background information to set the stage for the remaining chapters. In chapter 1, I share a historical perspective of physical education, psychology, and sport and exercise psychology to illustrate the evolution of sport and exercise psychology over time. In chapter 2, research terms and experimental designs are reviewed to ensure that students are well-versed in this language and prepared for exposure to empirical and meta-analytic findings from research. In chapter 3, theories, hypotheses, and mechanisms that have been proposed to explain multiple psychological benefits are explained. This will allow students to appreciate overlap in theories, hypotheses, and mechanisms across psychological outcomes while also recognizing those theories, hypotheses, and mechanisms that are unique to specific outcomes. Overall, these introductory chapters set the stage for a common appreciation of the history of exercise psychology, theories and mechanisms proposed to explain research terminology, and psychological benefits of exercise.

Chapters 4 through 14 cover the various psychological benefits of exercise, with each chapter devoted to a specific psychological outcome. Although each chapter is focused on a different outcome, they are all organized in a similar fashion. Each chapter begins with a vignette to give an example of why questions of exercise and this particular psychological outcome are important. Next, I provide definitions of terms, consider the prevalence of various mental health disorders, map out the mechanisms and causes that have been identified for the psychological outcomes, explore the impact of exercise on these mechanisms and causes, and then review both empirical (single study) and meta-analytic (statistical summaries of empirical studies) research to demonstrate our current state of understanding. This specific organization within each chapter allows students to become familiar with the psychological construct, to appreciate its importance as an outcome, to learn about the causes of the psychological construct, to understand how exercise might affect those causes, and to be exposed to some of the key research that has been conducted to explore the potential benefits of exercise for that specific outcome. By using this same organizational scheme in each chapter, students can find their rhythm with respect to remembering and mastering the content.

Features

One unique feature of the book is the inclusion of sidebars that introduce thought-provoking ideas, provide opportunities for self-reflection, or describe interesting research studies. An example of a self-reflection sidebar comes from chapter 4, Exercise and Stress. In this sidebar, students are asked to consider the stressors in their lives and to identify those that are related to their studies, their job, or their home life. These self-reflection sidebars will enhance students' understanding of the relevance of the material to themselves as a way to foster interest in the outcome being discussed. An example of a sidebar focused on an interesting research study can be found in chapter 13, Exercise and Sleep, which describes a study comparing quality of sleep between two villages in the Republic of Fiji. In this study, one of the villages has electricity and the other does not, so the comparison informs our understanding of how artificial light affects sleep quality. These sidebars serve to expand students' thinking about the topic through relevant and entertaining material. By self-reflecting and considering interesting ideas and research, students will become more engaged in the material, which will contribute to their ability to learn and retain the information. Another unique feature of this book is that each chapter also includes definitions of key terms to make these readily available to students as they master the material. Lastly, discussion questions are provided at the end of each chapter to prompt continued conversation, which again contributes to engagement and retention.

Instructor Materials

In addition to the textbook itself, PowerPoint slides have been created to parallel the chapters and to give the instructor a starting point for presenting the material. Also provided are paper or activity ideas for each chapter that might be used as in-class activities or as out-of-class assignments to facilitate a more in-depth consideration of the topic area. For each chapter, at least five multiple-choice questions, five true-false questions, three to five short-answer questions, and one or two essay questions and correct answers are provided as well. The provision of these materials allows the instructor more time to focus on preparing to teach the class content and less time on preparing the actual PowerPoint presentations and evaluative components.

Acknowledgments

First and foremost, I would like to acknowledge my partner, Paige Wagner, and our children, Payton, James, and Max Wagner. It is an incredible professional honor to be offered the chance to write a textbook, and I relish having the opportunity to infuse an excitement for exercise psychology into future generations. But it is important to recognize that when one accepts an opportunity to write a textbook, it can only be successfully accomplished with the support of family, because of the enormous time commitment required. At times, I have had to sacrifice being home for dinner on time, helping to rake leaves with my family on a beautiful Saturday, or enjoying other family events in order to meet deadlines necessary for staying on schedule. For the past two and a half years, I have spent most weekends and much of the summer and winter holidays working on this textbook. Despite missing family events and often being tied to my computer, my spouse and my children have always been understanding, and I thank them for their continued and unwavering support in all that I do.

I also want to acknowledge my parents, David and Liz Etnier, who set the wheels in motion for me to be a professor and to have this opportunity. As a professor himself, my dad radiated with the joy he had for his work. As an ichthyologist and aquatic insects expert, he was an enthusiastic and passionate teacher and a committed scientist who spent days collecting fish and aquatic insects in streams, rivers, and light traps and spent hours peering into his microscope to identify his finds. Ever eager to make contributions to science, he was an incredible role model for finding a career that you love enough that you will want to work hard. In addition to our incredible and enduring friendship, my mom has always been my strongest supporter and my best editor. I feel quite confident that I have received more "red ink" from my mom than from any other person helping me learn the art of writing. Those skills are invaluable in pursuing life as a college professor and have certainly contributed to my interest in and ability to write this textbook and I am thankful for her support.

In writing this textbook, I also want to acknowledge the work of my colleagues. In presenting what we know in the area of exercise psychology, I am reliant on the work of scholars interested in advancing our understanding of the potential of exercise to benefit mental health. It is through their committed efforts that we have learned much about how exercise can yield psychological benefits through both single sessions of exercise and a regular commitment to exercise. I look back historically and recognize the many individuals whose contributions laid the groundwork for the research that I am able to pursue today. We are all standing on the shoulders of those who go before us, and it is with humility that I attempt to summarize and synthesize the work of others. As such, I give thanks to the physical educators, psychologists, kinesiologists, and sport and exercise psychologists who have contributed so much to what we know today.

Several graduate students at the University of North Carolina at Greensboro provided invaluable assistance in the early drafts of this textbook. I want to express my sincere thanks to Sam DuBois, Sam Kibildis, Aiko Ueno, and Jarod Vance, who created summary tables collating information from meta-analytic reviews. I also want to acknowledge Frank Gerdine and Zachery Barnes, who added references into the EndNote library and incorporated citations into each chapter. I had the good fortune of serving as the graduate mentor to these students, which was incredibly rewarding, and I appreciate the help and support they provided during their time at the University of North Carolina at Greensboro.

Lastly, I thank Human Kinetics for inviting me to write this textbook. I have had numerous opportunities to work with the great folks at Human Kinetics and always find them to be professional and collegial. I especially recognize Diana Vincer, who provided important guidance and input during the planning stages of the textbook, and Melissa Feld, who has shepherded this textbook through several rounds of edits and who has consistently shown a great eye for detail and consistency.

Introduction

OBJECTIVES

After studying this chapter, you should be able to do the following:

- Describe the historical reasons for the emergence of physical education
- Understand that physical education and psychology were developing along similar paths that converged to produce the first sport psychology research
- Summarize the history of the development of sport psychology and distinguish sport psychology from exercise psychology
- Recognize the historical figures who made important contributions to physical education, psychology, sport psychology, and exercise psychology

KEY TERMS

kinesiology

discipline

subdisciplines

sedentary behaviors

accelerometer

experiment

exercise psychology

Jamie is a sophomore in college, and although he is currently listed as a psychology major, he hasn't decided on a clear career path. Jamie schedules an appointment with an academic adviser to talk about his interests, experiences, goals, and skill sets. Jamie was heavily engaged in youth sports through high school and still participates in intramurals in college. He enjoys working with kids and is currently volunteering at a local boys and girls club as a youth sports coach. Jamie is an avid exerciser and recognizes the value of physical activity for himself and for the children with whom he is working. He envisions a future in which he is somehow engaged in the promotion of physical activity, but he doesn't have a clear endpoint in mind. As Jamie shares his thoughts, the adviser starts to consider various career possibilities. The adviser thinks that Jamie might be happy as a physical educator, a sport coach, a strength and conditioning coach, an exercise instructor, a sport psychologist, or an exercise psychologist. As the adviser starts to talk about these various careers and the educational paths associated with each, the adviser mentions kinesiology, explaining its evolution as a discipline and how it consists of various subdisciplines that are linked to other parent disciplines. The adviser ends by talking about sport and exercise psychology and explains that this subdiscipline is often housed in kinesiology departments rather than psychology departments at universities and colleges. Jamie wants to learn more; the adviser has opened his eyes to a number of career paths that he hadn't previously considered.

To answer Jamie's questions and to better explain the distinctions between sport and exercise psychology, it is helpful to first provide a brief history of kinesiology. This serves to illustrate the close ties between kinesiology and physical education and the relatively recent emergence of sport and exercise psychology as an important subdiscipline within kinesiology. It is also valuable to consider how physical activity behaviors have evolved over time, leading to a recognized need for physical education in the 1800s and to a present-day interest in using psychological tools to promote exercise and using scientific methods to explore the psychological benefits of exercise. In this chapter, we will cover the history of kinesiology as linked to the history of physical education, give examples to demonstrate why the study of human movement is an important area of study, and describe the development and evolution of sport and exercise psychology as a unique subdiscipline within kinesiology. In subsequent chapters, we will learn how to measure physical activity and the various psychological outcomes that are influenced by exercise, we will discuss explanations for the positive benefits of exercise, and we will then systematically consider what we currently know about the effects of exercise on various psychological outcomes.

History of Kinesiology

The history of kinesiology is encompassed by the history of fitness and of physical education. *Kinesiology* is the name that has most recently been used by many academic departments, but historically, these departments evolved from departments of physical education and many retain the words *physical education* in their name. Interestingly, departments of physical education came into existence in response to the dramatic declines in fitness that were observed as a consequence of the industrial revolution. Although it is only relatively recently that *kinesiology* has become the name of choice for many academic departments, the first department of kinesiology was established in 1967 (Coakley, 2021), and the word *kinesiology* itself has roots in antiquity, deriving from *kinein* or *kinesis*, which is the Greek word for "movement," and *ology*, which means "the study of." As defined by the American Kinesiology Association (AKA), the academic discipline of **kinesiology** "involves the study of physical activity and its impact on health, society, and quality of life" (American Kinesiology Association, 2020). A **discipline** is defined as a branch of scientific study, so kinesiology is recognized as a science. Kinesiology also can be very simply described as the study of human movement.

---

kinesiology—Kinesiology is a science-based discipline focused on the study of physical activity and its impact on health, society, and quality of life.

discipline—A discipline is a branch of scientific study.

The term *kinesiology* was formally proposed by Karl Newell in 1990 as being the most appropriate name for academic departments (Newell, 1990a). Although George Sage had used the term in a paper presented at the American Alliance for Health, Physical Education, and Recreation (AAHPER) in 1968 ("Emerging Directions in Kinesiology") and his department at Colorado State University adopted this name early (Sage, 2013), most departments across the United States were using names such as *health and exercise science*, *exercise and sport science*, *human performance*, *movement studies*, and *leisure studies*, and prior to the use of those names, most were using the name *department of physical education* (Newell, 1990b). Kinesiology departments typically include various subdisciplines such as physical education, biomechanics, motor behavior, sport and exercise psychology, exercise physiology, athletic training, sport history, and sport sociology (see figure 1.1). **Subdisciplines** are defined as smaller branches of scientific study within a broader area of study. Although kinesiology has become the most common name for departments that house one or more of these subdisciplines and that offer doctoral-level training, debate is ongoing about the focus of these departments relative to the value of the humanities (e.g., history, ethics, sociology), the training of professionals (e.g., physical educators, personal trainers, health coaches, athletic trainers), and the importance of theoretical and scientific research (Twietmeyer, 2012). It remains to be seen how this continues to evolve as academic departments work to satisfy the overlapping yet competing demands of professional training and disciplinary study. If you are in a department of kinesiology, you might ask your professor about the evolution of names of your own department and about the make-up of the subdisciplines that are housed within your department. If your department is one of the over 600 members of the American Kinesiology Association (AKA) but does not include kinesiology in its name, you might also find it interesting to discuss this with your professor to understand your own department's rationale for using a different descriptor. Currently, almost 20% of departments affiliated with the AKA include kinesiology in their name, but that means that approximately 80% go by other names, none of which are particularly common (the next most common name, used by just 6% of departments, is *exercise science*).

Why Study Human Movement?

You might be wondering why the study of human movement is important and how this topic has so many subdisciplines. At first glance, it might seem that human movement is so natural and such an inherent part of our lives that there wouldn't be a need to study it. Actually, human movement

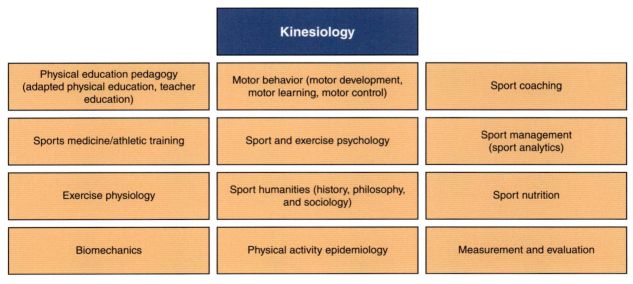

FIGURE 1.1 Subdisciplines of kinesiology.

---

subdisciplines—Smaller branches of scientific study within a broader area of study are described as subdisciplines.

is extremely complex. Think about it from the perspective of locomotion and gross motor skills. Infants learn to sit up, roll over, crawl, stand, cruise (walking while holding on to a stationary object), and ultimately walk independently. A child learns how to coordinate their body to kick a soccer ball, climb a tree, ride a bicycle, or jump on a pogo stick. Consider that, despite how complex and challenging those various activities are, children are able to learn to perform them well. An adult can learn new motor skills such as water skiing or playing pickleball despite never having done those activities before. And many older adults are able to continue to be physically active in pursuits such as walking, playing golf or tennis, hiking, and skiing despite age-related challenges such as arthritis, sarcopenia, and cognitive decline. By contrast, some older adults must work hard to simply rise out of their chair, to navigate uneven surfaces when walking, and to maintain activities of daily living as their physical and mental capabilities begin to decline with advancing age and failing health.

The Complexities of Human Movement

Human movement is so amazingly complex that scientists have only recently had success in programming robots to perform such movements. Programming a robot to walk has become newly possible, and so far even the most advanced robots are unable to navigate the simplest of paths or to perform a ball-catching task well. Intriguingly, recent advances in artificial intelligence might result in more rapid advances in this regard as evidenced by a robot teaching itself to navigate an obstacle course.

It is fascinating to consider the complexities involved in human locomotion, physical activity, and sport that make these behaviors of interest to kinesiologists. Now, let's consider how the various subdisciplines of kinesiology might approach a common topic to briefly illustrate the questions that might be of interest to each area. Have you heard of or played pickleball? Pickleball is a relatively new sport activity that was initially conceived in 1965. Pickleball has commonalities with badminton, tennis, and table tennis. The game is played on a small-sized court that looks like a tennis court with a low net across the middle. Solid paddles are used to hit a ball that looks like a Wiffle ball. The game can be played as singles or doubles. Consider an older adult who learns to play pickleball and becomes increasingly committed to this activity. This behavior might be of interest to scientists from any of the subdisciplines in kinesiology. Motor behaviorists (including motor control, motor development, and motor learning) would be fascinated by the actual learning of this new skill. They might focus on the translation of skills from other relevant sports to this specific racket sport. But this scenario might also be of interest to exercise physiologists who would consider changes in muscle type distribution in conjunction with sport participation or in fitness gains in response to the increased physical activity. The topics also could be of interest to physical educators who are most typically interested in the teaching of skills to children as a way of giving them foundational skills for sport participation and lifelong engagement in physical activity. These physical educators might be interested in the translation of teaching the skills of striking an object with an implement in childhood to the propensity to learn to play pickleball in older age. These topics also could be intriguing to sport psychologists who are interested in using mental skills to enhance sport performance by these pickleball players as they begin to become more competitive in the game. Finally, exercise psychologists might explore how older adults can use pickleball to help them preserve mental acuity into advancing age through the combination of physical and social activities that are a part of the game. This example provides a good illustration of the specific interests of researchers and practitioners in the various subdisciplines of kinesiology.

A Historical View of Physical Activity Behaviors

Let's shift our focus now to consider how participation in physical activity has changed over time. This is important because the genesis of physical education, which is encompassed in the field of kinesiology, was at least partially reflective of changes in physical activity behaviors across history and the concomitant impact on the health of modern humans. In our modern society, large numbers of individuals are not regularly engaged in physical activity but rather spend a substantial portion of

CHAPTER 1 • Introduction | 5

Pickleball exemplifies how scientists from across the subdisciplines of kinesiology might all be interested in studying a sport from their different perspectives.

their day participating in sedentary behaviors (Yang et al., 2019). **Sedentary behaviors** are ones that are performed while we are awake but that do not require substantial energy expenditure. Examples are sitting, reclining, or lying down while awake. Consider your own behaviors during the day. How much of the day do you spend in sedentary behaviors? As a student, common sedentary behaviors would likely include sitting in class, watching television, studying, interacting with social media on a cell phone, and playing video games.

Consider how our physical activity behavior today contrasts with bygone eras when humankind lived as hunter-gatherers. During the time of hunter-gatherers, physical activity and movement were critical for survival, so being sedentary was not an option. To be active meant survival, but to be sedentary would certainly result in death. In fact, estimates based on anthropological records suggest that hunter-gatherers typically covered between 4 and 10 miles (6-16 km) daily (O'Keefe et al., Vogel, Lavie, & Cordain, 2010) and suggest that a typical American man today weighing 155 pounds (70 kg) would have to walk an additional 12 miles (7 km) per day to approximate the level of energy expenditure displayed by early mankind (Cordain et al., 1998).

As humans moved into more agrarian societies such that their survival depended on the production of crops and the maintenance of farmland, physical activity continued to be attained through behaviors required by the demands of daily life, which might have included fetching water, clearing land for farming, working a plow, or harvesting a crop. Thus, physical activity behaviors were largely performed as a function of work demands. In addition to these demands, during the 17th and 18th centuries, many Americans followed Puritan beliefs and believed that play was forbidden as the work of the devil. Hence, physical activity was not pursued for leisure during this era.

As countries evolved into industrialized nations, work responsibilities began to change yet again, resulting in more specialization of skill sets such that the amount of physical labor required in different jobs increasingly varied. As a result of the Industrial Revolution, distinctions began to arise between those with professional jobs that did not require physical labor and those who still had very labor-intensive jobs. In the United States, the influence of "industrialization, urbanization, and immigration" was leading to a new vision of the role of sport and the need for physical education for the health of the nation and the acculturation

---

sedentary behaviors—Behaviors such as sitting, reclining, or lying down that are performed while we are awake but that do not require substantial energy expenditure are referred to as sedentary behaviors.

> ### Physical Activity Behavior in Hunter-Gatherer Communities
>
> A recent research study conducted with a modern-day group of hunter-gatherers provides a fascinating glimpse of the amount of physical activity performed by humans who live more simple lives, as was common in historical periods (Raichlen et al., 2017). The individuals in this study were defined as hunter-gatherers because they obtained at least 90% of their food from the wild environment. The members of a hunter-gatherer community in Tanzania agreed to wear an accelerometer for 14 days during four different time periods relative to the rainy season. An **accelerometer** is a device that can be worn on the hip or on the wrist and that collects movement data used to assess how much physical activity the person is doing. Data from the accelerometers indicated that both men and women (regardless of age) averaged over 2 hours of moderate to vigorous physical activity per day in addition to almost 4 hours of light-intensity physical activity. Light physical activity involves moving around while standing up and for people living in modern societies would include activities such as walking slowly, doing housework, or mowing the lawn. Moderate physical activity is performed at an intensity level similar to a brisk walk or bicycling, and vigorous physical activity in modern societies includes jogging, aerobic dance, or bicycling uphill. So if we translate the Tanzanians' activities to activities we might perform, this would be like spending 4 hours doing housework and yard work and then bicycling or jogging for 2 hours each day for 2 weeks. Contrast this amount of activity to the current recommendations that adults perform at least 150 minutes of moderate physical activity over the course of an entire week (U.S. Department of Health and Human Services, 2018).

of immigrants into society (McCullick & Lomax, 2000, p. 50). With increasing industrialization, the wealthy elite began to have more free time and greater amounts of discretionary income, and physical activity through sport and exercise became viewed as important for the maintenance of physical health. As a result, members of the upper class began to pursue physical activity during their leisure time. As physical activity began to be experienced through leisure pursuits as opposed to physical labor, the 1800s saw the initial development of many sports that continue to be popular today, including rugby, baseball, boat racing, cycling, canoeing, hockey, badminton, and football (King et al., 1995).

During the 1800s, in addition to the popularization of sport activities, physical activity participation was dramatically influenced by immigrants to the United States who brought with them the training that they had experienced in their countries of origin. In 1823 German gymnastics (called *Turnen*) was introduced in the United States, and these training organizations (called *Turnverein*) became popular in urban centers by the mid-1850s. Gymnastic training was also promoted by immigrants from Sweden in the 1880s through the Swedish Movement Cure, which was focused more on medical values than sport performance and hence consisted of activities expected to specifically improve physical health. In the 1890s French immigrants got into the action when they introduced the Delsarte System of Physical Culture that focused on physical activities emphasizing artistic abilities (e.g., singing, drama, dance).

The History of Physical Education

During the 1800s, numerous people were critically important in the establishment of physical education as a part of the school system in the United States. One such person is Catharine Beecher, who in 1828 began to incorporate physical education into her curriculum by setting calisthenics to music (the original Jazzercise!). She founded the American Women's Education Association in 1852 and is credited as "the originator of the first system of physical education by an American" (Barrow & Brown, 1988, p. 78). This is important because it represented a shift toward the belief that schools should be responsible for providing opportunities for physical activity for children.

In 1859 Aaron Molyneaux Hewlett was the first Black instructor ever hired at Harvard University, where he held the first academic position in the profession of physical education. He maintained the role of director of physical education at Harvard University until 1871. However, indicative of the segregationist and racist views surrounding sport, physical education, and education, it was over 90 years before another Black physical educator was

---

accelerometer—An accelerometer is a device that can be worn on the hip or on the wrist and that collects movement data used to assess how much physical activity the person is doing.

Immigrants to the United States brought with them an interest in physical activities that today would be considered gymnastics.

hired at any predominantly White university (Weiss & Jamieson, 2017).

In 1861 Edward Hitchcock Jr. was named a professor of hygiene and physical education at Amherst College in Massachusetts and established a gymnasium in which he collected anthropometric data and developed individual fitness training plans for students (Vertinsky, 2017). That same year, Diocletian (Dio) Lewis established the first school in America for physical educators, The Boston Normal Institute for Physical Education. This was important because Lewis stressed the need for teachers to be well prepared as physical educators for people with different skill and fitness levels and emphasized the value of focusing on general movement skills rather than sport skills per se. In 1862 Lewis published a book titled *New Gymnastics for Men, Women, and Children*, which satisfied the public's interest in exercise for health benefits (King et al., 1995). Dudley Sargent is credited with establishing a scientific foundation for physical education practices in 1881. Sargent brought his medical school training and a scientific approach to physical education and was passionate about the need to provide physical activity opportunities to students for their health and well-being. Sargent focused on hygiene, education, recreation, and restoration as goals of physical education (Bennett, 1978). He established the Sargent School for Physical Education in 1881 and developed some of the first exercise training equipment that reflects the early foundations of what is now known as the Cybex training system (Vertinsky, 2017). In 1885 Dr. William G. Anderson created the first professional organization for physical educators when he organized a meeting for the Association for the Advancement of Physical Education. This organization evolved into AAHPER in 1938 when the R was added for recreation, added dance to become AAHPERD in 1974, and is now called SHAPE America. SHAPE America is the professional organization that physical educators and faculty members in pedagogy (physical education) most typically attend.

It is important to point out that other women in addition to Catharine Beecher played important roles in the establishment of the profession of physical education. In 1889 Mary Hemenway established the Boston Normal School of Gymnastics and appointed Amy Morris Homans as director. Homans founded the Association of Directors of Physical Education for Women in 1915 as a means of specifically focusing on the professional development of female physical educators (Liberti, 2017). She also helped develop one of the first graduate programs in physical education at Wellesley College (Ransdell, 2014). From 1895 to 1897, Anita Julurness Turner attended the Harvard Summer School run by Sargent. This school was important because of its place in furthering women's interests in physical education and providing a school where female physical educators could receive training. Anita Turner was a teacher from 1891 to 1902 and then was the director of physical education responsible for physical education in the public schools of Washington, DC, from 1924 to 1936.

In the early 1900s physical education began to be seen as important for the development of personality and to contribute to the education of young people—that is, as "education through the physical" rather than "education of the physical." Importantly, historians have argued that physical education was actually used as a means of cultural assimilation for immigrants to the United States (Lawson, 2018). In other words, physical education emphasized American sports, games, and exercises, and a movement away from the German, Swedish, and French gymnastics that were previously popularized by those nations' immigrants. In 1890 Luther Gulick led the way in recognizing that physical education was a new profession. As a result, the formal education of physical educators by colleges and universities became more common in the early 1900s, with the University of Illinois (1905) and the University of Oregon (1907) leading the way. Gulick is also important because he organized an Academy of Physical Education in 1904 to bring together scientists exploring questions related to physical education (Liberti, 2017). This academy exists today as the National Academy of Kinesiology, with membership limited to those who are nominated and elected in recognition of their consistent and significant contributions to the professional or scholarly literature and their leadership in the field of kinesiology.

Although the professionalization of physical education was an important first step, it wasn't until the federal government recognized the poor health of Americans that physical education began to flourish. The dismal state of the fitness of American men was revealed during the draft for World War I. Concerns over low fitness revealed an increasing need for an emphasis on physical education. In fact, in 1918 the federal government listed health at the top of the Seven Cardinal Principles of Education including an explicit focus on "an effective program of physical activities" (Department of the Interior, 1918). At this point, many states began to require physical education in the schools. By the 1920s undergraduate training of 4 years was required for physical educators, and graduate-level coursework became available at a few universities including New York University, Columbia University, and the YMCA Graduate School of Nashville.

Despite the increase in physical education in the schools, the country remained concerned with the inactivity of Americans in the mid-1900s. At that time, Kraus and Hirschland (1954) published a study indicating that American children failed a test of muscular strength and flexibility at a dramatically higher rate (57.9%) than children from Austria (9.5%), Italy (8.0%), and Switzerland (8.8%). Based on this information, President Dwight D. Eisenhower established the President's Council on Youth Fitness in 1956 as a means of bringing attention to this concern. When President John F. Kennedy was elected, he contributed an article to *Sports Illustrated* called "The Soft American" (Kennedy, 1960), and he quickly worked to elevate the status of the President's Council. In his article, Kennedy expressed his view of the importance of physical fitness by stating that "the physical vigor of our citizens is one of America's most precious resources" (p. 16). He then went on to acknowledge the psychological benefits: "For physical fitness is not only one of the most important keys to a healthy body; it is the basis of dynamic and creative intellectual activity" (p. 16). You might be familiar with the President's Council (now called the President's Council on Sports, Fitness, and Nutrition), which promotes the Presidential Youth Fitness Program (www.pyfp.org) that is often administered in schools. Importantly, and partially in response to the Kraus and Hirschland study, the American College of Sports Medicine (ACSM) was established in 1954 through a joint effort of physical educators and physicians. This organization is currently the largest professional organization for sports medicine practitioners and provides for valuable cross-disciplinary interactions because it is attended by clinicians and scientists together.

Given its ties to the profession of physical education, it took some time for physical education to evolve into a recognized scientific discipline. As a profession, modern-day physical educators perceive that they have "the common aspiration of preparing young people for a lifetime of meaningful physical activity participation" (McEvoy, Heikinaro-Johansson, & MacPhail, 2017, p. 817). This is consistent with the view of physical education as a profession that is tasked with the development of motor and sport skills and the promotion of fitness and healthy lifestyles. However, some argue that physical education is a science-based discipline. In 1964 Franklin Henry published an article titled "Physical Education—An American Discipline" in which he argued that physical education is grounded in science and scholarship and should be considered a discipline rather than a profession. Although Henry initially trained as a psychologist, he was hired as an assistant professor in the department of physical education, and he conducted research in exercise physiology and motor behavior. Reflective of the fact that he trained many graduate students to pursue their own careers in motor behavior, Henry became known as the "Father of Motor Behavior Research."

The establishment of physical education as a discipline was important because it created an avenue for both the professional practice of teaching human movement and for the scientific study of human movement. Physical educators had an interest in developing evidence-based practice to support their teaching methodologies. This paved the way for the genesis of subdisciplines related to physical education, including exercise physiology, biomechanics, motor behavior, and sport and exercise psychology.

The History of Sport and Exercise Psychology

Although many people consider sport and exercise psychology to be a new subdiscipline housed within kinesiology, the fact is that people have appreciated the potential ties between the mind and the body for millennia. That is, people have long understood that our physical body can have an impact on our mind, brain health, and general affect. In the fifth century BCE, a Greek physician named Herodicus hypothesized that illness was the result of an imbalance between movement and nutrition (Georgoulis et al., 2007). He further postulated that bad digestion resulted in the spread of fluids throughout the body, which he theorized then reach the brain and cause illness. In other words, he thought that nutrition and movement were both important for brain health and the prevention of physical and mental illness. Because of this belief, he advocated for an empty abdomen, a properly functioning digestive system, proper diet, and exhaustive physical training. It is intriguing to think that Herodicus' ideas might have foreshadowed the subdiscipline of exercise psychology and an incredibly recent line of research that is focused on the role of a leaky gut in chronic neurological illnesses (e.g., Alzheimer's, Parkinson's, amyotrophic lateral sclerosis [ALS, commonly known as "Lou Gehrig's disease], depression and anxiety, autism, schizophrenia, chronic fatigue syndrome) (Camilleri, 2019; Fasano, 2020).

Centuries later, in the 17th century CE, René Descartes is credited with being the first to clearly hypothesize that the mind and the body interact in both directions. That is, he acknowledged that the body could affect the mind (or brain), but he also promoted the possibility that the brain could affect the body. Although he recognized that the mind and the body could be considered distinct in some ways, he emphasized that the two worked together to create a unified whole (Urban, 2018). This belief is referred to as *dualism* and continues to be a point of philosophical debate today as scholars consider the meaning of consciousness.

> What are some examples of how the body affects the mind? What about examples of the mind affecting the body?

Historical Figures in Psychology

Skipping ahead several centuries, three names relative to the discipline of psychology are worthy of note because they laid the foundation for psychology, which is considered a parent discipline of sport and exercise psychology. Wilhelm Wundt is credited with founding the first psychology lab in 1879 at the University of Leipzig in Germany (Vealey, 2006) and has been identified as the "Father of Experimental Psychology" (Bunn, 2017). Because of his own training in physiology, Wundt's work clearly moved psychology away from philosophy and toward a pursuit of understanding the workings of the mind from an experimental (although self-reflective) approach. G. Stanley Hall was important because of the role he played in the development of psychology in the United States. Hall established the first psychology laboratory in the United States at Johns Hopkins University in 1883, founded the *American Journal of Psychology* in 1887, and in 1902 cofounded the American Psychological Association (APA) with Edward Scripture (one of Wundt's students). The APA is now the leading professional organization for psychologists, researchers, and educators, with over 122,000 members. The third important early person in the field of psychology in the United States was William James, who was trained as a physiologist, psychologist, and philosopher. In 1875 James proposed that a person's emotional responses are actually caused by (in reaction to) the body's physical responses. In other words, he proposed that individuals see a threat, have an adrenaline response as they prepare for fight or flight, and then interpret that bodily reaction as fear. In 1890 James published the seminal book *Principles of Psychology*, which had a profound impact on other psychologists of the time.

> "If a moderate amount of physical exercise could be secured to every student daily, I have a deep conviction . . . that not only would lives and health be preserved, but animation and cheerfulness, and a higher order of efficient study and intellectual life would be secured."
> —Reverend William Augustus Stearn, President Amherst College, 1895
> What is important about this quote?

Connection Between Physical Education and Psychology

Although psychology is considered the parent discipline of sport and exercise psychology, it is intriguing to recognize that physical education (which is now considered a subdiscipline of kinesiology) and psychology were developing along parallel and somewhat intertwined paths. In the late 1800s and early 1900s both psychology and physical education were beginning to move from professions to disciplines (i.e., from being exclusively focused on practice to basing their practice on scientific study), both were becoming professionally organized, and psychologists and physical educators were working together to conduct experimental research at Yale and Harvard. In 1885 William Anderson, director of the Yale University Gymnasium, led the formation of the Association for the Advancement of Physical Education (AAPE) (Vealey, 2006). In 1894 Edward Scripture, director of the Yale University Psychology Laboratory, conducted one of the first studies looking specifically at athletes in a psychology lab, which provides a clear link between sports and psychology. He used a pendulum chronometer (see figure 1.2) to assess reaction time in fencers and assessed measures of simple reaction time (i.e., reaction time in response to a single stimulus) and discriminant reaction time (i.e., reaction time in response to one of two or more stimuli) in novice and elite fencers. Assisting him in the conductance of this early sport psychology experiment was William Anderson. Clearly, as physical education and psychology were both moving toward the development of a scientific basis for understanding, ideas were cross-pollinated, epitomized by psychologists giving presentations at physical education conferences in 1894 and 1901 (Kornspan, 2007a). In particular, in 1901 Scripture, the psychologist, gave the presentation "The Psychological Aspects of Physical Education" at Anderson's Association for the Advancement of Physical Edu-

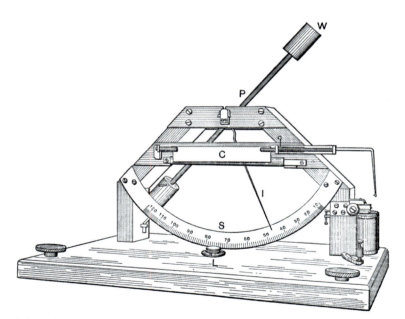

FIGURE 1.2 The pendulum chronoscope was a measurement device used by psychologists and physical educators to measure reaction time in athletes.

Fitz, G. W. (1895). A location reaction apparatus. Psychological Review, 2(1), 37-42. Retrieved from the NIH Digital Collections.

cation conference. This is indicative of the fact that scholars from psychology were beginning to conduct research that was of interest to physical educators and that today would be considered as falling within the realm of motor behavior or sport psychology in the field of kinesiology.

Another important figure in this time period was George Wells Fitz of Harvard, who is credited with establishing the first scientific laboratory focused on physical education in North America (Wiggins, 1984). He conducted experiments similar to the work of Scripture, and in 1895 Fitz published a study on reaction time for stimuli that appeared in unexpected locations. He predicted that the findings would have implications for athletic performance in sports such as fencing and tennis (Fitz, 1895).

Early Examples of Sport and Exercise Psychology

Although the publications by Scripture and Fitz precede that of Norman Triplett, these two studies were purely descriptive in nature, meaning that average performances were simply described. Thus, Triplett is widely credited with conducting the first sport psychology experiment in the United States in 1897. An *experiment* involves the manipulation of a variable (the independent variable) to examine differences in another variable of interest (the dependent variable) between levels of the independent variable. Triplett was an accomplished athlete and an avid sports fan who became interested in the performance of competitive cyclists when cycling alone or with pacesetters (i.e., cyclists who were freshly added on at each lap to help keep the pace). One of the things that he discovered in the official race records from the Racing Board of the League of American Wheelmen was that the cyclists were faster when performing with the pacesetters than when performing alone. As a result of this observation, Triplett hypothesized that people, in a wide variety of settings, would perform better when performing with others than when performing individually. To test this, he built a miniature track in his laboratory that allowed individuals to reel a fishing rod to make a small flag move around the track. The flag was responsive to the speed of reeling so would go faster when reeled faster. He manipulated the independent variable of the presence of co-actors (none present or one present) and measured the speed of performance in each of these conditions.

Triplett asked participants to perform alone and in pairs. His results supported his hypothesis by showing that performance was faster when in pairs than when alone (Triplett, 1898).

This historical event reveals several intriguing things. First, Triplett observed something in a set of data (the race records) and then was curious enough about the phenomenon to develop a hypothesis to explain the observation. He then used an experiment to test his hypothesis in a laboratory setting, which allowed him to control for other important variables that might have explained the results (e.g., drafting, which is following a cyclist closely enough to gain an advantage from the reduced wind resistance). This example demonstrates how observation and curiosity can come together to form the genesis of experimental studies. Second, this finding, which might seem trivial, actually paved the way for an entire body of research focused on social facilitation (i.e., the effects of co-actors on performance).

Want to Race? Social Facilitation in Nonhuman Animals and Insects

Social facilitation is defined as an increased display of effort in response to the real or perceived presence of others. Social facilitation is not unique to humans but rather is ubiquitous across many animal kingdoms. For example, it has been demonstrated in *Blatta orientalis* cockroaches (Zajonc et al., 1969), in the albino rat (Harlow, 1932), and in cows (Ralphs et al., 1994). You may have seen social facilitation in action in your own experiences. Think about a scenario where a lot of people are milling around waiting for booths to open up to make available a limited number of something that is of value (e.g., free pizzas or tickets to a concert). In this situation, people will move quickly and maybe even aggressively to position themselves for success. If they were alone in this scenario, there would be no need to compete.

Other early scientists also had interests that would now be considered examples of exercise psychology. For example, William James alluded to the psychological benefits of physical activity in a presentation at the American Philosophical Association meeting in 1907 when he said, "Ordinarily, we stop

---

experiment—An experiment is a scientific study that involves the manipulation of a variable (the independent variable) to examine differences in another variable of interest (the dependent variable) between levels of the independent variable.

when we meet the first effective layer, so to call it, of fatigue. We have then walked, played, or worked 'enough,' and desist. . . . But if an unusual necessity forces us to press onward, a surprising thing occurs. The fatigue gets worse up to a certain critical point, when gradually or suddenly it passes away, and we are fresher than before" (James, 1907, p. 4). This intriguing comment acknowledges an effect now recognized as the "feel-good phenomenon," which is sometimes experienced after an optimally challenging workout. Clearly, early psychologists were interested in psychological responses to physical activity and presaged the establishment of the subdiscipline of exercise psychology.

At this time, efforts also were ongoing in other countries around the world that would ultimately have an impact on sport and exercise psychology. One example comes from the work of Pierre de Coubertin, who was the founder of the modern Olympic Games in Athens, Greece, in 1896. Throughout his life, de Coubertin was a prolific writer, publishing articles focused on the psychological aspects of sport and, in fact, publishing an article titled "La psychologie du sport" in 1900 (Kornspan, 2007b). Because de Coubertin viewed the Olympics as also having an educational purpose, he regularly organized Olympic Congresses in conjunction with the competitions. In 1897 the Second Olympic Congress included conversations about the psychological benefits and moral effects of sport participation on children (Kornspan, 2007b). Clearly, this work was an important precursor for current studies focused on how sport engagement can benefit children. Indicative of the level of interest in sport and exercise psychology, in 1913 de Coubertin organized the first congress specifically focused on sport psychology, which was held in Lausanne, Switzerland (Kornspan, 2007b).

Following Triplett, the next important figure in the history of sport and exercise psychology in the United States was Coleman R. Griffith. He is important because he was the first person to conduct systematic research in the area of sport psychology over an extended period of time (1925-1938), and he also trained graduate students who made future impacts on physical education (Gould & Pick, 1995). As a result, he has been referred to as the "Father of American sport psychology" (Kroll & Lewis, 1970). Griffith initially focused on studying reaction time data from football players at the University of Illinois. As a result of his work, in 1925 he was named director of the Research in Athletics Laboratory, which consisted of space for both exercise physiology and sport psychology research. Over the course of the next two decades, Griffith conducted research focused on sport performance, coaching, personality, and motor learning. Griffith also published two classic books, *The Psychology of Coaching* (1926) and *The Psychology of Athletics* (1928), that brought this growing knowledge base to the attention of the general public. Interestingly, Griffith was also likely the first academic to be paid significantly for sport psychology consulting, demonstrating how the discipline of sport psychology also could be pursued as a profession. Griffith was hired in 1938 by the Chicago Cubs baseball organization to assess and observe the athletes during spring training and the baseball season so that he could offer them advice to improve performance. Unfortunately, the Cubs' managers were not enamored with the idea of a sport psychologist and reportedly ignored and mocked Griffith as being a "headshrinker" (Green, 2012). Opinions have clearly changed relative to the benefits of working with sport psychologists; most Major League Baseball teams now employ mental skills coaches.

It is fascinating to realize that in addition to work being conducted with sport performance as a focus, the early part of the 20th century also provides evidence of research focused on the mental health benefits of physical activity and exercise. In 1905 the beneficial effects of exercise on depression in individuals with learning disabilities were reported (Franz & Hamilton, 1905), and empirical work on this topic became more apparent in the 1920s and early 1930s (Layman, 1974). In 1955 Emma McCloy Layman published the first text that included a focus on exercise and mental health (Layman, 1955). Despite this early attention to exercise psychology topics, a more committed focus on these topics was not observed for several decades, because the subdiscipline of sport psychology became more firmly established with an initial focus on research questions relevant to sport and performance outcomes.

The Formative Years of Sport Psychology

The period from 1950 to 1980 has been referred to as the formative years in the development of sport psychology because of the proliferation of sport psychology texts for the lay public and because researchers began to pursue the study of sport psychology research questions more systematically. For example, Rainer Martens and Dan Landers explored the influence of social facilitation on sport performance, Albert Carron was interested in team cohesion, Glyn Roberts made contributions to our understanding of achievement motivation and attributions, and Ron Smith and Frank Smoll developed assessments and interventions for youth sport coaches (Landers, 1995). All of these researchers were important to the development of the subdiscipline of sport and exercise psychology in that they trained numerous graduate students who went on to make valuable contributions themselves, were important leaders in the field, and ultimately were inducted into the National Academy of Kinesiology. You might also be interested to know that Rainer Martens founded Human Kinetics, the publisher of this textbook, in 1974.

In the 1960s and 1970s we began to see the proliferation of professional organizations and journals devoted to sport psychology. These organizations were (and still are) important because they provide a venue for scholars to come together to share scientific findings, explore future research questions, debate, and continue their own professional growth. The International Society of Sport Psychology (ISSP) was created in 1965 and hosted the first international congress in Rome that same year. The North American Society for the Psychology of Sport and Physical Activity (NASPSPA) was founded in 1966 and was shortly followed by the establishment of the Canadian Society for Psychomotor Learning and Sport Psychology (CLPLSP) in 1969. These two societies had an enormous impact on the field as noted by Wiggins (1984, p. 21):

> To say that the formation of NASPSPA and CSPLSP has had a significant influence on the development of sport psychology in North America would be an understatement. Since the genesis of these two organizations, there has been a proliferation of systematic research conducted in sport psychology. This research has appeared in the form of articles in sport psychology journals, conference proceedings, book chapters, and books.

As these societies were being created in North America, other countries were also following suit, resulting in the establishment of the British Society for Sports Psychology (1967), the French Society of Sport Psychology (1967), the German Association of Sport Psychology (1969), and the European Federation of Sport Psychology (FEPSAC) (1969). Again, these societies were important to the development of sport and exercise psychology because their annual meetings gave researchers the opportunity to share their findings and ideas with one another. Because attendance is not limited to those from a particular country, these meetings also gave rise to the sharing of ideas across institutions and countries. The establishment of professional organizations was then followed by the founding of scientific journals specifically focused on sport psychology. These journals were equally important for establishing sport psychology as a viable subdiscipline because they provided outlets for the dissemination of research. In 1970 the *International Journal of Sport Psychology* (IJSP) published its first volume. This era also saw the creation of the *Journal of Sport Psychology* (JSP, 1979), the *Sport Psychologist* (1986), and the *Journal of Applied Sport Psychology* (1989). Notably, all of these journals had a focus on sport and performance outcomes and were not, upon inception, focused on the work of exercise psychologists.

Use a search engine to look up one of these professional organizations to learn more about their membership, mission, meeting schedule, and scientific programs.

- North American Society for the Psychology of Sport and Physical Activity (NASPSPA)
- American College of Sports Medicine (ACSM)
- Association for Applied Sport Psychology (AASP)
- International Society of Sport Psychology (ISSP)

It was also during this era that graduate programs with specializations in sport psychology began to appear in the United States mostly under the mentorship of researchers who initially would have categorized themselves as motor learning researchers. In the 1980s exercise psychology began to develop as a distinct aspect of sport psychology. At NASPSPA, members voted to limit the presentations at the conference to those that were focused on research as opposed to those focused on professional issues or consulting practices. As a result, in 1986 the Association for the Advancement of Applied Sport Psychology (now the Association for Applied Sport Psychology, AASP) was formed with a focus on the profession of sport psychology or sport psychology consulting (i.e., working with athletes to improve their sport experience and performance). In 1988 Rejeski and Brawley defined exercise psychology as "the application of the educational, scientific, and professional contributions of psychology to the promotion, explanation, maintenance, and enhancement of behaviors related to physical work capacity" (Rejeski & Brawley, 1988, p. 239). Two important figures in the development of exercise psychology were Bill Morgan and Dan Landers, who took research on exercise psychology to a new level. Morgan was the first president of Division 47 Exercise and Sport Psychology of the APA and trained numerous students who themselves went on to conduct important research in the area of exercise psychology. Landers also trained graduate students who made valuable contributions to exercise psychology, and he is important because he was influential in bringing the technique of meta-analysis to sport psychology with a review of the mental imagery literature (Feltz & Landers, 1983) and then to exercise psychology with a review of the literature on exercise and stress reactivity (Crews & Landers, 1987). He subsequently was coauthor on several meta-analyses, making additional substantive contributions to the field (Etnier et al., 2006; Kubitz et al., 1996; Petruzzello et al., 1991; Rethorst et al., 2009; Wipfli et al., 2008; Rethorst, 2008). As the distinction between exercise psychology and sport psychology became clearer, existing journals gradually changed their names to include the word *exercise*, and new journals that included a focus on exercise psychology began to emerge in the 2000s. This included the *International Journal of Sport and Exercise Psychology* (*IJSEP*) in 2002, the *Journal of Sport and Exercise Psychology* (*JSEP*) in 1988, the *Psychology of Sport and Exercise* (*PSE*) (the official journal of the European Federation of Sport Psychology established in 2000), and *Sport, Exercise, and Performance Psychology* (*SEPP*) (the official journal of Division 47 of APA established in 2011).

Women in Sport Psychology

At the end of the 20th century and the start of the 21st century we also began to see larger numbers of female academics developing in the field of sport and exercise psychology. Krane and Whaley (2010) identify female academics and scientists who made important contributions to sport and exercise psychology (table 1.1). They include Joan Duda, Deb Feltz, Diane Gill, Dorothy Harris, Thelma Horn, Penny McCullagh, Carole Oglesby, Tara Scanlan, Maureen Weiss, and Jean Williams, who presented regularly at NASPSPA, made important contributions to research, and were authors of numerous book chapters and textbooks (Gill, 1986; Harris & Harris, 1984; Weiss, 2004; Williams, 1986) that helped disseminate sport and exercise psychology research. All of these scholars trained their own graduate students, held important positions of leadership as presidents and fellows within professional organizations, and provided substantial professional service to journals as editorial board members and editors. Although I do not take the time to detail their accomplishments and contributions here, the interested reader should see Krane and Whaley (2010) and Vealey (2006) for additional information regarding women in sport and exercise psychology and the history of the field, respectively.

> One of the things about sport and exercise psychology that I hope you will find interesting is that many of the names included in this history are either still active in the field or have recently retired but still attend conferences. If you are interested in a career in sport and exercise psychology, I encourage you to consider attending a local or national conference (e.g., NASPSPA, AASP, ACSM), where students are always welcome, and you might have the chance to interact with some of these individuals who are so important to the field.

Sport and Exercise Psychology Today

As you recall, Rejeski and Brawley defined exercise psychology as "the application of the educational, scientific, and professional contributions of psychology to the promotion, explanation, maintenance, and enhancement of behaviors related to physical

TABLE 1.1   Selected Roles and Accomplishments of Notable Women in Sport and Exercise Psychology

Scientist	President or *editor*	Research focus and important accomplishments
Joan Duda	AASP, *JASP*	Motivational processes and physical activity; published *Advances in Sport and Exercise Psychology Measurement* and *Handbook of Applied Sport Psychology Research*
Deb Feltz	AAKPE, NASPSPA	Self-efficacy and physical activity
Diane Gill	APA Division 47, NASPSPA, *JSEP, Quest, Women in Sport and Physical Activity*	Social psychology and physical activity; published *Psychological Dynamics of Sport* (now *Psychological Dynamics of Sport and Exercise*)
Dorothy Harris	NASPSPA	First American and first woman member of ISSP; first resident sport psychologist at USOC training center
Thelma Horn	*JSEP*	Social influences on youth sport experiences; published *Advances in Sport Psychology*
Penny McCullagh	AASP, AKA, APA Division 47, NASPSPA	Observational learning
Carole Oglesby	AIAW, NAGWS	Published numerous books including *Foundations in Kinesiology; Women, Gender Equity, and Sport; Black Women in Sport*
Tara Scanlan	AASP, NASPSPA	Talent development in sport and other venues
Maureen Weiss	AAKPE, AASP, NASPSPA, *Kinesiology Review, RQES*	Psychological development of children through physical activity and sport; published *Developmental Sport and Exercise Psychology: A Lifespan Perspective*
Jean Williams	AASP	Published *Applied Sport Psychology: Personal Growth to Peak Performance* and *Key Studies in Sport and Exercise Psychology*

Note: AASP = Association for Applied Sport Psychology, *JASP* = Journal of Applied Sport Psychology, AAKPE = American Academy for Kinesiology and Physical Education, NASPSPA = North American Society for the Psychology of Sport and Physical Activity, APA = American Psychological Association, *JSEP* = Journal of Sport and Exercise Psychology, USOC = United States Olympic Center, AKA = American Kinesiology Association, AIAW = Association for Intercollegiate Athletics for Women, NAGWS = National Association for Girls and Women in Sport, *RQES* = Research Quarterly for Exercise and Sport.

Adapted from Krane & Whaley (2010).

work capacity" (Rejeski & Brawley, 1988, p. 239). This definition focuses on the use of psychological theory and techniques intended to affect the behavior of physical activity. This obviously is an important topic of study because increasing physical activity behavior is a public health imperative. However, this definition ignores the aspect of exercise psychology that focuses on the psychological benefits of exercise. These psychological benefits of exercise are important in their own right and also might have implications for the adoption and maintenance of physical activity behaviors. Thus, a complete definition of exercise psychology should include the psychological benefits of exercise. That is, **exercise psychology** is defined as the study of psychological outcomes in response to single and repeated participation in physical activity and of the application of psychological theory to the adoption and maintenance of physically active behaviors. Although both aspects of exercise psychology are of value, the focus in this text is on psychological outcomes in response to physical activity (or exercise). In the following chapters, you will learn about the breadth of psychological benefits that can be observed in response to both single sessions of exercise and regular participation in physical activity.

---

exercise psychology—Exercise psychology can be defined as the study of psychological outcomes in response to single and repeated participation in physical activity and of the application of psychological theory to the adoption and maintenance of physically active behaviors.

Summary

The industrial revolution resulted in a decline in physical activity, which then led to the genesis of physical education because instructors were needed to teach people the skills that would help them be physically active in their leisure pursuits. This then led to the recognition that physical educators needed training to be able to effectively teach children to be physically active. At the same time, psychology was also developing as a profession and a science. As physical educators and psychologists began to interact, they recognized that they had intersecting interests: athletic performance and success. Ultimately, sport and exercise psychology arose from these exchanges. Sport and exercise psychology is a subdiscipline of kinesiology that focuses on the use of psychological tools to promote physical activity and sport performance and the psychological benefits of physical activity. Sport and exercise psychology is typically housed in kinesiology departments along with the associated subdisciplines of physical education, biomechanics, motor behavior, exercise physiology, athletic training, sport history, and sport sociology. Given its dramatic growth over the past several decades, numerous conferences and journals are focused on the scholarship conducted in the area of sport and exercise psychology.

Discussion Questions

1. If you are a regular exerciser, how does exercising make you feel? Do you notice a difference in how you feel during exercise as compared to after exercise? Consider your behaviors during the day. How much of the day do you spend in sedentary behaviors? Could you change these behaviors to be more active?

2. Do you notice any mental health differences between elders in your family who are regular exercisers and those who are not? If so, explain the differences that you see. If not, how about between your family members and neighbors who differ in terms of their physical activity behaviors?

3. What is the name of your department? If it is a kinesiology or similar department, what subdisciplines are housed within your department? If it is not a kinesiology (or similar) department, identify the closest university to you that has a kinesiology (or similar) department and the subdisciplines it houses.

4. What were the driving factors behind the development of physical education in the 1800s? Why did so many sports that are still popular today (e.g., cycling, hockey, badminton, football) develop in the 1800s?

5. People often say that sport and exercise psychology is a new field of study, but this is not true. Give three examples supporting that sport and exercise psychology has been around for a fairly long time.

Answering Research Questions

OBJECTIVES

After studying this chapter, you should be able to do the following:

- Understand the distinction between independent, dependent, and confounding variables and recognize the importance of using valid and reliable tests
- Explain the difference between and contrast the strengths and limitations of cross-sectional, prospective, and experimental studies
- Understand what statistical significance means
- Relate narrative, systematic, and meta-analytic reviews and understand their strengths and limitations
- Articulate the meaning of mediators, mechanisms, and moderators
- Describe common theories, hypotheses, and mechanisms in the exercise psychology literature

KEY TERMS

empirical
independent variable
dependent variable
confounding variables
validity
reliability
internal consistency
statistically significant

correlational study
cross-sectional study
prospective studies
true experimental studies (randomized clinical trials [RCTs])
within-subjects design
between-subjects design
quasi-experimental study

mixed-design study
narrative review
systematic review
meta-analytic review
mediators
mechanisms
moderators

> Sometimes I hear people say that they have "conducted research" when, in fact, they are describing their efforts to do something such as figuring out which is the best television or the most fuel-efficient used car to buy. When the term *research* is used in this way, the speaker typically is trying to convey that they have sought out information from reviews on the Internet, visited stores to speak with salespeople, or talked with their friends to get their opinion. In this case, the speaker is acting as a consumer and is taking in information that was generated by others in some way. When we talk about research in this textbook, we are using the term in a different way. We'll discuss actual specific studies that have been conducted by scientists to answer a research question to make contributions to our understanding. In this case, we'll be talking about research in which a researcher designed a study with the purpose of collecting data to inform the research question by either supporting the researcher's hypothesis or failing to support the hypothesis relative to the research question. The hypothesis is the researcher's expectation of what will happen when the study is conducted.

In this textbook, we will examine the various psychological benefits of exercise. In so doing, we will learn about the psychological outcome itself (what are its causes, why it is important to consider, what are the implications), we will explore potential theories and hypotheses that explain why exercise might benefit this psychological outcome, and we will consider research evidence relative to this relationship. Because we will consider research evidence, it is important to provide foundational information relative to research terms and designs. In addition, we will consider variables that have been proposed to explain how and why exercise benefits psychological outcomes. We will conclude with an introduction to hypotheses and theories that are commonly proposed in the exercise psychology literature to explain the psychological benefits of exercise.

Research Terms

In this chapter, you will learn many terms that are important for establishing a common language relative to research and for understanding more about how to judge the quality of a research study.

> If you were going to do some research to figure out the next used car you would like to purchase, what sources would you use? Would you ask your friends or family for their advice? Would you start picking up auto magazines and using an Internet search engine to learn more about various options? Would you look up safety data provided by the National Highway Traffic Safety Administration? Following these steps would make you a more informed buyer and provide different kinds of information. But if you were interested in conducting your own research to answer a research question, how would you approach that? Imagine that you want to figure out if taking a preworkout supplement improves strength gains over a 1-month period, how would you answer this question? This type of research question could be addressed using an experimental design that would allow you to test hypotheses about cause-and-effect relationships.

Empirical

The word **empirical** describes evidence that is based on verifiable observations. In the scientific literature, empirical articles are those that describe findings based on data collected in a research study. This type of evidence is in contrast to that which is based on logic, opinion, conjecture, or anecdotes. As such, when we consider evidence relative to relationships between exercise and psychological outcomes, we will rely on the empirical evidence or empirical data. In addition to being based on data, another characteristic of empirical articles is that they are typically published in peer-reviewed journals. This means that most empirical studies have been subjected to impartial review by individuals who have expertise in this area and who judge the quality of the work to ensure that limitations of the research are clearly identified when a study is published. When research studies are identified in

---

empirical—Empirical is the word used to describe evidence that is based on verifiable observations.

this textbook, they will be identified by the authors' names when there are one or two authors or by the first author's name and "et al." for works by three or more authors and by the study year. This is how you should refer to studies when you use them to support any answers that you give for this class. That is, to identify a specific study you would use the authors' last names and the publication year; for example, Yerkes and Dodson (1908) or Lesnewich et al. (2019).

Independent and Dependent Variables

An **independent variable** is the variable in a study that we think of as the cause of some effect. The **dependent variable** is the variable in which we expect to see a change in response to the independent variable. In other words, the independent variable is the variable that we would like to manipulate to observe its effect on the outcome variables of interest (i.e., the dependent variables). In the broad exercise psychology literature, physical activity (or exercise) often is considered to be the independent variable (i.e., the variable that is causing a change in some other variable). For example, we might be interested in understanding how participation in physical activity (independent variable) affects perceived stress, cognitive performance, or quality of life (dependent variables). In other cases, physical activity (or exercise) can be considered to be the dependent variable (i.e., the variable that we are trying to affect). For example, we might want to study the effects of a phone-based app on walking behavior by expectant mothers or the use of social support groups to increase physical activity behavior by older adults. In this exercise psychology textbook, our focus is on physical activity (or exercise) as an independent variable, so we will consider evidence from research studies in which physical activity (or physical fitness) is manipulated or measured so that its relationship with other outcome variables (also called *dependent variables*) such as perceived stress, cognition, and quality of life can be ascertained.

Confounding Variables or Covariates

Confounding variables are another group of variables that are relevant to research questions. These are variables that could influence the relationship between the independent variable and the dependent variable but that are not of primary concern to the researcher. For example, imagine that we are interested in the relationship between physical activity behavior and mood. It would be important to think of other variables that could also influence mood and that might or might not be related to physical activity. For instance, income levels might be related to mood because those who are less financially well off might have numerous stressors in their lives that influence both mood and the ability to be physically active. Thus, income levels could be an important potentially confounding variable. As a result, researchers interested in this relationship would want to either measure income so that they could statistically control for it in their analyses (i.e., treat it as a statistical covariate) or attempt to hold income constant by only recruiting individuals of a particular income level. Either of these choices effectively makes income a constant so that it cannot have an effect on the outcome. Because one of the goals of an experimental study is for the sample we recruit to be representative of the population, our decision of how to manage this potential covariate has important implications in terms of generalizability. Generalizability is the extent to which we can generalize the findings of our study back to the population. In this example with income levels, the choice to use income level as a covariate is likely the best because it would allow for the results to be generalized to everyone. By contrast, if we only recruit individuals of a certain income level, that controls for income level, but the results would only generalize to people at that same level of income.

> Now that you've been introduced to the concepts of independent, dependent, and confounding variables, let's go back to the research design question posed at the beginning of the chapter. Imagine that you want to figure out if a preworkout supplement improves strength gain over a 1-month period. In this example, what is the independent variable? What is the dependent variable? What confounding variables would you need to consider?

Psychometric Properties

When we speak of the psychometric properties of a measurement tool, we are talking about two critical aspects of a test: validity and reliability. Meas-

---

independent variable—An independent variable is the variable in a study that we think of as the cause of some effect.

dependent variable—The dependent variable is the variable in which we expect to see a change in response to the independent variable.

confounding variables—Variables that could influence the relationship between the independent variable and the dependent variable but that are not of primary concern to the researcher are called confounding variables.

urement tools must be both valid and reliable for researchers to be able to trust the data they provide.

Validity

Validity describes the extent to which we can be confident the measure actually assesses the desired construct. For example, if I ask participants to wear an accelerometer, can I be confident that the data provided by the accelerometer is an accurate reflection of a person's physical activity behavior? Given this example, several things must be considered when answering this question. First, what types of physical activity behavior do I hope to capture? Accelerometers cannot be worn in swimming pools, are not very accurate for activities such as cycling and skateboarding, and might not be allowed to be worn in competitive sports. Therefore, I have to figure out a way to account for those shortcomings. If I am using the accelerometer to measure walking behavior by older adults, then cycling and skateboarding are not a concern, and the accelerometer is likely to provide a valid measurement. But if I am interested in the physical activity behavior of teenagers, the inability to measure cycling, skateboarding, and physical activity during sporting events might be problematic such that this particular tool would not be valid.

Reliability

Reliability expresses the consistency of the measurement. A reliable measure will provide the same data when assessed across time and when taken by different experimenters. If I have a reliable measure, it will provide me with the same data today as it does tomorrow (assuming that constructs are stable and that no intervention has occurred). Blood pressure measurement is an example of a measurement that can have reliability challenges. If two different experimenters assess the same person's blood pressure or if blood pressure is assessed using different automated systems, slightly different measurements are likely to be reported. If this is the case, typically a scientist might require that the blood pressure measurements be averaged for reporting in the data or that additional measurements be taken until two measurements are obtained that are within some acceptable level of accuracy.

As an example of both validity and reliability, if I were interested in measuring height, most people would agree that a tape measure would be considered a valid measurement tool. But how reliably can the measurement be taken? If an experimenter who is 5'1" tall and an experimenter who is 6'2" tall both use a tape measure to assess the height of a 5'11" participant who is standing with their back to the wall, which experimenter do you think will be more accurate? If their measurements differ, the method is clearly not reliable. But one might be able to improve the measurement process to ensure better accuracy (and hence reliability). One solution is simply to provide a stool for the 5'1" person to stand on so that they are at eye level with the height they are measuring. Another option is to replace the tape measure with a stadiometer (i.e., the tool used at a doctor's office where they adjust the bar to your head height and read your height on the scale). This would be more reliable than a tape measure irrespective of the height of the experimenter. In other words, if these same two experimenters use the stadiometer, their measurements will be more reliable, and if the same participant is measured on two different days of the same week, the measurement should still be reliable.

> Now that you've learned about validity and reliability, let's consider again a research study designed to test if a preworkout supplement helps with strength gain over a 1-month period. In this example, how would you measure strength gain? Would you ask the participant for their perception? Would you try to measure strength? If you were going to measure strength, how would you do this? For which muscle groups?

Internal Consistency

Another psychometric property to consider relative to reliability is internal consistency. Internal consistency is relevant when considering surveys (questionnaires) or interviews. This describes the extent to which the items measure the same variable, which then has implications for the appropriateness of calculating a total score. For example, if I administered a 20-item scale designed to assess self-esteem, the responses to the 20 items should be relatively consistent within a person. This would then support my ability to sum the responses to provide a total self-esteem score. In cases where surveys or interviews are purposefully designed to assess constructs that are not unidimensional, the statistical tool of factor analysis can be used to identify the questions

---

validity—Validity describes the extent to which we can be confident the measure is actually assessing the desired construct.
reliability—The consistency of the measurement is known as reliability.
internal consistency—Internal consistency is a specific type of reliability that describes the extent to which the items in a survey (questionnaire) or interview measure the same variable.

that are tapping into the same subdomain, and then the question of internal consistency would be levied at the level of the subscale. In other words, if the 20-item self-esteem scale were designed to assess self-esteem for physical activity and self-esteem for academics, the scale would include questions specific to each. The internal consistency then would be expected to be observed for those questions measuring physical activity self-esteem as distinct from those measuring academic self-esteem. This would mean that we could sum the scores for the questions for each subscale to present a score for each.

Statistical Significance

Another concept that is important for you to be familiar with is statistical significance. If a finding is **statistically significant**, this tells us that the finding is not likely to be due to chance. When scientists conduct studies, they should have a hypothesis that is guiding their work. This hypothesis is the expected outcome of their study. In the exercise psychology literature, the expected outcome is typically that exercise will benefit the psychological construct being explored. After researchers conduct their study and collect their data, they then use statistical tests to determine if any observed difference or change is statistically significant. If a finding is statistically significant, that means that the finding is not likely (the probability is less than 5%) to have occurred due to mere chance. For a scientific study to advance understanding, the data from the study must lead to the researcher being able to draw a conclusion of statistical significance indicating that the effect of exercise on the psychological construct is not a chance finding, but rather is likely to represent the true nature of the relationship. In other words, when their hypothesis is supported, they should be able to say, for example, that the exercise group had significantly more positive mood states than did the control group, and they would expect that this should be true if the experiment were replicated or simply when this same treatment is applied in a real-world setting.

It is important to understand that the results of any individual study are typically insufficient to wholeheartedly accept the finding as true. This is because the findings of any individual study are constrained by the specific design that is used, any threats to the validity of the study, the strength of the measurement tools, and the sample size of the study. In some cases, the anticipated effects might be observed, but the small sample size might result in the finding *not* being deemed statistically significant. This is an ongoing challenge in exercise psychology because the conductance of studies with large sample sizes is difficult. As such, many studies have sample sizes that are too small (these studies are called *underpowered*), and scientists are left unsure if observed differences between the treatment and control groups are likely to be due to chance or not. This limitation of individual studies is a primary reason why meta-analytic reviews (to be described later in this chapter) are important to our understanding of relationships.

Research Designs

A multitude of experimental designs are used in research studies. The ones that are most commonly used in the exercise psychology literature include correlational studies, cross-sectional studies, prospective studies, and true experimental studies (also called *randomized clinical trials*).

Correlational Studies

A **correlational study** is one in which measurements on the independent and dependent variables are taken at a single point in time from a single sample of participants. For example, researchers might measure physical activity levels and depression in a large group of participants at a single point in time. They would then examine the relationship between physical activity and depression. If they find that those who are more active report less depression, they have established a negative correlation between the two variables. The correlation is negative because as a person's score on one variable goes up (physical activity), their score on the other variable goes down (depression). Other relationships we might expect to observe could be positively correlated. For example, we would expect that people who are more physically active will report a better quality of life. Thus, we expect physical activity to be positively correlated with quality of life.

Cross-Sectional Studies

A **cross-sectional study** is one in which measurements are taken at a single point in time and compared between two or more samples distinguished by levels of the independent variable. This

---

statistically significant—If a finding is judged to be statistically significant, that means it is not likely to be due to chance.
correlational study—A correlational study is one in which measurements on the independent and dependent variables are taken at a single point in time from a single sample of participants.
cross-sectional study—A cross-sectional study is based on measurements that are taken at a single point in time and compared between two or more samples distinguished by levels of the independent variable.

is sometimes referred to as a *snapshot*. For example, researchers might take a snapshot of physical activity levels and depression in a large group of participants at a single point in time, then categorize participants into those who meet and those who do not meet physical activity guidelines. They would compare depression levels between the two groups with an expectation that individuals who are more physically active will report less depression.

Correlational and cross-sectional studies are valuable for the initial identification of relationships between variables because they are relatively easy to conduct and can help elucidate potential relationships. However, they are limited by the very fact that they are correlational in nature. This means that we can never determine the order of cause and effect from a correlational or a cross-sectional study. For example, it is just as likely that physical activity causes reductions in depression as it is that being depressed reduces a person's ability to be physically active. Neither correlational nor cross-sectional data allow us to determine which comes first. Similarly, it is equally plausible that increased physical activity improves quality of life as it is that people with a higher quality of life are more able to be physically active. Again, there is a chicken-and-egg problem in that this design does not allow us to determine which (if either) variable is causing the change in the other. This is an important distinction to keep in mind as we consider research in exercise psychology.

Prospective Studies

In prospective studies, participants are assessed on the independent and dependent variables at baseline and then are followed over time so that changes in the dependent variable can be observed in association with changes in the independent variable. For example, I might assess physical activity levels and cognitive performance at baseline. After ensuring that everyone in the sample is cognitively normal and thus has essentially the same level of cognitive performance at baseline, I could wait several years and then ask those same participants to be tested again. At that point, I'd look to see if changes in physical activity from baseline were predictive of changes in cognitive performance over the same time frame. Although these types of studies still do not allow for conclusions about cause and effect, they are slightly better than cross-sectional studies because I have ensured that cognitive performance was the same at baseline. That way, it is not likely that differences in cognitive performance were the impetus behind differences in physical activity. Rather, the more likely conclusion is that the changes in physical activity contributed to the changes in cognitive performance.

True Experimental Studies

True experimental studies, also referred to as randomized clinical trials (RCTs), are the gold standard in research. In these studies, participants are randomly assigned into groups, the independent variable is manipulated for one or more of the groups, the dependent variable is measured, and potential confounding variables are controlled. For example, first the researcher recruits participants from the population of interest (e.g., a university campus, a senior center, the general population). Next, the dependent variable is measured in participants at the start of the study (often called the *pretest* or *baseline measurement*). Participants are then randomly assigned to either a treatment group (e.g., an exercise group that will exercise for 1 hour per day, at moderate intensity, 3 days per week for 6 months) or a control group (e.g., a group that is asked not to exercise for 6 months). For that 6-month period, participants are asked not to make any other substantive changes to their lives (e.g., not to start a diet, change their medications, or change their smoking status). This is done because any of these variables might influence the dependent variable, which would make it harder to identify any potential benefits of exercise. At the conclusion of the treatment (i.e., at the end of 6 months), the dependent variable is measured in both groups again. If the researchers find improvements in the dependent variable in the exercise group that are not observed in the control group, they can then conclude that exercise *caused* those changes. This is the most powerful research design because of the ability to determine causation.

Participant Assignment to Groups

In conducting empirical studies, researchers must consider whether they want all participants within

---

prospective studies—When participants are assessed on the independent and dependent variables at baseline and then are followed over time so that changes in the dependent variable can be observed in association with changes in the independent variable, this is called a prospective study.

true experimental studies (randomized clinical trials [RCTs])—The gold standard in research is a true experimental study also known as an RCT. In an RCT, participants are randomly assigned into groups, the independent variable is manipulated for one or more of the groups, the dependent variable is measured, and potential confounding variables are controlled.

the study to experience all of the levels of the independent variable (a within-subjects design) or they want to assign participants to a level of the independent variable (a between-subjects design) so that each participant only experiences one level of the independent variable. These designs have pros and cons that are important to consider.

Within-Subjects Design

In a within-subjects design, all participants are exposed to all possible levels of the treatment (including the control condition). The use of a within-subjects design has numerous advantages. The most important is that because all participants experience all levels of the independent variable, any differences between individuals are effectively controlled for. For example, if I used a within-subjects design to explore the effects of a single session of exercise on memory but I had a wide range of memory abilities among my participants, my statistical analyses would focus on changes within an individual rather than comparing differences between different individuals. In other words, imagine that I have a sample of 20 people and within this sample are 4 people who are fantastic at memory tasks. If I randomly assign them to an exercise group and a control group and 3 of the 4 end up in the control group (or even worse, all 4), I might not observe any benefits due to exercise because the control group would perform so well. By using a within-subjects design, all 20 participants would perform the control condition and the exercise condition, and then I'd examine the memory improvement for individuals after exercise compared to their own performance in the control condition.

One of the biggest benefits of using a within-subjects design is that it dramatically increases the likelihood of reporting statistically significant results if, in fact, the researcher is testing a real difference (this is referred to as *statistical power*). Within-subjects designs have relatively high levels of statistical power because individual differences are not relevant to the analyses for the reasons just described. Because of the high statistical power, this then gives the researcher the ability to use a smaller sample size and still achieve statistical significance. Hence, for research conducted with groups that might be hard to recruit (e.g., individuals with specific health conditions, older adults), the use of a within-subjects design might be a good choice.

One potential shortcoming of a within-subjects design is that the researcher must consider the possibility of order effects that could have an impact on the findings due to variables such as fatigue, learning, and maturation. For example, if you were interested in comparing the effects of a high-intensity interval exercise (HIIE) session to those of a control condition, the use of a within-subjects design would require careful consideration because the performance of the HIIE is expected to cause fatigue that might be relatively long-lasting. One solution is to space the testing sessions far enough apart to ensure this doesn't happen—that is, have participants perform both conditions but with the testing days separated by several days of rest. Another consideration is that the memory task could be influenced by learning. Because of this, it is important to ensure that all participants do not perform the two conditions in the same order. In other words, if you always have the HIIE condition first but participants improve on the task due to learning, they might actually do better on the control day because of the learning. Conversely, if they always do the control condition first followed by the HIIE condition, improvements due to learning might exaggerate the effects that are due to the HIIE itself. So if participants do HIIE on one day and then a no-exercise control on another day, you would want to ensure that half of the participants did HIIE first followed by control while the other half did control first followed by HIIE. This is called a *counter-balanced design* because the order of presentation of the experimental conditions is presented in a balanced way across participants. And, as previously mentioned, you would want to include several days of rest between sessions to eradicate fatigue effects. In sum, when using a within-subjects design, it's important to consider and control for these types of effects.

Between-Subjects Design

In a between-subjects design, participants are assigned to groups that experience different levels of the treatment. If they are assigned randomly, then the study meets one of the criteria necessary to be deemed an RCT. If they are not assigned randomly to treatment conditions, for instance in a case where there are preexisting groups that are assigned to treat-

---

within-subjects design—If all participants are exposed to all possible levels of the treatment (including the control condition), this is called a within-subjects design.

between-subjects design—If all participants are assigned (usually randomly) to groups that experience different levels of the treatment, this is called a between-subjects design.

ment conditions, then this would be called a *quasi-experimental study*. In the example described earlier, a sample of 20 participants is randomly assigned so that 10 participants experience the control condition and 10 experience the treatment condition. Typically, we can assume that random assignment will result in the two groups being equivalent, but it can be a good idea when using this design to assess the groups to ensure their equivalence before administering a treatment. For example, if you learned that the control group had better memory than the exercise group before the study even started, you might then use memory performance as a covariate to statistically control for the difference. Another choice would be to randomly assign participants but to first match them by their baseline memory performance. Using the previous example, you might identify those four participants with the exceptionally high memory scores, match them for their high scores, and then randomly assign pairs to ensure that two participants are assigned to each of the groups.

Mixed Design

A *mixed-design* study combines a within-subjects design with a between-subjects design. The description of the RCT provided earlier is a mixed design because participants were randomly assigned to conditions (between-subjects variable) and the dependent variable was measured at pretest and posttest (within-subjects variable). So, a study is a mixed-design study when participants are randomly assigned to treatment conditions (the between-subjects variable) and measurements are taken at several different time points like pretest, midtest, and posttest (the within-subjects variable). This design allows the researcher to control for individual differences both by random assignment and by comparing each participant to themselves. This is a very statistically powerful experimental design that is common in RCTs.

> Let's pick up again with a study designed to see if a preworkout supplement helps with strength gain over a 1-month period. How might we design a study to test this? Would we randomly assign participants to take the supplement or not? If they didn't take the supplement, would they take a placebo? How often would they take the supplement (or the placebo)? When would we measure strength? At the beginning and end of the month or only at the end of the month? All of these considerations would be important for providing the best test of the research question.

Methods of Reviews of Empirical Studies

Now that you have an understanding of how individual research studies are conducted, let's turn our attention to the various types of reviews that are published in the scientific literature. Once several empirical studies have been conducted to answer a particular research question, it often becomes valuable to provide a review of this evidence to summarize the results. The summarizing of results to draw firm conclusions can be challenging when results are not consistent. Because the benefits for exercise on psychological outcomes tend to be small to moderate in size, reviews are helpful in terms of understanding the overall research findings relative to a particular research question. The three most common types of reviews are narrative reviews, systematic reviews, and meta-analytic reviews.

Narrative Review

A *narrative review* of the literature is simply a written description of a body of literature typically provided by an expert in this area. In a narrative review, authors are likely to share the studies they believe are most important in offering insights into the topic. Typically, in these types of reviews, authors discuss theories and mechanisms, identify shortcomings with the literature, and offer directions for future research. In fact, the chapters in this book are essentially narrative reviews because they present a description of specific studies deemed relevant to a topic area and then conclude with a summary and implications. Narrative reviews have been criticized for the following reasons:

1. They typically involve a narrow literature search (i.e., only a small subset of existing studies are included).
2. The small subset of studies means that large amounts of data might be overlooked or ignored.

---

quasi-experimental study—A quasi-experimental study is one in which participants are not assigned randomly to treatment conditions but instead preexisting groups are assigned to treatment conditions.

mixed-design study—A mixed-design study combines a within-subjects design with a between-subjects design; an example is when participants are randomly assigned to treatment conditions (the between-subjects variable) and measurements are taken at three different time points like pretest, midtest, and posttest (the within-subjects variable).

narrative review—A narrative review of a body of literature is one that relies on a written description of selected studies and is typically provided by an expert in this area for research.

3. Reviewers by necessity weight their conclusions with regard to what they review (instead of the entire body of existing literature).
4. Reviewers often use a vote count method (i.e., how many studies reported statistically significant results as compared to how many failed to report significance), and they therefore overlook low statistical power as a possible explanation for nonsignificant findings.
5. Authors often make a lot of methodological commentary by, for example, concluding that the findings are mixed due to the inclusion of low-quality studies using a variety of exercise interventions.

Despite their shortcomings, narrative reviews that are well done have the potential to provide a nice overview of a research area that can give the reader an initial idea of what the research shows.

Systematic Review

A **systematic review** is one in which the authors provide a clear explanation of their search strategy for empirical articles and attempt to include all articles that meet their criteria. The authors then describe the body of research in terms of variables that are relevant to the research question. These reviews are an improvement over a narrative review because they include all studies that meet the inclusion criteria. However, when the authors merely list numbers of studies fitting certain criteria (e.g., 20 studies were conducted using all female samples, 15 studies were conducted using all male samples, 30 studies included samples with both sexes), they do not contribute to our understanding of the evidence. When the authors provide a thoughtful synthesis and integration of the findings including insights into the cumulative results across studies, these types of reviews can then be stronger than narrative reviews in terms of their contribution to the literature because of their inclusion of all of the evidence relative to the research question.

Meta-Analytic Review

A **meta-analytic review** is a statistical summary of the data from a group of individual studies (also called *empirical studies*). As previously mentioned, individual studies often have a relatively small number of participants, which results in them being statistically underpowered to test their hypotheses. The result is that the authors of these individual studies sometimes conclude, for example, that exercise did not have a beneficial effect on the outcome variable. There are two solutions to this problem. One is to conduct studies with larger sample sizes so that the expected positive effects of exercise will be deemed statistically significant if they are, in fact, observed. The second is to use meta-analysis to statistically summarize the results of multiple studies. This increases the statistical power because the authors are effectively combining the sample sizes from all of the studies (i.e., instead of having a single study with $n = 80$, there are five studies with n's = 80, 120, 90, 60, and 40 for a total of $n = 390$).

Meta-analyses are possible because the finding from each study can be converted to a standard metric called *effect size*. An effect size (ES) tells us how different the treatment and control groups (or the pretests and posttests) are from one another relative to the amount of variability observed in the scores. Effect sizes are interpreted as small (ES = 0.20-0.50), moderate (ES = 0.50-0.80), and large (ES >0.80) with the descriptors providing an apt illustration of the relative magnitude of the effect. In this textbook, positive effect sizes always indicate a benefit of exercise. This will be true for all topics in this textbook, so, for example, positive effect sizes will indicate a benefit of exercise whether we are talking about depression (where a decrease would be beneficial) or about cognitive performance (where an increase would be beneficial). Importantly, the magnitude of the effect does not tell us anything about the importance or clinical significance of the effect. That requires one to understand how much of a change is likely to make a meaningful difference or how much of a change is typical in response to other types of treatments.

Let me provide a sport example, which is perhaps easiest to understand. Imagine that we conduct a meta-analytic review of the literature on mental imagery and basketball performance, and we find that mental imagery improves basketball free-throw shooting performance with an ES of 1.00. If we know that the average point difference in NBA basketball games is typically 3 points, the question is whether

---

systematic review—A systematic review is one in which the authors provide a clear explanation of their search strategy for empirical studies, attempt to include all articles that meet their criteria, and then provide descriptive information about the studies.

meta-analytic review—A meta-analytic review (also called a meta-analysis) is one in which the authors provide a clear explanation of their search strategy for empirical studies, attempt to include all articles that meet their criteria, and then provide a statistical summary of the data from these studies.

this improvement in free-throw shooting performance in response to mental imagery is important. Importance would likely be judged by understanding whether or not this improvement would change a large number of final outcomes of games. If we know that the average free-throw shooting percentage for NBA basketball players is 77.8%, and we assume a hypothetical standard deviation of 10%, this would mean that an ES of 1.00 equates to raising a team's (or player's) free-throw shooting percentage by 10% (because an ES of 1.00 equates to improvement of a full standard deviation). Given that NBA teams average between 17 and 26 free-throw attempts per game, an increase of 10% would move teams from scoring 77.8% of their attempts to 87.8% of their attempts, which would increase their score by 1.7-2.6 points depending upon how many free throws they took during the game. This might not matter in some games but could obviously make a difference in close competitions. So, as an example, if we look at the 1,230 games played in the NBA in 2022-2023, 123 were decided by 1-2 points. So, in this case, the large ES of 1.0 also would be a clinically meaningful effect because it could result in a real difference in a relatively large number of sport outcomes.

Another benefit of meta-analyses is that they allow for an examination of moderator variables. Sticking with the previous example, if studies have been conducted separately for the NBA and the WNBA, then we could compare the effects of mental imagery for women and men through meta-analytic techniques. This might show us that the effects are not significantly different, with both NBA players (ES = 1.02) and WNBA players (ES = 0.98) showing a large effect in response to mental imagery. As we consider the potential psychological benefits of exercise, meta-analytic reviews will be considered to provide a sense of the overall effect size and of the influence of any potential moderators.

Some criticisms have been raised relative to meta-analyses. Some have suggested the criticism of "garbage-in, garbage-out," which is to say that if the studies included in a meta-analytic review are of low quality, the results of the meta-analysis will also be of low quality. This criticism can be fairly levied against all reviews, but it is possible with meta-analyses to code for study quality so that effect sizes can be examined relative to this important variable and implications can be considered. Another criticism is the apples-and-oranges concern, which is that one should not combine effect sizes from studies that are very different. This is also a fair criticism, but again, it can be dealt with through steps taken in the review. For instance, it would not make sense to combine effect sizes for animal studies with those from human studies. However, studies can be meta-analytically reviewed separately for these two paradigms. It also might not make sense to combine findings from studies using aerobic exercise with studies using resistance training, but the impact of this variable on the effect sizes can be tested by coding and testing the moderator variable of exercise mode. Overall, when well done, meta-analytic reviews are the strongest type of review of the literature, particularly when the authors demonstrate an ability to interpret their findings relative to proposed theories, hypotheses, and mechanisms. As such, in this textbook, meta-analyses will be presented to summarize the body of evidence for each topic.

Summary on Reviews

Reviews of the scientific literature can be extremely valuable because they provide an overview of the current state of the knowledge. Narrative reviews tend to cover a smaller body of literature and provide the authors' subjective interpretation of the overall state of the evidence. When these are done well, the authors provide a good sense of the strengths and limitations of the literature. Systematic and meta-analytic reviews include all of the literature that meets inclusion criteria, which gives a broader sense of the evidence. When systematic reviews are done well, the authors demonstrate their ability to integrate and synthesize the evidence to provide a compelling conclusion regarding what the evidence shows. When meta-analytic reviews are done well, an overall measure of ES is provided and relevant moderator variables are explored to understand the variables that impact the size of the effect. Importantly, some systematic and meta-analytic reviews focus on topic areas that are so new that there is no existing research or use inclusion criteria that are so narrow that they end up including no studies in their review (Yaffe et al., 2012). These empty reviews make no contribution to the literature other than perhaps to draw attention to an area in need of research.

Mediators, Mechanisms, and Moderators

Now that we have learned about the basics of research design and the types of reviews that you might read in the literature, let's discuss some more sophisticated considerations such as the variables that might explain the effects of the independent variables (physical activity or exercise) on psychological outcomes. These variables are called *mediators* or *mechanisms* and are important for understanding how and why exercise has benefits for psychological outcomes. We will also consider variables that might influence the nature of the relationship between exercise and a psychological outcome. These variables are called *moderators*.

Mediators

Psychological variables that explain a relationship between an independent variable (or a predictor variable) and a dependent variable (also called a *criterion variable*) are called mediators. Remember that the independent variable is the one we see as a cause of change, the dependent variable is the variable we expect to change, and confounding variables are those that might influence this relationship but aren't of primary interest. Mediators are a group of variables that are of interest because they explain how the independent variable influences the dependent variable. Mediators are psychological constructs that cannot be directly measured but rather rely on a participant's self-report.

Mechanisms

Mechanisms are another group of variables that explain a relationship between an independent variable and a dependent variable. Mechanisms are biological or physiological variables that can often (but not always) be directly measured and are not reliant on self-report. An example of a mechanism we can directly measure is muscular strength because we can measure how much weight a person can lift at a maximal level of exertion. An example of a mechanism we cannot directly measure is cerebral blood flow because we do not currently have assessment techniques that allow us to safely assess blood flow directly within the brains of humans.

Understanding the Difference Between Mediators and Mechanisms

To provide an example of the distinction between mediators and mechanisms, let's consider the positive effects of physical activity on cognitive performance. These effects might occur because of the beneficial effects of exercise on self-efficacy (our confidence in our ability to perform a specific task), and they might also be a result of the effects on brain-derived neurotrophic factor (a chemical produced in the brain that is thought to improve brain health). In this example, self-efficacy would be viewed as a mediator, and brain-derived neurotrophic factor (BDNF) would be considered a mechanism. This is because self-esteem is not directly measurable (i.e., it can only be indirectly assessed through self-report), while BDNF can be assayed using standardized assessment techniques performed on blood samples.

When thinking about how we might explain the effects of exercise on psychological outcomes, it is important to recognize that we might have a single mediator or mechanism, multiple mediators or mechanisms, or a model that includes a chain of mediators or mechanisms. As an example of multiple mediators or mechanisms, it is possible that the benefits of exercise for body image are due to improvements in aerobic fitness (a mechanism) and increases in self-efficacy for exercise and perceived fitness (mediators). An example of a chain of mechanisms is if physical activity leads to reductions in a person's response to stressors (stress reactivity), which results in less circulating cortisol, which then mitigates the detrimental effects of cortisol on cerebral structure, which ultimately benefits cognitive performance. In this example, a chain of mechanisms (i.e., stress reactivity, cortisol, cerebral structure) explains how exercise results in a culminating effect on the outcome of interest (cognitive performance) (see figure 2.1).

FIGURE 2.1 A chain of mechanisms might explain the link between physical activity and cognitive performance.

---

mediators—Psychological variables that explain a relationship between an independent variable (or a predictor variable) and a dependent variable (also called a *criterion variable*) and that cannot be directly measured are called mediators.

mechanisms—Biological or physiological variables that explain a relationship between an independent variable and a dependent variable and that often can be directly measured are referred to as mechanisms.

The identification of mediators and mechanisms is extremely important from the standpoint of simply understanding how an independent variable has its effects. But it is also important because of the insights they can provide with respect to specific interventions. That is, if we know that a certain variable is a mediator or a mechanism for the beneficial effects of the independent variable on the dependent variable, then we can focus on designing our intervention to maximally affect that particular variable. Using the example from Understanding the Difference Between Mediators and Mechanisms, if self-efficacy is known to be a mediator for the effects of exercise on cognitive performance, we would design our exercise intervention to maximally improve self-efficacy with the expectation that this would yield the largest benefit for cognition. The implication of this knowledge is that we would need to look at the existing research evidence to understand the aspects of an exercise intervention that maximally increase self-efficacy. This might mean that we start at a very low intensity level and a short duration to ensure success and mastery, and that we provide positive feedback for accomplishing the exercise session. By taking these steps, we imagine that we would maximally benefit self-efficacy to maximally benefit cognition.

In addition, knowledge about mediators and mechanisms might suggest additional dimensions for our interventions that could result in greater change in the variables. To offer a slightly different example, if we know that sleep quality is the mediator between exercise and a decrease in depression and if we had a pill that people could take to increase their sleep quality independently from exercise, we might design an intervention that combined the two treatments. The goal would be to maximally benefit sleep quality because of its ultimate effect on depression. Understanding of mediators and mechanisms can be important from a purely scientific standpoint, but it might also guide our prescription of exercise and the use of other therapies simultaneously.

Moderators

A variable that affects the nature of the relationship between the independent variable and the dependent variable is called a **moderator**. Moderators affect either the direction or the magnitude of the relationship between the independent variable and the dependent variable. It is easier to visualize moderators that are categorical (e.g., biological sex) rather than those that are continuous (e.g., age or weight). For example, if we are interested in the effects of exercise on body image, we might predict that the nature of the relationship would be more positive for women than for men (figure 2.2). In other words, we'd expect the magnitude of the relationship to differ between women and men. In this case, if our results supported our hypothesis, we would describe biological sex as a moderator of the relationship because it influences the magnitude of the relationship between the independent variable (exercise) and the dependent variable (body image).

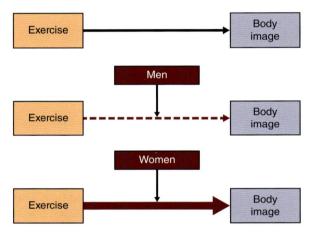

FIGURE 2.2 Visual depiction of biological sex as a moderator of the relationship between exercise and body image. The dashed line demonstrates a small positive relationship, and the solid line demonstrates a strong positive relationship.

The identification of moderators is also important for both scientific and practical reasons. Scientifically, understanding moderators might actually give us hints as to what potential mechanisms might be. For example, if we find larger benefits for the effects of exercise on stress in postmenopausal women than in normally menstruating women, we might guess that estrogen plays some kind of a role in the relationship. From a practical standpoint, moderators might also give us insights in terms of targeted interventions. Sticking with the same example, if exercise is found to be more beneficial for postmenopausal women, we could target our exercise interventions to this group while also working to discover alternative or modified interventions that could provide more benefits in terms of reducing depression in premenopausal women.

---

moderator—Variables that affect the nature of the relationship between the independent variable and the dependent variable are known as moderators.

Moderated Mediation

In recent research, scientists have begun to explore moderated mediation models to understand both the variables that explain and the variables that modify the relationship between the independent variable and the dependent variable. This is more common in studies focused on behavioral change (e.g., Baranowski et al., 1998; Lee, 2020; Zhu et al., 2017), but it has been used in a few studies focused on psychological outcomes (e.g., Sylvester et al., 2018). As an example of a study testing a moderated mediation model, Zhu and colleagues (2017) conducted a secondary data analysis using data previously collected in a longitudinal study exploring the effects of an online exercise intervention on physical activity behavior. In the original study, community-dwelling older adults were randomly assigned to a control (no intervention), the Bone Power program, or the Bone Power program plus a 10-month booster program. The Bone Power program was a 2-month online exercise intervention that consisted of 11 modules including discussion boards and video libraries. The booster program was a biweekly health newsletter and follow-ups. Results presented in the initial study indicated that Bone Power increased self-efficacy, outcome expectations, and physical activity behavior (Nahm et al., 2015), and this effect was maintained at 12 months in the booster group. The purpose of the moderated mediation analysis was to see if this observed effect was mediated by changes in self-efficacy and if this was then further moderated by age group (because of age group's anticipated effect on Internet use). Figure 2.3 provides a simplified conceptual depiction of the model being tested. In this figure, the authors illustrate that they were interested in testing the effects of the intervention on the changes in self-efficacy over time and whether this explained the effects on changes in exercise over time. To test moderation, they then calculated a term to represent the interaction between the exercise intervention and age and tested its effects on the previously described relationships.

Limitations in the Study of Mediators and Mechanisms in Exercise Psychology Research

One of the challenges in the exercise psychology literature is that researchers are still in the early stages in terms of designing studies to appropriately test mediators and mechanisms and then using the requisite statistical tests to assess these variables as providing a causal explanation of changes in the dependent variable. An example of this shortcoming is that aerobic fitness is often proposed as a potential mechanism explaining the effects of exercise on psychological outcomes. The idea is that the changes in cardiorespiratory fitness are responsible for the improvements in the psychological outcome. To test this hypothesis, researchers might randomly assign participants to an exercise intervention or a control condition and then measure the psychological outcome and aerobic fitness at the pretest and the posttest. This has been done in the literature, but often the researchers don't then use the appropriate statistical tools to test the proposed mechanism to see if it actually explains changes in the dependent variable. Often, they will report improvements in both the psychological outcome and aerobic fitness for the exercise group but not for the control group. They will use this as a reason to suggest that the changes in fitness caused the changes in the psychological outcome. You might see the shortcoming of this reasoning. In this example, because they haven't actually statistically tested the role of aerobic fitness in predicting the relationship between

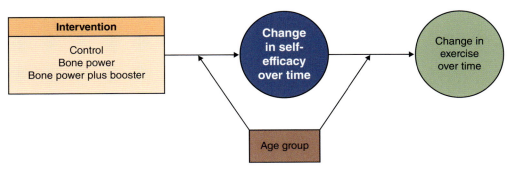

FIGURE 2.3 Visual depiction of mediator and moderator tested in Zhu and colleagues (2017).
Adapted from Zhu et al. (2017).

the intervention and the psychological outcome, then all that has been shown is that both variables are responsive to exercise (see figure 2.4a). In this example, no evidence supports aerobic fitness as the explanation for observed changes. This is a sophisticated point, but it will be important as we move forward in exploring the exercise psychology literature. To actually test fitness as a mechanism (see figure 2.4b), techniques need to be used to test the path from exercise to fitness, from fitness to the psychological outcome, and from exercise to the psychological outcome controlling for the effects of fitness on the psychological outcome. When these statistical steps are taken, we can put more faith in conclusions about the role of the proposed mechanisms.

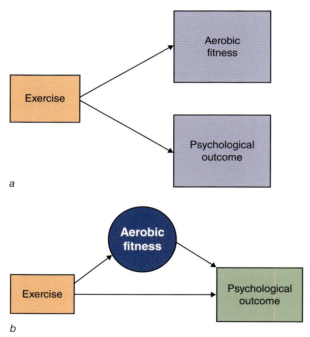

FIGURE 2.4 (a) Depiction of a study testing the effects of exercise on fitness and on a psychological outcome. (b) Depiction of a study testing fitness as a mechanism of the relationship between exercise and a psychological outcome.

Mechanisms, Mediators, Theories, and Hypotheses in the Exercise Psychology Literature

Now that you can distinguish between independent variables, mediators, mechanisms, moderators, confounding variables, and dependent variables, I will introduce some common mediators and mechanisms in the exercise psychology literature. After that, we'll turn our attention to some of the mechanisms, hypotheses, and theories that are commonly considered in exercise psychology. Typically, the studies we review have tested the effects of physical activity or exercise (the independent variable) on psychological outcomes (the dependent variable) and have proposed how these effects are realized (the mediators or mechanisms) and in what groups they are most evident (moderators).

Psychological Mediators

As we begin to learn about the effects of exercise on various psychological outcomes, you might find it surprising to know that some of these effects might be mediated by other psychological constructs that we will also learn about in this textbook. The example given previously with sleep quality as a potential mediator of the effects of exercise on depression illustrates this because both depression and sleep quality are outcomes we will discuss. This is both interesting and challenging as we recognize that we might be interested in variables that could be viewed as the outcome of interest or as a mediator of some other outcome of interest or that the two might have a reciprocal relationship (depending on the research question). This makes sense conceptually. For example, if we find that exercise has benefits for depression, it is possible that those effects might be mediated by the benefits of exercise on sleep. Intriguingly, depression might also be a mediator and sleep might also be an outcome, so the benefits of physical activity on sleep quality might be explained by the fact that physical activity reduces depression, which means that depression would be a mediator. Thus, many psychological variables could be viewed as the outcome variable of interest or as a relevant mediator.

Physiological Mechanisms

Numerous physiological mechanisms have been forwarded to explain the effects of physical activity or exercise on psychological outcomes. When discussing physiological mechanisms, this invariably opens the door for micromediational chains because the human body is so complex in terms of physiological interactions. Often, the question of which physiological mechanism is being explored depends on the level of analysis at which the researcher is interested. For example, if I am interested in the effects of chronic exercise on cognitive performance, I might initially focus my attention on the changes in blood-based factors. I might discover that individuals who are randomly assigned to an exercise condition experience increases in brain-derived neurotrophic factor (BDNF) as measured in the blood. But that doesn't actually explain how or why exercise might be benefiting cognitive performance. Because I know that BDNF is important for the development of neurons in the brain, I could focus my next study on the changes in hippocampal volume in participants who exercise as compared to those who don't. If I find differences, this might provide a more proximal explanation of why exercise benefits cognitive performance. But I could go even further to then look at the impact of this increase in hippocampal volume on the availability of N-methyl D-aspartate receptors that are known to be important for memory and learning (Bloodgood & Sabatini, 2009). Hence, in the consideration of physiological mechanisms, it is fascinating to consider how the level of analysis can move from a more holistic view of the organism to one that is focused at the level of neurotransmitters.

Cognitive Theories

Now let's consider the theories that have been proposed to explain why exercise has positive effects for psychological outcomes. The theories described in this chapter have been applied to explain more than one outcome. By introducing you to some of the most commonly proposed mediators and mechanisms in exercise psychology, this will allow us to more efficiently discuss novel mediators, mechanisms, hypotheses, and theories pertinent to specific outcomes in subsequent chapters.

Dual Mode Theory

The dual mode theory (Ekkekakis, 2009) is particularly beneficial for considering the expected benefits of a single session of exercise relative to its intensity level. Grounded in evolutionary theory, this theory considers moderate intensity exercise (exercise that is below the anaerobic threshold and therefore does not result in a buildup of lactate acid) to be adaptive with an expectation of favorable responses that would thus serve to reward this behavior. By contrast, exercise that is predominantly at an intensity at which lactate acid accumulates (i.e., above the anaerobic or lactate threshold) is thought to be maladaptive and, hence, expected to result in negative responses, which would serve to discourage the organism from continuing to perform this high-intensity form of exercise. This theory has been discussed mostly in the affect and mood literature.

Time-Out or Distraction Hypothesis

The time-out or distraction hypothesis suggests that the beneficial effects of a single session of exercise are a result of the exercise distracting an individual from their cares or providing a time-out from their daily responsibilities and stressors. In other words, proponents of this hypothesis think that the benefits of exercise are due simply to the mental and physical break from a person's normal stressors that an exercise session provides. This hypothesis is most typically proposed when explaining increases in positive moods and decreases in negative moods, depression, anxiety, and stress.

Biologically Based Theories

In exercise psychology, numerous biologically based theories have been proposed to explain psychological benefits, and some of these are proposed for various psychological outcomes. Let's consider some theories that are commonly discussed relative to the effects of exercise on psychological outcomes and also look at how these variables are measured.

Inverted-U Hypothesis

The inverted-U hypothesis was initially proposed by Yerkes and Dodson (1908) based on animal research and has been adapted to consider relationships between physiological arousal and performance by humans. The hypothesis suggests that increases in physiological arousal (envisioned on the *x*-axis) are related to improvements in performance (envisioned on the *y*-axis) in an inverted-U-shaped pattern (see figure 2.5); that is, at lower levels of

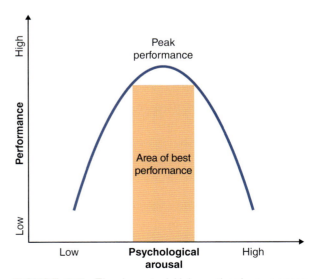

FIGURE 2.5 The inverted-U hypothesis suggests that the relationship between physiological arousal and performance assumes the shape of an upside-down U.

arousal, increases in arousal are thought to benefit performance. But this only holds true until one reaches the peak in terms of performance (at some relatively moderate level of arousal). After that point, further increases in arousal are thought to have a negative impact on performance. This hypothesis is frequently cited in the sport psychology literature but has also been applied to the exercise psychology literature particularly when considering the effects of acute exercise on cognitive outcomes or mood.

Cardiovascular Fitness Hypothesis

Cardiovascular fitness, aerobic fitness, or cardiorespiratory fitness are all terms that describe the body's ability to use oxygen to do physical work. Scientists have proposed the cardiovascular fitness hypothesis, which posits that the changes in aerobic fitness in response to chronic exercise are responsible for observed psychological benefits. This hypothesis has been proposed frequently for cognitive outcomes in part because of the anticipated link between cardiovascular fitness, circulation of blood in the brain, and the availability of oxygen and other resources to the brain. Proponents of this hypothesis believe that it is necessary to increase cardiovascular fitness to observe psychological benefits.

Thermogenic Hypothesis

The thermogenic hypothesis suggests that increases in body temperature in response to exercise might explain psychological benefits. This hypothesis has typically been forwarded for the mood-enhancing effects of exercise and for reductions in negative psychological constructs (e.g., stress, depression, anxiety). In particular, it is hypothesized that increases in body temperature translate to increases in the temperature in certain brain regions associated with muscle tension and relaxation, resulting in an overall reduction of stress, depression, and anxiety.

Neurovisceral Integration

Thayer and Lane (2000) proposed the neurovisceral integration model to explain the relationship between heart rate variability, attentional regulation, and affect. Heart rate variability (HRV) is a measure of the variability in the beat-to-beat intervals of a person's heart and provides an index of the efficiency of feedback loops between central (brain) and autonomic nervous systems. High levels of HRV are indicative of higher vagal tone, which has been shown to be reflective of better self-regulation and behavioral flexibility. Higher levels of HRV (better vagal tone) are achieved with physical activity participation. Thus, in exercise psychology, HRV has been used as an index of vagal tone and explored as a potential mechanism of the effects of exercise on depression (e.g., Lesnewich et al., 2019), stress (e.g., Zou et al., 2018), and cognition (e.g., Alderman & Olson, 2014; Ludyga et al., 2020).

Cognitive Reserves Theory

The cognitive reserves theory actually implicates several biological mechanisms that might explain the benefits of exercise for cognitive performance. This theory proposes that a person's cognitive reserves determine their ability to perform cognitive tasks. According to this theory, cognitive reserves can be increased by educational opportunities, stimulating work, and physical activity. Cognitive reserves are also thought to decline due to advancing age and in response to chronic illness or poor health. Importantly, because physical activity is thought to increase cognitive reserves, this theory has been proposed to explain both improvements in cognitive performance and why physical activity might be protective against clinical cognitive impairment. Essentially, the premise is that increases in cognitive reserves result in a higher starting point against which normal age-related declines might not result in a sufficient decrease in cognitive reserves for behavioral changes to be evident.

Other Biological Mechanisms

In addition to the aforementioned explanations for exercise benefits on psychological outcomes, other biological mechanisms have been identified as potentially important, including cortisol, neurotrophic factors, brain structure, endorphins, and endocannabinoids. These are described briefly here and then in more detail for relevant psychological outcomes.

Cortisol

Cortisol plays an important role in the provision of energy stores for performance and in the maintenance of blood pressure during exercise, but it is also considered to be the body's stress hormone. The release of cortisol is controlled by the hypothalamic pituitary axis, and it has both acute and chronic effects. In the acute sense, the release of cortisol is a critical component of the fight-or-flight response because it prepares the body's energy system for a response. In the chronic sense, relatively high levels of cortisol in the long term have a negative impact because cortisol decreases neurogenesis and might ultimately have an impact on brain structure (i.e., reduced hippocampal volume). The effects of chronic exercise in terms of controlling the cortisol response make this hormone a putative mechanism for beneficial effects of chronic exercise on any psychological outcomes affected by hippocampal function (e.g., depression or cognition). Furthermore, because cortisol is the stress hormone, it is implicated in studies exploring the potential stress-reducing benefits of exercise.

Neurotrophic Factors

Neurotrophic factors include BDNF, vascular-endothelial growth factor (VEGF), and insulin-like growth factor (IGF). These factors are important for maintaining brain health through their impact on neurogenesis. As such, these factors are again implicated for psychological outcomes likely to be directly influenced by brain structure. Most commonly, these factors are mentioned for cognition.

Brain Structure

Changes in brain structure could be the mechanism for any conceivable psychological outcome. Essentially, the idea is that over an extended period of time, regular exercise actually results in a restructuring of the brain's architecture. You have likely heard the brain referred to as being "plastic." This is because the structure of the brain itself is changeable, with evidence suggesting that while it is more malleable during the early years of development, it can still be modified even into older age. This happens through a process called *neurogenesis*, which occurs in the dentate gyrus of the hippocampus. The hippocampus is an important brain structure because it is involved with learning and memory and because it recently has been implicated in major depressive disorder.

Endorphin Hypothesis

The endorphin hypothesis typically is proposed to explain the feel-good effects of exercise—that is, the enhancement of positive moods and the reduction of negative moods. Endorphins are referred to as the *body's natural opioids* and hence have been implicated in the relationship between exercise and pain. The primary challenge relative to testing this hypothesis is that we are unable to measure endorphins in the brain and so are forced to rely on measures taken from blood samples. As such, it is difficult to truly assess the extent to which endorphins might be responsible for mood-altering or pain-reducing effects of exercise.

Endocannabinoid Hypothesis

Another physiological mechanism that has been proposed to explain positive affective responses to exercise is endocannabinoids. These are molecules created by the body that have similar effects to what someone might experience from external cannabis (i.e., marijuana). The endocannabinoid system is important for regulating a variety of processes in the human body, including sleep and mood. Research testing this hypothesis relative to exercise is in its infancy.

Summary

You've been introduced to the different variables that are important to consider when reading empirical (data-based) literature; the various research designs that might be used to answer research questions; the types of reviews of the scientific evidence that you might read; and some of the common mechanisms, hypotheses, and theories that have been proposed in the exercise psychology literature. As an exercise professional, it will be important that you are comfortable reading research evidence so that you can make evidence-based decisions in your interactions with students, clients, and colleagues. For example, if you intend to become a physical educator, it will be great for you to recognize the mental health benefits that you can help your students achieve. If you plan to be a fitness trainer, being able to articulate these benefits to your clients and to understand which are most important to them will help you focus on these benefits as reinforcers of physical activity behavior. If you envision going into health care or becoming a scientist yourself, this evidence will hopefully spark additional interests in understanding the psychological benefits of exercise, considering how to prescribe exercise to achieve these benefits, and understanding how and why these benefits occur.

Discussion Questions

1. What is a moderator, and why is the study of moderators important in exercise psychology? Give a single example that you have not read about in this chapter that demonstrates your understanding of moderators.

2. What is a mediator, and how does it differ from a mechanism? Give a single example that you have not read about in this chapter that demonstrates your understanding of mediators.

3. Which research design is considered the gold standard and why? In explaining why, describe the aspects of the design that are critical.

4. Provide a conceptual explanation of what a researcher would need to do to establish sleep quality as a mediator of the effects of a chronic exercise study on depression. Be sure to consider both the study design and the statistical analyses required.

5. Explain the difference between independent, dependent, and confounding variables. Give an example that demonstrates that you understand the distinctions between these variables.

Methods and Measurement for Exercise Psychology

OBJECTIVES

After studying this chapter, you should be able to do the following:

- Define terms that describe physical activity behaviors
- Describe common measures of physical activity and fitness
- Understand the distinction between acute and chronic exercise paradigms
- Identify the current physical activity recommendations and the variables associated with physical activity behavior
- Appreciate the various ways in which psychological outcomes can be assessed

KEY TERMS

physical activity

resting metabolic rate (resting energy expenditure)

very light– or light-intensity physical activity

moderate-intensity physical activity

vigorous-intensity physical activity

exercise

sport

aerobic activities

anaerobic activities

resistance activities

exercise prescription

physical fitness

aerobic fitness

$\dot{V}O_2$max

body mass index (BMI)

ratings of perceived exertion (RPE)

exercise bouts

acute exercise

chronic exercise

experimenter burden

participant burden

self-report measures

nanotechnology

Freya is taking a class that requires her to complete a small research study. Freya has always been an avid cyclist. Recently, she's been unable to find time to get on her bike because of the demands of school and work. She recognizes that she is more irritable than usual and is even starting to experience feelings of depression which she hasn't experienced since high school. She wonders if this is a result of her inability to exercise at her normal levels and decides to use this as motivation for her research question. She meets with her professor, Dr. Pearson, to talk about her idea and how she might design a study to answer her question.

Dr. Pearson and Freya talk about conducting a cross-sectional study to see if the amount of physical activity a person participates in is predictive of their experience of depression. Dr. Pearson points out that physical activity can be very difficult to measure because it includes such a wide range of activities from low-intensity, short-duration activities completed as a part of normal daily activities to more focused exercise sessions that are designed to increase fitness. They talk about measuring physical activity by using questionnaires, fitness apps on smartphones, and accelerometers. Given that Freya doesn't have money to buy accelerometers and that she wouldn't be able to access the data from fitness apps on people's personal phones, they decide that a questionnaire is the best method to use. They then focus on the measurement of depression. Dr. Pearson points out that depression is a clinical mental health experience and that its assessment requires clinical training. But she also explains that depressive symptoms can be measured with a questionnaire administered by a person who does not have clinical training. Freya leaves the meeting excited to learn more about the existing questionnaires for the measurement of physical activity and depressive symptoms and looks forward to finding appropriate measures for use with college students so she can administer them to a group of her peers to see if any relationships are evident.

In the previous chapter, we learned about research from a point of view that was not yet specific to exercise and physical activity. Let's now turn our attention to definitions specific to exercise and physical activity, exercise paradigms, and measurement issues in exercise psychology. These definitions and explanations will provide important background for our discussions in subsequent chapters so that we have a common understanding of terms. You might be surprised by how challenging it is to describe the behaviors of physical activity and exercise. Because these behaviors are so complex and can be performed in such a wide variety of ways, this has implications for our ability to measure exercise and physical activity. Before reading further, take a moment to consider how you would define physical activity and what types of activities you would consider to fall under this category of behavior. Now, consider how you would define exercise. Similarly, what types of activities fall under this category?

Definitions

Given that this course is focused on the psychological outcomes of exercise, it is important to define relevant terms related to exercise. The most commonly used terms to consider are *physical activity*, *exercise*, *sport*, *aerobic activities*, *anaerobic activities*, *resistance activities*, *sedentary behavior*, *physical fitness*, and *body mass index*. As we move through each chapter, the definition of the specific psychological outcome being considered will be provided.

Physical Activity

The American College of Sports Medicine (ACSM) defines **physical activity** as "any bodily movement produced by the contraction of skeletal muscles that results in an increase in caloric requirements over resting energy expenditure" (American College of Sports Medicine, 2022, p. 1). Let's dig deeper into what this means. **Resting metabolic rate** (or rest-

---

physical activity—The definition of physical activity is that it is "Any bodily movement produced by the contraction of skeletal muscles that results in a substantial increase in caloric requirements over resting energy expenditure" (American College of Sports Medicine, 2022, p. 1).

resting metabolic rate (resting energy expenditure)—The energy expended (in calories) to maintain bodily functions when at rest is known as resting metabolic rate; it is approximated as 3.5 milliliters per kilogram per minute.

ing energy expenditure) is defined as the energy expended (in calories) to maintain bodily functions when at rest. The resting metabolic rate is equivalent to the caloric consumption of 1 kilocalorie per kilogram per hour and is also referred to as 1 metabolic equivalent (or 1 MET). Although resting metabolic rate varies with age, sex, height, and weight, it is approximated as 3.5 milliliters per kilogram per minute of oxygen consumption and accounts for approximately 50% to 75% of daily energy expenditure. Since physical activity substantially increases energy expenditure beyond what is needed for rest, physical activities are those with metabolic equivalents substantially greater than 1 MET. Behaviors such as walking, playing tennis, gardening, cleaning house, and lifting weights would all be considered examples of physical activity because they all require substantially more energy than is needed at rest. Based on their specific intensity level, we could estimate the exact amount of energy needed to perform each activity. This is expressed in METS, which tell us the ratio of energy expended relative to rest. In fact, compendiums of physical activities list a multitude of behaviors and their estimated energy expenditure in METS for adults (Ainsworth et al., 2011) and for youth (Butte et al., 2018). It is also possible to use METs to help us understand how to describe intensity levels of activities. **Very light– or light-intensity physical activity** are those activities that result in energy expenditure that is >1.0 but <3.0 METs (e.g., yard work at light effort or walking at <2.0 miles per hour), **moderate-intensity activities** result in 3.0 to 5.9 METs (e.g., walking at 2.5 miles per hour or playing doubles tennis), and **vigorous activities** result in ≥6.0 METs of energy expenditure (e.g., bicycling at >9.5 miles per hour or running at >4.0 miles per hour) (American College of Sports Medicine, 2022).

> Use a search engine to search for "adult compendium of physical activities" and "youth compendium of physical activities." Identify the predicted energy expenditure for adults and children who walk, play singles tennis, garden, clean house, or lift weights for 30 minutes. Choose two other activities of particular interest to you and look up their METs in the compendium.

Exercise

A related term that is equally important to understand is *exercise*. ACSM defines **exercise** as a specific subset of physical activity that consists of behaviors that are planned and structured and that are performed repeatedly, with a goal of improving or maintaining physical fitness. This definition is important because of the distinction it makes between physical activity and exercise. According to this definition, exercise must be done purposefully with a goal of improving fitness. This is likely consistent with how we think of exercise; that is, jogging and lifting weights would be considered exercise. But the challenge with this definition comes from the fact that the same activity—for example, walking—could be considered a form of physical activity (e.g., if a person is walking to go to the grocery store) but might also be a form of exercise (e.g., if a person is walking to maintain cardiorespiratory fitness). A consideration with this definition, then, is that to measure a behavior and count that behavior as exercise, we would have to ask the participant what their reason was for performing the activity.

Sport

It is also interesting to consider the definition of sport and how it relates to exercise and physical activity. Eitzen and Sage (1997, p. 16) define **sport** as "any competitive physical activity that is guided by established rules." Obviously, this includes activ-

American College of Sports Medicine

The American College of Sports Medicine (ACSM) is a professional organization of more than 50,000 sports medicine professionals, researchers, and academics. This organization hosts regional and national meetings and provides certifications and other education opportunities for professionals in the sport sciences.

---

very light– or light-intensity physical activity—Very light– or light-intensity physical activity consists of those activities that result in energy expenditure that is >1.0 but <3.0 METs. Examples include yard work at light effort or walking at <2.0 miles per hour.

moderate-intensity physical activity—Moderate-intensity physical activity includes those activities that result in 3.0 to 5.9 METs. Examples include walking at 2.5 miles per hour or playing doubles tennis.

vigorous-intensity physical activity—Vigorous-intensity physical activity is defined as those activities that result in ≥6.0 METs of energy expenditure. Examples include bicycling at >9.5 miles per hour or running at >4.0 miles per hour.

exercise—Exercise is a specific subset of physical activity that consists of behaviors that are planned and structured and that are performed repeatedly, with a goal of improving or maintaining physical fitness.

sport—A definition of sport is "Any competitive physical activity that is guided by established rules" (Eitzen & Sage, 1997, p. 16).

38 | The Psychological Benefits of Exercise and Physical Activity

Would both of the activities be considered physical activity and exercise?

ities such as soccer, basketball, tennis, and golf. It is true that all sports are also physical activity, but these would also be considered forms of exercise if a participant had fitness goals as a motivation. So, for example, if a person competes in triathlons or 5K races as a way to stay fit, the activities used for training could be considered physical activity, exercise, and sport. From an exercise psychology point of view, sport can have commonalities with physical activity and exercise, but it also can include other variables that could be uniquely relevant to the psychological outcome of interest. For example, if a researcher were interested in the anxiety-reducing effects of physical activity, the choice to examine these benefits in response to competitive sport might not make sense because of the unique impact of competition on anxiety.

Aerobic and Anaerobic Activities

When we consider physical activity, exercise, and sport, we might also think about the nature of the activities being performed relative to their energy demands, which are determined by the intensity level of the activity. Activities can be described as being either aerobic or anaerobic. **Aerobic activities** are those performed at an intensity level that results in the muscles being able to rely on oxygen to perform. As a result of being oxygen dependent, these activities can be performed for extended periods of time. These activities increase the use of energy above that which is required at rest but, by definition, are performed below the anaerobic threshold. However, once the intensity level goes above the anaerobic threshold, the activity is by definition anaerobic, and performance will require the use of energy stores that are not dependent on oxygen. Purely **anaerobic activities** are performed at a high intensity level and therefore can only be maintained for 10 to 15 seconds because of the limited energy stores used in these activities. For example, walking and jogging would be considered aerobic, but running a 100M dash in 14 seconds would be anaerobic. Importantly, the demands on the aerobic and anaerobic energy systems are on a continuum, and both systems can be trained to improve that specific form of fitness. In the exercise psychology literature, most studies have focused on aerobic activities, but more recent work has begun to examine high-intensity interval exercise (HIIE) or high-intensity interval training (HIIT), in which short bouts of high-intensity exercise (often anaerobic) are interspersed with rest breaks.

---

aerobic activities—Activities performed at an intensity level that results in the muscles being able to rely on oxygen to perform are known as aerobic activities.

anaerobic activities—Activities that are performed at a high intensity level and therefore can only be maintained for 10 to 15 seconds because of the limited energy stores used are described as anaerobic activities.

Resistance Activities

Resistance activities are described as activities that are specifically designed to increase muscular fitness through the use of free weights, exercise machines, body weight, resistance bands, or any other objects that require the use of force against a resistance (e.g., kettle bells or ropes). Resistance exercise is typically described in terms of the amount of resistance (or weight) and is performed in sets of repetitions. The body of evidence is growing relative to the potential role of resistance activities in benefiting psychological outcomes.

Sedentary Behavior

Sedentary behavior is consistently viewed as behavior performed during "awake" time but has been defined in different ways including literally as sitting and as activities that result in fewer than 100 counts on an accelerometer per minute (Shiroma et al., 2013) or result in energy expenditure <1.5 METS (Haskell, 2012). Researchers have begun to explore the effects of sedentary behavior on health outcomes. Some evidence shows that these effects are independent of the effects of physical activity such that a person who spends more time in very light physical activity might have better health outcomes than someone who replaces that time with purely sedentary behavior. Although the extant literature on sedentary behavior and psychological outcomes is limited at this time, be on the lookout for future research exploring this interesting question.

Changes in Response to Physically Active or Sedentary Behaviors

The behaviors just described (physical activity, exercise, sport, aerobic activities, anaerobic activities, resistance activities, and sedentary behavior) can result in measurable psychological and physiological changes when a person participates in them for a sufficient amount of time. The possible psychological changes are the focus of the remainder of this textbook. With respect to the physiological changes, fitness will increase in response to physically active behaviors, with the nature and the amount of the change dependent on the modality (the type of physical activity) and the intensity and duration of the behavior. Of course, sedentary behaviors will have the opposite effect, resulting in decreases in fitness over time. Exercise prescription refers to the development of an exercise plan designed spe-

Sit-to-Stand

Based on a growing body of research evidence, the *British Journal of Sports Medicine* published an expert consensus statement arguing for changes to sedentary office environments (Buckley et al., 2015). In this paper, experts proposed that office workers should organize their work day to begin to accumulate 2 hours per day of standing and light walking and that they should gradually progress toward 4 hours per day. Based on this, sit-to-stand desks and even desks that are incorporated with a treadmill are recommended with the recognition that it takes time to adjust to working in a standing position and that ergonomic adjustments might be necessary.

---

resistance activities—Resistance activities are those specifically designed to increase muscular fitness through the use of free weights, exercise machines, body weight, resistance bands, or any other objects that require the use of force against a resistance (e.g., kettle bells or ropes).

exercise prescription—An exercise plan designed specifically to improve a particular aspect of fitness is known as an exercise prescription.

cifically to improve a particular aspect of fitness. Let's learn more about physical fitness and exercise prescription.

Physical Fitness

Physical fitness is defined as "a set of attributes or characteristics individuals have or achieve that relate to their ability to perform [physical activity] and activities of daily living" (American College of Sports Medicine, 2022, p. 1). ACSM considers there to be two types of physical fitness. Health-related physical fitness includes cardiorespiratory (or aerobic) fitness, body composition, muscular strength, muscular endurance, and flexibility. Skill-related physical fitness includes agility, coordination, balance, power, reaction time, and speed. Clearly, measuring physical fitness is challenging if we want to measure it comprehensively. Most of the evidence presented in exercise psychology focuses on aerobic fitness (also referred to as *cardiorespiratory fitness*) as opposed to these other aspects of fitness. Aerobic fitness is defined as the body's ability to use oxygen to perform sustained exercise, and it tends to improve in response to the performance of aerobic activities of sufficient intensity, duration, and frequency.

The gold standard measurement of aerobic fitness is a graded maximal voluntary exercise test using a metabolic cart to capture exhalations as an individual gradually increases their exercise intensity until unable to continue. This is sometimes also referred to as a *maximal graded exercise test*. As the person is exercising, the metabolic cart captures and assesses the percent of oxygen that is being used relative to what is available in room air. In a maximal test, the person is encouraged to exercise as long as possible. The measure that derives from a maximal aerobic fitness test is called $\dot{V}O_2max$, where the $\dot{V}$ is the rate of change in volume and O_2 is oxygen, and the abbreviation *max* indicates that this was a maximal test. Other measures of aerobic fitness include $\dot{V}O_2$ peak, which is obtained when the exercise test does not reach maximal effort. For safety reasons, this measure is often used when measuring fitness in older adults. Other estimated measures of aerobic capacity can be derived from submaximal tests conducted with or without a metabolic cart. These tests include step tests, 6-minute walk tests, and 1/2-mile walk tests. In the absence of a metabolic cart, estimates are derived from the heart rate response to exercise in combination with individual characteristics (i.e., age and sex) with an approximation based on age-predicted maximal heart rate.

> When you were in middle school, junior high school, or high school, it is likely that you completed tests of physical fitness as a part of your physical education curriculum. For many of you, this might have included tests that are a part of the FitnessGram, including the 1-mile run, the PACER test, curl-ups, trunk lifts, push-ups, flexed arm hang, and the sit and reach. Each of these tests is expected to provide a measure of a specific aspect of fitness.

Body Mass Index

In the exercise psychology literature, the other measure of fitness that is often considered to provide an indication of health-related fitness is body mass index. Body mass index (BMI) is a ratio of a person's weight in kilograms relative to their height in meters squared. This index provides a rough indicant of body fat and is often used to provide an estimate of a person's overweight status relative to normative and health data. According to the Centers for Disease Control, BMI under 18.5 is underweight, between 18.5 and 24.9 is normal or healthy weight, between 25.0 and 29.9 is overweight, and over 30.0 is obese for adults. Although BMI provides a good estimate of weight relative to these health categories, its use is limited. In particular, BMI does not consider a person's percent body fat relative to their percent of muscle. This is important because differences in percent body fat are generally present relative to a person's race (Blacks have less body fat than Whites, who have less body fat than Asians), biological sex (men have less body fat than women), age (younger adults have less body fat than older adults), and athletic or exercise status (athletes have less body fat than nonathletes) (Camhi et al., 2011; Prentice & Jebb, 2001). As such, for example, trained body builders might have a high BMI but should not be considered overweight or obese because their BMI is not a good indicator of their body fat.

---

physical fitness—Physical fitness has been defined as "A set of attributes or characteristics individuals have or achieve that relate to their ability to perform [physical activity] and activities of daily living" (American College of Sports Medicine, 2022, p. 1).

aerobic fitness—Aerobic fitness is the body's ability to use oxygen to perform sustained exercise; tends to improve in response to the performance of aerobic activities of sufficient intensity, duration, and frequency.

$\dot{V}O_2max$— $\dot{V}O_2max$ is the maximum volume (V) of oxygen (O_2) a person's body is capable of using during exercise. It is the gold standard measurement of aerobic fitness and is measured during a graded maximal voluntary exercise test conducted while using a metabolic cart.

body mass index (BMI)—BMI is the ratio of a person's weight in kilograms relative to their height in meters squared.

Use a calculator to determine your BMI. Consider your BMI relative to the information provided earlier. If you are in the overweight or obese category and are not a trained athlete with the expected low percent body fat, you might want to consider making lifestyle changes to lower your BMI. This is because people who are overweight or obese have an increased risk of mortality, high blood pressure, type 2 diabetes, heart disease, stroke, cancer, mental illness, and difficulty with physical functioning. As a university or college student, you are likely to have resources available to you through your health center or student recreational center, and you might be able to take physical activity, lifetime fitness, or lifetime health courses at your institution to help you increase your physical activity and manage your eating behaviors for health.

$$BMI = \frac{weight\ (kg)}{height\ (m)^2}$$

Exercise Prescription

An exercise prescription is a specific plan designed to improve a certain aspect of fitness. According to the ACSM, the components that must be considered for exercise prescription are explained by the FITT principle. FITT is an acronym for frequency, intensity, time, and type. Frequency refers to how often exercise is performed, such as 3 days per week. Intensity can be expressed in several ways including as a rating of perceived exertion; as a speed (6 miles per hour); or as a percent of maximal heart rate, which can be directly assessed using a maximal exercise test or estimated as age-predicted heart rate max (220 − age). This variable can be challenging to consider because of the importance of making intensity level self-referenced. In other words, running at 6 miles per hour might not be hard for some people who are relatively fit, but it might be essentially impossible for someone who is more sedentary. Because of this, ratings of perceived exertion are often used in conjunction with descriptions of absolute intensity levels to express the participants' experience of the exercise relative to their own fitness levels. **Ratings of perceived exertion (RPE)** are subjective judgments people make about how hard they are working. RPE by adults are typically obtained using Borg's Rating of Perceived Exertion scale, while the OMNI scale (see figure 3.1) is more often used with children. Time describes the amount of time for a single session of the exercise (e.g., 20 minutes). Type is also called *modality* and for aerobic activities might fall into four different groups based on the ACSM guidelines. Group A describes relatively low-intensity aerobic activities that require little skill (e.g., walking or aqua aerobics). Group B is characterized as vigorous-intensity endurance exercises that require little skill (e.g., running or spinning). Group C are activities that require skill to perform such as swimming and cross-country skiing. Group D includes recreational sports such as racket sports, basketball, and soccer.

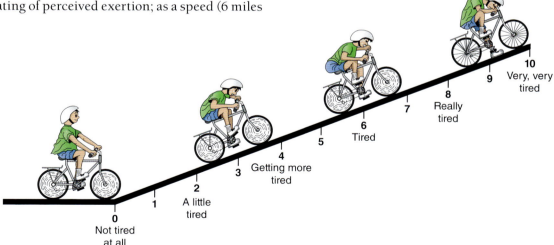

FIGURE 3.1 The OMNI scale for children is used to measure perceived exertion.

Reprinted by permission from R. J. Robertson, *Perceived Exertion for Practitioners: Rating Effort with the OMNI Picture System*, (Champaign, IL: Human Kinetics, 2004), 145.

---

ratings of perceived exertion (RPE)—Subjective judgments people make about how hard they are working are known as RPE.

Exercise Paradigms

In discussing physical fitness and exercise prescription, the focus was on chronic or regular participation in physical activity. In terms of physical fitness, we do not expect durable changes in response to a single session of exercise. However, when considering the exercise psychology literature, it is important to recognize that measurable psychological changes can be observed in response to both single sessions of exercise and repeated exposure to exercise. Thus, it is important to distinguish between acute exercise and chronic exercise. These terms reflect the extent to which the *exercise bouts* (sessions during which exercise is performed) are repeated and have important implications relative to potential benefits.

Acute Exercise

In the exercise psychology literature, some of the research has focused on the effects of a single session of exercise. Single sessions of exercise are also referred to as *acute exercise*. Researchers conducting studies on acute exercise are typically most interested in the relatively transient effects of the exercise session. That is, researchers looking at acute exercise questions typically focus on physical activity that is defined as exercise (paying close attention to mode, intensity, and duration) rather than on physical activity more broadly defined. These scientists also typically focus on outcome measures that are thought to be sensitive in the short term such as mood, cognitive performance, and sleep. For example, a researcher who is interested in examining the effects of acute exercise on a cognitive outcome such as memory might randomly assign participants to a treatment group (e.g., exercise for 20 minutes while watching a video) or a control group (e.g., watch a video for 20 minutes) prior to performing a memory task. Memory performance then would be compared between the two groups. If the researcher established that acute exercise benefited memory, the next step might be to design a study in which participants are randomly assigned to the control condition (watching a video) or to one of three intensity levels of exercise (low-, moderate-, or high-intensity exercise while watching a video). This design would allow the researchers to identify which of these intensity levels of exercise had the biggest benefit for memory. You'll note that in the studies described, both of the groups watched a video. This is important because you want the two groups to be the same in every way except the variable you're interested in (the independent variable). By making sure that all groups are watching the video, the only difference between the groups is the exercise itself.

Chronic Exercise

Other studies in the exercise psychology literature focus on regular (or chronic) exercise. *Chronic exercise* is defined as the regular performance of exercise bouts over an extended period of time such as weeks, months, or years. In this case, researchers are more likely to look at activities that would be considered physical activity in addition to studying exercise. In other words, researchers might be interested in the long-term effects of a physically active lifestyle on depression or might specifically examine the benefits of a 15-week group exercise class for self-esteem. You'll notice that the outcome variables of depression and self-esteem are more enduring in nature. Other dependent variables that might be explored in response to chronic exercise include quality of life, body image, and brain structure. When researchers set out to study the effects of chronic exercise (or physical activity) on a psychological outcome, they might initially use a design that is cross-sectional or prospective in nature. The reason for this is because these designs are less costly and time-consuming. It is much easier to recruit individuals who have been regularly active for 1 year and to compare them to individuals who have been sedentary for 1 year (i.e., to use a cross-sectional design) than it is to recruit sedentary individuals and randomly assign them to a 1-year exercise intervention or a control condition (i.e., to use an RCT design). Although not as strong from a scientific perspective, cross-sectional and prospective studies can provide initial evidence in support of conducting an RCT.

Dose Response

When considering exercise as an independent variable with putative psychological benefits, one of the questions that will be asked repeatedly is what amount (or dose) of exercise is needed to achieve benefits. This is an amazingly challenging question for two reasons. First, because exercise is a behavior, it can be performed in an infinite number of ways. As mentioned, the FITT principle describes that exercise is performed at a certain frequency (i.e., the number of days per week),

---

exercise bouts—Sessions (periods of time) during which exercise is performed are also called exercise bouts.

acute exercise—Acute exercise is a single session of exercise.

chronic exercise—Regular exercise performed over a period of weeks, months, or years is referred to as chronic exercise.

intensity, time (sometimes called *duration*, which is the length of each individual exercise session), and type (e.g., cardiovascular, resistance, anaerobic, or some combination). Thus, to truly be able to prescribe a particular exercise regimen, we would need to be able to answer questions about each of these aspects of the exercise. Second, and related, the only way to truly identify the dose required for benefits is to conduct RCTs that compare various doses of exercise to one another or to an appropriate control group. These studies can be challenging to conduct because they require so many treatment groups and because changing one variable according to the FITT principle could affect other variables. For instance, if you are interested in high-intensity exercise, by definition you will need to consider only exercise that is relatively short in duration. But to keep duration the same, that means you'd need to compare the short-duration high-intensity exercise to short-duration low-intensity exercise. But, a short-duration, low-intensity exercise session is probably not ideal because of the limited amount of work completed. In fact, some researchers have been arguing that the most important variable might be the total work completed (or volume) so that a long-duration, low-intensity exercise bout might have similar benefits to a short-duration, high-intensity exercise bout. Although studies exploring dose–response questions are relatively rare, they provide valuable guidance as we strive to move toward the provision of specific exercise recommendations to benefit psychological outcomes.

Measurement in Exercise Psychology

Now that you understand the distinctions between physical activity behaviors and physical fitness, you'll appreciate that exercise psychology researchers have an interest in measuring both. Because physical activity behaviors are related to physical fitness, both have been considered as the independent variable in studies examining potential psychological benefits. If physical fitness is found to be predictive of better psychological outcomes, the inference is that these relationships are reliant on higher levels of physical activity. Similarly, if a scientist is interested in changing physical activity behavior, improvements in fitness might be used as a manipulation check to assess the amount of physiological change observed. Given the close relationship between these two variables, the measurement of both is important in exercise psychology. Measures of psychological variables also are key because they serve as the dependent (or outcome) variable in exercise psychology.

Measurement of Physical Activity

Interestingly, in the exercise psychology literature, studies assessing behaviors as the independent variable have focused largely on physical activity rather than exercise. This is because *physical activity* is the more encompassing term and because it is expected that all forms of movement that increase energy expenditure will affect psychological outcomes. In studies that use RCT designs, the independent variable is typically exercise because the treatment condition is purposefully designed to administer a strong enough dose of exercise to observe changes in fitness.

The assessment of physical activity in real-world situations is surprisingly challenging. This is because physical activity is a behavior performed at any time and encompasses so many different types of behavior. It is also challenging because it is often important to know the specific type of physical activity performed (type or mode), how often it was performed (frequency; days per week), for how long it has been performed (duration; for how many minutes per day and for how many days), and at what level of energy expenditure (intensity). In measuring physical activity, a number of methods are available, with the most commonly used assessments falling under the categories of direct measurements and indirect (or self-report) measurements. A challenge with the assessment tools for physical activity is that those with higher levels of validity (i.e., evidence that they measure what they are supposed to measure) also tend to have lower levels of feasibility (i.e., their practical usefulness in a field setting) and vice versa.

The best measure of physical activity is one that is accurate, precise, objective, simple to use, nonreactive, socially acceptable, time efficient, applicable to large groups, causes minimal intrusion into habitual physical activity, and allows for continuous and detailed recording of behavior. Reading this list of criteria should illustrate how difficult it is to identify a measure of physical activity that will satisfy all of these needs. In a nutshell, these considerations are related to psychometric properties such as validity and reliability, but they also emphasize the importance of feasibility because researchers must consider factors such as experimenter burden, participant burden, sample size, and duration of measurement. **Experimenter burden** is the requirements of a research study for the experimenters and includes considerations such as how many experimenters will be needed, how much time will it take each experimenter, and how much data reduction is required. **Participant burden** is the requirements of a research study for the participants with respect to duration, invasiveness, and intensity that have implications for physical and psychological impacts on the participant. For example, this refers to how invasive the study measurements are, how much time it takes the participant, and how easy it is to participate. Sample size reflects how many participants we aim to assess, and duration of measurement is the window of time over which we would like to assess the behavior. Typically, researchers choose to use direct measures to assess physical activity when they have a relatively small sample (<100) whom they want to assess over a fairly short time frame (e.g., physical activity over 1 week). In this situation, direct measures would not place too much burden on the experimenters or the participants. If researchers are interested in a larger sample (>100) or a longer time frame (e.g., physical activity over a year), they would be more likely to use a self-report measure because of the desire to limit the burden on the participants.

Direct Measures of Physical Activity

Direct measures of physical activity behavior include observations, doubly labeled water techniques, and the use of wearable devices to assess movement. Of these, wearable devices are the most commonly used, but let's consider the other measurement options as well so that you understand what is possible.

Observation is a form of direct measurement that refers to an experimenter observing a person's behavior and recording events of interest. In the exercise psychology literature, observation is rarely used as the method for assessing physical activity behavior. This is because of the inability to measure intensity and the large amount of experimenter burden inherent in this technique. With observation, researchers cannot clearly distinguish the intensity level of the behavior being performed. This shortcoming might be addressed by combining observation with the wearing of accelerometers or heart rate monitors. However, the experimenter burden of this technique cannot be mitigated. Whether watching the participant in real time or using a recording of their behavior, an experimenter is required to use a checklist or scoring rubric to identify periods of activity and periods of inactivity. This is time-consuming and, in many cases, impractical. However, observation has been used in some studies focused on children's behavior in physical education classes. The System for Observing Fitness Instruction Time (SOFIT) (McKenzie, 2002; McKenzie et al., 1992) is an observational tool developed for this purpose. It has been shown to be valid and reliable for use with children from first to eighth grade (Rowe et al., 1997) and high school students (Rowe et al., 2004), and has been modified for use with preschool-aged children (Sharma et al., 2011). Overall, observation methods are valid and with training and checklists can be reliably used, but the experimenter burden and the inability to judge intensity level limit its usefulness in exercise psychology studies.

Doubly labeled water techniques provide a gold standard measurement of energy expenditure, but they are also rarely used in the exercise psychology literature. This technique is one in which the participant drinks water that has been doubly labeled (DLW) with radioisotopes ($^2H_2^{18}O$) in doses relative to body weight. All liquid that the participant eliminates is collected. Because hydrogen (^2H) is eliminated from the body as water and oxygen (^{18}O) is eliminated as water and CO_2, energy expenditure can be calculated based on CO_2 produced over a given period and using standard equations. Participants provide a baseline urine sample, are given the radioisotopes, and refrain from food or drink for 5 to 8 hours before providing another sample. Following this procedure, participants provide several urine samples during a period of 1 to 4 weeks. The positives of this technique are that it is extremely accurate and relatively nonintrusive. The cons are that it is expensive and provides only an overall measure of energy expenditure, so this technique can't be used to distinguish activities or times. As a result, this measure can only be used to assess chronic forms of physical activity (accumulated

---

experimenter burden—The requirements of a research study for the experimenters that includes considerations such as how many experimenters will be needed, how much time it will take each experimenter to collect the data, and how much data reduction is required.

participant burden—The requirements of a research study for the participants with respect to duration, invasiveness, and intensity that have implications for physical and psychological impacts on the participant.

over time) as a way of understanding the influence of physical activity on some outcome of interest.

The use of wearable devices designed to measure movement to assess physical activity behavior is by far the most common direct measurement and is rapidly evolving. Pedometers (which measure movement in the vertical plane) are worn on the hip, were used in many early studies, and continue to be used when researchers are interested in step counts. These are common in school-based research but are used less often in research with other populations. Accelerometers (which measure acceleration in three planes) are also typically worn on the hip, although some can be worn on the wrist. Accelerometers record acceleration in all three dimensions, allowing for data to be converted to step counts and to METs. Accelerometers have been the most commonly used direct measure to date (Prince et al., 2008); however, since the advent of smartphones and smart watches, researchers have also begun to use these devices to assess physical activity, which likely will become increasingly common. Both smartphones and smart watches allow for the inclusion of GPS data, which contribute to our ability to measure distance covered. This is useful for activities that cover measurable distances (e.g., hiking, biking, walking, jogging) but are not useful for activities performed in place (e.g., walking or running on a treadmill, using a stationary bicycle). Another limitation is that if we don't also include some kind of self-report, we don't know what the person is actually doing. If they are traveling at 15 miles per hour and that's the only information we have, we wouldn't know if they were on a bicycle, an electric bicycle, or a motorized scooter. Smart watches do often allow for the collection of heart rate data, which is a huge advancement for our ability to measure exercise intensity in real-world settings. The assessment of heart rate would allow us to distinguish between riding a bicycle and riding on a motorized scooter. The benefits of using these devices to measure physical activity are that they have acceptable validity, are reasonable in terms of financial cost, are minimally invasive and so have relatively low participant burden, and provide information about patterns of activity. However, there are also some downsides to these devices. That is, regardless of the device that is used, researchers have to contend with challenges such as determining the minimum hours of wear time necessary for inclusion, accounting for activities that might not be amenable to measurement by these devices (e.g., skateboarding, riding a stationary cycle, swimming), encouraging participants to be compliant with wearing the device, and conducting the necessary steps to convert the data provided by the device into usable data points for analyses. It is also critically important that any of these devices used for research be tested to establish validity and reliability with the particular sample to be studied. This is true for all devices but is particularly important for commercial products that often rely on proprietary algorithms that have not been subjected to scientific scrutiny.

Interesting Facts About Pedometers

- The first pedometers appear to have been used in Roman times when a gear-driven attachment on a pull cart was used by military troops to approximate the distances they covered.
- Images from the 15th century suggest that Leonardo da Vinci invented the first wearable pedometer. It was a gear-driven device with a pendulum arm (a mechanical pedometer) that was designed to improve the ability to measure distances for maps.
- Dr. Yoshiro Hatano is credited with naming a pedometer "the 10,000 steps meter" as a means of promoting daily activity for physical health. This led to the common mantra suggesting that 10,000 steps per day will benefit health.

Indirect Measures of Physical Activity

The most commonly used indirect measures of physical activity are self-report measures that might be in the form of questionnaires or interviews. Questionnaires are most common because they are cheap and easy to administer to large numbers of people (i.e., large samples). These measures have typically been shown to be reasonably valid as compared to DLW and to have acceptable levels of reliability. Although some researchers might use a technique of having participants report their activity daily using an exercise log, most of the time researchers ask participants to remember back over a certain time frame to report their physical activity behaviors. For example, the International Physical Activity Questionnaire (IPAQ) includes questions such as "During the last 7 days, on how many days did you do moderate physical activities such as carrying light loads, bicycling at a regular pace, or doubles tennis?" If the participant reports that they did moderate activity on 1 or more days, follow-up questions ask about how many days and for how much time per day.

As you can imagine, the use of questionnaires to assess physical activity has several shortcomings. One shortcoming is that participants sometimes have a hard time remembering what they did over the time interval they are asked to recall. This is more of a problem when reporting physical activity than exercise because it is more difficult to remember low-intensity activities that are not performed with a specific fitness purpose. That is, it is harder to remember physical activities such as doing housework, gardening, or walking than it is to remember structured, planned activities such as exercise that are performed at a higher intensity (Haskell, 2012). Across a variety of measures, overreporting is also a real problem, with recent evidence showing that the IPAQ results in an overestimation of the percent of adults who meet physical activity guidelines (Mama et al., 2019; Steene-Johannessen et al., 2016). Importantly as well, most of the self-report measures have not been validated in diverse samples. As a result, concerns have been raised that these measures might not be generalizable for use in more representative samples. Lastly, most of the questionnaires are unitless, meaning that they just provide a number to represent a person's physical activity behavior. This is a limitation because it means that you can't compare across studies that use different questionnaires. Some questionnaires, however, allow the researchers to calculate kilocalories or METs, which then provides a common metric allowing for comparisons across studies using different measures.

Studies that include large samples sizes often rely on self-report measures because the measures are readily available, inexpensive, and easy to administer. Importantly, a large number of self-report measures have acceptable psychometric properties (i.e., they are valid and reliable), so all empirical studies assessing physical activity should use previously established measures rather than creating measures of physical activity on their own for the study.

Physical Activity Recommendations

Let's consider the recommendations for physical activity and the extent to which people tend to meet these recommendations. The recommendations for physical activity have remained relatively consistent in recent decades and across various organizations. It is interesting to recognize that these recommendations are largely based on the goal of obtaining expected positive physical outcomes. Specific recommendations for psychological outcomes have not been developed and, therefore, the same recommendations are given because the benefits are simply expected to be similar. The U.S. Department of Health and Human Services (USDHHS) recommends 150 to 300 minutes of moderate-intensity aerobic physical activity per week and participation in strength-training activities ≥2 days per week for adults and ≥60 minutes per day of moderate to vigorous activity every day for children ages 6 to 17 years (U.S. Department of Health and Human Services, 2022). These recommendations are consistent with those offered by the World Health Organization (World Health Organization, 2020).

In the United States, data from 2019 indicate that the percentage of Americans meeting the 2018 federal guidelines for aerobic activity is approximately 47% and for muscle strengthening is only 31%. In fact, only 24% of adults in the United States meet both aerobic and muscle strengthening guidelines (National Center for Health Statistics, 2020). This is concerning because while we know that being physically active reduces the risk of chronic illness, morbidities, and mortality, the converse is also true: sedentary behavior increases mortality; the risk of chronic diseases such as cardiovascular disease, diabetes, and obesity; and the risk of various cancers (Park et al., 2020). The percentage of individuals in the United States who meet physical activity recommendations for both aerobic exercise and strength training generally decreases with advancing age, with approximately 28% of young adults (18-24 yr), 23% of adults (25-44 yr), 21% of middle-aged adults (45-65 yr), and 23% of older adults (65 and older) meeting the guidelines (Centers for Disease Control and Prevention, 2019). Differences also occur for those who self-identify by one race, such that Native Hawaiian or Other Pacific Islanders (27.2%) report meeting the guidelines more than do Non-Hispanic Whites (23.5%), Non-Hispanic Blacks (23.0%),

American Indians and Alaska Natives (22.5%), and Asians (22.1%), all of whom report more activity than do Hispanics (20.8%) (Centers for Disease Control and Prevention, 2019). Interestingly, the percentage of individuals meeting the guidelines increases with increasing levels of education (see figure 3.2) and with increasing socioeconomic status judged by family income (see figure 3.3).

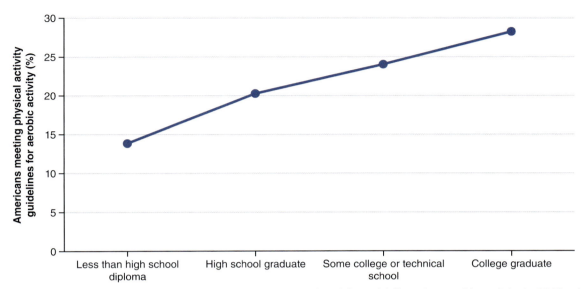

FIGURE 3.2 Percentage of Americans meeting 2018 physical activity guidelines for aerobic activity in 2019 relative to their education level (Centers for Disease Control and Prevention, 2019).

Adapted from Centers for Disease Control and Prevention (2019).

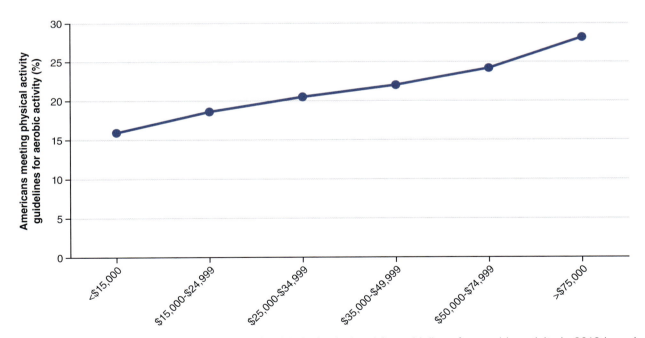

FIGURE 3.3 Percentage of Americans meeting 2018 physical activity guidelines for aerobic activity in 2019 based on family income (Centers for Disease Control and Prevention, 2019).

Adapted from Centers for Disease Control and Prevention (2019).

Measurement of Psychological Outcomes

When measuring the psychological outcomes that are of interest in exercise psychology, many different approaches can be taken. The choice of the particular measure to be used is largely dependent on the specific research question being addressed (e.g., Are we interested in the participant's *perception* of the psychological construct or a biological mechanism related to the psychological construct?). The choice is also influenced by factors such as the experimental design (e.g., Will the study be conducted in the field or in a laboratory?) and sample size (e.g., Will we use a small or a large number of participants?). Many researchers choose to use several different measures that provide various windows on the psychological outcome so that the overall nature of the effect of exercise can be triangulated to be best understood. For example, if we were interested in measuring sleep quality, we could measure this construct by self-report, which would provide a measure of perception, or by observation, monitoring devices, or neuroimaging measures that would provide more objective measures of variables indicative of sleep quality. This is true for most of the variables we will explore in this textbook—the psychological construct and the relevant mechanisms can be assessed in numerous ways. Importantly, every measurement has its strengths and limitations, so researchers must make informed decisions when they select the tools they want to use. The following are important considerations when using each of these types of measures.

Self-Report Measures

As mentioned, psychological constructs are often measured using self-report instruments designed to assess the person's perception of a particular construct. These instruments are commonly used to measure psychological outcomes such as depression, stress, mood, affect, sleep quality, self-esteem, body image, and quality of life. When we use **self-report measures**, we ask participants to report their perception of the psychological construct using a survey or through an interview. This probably seems logical. The questionnaires or surveys generally are designed to essentially answer the questions of "How do you feel?" (mood), "How would you rate your sleep quality overall?" (sleep quality), or "How do you think your health compares to others the same age and gender as you?" (quality of life). When reading studies that use these self-report measures, it is important to know if the validity and reliability (psychometric properties) of the measure have been previously established for the particular participants being studied. For example, if a measure of stress was developed and its psychometric properties were established with children, we would need to know that the psychometrics remained sound in a study focused on college-aged adults.

An important strength of self-report measures is that they provide us with the participants' perception rather than inferring their experience from more direct measures or behaviors. When considering psychological outcomes, this is a truly valuable aspect of these measures. Another strength of paper-and-pencil or electronic questionnaires is that they can be administered easily and to large numbers of people. Interviews are more time and staff intensive. They often provide stronger data but must be used with smaller samples of participants because of considerations of experimenter burden. One of the challenges of using self-report measures is that they rely on the participant having a true awareness of the construct being assessed and being able to report their perceptions accurately and honestly. For example, I have 15-year-old twin boys who have been participating in a longitudinal study since they were 10 years old. One purpose of the study is to explore how the ability to inhibit desired behaviors when children are 10 predicts risk-taking behaviors when they are teenagers. My boys were asked to complete a survey that asked them about their use of legal and illegal drugs, alcohol, and smoking products. Although the researchers and I have assured my boys that their answers are confidential and will not be shared with anyone other than the scientists, one of my boys said to me, "They're crazy if they think anyone would answer those questions honestly. This is an obvious trap for teenagers. The whole world is out to get teenage boys!" Clearly, if my son is doing any of those types of behaviors, his answers won't be honest on the survey. The more sensitive the nature of the questions, the more difficult it is to be confident that the answers are truthful. Although this is a recognized limitation of self-report instruments, the steps that are taken to ensure confidentiality and anonymity can help with securing honest answers and steps taken to establish validity and reliability provide us with some degree of confidence in the assessments.

---

self-report measures—Self-report measures are those that require participants to report their perception of the psychological construct using a survey or through an interview.

Behavioral Measures

Behavioral measures are commonly used in exercise psychology to measure constructs such as cognition and pain. A good example of a behavioral measure is the cold pressor task, which is used to measure pain tolerance. In this task, participants are asked to put their hand and arm into an ice-cold water bath. Over time, this will become painful to the participant, but they are asked to leave their hand and arm in the cold water for as long as they can bear while also likely providing judgments of their perception of the level or intensity of the pain. The measure of pain tolerance is how long they are able to leave their hand and arm in the cold water. One important consideration for behavioral tasks is to make sure that the task is implemented consistently across participants and that relevant variables are appropriately described to allow for comparisons across studies. Relevant to this example, and not surprisingly, Mitchell and colleagues (2004) provide data showing that pain tolerance times are significantly longer when the water is at 7 °C and 5 °C as compared to 1 °C. Hence, scientists using this task have to ensure that they can precisely regulate the temperature of the water bath. Another key for behavioral measures is that the participants must be equally motivated to leave their hand in the cold-water bath. If a participant is not at all invested in the research study and they put their hand in and immediately withdraw it, they likely have not provided a true measure of their pain tolerance. Researchers might use standard instructions or reasonable incentives to try to ensure relatively equal motivation and then likely also have criteria that must be met to determine if a participant appeared to comply with the instructions. In this example, if the scientists know that most people can tolerate the ice-cold water for 30 to 120 seconds (Mitchell et al., 2004), a participant who only keeps their hand in for 15 seconds might be excluded from the data analysis.

Wearable Technology Measures

Wearable technology also can be used to measure physiological variables that have implications for psychological outcomes. The possibilities in this realm have increased dramatically as technology has improved so that measurement devices are now smaller in size and have greater capabilities. In fact, smart watches are now being used to assess a variety of measures that are relevant to exercise psychology. For example, scientists who are interested in measuring stress might use heart rate obtained across the course of the day as recorded on a smart watch. Those who are interested in sleep quality might ask participants to wear a smart watch while they sleep. With the rapid advances in nanotechnology (i.e., the development of measurement devices that are on the nanoscale, which is 100 millionth of a millimeter—think Antman in the Quantum Realm), wearable technology is likely to enter a new era. I anticipate that researchers will increase their use of wearable technology to measure numerous variables such as temperature, tension, heart rate, and blood pressure. When coupled with self-report measures to confirm how the participant is perceiving the physiological signals that are being assessed, these are likely to be strong measures that are attractive to scientists.

Biological Measures

Some measures can be measured directly using biological assessments. Direct measures of constructs relevant to exercise psychology are predominantly evident when thinking about mechanisms. Scientists might collect samples of bodily fluids (e.g., blood, saliva, sweat), hair, or skin cells that can then be processed to provide for assessments of putative mechanisms such as cortisol or brain-derived neurotrophic factor (BDNF) or potential moderators such as a person's genetic risk for Alzheimer's disease. When the samples are handled properly and the processing techniques are conducted appropriately, this provides a very accurate way to assess variables of interest. Importantly, some of these measures also have limitations. For instance, if blood samples are drawn from a vein in the arm, researchers should make it clear that this is a peripheral measure and that the implications for central measures (from the brain) might not be certain.

Neuroimaging Measures

Recent exercise psychology research might include measures obtained from neuroimaging techniques such as electroencephalography (EEG), computed tomography (CAT) scans, positron emission tomography (PET) scans, and magnetic resonance imaging (MRI) (see figure 3.4). EEG measures electrical activity in the brain and is relatively inexpensive and noninvasive compared to the other neuroimaging techniques. It provides information relative to the brain's activation state (e.g., relaxed or stimulated) or

---

nanotechnology—Nanotechnology is defined as the development of measurement devices that are on the nanoscale, which is 100 millionth of a millimeter.

to the timing of specific brain processes (e.g., stimulus identification or recognition of an erroneous response). EEG is typically used in studies focused on brain function in response to acute exercise or chronic physical activity. CAT and PET scans are more invasive and costly because they require participants to receive an injection of a radioactive substance. For this reason, they are not commonly used in the exercise psychology research, but PET scans have been included in some studies focused on Alzheimer's disease because they allow for the imaging of neurofibrillary tangles and amyloid plaques implicated in the disease processes. Because they are less invasive and expensive, MRI scans have been more common in exercise psychology studies.

Structural MRI is sometimes used to allow for precise assessments of brain structure (see figure 3.4). Neuroimaging measures of brain structure are not as direct as could be obtained with a dissection (as is done in some animal studies), but it provides high-resolution images that clearly contrast between different tissues in the brain. MRI images are generated based on the magnetic properties of hydrogen ions in the brain, which provide extremely accurate images that allow for reliable measurement of specific brain structures. The images of the brain are taken as multiple, repeated "slices" so that measurements can be made directly on the images to allow for volumetric estimates in three dimensions.

Neuroimaging techniques can also be used to provide measures that allow for inferences about brain function. Measures of brain function with MRI (functional MRI, fMRI) are actually indirect measures in that the assessment reflects cerebral oxygenation and blood flow (blood oxygen level dependent, BOLD, signals) and inferences are made from these measures to brain function. Studies using fMRI might compare brain activity at rest with activity while doing a task, look at connectivity between various brain regions while at rest (resting state connectivity), or assess brain activation along white matter tracts using a technique called *diffusion tensor imaging*. fMRI measures are extremely accurate in terms of the location of the brain activation but are less accurate with respect to the timing of the activation because it is assessed across a time block of

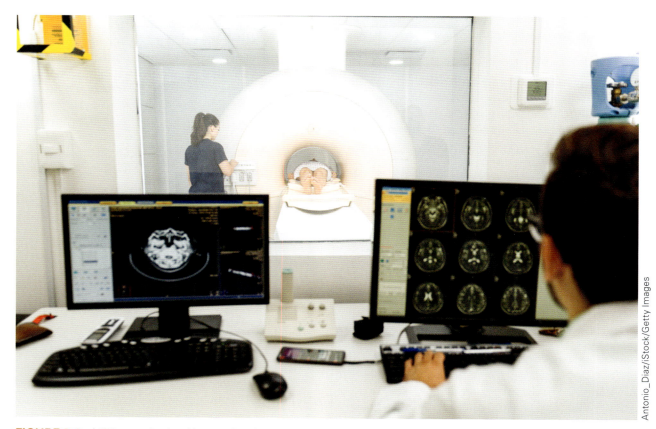

FIGURE 3.4 MRIs are obtained by moving the participant into the opening of an MRI machine, which uses magnets to provide images of brain structure and brain function.

30 seconds. Nonetheless, these measures have been incredibly valuable in allowing us to understand brain function relative to clinical conditions such as depression and Alzheimer's disease and hence have enormous potential in helping us understand the potential role of exercise in mitigating these diseases.

Summary

Before exploring the research evidence relative to the effects of exercise on various psychological outcomes, it is important to provide definitions of relevant terms. This allows us to have a clear understanding of the precise independent variables being considered that can reflect behaviors (e.g., physical activity, exercise, sport, sedentary behavior) or variables that change in response to physically active behaviors and are used to make inferences about physical activity (e.g., physical fitness, body mass index). In the exercise psychology literature, we will learn about research relative to single sessions of exercise (acute exercise) and regular physical activity participation (chronic exercise). In considering studies on exercise, we will be interested in understanding the influence of the particular mode of exercise (e.g., aerobic, high-intensity interval training, resistance) and in dose–response questions that relate to the duration and intensity of the exercise session and the frequency of participation for chronic exercise programs. In this chapter, we also learned about the various ways in which physical activity and physical fitness can be measured. Physical activity can be measured using direct measures such as observation, doubly labeled water, and wearable devices. It can also be measured using self-report measures like questionnaires or interviews. Psychological outcomes that might be influenced by physical activity are most commonly measured using self-report instruments but might also be assessed using wearable technology or with behavioral, biological, or neuroimaging measures. By introducing the various ways that physical activity, exercise, and fitness and the psychological outcomes can be assessed, you should now have an initial appreciation for the considerations that a scientist must make when deciding how to measure the constructs that are relevant to answer the research question.

Discussion Questions

1. If you were interested in measuring the relationship between physical activity and mood in a large sample of college-aged adults, which types of measures would you choose and why?
2. Consider the following scenarios: a couple walking their dog, an older person bowling, a postman delivering the mail by bicycle, a family downhill skiing, a woman attending a spin class. Which of these is sport? Which is exercise? Which is physical activity? Provide an explanation for each choice.
3. Explain the limitation of using heart rate during the day as the only measure of stress in a research study.

Exercise and Stress

OBJECTIVES

After studying this chapter, you should be able to do the following:

- Define stress and understand its biological impact on the organism
- Recognize the difference between positive stressors and negative stressors
- Describe the hypotheses and mechanisms that have been proposed to explain the benefits of exercise for stress
- Know how stress is measured in research and what the implications of the measurement choice are for our understanding
- Describe the empirical and meta-analytic evidence in support of exercise reducing stress

KEY TERMS

stressor

stress

peripheral nervous system

central nervous system

endocrine system

autonomic nervous system (ANS)

sympathetic nervous system (SNS)

parasympathetic nervous system (PSNS)

hypothalamic-pituitary-adrenal axis (HPA axis)

allostatic load

stress reactivity

stress recovery

stress pileup

heart rate variability (HRV)

> Krystal was a mid-level executive living in a city with tons of traffic but where some people still drive their cars to and from work (imagine Phoenix or Atlanta). She had a lot going on in her life. Her husband had just lost his job, so her own employment was critical for her family. Her parents were heavily engaged in her life but more in an overbearing sense than a supportive way, and they constantly were asking when Krystal and her husband were going to give them their first grandchild. She and her husband were renting a two-bedroom apartment in the suburbs, but the rent was going to increase soon and they hadn't yet found a good alternative relative to her commute. Krystal was an athlete in high school and had stayed active through college. But lately, she had not been able to find the time or willpower to maintain an exercise program. She'd started picking up dinner on her way home from work and joining her husband for cocktails before and after their meal.
>
> One day Krystal was driving into work for an important meeting. She was running late, and an accident had traffic backed up for miles. She had no alternative route. Time was passing. She had to get to this meeting. As she was sitting in traffic, she started methodically pounding her fist into her thigh in frustration. As she became increasingly late for the meeting, she got more upset and continued this abuse. She didn't stop to consider that she was hitting herself fairly hard and over an extended period of time. When she finally got to her office, she was not able to stand up as she exited the car. She had bruised her bone and had to seek medical treatment for her injury. Clearly, Krystal's coping mechanism of choice for the stress she was experiencing was neither effective nor healthy. Scenarios like this are common as people have increasing amounts of stress in their lives that result in them adopting a variety of coping mechanisms but also often results in them sacrificing time for themselves to be physically active when, in fact, being physically active might be a very effective way to cope with stress.

Krystal's story is an example of how stress levels can get out of control, leading people to perform behaviors or make decisions that might not help to alleviate the stress and ultimately might cause physical or psychological damage. Stress is ubiquitous, meaning that all people experience it to some degree. The coping methods we choose to help us manage stress are critical to navigating life's stressors as effectively as possible. Hence, it is important to consider if exercise or physical activity can provide a way of coping with stress or of reducing our responses to stressful situations.

What Is Stress?

When you read the word *stress*, how do you define it? Give yourself a minute or two to think about what the word *stress* means to you. You probably define stress as an experience—how you feel. Now consider what a stressor is. What ideas come to mind when you think about the stressors in your life? In this case, you probably think of a stressor as something that causes you to experience stress.

If you look "stress" up in the dictionary, you will find several different meanings. Some of the definitions focus on stress as a stimulus. Although this might not have been your first thought, a structural engineer would define stress in this way, as the pressure or tension that is exerted on an object. That's probably not what you thought of when trying to define the word *stress*, but it might be consistent with how you think about a **stressor**—that is, a stimulus that creates feelings of tension or that makes you feel pressure. Interestingly, when you thought of stress, you probably considered what you feel in response to stressors. That is, you might have defined stress as your body's reaction when faced with a stressor. This might include a physiological response (e.g., increased heart rate, respiration rate, blood pressure, or sweating) or a behavioral response (e.g., increased agitation, irritability, or anxiety). Another way to think of stress is as a process that involves an appraisal of the stressor relative to the resources you can use to meet the demands of the stressor. This is actually more consistent with a physicist's definition of stress, that stress is an inter-

---

stressor—A stressor can be defined as a stimulus that creates feelings of tension or that makes you feel pressure.

action between the applied force and the resistance to that force. In this case, you are exposed to a force that you judge as threatening to your well-being (the stressor), you muster resistance to that force (your coping mechanisms), and the process leaves you with a response due to the interaction (this will be experienced as a stressful response if your coping mechanisms are insufficient). These examples and definitions confirm one of the interesting things about stress, that it can be viewed as a stimulus (aka the stressor), a response (e.g., "I'm super stressed"), and an interactive process (the cognitive appraisal).

The formal definition of stress that is typically adopted by exercise psychologists is that **stress** results from an imbalance between a person's perception of demands (these can be physical or psychological, real or imagined) and an individual's perception of the resources they can bring to bear in response to those demands (Lazarus & Folkman, 1984). This is then expanded slightly by also noting that a cognitive appraisal must occur that results in a perception of threat (i.e., the experience of real or imagined harm). For example, if you perceive that an upcoming exam is going to be very challenging and that you are not adequately prepared, you might experience stress. But if you're a high school senior in your spring semester and you've already been accepted to your top choice for college, you might not experience any stress because as long as you pass the course, no potential threat or negative consequences exist for not doing well on the exam. A further expansion of the definition is to note that the experience of stress typically results in physiological and behavioral responses designed to alleviate the stress. So if you are not a high school senior, your exam is tomorrow, and you have a perception of threat from the exam, this will typically activate behavioral responses including rereading materials, reviewing your notes, studying, and practicing responses, and it might also activate feelings of energy and nervousness that help you stay awake late into the night or that keep you from getting a good night's sleep.

> Please think about the various stressors in your life that cause you stress. What do you think of? Do you have stressors related to being a student? To your job? To your home life?

If you are reading this chapter, you are likely a college student, which means that you undoubtedly experience at least some level of stress related to being a student. This might ebb and flow throughout a semester or a year but probably exists to some degree fairly consistently throughout a college career. In addition to your college classes being a source of stress, many of you might also be working a part- or full-time job and have stress at work. Or maybe you have additional stress due to your relationships with your roommate, significant other, or family. Or you might be experiencing significant stress due to the combined effects of all three—trying to maintain relationships while also working and being a student. These stressors typically represent a kind of low-lying, steady stress that you have learned to accept and that you deal with appropriately as you bide your time until the weekend or until your next break in the school year. You might also have larger sources of stress that require additional coping mechanisms. These might be relatively short-term such as when you reach that point in the semester when you have several exams and big assignments due in the same week. They might also be more long-term. Examples of this are moving to a new city to start your college experience, adapting to living with roommates, breaking up with a significant other, or facing health or financial challenges. These types of stress might require additional coping strategies to ensure that they do not become overwhelming.

> You've thought about some situations or things that cause you stress. Now answer these questions: How do you know when you're experiencing stress? What happens? What are the signs for you? What is your individualized stress response?

The way that people react to stress is somewhat individualized, meaning that responses to the same stressor might differ between individuals, particularly when the stressor is relatively mild or moderate in nature. The most common symptoms of stress are shown in figure 4.1. In response to a moderate stressor such as giving a public speech, you might experience an increase in blood pressure and begin to sweat profusely. But your friend might have a very different response; her face might turn fire-engine red and she might have trouble concentrating. If the stress is short-term as in the case of giving a

---

stress—The experience of stress results from an imbalance between a person's perception of demands (these can be physical or psychological, real or imagined) and an individual's perception of the resources they can bring to bear in response to those demands (Lazarus & Folkman, 1984).

public speech, these physiological responses will return to baseline fairly quickly. But if the stress is more long-term, as when the stress comes from job or school demands and the physiological responses continue unabated, you might begin to experience more chronic forms of wear and tear. You might begin to develop headaches or ulcers, become generally irritable with your friends and family, lose sleep, or adopt unhealthy styles of coping that end up exacerbating the situation. For all of us, our immediate responses to stress can be beneficial because they might give us the sense of urgency we need to get into action. For example, if you have an exam in 2 weeks, you probably are not experiencing much stress right now, but when the exam is the next day, your feelings of stress will be your signal to start getting serious about your preparations for that exam (and hopefully you haven't waited too long). If you have an exam in 2 weeks and you are already experiencing stress and ignoring those signals, you might begin to experience negative effects that result from keeping the body primed for action for an extended period of time when no action is actually being taken.

The first person to really consider the link between our immediate, short-term responses to stress, our more enduring responses to chronic stress, and the long-term impact of chronic stress on our health was Hans Selye. Selye was an accomplished scientist who published over 1,600 scientific articles and numerous books and who was nominated for the Nobel Prize in 1949. Although the initial acute response to stress (the fight-or-flight response) had been generally understood since 1915, Selye was responsible for identifying the role of stress in illness. His initial work with animals led him to propose the general adaptation syndrome (GAS) (Selye, 1950). The GAS explains that the body's response to a stressor is nonspecific (figure 4.2). Through his research, Selye found evidence to support his hypothesis that an individual's response to chronic stress would be the same regardless of the source of the stress. That is, for example, he expected the stress response to be the same whether the source of the stress was chronic noise exposure, financial challenges, or relationship stress. Although individuals' reactions to acute stressors might vary, such that one person might sweat and have a dry

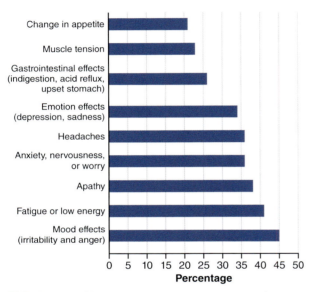

FIGURE 4.1 The most common symptoms of stress and the percentage of people in the United States who experience them.

Data from Patterson (2022).

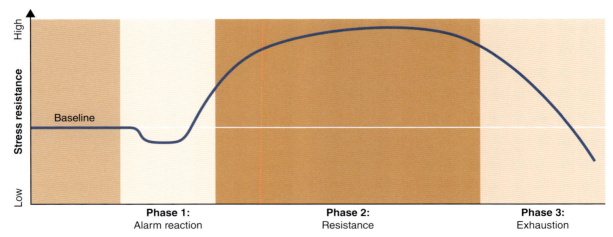

FIGURE 4.2 A visual representation of the general adaptation syndrome showing the three phases of the body's ability to mount resistance in the face of exposure to an ongoing stressor.

mouth while another might notice their heart racing, Selye expected the chronic stress response to be consistent across a variety of stressors for each individual. Selye described the GAS as consisting of three phases. The first phase is the alarm reaction, which is the immediate response to stress that involves mobilizing the body's resources through the release of epinephrine and norepinephrine. The second phase is resistance, which is when the stressor continues but is not severe enough to cause death as well as when the hypothalamic-pituitary-adrenal (HPA) axis kicks in. The third phase is exhaustion, which is when the prolonged stress response results in a weakened immune system, the depletion of the body's reserves, and, if left unabated, death.

Physical and Psychological Stressors

When you think about the stressors that exist in your life and that you are dealing with on a daily basis, would you consider them to be more physical or psychological in nature? An example of a physical stressor is if you have a very physically demanding job (e.g., as a college athlete, working in a warehouse). An example of a psychological stressor is if you aren't getting along with your roommate or if you have financial stress. Now, think about the most effective ways to cope with these stressors. Will your stress be reduced by a physical response (which does not include striking your roommate), a psychological response, or perhaps some combination? Many of us will choose to use a variety of coping mechanisms to deal with our stressors; we might use meditation at night to help ensure we get a better night's sleep to deal with our physical demands. Or we might invite our roommate to go to the gym to exercise together and to have a chance to come to an agreement about how clean to keep our shared spaces.

Let's expand on this notion of stressors being either physical or psychological. This is intriguing because of the way that the nature of our stressors has changed over time. Evidence shows that the remains of Homo sapiens (modern humans) can be traced back approximately 200,000 to 300,000 years. During that period, humans lived in caves or very simple dwellings, were able to construct tools, and survived as hunter-gatherers. For these humans, the stressors they faced threatened their very survival. Although they also might have experienced stress from their personal relationships, the more pressing stressors were the need to hunt successfully so that they could eat and the need to avoid becoming prey themselves. That is, when working together with others to take down a woolly mammoth, the need to be quick and strong and to react immediately if things went terribly wrong would have been critically important. When accidentally startling a saber-toothed tiger at a water hole, the ability to experience an immediate stress response resulting in effective fighting or fleeing might have meant the difference between life and death. As a result, those humans who had the most effective fight-or-flight response would have been the ones most likely to survive and to pass this effective and efficient response system on to their offspring.

What about the experience of stress now? In your life, you probably do not face physical stressors on a daily basis. Perhaps you've jumped when you've seen a snake in your path or felt ready to fight or flee when a barking dog ran at you. But hopefully this isn't a daily experience. Rather, your daily stressors are much more likely to be psychological stressors. An example is standing in the "wrong" line at the grocery store (the line where the cashier suddenly asks for a price check over the public announcement system and you know your wait time just increased dramatically), trying to get help from an automated phone system, or buying a car. Psychological stressors are more common in civilized postindustrial societies because most of us live in relative physical safety but must face the challenges that inevitably arise as we pursue our goals. The challenge for us from a health standpoint is that our bodily reaction to stressors is the same regardless of whether the stressor is physical or psychological—or even imagined. However, we typically do not do anything physical—that is, we neither fight nor flee—in response to the stressor. As a result, we have a lot going on internally that is physiologically preparing us to fight or flee but ends up being unnecessary because neither of these physical choices is appropriate when facing a psychological stressor. Since the body doesn't know the difference, the stress response might take an extended period of time to abate and, as a result, a negative health impact might result.

Prevalence and Costs of Stress

As previously mentioned, stress is ubiquitous. Since 2007, the American Psychological Association (APA) has conducted a national stress survey every year in which they ask questions about sources of stress, the intensity of the experience, and how people respond both mentally and physically. It is interesting to consider the sources of stress in recent years and relative to the global COVID-19 pandemic. The pandemic began to affect life in the United States in March 2020, and this was ultimately a shared major stressor that affected almost every person in the entire world. In the APA surveys, online questionnaires were collected from adults living in the United States in August and September 2019 (n = 3617), which was prior to the pandemic, and in August 2020 (n = 3409), which was about 5 months into the pandemic (see figure 4.3). In 2020, as you might imagine, the COVID-19 pandemic was identified as the top stressor, acting as a significant source of stress for 78% of adults, and almost 20% of adults reported that their mental health was worse than the year before. Importantly, in 2020, Gen Z adults (18-23 years of age) reported the highest stress levels of any age group, which reflects their stress regarding their education, their uncertainty about the 2020-2021 school year, and their perception of the impossibility of planning for their future. The experience of stress and the potential negative impact on mental health is so extreme that the APA described 2020 as a year of a "national mental health crisis that could yield serious health and social consequences for years to come" (APA, 2020, p. 1).

In considering the impact of stress, one might also think about the economic costs of stress. In the United States, it has been estimated that the impact of stress on the workplace through effects such as increased accidents, absenteeism, job turnover, and decreased productivity combined with direct costs due to medical, legal, and insurance expenses result in a total cost of $300 billion every year (Mohney, 2018). Clearly, it is important for us to identify ways to reduce the experience of stress in our society for personal and economic reasons.

Mechanisms of Stress

From a mechanistic perspective, the stress response involves the **peripheral nervous system** (made up of the autonomic and somatic nervous systems), the **central nervous system** (made up of the brain and spinal cord), and the **endocrine system** (glands that produce hormones). The autonomic nervous system (ANS) consists of the sympathetic nervous system (SNS) and the parasympathetic nervous system (PSNS). The first system to be engaged in response to a stressor is the SNS. The SNS reacts almost immediately to a stressor and signals the adrenal medulla glands (located on top of the kidneys) to release epinephrine and norepinephrine (also called

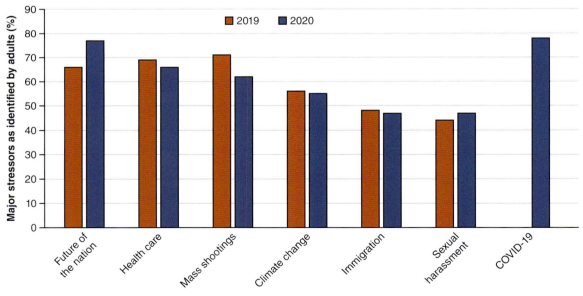

FIGURE 4.3 Percentages of adults identifying various sources of stress in 2019 prior to the COVID-19 pandemic as compared to 2020 at the beginning of the COVID-19 pandemic.

Data from American Psychological Association (2019). Stress in America: Stress and Current Events. American Psychological Association (2020). Stress in America 2020: A National Mental Health Crisis.

peripheral nervous system—The autonomic and somatic nervous systems make up the peripheral nervous system.

central nervous system—The brain and spinal cord make up the central nervous system.

endocrine system—The endocrine system consists of glands that produce hormones.

adrenaline and *noradrenaline*). The release of epinephrine and norepinephrine moves the organism away from homeostasis (the optimal zone of physiological functioning in the absence of stressors) and into a fight-or-flight response. This fight-or-flight response is designed to prepare the organism to do what is necessary to face the stressor. It includes increases in heart rate, respiration, and perspiration, and reductions in pain perception in preparation for a response. Within minutes of exposure to the stressor, the hypothalamic-pituitary-adrenal axis is also stimulated.

To remember the various aspects of the nervous system that are important for the stress response, use these mnemonics.

- The autonomic nervous system (ANS) is designed to respond automatically and so is important in producing a rapid and non-thinking response to stressors and in returning the body to homeostasis after the stressor has been removed. Within the autonomic nervous system:
  - The sympathetic nervous system (SNS) is responsible for our stress response because this system is "sympathetic" to our experience of stress and "wants to help us."
  - The parasympathetic nervous system (PSNS) helps to return the body back to normal and so is like the paramedics coming to save the day and calm everything back down.

When a person is exposed to a stressor, the hypothalamic-pituitary-adrenal axis is activated. The hypothalamic-pituitary-adrenal axis (HPA axis) includes parts of the central nervous system (the hypothalamus and the pituitary) and a part of the endocrine system (the adrenal glands). The stimulation of the HPA axis in response to a stressor results in a series of events. The hypothalamus releases corticotropin-releasing hormone (CRH), which stimulates the anterior pituitary to release adrenocorticotropic hormone (ACTH), which then stimulates the adrenal cortex to release cortisol. The increase in cortisol in response to a stressor typically peaks within 5 to 30 minutes of exposure, but the release of cortisol might continue for up to several hours. The HPA axis causes cortisol to be released because cortisol is important for further mobilizing the body's response to the stressor. The HPA axis increases blood pressure, cardiac output, and blood sugar (or glucose); decreases activities that are not critical for the fight-or-flight response (e.g., reproduction, digestion, growth); and communicates with areas of the brain that are important for the perception of fear. In a properly functioning HPA axis, the circulating cortisol ultimately reaches a level that signals the hypothalamus and anterior pituitary to shut the system back down. This is called a *negative feedback loop*, and its purpose is to help the individual calm back down (i.e., return to homeostasis) after the stressor is gone (figure 4.4).

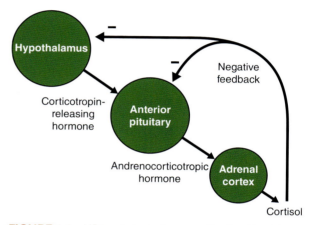

FIGURE 4.4 HPA axis including negative feedback loop.

The Stress Hormone

Cortisol is also known as the *stress hormone* because of the important role it plays in the stress response. Cortisol is a steroid hormone that is released by the adrenal glands and that affects almost every system in the body. When cortisol is in good balance, it helps the body to respond to acute stressors and to return to homeostasis afterward, to control blood pressure, to manage energy supplies, and to control the sleep–wake cycle. When a person has too much cortisol, this is called Cushing syndrome, and too little is called Addison's disease.

---

autonomic nervous system (ANS)—Designed to respond "automatically" to a stressor, the ANS is important in producing a rapid and nonthinking response to stressors and in returning the body to homeostasis after the stressor has been removed.

sympathetic nervous system (SNS)—A part of the ANS, the SNS is responsible for initiating our stress response.

parasympathetic nervous system (PSNS)—A part of the ANS, the PSNS is responsible for shutting down our stress response to return the body to homeostasis.

hypothalamic-pituitary-adrenal axis (HPA axis)—The HPA axis includes parts of the central nervous system (the hypothalamus and the pituitary) and a part of the endocrine system (the adrenal glands).

When an organism responds effectively and efficiently to stressors, this is called *allostasis* (Sterling & Eyer, 1988). That is, allostasis is the activation of physiological systems in response to a stressor that contribute to the organism surviving the stressor and that ultimately bring the body back to homeostasis. Clearly, this is important because organisms invariably will be exposed to stress and must be able to respond appropriately to the stressor and return the body to homeostasis. When the organism is overstimulated or not responding normally to a stressor, this is called *allostatic load* (McEwen & Stellar, 1993). Specifically, McEwen (1998) defines allostatic load as "the wear and tear on the body and brain resulting from chronic overactivity or inactivity of physiological systems that are normally involved in adaptation to environmental challenge" (p. 37). Three factors contribute to allostatic load:

1. Frequent stress (where the magnitude and the frequency have a combined effect)
2. Failed shutdown (when the negative feedback loop of the HPA axis becomes dysfunctional)
3. Inadequate response (when the HPA axis becomes dysfunctional in that it doesn't mount a sufficient response)

Is Stress Good or Bad?

Now that we've thought carefully about the definition of stress, learned how stress is experienced biologically, and considered the difference between acute (short-term) and chronic (long-term) effects, let's consider this question: Do you think stress is good or bad? The preceding conversation might have led you to answer the question by responding that stress is, by definition, bad. But if you haven't already done so, consider the possibility that certain stressors and even the experience of stress might also be good. What types of stressors are good? Can you think of ways that the experience of stress might be good?

When stressors are considered good, we call them *eustressors* (positive stressors). This would include things like getting married, giving a presentation at a meeting, starting college, or moving to a new town for a new job. All of these events are likely to cause us stress, but because the reason for the stressor is positive, our overall experience also might be positive. When stressors are considered bad, we call them *distressors*. This would include things like getting a divorce, a bad grade, or a traffic ticket. In fact, even the experience of distress also can be good

Allostatic Load and Mortality

Seeman and colleagues (2014) conducted an interesting study in which they examined the relationship between perceived control, perceived inequality, and allostatic load. English-speaking American adults (25-74 years) provided data in 1994 to 1995 and then again approximately 9 years later (range = 7.8-10.4 years). The researchers measured allostatic load by using biomarkers and physiological measures and by making inferences from medication use. These measures of allostatic load were taken for cardiovascular functioning; activity of the SNS, PSNS, and HPA axis; inflammation; lipid/fat metabolism; and glucose metabolism. Perceived control and perceived inequality were measured with questionnaires. Perceived control was defined as having a sense of control over aspects of one's life including work, finances, relationships with children, and marital relationship. Perceived inequality was assessed for work, home, and family as judged relative to other people. Results showed that lower perceptions of control and higher perceptions of inequality were predictive of greater allostatic load even after controlling for race, income, and sex. This suggests, then, that a relationship exists between two aspects of social status (perceived control and perceived inequality) and physiological measures indicative of an ineffective stress response (i.e., higher allostatic load). Importantly, in a follow-up study based on a subset of this same database, the authors found that participants who experienced an increase in allostatic load over a 2.5-year period had a higher risk of death (15%) over a 4.5-year period compared to those who experienced a decrease in allostatic load (5%) (Karlamangla et al., 2006). This means that lower perceived control and higher perceived inequality are predictive of greater allostatic load, which is predictive of higher mortality. This study demonstrates how understanding ways to reduce allostatic load can have critical health implications.

---

allostatic load—Allostatic load is defined as "The wear and tear on the body and brain resulting from chronic overactivity or inactivity of physiological systems that are normally involved in adaptation to environmental challenge" (McEwen, 1998, p. 37).

because it might motivate us to action that might then improve our life situation. For example, stress might motivate us to study, pay our bills, or have a hard conversation with a roommate who is irritating us. These actions could then lead to positive outcomes for us if we do well on our exam, do not have any late payments or lose services, or come to an agreement with our roommate over how late we will keep lights and music on at night.

Now that we've recognized that stress can be good or bad, let's consider some other important aspects of stress. These include that stress is unavoidable and that having a biological response to stress is necessary. As a young adult, you've probably developed numerous coping mechanisms to help you deal with stress (good and bad). You might use time management skills, be ultra-organized, talk with your friends and family, exercise, or listen to music. The coping skills that you choose to use might depend on the nature or the intensity of the stressor. You might listen to music as an avoidance mechanism to cope with a roommate who is driving you crazy, or you might seek out a social support group if you just learned that your mother has breast cancer. When you consider how stressors affect you, you probably realize that the extent to which events are stressful is dependent on several aspects of the event. In general, stress will be higher when the task is complex, decisions must be made rapidly, you have responsibility for the welfare of others whom you care about, you don't have control over an unpredictable outcome, the experience is new, and the degree of threat (psychological or physiological) is high.

As mentioned, it is important to understand ways to reduce stress responses because of the potential impact of stress on health. The short-term impacts of stress might be troublesome if a person has high blood pressure or heart complications or if the person chooses coping mechanisms that have a level of risk (e.g., binge drinking alcohol). The long-term impacts of repeated exposure to stress (allostatic load) exert their influence through biological dysregulation (i.e., a disruption of the negative feedback loop of the HPA axis), which might ultimately have a negative effect on immune function (Segerstrom & Miller, 2004) and hormone function (Miller et al., 2007). Another pathway by which chronic stress can affect health is through its impact on lifestyle behaviors. Stress might lead us to reduce our commitment to healthy lifestyle behaviors (e.g., exercise, healthy eating, sleep) and to increase the expression of unhealthy lifestyle behaviors through the adoption of negative coping behaviors (e.g., drinking alcohol, eating comfort foods, staying up late).

Exercise and Stress-Reduction Theories

One behavior that has been suggested as a possible way to cope with stress is exercise. Given what we learned earlier in this chapter, this makes good sense because when we are exposed to a stressful event, our body is primed to fight or flee, which means it is also primed for exercise. That said, when people are exposed to chronic stress, the deleterious effects of being in the resistance phase for an extended period of time might make participation in physical activity more challenging because of feelings of fatigue, frustration, low energy, and time pressure. Given that exercise is viewed as potentially having stress-reduction effects, let's consider the hypotheses proposed to explain this. The putative hypotheses are both physiological and psychological in nature.

Physiological Toughness Hypothesis

Dienstbier (1989) proposed the physiological toughness hypothesis, which suggests that physiological toughness is a characteristic that can be trained through either passive or active treatments. Passive

---

Factors That Affect the Impact of a Stressor

- Complexity of the task
- Requirements for rapid decisions
- Responsibility for welfare of others
- Lack of control
- Novelty
- Predictability
- Degree of threat

Considering the factors that contribute to the impact of a stressor, how might you reduce the stress of submitting a large written paper for a class that has a due date in 1 month? What methods of coping might help you to reduce the stress of moving to a new city to start a new job?

treatments include intermittent exposure to shock or cold, and active treatments include regular aerobic exercise. According to Dienstbier, these treatments result in changes to physiological mechanisms that then serve to protect the organism by reducing allostatic load. These physiological mechanisms include resistance to catecholamine depletion in the central nervous system, increased catecholamine responsivity in the periphery, increased beta-receptor sensitivity, and decreased cortisol. All of these responses would be considered positive and are expected to reduce the overall allostatic load. Thus, Dienstbier advises that participation in aerobic exercise is expected to increase physiological toughness, which results in a reduction in the stress response and a faster return to homeostasis.

Cross-Stressor Adaptation Hypothesis

The cross-stressor adaptation hypothesis is similar to the physiological toughness hypothesis in that it suggests that repeated exposure to a low-level stressor (in this case exercise) conditions the body so that it is better prepared to respond to other stressors. This is based partially on the notion proposed by Selye that the body's stress response is nonspecific. Hence, repeated exposure to exercise is thought to induce a low-level stress response that can become more efficient through training. Furthermore, and importantly, the body's systems also are thought to be trained for enhanced coordination of physiological systems, which then results in less disruption of homeostasis in response to exercise. The idea is that because the body's stress response to exercise is more efficient, the exerciser will have a decreased reaction to a novel stressor, a quicker recovery from the stressor, and hence an overall smaller stress response as compared to a nonexerciser.

Time-Out or Distraction Hypothesis

As previously described, the time-out or distraction hypothesis posits that exercise provides a distraction from daily stressors such that the body is able to resume normal functioning through this escape. This hypothesis is clearly not very specific in terms of the mechanisms of action but is testable. If the distraction hypothesis explains the beneficial effects of exercise on stress, we would expect other distracting activities to have a similar response. For example, going to the movies should have a similar stress-reducing effect as going for a walk.

Sense of Control Hypothesis

It has also been suggested that exercise might reduce stress because of the sense of mastery or control that it offers. By completing an exercise bout, one has demonstrated the ability to accomplish a challenging task. This might then boost a person's sense of having control over various aspects of their life and might also increase confidence in a way that carries over to other areas. Researchers who want to test this hypothesis could design their exercise intervention specifically to maximize a sense of control through, for example, starting at a low intensity level and a relatively short duration to ensure success and a sense of accomplishment.

Measurement of Stress

Before considering the empirical evidence relative to the effects of exercise on stress, it's important to think about how stress is measured. Because stress is experienced both psychologically and physically, measurements have been developed that are more subjective in nature (i.e., they assess perceptions) and that are more objective in nature (i.e., they assess objectively measured physiological responses to stress). In addition, because the events that cause stress can be both acute and chronic, measures exist for both situations. Finally, because the exact nature of the stress response relative to temporal factors and magnitude is important, researchers have also identified terms to capture this pattern of response: **stress reactivity** is the immediate response to a stressor, **stress recovery** is the time required for the person's stress response to return to baseline, and **stress pileup** is a pattern of repeated stress exposures (Smyth et al., 2018) (figure 4.5). Importantly, evidence shows that responses to laboratory stressors are indicative of a person's risk for the development of high blood pressure and heart disease thus suggesting that findings relative to laboratory stressors have implications for real-world physical responses and health impacts (Fredrikson & Matthews, 1990).

---

stress reactivity—The highest initial increase in physiological responses following exposure to a stressor is identified as stress reactivity.

stress recovery—The length of time required for physiological responses to return to baseline after exposure to a stressor is referred to as stress recovery.

stress pileup—The pattern of reactivity and recovery in physiological responses over a period of time (typically within a day or across several days) is known as stress pileup.

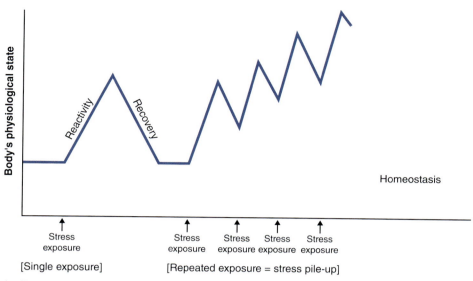

FIGURE 4.5 An illustration of stress reactivity, stress recovery, and stress pileup relative to stress exposures.

Psychological Measures

Psychological measures of stress are designed to assess perceptions of various events. We typically see two broad categories of self-report or questionnaire measures in the research literature: (1) those that are designed to assess overall exposure to stressors across some extended period of time (perhaps 1 month or 1 year) and (2) those that are focused more on daily hassles—the small hassles and irritants that we must deal with on a daily basis.

Questionnaires Measuring Major Stressors

The Schedule of Recent Experience (SRE) was developed based on years of exploring the relationship between life events that require change or adaptation and the experience of illness. The SRE was introduced by Holmes and Rahe in 1967. This survey provides an example of a measure for overall exposure to stressful events. It uses a relatively long reflection period (1 year), includes examples of 43 common life events, and is designed to assess relatively major life changes or events that are likely to be perceived as stressful. The survey includes values for the strength of the stressor that were generated from samples of adults. Table 4.1 shows two questions from this survey to which respondents are asked to describe how many times the event has happened to them in the previous year and then to multiply the number of events by the value for the strength of the stressor to get a subscore. Scores are then summed across the various stressors to calculate a total score.

Let's think about the two questions shown in this example. Would you consider these examples to represent eustress or distress? What else might you want to know before assigning the stressor a score to be calculated into a total stress experience? Do you think it's appropriate to multiply the value for the stressor by the number of exposures during the past year? According to Holmes and Rahe, these events are actually meant to assess the requirement for an adaptive behavior on the part of the

TABLE 4.1 Schedule of Recent Experience Sample Questions

	# of times	×	Mean value	= Your score
1. A major change in your social activities	3	×	18	= 54
2. Gaining a new family member to the household	1	×	39	= 39

individual; that is, they are asking about exposure to events that would require significant adaptation and hence might be presumed to predict a negative physiological response. The authors of this survey do not distinguish between eustress and distress but rather view all need for change as potentially contributing to a stress response. Thinking about these questions might help you recognize one of the challenges of assessing stress through questionnaires, because one person's distress may be another person's eustress and vice versa. In addition, the impact of the stressor on a person might range from small to large rather than being a consistent experience across individuals.

Another consideration in assessing stress in this fashion relates to a chicken-and-egg conundrum. That is, someone who is interested in the relationship between stress and illness and uses a survey like this to measure stress has no way of being sure that the experience of the illness isn't, in fact, causing the judgments of stress (or even the number of life changes). For example, if a person is battling cancer, that person might have a change in work hours or conditions and experience changes in terms of social activities, sleep, and exercise that are reflective of the ongoing experience of being sick with cancer. Using the SRE, all of these changes would be considered in the formula of the total stress experience, but they are actually reflective of the illness rather than suggesting a cause of the illness.

In response to these limitations of the SRE and other surveys using a similar approach, researchers have developed interview-based approaches that provide the opportunity to better understand the specific nature of the effects of a stressor on an individual. Although several of these have established reliability and validity, the high cost required for this type of measure prevents them from being commonly used in the exercise psychology literature.

Questionnaires Measuring Daily Hassles

Another way to approach the psychological assessment of stress is to look at daily hassles. On its own, a single hassle might not have an important impact on the individual, but when accumulated at a high rate relative to time, they might have an influence on health. Examples of daily hassles include trying to find a parking spot, finding out your key card for access to your room has expired, or oversleeping your alarm. The Revised University Student Hassles Scale (RUSHS) is a measure of daily hassles that was developed specifically for college students. This survey contains 54 questions with daily hassles in a variety of areas including time pressure, financial constraints, and friendships. Participants are asked to identify hassles they've experienced in the previous month and then to indicate the perceived severity of each particular hassle from "not at all severe" to "extremely severe." Scores include the number of hassles identified and the average severity scores for those hassles.

In summary, psychological measures of stress rely on self-report and can be obtained using written surveys or interview methods. These measures can be designed to focus on major life stressors that would be expected to have large and persistent effects on the individual or to consider things like daily hassles that result in relatively small reactions and from which the person tends to recover quickly. Given that the accumulation of daily hassles can contribute to a stress pileup, both major life stressors and daily hassles have important health implications, which is why valid and reliable measures have been developed and used in research on stress.

Physiological Measures

Physiological measures of stress are typically assessed in response to a specific stress-inducing event. Various measures of heart rate (HR), blood pressure, galvanic skin response (GSR; sweatiness), electroencephalographic (EEG; brain) activity, and electromyographic (EMG; muscle tension) activity are commonly used to assess stress. Measurements can be taken using either manual or automated measurement tools and are typically recorded at least once prior to and once following exposure to the stressor. When researchers are interested in the time course of the stress response, multiple measures would be taken after the exposure, allowing for measurement of the time of the peak response and an understanding of recovery.

In recent studies, assessments of heart rate variability have become more common. **Heart rate variability (HRV)** is a measure of the variability in the time intervals between heartbeats. A higher HRV is described as a higher vagal tone and is indicative of greater activation of the PSNS, which is the system responsible for bringing the body back to homeostasis. Because the PSNS serves to bring the body back to homeostasis after a stressful event, higher HRV is thus associated with a healthier system and is thought to be indicative of being calm and

---

heart rate variability (HRV)—HRV is a measure of the variability in the intervals (length of time) between heartbeats.

relaxed in the face of stress. By contrast, lower HRV is indicative of a "monotonously regular heart rate" (Kim et al., 2018, p. 235) and of a dampened ability to appropriately cope with stress.

High HRV = high vagal tone
= high PSNS activation

Decrease in HRV in response to stress
= decrease in vagal tone = low PSNS activation

In addition to self-report and physiological measures of stress, researchers might also collect saliva or blood samples to allow for the assessment of cortisol as an indicant of stress. As mentioned previously, cortisol is also known as the *stress hormone*, so high levels are associated with a large stress experience. One of the biggest challenges in using cortisol as an outcome measure is that it has a diurnal rhythm (i.e., cortisol levels change naturally across the course of the day for all individuals). This means that levels can vary significantly depending on the time of day at which they are assessed. As a result, within-subjects designs with strict controls on time of day, diet, and fluid consumption are best to account for individual and time-of-day variability when assessing cortisol. If those controls are possible, cortisol measurements provide an effective tool for understanding stress responses.

Stress Induction

In research studies, a wide number of events have been used to induce stress. These events can be categorized as those that are not influenced by a response (passive) or those that potentially could benefit from a response (active). The cold pressor task is an example of a passive stressor. In this task, participants are asked to immerse their arm in a cold-water bath and hold it there as long as possible (figure 4.7). If you've ever needed to ice an injury, you probably recognize that the cold pressor task would quickly become stressful as the experience becomes increasingly uncomfortable. Passive tasks tend to result in decreases in heart rate and increases in diastolic blood pressure (DBP). In this case, participants must use coping mechanisms to help them keep their arm in the frigid water, and the body will respond physically as long as the arm is in the tank. Active tasks include cognitively stressing tasks such as the Stroop task, solving math problems, or giving a presentation in front of your peers. In these tasks, the participant actively participates in the task, and the stress presumably can be reduced by performing well, but the tasks are usually designed to be difficult so that they evoke the desired stress response. Performance of active tasks typically results in increased heart rate and increased systolic blood pressure (SBP).

Patterns of Stress Responses

One exciting recent advancement in the area of stress measurement is the ongoing development of a technique that focuses more on the temporal nature of the stress response than the adoption of a snapshot approach that only focuses on a single point in time. Smyth and associates (2018) have

Measuring Cortisol

Using cortisol to assess stress is not as easy as you might hope. Cortisol has a diurnal rhythm, which means that cortisol levels fluctuate in a predictable way over the course of the day and relative to a person's waking time and the time when they go to sleep (figure 4.6). Although this pattern is predictable, it is also highly individualized, which can make it challenging to use cortisol as an outcome measure in a between-subjects research design.

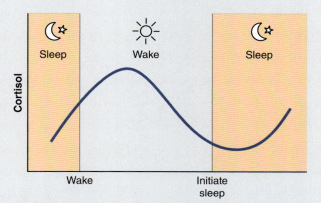

FIGURE 4.6 A visual representation of the diurnal cortisol response.

FIGURE 4.7 The cold pressor task is one that is used to create a stress response, and it is also used in studies to measure pain threshold and tolerance (see chapter 8).

proposed that researchers consider stress responses with a recognition of the temporal nature of the reaction. In particular, they consider stress reactivity, stress recovery, and stress pileup. Based on their model, they define stress reactivity as the highest initial increase following exposure to the stressor. They define stress recovery as the length of time required to return to baseline. Stress pileup is the pattern of reactivity and recovery over a period of time (typically within a day or across several days). In their work, they focus on the negative affective responses and the tendency to perseverate (worry) when exposed to stressors, and they propose that these measures are appropriate for reflecting both individual differences in responses and the temporal nature of exposure to a single stressor or to repeated stressors. This focus on a pattern of responses could be important because, for example, stress pileup has been linked to more negative affect (Schilling & Diehl, 2014) and negative affect has been linked to lower quality sleep (Brummett et al., 2006).

Evidence Relative to the Effects of Exercise on Stress

The potential benefits of exercise for stress have been explored through numerous individual studies and have also been examined through meta-analytic reviews. The empirical studies presented here offer an opportunity to consider the distinction between large-scale epidemiological studies and smaller lab-based studies. Both types of studies provide important information to advance our understanding, but they also have acknowledged shortcomings. In this section, we will also consider reviews focused on chronic and acute exercise, on tai chi and mind–body exercises in particular, and on RCTs.

Empirical Evidence

Perales, Pozo-Cruz, and Pozo-Cruz (2014) present data from an analysis of a remarkable data set. The Household Income and Labour Dynamics in Australia (HILDA) Survey has been administered annually for 12 years to a nationally representative sample of the same 17,080 adults. This large sample, its representativeness of the population, and the length of time over which data have been collected are what make this data set remarkable. In this study, physical activity was assessed as how many days per week a person generally participates in moderate to vigorous physical activity (MVPA) for at least 30 minutes. Psychological distress was measured at three time points across the 12 years using the Kessler Psychological Distress Scale, which consists of 10 questions regarding the regular experience of negative feelings and emotions associated with stress (e.g., hopelessness or worthlessness). On this scale, a lower number represents a more frequent experience of negative emotions (e.g., 1 = all the time; 5 = none of the time). Results showed that across the 12 years of the study, increases in the weekly frequency of MVPA were associated with significant reductions in psychological distress. In other words, those individuals who increased the amount of weekly physical activity also experienced decreases in their stress experiences. Although the design of this study means that we cannot conclude that MVPA *caused* these reductions in psychological distress, the prospective design of the study means that we can at least conclude that MVPA at one point in time is predictive of subsequent perceptions of distress.

In contrast to this large-scale prospective study looking at chronic forms of physical activity, Moreira and colleagues (2014) conducted a study looking at the effects of a single session of exercise on the stress response during the cold pressor task. Specifically, they explored the effects of a single session of circuit training on the blood pressure response of young, apparently healthy adults during and following the cold pressor task. In this within-subjects study, participants performed the cold pressor task on one day following a no-exercise condition and on another day following three circuits consisting of resistance and aerobic exercises. The results were supportive of exercise resulting in hypotension (reduced blood pressure). In the first 2 minutes following the cold pressor task, and for an entire hour following the task, SBP and DBP were significantly lower when participants had exercised as compared to when they had not. Furthermore, the extent to which their immediate blood pressure response to the cold pressor task was blunted by exercise (stress reactivity) was predictive of the magnitude of the benefits in the hour following the stress exposure. The implications of this study are that acute exercise has both immediate benefits through the reduction of the physiological reaction to a stressor and has enduring hypotensive effects that might then provide longer-term benefits in terms of a reduced overall stress response. This is exciting because it suggests that a single session of exercise can have stress-reducing benefits that are both short- and long-term.

Using an experimental design that allows for conclusions of cause-and-effect relationships, Chovanec and Gropel (2020) conducted an RCT with college females to explore the effects of a chronic exercise training program on stress reactivity. Fifty-two participants were randomly assigned to either an aerobic training group, a resistance training group, or a wait list control. For 8 weeks the training groups met 3 times per week for 60-minute exercise sessions. Questionnaires assessing perceived life stress and measures of stress reactivity and recovery in response to a 15-second visual and auditory stressful stimulus (images of spiders and snakes paired with an obnoxious noise) were obtained prior to and following the intervention. Results for both training groups were the same in that participants who participated in either aerobic training or resistance training had increases in aerobic fitness, decreases in body mass index (BMI), reductions in perceived life stress, and a faster return to baseline HR after exposure to the stressful stimuli. These results suggest that both resistance and aerobic exercise provide physical health benefits and that both also result in reductions in perceived and objectively measured stress.

These three studies provide excellent examples of the type of research studies that are conducted to explore the effects of exercise on stress. Using prospective and RCT designs, looking at a single session of exercise, an 8-week intervention, or physical activity participation across an entire year, results consistently support the potential of exercise to alleviate stress.

Meta-Analytic Evidence

Given the substantial amount of research that has been conducted on this topic, it is probably not surprising that numerous meta-analytic reviews have been performed. As you recall, a meta-analytic review is one in which the results of empirical studies are statistically summarized to provide an overall effect size and to allow for an examination of potential moderators. Because of the wide variety of designs that have been used, a particular challenge in this research area is to clearly define inclusion criteria to limit studies to those that are exploring the same research question (e.g., the effects of acute or chronic exercise).

The first meta-analytic review of this literature was conducted by Crews and Landers (1987). At that time, the empirical evidence consisted of only 7 chronic training studies and 26 correlational studies exploring the relationship between aerobic exercise or aerobic fitness and stress reactivity. Overall, the average effect size (ES) of 0.48 indicated that fit or exercised participants displayed significantly reduced responses to stressors as compared to unfit or unexercised participants. The authors conducted analyses to see if there was variability in the size of the effects that might be explained by moderator variables. However, in this case, the effect sizes were shown to be very similar to one another (homogeneous), so moderator variables were not explored. Thus, the authors concluded that the relationship between physical activity participation or fitness and the stress response is robust and consistently positive, thus supporting a positive association between regular participation in physical activity and stress reduction.

Almost 20 years later, Hamer and associates (2006) reviewed the evidence from studies in which a single session of exercise was administered and the blood pressure response to a cardiovascular stress-reactivity test was used as the outcome measure. The cardiovascular stress-reactivity tests included the Stroop task, a cold pressor task, and a public speaking task. Hamer and colleagues reported that across 15 RCTs, there was an average decrease in the blood pressure response to a stressor with an ES of 0.40 for DBP and an ES of 0.38 for SBP. These effects are considered small, but the authors took an important next step by converting these effect sizes back to the original measurement standard (i.e., blood pressure) and then linking this to clinical outcomes. The authors found that these effect sizes equate to approximately 3.0 mm HG for DBP (with a standard deviation of 2.7) and 3.7 mm HG for SBP (with a standard deviation of 3.9). They then provide evidence that for each standard deviation decrease in blood pressure reactivity to a stressor, there is a decrease in carotid artery thickness (Kamarck et al., 1997), which is itself related to a reduced risk of having a heart attack (Salonen & Salonen, 1993). Given that a decrease in DBP by 3.0 mm HG is bigger than the standard deviation of 2.7 and that the decrease in SBP by 3.7 mm HG approximates the standard deviation of 3.9, these findings have the potential to be clinically meaningful because they imply a decrease in the risk of a heart attack.

Two meta-analyses have focused on specific modes of physical activity. Wang and colleagues (2010) used meta-analytic tools to explore the effects of tai chi on stress. Results from eight studies conducted across a variety of populations indicated that tai chi participation significantly improved perceived stress management with a moderate effect size of 0.66. In the studies that were reviewed, tai chi was performed for between 60 and 120 minutes, 1 to 4 times per week, for 10 to 24 weeks. With a similar interest, Strehli and associates (2021) limited their meta-analysis to 26 studies looking at the effects of mind–body physical activity interventions on stress-related variables (i.e., heart rate, cortisol, blood pressure). The studies they included were mostly focused on yoga-based interventions, with qigong exercises the second most common. Results showed significant and large reductions for heart rate ($g = 1.71$), cortisol ($g = 1.32$), and blood pressure ($g = 1.04$) in response to the physical activity participation. Importantly, most of these physiological measures were taken at rest rather than in response to a stressor, which suggests that this type of physical activity is associated with reductions in baseline physiological stress markers. In combination, these two meta-analytic reviews suggest that tai chi and mind–body physical activity interventions have the potential to improve perceived stress management and to reduce resting indicators of physiological stress.

Stubbs and colleagues (2017) focused their review on studies exploring the benefits of exercise in terms of reducing anxiety in people with an anxiety disorder or a stress-related disorder. They found six RCTs in which a total of 262 adults had been randomized to either an exercise intervention or a control condition. In all studies, the exercise intervention was aerobic in nature, lasted between 6 and 12 weeks, and, when reported, was conducted at moderate intensity. The average effect size of 0.58 indicates that exercise reduces anxiety symptoms in people who are known to have high anxiety. The authors caution that this is a small number of RCTs and some of the RCTs were not of high quality, but this finding certainly supports further exploration of the potential of exercise in this population.

Summary

Stress is ubiquitous, but the impact of stress on individuals varies based on their social support network, their coping abilities, and their levels of exercise. When considering stress, we recognize the distinction between acute bouts of stress and more chronic exposure to stress. Both can cause harmful effects, but chronic exposure is most likely to have long-term health consequences. The increase in allostatic load primes the organism to react in a more stressful way to acute events but can also have an enduring deleterious effect on health. Fortunately, evidence supports that regular participation in exercise can positively affect perceived stress, physiological markers of stress, stress reactivity, and stress recovery. Evidence from prospective studies, acute exercise studies, and RCTs supports that exercise can reduce stressful responses. Meta-analytic reviews tell us that across this body of literature, the effects when assessed relative to exposure to a stressful event or at baseline in people with high levels of anxiety range from small to moderate, the effects of tai chi on perceived stress are moderate, and the effects of yoga and qigong for baseline measures of physiological stress are large. Future research is warranted in this area to advance our understanding of dose–response relationships, the durability of the effects, and the mechanisms underlying the effects.

Discussion Questions

1. In Perales and associates' (2014) study (HILDA), surveys were administered annually for 12 years. What did the authors measure, what did their results show, and what were the implications?

2. In Chovanec and Gropel's (2020) study, 52 college females were randomly assigned to an aerobic training group, a resistance training group, or a wait list control. Explain what was measured, what was found, and what the implications are.

3. Strehli and colleagues (2021) found large effects for mind–body physical activity interventions on biological indicants of stress, while Wang and associates (2010) report an overall moderate effect size for tai chi. Provide a thoughtful discussion of why these effect sizes might be different and how we should interpret these effects.

4. Define stress and discuss how it can be viewed as a stimulus, a response, or the stimulus–response process.

Exercise and Anxiety

OBJECTIVES

After studying this chapter, you should be able to do the following:

- Contrast state anxiety, trait anxiety, and generalized anxiety disorders and recognize the most common anxiety disorders
- Compare various ways of assessing anxiety in laboratory settings
- Understand the mechanisms that have been proposed to explain why exercise reduces anxiety
- Summarize what the research shows with regards to reducing anxiety in nonanxious samples and in clinically anxious samples

KEY TERMS

anxiety

state (acute) anxiety

trait (chronic) anxiety

generalized anxiety disorder

panic disorder

phobias

obsessive-compulsive disorder (OCD)

post-traumatic stress disorder (PTSD)

cognitive behavioral therapy (CBT)

somatic activation

anxiety-related behaviors

self-report measures

Bob was a Vietnam War veteran who was working as a musician and lived in a small home with his wife and two sons. Bob had recently injured himself, and the explanation of what happened was unique. He had been having trouble with nightmares from his military experiences in Vietnam, and they were affecting his ability to get a good night's sleep. He was upset about the vividness of the dreams, which were forcing him to relive both real and imagined situations in Vietnam. But he was also concerned for practical reasons because his thrashing about and vocalizations were keeping his wife up, making it challenging for her to be fully rested for her 7:00 a.m. to 7:00 p.m. shift as a nurse. One evening when his sons were away at a friend's house for a sleepover, Bob decided to sleep in the bottom bunk in his boys' bedroom. He thought the change in location for sleeping might help with his nightmares and also give his wife a chance to get a good night's sleep. In the middle of the night, Bob had another nightmare that involved him being trapped in a cage. In an effort to escape his dream prison, he began thrashing around. As the nightmare escalated, Bob kicked his legs out straight, knocking the footboard of the bed out. He was startled to wake up in excruciating pain when the footboard of the top bunk crashed down on his shins. Clearly, Bob was suffering from post-traumatic stress disorder and panic attacks, and this was his wake-up call to seek help. Following this episode, Bob contacted the Veterans Affairs agency and began treatment with a psychiatrist. The psychiatrist enrolled Bob in a therapy group program to focus on identifying triggers, reducing and managing stress and anxiety, and building self-esteem. The psychiatrist also prescribed drugs to treat his depression and anxiety.

The opening scenario focuses on a person who is experiencing post-traumatic stress disorder (PTSD), which is linked to panic attacks and anxiety. Although therapy and pharmacological interventions can be successful in treating anxiety, it is important to appreciate the potential role of exercise as well. In other words, in addition to the treatments prescribed, the question is if the psychologist should also recommend exercise. This might be particularly relevant in this example because upon retiring from the military, Bob experienced a transition toward being less physically active. We will consider how single sessions of exercise and chronic exercise can affect the experience of anxiety.

What Is Anxiety?

The American Psychological Association (APA) defines **anxiety** as "an emotion characterized by feelings of tension, worried thoughts and physical changes like increased blood pressure" (American Psychological Association, 2022). We have all experienced anxiety in an acute sense, and this is referred to as **state anxiety**. Examples might be when you have a big exam that you do not feel prepared for, when you are asked to give a public presentation, or when you have an important sport competition. In these situations you are likely to experience a variety of symptoms including sweaty palms, nausea, a racing heart, and tunnel vision. The experience of feelings of anxiety in the face of these types of evaluative situations is common and natural, and the symptoms typically abate relatively quickly either during or following the event. These episodes of state anxiety are experienced by everyone and can be managed with various coping techniques including deep breathing, controlling negative thoughts relative to the situation, and even imagining yourself being successful.

Although the experience of state anxiety is normal and ubiquitous, the experience of chronic anxiety is less common. When anxiety is experienced over an extended period of time, it is considered **trait anxiety**. When trait anxiety is particularly long-lasting (6 months is often the criterion), is irrational or disproportionate to the threat, and affects daily living, it is considered to be a clinical form of anxiety or an anxiety disorder. Within any given year, approximately 19% of Americans are affected by various forms of anxiety disorders in ways that have a significant impact on their daily functioning.

---

anxiety—Anxiety is defined as "An emotion characterized by feelings of tension, worried thoughts and physical changes like increased blood pressure" (American Psychological Association, 2022).

state (acute) anxiety—Anxiety that is experienced over a short period of time is called state or acute anxiety.

trait (chronic) anxiety—Anxiety that is experienced over an extended period of time is also called chronic anxiety.

American Psychological Association

The American Psychological Association (APA) is an important scientific and professional organization that has more than 100,000 members and affiliates including researchers, practitioners, and students. The organization hosts an annual meeting at which research papers are presented. It advocates to promote the unique benefits of psychology in terms of both the science of behavior and the benefits to individuals in their daily lives. In particular, APA is engaged in advocacy on a variety of topics including health disparities, federal funding for psychological research, civil rights, criminal justice, gun violence, suicide, and substance use disorders. Within the APA is a division called Division 47: Society for Sport, Exercise, and Performance Psychology, which is an interest group that focuses on topics related to exercise psychology.

What Are Anxiety Disorders?

The APA identifies several major types of anxiety disorders including generalized anxiety disorder, panic disorder, phobias, obsessive-compulsive disorder, and PTSD. Although these disorders have anxiety in common, they differ in terms of the specific nature of the experience (figure 5.1).

Generalized Anxiety Disorder

Generalized anxiety disorder is defined by the experience of recurring fears or worries that often have unclear specific causes and that affect a person's ability to perform daily tasks. The target of the fear or worry might seem rational, such as being worried about finances or performing well at work, but the anxiety is considered a disorder when the fears or worries are persistent or out of proportion to the actual potential consequences of an event. For example, if a 36-year-old man is living paycheck to paycheck and is losing sleep and experiencing anxiety related to his finances, this is a reasonable response. But if a 36-year-old man who has stable employment, makes a good salary, and has a reasonable amount of money in a savings account is losing sleep and experiencing anxiety related to his finances, this is probably disproportionate to the actual threat. Generalized anxiety disorder can manifest as paralysis through analysis, where people are unable to function because they are considering every possible negative outcome relative to a decision they might need to make. These worries often result in difficulties handling uncertainty, indecisiveness, and sensing threat in a wide range of situations. To meet the definition of generalized anxiety disorder provided by the APA, this sense of anxiety has to be experienced on most days for at least 6 months.

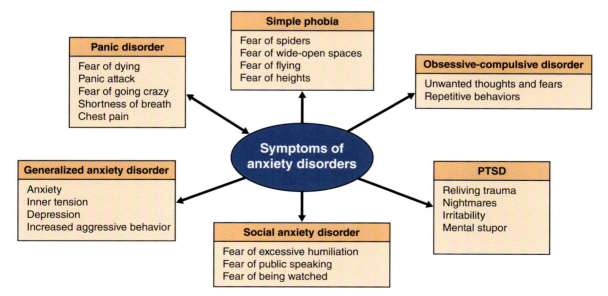

FIGURE 5.1 Visual representation of the various anxiety disorders and common symptoms.

---

generalized anxiety disorder—The experience of recurring fears or worries that often have unclear specific causes and that affect the ability to perform daily tasks characterizes generalized anxiety disorder.

Panic Disorder

Panic disorder is characterized by the experience of sudden, intense feelings of terror that have no obvious or justifiable cause. These perceptions are accompanied by physiological responses or symptoms that include shortness of breath, heart racing, sweating, and feeling dizzy or faint. They typically reach maximum intensity after about 10 to 15 minutes. Although many people might experience an occasional panic attack, this would be diagnosed as a mental health disorder according to the APA if the panic attacks were recurring on a regular or semi-regular basis and were accompanied by concern about future attacks and evidence of maladaptive changes in behavior related to the panic attacks. In some cases, individuals are able to identify the triggers for their panic attacks and might self-select to avoid those triggers as a way to minimize the likelihood of an attack. Common triggers include caffeine, a traumatic situation, a reaction to medication, and life stressors. In other cases, there are no identifiable triggers, and the panic attacks occur seemingly at random. Panic attacks sometimes can occur during sleep as in the example of Bob provided at the start of this chapter.

Phobias

Phobias are another type of anxiety disorder, and they are experienced by about 19 million Americans. A phobia is an unrealistic and debilitating fear of something specific. Phobias can be experienced relative to almost any stimulus, but common phobias include fears of spiders (arachnophobia), snakes (ophidiophobia), dogs (cynophobia), heights (acrophobia), wide-open spaces (kenophobia), and small spaces (claustrophobia). One distinction between panic disorder and a phobia is that with a phobia, the cause is always identifiable but doesn't warrant the extreme feelings of fear that are experienced. For example, consider Rene, who has a phobia about mice. This phobia controls many decisions she makes; she will not consider staying at a state park cabin because she once saw a mouse at a state park when she was a teenager. One day Rene saw a mouse in her home and immediately panicked. She jumped up on a sofa and started hyperventilating while simultaneously screaming uncontrollably. She picked up a pillow to beat off her perceived attacker. Luckily, her son came to her rescue and was able to escort her out of their home. But she was unable to return to her home until the pest-control people were called, had treated the home, and had repeatedly assured her that they had taken care of all mice. Even with these reassurances, she was on high alert for weeks in fear of seeing another mouse in her house.

> Do you have any phobias? What are they? How long have you had them? How do you react when faced with the trigger of your phobia? Have you done anything to reduce your phobia? If you don't have a phobia, imagine how you feel when you are watching a really scary movie—perhaps on the edge of your seat, nervous, jumpy, and ready to flee. Imagine experiencing these feelings in an ongoing fashion or in response to situations you encounter frequently in your life. This gives you an idea of the experiences of individuals with clinical anxiety disorders.

Obsessive-Compulsive Disorder

Obsessive-compulsive disorder (OCD) is evident when a person has thoughts or feelings (obsessions) that are persistent, unwanted, and uncontrollable. To reduce the anxiety caused by these obsessions, the person participates in repeated behaviors such as hand washing that become compulsive. The person's behaviors then come to reflect perfectionism, excessive orderliness, and a need for control of situations and relations with others. Although we all might have habits that we repeat such as biting our nails or double- and triple-checking our alarm clock the night before an important event, these are not compulsions unless we spend at least an hour per day doing these things, they feel uncontrollable and unenjoyable, and they interfere with our normal activities. OCD has a stronger familial link than other anxiety disorders, meaning that children of parents with OCD are themselves more likely to have OCD.

PTSD

PTSD is experienced when a person has previously been exposed to a traumatic event and then relives

---

panic disorder—Panic disorder is characterized by the experience of sudden, intense feelings of terror that have no obvious or justifiable cause.

phobias—An unrealistic and debilitating fear of something specific is known as a phobia.

obsessive-compulsive disorder (OCD)—OCD is when a person has thoughts or feelings (obsessions) that are persistent, unwanted, and uncontrollable, and to reduce the anxiety caused by these obsessions, the person participates in repeated behaviors such as hand washing that become compulsive.

post-traumatic stress disorder (PTSD)—PTSD is experienced when a person has previously been exposed to a traumatic event and then relives that trauma when exposed to reminders of the event (triggers).

that trauma when exposed to reminders of the event. PTSD is common in military veterans and in people who have lived through natural disasters or who have witnessed horrific events such as a deadly car accident or a shooting. It is estimated that 3.5% of Americans have PTSD, and 7.6% of veterans experience PTSD (Hegberg et al., 2019). The symptoms of PTSD include reliving of the traumatic episode, negative thoughts and feelings, avoidance of reminders (triggers) of the event, and heightened arousal. PTSD is characterized by intense feelings of sadness, fear, or anger and might be typified by excessive reactions to ordinary events that serve as triggers. For example, the sound of a car backfiring or seeing a news story about a shooting might serve as a trigger for anxiety, depression, and panic in a person with PTSD. Although PTSD resolves on its own in approximately 50% of individuals, it can last for years in other people. Individuals with PTSD have higher chronic health issues including diabetes and obesity and show reductions in their physical activity participation as compared to their behavior prior to the experience of PTSD.

Reflective of the fact that so many different types of anxiety disorders exist, empirical evidence is limited specific to the effects of exercise for many of these forms of anxiety. Instead, the vast amount of research is focused either on anxiety as a state-level emotional response or on generalized anxiety disorder. The body of evidence on PTSD and panic attacks is growing, but research on exercise and OCD or phobias is extremely limited.

> Do you know anyone who has been diagnosed with one of these clinical disorders? If so, you likely have a sense of how life-altering these disorders can be as the person tries to navigate their lives. Individuals with anxiety disorders are known to report lower quality of life, to have challenges in their personal relationships, and to have difficulty meeting demands of their employment. If you know someone with a clinical disorder, do you know if they have ever tried exercise as a way to mitigate their anxious reactions? We'll learn more in this chapter about the potential role of exercise in treating anxiety disorders.

Separation Anxiety Disorder

In addition to the anxiety disorders listed here, you might be familiar with one other anxiety disorder. Separation anxiety disorder typically becomes evident during childhood and, therefore, is considered by APA to fall under a separate section of disorders specific to diagnoses that take place in infancy, childhood, or adolescence. You might have seen this in a toddler left at school for the first time. The child might cry and cling to her parents when they attempt to leave the child at school. To be considered a disorder, it would be characterized by excessive distress relative to a child's developmental age and in response to anticipated or actual separation from loved ones. If the distress is intense or prolonged and interferes with normal activities, this might meet the criteria for a clinical disorder.

Prevalence and Costs of Anxiety

Clinical anxiety disorders are relatively common, with estimates that approximately 19% of adults in the United States have experienced an anxiety disorder in the past year (Harvard Medical School, 2007b) and with an estimated 31% of adults having an anxiety disorder at some point in their lives (Harvard Medical School, 2007a). When examined at the level of the specific anxiety disorder, evidence suggests that phobias are the most commonly experienced (see table 5.1). During the COVID-19 pandemic, the

TABLE 5.1   Prevalence Estimates for Anxiety Disorders in the U.S. Population

	Estimated number of Americans	Estimated % of US population
Generalized anxiety disorder	6,800,000	3.1%
Panic disorder	6,000,000	2.7%
Phobias	19,000,000	8.7%
Obsessive-compulsive disorder	2,200,000	1.0%
Post-traumatic stress disorder	7,700,000	3.5%

Adapted from Anxiety and Depression Association of America (2022).

numbers of people experiencing anxiety and depression increased dramatically. Mental Health America (2021) reported increases from 2019 to 2020 of 93% and 62% for anxiety and depression, respectively, in terms of the numbers of people completing an online screening form as a first step in seeking help (Mental Health America, 2021). Data from repeated measures of anxiety and depressive symptoms from the first half of 2019 (before the COVID-19 pandemic) to May and April of 2020 (the early months of the COVID-19 pandemic in the United States) showed that people were three times more likely to be identified as having an anxiety or depressive disorder (Twenge & Joiner, 2020). Time will tell if the COVID-19 pandemic has a lasting impact on the prevalence of these disorders on a national or even international scale.

In terms of prevalence relative to demographic factors, data support higher prevalence in women (23.4%) than in men (14.3%), with Whites demonstrating more symptoms of anxiety than ethnic minority groups for all disorders except PTSD, for which Blacks had the highest prevalence (8.6%) (The Recovery Village, 2022). There is a significant interaction among age group and sex (figure 5.2) such that women report a higher prevalence than men across older age groups, but the magnitude of this difference decreases across older age groups and are equivalent in the 85-plus group (Reynolds et al., 2015). Importantly, individuals with anxiety disorders often also experience major depressive disorder or have a substance use disorder. These co-occurring disorders make treatment more challenging.

The implications of having an anxiety disorder are important to consider. Individuals who have anxiety disorders are likely to experience functional impairment as they try to limit exposure to events that will cause anxiety. This might then limit their vocational options or their ability to be successful in their careers. They often have other comorbidities including depression and substance abuse. They have an increased risk of suicide and cardiovascular disease and reduced quality of life. Marciniak and colleagues (2005) estimated that the medical cost of treatment for individuals with an anxiety disorder is $6,475 (approximately $9,583 in 2023 dollars), with additional costs of $2,138 (approximately $3,164 in 2023 dollars) for generalized anxiety disorder, $1,603 (approximately $2,372 in 2023 dollars) for panic disorders, and $3,940 (approximately $5,831 in 2023 dollars) for PTSD. In total, recent estimates of the overall economic burden of anxiety disorders are difficult to find, but it previously was estimated that anxiety disorders account for 31.5% of the total economic costs of mental health in the United States (approximately 46.6 billion in 1990 dollars, Rice & Miller, 1998), and that worldwide the combined economic impact of depression and anxiety amounts to an estimated $1.15 trillion per year, which includes health care costs, the cost of pharmacological treatments, and lost productivity (Chisholm et al., 2016).

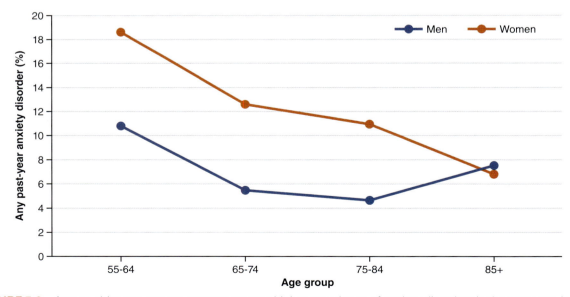

FIGURE 5.2 Across older age groups, women report a higher prevalence of anxiety disorders in the past year, but this difference decreases across age groups and is relatively low in both men and women who are over 85 years of age.
Adapted from Reynolds et al. (2015).

Treatment of Clinical Anxiety

When a person has a clinical anxiety disorder, they should seek help from a medical professional. This medical professional likely will consider psychotherapy and medications as part of a treatment plan. Psychotherapy can take a variety of different forms, with cognitive behavioral therapy being the most common choice among clinicians because it is considered the most effective method for people with anxiety disorders. In **cognitive behavioral therapy (CBT)**, the therapist helps the patient to identify the triggers of their anxiety and to learn different ways of thinking and behaving in response to the triggers so that they can manage their anxiety symptoms. In addition to psychotherapy, clinicians also are likely to prescribe medications (see table 5.2). Medications do not cure anxiety disorders, but they have been shown to reduce symptoms. Benzodiazepines are often prescribed for a short period of time to help patients manage the symptoms of their anxiety. Because this medication can be addictive and can worsen preexisting depression, it is not typically used in the long term. Antidepressants such as selective serotonin reuptake inhibitors (SSRIs) and serotonin and norepinephrine reuptake inhibitors (SNRIs) might seem an odd treatment, but these antidepressants are a common first choice in the treatment of anxiety because of the expected role of monoamines in anxiety. Beta-blockers, which are effective at managing high blood pressure, can also be helpful in reducing the physical symptoms of acute bouts of anxiety and are particularly useful in the face of predictable types of anxieties. In other words, if someone knows they are likely to become anxious on an airline flight but they need to fly somewhere, their doctor might prescribe a beta-blocker to help them manage their symptoms while they travel. Anxiety disorders are relatively treatable, but only about 37% of those with clinical anxiety disorders actually seek treatment (Anxiety & Depression Assocation of America, 2022).

Mechanisms of Anxiety

The causes of anxiety disorders are numerous and might not be precisely the same for each specific disorder. Researchers believe that anxiety disorders have biological causes including heredity and neurotransmitter imbalances, social causes including stress and adverse life experiences, and psychological causes including low self-esteem (Shri, 2010) and neuroticism (Gottschalk & Domschke, 2017). Although human studies have not provided evidence for a direct link between specific genes and anxiety disorders, evidence from family, twin, and adoption studies do support the idea that genetic factors explain approximately 30% of the variability in anxiety-related traits (Gottschalk & Domschke, 2017). In other words, if we compare the likelihood of identical twins both having clinical anxiety to the likelihood of fraternal twins both having clinical anxiety, results show that the likelihood is greater for the identical twins who share the same genetic code. This is evidence in support of a genetic component to the experience of clinical anxiety. Other evidence suggests that neurotransmitter imbalances might play a role. For example, serotonergic transmissions are implicated in the experience of anxiety. Much of this evidence for neurotransmitter imbalance is considered indirect because it is based on evidence showing that treatment with drugs that act on these receptors can be effective in the treatment of anxiety (Bandelow et al., 2017).

TABLE 5.2 **Pharmacological Treatments for Anxiety**

Type of treatment	Examples
Benzodiazepines (tranquilizers)	Xanax (alprazolam), Valium (diazepam), Ativan (lorazepam)
Beta-blockers	Inderal (propranolol), Sectral (acebutolol), Zabeta (bisoprolol)
Selective serotonin reuptake inhibitors (SSRIs)	Prozac (fluoxetine), Celexa (citalopram), Lexapro (escitalopram)
Serotonin and norepinephrine reuptake inhibitors (SNRIs)	Effexor (venlafaxine), Cymbalta (duloxetine), Pristiq (desvenlafaxine)

cognitive behavioral therapy (CBT)—CBT is therapy that involves the therapist helping the patient to identify the triggers of their anxiety and to learn different ways of thinking and behaving in response to the triggers so that they can manage their anxiety symptoms.

Theories and Mechanisms of Exercise and Anxiety

As with stress, numerous mechanisms have been proposed to explain why both acute exercise and chronic exercise can lead to reductions in anxiety. Mikkelsen and colleagues (2017) categorize these mechanisms into physiological mechanisms and psychological mechanisms.

Physiological Mechanisms

Physiological mechanisms focus on the underlying biological reaction in response to an anxiety-provoking situation. These include the thermogenic hypothesis and other less well studied mechanisms reflecting an interest in hypothalamic-pituitary-adrenal (HPA) axis dysfunction, neurotransmitters, and endorphins.

Thermogenic Hypothesis

One of the hypotheses initially proposed to explain the anxiety-reducing effects of acute exercise was the thermogenic hypothesis. This hypothesis suggests that increases in body temperature in response to exercise are responsible for reductions in anxiety. The premise underlying this is that the hypothalamus is linked to the regulation of body temperature and also influences emotions. Thus, by increasing body temperature, the hypothalamus is expected to be affected in a way that leads to the experience of more positive and less negative emotions. As such, this hypothesis would suggest that you might expect a similar anxiety-reducing effect in response to spending time in a hot tub, relaxing under a heated blanket, or exercising.

Other Proposed Mechanisms

Surprisingly little evidence has been published relative to some of the mechanisms purported to underlie anxiety disorders, but these mechanisms might be implicated in the anxiety-reducing effects of exercise, so they are briefly mentioned here (figure 5.3). Evidence suggests that HPA dysfunction is a general feature in individuals with a variety of anxiety disorders (Faravelli et al., 2012). In particular, scientists believe that stress exposure in childhood might create a vulnerability in HPA axis function such that exposure during adulthood to additional stressors (e.g., life events or comorbidities) or more enduring factors (e.g., genetic vulnerability or cognitive appraisal skills) can combine to affect the way in which anxiety is experienced. Furthermore, the dysregulation in the HPA axis might result in heightened responses during exposure to acute anxiety-inducing stimuli. The neurotransmitter hypothesis is also applied relative to the anxiety-reducing effects of exercise. This link is logical given the evidence of monoamine irregularities in

---

Testing the Thermogenic Hypothesis

Petruzzello and Landers (1983) conducted a study designed to test the thermogenic hypothesis by manipulating core body temperature during an exercise bout. They asked 20 male participants to wear an internal body thermometer while exercising under three temperature conditions. The conditions consisted of normal (no manipulation), cooler (a decrease in the normal rise in temperature), and warmer (an increase in temperature beyond normal temperatures) temperatures. In all three conditions, participants ran for 30 minutes at 75% $\dot{V}O_2max$. In the normal condition, participants ran wearing shorts, a T-shirt, socks, and shoes. In the warmer condition, participants ran wearing full-length tights, a long-sleeve T-shirt, a nylon running jacket and pants, and with a terry cloth across their neck. In the cooler condition, they wore an ice-filled terry cloth across their neck and ran in the same clothing as in the normal condition, but the T-shirt and shorts had been dampened with cold water. The manipulations were effective in that core temperature and perceived temperature were lowest during the cooler condition, next for the normal condition, and warmest for the warmer condition. However, counter to the thermogenic hypothesis, anxiety was highest during the warmer condition and not different between the cooler and normal conditions. The authors concluded that an increase in body temperature is not necessary to observe reductions in anxiety but that increasing body temperature above a threshold might actually increase anxiety. The authors caution that their study isn't a pure test of the thermogenic hypothesis because they were not able to assess brain temperature. Nonetheless, at this point in time, no evidence supports the thermogenic hypothesis as a viable explanation of the benefits of exercise for anxiety.

people with anxiety disorders. Similarly, the endorphin hypothesis has been proposed to explain the reduction in anxiety in response to exercise. The expectation is that following exercise, the release and binding of beta-endorphins increases, which leads to an increase in positive mood, a decrease in negative mood, and a reduction in the perception of pain. All of these mechanisms have been implicated in anxiety disorders and also have been shown to be responsive to both single exercise bouts and repeated exercise sessions. As such, any or all of these physiological mechanisms can play a role in the anxiety-reducing effects of exercise (figure 5.3).

Psychological Mediators

In addition to physiological mechanisms, psychological mediators have been proposed to explain the effects of exercise on anxiety. One of these hypotheses is unique to the effects of exercise on anxiety because it focuses on the impact of exercise on anxiety sensitivity. The other hypothesis focuses on self-efficacy, which is a psychological mediator commonly proposed as a link between exercise and a variety of psychological outcomes.

Anxiety Sensitivity

Among the psychological mechanisms for anxiety, one hypothesis is unique to the exercise-related benefits for anxiety. This hypothesis is focused on anxiety sensitivity and the notion of repeated exposure (Anderson & Shivakumar, 2013). The idea is that individuals who are high in trait anxiety are also high in sensitivity such that they tend to exaggerate anxiety-related sensations to the level of anticipating disastrous outcomes. This hypothesis suggests that exercise provides a desensitization paradigm in that repeated exposure to heightened physiological symptoms in response to exercise allow the anxious person to recognize that disastrous outcomes do not follow. Thus, over time, the anxious person can become habituated to physiological responses to exercise, and this can generalize to physiological responses to other stimuli. Hence, this hypothesis suggests that exercise training essentially trains the anxious individual to experience physiological symptoms indicative of increased arousal without attributing these to an anxiety response.

Self-Efficacy Hypothesis

The self-efficacy hypothesis is applied to anxiety in much the same way as it is applied to other mental health outcomes. In particular, repeated completion of exercise bouts provides a person with a sense of mastery and accomplishment, which then contributes to their self-efficacy. This heightened self-efficacy then provides a sense of an ability to manage potential threats that can be generalized to other stimuli. Hence, according to this hypothesis, a person's self-efficacy increases in response to exercise, and this increased self-efficacy results in the experience of less anxiety across a variety of threatening situations.

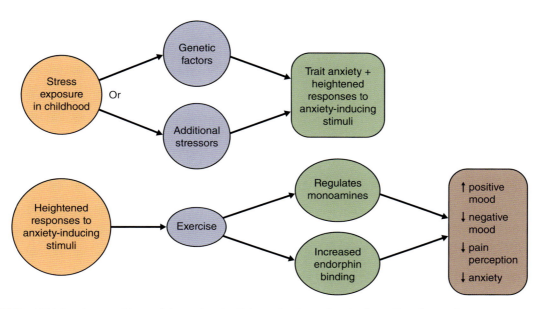

FIGURE 5.3 HPA involvement in anxiety and potential mechanisms for the benefits of exercise.

Measurement of Anxiety

The assessment of anxiety can be challenging in part because some anxiety disorders require certain triggers that might be unknown. Hence, we cannot predict when the person might actually experience the anxiety symptoms. Another measurement challenge is that anxiety and depression are comorbidities, with approximately half of patients with anxiety disorders also experiencing depression (Salcedo, 2018). Thus, it can be hard to distinguish symptoms that are specific to these illnesses as independent constructs. Assessment of trait anxiety is, however, guided by theoretical explanations that consistently include cognitive, behavioral, and physiological components of anxiety. For example, the affective information processing theory (Lang & Cuthbert, 1984) proposes that anxiety responses reflect three different categories: somatic activation, anxiety-related behaviors, and self-reports. As a result of these theoretical expectations, measurement tools have been developed to assess anxiety in each of these categories. Let's consider each of these in turn.

Somatic Activation

Somatic activation is the body's physiological response to a stimulus. Somatic activation is considered to be central to the experience of trait anxiety and can serve as a stimulus for the cognitive appraisal and resultant emotional response to stimuli that are perceived as threatening. This is consistent with William James's hypothesis that a person's emotions are actually a response to the body's physical reaction. Various measures have been used to assess the somatic (or physiological) responses associated with anxiety. These include measures of heart rate, heart rate variability, galvanic skin response (which provides a measure of sweat gland activity on the skin), and blood pressure. It is interesting to note that when we look at responses to an acute, real threat, the nature of the somatic response does not differ between high and low trait anxious individuals. This is because it is appropriate and adaptive to have a preparatory response to an acute, real threat (Elwood et al., 2012). In other words, if you were walking down the street and were suddenly charged by a barking dog that seemed prepared to attack, the anxiety response you experience would not differ based on whether you had low or high levels of trait anxiety. Everybody is likely to have a very similar response in this situation. The difference that we would expect to see in somatic activation is more relevant to exposure to chronic threats or to perceived threats. That is, with exposure to chronic threat, we would expect to see faster habituation of the physiological response in low trait anxious individuals as compared to high trait anxious individuals. For example, in coping with the challenges of the COVID-19 pandemic, a high trait anxious person would be expected to have a heightened physiological response over the months of the pandemic, while a low trait anxious person would be expected to return to normal physiological levels after a few days, weeks, or months. Finally, with exposure to a hypothetical stressor, we would expect high trait anxious individuals to have a larger and longer-lasting response than low trait anxious individuals. So, an upcoming final exam would be expected to differentially affect a high trait anxious person relative to a low trait anxious person even if we control for factors such as study time and academic preparedness.

Anxiety-Related Behaviors

Anxiety-related behaviors include avoidance behaviors (to minimize exposure to the threat), hypervigilance (to be on the lookout for a threat), and hyperarousal (disproportionate to the threat). Anxiety-related behaviors often are assessed using computerized tasks performed in a laboratory setting. The goal of these tasks is to assess the extent to which a person uses avoidance behaviors, displays sustained hypervigilance, or shows hyperarousal across a variety of situations (Elwood et al., 2012). The laboratory task that is used often includes the presentation of an image that is threatening or nonthreatening (see figure 5.4). Following presentation of that image, a stimulus appears either on the same side as the threatening image (figure 5.4a) or the opposite side (figure 5.4b). Reaction time is then assessed and analyzed relative to the nature of the image. Evidence from these types of studies is relatively consistent in showing that highly anxious individuals have an attentional bias such that they are more sensitive to the threatening images than are people who are low anxious (Shechner & Bar-Haim, 2016). This is evidenced by the highly anxious individuals responding more quickly to stimuli that appear on the same side as the threatening image as compared to when the stimuli are on the same side

---

somatic activation—The body's physiological response to a stimulus is referred to as somatic activation.

anxiety-related behaviors—Anxiety-related behaviors include avoidance behaviors (to minimize exposure to the threat), hypervigilance (to be on the lookout for a threat), and hyperarousal (disproportionate to the threat).

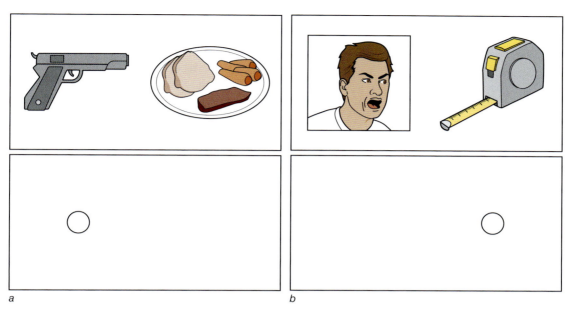

FIGURE 5.4 A series of computer screens illustrate this task (dot probe): *(a)* threatening image on the same side as the stimulus, and *(b)* threatening image on the opposite side from the stimulus.

as the nonthreatening image (Van Bockstaele et al., 2014). In contrast to their bias toward attending to threat, highly anxious individuals avoid confronting threat and are more likely to judge a situation to be threatening (Elwood et al., 2012).

Self-Report Measures

Self-report measures allow for the assessment of anxiety by recording participants' perceptions of anxiety responses using semi-structured interviews or self-report measures. With adults, the most commonly used measure is the Spielberger State-Trait Anxiety Inventory (STAI). Form X of this survey was criticized because it overlapped too much with depression. As a result, Form Y was developed to allow for a clearer focus on anxiety, Form Y-1 assesses state anxiety, Form Y-2 assesses trait anxiety. All forms of the survey consist of 20 statements with responses given on a 4-point scale including *Not At All*, *Somewhat*, *Moderately So*, and *Very Much So*. The STAI-Form Y is commonly used in research studies, and normative data is available so that we can understand the average STAI score of a sample in relation to the average that is observed in the general population. If you are interested in learning more about the STAI, you can find the Y forms of the survey by searching on the Internet for "State Trait Anxiety Inventory Y form."

In a review of instruments used with adolescents (Brooks & Kutcher, 2003), it was reported that self-report measures were used both to diagnose anxiety disorders and to identify the frequency or severity of anxiety symptoms. The Schedule for Affective Disorders and Schizophrenia for School-Age Children (KSADS) and the Anxiety Disorders Interview Schedule for Children/Parents (ADIS-C/P) were the most commonly used assessment tools for diagnosis, and both were judged to have well-established reliability and acceptable validity. With regards to anxiety symptoms, the two most commonly used instruments were the Revised Children's Manifest Anxiety Scale (RCMAS) and the Spielberger State-Trait Anxiety Inventory version for children (S-TAIC). Both measures have been used widely in research, making comparisons across studies possible. The RCMAS includes physical, cognitive, affective, and behavioral symptoms of anxiety, making it very useful as an outcome measure relative to treatment, but it does not discriminate well between depression and anxiety. The S-TAIC only assesses cognitive and affective symptoms, but it does discriminate better from depression.

The assessment of anxiety in older adults presents unique challenges for several reasons. First, normal concerns relative to the aging process might be confused with symptoms of anxiety. Second,

---

self-report measures—The assessment of anxiety through the recording of participants' perceptions of anxiety responses using semi-structured interviews or self-report measures is a self-report measure.

an increased number of medical disorders might influence reports of somatic symptoms. Third, the experiences and sources of worry for older adults might differ from younger adults (Balsamo et al., 2018). The STAI has been adapted for use with older adults and is the most commonly used measure in this population (Therrien & Hunsley, 2012). The STAI has acceptable reliability with older adults but might not be the best choice because it does not discriminate well between anxiety and depression in older adults. Better choices might be measures developed specifically for older adults including the Adult Manifest Anxiety Scale, the Geriatric Anxiety Inventory, and the Geriatric Mental State Examination. The Adult Manifest Anxiety Scale can be a good choice for researchers adopting a life span approach because three versions of this scale were developed independently for younger adults (19-59 yr), college students, and older adults (≥60 yr), allowing for comparisons across age groups.

Evidence Relative to the Effects of Exercise on Anxiety

In considering the potential benefits of exercise for anxiety, it is necessary to examine the evidence relative to the precise purpose of the exercise. In other words, exercise might be used to reduce anxiety symptoms for people who have not been clinically diagnosed with an anxiety disorder or to treat anxiety specifically in those who have been clinically diagnosed with anxiety. Prior to exploring these various topics, it is interesting to recognize that early research on the potential effects of exercise on anxiety adopted the point of view that exercise was likely to have negative effects. This is because of two relatively early studies described in 1967 and 1971 that I will explain briefly (Pitts, 1971; Pitts & McClure, 1967).

Historically Important Research

In 1967 Pitts and McClure published findings from a study in the *New England Journal of Medicine*, a particularly well-read and influential outlet. In their study, they infused sodium lactate into 10 healthy people and 14 people with clinical anxiety. They found that those with anxiety experienced increases in anxiety and that their anxiety symptoms persisted for 2 to 5 days. In fact, even some of the healthy individuals reported symptoms of anxiety. The authors described this as a causal effect and made the inference that participation in exercise that would raise lactate levels would be expected to increase anxiety in a similar fashion. In a subsequent review, Pitts (1971) described results from four investigations showing that when individuals with clinical anxiety performed exercise, they experienced increases in anxiety symptoms that appeared to co-occur with increases in blood lactate. The impact of these two studies on research related to exercise and anxiety was profound. Because of this hypothesized link between exercise or increased lactate and an increase in anxiety, researchers and medical professionals were concerned that participation in exercise by clinically anxious participants might actually worsen symptoms. Importantly, other researchers eventually began to question the inferences and the causal link between sodium lactate and the observed symptoms. In particular, Grosz and Farmer (1972) demonstrated that the effects attributed to the increased lactate in the Pitts and McClure study were plausibly attributed to the change in the pH of the blood, which created alkalosis (i.e., when the pH balance of body fluids becomes too basic), inciting a feeling of anxiety. They further demonstrated that the changes could not be attributed to increases in blood lactate based on the timing of the symptoms and the infusion rate that was used. Researchers also began to recognize that the exercise prescribed in the studies described by Pitts was at an extremely high intensity level. This high intensity level might be perceived as anxiety provoking for anyone and particularly so for relatively inactive participants. Thankfully, these arguments carried the day, and scientists began again to explore potential positive effects of exercise in the reduction of anxiety symptoms in healthy, normal adults.

Reducing Anxiety Symptoms in Nonanxious Samples

Smith (2013) conducted a study in which healthy college students were asked to complete a bout of acute exercise or a session of quiet rest prior to exposure to emotional pictures designed to increase state anxiety. The exercise was 30 minutes of moderate-intensity cycling. Participants completed the STAI-Y1 before their assigned condition, 15 minutes after the assigned condition, and then again after viewing 90 images that consisted of equal numbers of pleasant, neutral, and unpleasant images. Results showed that state anxiety decreased in both groups from pretest to posttest, providing some support for the distraction hypothesis. However, after exposure to the anxiety-provoking images, anxiety increased significantly after the control condition but remained reduced after the exercise condition. This is a fascinating finding because it suggests that the anxiety-reducing effects of exercise are protective against anxiety and somewhat enduring (i.e., they were evident 45 minutes after the exercise bout).

Studies focused on the reduction of anxiety symptoms in the general population have been meta-analytically reviewed on several occasions. Petruzzello and colleagues (1991) presented the first summary review of the literature and reported that acute exercise (ES of 0.24) and chronic exercise (ES = 0.34) resulted in small reductions in measures of state and trait anxiety, respectively. A criticism of this review is that only 13 of the 104 studies included in the review were RCTs. Thus, Wipfli and associates (2008) conducted a meta-analysis in which they only included RCTs so that judgments about cause and effect could be rendered. Overall, results showed that across 49 studies, anxiety was moderately reduced in exercise groups as compared to no-treatment control groups (ES = 0.48), the reduction in anxiety was larger for the exercise group than for groups receiving other anxiety-reducing treatments (ES = 0.19), and equated to a decrease of 3.42 points more on anxiety scales for the exercisers than for the no-treatment control participants. Importantly, in this study Wipfli and associates combined effects from studies using acute exercise paradigms and those using chronic exercise paradigms. This is a limitation of this review because it is not logical to combine effects from studies using such different paradigms. From data presented in their study, however, one can see that the average ES for acute exercise studies was 0.39, and the ES for chronic exercise studies of varying lengths was also small to moderate in size (4-9 weeks: ES = 0.59; 10-14 weeks: ES = 0.40; >15 weeks: ES = 0.38). Their review did include studies using clinically anxious populations and nonanxious populations with beneficial effects reported for both groups (ES = 0.52 clinically anxious; ES = 0.40 nonanxious). These results can be generally assumed to represent the results we should expect in both clinically anxious and nonanxious samples; however, this review only included three effects for clinically anxious samples, so this effect should be interpreted with caution.

Even more recently, Ensari and colleagues (2015) addressed some of the limitations of both previous reviews by including only studies on acute exercise and only studies in which adults were randomly assigned to conditions. This review had relatively equal representation of studies with healthy samples and those with samples reporting psychiatric disease (e.g., panic disorder or mood disorder), nonpsychiatric disease (e.g., iron deficiency or type 2 diabetes), or both. Results suggested a small positive effect of exercise in reducing anxiety symptoms (ES = 0.16) and that these effects were larger for those with both psychiatric and nonpsychiatric disease (ES = 0.61) as compared to all other groups (healthy: ES = 0.13; psychiatric disease: ES = 0.22; nonpsychiatric disease: ES = 0.31). Thus, overall these meta-analytic reviews suggest that a single session of exercise can cause a small reduction in anxiety symptoms for people who are clinically anxious and for people who are not clinically anxious. Some evidence suggests that effects might be the most robust for individuals who are coping with both psychiatric and nonpsychiatric illness.

Reducing Anxiety Symptoms in Clinically Anxious Samples

Rosenbaum and associates (2015) published an empirical study focused on the effects of exercise on anxiety symptoms in hospitalized patients with PTSD. In this study, the researchers compared those who received usual care (a combination of psychotherapy, medications, and group therapy) to those who received usual care plus an exercise program. The exercise program was performed for 12 weeks and consisted of one supervised session and two unsupervised sessions per week conducted at home and a walking program encouraged through the use of a pedometer and exercise log. Participants (n = 81) were randomly assigned to one of the two conditions. From pretest to posttest, both groups experienced a reduction in PTSD symptoms, but the reduction was significantly larger for the exercise group. This benefit was also significant for measures of depression, anxiety, and stress, with results consistently showing that the exercise group experienced the greatest declines in symptoms. Furthermore, the reductions in PTSD and depression were deemed to be clinically significant. This study provides an important demonstration of the potential of exercise to provide benefits for individuals with PTSD that go above and beyond what can be achieved with standard treatments. In other words, exercise provides added benefits above and beyond what is attained with recommended methods of care.

Stubbs and colleagues (2017) conducted a meta-analysis of RCTs testing the effects of an aerobic exercise intervention on anxiety symptoms in people who had been clinically diagnosed with an anxiety disorder based on established criteria. They summarized the results of six studies that had compared exercise to a nonactive control group (i.e., they excluded studies that compared exercise to other treatments that would be expected to reduce anxiety such as pharmacological interventions or electroconvulsive therapy). In this meta-analysis, they calculated ES for the pre- to postintervention change for those in the control conditions and those in the exercise conditions. Results showed that participants in the exercise conditions experienced significant reductions in anxiety (ES = 0.58), while those in the control conditions demonstrated no significant change in their anxiety. Aylett and colleagues (2018) also reviewed RCTs conducted with adults with clinically elevated symptoms or a formal diagnosis of an anxiety disorder. They found an overall average effect size of 0.41, indicating that those randomly assigned to an exercise condition had greater reductions in anxiety than did those in a wait-list control condition. They found no difference in the size of the effect for patients with clinically elevated symptoms (n = 7 studies; ES = 0.46) as compared to the effect for patients with a clinical diagnosis (n = 8 studies; ES = 0.32). Overall, these two meta-analytic reviews support that exercise reduces anxiety in individuals with heightened anxiety to begin with.

PTSD is a particular anxiety disorder that might benefit from exercise, an idea that researchers have explored. Although this body of evidence is currently small, this is an important direction for research because individuals experiencing PTSD could benefit from this accessible and free behavior of exercise participation. Rosenbaum and colleagues (2015) meta-analytically analyzed findings from 4 RCTs conducted with 200 adults (34-52 yr) that compared the effects of exercise to usual-care or wait-list control conditions. The included trials were 10 to 12 weeks in length and consisted of yoga (2 studies), aerobic exercise (1 study), and a combination of aerobic and resistance exercise (1 study). Results showed that exercise significantly reduced PTSD symptoms (ES = 0.35) and also had a beneficial effect on depressive symptoms (ES = 0.37). These effects are promising given the challenges that individuals with PTSD face, that other treatments tend to be expensive (i.e., trauma-focused psychotherapies), and that exercise has added benefits relative to the risks of diabetes and obesity.

The body of evidence for exercise and anxiety is so large that two meta-analytic reviews of meta-analyses have been published. These "super" meta-analyses are sometimes also called *umbrella reviews*, and they pull together ES from an even larger body of literature than does a typical meta-analysis. Wegner and associates (2014) conducted an umbrella review of 18 meta-analyses focused on the anxiety-reducing effects of exercise. In this review, they included ES from studies using prospective-longitudinal or cross-sectional designs. The overall ES was small and positive (ES = 0.34), and benefits were observed for clinically diagnosed patients (ES = 0.36) and for normal participants (ES = 0.31). This finding is consistent with that reported by Rebar and colleagues (2015), who limited their umbrella review to meta-analyses focused on acute exercise in healthy, nonanxious populations. From four meta-analytic reviews, across 306 effects from studies providing data from 10,755 participants, they found a significant, small ES of 0.38, showing that exercise reduces anxiety symptoms.

Summary

As we review the evidence relative to the potentially anxiety-reducing effects of exercise, we explore effects for nonanxious individuals and for clinically anxious individuals. In both cases, exercise has a small, positive benefit that can be observed shortly after a single session of exercise, after a single session of exercise and exposure to anxiety-provoking stimuli, and after chronic exercise training. Some studies have begun to explore the potential synergistic effects of exercise in combination with either psychotherapy or medication. Although limited, the results are promising in suggesting that exercise can augment benefits from these traditional treatments and compares favorably with these treatments when presented in isolation. As we've seen in other chapters, it's important to recognize that exercise has benefits that traditional treatments do not. Exercise results in physical health benefits, can be performed at low or no expense, and does not have negative side effects like some medications. Current evidence supports that exercise should be recommended for individuals experiencing clinical anxiety disorders and to manage anxiety symptoms in normal, healthy adults.

Discussion Questions

1. What challenges do individuals with anxiety disorders face (i.e., what are the implications)?

2. In the Petruzzello and Landers (1983) study, they manipulated body temperature during exercise and found that anxiety actually increased in the condition where body temperature was highest. Why did they suggest this doesn't rule out the thermogenic hypothesis?

3. What did Pitts and McClure (1967) and Pitts (1971) find, and why was this such a challenge for the research area of exercise and anxiety?

4. What do the results tell us overall about the possible anxiety-reducing effects of exercise? Have potential synergistic effects of exercise and traditional treatments been explored, and what do results show?

Exercise and Depression

CHAPTER OBJECTIVES

After studying this chapter, you should be able to do the following:

- Understand the distinction between depressive symptoms and the experience of clinical depression
- Recognize the implications of the high prevalence of depression
- Identify mechanisms that explain why people experience depression
- Describe the potential role of chronic physical activity in preventing and treating clinical depression

KEY TERMS

depressive symptoms

clinical depression

monoamine neurotransmitters

brain-derived neurotrophic factor (BDNF)

Logan is a 25-year-old carpenter who had been dating the same young woman, Sarah, for 5 years. In fact, they had gotten engaged in March, and they were beginning to plan their wedding for the following spring after she graduated from college. But in September, Sarah suddenly called off the engagement when she met another man in one of her classes. Logan was devastated. He had battled depression during his late teens but had felt really good about himself and been doing great during the 5 years he was with Sarah. In fact, he had gradually weaned himself off of his antidepressant medication and hadn't seen a therapist in years. But this sudden breakup with Sarah threw Logan into a very dark place. Logan became apathetic about everything including his job. He started leaving work early to avoid walking to his car with others who might try to talk with him about his troubles. He stopped playing soccer with his friends and became a recluse. He was sharing a home with two friends but cut them off from communication and began to just hole up in his bedroom. At one point, his car ran out of gas and instead of seeking help from his friends, he simply walked home and left his car on the side of the road. Of course, his car was towed, which meant that he had to pay an impoundment and towing fee to get his car back. Rather than do that, Logan quit going to work and left his car at the pound. His life was quickly spiraling out of control.

One Saturday his friends stormed his bedroom and dragged him with them to play pickup soccer at the park behind their house. This was something they'd done every Saturday for years, and the group was well known to Logan. Although he didn't want to go, his friends would not be denied, so he found himself outside and ended up joining in the soccer game. In hindsight, it was amazing to Logan how that one day of activity seemed to provide a small light in his darkness. He felt good to be running around, and he actually felt a small twinge of joy when he scored a goal. This one opportunity to get outside and exercise certainly didn't cure Logan, but it provided an initial impetus. Logan recognized that he had a problem and reached out to his therapist for help that evening. He started back on antidepressants, which helped enable him to rejoin his normal activities. He became active in soccer and started running on days when he didn't have an opportunity to play pickup with his friends. He eventually went back to carpentry and after several years met and fell in love with another woman with whom he was able to start his family.

Clearly, Logan's happy ending isn't how all stories of depression end, but it does provide an example of the potential role of exercise and physical activity in combating this mental health disorder. People who experience clinical depression that is not well managed suffer from a truly debilitating mental illness. They might struggle to get out of bed to start the day, they might be unable to tend to their responsibilities and might be so apathetic that they are not troubled by the consequences, and they might be unable to interact with others to receive any kind of social or family support. Given the severity of the consequences of untreated depression, it is worth considering the role of exercise as a potential preventative or a treatment option.

What Is Depression?

Similar to anxiety, depression is an experience that can be either short or long term and can range from relatively mild experiences to debilitating experiences that might require clinical intervention. All of us are depressed from time to time when we experience sadness. During these times we experience **depressive symptoms**, which include feelings of sadness, low motivation, and apathy. Sometimes we are depressed for longer periods of time in response to a major negative event such as losing a loved one, breaking up from a serious relationship, or losing a job. These types of depression are common and natural and typically don't require intervention or

---

depressive symptoms—Depressive symptoms include feelings of sadness, low motivation, and apathy that are commonly experienced by everyone but that typically resolve with the passage of time and the use of coping methods.

treatment; rather, they gradually resolve on their own with the passage of time and the use of coping strategies. However, when depression is severe, long-lasting, and not directly tied to a specific event or extends well beyond a typical coping period for that type of event, it might be considered a serious medical illness.

> ### Like the Weather
>
> The 10,000 Maniacs perform a song called "Like the Weather" that provides a clear illustration of the experience of clinical depression. You can find the lyrics or the song on the Internet. These lyrics paint the picture of a person who is unable to get out of bed, who sees the world as being gray and miserable, who isn't able to work in a job because of their depression, who doesn't know how to get out of the situation, who has dealt with it for a long period of time, and who fervently hopes and prays that the experience will pass. One of the real challenges of depression is that it puts a person into a vicious cycle where they become unable to participate in activities or to interact with others in ways that might bring joy, satisfaction, and a sense of accomplishment, and it is exactly these missing experiences that contribute further to their depression.

When experiencing **clinical depression** (which is also called *major depressive disorder*), individuals feel depressed most of the time for at least 2 weeks, they often have feelings of low self-worth and self-loathing, and they are challenged to find ways to cope with their extreme negative emotions. A person's behaviors and thoughts provide evidence that they are depressed. The American Psychological Association explains that people who are depressed "may experience a lack of interest and pleasure in daily activities, significant weight loss or gain, insomnia or excessive sleeping, lack of energy, inability to concentrate, feelings of worthlessness or excessive guilt and recurrent thoughts of death or suicide" (American Psychological Association, 2022). Depression is distinct from grief. With grief, feelings of sadness tend to come in waves rather than being present essentially all of the time as is the case with clinical depression. With grief, there is not typically a concomitant decrease in self-esteem, but with depression feelings of low self-esteem and even self-loathing are common. The focus of this chapter is on clinical depression with an interest in identifying the potential of exercise to mitigate depressive symptoms and potentially help combat the experience of clinical depression.

> If you are experiencing depression, please seek help. You almost certainly have resources available at your university or college. Search for student counseling or student health, or reach out to your dean of students for direction. National resources also are available through the Substance Abuse and Mental Health Services Administration (SAMHSA), which is available at 1-800-662-HELP (4357) or 1-800-487-4889.

Prevalence and Costs

In the United States, clinical depression is estimated to affect approximately 8% of adults each year (Brody et al., 2018), and roughly 30% of people are predicted to experience clinical depression at some point in their lives (Kessler et al., 2012). This equates to approximately 26 million Americans per year dealing with clinical depression in an ongoing way and approximately 99 million experiencing clinical depression at some point in their lifetime. Globally, an estimated 322 million people were experiencing clinical depression in 2015 (World Health Organization, 2017) with evidence that prevalence is increasing over time (Moreno-Agostino et al., 2021) and increased by an estimated 53.2 million cases in response to the COVID-19 pandemic (Santomauro et al., 2021). Considering the prevalence of this mental health disorder and knowing the devastating effects it can have on a person's ability to simply function in life, this disorder merits our full attention in terms of identifying potential preventative therapies and treatments.

Important differences in the experience of clinical depression are observed based on sex, race, ethnicity, and income. Women are more often afflicted than men; clinical depression is experienced significantly more by Hispanic, non-Hispanic White, and non-Hispanic Black Americans than by non-Hispanic Asian Americans; and the percentage of individuals diagnosed with clinical depression decreases with increasing income (Brody et al.,

---

clinical depression—An enduring experience of depressive symptoms such that the person feels depressed most of the time for at least 2 weeks, has feelings of low self-worth and self-loathing, and feels challenged to find ways to cope with their extreme negative emotions are the criteria for clinical depression.

2018). Clinical depression typically first appears in young adults, but the prevalence of depression does not differ significantly by age, meaning that its prevalence is similar in young adults, middle-aged adults, and older adults. Importantly, and of concern, mental health disorders have a worldwide prevalence of 13.4% (Polanczyk et al., 2015), and depression is one of the most common mental health concerns of children and adolescents (Wegner et al., 2020). Furthermore, evidence shows that depression rates are on the rise across all ages, with the most rapid increase observed in adolescents ages 12 to 17 years (Weinberger et al., 2018). It is frightening to recognize that depressive symptoms reported among adolescents have risen dramatically for females, with 58% more females reporting high levels of depressive symptoms in 2015 than in 2009-2010 and with increasing suicide rates for both males and females (Twenge et al., 2018). Because of the link between clinical depression and attempted suicide, this increase in high levels of depression is likely a factor in the increases in suicide that have been observed in recent decades. For females, the suicide rate doubled between the late 1990s and 2015, and it's still less than half the suicide rate observed for teenage boys (in 2015, boys = 9.43/100,000; girls = 3.7/100,000) (Twenge et al., 2018).

Globally, little variance is observed in the prevalence of depression across various countries, and depression is the most influential factor in determining years lived with disability (World Health Organization, 2017). Years lived with disability (YLDs) are an indicant of the cost of an illness and are calculated by considering the impact of the disease on both short- and long-term health. In other words, depression is the most important factor across the world in determining the relative health of a population because of the magnitude of its effects on a person's ability to live a healthy life. People with clinical depression are two to three times more likely to attempt suicide. Based on data in the United States from 2019, suicide was the second leading cause of death for people aged 10 to 34 years, the fourth leading cause for people aged 35 to 44 years, and the tenth leading cause of death across all ages (National Institute of Mental Health, 2022b). In fact, in 2019 there were more deaths by suicide than by homicide for those aged 10-64 years (Heron, 2021). These data emphasize the importance of identifying ways to mitigate depressive symptoms using any combination of treatments available. In the United States, suicide rates across states vary, with a particularly high suicide rate observed in what is referred to as the *suicide belt* (figure 6.1). It

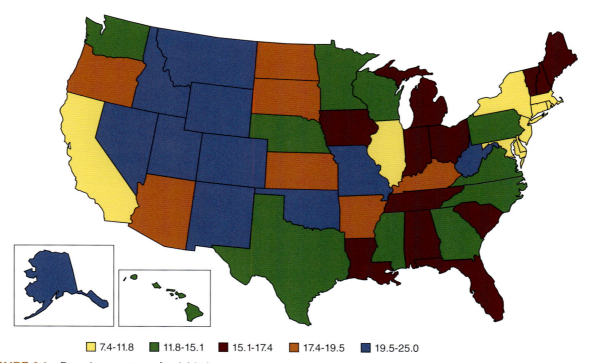

FIGURE 6.1 Prevalence rates of suicide by state.
From NIMH (2020).

is thought that rates might be particularly high in these states because their populations are disproportionately middle-aged, White, single men who have access to guns. The fact that this disproportionality is also evident in Alaska and that suicide rates are high in this state as well lends credence to this possible explanation because Alaska has similar characteristics to the states in the suicide belt.

Clearly, the costs of depression are enormous in terms of personal, societal, and economic impacts. Do you know anyone who has clinical depression? Have you observed their behavior? What are their interactions with friends, family members, and the broader community like? Are they able to hold a job? The impact on the individual who is suffering from depression is enormous, and the effect on their friends, coworkers, and family members is real. In addition to these personal costs of depression, the economic costs of depression are staggering. In the United States, depression accounts for approximately 400 million disability days per year (days of work lost due to depression) and had total costs estimated at $210.5 billion in 2010 (Greenberg et al., 2015). Approximately half of these costs are due to the direct costs of medical treatment and another approximately half of these costs are due to losses in productivity from absenteeism (missing days from work) and presenteeism (reduced productivity while at work). A small part of this cost is from the projected economic impact of suicide (5%).

> If you are having suicidal thoughts, please seek help. I urge you to reach out to someone in your family, your friend group, your university or college, or through a national hotline. If you want to contact someone trained to talk with individuals having suicidal thoughts, you can call the National Suicide Prevention Lifeline by simply dialing 988 at any time of the day or night.

Mechanisms and Mediators of the Effects of Exercise on Depression

Depression is known to be caused by a combination of genetic and environmental factors. An analysis of data from over 21,000 individuals showed that the experience of clinical depression was 40% due to heritability (i.e., genetic factors) and 60% related to individual environmental factors (Sullivan et al., 2000). In other words, your likelihood of experiencing clinical depression is influenced almost equally by your family's history of depression and by what you are experiencing or have experienced in your life and the support system you have or had available to you. When we consider the influence of environment, researchers know that early childhood experiences can have a lasting effect on the way that individuals interpret experiences in the present, which has a mechanistic explanation. The experience of childhood trauma results in a dysregulation of the hypothalamic-pituitary-adrenal (HPA) axis such that the body's stress response is not appropriately controlled (Menke, 2019). This then means that traumatic childhood experiences condition the person in a way that makes them at risk for depression because of the way their body has essentially been trained through previous experiences to react to stressful situations. Evidence supports that the experience of childhood trauma is associated with a diagnosis of depression and with higher depressive symptom scores (Humphreys et al., 2020). In addition to experiences potentially priming a person to experience depression, we also know that differences in physiological functioning and psychological mediators can serve as causal mechanisms underlying depression. Commonly identified physiological mechanisms include monoamines, HPA axis dysfunction, differences in cerebral structure, and endocrine dysfunction. Psychological mediators include mastery, self-esteem, and self-efficacy. Having an understanding of these mechanisms will allow us to explore how and why exercise could be beneficial in terms of reducing depressive symptoms, preventing depression, or treating depression. Let's consider each of these individually.

Physiological Mechanisms

In addition to the link between childhood trauma, HPA axis dysfunction, and depression, evidence supports additional physiological mechanisms. Some of this evidence is indirect because it comes from an understanding of the pharmacological interventions that reduce depressive symptoms. Other evidence has been generated using animal models. Recent evidence has emerged from neuroimaging studies that allow for an understanding of differences in brain structure and function linked to depression.

Monoamine Deficiency Hypothesis

The monoamine neurotransmitters consist of serotonin, norepinephrine, and dopamine. These neurotransmitters are known to play a role in many of the symptoms of depression such as mood, motivation, and fatigue. There are also known associations of clinical depression with high levels of monoamine oxidase enzyme activity (this activity reduces the availability of monoamines) and with low levels of the monoamines themselves. In addition, evidence suggests that deficiencies in the functioning of serotonin receptors, which would result in dampened benefits of circulating serotonin, are linked to depression. Given these various associations, monoamines have been proposed to be causally related to depression with deficiencies in their availability or function being posited as a mechanism for depression. This hypothesis is supported by studies in which these transmitters have been manipulated and decreases in depression have been observed. In fact, many of the pharmacological interventions that are effective in treating depression target monoamine availability. These include monoamine oxidase inhibitors (which inhibit the breakdown of monoamines, resulting in greater circulating monoamines), selective serotonin reuptake inhibitors (SSRIs, which result in greater circulating serotonin levels), and serotonin and norepinephrine reuptake inhibitors (SNRIs, which result in greater circulating serotonin and norepinephrine levels). Although monoamine deficiencies are clearly implicated in the depressive experience for many individuals, these relatively broad acting pharmacological interventions have substantial side effects and are ineffective for approximately 33% of patients.

Animal studies provide support for the idea that exercise results in the production of monoamines, which then bolster these neurotransmitters from the low levels typically observed in depressed individuals (Lin & Kuo, 2013). However, this area of research is limited because we are not yet able to directly measure these neurotransmitters in the brains of humans. By relying on animal studies, we are limited to protocols that involve voluntary wheel running or forced treadmill running in laboratory settings. These settings provide the benefit of strict control over the environment but have the shortcoming of including stress-inducing scenarios and forced exercise that might not reflect the human experience (see Dishman, 1997, for review).

HPA Axis

Abnormal function of the HPA axis is a hallmark of depression (Menke, 2019). As mentioned, this might be triggered by a traumatic childhood experience, but it also could be an inherent dysfunction that might then explain the strong genetic link for depression. In particular, the HPA axis dysfunction manifests as an impaired sensitivity of the glucocorticoid receptors that are expected to initiate the negative feedback loop to shut down HPA axis activity. If you remember back to the chapter on stress, the HPA axis naturally becomes activated in response to a stressor to prepare the body for a response. This results in a cascade of physiological effects in the body that culminate in the release of cortisol. In depression, the problem is that the feedback loops that should be triggered to shut down the HPA axis response are malfunctioning. This results in heightened levels of circulating cortisol, which has a host of negative effects, ultimately resulting in changes in brain structure that are implicated in depression (i.e., reductions in hippocampal volume). Given the purported beneficial effects of exercise on HPA axis function, this is a logical mechanism to explain the antidepressant effects of exercise. Beserra and colleagues (2018) conducted a meta-analytic review of five studies that tested the effects of exercise on cortisol in persons with clinical depression. Results showed that on average, exercise programs lasting 8 to 16 weeks and exploring various modes of exercise resulted in a moderate decrease in cortisol levels (ES = 0.65). Further analyses showed that these effects were evident for aerobic forms of exercise (ES = 0.76) and that a dose–response relationship existed relative to exercise frequency, with effects going from largest to smallest for five times per week (ES = 2.18), three times per week (ES = 0.64), and two times per week (ES was not significant). These results suggest that exercise can have a positive effect on HPA axis function, which then might have implications for circulating levels of cortisol, which affect neurogenesis and hippocampal structure.

Cerebral Structure and Neurogenesis

Research has shown that changes or differences in cerebral structure might be causally linked to depression. Studies consistently show that a smaller hippocampus is associated with clinical depression (Gujral et al., 2017; Schmaal et al., 2016; Videbech & Ravnkilde, 2004), and antidepressant medications

---

monoamine neurotransmitters—Monoamine neurotransmitters include serotonin, norepinephrine, and dopamine and are known to play a role in many of the symptoms of depression such as mood, motivation, and fatigue.

and electroconvulsive therapy have been shown to increase hippocampal neurogenesis (Ernst et al., 2006). A recent meta-analytic review shows that older adults with late-onset depression (i.e., they were clinically depressed when >50 years of age) have smaller total brain volume and smaller hippocampal volume (Geerlings & Gerritsen, 2017). The neurogenesis hypothesis posits that a decrease in neurogenesis (the creation of new neurons) is implicated in clinical depression and that this is a contributing factor to the reduced hippocampal volume (Ernst et al., 2006). The impact on neurogenesis might be largely due to the role of brain-derived neurotrophic factor (BDNF) (Phillips, 2017). **BDNF** is a neurotrophic factor that is found in the brain (central nervous system) and in the periphery (i.e., it can be measured in plasma or serum from a blood sample). BDNF is important for neurogenesis and for the differentiation and survival of the new neurons. Peripheral levels of BDNF (i.e., when BDNF is measured in the blood) have been shown to be reduced in persons with depression (Lee et al., 2007; Yoshida et al., 2012) and also in those who have tried to commit suicide (Kim et al., 2007). Meta-analytic findings show lower levels of BDNF in clinically depressed patients who are not taking antidepressants as compared to healthy controls (Molendijk et al., 2014). Furthermore, postmortem studies of persons with clinical depression show reductions in BDNF in the hippocampus (Duman & Monteggia, 2006). Additional indirect support for the neurogenesis hypothesis is provided by the fact that it takes approximately 4 to 5 weeks for new neurons to become fully functional, and it typically takes a similar amount of time for antidepressants to have an effect. This temporal link then implies a common underlying mechanism, which is that antidepressants might be effective because they increase BDNF, which then promotes hippocampal neurogenesis, which then helps alleviate depression.

Evidence consistently shows an association between exercise or measures of aerobic fitness and hippocampal volume, and some promising evidence has shown a causal link in randomized clinic trials (RCTs). As an example of correlational evidence, a prospective study performed by Erickson and colleagues (2010) found that the number of blocks walked per week at baseline was predictive of greater hippocampal volume when measured 9 years later. Using an RCT design, Erickson and colleagues (2011) also showed that adults randomly assigned to a 12-month aerobic exercise program experienced an increase in hippocampal volume (approximately 2%) not observed in the control participants. Research in this area also has focused on the effects of exercise on BDNF. In a narrative review, Phillips (2017) described evidence with humans showing that physical activity participation (typically 3-7 days/week for 5-60 weeks) increases plasma and serum levels of BDNF and the size of the hippocampus. Specific to depression, physical activity increased BDNF in patients who were unmedicated and diagnosed with clinical depression (Gustafsson et al., 2009) and in older adults who were in remission from clinical depression (Laske et al., 2010). Although this body of evidence is relatively small, the results are promising in suggesting that exercise might impact neurotrophic factors implicated in neurogenesis and might alter brain structure and function in ways that would be expected to result in decreases in depression.

Endocrine Function

Abnormalities in the function of the endocrine system have also been implicated as relevant to depression (Jesulola et al., 2018). Evidence shows that growth hormone release is dysfunctional in persons with depression. Furthermore, when examining responses to tests that are designed to increase growth hormone, depressed individuals show blunted responses that are markedly different from responses seen in healthy, nondepressed controls. Evidence also implicates thyroid hormones in some of the symptoms of depression, including weight loss and sleep disturbances. In addition, a link is seen between thyroid hormones and serotonin, and evidence suggests that the administration of a particular thyroid hormone (tri-iodothyronine) is an effective treatment for some patients with depression. Finally, evidence suggests the potential role of endorphins (the body's natural opiates) in the etiology of depression (Berrocoso et al., 2009). These observed relationships suggest that endocrine dysfunction may also be implicated in the etiology of depression.

Evidence supports the potential role of endorphins in explaining the antidepressant effects of exercise. Specifically, studies have shown that exercise results in the release of beta-endorphin, which is an endogenous opiate. Endogenous opiates

---

brain-derived neurotrophic factor (BDNF)—BDNF is a neurotrophic factor that is found in the brain (central nervous system) and in the periphery (i.e., it can be measured in plasma or serum from a blood sample) and that is important for neurogenesis and for the differentiation and survival of the new neurons.

are opiates that are produced by the body and have effects that are similar to those experienced when a person takes exogenous opiates such as heroin or morphine, although on a much smaller scale. Hence, the release of endorphins in response to exercise produces a feel-good effect. This effect has been cited as a possible explanation for the effects of exercise in terms of reducing negative moods and enhancing positive moods. Very limited evidence also supports that a single session of exercise increases growth hormone in individuals with clinical depression (Kiive et al., 2004).

Psychological Mediators

In addition to the physiological mechanisms described, psychological variables also might be important mediators in terms of the effects of physical activity on depression (Lubans et al., 2016). For example, the mastery hypothesis suggests that feelings of mastery or a sense of accomplishment in response to physical activity participation might be associated with increases in self-efficacy and self-esteem and might be important for the antidepressant effects of exercise. Similarly, achieving a sense of social connectedness through interactions with others during the performance of physical activities can be important for reducing depressive symptoms. Finally, exercising outdoors might hold particular benefits due to the restorative properties of being in the natural environment, which is associated with positive mental health outcomes. Early researchers thought that the benefits of exercise for depression might be simply due to the time-out that exercise provides from daily worries and negative thoughts. Research has not typically supported this hypothesis because the benefits of exercise tend to supersede those of other activities that might also provide a time-out (e.g., watching a movie or soaking in a hot tub). Another psychological hypothesis that has been proposed is the self-esteem hypothesis. Because we know that exercise improves self-esteem (see chapter 12) and because we know that depressed individuals tend to have low self-esteem, it has been suggested that these increases in self-esteem might mediate the benefits of exercise for depression. Although the role of self-esteem as a mediator has been supported by findings of cross-sectional studies (Dishman et al., 2006; McPhie & Rawana, 2012), this has not been established using causal designs that would allow one to truly test the causal role of self-esteem in this relationship.

Treatment of Clinical Depression

Individuals who experience clinical depression often do not seek treatment. In fact, it was estimated in 2020 that approximately 35% of U.S. adults (18 years and older) and approximately 60% of U.S. adolescents with clinical depression do not receive treatment (National Institute of Mental Health, 2022a). This might be due to the social stigma of seeking treatment for mental illness, concerns about side effects of pharmacological treatments, or the expense of many of the available treatments. For people who do seek treatment, the most common intervention is pharmacological, but psychotherapy, electroconvulsive therapy, and exercise also have been shown to be effective.

Pharmacological Treatment

Given our understanding of the causes of depression, early pharmacological interventions were focused on monoamine oxidase inhibitors and tricyclic antidepressants. As mentioned earlier, monoamines include serotonin, dopamine, and norepinephrine, and low levels of these neurotransmitters are implicated in depression. Given the expected role of monoamines in depression, treatments with monoamine oxidase inhibitors are designed to increase monoamine availability. The name *monoamine oxidase inhibitor (MAOI)* is understood by remembering that "oxidase" refers to the breaking down of a substance. Thus, a drug that is an inhibitor of the oxidase (the breaking down) of monoamines results in greater availability of monoamines. One limitation of MAOIs is that they are nonspecific, which means that they affect all monoamines (i.e., their effects are broad). So although they can be effective in reducing depression, they often have substantial side effects (e.g., weight gain, sleep problems, agitation) and might require diet restrictions and avoidance of other medications because of the potential for a dramatic and dangerous increase in blood pressure. As a result of these limitations, more targeted pharmacological interventions have been developed that focus specifically on single monoamines. These more targeted pharmacological treatments include selective serotonin reuptake inhibitors (SSRIs), norepinephrine reuptake inhibitors (NERIs), and serotonin and norepinephrine reuptake inhibitors (SNRIs) (table 6.1). By parsing out the names of these categories of drugs, you can understand that they are specific

TABLE 6.1 Single Monoamine Pharmacological Treatments

Type of treatment	Examples
Selective serotonin reuptake inhibitors (SSRIs)	Prozac (fluoxetine), Paxil (paroxetine), Celexa (citalopram), Lexapro (escitalopram), Zoloft (sertraline hydrochloride)
Serotonin and norepinephrine reuptake inhibitors (SNRIs)	Effexor (venlafaxine), Cymbalta (duloxetine), Pristiq (desvenlafaxine)
Norepinephrine and dopamine reuptake inhibitors (NDRIs)	Wellbutrin (bupropion)

to either serotonin or norepinephrine or both, and they inhibit the reuptake of this neurotransmitter resulting in more of that neurotransmitter being freely available. If the SSRIs, NERIs, or SNRIs are not effective, tricyclic or tetracyclic antidepressants can be used, but these cyclic antidepressants affect numerous chemical messengers and cause even more side effects, making them generally a last choice for treatment.

Unfortunately, approximately 50% of patients with clinical depression do not respond to their first course of treatment (Ruhe et al., 2006), and more than 65% never achieve remission even after multiple treatments (Rush et al., 2006). In addition, the negative side effects of antidepressants can be substantial, resulting in poor rates of adherence. As a result of these limitations, alternative therapies are often pursued by persons suffering from depression.

Psychotherapy

Psychotherapy (also called simply *therapy*) is a treatment option for depression (and other mental health disorders) that involves talking with a trained mental health care provider who assists in identifying ways to mitigate the depression through learning coping methods. There are numerous types of therapy that have been used with depression, including cognitive therapy, behavioral therapy, cognitive behavioral therapy, and dialectical behavior therapy. These psychological approaches to the treatment of depression have been shown to be effective with a moderate ES ($g = 0.72$) for depression between a treatment group and a control group at the posttest (Cuijpers, Karyotaki, de Wit, & Ebert, 2020). In their meta-analytic review, Cuijpers et al. reported that cognitive behavioral therapies were the most commonly used, with an average ES of 0.73. However, tests of the specific psychotherapy approach being used did not identify any significant differences between treatments. Hence, the results of this review suggest that psychotherapeutic treatments are effective overall with no distinctions between particular methods.

Electroconvulsive Therapy

A treatment for clinical depression that consistently has been shown to be effective is electroconvulsive therapy (ECT). This probably sounds terrible, but this treatment has been used for over 70 years with great effect, particularly for patients who don't respond to pharmacological interventions. ECT is conducted under general anesthesia and involves the administration of small electric currents through the brain that are purposefully designed to cause a brief seizure. This apparently serves to reset the brain in a way that has been shown to be effective for severe depression and treatment-resistant depression. A recent review of the empirical studies focused on this technique found that ECT resulted in significant increases in hippocampal volume, and the authors concluded that this likely was due to a positive impact on neurotrophic factors important for neurogenesis (Gbyl & Videbech, 2018). When compared to other treatments, Lima and colleagues (2013) concluded that ECT also can be used effectively and safely with adolescents (13-18 years of age). In sum, ECT is a good approach to take for those who have not benefited from or who cannot tolerate the side effects of pharmacological interventions or for pregnant women who cannot take medications that might harm their fetus.

Treatment Selection

Treatment selection is a relatively new approach to the treatment of depression and is based upon the premise that with multiple treatment options available, it is important to be able to identify the specific treatment or combination of treatments that will be most efficacious for a specific individual (Cohen & DeRubeis, 2018). The National Institute of Health recently created a Precision Medicine Initiative (Collins & Varmus, 2015), designed to advance our understanding of how to select the most appropriate treatment for a given individual. Precision medicine has had important positive outcomes in cancer research, where knowledge about the specific type of cancer allows for a targeted treatment approach particularly with regards to the standard cancer treatment that will be most beneficial (e.g., some specific and tailored combination of surgery, radiation, chemotherapy, hormone therapy, and immunotherapy) and even the specific chemotherapy drugs and regimens to be prescribed. Similarly, with respect to depression, because numerous underlying mechanisms could be implicated to varying degrees for any given individual, clinical diagnostics that could identify the root cause for that individual might lead to a matching of the best treatment to suit their needs and, hence, the best outcomes.

Measurement

The assessment of depression is challenging because it is important to be able to distinguish between measures of clinical depression (which are most capably performed by a researcher with clinical training) and measures of depressive symptoms. The physical activity literature includes studies that look at the influence of physical activity on depressive symptoms in nondepressed individuals and in clinically depressed individuals, as well as studies examining the influence of physical activity on the future diagnosis of depression (i.e., as a preventative or as a treatment). At the present time, most studies are focused on depressive symptoms, which likely reflects three facts. First, the studies are not being conducted with research teams that include both clinical psychologists (who can assess clinical depression) and exercise psychologists (who can design an appropriate exercise intervention). Second, it is harder to gain access to persons who are clinically depressed, whereas depressive symptoms can be assessed in the general population. Third, exercise interventions are typically relatively short term (i.e., weeks or months in length), while a long-term effect on clinical depression is likely to take more time to realize.

Depression instruments consist of semi-structured and fully structured interviews and observer-rated measures that are typically used for diagnostic purposes (i.e., to assess clinical depression) or self-report measures used to assess depressive symptoms. Semi-structured interviews are those that begin with a series of broad questions that allow for specific follow-up questions dependent on the participant's response. Fully structured interviews are more stringent in that the specific questions to be asked are all determined prior to interacting with the participant. Observer-rated measures are those that require an experimenter to record and evaluate behaviors observed in the participant and can be conducted relative to the administration of an interview. Interviews and observer-rated measures are almost always conducted by a person who has clinical training relative to the diagnosis of depression. Self-report measures are, of course, measures that ask the participant to report on their own symptoms and can be administered by any trained researcher.

As previously mentioned, studies exploring the effects of physical activity or exercise on depression typically have focused on depressive symptoms as the outcome of interest. Commonly used self-report measures of depressive symptoms that have been used in adults include the Hamilton Depression Rating Scale (HDRS), the Beck Depression Inventory (BDI), the Profile of Mood States – depression questions, and the Center for Epidemiological Studies Depression scale (CESD). Of these measures, the BDI and CESD are most commonly used as initial screening measures (Sharp & Lipsky, 2002).

When assessing depressive symptoms in adolescents, the most commonly used measures are the Hamilton Rating Scale for Depression (HRSD) and the Children's Depression Rating Scale-Revised (CDRS). The HRSD is scored through an interview with the child, while the CDRS is administered to the child, a parent, and one other adult (e.g., the child's teacher). Neither of these require the interviewer to be clinically trained, but more general training of procedures is necessary to ensure reliable administration and scoring. The Children's Depression Inventory (CDI), the BDI, and the CESD are other commonly used self-report measures of depression in studies with adolescents. Although the CDI and the BDI have acceptable psychometrics, the CESD is not recommended for use with children (Brooks & Kutcher, 2003).

Evidence on the Benefits of Exercise for Depression

The body of evidence relative to exercise and depression is one of the more developed topics of research, with over 33,000 studies focused on exercise or physical activity and depression. This evidence can be reviewed at the level of the individual study (the empirical evidence) or through meta-analytic summaries of empirical studies. We consider both types of evidence here.

Empirical Evidence

As we consider the empirical evidence relative to depression, it is important to remember that this question can be approached from a variety of vantage points similar to our viewpoint for anxiety. One approach is to consider the potential of exercise to reduce depressive symptoms in people who are not clinically depressed. When considering this line of research, both acute and chronic exercise interventions conceivably could have an impact; however, the focus in the research literature has been almost exclusively on chronic exercise. Another approach is to think about exercise as a means to prevent the experience of clinical depression. Relative to this question, only chronic exercise programs are relevant. Lastly, we can look at exercise as a means of treating clinical depression, which also would require a chronic intervention to have long-lasting effects. Before turning our attention to the meta-analytic summaries of these bodies of literature, we will first learn about an exemplar study for each of the outcomes of interest.

Reducing Depressive Symptoms

Resnick and colleagues (2008) used a between-subjects design with senior centers to explore the effects of an exercise program on self-efficacy, mental and physical quality of life, depressive symptoms, and pain in community-dwelling older adults. Six senior centers were randomly selected to receive the Senior Exercise Self-Efficacy Project (SESEP), and seven were selected for the control group. The SESEP consisted of stretching, resistance training, and aerobic exercises combined with an education program designed to increase self-efficacy for being physically active while also providing educational information about goal setting and nutrition. The control group was offered the same number of sessions but focused only on nutrition during their sessions. The programs were offered 2 days per week for 1 to 1.5 hours for 12 weeks. Participants consisted of 166 older adults (M = 73.0 yr), with the majority being female (81%), unmarried (86%), with at least a high school education (64%), and retired (77%). Importantly, this sample was racially diverse, with 73% of participants identifying as Black, 20% as Latino, and 7% as other races. Of the psychological constructs assessed, depression was the only one for which a significant impact was observed for the exercise group but not for the control group. Although the number of depressive symptoms was low at baseline, the reduction in depressive symptoms for the exercise group exhibited a moderate effect size (ES = 0.50), and at the posttest, the difference in depressive symptoms between the groups was in the small to moderate range (ES = 0.41). The authors concluded that the results support the successful implementation of the SESEP in a low-income area through community centers with the results that ethnic minority older adults experienced significant reductions in depression.

Preventing Clinical Depression

The Nurses' Health Study is one of the largest investigations of risk factors for chronic diseases in women. The original Nurses' Health Study was established in 1976 and was designed to explore long-term consequences of the use of oral contraceptives. The researchers imagined that nurses would be an ideal group to study because they would be able to answer technical questions about their health and would be motivated to stay engaged in this long-term study. Because of the focus of the original study and the potential sensitivity of the subject matter at that time, the initial sample included only married, female, registered nurses between the ages of 30 and 55 who lived in the 11 states with the highest populations. For the baseline measure, 121,700 women returned completed surveys. These women have been contacted every 2 years to collect additional information.

Chang and associates (2016) report on prospective relationships between physical activity and depression using data from a subsample of the Nurses' Health Study. Given the age of the participants at this point in time (M = 71.4 years), the focus of this study was on late-life depression, which was defined as clinical depression that occurred for the first time after age 65. The Nurses' Health Study included questions about doctor-diagnosed depression in 2000, making that the baseline for this study, but did include questions about a history of depression in earlier years. To be included in this study, participants had to be older than 65 in 2000, have no prior indication of depression, and provide all necessary data, resulting in 21,728 women included in the analyses. Data that were used in the analyses were collected at 2-year intervals for 10 years. Results showed a dose–response relationship between the amount of moderate to vigorous physical activity performed and the risk of depression. In particular, women who exercised for 5 or more hours per week were considered to represent a normal risk level. Compared to this group, the risk of depression increased with decreasing physical activity such that those exercising 2.5 to 4.99 hours per week had an 11% increased risk, those exercising 1.0 to 2.49 hours per week had a 23% increase in risk, those exercising 0.1 to 0.99 hours per week had a 47% increase in risk, and those who were completely sedentary had a 60% increase in risk (figure 6.2). Importantly, the researchers were able to conduct additional analyses to test the possibility that depression was actually leading to less physical activity. These analyses supported that this explanation was not likely and that the evidence supported that the low levels of physical activity preceded the incidence of depression. This study provides powerful evidence that physical activity participation is protective against clinical depression at least in older women who were nurses for at least a portion of their careers.

Treating Clinical Depression

Dunn and colleagues (2002, 2005) conducted an important RCT in this area that was called the Depression Outcomes Study of Exercise (DOSE). The scientists recruited eighty 20- to 45-year-olds who were clinically diagnosed with mild to moderate clinical depression. Participants were randomly assigned to one of five conditions. The conditions included two doses of exercise: (1) a dose that matched the current public health recommendations of 180 minutes of moderate-intensity physical activity per week (called the *public health dose*) (17.5 kcal/kg/wk) or a low dose (7 kcal/kg/wk) and two frequencies of exercise (3 days/wk or 5 days/wk) to create four possible exercise groups, and (2) an exercise placebo control group that met 3 days per week to do approximately 20 minutes of light-intensity stretching (see table 6.2).

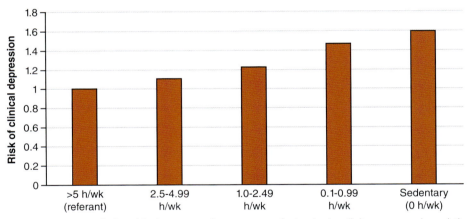

FIGURE 6.2 Dose–response relationship between the amount of physical activity per week and the risk of clinical depression in the future.
Adapted from Chang et al. (2016).

TABLE 6.2 Conditions Used in the DOSE Study

		DOSE		
		Placebo control	**Low dose = 7.5 kcal/kg/wk**	**Public health dose = 17.5 kcal/kg/wk**
FREQUENCY	**3 days/wk**	Light stretching 20 min daily	Low dose obtained over 3 days	Public health dose obtained over 3 days
	5 days/wk		Low dose obtained over 5 days	Public health dose obtained over 5 days

From Dunn et al. (2002). From Dunn et al. (2005).

The public health dose of exercise equated to a total of approximately 180 minutes (i.e., approximately 60 min/day for the 3 days/wk group or approximately 35 min/day for the 5 days/wk group), and the low dose equated to approximately 80 minutes of moderate-intensity exercise per week (i.e., approximately 25 min/day for the 3 days/wk group or approximately 15 min/day for the 5 days/wk group). Participants attended supervised exercise sessions for the first 12 weeks of the study, at which point the four exercise groups were allowed to exercise on their own at home and the control group was allowed to start an exercise program. Depression was assessed using the HRSD administered weekly for the first 12 weeks. Results at 12 weeks showed that significant decreases in depression were evident for the two groups receiving the public health dose of exercise (figure 6.3). For these two groups, HRSD scores decreased by 47% on average for the entire group. In addition, 46% of the participants showed a therapeutic response to treatment (a decrease in HRSD scores by at least 50%), and 42% experienced a remission in symptoms. Thus, these findings tell us that participation in 180 minutes of exercise per week (regardless of whether this is performed across 3 days or 5 days) results in significant reductions in depressive symptoms and full remission in almost 50% of participants. The authors point out the importance of this by comparing it to other depression treatments. In particular, previous research has found that cognitive behavioral therapy (CBT) resulted in 36% remission, and an antidepressant medication resulted in 42% remission. Hence with 42% remission observed in the 180 minutes per week group, exercise was shown to be more effective than CBT therapy and as effective as antidepressant medications (Elkin et al., 1989).

Meta-Analytic Evidence

As mentioned earlier, given the substantial interest in the effects of exercise on depression, this topic has been well studied, with a plethora of empirical studies exploring effects on symptoms and clinical diagnoses. Given the large number of empirical studies and their different foci, it is not surprising that many meta-analytic reviews have been conducted in this area. In fact, this literature has been reviewed in at least 39 meta-analytic reviews. As a result, in some of the areas of research, we will be able to present findings from umbrella reviews (i.e., meta-analyses of meta-analytic reviews), hence providing summary data from a very large number of empirical studies.

Reducing Depressive Symptoms

Researchers have explored the potential impact of exercise on depressive symptoms in people who are not clinically depressed. Over the years, this body of evidence has been reviewed meta-analytically on numerous occasions, and here we discuss findings of three umbrella reviews.

Wegner and colleagues (2014) conducted a review of 32 meta-analyses focused on the depressive-reducing effects of exercise. They included meta-analyses focused on a variety of populations (e.g., patients with chronic illnesses, clinical popu-

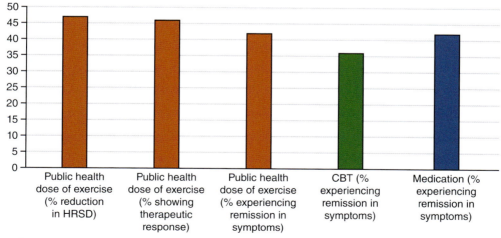

FIGURE 6.3 Results from the DOSE study demonstrating reductions in clinical depression in response to the public health dose of exercise. Remission in symptoms is comparable between exercise and medication use and better for exercise than CBT.

Adapted from Dunn et al. (2005).

lations, nonclinical populations, cancer survivors). The overall effect size was moderate (ES = 0.56) but was larger for RCTs (ES = 0.65), suggesting that evidence for a causal relationship is strong. It is encouraging that their results also showed that effects were larger for studies with clinically depressed samples (ES = 0.73) than for studies with nondepressed samples (ES = 0.41).

Wegner and associates (2020) conducted an umbrella review of four meta-analyses summarizing results from 30 studies focused on the effects of exercise on depressive symptoms in children and adolescents. Results showed that depressive symptoms were significantly reduced in response to exercise in children and adolescents when clinical and nonclinical samples were combined (ES = 0.50). Given that they combined results from clinical and nonclinical samples, it is important to point out that the results for the clinically depressed (ES = 0.48) were not substantially different from the overall mean, suggesting that effects were similar across the two samples.

Hu and colleagues (2020) conducted a systematic review of the published meta-analytic reviews focused on the effects of exercise on depressive symptoms in the general population, and they identified eight meta-analyses meeting their inclusion criteria. In total, the reviews considered 134 individual studies with relatively little overlap across the reviews, and all used depressive symptoms as the outcome. Of the eight meta-analyses, all reported beneficial effects of exercise in the reduction of depressive symptoms, and these effects were significant in six of the reviews with small to moderate effect sizes reported (ES = 0.35-0.81). Intriguingly, the meta-analysis reporting the largest overall ES (ES = 0.81) limited the studies to only those looking at resistance exercise training. This might suggest that this mode of exercise has specific benefits relative to the reduction of depressive symptoms in individuals who are not clinically depressed.

Overall, these small to moderate reductions in depressive symptoms are impressive given that they were found in samples that were not depressed as well as in clinical samples. This suggests, then, that exercise is important for the management of depressive symptoms in the general population and in those experiencing clinical depression, and this has been observed in studies across the life span.

Preventing Clinical Depression

Research focused on the prevention of clinical depression is typically prospective in design. That is, participants are recruited from the general population, their physical activity behavior is assessed, and they are followed forward in time to gauge if they develop depressive symptoms or become clinically diagnosed with depression. This literature is relatively robust and therefore has been reviewed meta-analytically on numerous occasions.

Mammen and Faulkner (2013) analyzed findings from 30 prospective studies and reported that 25 yielded significant inverse relationships between baseline levels of physical activity and clinical depression. In other words, people with higher levels of baseline physical activity had a decreased likelihood of becoming depressed in the future. They also reported that in four high-quality studies, a reduction in physical activity over time was predictive of an increased risk of depression, while maintenance of a physically active lifestyle or increases in physical activity were associated with a decreased risk of depression. This provides strong evidence in support of physical activity protecting against depression.

Schuch and associates (2018) meta-analyzed findings from 49 prospective studies, resulting in a summary analysis of data from 266,939 individuals who were followed for an average of 7.4 years. Studies were included only if participants were not depressed at baseline. Results showed that men and women with higher physical activity levels at baseline had a 17% to 41% reduction in the risk of being diagnosed with depression relative to those with lower physical activity levels. Although slightly smaller, the risk of depression remained at 15% even after adjusting for various biases to ensure the highest quality of results are being presented. This evidence supports that participation in physical activity is protective against clinical depression with benefits observed for men and women.

Thus, in two meta-analyses, results consistently show a protective effect of physical activity participation against a future diagnosis with clinical depression. This suggests the importance of physical activity as preventative, which might be attractive for anyone whose risk of depression is increased due to a family history of depression.

Treating Clinical Depression

In 2020, Ashdown-Franks and colleagues (2020) systematically reviewed eight meta-analyses with a focus on samples of children, adolescents, and adults who had been clinically diagnosed with depression. They reported that exercise was beneficial for children and adolescents (ES = 0.43-0.95), adults (ES = 0.57-1.14), and older adults (ES = 0.90). They described their findings as being relatively consistent across the meta-analyses reviewed, and based on this evidence, they suggested that structured exercise at moderate to vigorous intensity can positively affect depressive symptoms among the clinically depressed when used as an add-on to existing treatments.

> **Consensus Statements From Around the World**
>
> In 2018 a consensus statement was published jointly by four major professional organizations (Exercise and Sports Science Australia, the American College of Sports Medicine, the British Association of Sport and Exercise Science, and Sport and Exercise Science New Zealand). The point of the consensus statement was to promote "the role of exercise interventions as a key component of a global strategy toward achieving a 50% reduction in the life expectancy gap of people experiencing mental illness by 2032" (Rosenbaum et al., 2018, p. 73). Simultaneously, the European Psychiatric Association reviewed the evidence, concluded that exercise reduces depressive symptoms in people with clinical depression, and recommended moderate exercise for 45 to 60 minutes, 2 to 3 days per week (Stubbs et al., 2018).

Bidirectional Relationship

In considering the extant literature on exercise and depression, one interesting point to consider is the possibility that this is actually a bidirectional relationship. In other words, it is plausible that those with less depression are able to be more physically active and that this physical activity provides protection against depression. However, the converse is also true, which is that people who are more depressed are less likely to be active, which can then exacerbate the depression. This possibility of a bidirectional relationship is a major limitation for studies using cross-sectional designs. That makes a study conducted by Vella and associates (2017) especially informative because they specifically examined the bidirectional nature of this relationship in adolescents relative to their participation in organized sport. As a part of the Longitudinal Study of Australian Children, they collected data on sport participation and mental health in over 4,000 adolescents when they were 12 years old and again when they were 14 years old. Results showed that those who participated in more sport at age 12 had better mental health at age 14. Results also showed that those who had worse mental health at age 12 were less likely to participate in sport at age 14. This is an important set of findings because it argues for the value of sport participation while also demonstrating that adolescents who are already experiencing mental health challenges might be less likely to join organized sport activities. Interesting as well is the fact that no differences were observed between girls and boys or between different types of sport activities (individual versus team). Overall, this finding confirms the importance of recognizing the potential for a bidirectional relationship such that lower physical activity is predictive of greater depression, but also greater depression is predictive of lower physical activity.

Specific Populations

In addition to studies focused on the benefits of exercise for the general population, increasingly more studies have focused on the potential benefits of exercise on depression with specific, potentially unique populations. These bodies of evidence are large enough in some cases that meta-analytic reviews have begun to be published. Meta-analytic reviews have been conducted for studies focused on cancer survivors (Duan et al., 2020), people with dementia (Watt et al., 2021), people living with HIV (Heissel et al., 2019), and people with schizophrenia (Dauwan et al., 2016). In general, the results of these meta-analytic reviews support that exercise reduces depression in these various specific populations. This could be particularly important given that depression is a common comorbidity in these illnesses and complicates clinicians' ability to address the underlying chronic disease. Exercise also has been found to be beneficial to women experiencing postpartum depression (Daley et al., 2009), which is important given that postpartum depression occurs in approximately 13% of new mothers and can have negative effects on the bonding between the mother and her baby. Overall, research supports positive effects of exercise on depression in specific populations that might experience depression as a comorbidity or as a consequence of childbirth.

Summary

In considering the role of exercise in combating depression, we recognized that we have to consider whether we are talking about reductions of depressive symptoms in nondepressed individuals, the prevention of depression, or the treatment of depression in clinically depressed individuals. The prevalence of depression is on the rise, and the societal and economic costs of clinical depression for individuals and their families are very high. Evidence strongly suggests that exercise can have a positive effect on all of the outcomes of depression. That is, it has been shown to reduce depressive symptoms, to protect against clinical depression, and to effectively treat those who are clinically depressed when offered in isolation or in conjunction with other treatments. Exercise also has been found to be effective at reducing the experience of depression in people who are dealing with other chronic illnesses such as cancer, dementia, HIV, and schizophrenia, and it benefits women who are experiencing postpartum depression. As such, exercise should be recommended for all as a way of protecting against clinical depression and might be particularly beneficial for people already experiencing clinical depression or depressive symptoms. Research exploring the mechanisms underlying these benefits is still in its infancy. Future research designed to identify mechanisms of these benefits will be important for furthering our understanding of how exercise can be used to prevent and treat depression either in isolation or in combination with other forms of treatment.

Discussion Questions

1. What is the difference between depressive symptoms and clinical depression?
2. Name and describe three psychological mediators that could explain the benefits of exercise for depression.
3. The DOSE study was important for advancing our understanding of how much physical activity is necessary to reduce depressive symptoms in young people (ages 20-45) with clinical depression. Describe the design of the study, explain what was found, and provide some context by comparing the results to what we know from other forms of treatment.
4. Explain why physical activity could be important for breaking the cycle of depression.

Exercise and Affect, Mood, and Emotions

OBJECTIVES

After studying this chapter, you should be able to do the following:

- Distinguish between affect, mood, and emotion
- Explain the various ways in which affect, mood, and emotion are measured and specific instruments used in exercise psychology
- Describe early theories of mood and understand the dual mode theory and how it is applied to exercise and affect
- Understand how endorphins and endocannabinoids can explain the benefits of exercise for affect and provide evidence to support both
- Discuss empirical and meta-analytic evidence relative to the effects of acute exercise and chronic exercise on affect

KEY TERMS

runner's high
exercise addicts
affect
mood
emotion

ventilatory threshold (VT)
endorphins
endocannabinoid (eCB) system
exercise-specific measures
circumplex model of affect

Michael has been a regular exerciser for his entire life. He participated in a variety of sports during his childhood, played basketball and soccer in high school, continued with recreational sports in college, and then in his late 20s and 30s became a regular runner. He participates in three or four road races each season and trains regularly so that he's prepared to be competitive in those events. Recently, he's begun to suffer from plantar fasciitis, which is when the tissue surrounding the muscle and tendons in the arch and heel of the foot becomes injured through overuse. It's incredibly painful, and the best way to treat it is through rest, ice, and the use of anti-inflammatories. Michael has been treating his plantar fasciitis for a month so has not been exercising at all in an effort to get past this overuse injury once and for all. Lately, though, he's noticed that his mood has been kind of sour, and his boyfriend has been pointing out that he's been irritable and down. He seems to snap back at people for small things and to have lower energy levels and less patience than normal. He recognizes that the lack of exercise might be the reason for his poor mood. He decides to join the Y to start swimming. Although it's not his favorite mode of exercise, he is a strong swimmer and is able to get back into a regular exercise routine that does not exacerbate the plantar fasciitis. Within a couple of weeks of swimming, both Michael and his boyfriend are excited to notice that his mood has improved, and he's feeling happy and positive again. To ensure that he can maintain a regular exercise regimen, Michael envisions that he will do both swimming and running in upcoming months and will even consider adding in other forms of training such as cycling and cross-country skiing to allow him to maintain his fitness and his positive mood while also minimizing the likelihood of overtraining injuries.

The story about Michael provides an example of how exercise can be used as a way to improve mood. Have you ever experienced the feel-good phenomenon after exercise? This phenomenon is often sensed by regular exercisers in the period of time following an exercise session. It is typically described as feeling better and having a sense of reduced tension. At its extreme, this experience is sometimes referred to as a *runner's high*, which is most commonly perceived by those who exercise in ways that require the repetitive use of large muscle groups through a variety of activities such as running, biking, and swimming for longer distances. A **runner's high** has been described as a feeling of euphoria in response to running during which a person feels extreme joy, reduced pain, and a sense of the running being effortless. If you have ever enjoyed the feel-good phenomenon or a runner's high, consider what it felt like and the circumstances that surrounded that particular event. Was your experience a strong positive mood or more of a subtle change in your general feelings? How long did the experience last? Was there anything in particular about the experience that you think would be important for re-creating that feeling?

Runner's High

The runner's high is a euphoric response to physical activity that is sometimes experienced by regular runners after an extended exercise session. It is typically experienced on days when the temperature and humidity are such that the weather itself feels good and when the runner is able to run automatically without having to make decisions about directions or distance. When a runner experiences a runner's high, they feel that their running is effortless and that they could go on forever. This feeling might contribute to their desire to stay regularly active as they hope to re-create this feeling.

Many people who exercise regularly say that they experience a general positive response after completing an exercise bout and that it is this positive experience that helps them maintain their commitment to regular exercise. In fact, some regular exercisers will tell you that if they miss a couple days of activity, they notice that their mood begins to become more negative as in the story at the begin-

---

runner's high—A feeling of euphoria in response to running during which a person feels extreme joy, reduced pain, and a sense of the running being effortless are characteristics of a runner's high.

ning of this chapter. In the event of a runner's high, the exercise bout itself might feel more effortless than usual, and the postexercise feelings might be described as euphoric. In fact, some have suggested that the feel-good phenomenon can contribute to the potential for exercise addiction as hard-core exercisers strive to maintain that extremely positive feeling. Anecdotal evidence suggests that exercise can have powerful positive effects in the case of a runner's high, but some evidence also suggests that regular exercise can result in smaller, less long-lasting benefits to mood, and we've already discussed the evidence supporting that exercise can reduce negative moods such as depression and anxiety. However, one of the perplexing aspects of exercise psychology is that if these feel-good effects were ubiquitous, presumably more people would be regularly physically active since people tend to repeat behaviors that have positive consequences. Clearly, given the large number of people who do not meet the physical activity recommendations, this question of whether exercise leads to positive mood must be a bit more complex and is likely to be dependent on the dose of the exercise, factors in the environment, and individual differences. It is important to identify the factors that are critical for ensuring a positive affective response to exercise because evidence supports that the affective response to a single session of exercise is predictive of physical activity participation over a period of 6 to 12 months (Williams et al., 2008; Williams et al., 2011).

When we switch our focus to the effects of exercise on affect and mood, we move away from the clinical psychological outcomes we have previously considered (e.g., depression and anxiety) and instead focus on a more short-term effect that might last minutes, hours, or days rather than months or years and that can range from being quite specific to being broader in nature. One of the great challenges in this area of research is with defining the terms *affect*, *mood*, and *emotion*, which are familiar to us and yet are often unspecified such that we might not readily be able to distinguish between them. After defining these terms, we will consider how affect, mood, and emotion are measured; review theories and mechanisms; and consider the evidence relative to the effects of exercise on these outcomes.

What Are Affect, Mood, and Emotion?

In the psychology literature, **affect** is viewed as a very broad and unspecified experience that has both a valence and an intensity level. In terms of valence, two-dimensional models of affect categorize affect as generally positive (indicative of pleasure) or generally negative (indicative of displeasure). Importantly, affect is viewed as motivational so that positive affect is expected to increase the likelihood of a behavior, while negative affect is anticipated to decrease the likelihood of a behavior. Thus, a positive affective response to exercise should motivate a person to

---

Exercise Addiction

Exercise addiction is not officially recognized by the American Psychological Association in the most recent *Diagnostic and Statistical Manual* (American Psychiatric Association, 2022) because evidence is not yet sufficient for the diagnostic criteria. However, exercise psychologists have observed characteristics that would seem to argue that this is a real behavioral addiction. In particular, although exercise behavior has benefits for both physical and mental health, when the behavior becomes controlling, it might shift to a pathogenic behavior that can become addictive (Egorov & Szabo, 2013). People who might be described as **exercise addicts** demonstrate symptoms such as mood modification in the absence of exercise, tolerance for increased levels of exercise, symptoms of withdrawal in the absence of exercise, and prioritizing exercise over other important aspects of life. An example of someone with an exercise addiction is a person who increases their exercise volume despite battling an overtraining injury, who misses important family events rather than skip an exercise session, and who is irritable and moody when unable to exercise. Do you know anyone who exhibits these behaviors? In terms of prevalence, it appears that approximately 5% of college students, 5% of amateur competitive athletes, and 8% of general exercisers might suffer from exercise addiction (Trott et al., 2020).

---

exercise addicts—People who demonstrate symptoms such as mood modification in the absence of exercise, tolerance for increased levels of exercise, symptoms of withdrawal in the absence of exercise, and prioritizing exercise over other important aspects of life might be considered exercise addicts.

affect—Affect is a very broad and unspecified experience that has both a valence and an intensity level.

continue to exercise (an approach response), and a negative affective response to exercise, conversely, should motivate a person not to exercise (an avoidance or withdrawal response). As mentioned, affect is also thought to exist along a continuum in terms of its intensity level, and the intensity level then affects the strength of the motivational push with regards to its impact on behavior (Velasco & Loev, 2020). That is, a more intense affective response should be more motivational than a less intense affective response.

Mood is influenced by affect and is itself considered to be a broad experience that is not typically attributable to a specific event. Moods are of relatively low intensity and long duration in that they can last for hours or days. This is probably consistent with your own experiences when you judge that you are in a bad mood or a good mood and can't think of a specific event that caused that feeling. Perhaps you had a fight with your roommate a few days ago or broke off a long-term relationship last week. This type of event might put you in a negative mood that lasts for days. In response to your mood, people who are around you might ask, "Did you wake up on the wrong side of the bed?" Clearly, this suggests that we can start the day in a bad mood, and this can then affect how we interact with others and our perception of events throughout the day. Importantly, moods can bias the emotions that are experienced such that a person in a bad mood might respond more negatively and experience more negative emotions in response to a situation as compared to a person in a good mood who is responding to the exact same situation. For example, imagine that you are looking forward to an afternoon barbeque with friends, but a thunderstorm builds and the event gets canceled. If you were in a bad mood to start with, this might tilt your emotions so that you are upset, sad, and irritable for the rest of the evening. But if you were in a good mood to start with, you might interpret the rained-out event as a chance to call your best friend to catch up since you haven't visited in a long time or to binge-watch a favorite television series, and your emotions might be much more positive.

Emotion is a higher-order experience than either affect or mood, meaning that it is reliant on cognitive processing that occurs in higher-order levels of the brain and in response to a specific event. The experience of an emotion requires paying attention to the stimulus, is reliant on some level of cognitive appraisal prior to a judgment of the experience, and is typically accompanied by observable facial expressions that are thought to be somewhat consistent across cultures. Emotions are relatively short in duration, lasting for seconds or minutes, and are usually closely tied to a specific, identifiable stimulus. Emotions are well described by specific familiar adjectives such as *happy*, *sad*, *proud*, *excited*, and *angry*. Emotions provide us with an overall indication of how an individual is adjusting to constantly changing demands, and they provide the impetus for goal-directed behaviors (Thayer & Lane, 2000). Finally, the experience of an emotion might also contribute to the more generalized mood a person is feeling. For example, if you are very excited and happy over news of a pay raise, this might translate to a positive mood for an extended period of time.

Theories and Mechanisms of Mood and of the Effects of Exercise on Mood

Mood has been a construct of interest for centuries, with numerous psychologists proposing theories to explain the experience of mood and with theories evolving with increasing knowledge. These theories typically fall into three main categories: physiological theories, neurological theories, and cognitive theories (figure 7.1). The James-Lange theory of mood was described independently and simultaneously by William James and Carl Lange in 1884 and provides an early example of a physiological theory. This theory suggests that an event triggers a physiological response that is then interpreted as a mood. For example, imagine that you are walking in the woods and realize that you are being followed (stalked, perhaps) by a mountain lion. You begin to tremble. According to this theory, you then realize that because you are trembling, you must be afraid. Thus, the physiological response happens first and is interpreted based on the situation to result in an emotional response. Several decades later, Walter Cannon and then Philip Bard proposed a neurological theory of emotion. The Cannon-Bard theory presents a slight modification of the James-Lange theory because it suggests that the physiological response and the experience of emotion happen simultaneously. According to this neurological theory and sticking with the previous example, the recognition that you're being stalked

---

mood—Mood is influenced by affect and is considered to be a broad experience that is not typically attributable to a specific event.

emotion—An emotion is a higher-order experience than either affect or mood, meaning that it is reliant on cognitive processing that occurs in higher-order levels of the brain and in response to a specific event.

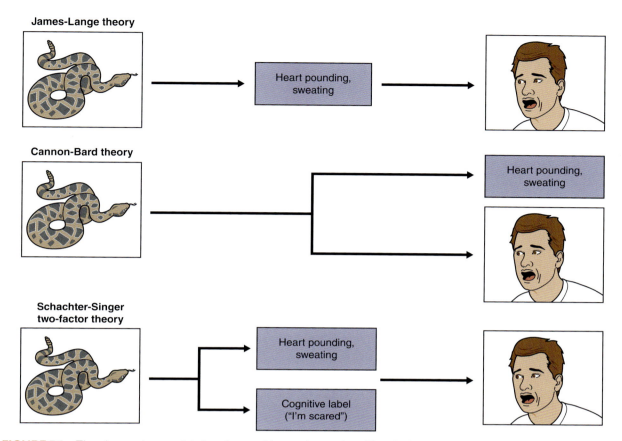

FIGURE 7.1 The circumplex model showing positive and negative affect (valence) on the x-axis and activation (intensity) on the y-axis with example emotions shown in each quadrant
Based on Russell (1980).

by a mountain lion leads to changes in subcortical brain activity. These changes in brain activity then trigger the physiological response and the simultaneous experience of the emotion of fear. Again, several decades would pass before another important theory of emotion would be proposed. In 1962 Schachter and Singer proposed a two-factor theory of emotion. This theory suggests that the event leads to a physiological response, which is then cognitively appraised to allow for an interpretation of the physiological response, which results in the experience of a particular mood. According to this theory, the physiological response is affectively neutral and therefore can result in any mood experience. It is the cognitive appraisal that drives the specific emotion that is experienced, and this is what differentiates this theory from the James-Lange theory. The two-factor theory is considered to be a cognitive theory because the cognitive appraisal is necessary to explain the emotional experience.

For example, imagine that your heart is racing, your palms are starting to sweat, and your breathing has become fast and shallow. In the absence of any further information, you might not be able to imagine a mood state that goes with those physiological experiences. But imagine two different situations that might evoke this physiological response and think how your mood would differ in these two scenarios. First, imagine that your palms are sweaty, your breathing is fast, and your heart is racing. You are standing at the top of one of the largest waterslides in the world and are getting ready to plunge over 100 feet (30 m) and to exceed 60 miles per hour (96 km/h). The ride attendant has just instructed you to cross your legs and to cross your arms over your chest and is about to hit the button sending you flying. In this scenario, you would likely interpret the physiological symptoms as delight, excitement, and joy. Now, imagine again that your palms are sweaty, your breathing is fast, and your heart is racing. You are getting ready to give a presentation to an audience of 150 people, who will be asking you questions at the end of your talk. Your performance in this talk will determine if you

What Do Facial Expressions Tell Us?

The facial expressions that are tied to emotions were long thought to be ubiquitous across cultures. This was named the *universality hypothesis of facial expressions*. Based on research conducted in the 1960s and 1970s, it was thought that six basic emotions (happiness, surprise, disgust, fear, sadness, and anger) were linked to unique facial expressions that could be recognized by all cultures. More recently, researchers have suggested that these earlier conclusions are an artifact of methodological choices made in conducting the research to support the universality hypothesis. In particular, the initial research was limited to studies of Pacific Islander communities and used tasks that were constrained such that participants had to select an emotion from a limited number of choices. To address these methodological limitations, researchers in the 21st century began to use emotion identification tasks that allowed for more freedom of choice and tested the hypothesis in indigenous groups who lived in relatively isolated communities around the world. When tested in this way, scientists have found support for the minimal universality hypothesis, which predicts that across cultures, the ability to recognize the valence of an emotion is consistent, but that the specific emotion perceptions are not consistent across cultures (Gendron, Crivelli, & Barrett, 2018). Essentially, these findings tell us that facial expressions that are linked to emotions might be partially socially influenced.

are hired for a job in which you are very interested. In this case, you might experience emotions such as tension and nervousness. The physical response in both situations is the same, but the mood that is being experienced (and that will be experienced following the event) might be very different depending on your cognitive appraisal of the situation.

In considering how these theoretical models apply to exercise, Ekkekakis (2009a) pointed out that these early theories are not ideal for under-

In response to both of these situations, you might experience a racing heart; rapid, shallow breathing; and sweaty palms; but the emotions you are likely to experience can differ dramatically because of the different cognitive appraisal of the situation.

standing the influence of exercise on emotion, mood, and affect. This is because these theories were developed to explain affective responses to external stimuli that might be real or symbolic and that are culturally framed but are decidedly not themselves somatic events (i.e., events that are inherently of the body). In other words, these theories were not developed to explain affective responses to exercise, which is largely a somatic event. Ekkekakis and his colleagues have provided important criticisms of these past theories as applied to exercise psychology and present an alternative theoretical explanation of emotion in response to exercise.

The Dual Mode Theory

The dual mode theory (Ekkekakis, 2003, 2005) is based on key tenets from evolutionary theory. Evolutionary theory proposes that physical activity is a critical component of the factors that contributed to human evolution, that affective responses were shaped through evolution so that they serve functional roles in behavioral choices necessary for survival, and that physical activity behaviors that serve a clear function related to survival (e.g., moderate-intensity exercise for hunting and gathering; very high-intensity exercise for fleeing) are likely to result in more consistent affective responses across people than are physical activity behaviors that aren't as clearly advantageous (i.e., high-intensity exercise). Let's unpack all of this a bit.

The premise of the dual mode theory is that physical activity played such a critical role in survival when humans lived as hunter-gatherers that responses to the behavior of physical activity would have evolved to be suited to benefit the individual from a survival perspective. With respect to affect, the affective responses to physical activity are expected to be positive when the physical activity behavior would contribute to survival but would be predicted to be negative when the physical activity behavior might jeopardize survival. This makes clear sense for low- and moderate-intensity exercise because a positive affective response would encourage more of this behavior, which was necessary to acquire food as a hunter-gatherer. It is perhaps less intuitive for very high-intensity exercise needed to flee a dangerous animal but does still make sense. This type of activity is necessary in the short term to escape the danger, but because it cannot be maintained for a long period of time, it makes sense that the affective response would be negative to help dissuade the organism from persisting in the behavior any longer than necessary. Thus, the dual mode theory hypothesizes that affective responses to exercise will be positive when the exercise is at a sustainable level in terms of intensity and duration but would be negative when the exercise is not sustainable.

In addition to proposing the dual mode theory, Ekkekakis has made other important contributions to our understanding of the effects of exercise on emotion. Ekkekakis (2009a) argued for the use of a circumplex approach to measure affect, the inclusion of multiple time points of measurement to capture the full temporal pattern of the response, the importance of standardizing exercise intensity

> ### Ventilatory Threshold
>
> **Ventilatory threshold (VT)** is the exercise intensity level at which the energy source for completion of the exercise shifts from being aerobic (reliant on oxygen) to anaerobic (not reliant on oxygen). If you think of this for yourself, this is the point at which you shift over from a running intensity that you could maintain for perhaps an hour to one that you can only maintain for perhaps 15 minutes. Therefore, exercise above VT being deemed high intensity would be expected to produce a negative affective response, and exercise below VT being considered low- or moderate-intensity exercise would be expected to result in positive affective responses. These affective responses would reinforce low- to moderate-intensity exercise but would deter high-intensity exercise, and these affective responses would be expected to benefit the organism overall.

relative to the individual's fitness level, and the importance of analyzing data at the level of the individual rather than relying solely on group averages.

Biological Mechanisms

Although researchers are still helping us understand the nature of brain activation that is critical for the experience of affect, mood, and emotions, we do have some understanding of the regions of the brain that are relevant. Affect and mood are at least partially determined by activation of cerebral structures that make up the limbic system. These include the prefrontal cortex, hippocampus, amygdala, and anterior cingulate cortex. We have a good understanding of the specific brain regions that are activated during emotional processing and for experiences of the five basic emotions of fear, sadness, anger, disgust, and happiness. In fact, Vytal and Hamann (2010) conducted a meta-analytic review of 83 neuroimaging studies exploring patterns of brain activation captured with functional magnetic resonance imaging (fMRI) in response to the five basic emotions. Their results showed a consistent brain pattern of activity in response to the induction of each of these emotions and that this pattern of response allows for the discrimination of these emotions from one another. These findings support the notion of specific activation patterns of brain regions that are matched with the experience of the five basic emotions.

Additionally, evidence from studies using electroencephalography (EEG) support that differences in hemispheric activation are associated with positive and negative emotions. In particular, greater activation in the left hemisphere is observed when positive images are viewed, and greater activation in the right hemisphere is observed when negative images are observed. Interestingly, it also appears that individuals can be either left- or right-hemisphere dominant. In other words, their baseline levels of activation can show a bias toward greater activation of the left hemisphere (positive emotions) or right hemisphere (negative emotions). This baseline bias then affects their behavioral responses to emotional stimuli. Those who are left-hemisphere dominant typically respond with more approach behaviors, meaning that they are more likely to experience positive emotions in response to a relatively neutral or slightly positive event. By contrast, those who are right-hemisphere dominant tend to respond with more avoidant behaviors, such that they are more likely to experience negative emotions in response to neutral events and to have less positive emotions in response to positive events.

Research using fMRI and EEG can be useful to help us to further understand the roles of these emotion-linked brain structures in the experience of emotion. However, relative to the effects of exercise on affect, we are still limited in the extent to which neuroimaging measures can be used during exercise because of the movement artifact created during exercise. Thus, this work has so far been limited to a focus on postexercise experiences rather than on the experience during exercise. As a result of this limitation of neuroimaging measures, the focus in this area of study has been on identifying blood-based biological mechanisms, which can be measured peripherally in human studies.

The most prevalent biological mechanism that has been proposed to explain the benefits of exercise on mood is the endorphin hypothesis. This hypothesis suggests that exercise causes a release of **endorphins** (the body's natural opioids) or an increase in binding of endorphins in the brain and that this results in the observed exercise-induced mood changes. Evidence in support of this hypothesis comes from studies showing increased levels of norepinephrine in the periphery (i.e., in the blood)

---

ventilatory threshold (VT)—The exercise intensity level at which the energy source for completion of the exercise shifts from being aerobic (reliant on oxygen) to anaerobic (not reliant on oxygen) is referred to as VT.

endorphins—Endorphins are the body's natural opioids.

and in the cerebrospinal fluid in response to exercise. However, because endorphins cannot cross the blood-brain barrier, critics of the hypothesis raise the fair point that these peripheral measures of endorphins are not necessarily indicative of what is happening in the brain itself. That being said, some studies show effects on endorphins in the brain that are linked to exercise including a study conducted by Boecker et al. (2008).

Boecker and colleagues (2008) conducted a fascinating within-subjects study in which they used positron emission tomography (PET) scans to directly assess the binding of endorphins in the brain in a group of very accomplished runners. They recruited 10 trained male athletes who indicated that they had previously experienced a runner's high in response to running and who had trained a minimum of 4 hours per week for the previous 2 years. This high level of training was necessary because the protocol required that participants run for 2 hours prior to the PET scan on one day of testing. On the other day of testing, they were asked to abstain from running for 24 hours prior to the PET scan to serve as a control condition. Measures of affect including euphoria were assessed on both of these experimental days and on 2 additional days when participants also ran for 2 hours in their normal environment. Results showed that athletes experienced significant increases in happiness and euphoria in response to the runs. They also showed significant increases in opioid binding in several areas of the brain that are important for emotional processing including the prefrontal cortex, cingulate cortex, hippocampus, and sensorimotor regions. Importantly, as well, significant relationships were observed between the amount of increase in opioid binding and the amount of improvement in mood. Although future studies will be necessary to confirm this finding, this study design and methods provide important support for the endorphins as a potential mechanism of the positive affective effects of exercise.

Another biological mechanism that is receiving increasing attention relative to the feel-good phenomenon and the runner's high is the endocannabinoid system. The endocannabinoid (eCB) system is important for the maintenance of homeostasis in the brain and body and plays a role in energy metabolism, cognition, sleep, and stress responses. Receptors for eCB are found throughout the brain, but type-1 receptors are most dense in the limbic regions, which we know are important for the experience of emotions. These molecules are able to cross the blood-brain barrier, and hence peripheral measures might be indicative of changes that are happening centrally.

In a systematic review of 17 acute exercise studies conducted with humans, Siebers and associates (2022) found consistent increases in eCBs in response to acute moderate-intensity exercise. These authors concluded that increases in eCBs in response to exercise were associated with decreased anxiety, increased euphoria, and decreased perceptions of pain after exercise. Because most of the research was conducted in laboratory settings, they limit their discussion of implications to those scenarios and recommend running at 70% to 85% of age-adjusted maximal heart rate (AMHR) (a vigorous intensity) for 20 or more minutes for experienced runners to experience a runner's high in a laboratory setting. This limitation of their conclusion to laboratory settings is interesting because it suggests that we don't have a strong understanding of how to increase the likelihood of experiencing a runner's high in a natural exercise environment. Future research will be necessary to see if these recommendations for lab-based settings generalize to natural environments.

Measurement of Affect, Mood, and Emotion

Affect, mood, and emotion are most commonly measured using self-report instruments. The instruments typically include words that describe specific emotions. Early research on exercise and mood commonly used measures like the Profile of Mood States (POMS) (McNair et al., 1971), the Positive and Negative Affect Schedule (PANAS) (Watson et al., 1988), and the State-Trait Anxiety Inventory (STAI) (Spielberger et al., 1970). However, in the 1990s, exercise psychologists began to recognize that these measures that had been adopted from the broader field of psychology were not particularly well suited for studies looking at responses to exercise. This is because they included specific emotions that made sense in the absence of exercise but that didn't make sense as a response to exercise because of the specific nature of the terms (e.g., emotion terms such as *jittery* and *afraid*). Although these measures

---

endocannabinoid (eCB) system—The eCB system is important for the maintenance of homeostasis in the brain and body and plays a role in energy metabolism, cognition, sleep, and stress responses.

have been used extensively and continue to be used today, each measure has shortcomings that lessen the effectiveness for assessing exercise outcomes.

The primary limitation of the POMS is that it is heavily focused on negative mood states. Respondents indicate the degree to which each of 65 emotional descriptors reflects their feelings during the past week or after performing an exercise session. Based on these responses, which can range from "not at all" to "extremely," scores are tallied for six moods including tension, depression, anger, fatigue, confusion, and vigor. Clearly, the emphasis with this scale is on potential negative responses given that only one of the six dimensions (vigor) is positive. This is a critical shortcoming because evidence supports that exercise has mood benefits both in terms of reducing negative moods and increasing positive moods, and these more positively valanced changes might not be captured adequately with the POMS. In addition, the POMS actually provides measures for only five different moods (confusion is not a mood), which is not likely to reflect the range of possible moods that might be affected by exercise.

Although the PANAS is more balanced in its assessment of positive and negative affect (with 10 items for each), it is still not ideal for assessing affective responses to exercise. The primary shortcoming with the PANAS is that this is a broad measure of affect and does not adequately assess more specific emotional responses to exercise. In addition, the PANAS only measures affective states that are high-activation states and purposely excludes low-activation states that might actually be relevant to exercise such as calmness, relaxation, tiredness, and fatigue (Ekkekakis & Zenko, 2016). Lastly, the more specific descriptors that are used are not emotional responses we might typically associate with exercise participation (e.g., joy, enthusiasm, irritation, nervousness).

The state form of the STAI has been used in the literature described as measuring exercise and mood, but in fact the STAI was designed to be a measure of anxiety in response to a perceived threat. This is problematic because most exercise studies result in the participant experiencing an increase in physiological arousal but do not typically focus on the manipulation of the sense of threat. An exception to this would be studies focused on constructs such as social physique anxiety in response to, for example, mirrored walls in a group exercise facility. Furthermore, the STAI might not appropriately measure mood at all relative to exercise because of the specific descriptors that are used. For the STAI, participants are asked to indicate the extent to which certain statements describe their feelings right now (for the state measure) or in general (for the trait measure). Although the trait measure can be useful for assessing changes in anxiety in response to chronic exercise programs, the state measure is not as well suited for measuring the anxiolytic (anxiety-reducing) effects of acute exercise. This is because some of the statements that evoke negative emotions are closely linked to feelings that might be triggered by the high levels of arousal associated with an acute session of exercise. That is, it is difficult to discern the difference between a perception of increased arousal (i.e., heart rate, blood pressure, breathing rate) and increases on the descriptors provided on the STAI (e.g., "I feel jittery," "I feel anxious") or improvements in feelings of tranquility (e.g., "I am relaxed"). Hence researchers argue that the STAI is not the best tool for distinguishing between increases in arousal and true changes in mood in response to a single session of exercise (Rejeski et al., 1991).

In response to these concerns, exercise psychologists and other researchers interested in studying the effects of exercise on mood began to develop **exercise-specific measures**, which are measures that have been specifically designed to assess responses to the exercise experience. Some researchers moved to a measurement technique that was based on the circumplex model of affect. The **circumplex model of affect** was first proposed by Russell (1980) as a way to describe the systematic fashion by which emotions are related to one another. Russell proposed that emotions can be identified as falling along a circle that is prescribed by a vertical axis representing activation level (or the intensity level) and a horizontal axis representing the valence (positive or negative affect) of the emotion. The activation or intensity level conveys information as to whether this experience is important or trivial. The valence gives an indication of the value (good or bad) of the emotion. Emotions can then be identified as falling in specific places around this circle as judged based on the valence and arousal level that correspond to the emotion label (figure 7.2). Based on this model, some researchers began to use the Felt Arousal Scale and the Feeling Scale (Hardy & Rejeski, 1989) in

---

exercise-specific measures—Measures that have been specifically designed to assess responses to the exercise experience are called exercise-specific measures.

circumplex model of affect—Russell (1980) proposed the circumplex model of affect, which proposes that emotions fall along a circle prescribed by a vertical axis representing arousal level (or intensity level) and a horizontal axis representing the valence (positive or negative) of the emotion.

combination to ascertain emotional responses relative to the circumplex model. The Felt Arousal Scale is used to assess the intensity level of the heightened arousal experienced in response to exercise ranging from Low Felt Arousal to High Felt Arousal. The Feeling Scale is used to assess the valence of a person's emotional experience ranging from Very Good to Very Bad. The responses to these surveys are then used to plot a person's emotional response based on the circumplex model, with the Feeling Scale providing the coordinate on the *x*-axis and the Felt Arousal Scale providing the coordinate on the *y*-axis (see figure 7.2).

Other researchers chose to develop and establish the psychometric soundness of measures that were specifically designed to reflect emotions anticipated to be experienced in response to exercise. In the development of these scales, researchers started by identifying the specific emotional experiences that were particularly attributed to feelings after exercise. To do this, they started with a long list of words that had been used in previous mood, affect, or emotion questionnaires, and then they asked people with substantial exercise experience or who worked in the field of kinesiology to narrow the list down. Once they'd identified this shorter list of emotions, they asked college students to identify which of these words were relevant to their exercise experiences. Using this data, they identified factors that seemed to represent common emotional experiences to create relatively brief questionnaires capturing affective responses to exercise. These methods were used by Gauvin and Rejeski (1993) and by McAuley and Courneya (1994) to create two exercise-specific measures.

> Think about how you feel following an exercise session. What are the emotion- or mood-related terms that you would use to describe your experience? Are they mostly positive or mostly negative? Does your emotional response change as a function of time from during exercise to immediately following exercise to an hour following exercise?

Gauvin and Rejeski (1993) created a measure called the Exercise-Induced Feeling Inventory. Through a series of five studies, the authors established the validity of this scale. The scale gauges how a person feels at a particular moment in time on 12 emotion descriptors using a 5-point range from "do not feel" to "feel very strongly." These emotion descriptors reflect four categories of responses to exercise: revitalization, tranquility, positive engagement, and physical exhaustion. Note that these categories reflect the expectation that mood responses to exercise would be more positive than negative, because three of the four categories describe positive reactions. At approximately the same time, McAuley and Courneya (1994) described three studies used to create and establish the psychometric properties of the Subjective Exercise Experiences Scale (SEES). This survey also consists of 12 descriptors of emotions that might be experienced after exercise. Participants are asked to indicate "the degree to which you are experiencing each feeling *now*" (p. 176) on a 7-point scale ranging from "not at all" to "very much so." Emotional descriptors come from three categories of emotions: positive well-being, psychological distress, and fatigue. This scale clearly reflects an expectation of more negative mood responses given that two of the three categories of emotions are negative. The development of these exercise-specific measures of mood was important because it promoted the understanding that emotional responses to exercise are unique relative to other behaviors, and these particular instruments have allowed researchers to more clearly describe the positive affective experiences that have been associated with exercise participation.

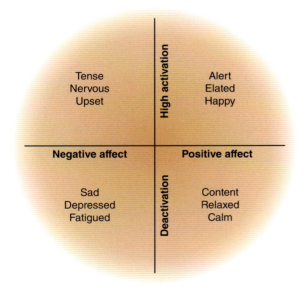

FIGURE 7.2 Visual representation of three theories of the experience of emotion.

Empirical and Meta-Analytic Evidence on the Effects of Exercise on Mood

A substantial body of evidence is focused on the effects of exercise on mood. This evidence is considered separately for the effects of a single session of exercise compared to regular engagement in exercise.

Acute Exercise and Mood

Ekkekakis and colleagues (2008) published a study that is a great example of the type of research that is needed to advance our understanding of the effects of acute exercise on affect. As you might expect, the authors of this paper adhered to the recommendations Ekkekakis made formally in 2009 and also provided a test of the hypotheses of the dual mode theory that previously had been proposed by Ekkekakis (Ekkekakis, 2009a, 2009b). Thirty young (college-aged) adults participated in a within-subjects design such that they experienced all of the treatment conditions. To ensure that exercise intensity was standardized relative to each individual's fitness level, participants first completed a maximal exercise test to identify VT. The conditions were randomly assigned across visits and consisted of 15 minutes of treadmill exercise performed at moderate intensity (20% <VT), high intensity (at VT), and very high intensity (10% >VT). Affect was measured using the Feeling Scale and Felt Arousal Scale so that the affective response could be observed using a circumplex model, and measures were taken during the warm-up, every 3 minutes during exercise, and during the cool-down.

In the moderate-intensity condition, participants maintained a relatively stable affective response but showed an increase in activation. In the high-intensity condition, participants similarly showed an increase in activation, but this time affect became more negative. In the very high-intensity condition, participants showed an even larger increase in activation and an even larger shift toward negative affect. Thus, these results support that during exercise, participants consistently experienced a perceived increase in activation and that the highest level of intensity moves the participant toward the experience of distress and tension as affect becomes more negative. Noticeably and importantly, a shift back to more positive affect is observed from minute 15 to the end of the cool-down for all conditions, with the largest improvement observed for very high intensity ($M = 2.63$) followed by high intensity ($M = 1.20$) and moderate intensity ($M = 0.83$). These increases following exercise are the positive affective responses that might be described as the postexercise feel-good phenomenon but that are presaged by feelings of negative affect during a high-intensity exercise bout that might influence a person's future interest in exercising.

Finally, in addition to their presentation of group means to answer their research questions, Ekkekakis and colleagues also examined the changes in affective valence person by person to identify which intensity levels resulted in the most consistent affective response (table 7.1). The data clearly show that the higher levels of exercise intensity (at VT, >VT) result in a negative affective response during exercise for most people (experienced by 77% to 80% of participants, respectively). This is consistent with the predictions of the dual mode theory because these higher levels of exercise cannot be maintained for an extended period of time so a negative affective response is predicted to be important to dissuade the individual from continuing this activity that is anticipated to have a negative consequence on the body. By contrast, the moderate-intensity exercise (<VT) resulted in much more variability in the affective response experienced by the exercisers. Almost equal numbers had more negative affect as those who had no change in affect, and some had a positive response. This suggests that individual-level

TABLE 7.1 Display of Participant Distribution Across Categories of Affective Change (More Negative, No Change, More Positive) Relative to the Intensity of the Exercise Performed

Intensity of exercise	Affect more negative	No change in affect	Affect more positive
<VT	43% ($M = 1.69$)	50%	7% ($M = 1.50$)
At VT	77% ($M = 2.17$)	10%	13% ($M = 2.75$)
>VT	80% ($M = 3.17$)	10%	10% ($M = 2.00$)

From data presented in Ekkekakis et al. (2008).

cognitive interpretations of the experience might determine whether the person would decide to continue to exercise because the affective response to the moderate-intensity exercise is not so strongly or consistently negative.

Overall, these findings provide support for the predictions of the dual mode theory in suggesting that exercise at high intensity will result in negative affect during exercise. Importantly, however, all intensity levels of exercise resulted in positive affective responses after cessation of the exercise bout.

Reed and Ones (2006) published a meta-analytic review of 158 studies exploring the effects of a single session of exercise on positive activated affect. Positive activated affect was defined as affective responses in the upper right quadrant in the circumplex model. Thus, in this review, the authors focused on outcomes reported explicitly for instruments and subscales that provided an assessment of this particular category of affective responses and were only interested in improvements in positive affect rather than reductions in negative affect. Examples of positive activated affect include vigor from the POMS, positive engagement and revitalization from the EFI, positive affect from the PANAS, and positive well-being from the SEES. When examining the change in positive activated affect from a pretest assessment to a posttest assessment, results showed that the control participants experienced a small decrease (ES = –0.17), while the exercise participants experienced a moderate increase (ES = 0.47) in positive activated affect. One intriguing finding from their analyses of moderators was that participants who were in the lower third of the distribution with respect to their pretest affect experienced significantly larger improvements (ES = 0.63) in response to exercise than did those who were moderate (ES = 0.34) or high (ES = 0.39) in terms of their baseline levels of positive activated affect. This suggests the potential role of exercise as a means of self-regulating mood to achieve more positive mood states when one is experiencing a negative mood. With respect to the dose of exercise that is ideal to achieve these positive effects, results from this review are somewhat tenuous because of the relatively small sample sizes for these comparisons. However, they do suggest that lower-intensity exercise and exercise that is shorter in duration than 35 minutes result in the most consistently positive benefits. This is consistent with predictions of the dual mode theory and suggests the value of prescribing low-intensity exercise of durations that meet physical activity recommendations (i.e., up to 60 min daily) to achieve maximal affective benefits. Consistent with the predictions of the dual mode theory, exercise at a higher volume (i.e., either higher intensity or duration longer than 75 min) resulted in negative affect (ES = -0.98) in response to these higher loads.

Chronic Exercise and Mood

Mechanisms for the effects of chronic exercise on mood are unknown. Reed and Buck (2009) offer a maintenance explanation, which proposes that each acute bout of exercise causes an improvement in positive activated affect and that chronic exercise merely reinforces this improvement on a regular basis.

A study by Belitardo de Oliveira and associates (2019) provides an interesting example of the potential link between chronic exercise and mood, with a focus on eCBs as a mechanism of the effects. Sedentary adults (n = 34; 18-65 yr) were tested at baseline and then randomly assigned to an exercise intervention or a wait-list control condition for 12 weeks. The exercise intervention consisted of 40 minutes of exercise on a treadmill performed at the perceived effort level previously identified as VT. In response to the exercise intervention, the exercisers showed a decrease in plasma eCB concentration not observed in the control participants. The exercisers also showed significant decreases in anxiety, anger, and body weight and significant increases in fitness that were not evident in the control group. Importantly, the results of regression analyses showed that the observed changes in anger, in total mood disturbance (a total score calculated from the POMS), and in body weight were significantly predicted by the amount of decrease in eCB (R^2 = 13.1%, 27%, 12.2%, respectively). These results might seem counterintuitive because the results for acute exercise suggest that exercise increases eCB. However, the authors explain that regular physical activity leads to increased eCB metabolism in response to exercise, which is the cause of the reductions in circulating levels of eCB. This might explain why the amount of reduction in eCB from pretest to posttest was predictive of the amount of improvement in mood (i.e., greater reduction in eCB = greater metabolism of eCB = greater benefits for mood).

Reed and Buck (2009) conducted a meta-analytic review of studies exploring the effects of chronic exercise on positive activated affect. Results from 105 studies showed a significant moderate benefit of exercise relative to control conditions after intervention (ES = 0.51), and results from 115 studies showed a significant moderate improvement in affect from before to after intervention (ES = 0.49) for the exercisers. Thus, both between-subjects and within-subjects designs support a moderate benefit of long-term exercise on affect. Consistent with the findings of Reed and Ones (2006) in the meta-analysis on acute exercise, a dose–response relationship was observed between baseline affect and the benefits obtained such that the largest benefits were observed for those with the least positive baseline affect (ES = 0.81) followed by those with moderate levels of baseline affect (ES = 0.45) followed by those with the most positive affect at baseline (ES = 0.26). This is exciting because it suggests that while everyone can achieve improvements in affect in response to exercise, those who are starting with relatively low levels of positive activated affect can experience the greatest benefits.

Arent and colleagues (2000) conducted a review of the studies exploring the potential of exercise for older (study inclusion criteria requires participants to be >60 yr or the mean age of the sample was >65 yr) adults. The average effect size for posttest comparisons between studies in which the experimental (exercise) and control groups were equivalent in terms of mood at the pretest was 0.34, suggesting that the exercise groups had more positive mood at the posttest than did the control groups. This finding was consistent with what was reported when examining only the magnitude of the improvement in positive affect for the exercise group (ES = 0.38). Thus, consistent with Reed and Buck's (2009) meta-analysis, whether comparisons are made between exercise and control groups at the posttest or between the pretest and posttest for the exercise group, summary statistics across studies support a small positive benefit of exercise. Importantly, in the analysis of pretest to posttest gains for the exercise group, the authors confirmed that the benefits were essentially equivalent, whether looking at measures of positive affect that showed increases (ES = 0.35) or negative affect that showed decreases (ES = 0.39). Thus, chronic exercise by older adults increases reports of positive affect and decreases reports of negative affect.

Puetz and associates (2006) conducted a meta-analysis focused specifically on feelings of energy and fatigue. They justified the importance of the review based on the facts that approximately 20% of adults report persistent fatigue, that fatigue is a common reason for physician visits, and that numerous medical conditions are associated with feelings of fatigue (e.g., those with fibromyalgia, those undergoing cardiac rehabilitation, cancer patients and survivors). They included studies that used experimental designs and used a measure of energy or fatigue as an outcome (e.g., as assessed in the subscales of the POMS). Of the 70 studies included in their review, 77% were from patient groups and 23% were from groups without a medical condition. Samples had an average age of 50 years and the exercise programs were on average 13 weeks in duration with 3 sessions per week lasting 45 minutes and performed at moderate intensity (54% of maximal aerobic capacity). The average effect size indicated a small to moderate effect (ES = 0.37), supporting increases in energy and decreases in fatigue in response to the chronic exercise programs. Importantly, the magnitude of the effect was consistent across the various patient groups and the nonpatient groups. This average effect was interpreted as being clinically significant and was observed to be larger than that reported in studies of cognitive behavioral therapy in Gulf War veterans (ES = 0.19) and of a pharmacological intervention in patients with multiple sclerosis (ES = 0.23). Thus, results from this review indicate that exercise is a powerful behavioral intervention in terms of reducing fatigue and increasing energy and that these benefits exceed those observed in response to some other forms of treatment.

Summary

Given that we all experience positive and negative affect, moods, and emotions, the findings regarding the effects of exercise on these is of clear relevance to all of us. Furthermore, it is likely that a person's affective response to single sessions of exercise is an important determinant of their willingness to adhere to chronic exercise programs. Across numerous studies, clear evidence can be found that a single session of exercise has a moderate beneficial impact on affect and that chronic exercise has a small to moderate benefit. Importantly, larger benefits in terms of this feel-good response to exercise are expected for those who start off in a less positive place. So, if you are in a bad mood or having a bad day, a bout of exercise is likely to help you cheer up. Importantly, exercise both increases positive affect and decreases negative affect, so exercise increases your likelihood of using positive emotional labels such as *happy*, *energized*, and *calm* to describe how you feel while also decreasing your use of negative emotional labels such as *sad*, *fatigued*, and *anxious*. The dual mode theory and empirical evidence suggest that low and moderate intensities of exercise are most likely to result in positive responses during exercise but that all intensities of exercise result in benefits after exercise. As a slight modification to this advice, evidence for the runner's high suggests that exercising at 70% to 85% AMHR for 20 or more minutes is most likely to provide a runner's high for experienced exercisers. Although the mechanisms underlying this benefit are not known, some evidence supports the role of endorphins and endogenous endocannabinoids. Understanding the mechanism of action for the mood-enhancing benefits might help us to further refine our recommendations regarding the intensity and duration of exercise most likely to provide these benefits.

Discussion Questions

1. Briefly explain the three early models of emotion (James-Lange, Cannon-Bard, and Schacter and Singer) and why they might not be well suited to explain the effects of exercise on emotion.

2. Provide meta-analytic evidence supporting this statement: "Exercise results in a positive affective response following acute and chronic exercise."

3. Talk about the various self-report measures of affect, mood, and emotions, and explain why researchers developed exercise-specific measures of mood.

4. Explain what ventilatory threshold (VT) is, and describe the study by Ekkekakis and associates that used VT to explore benefits to affect. What did they do, and what did they find?

Exercise and Pain

OBJECTIVES

After studying this chapter, you should be able to do the following:

- Understand that pain experiences differ and recognize the prevalence and implications of experiencing chronic pain
- Explain how pain is perceived and how this knowledge leads to potential treatment options
- Describe methods of measuring pain and the difference between pain threshold and pain tolerance
- Discuss the evidence for exercise reducing the experience of pain by healthy participants and by those experiencing various forms of chronic pain

KEY TERMS

pain	C fibers	local anesthetics
acute pain	cupping	regional anesthetics
chronic, recurrent pain	transcutaneous electrical nerve stimulation (TENS)	centrally acting analgesics
chronic, intractable, benign pain	biofeedback	sensation threshold
chronic, progressive pain	relaxation	pain threshold
nociceptors	acupuncture	pain tolerance
A-delta fibers	peripherally acting analgesics	lactate threshold
		isometric exercise

Have you ever been injured during a sport competition and not realized the extent of your injury until the event concluded? Perhaps the most famous example of this occurred in the 1996 Olympics. In that competition, the United States gymnasts were the last to perform for the all-around gymnastics team contest. They were vying with Russia for the gold medal, with Russia performing floor exercises and the United States performing the vault simultaneously, and the outcome dependent on these last events. At this point, the United States had never won a team gold in the women's Olympics competition, while the Russians historically had dominated the event. The initial competitors for the United States did not perform well. Dominique Moceanu performed second to last for the United States and fell on both of her vaults. The final vaulter for the United States was Kerri Strug, and she needed a 9.430 on one of her two vaults to pull the United States into first place. On her first vault, she made an awkward landing and heard a pop. Although at the time, no one was certain of the extent of her injury, Kerri learned later that she had torn two ligaments in her ankle. Reflective of the poor landing, the vault was only scored as a 9.162, which meant the United States was currently not likely to win gold. Kerri had one more vault to go, but how could she possibly perform with a seriously injured ankle? As a testament to her force of will and determination, she went back to the line to perform her second vault. The vault required that she sprint to the springboard from a distance of approximately 155 feet (47 m), vault using a two-foot takeoff, perform her aerial gymnastics, and land on both feet from a height of approximately 15 feet (4.6 m). It is remarkable that she could perform despite the excruciating pain she must have felt with every step and the anticipation of even worse pain on hitting the springboard and then making the landing. Remarkably, Kerri stuck the landing on both feet only to immediately take all of the weight off of her injured ankle and fall to the mat in pain. She was given a score of 9.712, which mathematically clinched the gold medal for the United States.

Although Kerri's decision to perform despite the injury is one that many might question because of the risk of permanent damage, it is clear that in that moment, the excitement, pressure, and sense of opportunity and maybe even destiny made important contributions to this athlete's ability to perform. This happens in much less prestigious athletic events and even with recreational or weekend warriors. Regular exercisers often push through or ignore sensations of pain to complete a practice or a performance. In fact, many athletes purposefully push themselves through the experience of pain on a regular basis to stimulate gains in fitness, strength, endurance, and so on. Of interest relative to this chapter is the role that chronic exercise might play in terms of pain tolerance in a person's daily life. In this chapter, we will consider definitions of pain and explore the prevalence and costs of chronic pain, learn about the mechanisms and theories of pain experiences, and review the empirical and meta-analytic evidence relative to the potential of both acute and chronic exercise to mitigate pain experiences.

Defining Pain

Although it's likely none of you have experienced the extreme pain that Kerri Strug endured, pain is a ubiquitous experience in that we have all felt at least short-term bouts of pain in response to acute tissue injury. For example, all of you have undoubtedly skinned a knee, had a splinter, or experienced a paper cut, but some of you might have experienced more intense experiences of pain such as from cutting your finger with a sharp knife, breaking a bone, or tearing a ligament or tendon. Others of you might suffer from more chronic forms of pain such as lower back pain, arthritis, or migraines. These examples emphasize how varied the experience of pain is in terms of the cause, duration, and intensity. The variety of experiences of pain is also evident from the range of terms that can be used to describe pain. Most likely, you've been asked in the past by your parent, a friend, a coach, or a doctor to describe the pain you are feeling. When asked this question, the responses can include descriptors such as *sharp, throbbing, dull, intense, knife-like*, and *shooting*. One of the big challenges in research focused on pain is to provide a definition of pain that encompasses and adequately describes such a subjective experience.

> **Caveat to Statement That the Experience of Pain Is Ubiquitous**
>
> There is a very rare condition know as congenital insensitivity to pain and anhidrosis (CIPA), which results in individuals not being able to feel pain. In these individuals, the nerves that sense pain are not able to communicate properly with the brain. This disorder occurs in approximately 1 out of 125 million individuals worldwide. For more information, enter these search terms into a search engine: BBC future the curse of people who never feel pain.

Pain was defined in 1979 by the International Association for the Study of Pain (IASP) as "an unpleasant sensory and emotional experience associated with actual or potential tissue damage, or described in terms of such damage" (Merskey et al., 1979, p. 250). One of the criticisms of this definition was the use of the word *unpleasant*, which might seem to unintentionally trivialize the experience. This definition has since been reviewed and refined by the IASP so that the current definition of **pain** is the following: "An aversive sensory and emotional experience typically caused by, or resembling that caused by, actual or potential tissue injury" (Raja et al., 2020, p. 1979). The strengths of this definition are that it recognizes that pain is aversive, that it consists of both the sensory response and the emotional effects, and that it acknowledges both the experience of pain that can be clearly attributed to a noxious stimulus and the experience of pain that mimics what would be felt in response to an actual stimulus. This latter aspect of the definition is critically important as we recognize that even in the absence of a clearly identified stimulus, the experience of pain can be real and debilitating.

As mentioned earlier, several types of pain exist, and they can be categorized based on how long-lasting the pain is and the cause of the pain. The four

> **Important Information About Pain**
>
> In addition to the definition of pain, the IASP also provides accompanying notes to further explain how pain should be conceptualized. These include that pain is always subjective, that the concept of pain is learned through experiences, that reports of pain should be accepted and respected, that verbal communication is not necessary to indicate a pain experience, and that pain might not always be adaptive. These notes are important because they further clarify key aspects of the pain experience, assisting clinicians in better understanding pain as a lived experience.

categories of pain are acute; chronic and recurrent; chronic, intractable, and benign pain; and chronic and progressive pain. Although it probably doesn't seem acute to the person experiencing it, by definition pain is considered to be **acute** if it lasts less than 3 months. This would include both a one-day headache and a sprained ankle that takes weeks to heal. Pain is described as **chronic and recurrent** if it is the result of benign causes and is characterized by regular, intense periods of pain interspersed with pain-free periods of time. A good example of chronic, recurrent pain is that which is caused by migraine headaches. **Chronic, intractable, and benign pain** is a constant pain that varies in intensity and that has benign yet relatively permanent causes such as low back pain due to a herniated disc. Lastly, **chronic and progressive pain** is a constant pain that is progressive in nature because it is due to an underlying malignant condition such as cancer or rheumatoid arthritis. When we begin to consider the effects of exercise on pain, it will be important to remember that the impacts of exercise can differ depending on the category of pain being considered.

Prevalence and Costs

Although acute pain is a critical defense mechanism that protects individuals from further damage, chronic pain does not serve the same purpose. Acute pain is typically indicative of soft tissue damage

---

pain—Pain has been defined as "An aversive sensory and emotional experience typically caused by, or resembling that caused by, actual or potential tissue injury" (Raja et al., 2020, p. 1979).

acute pain—Pain that lasts less than 3 months is considered to be acute.

chronic, recurrent pain—Pain that is due to benign causes and is experienced as regular and intense experiences of pain interspersed with pain-free periods of time is referred to as chronic, recurrent pain.

chronic, intractable, benign pain—Pain that is due to benign but relatively permanent causes and is constant is called chronic, intractable, benign pain.

chronic, progressive pain—Pain that is due to progressive causes that are not benign and is constant is called chronic, progressive pain.

that will heal over a period of time. The purpose of acute pain is to alert the organism to the risk of damage so that they can remove themselves from the cause of the pain or can work to return the body to homeostasis. For example, if you feel the sensation of pain when you pick up a pot on the stove, you will immediately recognize that the handle is hot and put it down or even drop it as quickly as possible to prevent or minimize tissue damage. By contrast, chronic pain tends to be due to an underlying condition that might change over time. Although the prevalence of chronic pain varies across countries (range = 5.5-60.4%), it is estimated that worldwide approximately 30% of adults suffer from chronic pain (Elzahaf et al., 2012). In the United States, data from 2016 show that approximately 20% of adults were experiencing chronic pain and 8% of adults had chronic pain that was considered to have a high impact on their lives. High-impact chronic pain is that which limits life or work activities on most or every day for a period of 6 months or longer. This data showed greater prevalence of both chronic pain and high-impact chronic pain with advancing age, for women, for those living in or near poverty, and for those living in rural communities. No significant differences were observed as a function of race or ethnicity (Dahlhamer et al., 2018). Evidence also supports that children experience both acute and chronic pain; survey data collected from 9- to 13-year-olds showed that 96% had experienced acute pain in the previous month (with headaches and muscle pain most common), that 57% of children had experienced one or more recurrent pains (e.g., headaches, stomachaches, growing pains), and 6% were dealing with chronic pain (e.g., long-lasting illness, broken bones, back pains) (van Dijk et al., 2006). This data clearly supports the notion that the experience of pain is ubiquitous.

When considering chronic pain, lower back pain and migraines are the most commonly reported. Low back pain is experienced by approximately 13% of the US population, with approximately 30% of adults reporting back pain in the previous 3 months (Lo et al., 2021). The total for back pain–related costs is $56.5 billion annually for medical expenditures and increases to $315.0 billion annually when all health care costs are considered (Lo et al., 2021). Migraines also are prevalent, with reports that 15.9% of Americans have experienced migraines in the previous 3 months. Prevalence is higher for women (20.7%) than men (9.7%) and is higher in younger age groups (17.9% in 18- to 44-year-olds, 15.9% in 45- to 64-year-olds) as compared to older age groups (7.3% in 65- to 74-year-olds, 5.1% in those over 75 years) (Burch et al., 2018).

Chronic pain is a major burden on society because of the associated medical costs, absenteeism from work, and higher morbidity rate. It is one of the most common reasons that people will seek out health care and can result in limits in the ability to perform daily activities, increased anxiety and depression, decreased quality of life, and dependence on pain killers such as opioids, which have known risks of addiction. Data from the Global Burdens of Diseases, Injuries, and Risk Factors Study (2016) indicate that low back pain and migraines were the leading causes of years lived with disability (YLD) in 1990, 2006, and 2016, demonstrating the impact that these have worldwide. The economic costs of all medical expenditures and losses in productivity due to forms of pain in the United States have been estimated to range from $560 to $650 billion (Gaskin & Richard, 2012).

Given the personal, societal, and economic impact of chronic pain, Healthy People 2030 includes three goals related to chronic pain. These goals include reducing the percent of adults living with high-impact chronic pain, increasing the ability of those living with high-impact chronic pain to self-manage their pain, and reducing the impact of high-impact chronic pain on loved ones. The inclusion of these goals in Healthy People 2030 is indicative of the high priority of these objectives and supports our need to learn more about behavioral interventions (e.g., exercise) that might help reduce pain experiences.

Theories and Mechanisms of the Experience of Pain

The experience of pain is a hard-wired phenomenon that is expected to help us avoid situations that might cause tissue damage. As previously described, if you accidentally touch something hot like a handle on a pot, the pain you experience is a critical signal telling you to move away from the heat source to minimize tissue damage. In this example, the heat provides a noxious stimulus that signals the brain to respond. Noxious stimuli can be thermal (hot or cold), chemical (internal or external), or mechanical (force or pressure).

> *I triple-dog dare you.* Thinking of the noxious stimulus of cold reminds me of the scene in *A Christmas Story* where Flick, Ralphie's friend, was triple-dog dared to touch his tongue to the school flagpole when the temperature outside was well below freezing. Although this scene was shot using movie magic so that the actor playing Flick wasn't actually hurt, we can all probably imagine the sensation of your tongue being frozen to something metal. The painful experience portrayed by Flick was very believable and relatable.

When we consider the physiology of pain, a series of events happens in response to a noxious stimulus (figure 8.1). When tissue is damaged, algogenic substances are released in the tissue at the point of the stimulus. These substances promote immune system activity, cause inflammation, and activate the nerve endings of the nociceptors to signal pain. **Nociceptors** are specialized free nerve endings or neurons that are present in nearly all of our tissues and serve the explicit and unique function of transmitting a pain signal. When nociceptors are exposed to a noxious stimulus, they generate electrical signals that transmit information to the spinal cord via the afferent nerves (peripheral nerves that deliver a signal to the central nervous system) to be delivered to the brain for interpretation. The speed at which the information is transmitted along the afferent nerves is dependent on the specific fiber type that is transmitting the information. The myelinated **A-delta fibers** are used for the rapid transmission of a pain message for sharp, localized, and distinct pains. These fibers pass through the thalamus on the way to the motor and sensory areas of the cortex. This allows for a quick response. By contrast, the unmyelinated **C fibers** provide a slow transmission of pain messages in response to noxious stimuli that are more diffuse and that would be described as dull or aching. Once transmitted to the dorsal horn of the spinal cord, substance P (a neuropeptide) and glutamate (a neurotransmitter) are released in the dorsal horn, which facilitates the transmission of the pain signal up the ascending tracts of the spinal cord to areas of the brain including the brainstem, thalamus, cerebral cortex, and limbic system. It is in these regions that the pain signal is interpreted, resulting in behavioral, emotional, and cognitive responses.

The gate-control theory of pain (Melzack & Wall, 1965) proposes that the spinal cord has a gating mechanism that can be opened or closed to influence the amount of signal transmitted to the brain. The gate is thought to be housed in the spinal cord dorsal horn and to exert its effects on the small-diameter A-delta and C fibers that deliver the signal of pain up the spinal cord to the brain. The aperture

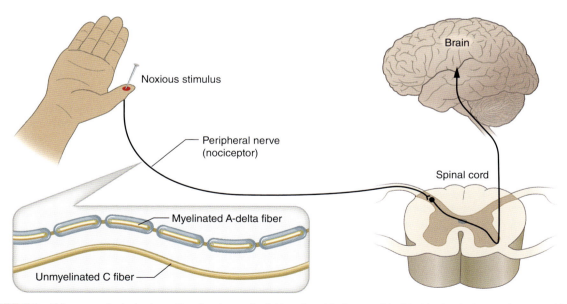

FIGURE 8.1 When a pain-inducing stimulus is applied, the signal is transmitted to the brain by nociceptors (A-delta fibers and C-fibers) through the spinal cord to the brain.

nociceptors—Specialized free nerve endings or neurons that are present in nearly all of our tissues and serve the explicit and unique function of transmitting a pain signal are called nocicepters.

A-delta fibers—A-delta fibers are myelinated fibers used for the rapid transmission of a pain message for sharp, well-localized, and distinct pains.

C fibers—C fibers are unmyelinated fibers that provide a slow transmission of pain messages in response to noxious stimuli that are diffuse and described as dull or aching.

of the gate is thought to be controlled by inhibitory neurons in the spinal cord that might attenuate the pain signals being delivered by narrowing the gate. According to this theory, when more activity or a stronger signal is transmitted via the pain fibers, this causes the gate to open. This makes sense because a more intense noxious stimulus (e.g., a hotter iron, a harder blow, a louder noise) needs to be responded to as quickly as possible. The gate is also thought to be controlled by a person's emotions, with positive emotions (e.g., joy or happiness) closing the gate and negative emotions (e.g., anxiety or sadness) opening the gate. This theoretical hypothesis is supported by the anecdote about Kerri Strug, which illustrates how a person who is focused completely on their competitive performance might not feel the pain of an injured ankle as strongly because the intense focus is serving to narrow the gate.

Mechanisms and Theories Explaining How Exercise Reduces Pain

Exercise might reduce the experience of pain through physiological mechanisms including increases in beta-endorphins, serotonin, and endocannabinoids (eCB); increases in activation of eCB receptors; and reductions in inflammation (Lima et al., 2017). Beta-endorphins and serotonin are increased in response to both acute and chronic exercise. Beta-endorphins are endogenous opioids that are known to decrease substance P in the periphery. As previously explained, substance P is a neuropeptide involved in the pain response (e.g., a decrease in substance P would result in a dampening of the pain experience). Evidence also suggests that increases in serotonin and beta-endorphins in response to exercise interact to promote the reduction of pain. Another pathway by which exercise can reduce pain is through its impact on eCB receptors. These receptors are present in areas of the brain and spinal cord responsible for pain modulation, and these receptors are activated by exercise. When these receptors are activated, an analgesic (pain-reducing) effect is experienced. Circulating levels of eCBs are also increased in response to both aerobic exercise and resistance training, and these work synergistically with opioids to reduce the sensation of pain. With respect to inflammation and specific to migraine headaches, numerous inflammatory markers are implicated in the experience of migraines, and exercise has been shown to lead to a reduction in these inflammatory markers (Song & Chu, 2021). All of these mechanisms can play a role in the pain-reducing effects of exercise.

> Think about the times when you have experienced pain. It is likely that you have experienced many different kinds of pain: acute pain such as from a paper cut or your leg falling asleep, or longer-term pain such as a headache, broken bone, or pain experienced following a surgery. Think about exercise relative to these experiences. In which cases do you think exercise is likely to be the most beneficial? This might be prior to the insult or following the insult. In other words, exercise might reduce your frequency of headaches in advance of the experience or if you can exercise while you have a headache, it might go away faster. Consider your choices with respect to exercise and whether you use exercise as a way to reduce pain perceptions.

Treatment

Treatments for pain have been developed based on theory and an understanding of the mechanisms of pain. When considering treatments, we have to recognize that their efficacy is likely to differ depending on the nature of the pain. Many techniques that are used to manage pain are primarily effective with acute pain, and some should only be used for a limited period of time. For example, pharmacological interventions should only be used for relatively short periods of time because they can have potential damaging effects (e.g., liver failure, ulcers, anemia) or because they can become addictive (e.g., opioids). That said, pharmacological treatments play an important role in pain management for both acute and chronic pain.

Transcutaneous electrical nerve stimulation (TENS) is the process of putting electrodes on the skin near where a person is experiencing pain and then giving a mild electric current. TENS use is predicated on the gate theory of pain, but it is also expected to have an impact on beta-endorphins.

---

transcutaneous electrical nerve stimulation (TENS)—TENS is the process of putting electrodes on the skin near where a person is experiencing pain and then giving a mild electric current with the purpose of reducing pain.

Cupping

Cupping is the practice of heating a glass and then putting it on your skin to reduce the sensation of pain from other sources. As the glass cools, a vacuum is created that pulls the skin up into the cup and bruises it. Olympic athletes have taken to using this technique as evidenced from images of swimmers at the 2016 Olympics including Michael Phelps. The mechanisms underlying its effectiveness aren't clear. It might be effective because it closes the pain gate as in the gate control theory. Alternatively, it might increase blood flow to promote healing and it might break down chemical toxins that delay healing.

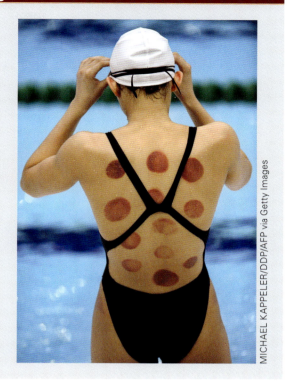

This treatment has been popular since the 1970s, but empirical evidence in support of this method is mixed and might depend on the particular context of use. For instance, Brosseau and colleagues (2002) reviewed a small number of studies ($n = 3$) looking at the effectiveness of TENS in lower back pain. Although none of the results were statistically significant (likely due to the small number of participants in each study), the TENS group reported reductions in pain intensity, improved functional status, and greater patient satisfaction as compared to a sham treatment group. More recently, results from a systematic review support positive effects compared to placebo treatments for patients experiencing acute pain when TENS was administered by ambulance staff (Simpson et al., 2014). Overall, TENS continues to be used to reduce pain, but empirical evidence supporting its efficacy is limited.

Other physical methods of pain management include the use of biofeedback, general relaxation, and acupuncture. **Biofeedback** is particularly effective with muscle tension headaches. When using biofeedback, a person is trained to reduce muscle tension through monitoring and responding to feedback provided by electrodes placed on the muscles suspected of being the root cause of the headaches. By gaining an awareness of the existing muscle tension and learning techniques to reduce muscle tension, patients ultimately can gain some control over their headaches. General **relaxation** also might be effective and is a less expensive therapy because it can be learned without equipment. **Acupuncture** is another treatment that has been used effectively to control pain. Acupuncture, or the use of small needles to stimulate specific places in the body, has been used in traditional Chinese medicine for over 3,000 years. In 1976, acupuncture needles were approved by the United States Food and Drug Administration as medical devices for general use. Recent evidence supports its effectiveness in reducing pain from chronic musculoskeletal pain (e.g., low back, neck, shoulder, knee), headache, and arthritis as compared to sham acupuncture (ES = 0.20) and no acupuncture (ES = 0.50) controls (Vickers et al.,

---

cupping—The practice of heating a glass and then putting it on one's skin with the purpose of reducing the sensation of pain from other sources is called cupping.

biofeedback—The process of reducing muscle tension through monitoring and responding to feedback provided by electrodes placed on the body is known as biofeedback.

relaxation—Relaxation is a technique used to reduce muscle tension and manage pain without equipment.

acupuncture—Acupuncture involves the use of small needles to stimulate specific places in the body to control pain and have been used in traditional Chinese medicine for over 3,000 years.

2018). According to traditional Chinese medicine, acupuncture is effective when used at one of the 365 meridians in the body to release qi and thus restore balance between yin and yang, which are the two interrelated forces that are foundational to Eastern medicine. Researchers from Western countries have attempted to identify physiological mechanisms to explain the benefits of acupuncture. In brief, Western researchers believe that acupuncture works because the needles stimulate both local and central pain-control mechanisms (Coutaux, 2017).

Many pharmacological interventions are effective for reducing the experience of pain. **Peripherally acting analgesics** (pain relievers) work by inhibiting the production of the neurochemicals that are needed for the nociceptors to sense the release of algogenic substances. Hence, these painkillers stop the signal right at its source. Examples of this type of pain reliever include acetaminophen and nonsteroidal anti-inflammatories (NSAIDs). These pain relievers are systemic in that they are typically taken orally and can reduce pain anywhere in the body. Because of the mechanism of action, NSAIDS also reduce inflammation. **Local anesthetics** are used to block the afferent nerve cells from generating impulses to deliver to the spinal cord. As you might guess, local anesthetics result in pain relief in a localized area. Examples of these include morphine, Novocain, and lidocaine, which are used for relatively minor surgical procedures such as having a cavity filled. **Regional anesthetics** can be used to block pain sensations in a larger region of the body. For example, an epidural is when pain medicine is injected into the fluid around the spine; some women request an epidural when giving birth. This regional pain medicine provides relief, but the person remains conscious. **Centrally acting analgesics** affect the entire body. Examples include codeine and morphine, which would be used for major surgeries where the pain is likely to be more severe and pervasive, as with spinal surgery.

Another method of pain management is to perform surgery to intervene when there is a physical cause for the pain. This is used in many situations such as to stop a toothache (e.g., removing decay and filling a cavity), to alleviate back pain (e.g., discectomy for a herniated disk), or to treat arthritis (e.g., a synovectomy to remove membranes that line a joint to reduce inflammation). These surgical methods can provide relief that can be temporary or permanent, and people tend to recover fairly quickly and manage postoperative pain using the pharmacological interventions previously discussed.

Additionally, numerous cognitive methods can be used to help control the experience of pain. These are most effective for acute forms of pain that are mild to moderate in terms of their severity. When using these methods, a person focuses on something in the environment that is nonpainful and that can serve as a distraction. An example is listening to music while at the dentist or focusing on a picture of the baby's ultrasound during labor. Another example is using mental imagery to visualize a relaxing and peaceful scene that serves as a means of distraction from the source of the discomfort. Coping statements also can be effective, such as saying to oneself, "I can endure" or "It's not that bad."

Measurement

Given how challenging it has been to define the term *pain*, you can imagine that the assessment of this purely subjective experience is equally challenging. The most typical way to assess pain has been through self-report. The McGill Pain Questionnaire is a fairly complex measure that asks participants to describe the pain they are experiencing using groups of adjectives such as *tingling*, *itchy*, *smarting*, or *stinging*; to identify the location on the body; to rate the pain intensity as none to excruciating; to identify accompanying symptoms such as nausea or dizziness; to identify the effect on sleep and activity levels; and to indicate if the pain is constant, periodic, or brief. This is in contrast to the much simpler pain scale you might have seen at the doctor's office, which is called a visual analog scale. This scale might consist only of words and the numerical response options but might sometimes also include faces depicting emotions (see figure 8.2). Typically, however, this type of scale only requires a single response representing an overall experience of pain.

In addition to self-report measures, researchers also have validated behavioral measures of pain that are sometimes referred to as *experimental pain paradigms*. When using these paradigms, a pain exposure is administered to the participant and then

---

peripherally acting analgesics—Pain relievers that inhibit the production of the neurochemicals needed for the nociceptors to sense the release of algogenic substances are called peripherally acting analgesics.

local anesthetics—Local anesthetics are used to block the afferent nerve cells from generating impulses to deliver to the spinal cord, and they result in pain relief in a localized area.

regional anesthetics—Regional anesthetics are used to block pain sensations in a large region of the body.

centrally acting analgesics—Pain relievers that affect the entire body are known as centrally acting analgesics.

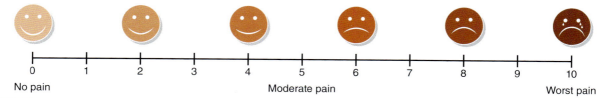

FIGURE 8.2 Visual analog pain scale.
Source: https://assessment-module.yale.edu/im-palliative/visual-analogue-scale

the person's responses are recorded. Regardless of the stimulus, the responses that are recorded can include the **sensation threshold** (the first notice of the sensation), the **pain threshold** (when the sensation is first described as painful), **pain tolerance** (when they first ask for the experience to stop), and pain tolerance with encouragement. Pain exposure has been induced using various noxious stimuli including electrical, pressure, and thermal. In all cases, the induction of pain is temporary and does not result in any permanent tissue damage. In the exercise psychology literature, a commonly used electrical stimulus is called the *noxious dental pulp stimulation technique*, which is when the researcher attaches a cathode to an upper tooth so that a small electrical pulse can be administered. With regards to a pressure stimulus, researchers have applied pressure to a specific focal point (e.g., a finger) to measure pain threshold and tolerance (figure 8.3). An example of a thermal stimulus is the cold pressor task, which requires that participants immerse their hand in a bucket of ice-cold water.

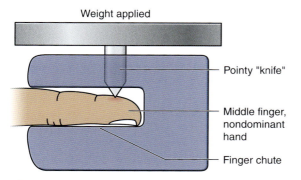

FIGURE 8.3 Example of equipment used to apply pressure to the finger to measure pain.

Empirical and Meta-Analytic Evidence for Exercise and Pain

When considering the role of exercise in the experience of pain, we must consider how exercise might be used to reduce the sensation of both acute and chronic pain following the cessation of exercise. We also need to separate out the evidence relative to whether we are concerned with the potential benefits of exercise in adults who are not experiencing chronic pain (healthy adults, for the purpose of this chapter) or if we are exploring its usefulness as a way to mitigate pain experiences in adults living with chronic pain.

Acute Exercise and Acute Pain: Evidence From Healthy Adults

When considering healthy adults, research designs typically have explored how exercise affects the perception of laboratory-induced acute pain experiences. Thus, the results usually provide data in terms of changes to pain threshold and pain tolerance. Many researchers have been interested in the potential for a single session of exercise to reduce the perception of pain. This phenomenon is referred to as *exercise-induced analgesia*. Schmitt and associates (2020) conducted a study designed to look at the combined effects of exercise intensity and fitness on pain threshold and pain tolerance. Thirty-three sedentary or active (defined as cycling at least 3 days/wk for approximately 60 min for the previous 2 yr) young adult (18-40 yr) men participated in the study. Maximal fitness was assessed and lactate threshold was identified to control the exercise intensity relative to an individual's fitness. **Lactate threshold** is the point at which the intensity of exercise is so high that the production of lactate exceeds

---

sensation threshold—The first notice of a sensation is identified as the sensation threshold.

pain threshold—Pain threshold is the point at which the sensation is first described as painful.

pain tolerance—Pain tolerance is when a pain stimulus reaches the point that a participant asks for the experience to stop.

lactate threshold—Lactate threshold is the point at which the production of lactate exceeds the body's ability to clear the lactate, resulting in an increase of lactate in the blood.

the body's ability to clear the lactate, resulting in an increase of lactate in the blood. The exercise intensity at which lactate threshold is reached is very similar to that at which ventilatory threshold occurs (VT), so it represents a point where exercise is switching from aerobic to anaerobic. Using a within-subjects design, participants completed three testing sessions: no exercise, high-intensity exercise (20% above lactate threshold), and low-intensity exercise (20% below lactate threshold). Both exercise sessions included a 5-minute warm-up, 20 minutes of exercise at the target intensity level, and a 5-minute cool-down. Pain threshold was determined relative to a thermal pain stimulation device with instructions to identify when the perception of heat became a painful sensation; the temperature in °C was the dependent variable. Pain tolerance was assessed using a cold pressor task with instructions to remove the hand when the pain became intolerable; the dependent variable was measured as time in seconds. Pain threshold and pain tolerance were measured before and after each condition. Results showed a dose–response relationship between exercise intensity and the change in pain threshold and tolerance from pretest to posttest (see table 8.1), but differences between groups were only significant for the high-intensity exercise group compared to the control condition. Interestingly, the increase in pain threshold was positively related to fitness for the high-intensity exercise session. This tells us that when considering the high-intensity condition, a person's fitness predicted their pain threshold such that fitter individuals had a higher pain threshold.

This literature exploring the effects of a single session of exercise on pain perceptions by healthy adults has been meta-analytically reviewed by Naugle and colleagues (2012) to summarize the results of studies looking at the effects of acute exercise on pain threshold and pain ratings in response to experimental pain paradigms (i.e., when the pain is induced in a laboratory setting). Eight studies were reviewed that used aerobic exercise, and these studies yielded a significant benefit across a variety of pain stimuli for pain threshold (ES = 0.43) and for pain ratings (ES = 0.64). These effect sizes indicate that exercise results in a small to moderate benefit in terms of reductions in the perception of pain (increased pain threshold, decreased pain ratings) with some evidence that effects for pain ratings last for up to 30 minutes after exercise (Hoffman et al., 2004). Naugle and colleagues also reviewed studies that studied **isometric exercise** (exercise involving a static contraction), which also resulted in benefits in response to exercise with participants reporting a higher pain threshold (n = 9 studies; ES = 1.05) and a lower pain rating (n = 7 studies; ES = 0.72). These effects in response to isometric exercise are moderate to large. Benefits for threshold and pain ratings were observed to last for up to 15 minutes in the exercised limb (Kosek & Lundberg, 2003).

Wewege and Jones (2021) also reviewed the literature on acute exercise and exercise-induced reductions in pain perceptions in healthy individuals in response to experimental pain. Results from RCTs showed that aerobic exercise (n = 7 studies; N = 236) caused large reductions in pain perception (ES = 0.85), and resistance exercise (n = 2 studies, N = 23) caused moderate reductions in pain perception (ES = 0.45). Although these results are consistent with those of Naugle and colleagues and supportive of exercise-induced hypoalgesia, Wewege and Jones point out that the studies reviewed were typically of poor quality and that the small number of studies in this area is concerning. Although these effects are promising, given the small and lackluster body of evidence, more research is needed on the potential of acute exercise to reduce pain perceptions by healthy adults.

Chronic Exercise and Acute Pain: Evidence From Healthy Adults

Although it represents an indirect approach to the question of whether chronic exercise benefits pain perception, researchers have explored the possibility that athletes have higher pain thresholds and pain tolerance than nonathletes. The premise is that

TABLE 8.1 Differences in the Change in Pain Threshold and Pain Tolerance in Response to Treatment

	Control	Low	High
Change in heat pain threshold (temperature)	0.1	0.5	0.8
Change in pain tolerance (s)	1.5	13	21.2

Data estimated from Schmitt et al. (2020).

isometric exercise—Exercise involving a static contraction is called isometric exercise.

repeated exposure to the pain that is inherent in high-level physical training provides either physiological or psychological training that prepares athletes to better face other noxious stimuli. As an example of this type of research, Flood and associates (2017) compared perceptions of pain between 15 athletes and 15 nonathletes. Athletes in this study were highly competitive (state and national level) and training at high volumes (14.8 hr/wk). Nonathletes were recreational athletes training <4 hours per week or did not participate in physical training at all. In the pressure pain threshold (PPT) task, participants put their hand on a table palm down and increasing pressure was applied to their index finger until they reported the first perception of pain. Next, they performed the conditioning stimulus by putting their left hand and wrist in a cold-water bath for up to 4 minutes. They were instructed to remove their hand when the pain became unbearable. Immediately following the cold pressor task, they performed the PPT task again. Results showed that athletes had a higher pain threshold during the PPT task, had lower perceptions of pain during the cold pressor task, and had greater increases in pain threshold after the cold pressor task as compared to nonathletes. The major limitation of this study is the cross-sectional design, which means that we cannot determine if the increased pain capacity is a result of the regular exercise. Although this is one possible explanation, it is also possible that some innate ability predisposes athletes to be able to handle high levels of physical training and also makes them more pain tolerant or that the effects are due to some third-order variable such as an increased previous exposure to icing techniques that might be expected for high-level athletes.

The literature comparing athletes to nonathletes in terms of pain perception was meta-analytically reviewed by Tesarz and associates (2012). They reported significant effects for pain threshold (n = 9 studies; ES = 0.69) and tolerance (n = 12 studies; ES = 0.87). After limiting the analysis to only the high-quality studies, the findings for pain threshold were no longer significant, but the data on pain tolerance remained significant. Hence, the authors described the findings for pain tolerance as relatively robust. The authors provided an explanation for why they saw effects for pain tolerance but not for pain threshold when they limited their review to the high-quality studies. They suggested that pain threshold is relatively constant because it is more perceptually linked but that pain tolerance is reliant on coping skills that might be developed in response to the "systematic exposure to brief periods of intense pain" that can be a part of athletic participation (Tesarz et al., 2012, p. 1259). Thus, they thought that athletes learned coping mechanisms as a result of their sport participation and these methods helped them better tolerate pain.

Other studies have focused on comparisons between exercisers (who are not specifically athletes) and nonexercisers. Jones and colleagues (2014) conducted a quasiexperimental study to test the effects of a 6-week exercise program on pain perceptions by healthy adults. Twenty-four adults (18-50 yr; M = 24.4 yr) were invited to join a 6-week exercise intervention or to maintain their regular physical activity for 6 weeks. The exercise program was cycling on an ergometer at 75% of heart rate reserve 3 days per week for 30 minutes per day. Participants were not randomly assigned but were asked to indicate their preference for group assignment (this is why this is called a quasiexperimental study). Pain threshold was assessed using the application of pressure with a handheld algometer to four muscular sites (trapezius, biceps brachii, rectus femoris, tibialis anterior). Pain tolerance was assessed using an ischemic test. Participants first performed a maximal handgrip on a dynamometer using their dominant hand. A blood pressure cuff was then applied to that arm while it was raised above the heart, and the pressure was increased to 200 mm Hg. At that point, the arm was returned to horizontal and the participant was asked to contract the handgrip at 30% of their maximum for repeated contractions (alternating 4-s contraction with 4-s rest) for as long as tolerable. Results showed no differences in pain threshold as a result of the exercise, but a significant increase in pain tolerance for the exercise group that was not observed for the control group. This is consistent with the results of Tesarz and associates (2012) with benefits observed for tolerance but not threshold. Because participants were not randomly assigned to groups, we cannot draw firm conclusions about cause and effect. However, because the design of this study is stronger than a cross-sectional design, the findings provide more solid support for the direction of causation such that participation in regular exercise is associated with alterations in perceptions of pain when assessed as pain tolerance.

Pacheco-Barrios and colleagues (2020) conducted a meta-analytic review of 36 studies that used either quasiexperimental or RCT designs to assess the impact of regular exercise on pain threshold reports by healthy adults. Results showed a small positive benefit of chronic exercise on pain threshold (ES = 0.19), with moderator analyses showing that larger effects were evident for women (ES = 0.36), for moderate-intensity exercise (ES = 0.27), and for strength-training exercises (ES = 0.34). Interestingly, when the authors looked only at studies using moderate-intensity strength-training exercises, larger effects were observed (ES = 0.45), and when they looked at strength-training exercises performed by women, the largest effects were evident (ES = 0.67). These findings have to be viewed cautiously because of the inclusion of studies with quasiexperimental designs, because of the small sample sizes used in the studies, and because of the relatively small number of studies included when moderators were examined. Nonetheless, they provide further support for a causal link between exercise participation and reductions in perceptions of experimental pain, with some suggestions regarding the best mode (i.e., strength training) and intensity (i.e., moderate) to use and for whom effects might be strongest (i.e., women).

Chronic Exercise and Chronic Pain: Evidence From Adults Living With Chronic Pain

The body of evidence on chronic exercise and chronic pain is large and varied. Considering all the potential causes of pain, this makes sense because you wouldn't necessarily expect exercise to have the same benefits for chronic pain from, for example, fibromyalgia syndrome (a rheumatoid disorder of the muscle and bones) as from lower back pain (pain resulting from a variety of sources including muscle or ligament strains, arthritis, herniated disks). In these studies, pain is typically assessed using a questionnaire to measure perceptions of pain in the absence of a pain manipulation.

Exercise and Pain Following Breast Cancer Treatment

Osypiuk and associates (2020) published a study looking at the potential for qigong (a mind–body exercise) to reduce persistent pain in breast cancer survivors. They recruited 21 women who had surgery to treat their stage 0 to III breast cancer and were still experiencing pain at least 3 months after completing all treatment including the surgery, chemotherapy, or radiation. In this study, all participants received the qigong intervention delivered one time per week for 1.25 hours for 12 weeks and were asked to perform an additional 2 to 3 hours of the qigong exercises on their own using an instructional video. Results showed that participation in exercise was associated with reductions in pain measures that were evident after the 12-week intervention and that were maintained 3 months following the intervention. The authors concluded that a mind–body exercise intervention might be of particular benefit to breast cancer survivors who continue to experience pain after treatment.

Lower Back Pain

Lower back pain is pain and discomfort that is localized to the lower back and that might include leg pain. Lower back pain is, by far, the most commonly studied chronic pain condition for which the potential benefits of exercise have been explored. In fact, this literature has been reviewed in eight meta-analyses. Results from these reviews consistently support that participation in exercise reduces the experience of lower back pain. Searle and colleagues (2015) made an important contribution because they specifically compared the effects of various modes of exercise. They reviewed 39 RCTs testing the effects of exercise programs including coordination and stabilization ($N = 12$), strength and resistance ($N = 11$), cardiorespiratory ($N = 6$), and combined programs including multiple exercise components ($N = 14$) on pain in individuals with lower back pain. In this review, the positive effects were most evident for the coordination and stabilization and the strength and resistance exercise programs, with much less consistent findings for cardiorespiratory and combined programs. Overall, they reported that most (approximately 77%) of the studies reported positive effects with a small average effect size (ES = 0.32). More recently, Owen and associates (2020) used network meta-analysis techniques to compare between exercise program types. Similar to Searle and colleagues, they reported positive effects for resistance and stabilization exercise programs. However, different from Searle and colleagues, they also found benefits from aerobic exercise and Pilates exercises, which were not specifically tested in Searle et al.'s review. In fact, based upon their findings, Owen and coauthors argued that the best interventions for lower back pain are Pilates, aerobic, and stabilization exercises.

Fibromyalgia Syndrome Pain

Fibromyalgia syndrome (FMS) is a pain disorder that is characterized by widespread pain and tenderness that is accompanied by fatigue and other symptoms. Although the empirical evidence testing the efficacy of exercise for the reduction of pain and other FMS symptoms is limited in quantity and is characterized by studies with small sample sizes, meta-analytic reviews consistently support beneficial effects of exercise. Summarizing findings from 28 RCTs (N = 2,494 participants), Hauser and associates (2010) reported that aerobic exercise significantly reduced perceptions of pain (ES = 0.31). Based on the studies reviewed, they recommended that FMS patients should perform land- or water-based exercise at light to moderate intensity, 2 or 3 times per week, for a minimum of 4 weeks to experience benefits. Averaged across 16 studies (N = 832 participants), Mist and colleagues (2013) reported a reduction in pain for participants in an exercise condition compared to a control condition, with most of the results in their review coming from studies using qigong or tai chi for the exercise intervention. Sosa-Reina and associates (2017) included 14 RCTs exploring the effects of exercise (but excluding studies using yoga or tai chi) and found a significant and large benefit for reported pain (ES = 1.11). Based on their review, they recommend that persons with FMS perform aerobic exercise 2 or 3 times per week for 30 to 60 minutes at moderate to vigorous intensity, with the expectation that significant reductions in pain will be observed after 4 to 6 months. In summary, results of meta-analytic reviews of this literature consistently support the analgesic benefits of exercise for individuals suffering from FMS and suggest that both aerobic exercise and lighter modes of exercise (e.g., tai chi and qigong) can be beneficial.

Knee Osteoarthritis

Knee osteoarthritis occurs when knee cartilage is compromised, resulting in bones rubbing together, which causes pain, swelling, and stiffness in the knee joint. Tanaka and colleagues (2013) reviewed RCTs with exercise programs that were 8 weeks or longer, with 3 or more sessions per week, and that were focused on older adults (>55 yr) who had been diagnosed with knee osteoarthritis. Their results showed that exercise of any type resulted in the experience of significantly less pain as compared to any control condition (ES = 0.94). In a moderator analysis, findings further showed that while aerobic exercise (ES = 0.45) and weight-bearing strengthening exercises (ES = 0.70) were both effective, nonweight-bearing strengthening exercises resulted in the biggest reduction in pain (ES = 1.42). These effects are remarkably strong and robust and obviously point to the value of exercise for these individuals.

Migraines

Migraines are severe headaches that typically occur on one side of the head and are often accompanied by light and sound sensitivity and nausea. Participation in regular exercise can reduce the experience of migraines. Research in this area is fairly limited, but results are promising. Cross-sectional studies with large sample sizes show that individuals who are more physically active report fewer recurrent headaches or migraines (Molarius et al., 2008; Queiroz et al., 2009). In addition, Hagen and associates (2016) measured $\dot{V}O_2$peak in 3,899 participants and found that in participants aged 20 to 50 years, those who reported migraines were 3.7 times more likely to be in the lowest fitness quintile. That is, higher aerobic fitness levels were found to be related to reduced experiences of migraines. Interestingly, those in the lowest quintile were also 4.1 times more likely to experience a migraine aggravated by physical activity. This is important because of the concern that a single session of physical activity might trigger migraines. That is, evidence suggests that exercise has been a trigger for approximately 20% of migraine sufferers (Kelman, 2007). But other evidence from a headache-diary study shows that exercise was a trigger only a small percentage (<2%) of the time for migraine and nonmigraine-type headaches (Park et al., 2016). Hagen and associates' finding might help explain these seemingly conflicting results because they suggest that exercise might be a trigger for relatively inactive individuals but that it is less likely to be a trigger for those who exercise regularly, and for these individuals exercise might actually decrease migraines. Much more research is needed to identify the specific prescription of exercise that might benefit sedentary individuals who want to exercise for health reasons and potentially as a way to manage their migraines.

Meta-analytic reviews of this literature are particularly promising. La Touche and colleagues

(2020) reviewed findings from seven RCTs and three quasiexperimental studies exploring the effects of aerobic exercise on experiences of migraines. They found an average decrease in frequency of migraines that was of moderate clinical significance (ES = 0.76; N = 6), a decrease in reported intensity that was considered to be of large clinical significance (ES = 1.25; N = 5), and an average reduction in the duration of migraine episodes that represents a small clinical effect (ES = 0.41; N = 4). These findings of benefits are consistent with those reported by Lemmens and associates (2019), who reviewed results from six RCTs exploring the potential role of aerobic exercise in the experience of migraines. Their results showed that aerobic exercise resulted in reductions in pain intensity of 20% to 54% (N = 3), decreases in attack duration of 20% to 27% (N = 3), and a decrease in the number of days with a migraine over a 30-day period by 0.6 days (N = 4). Thus, overall, results from cross-sectional studies and from meta-analyses of RCTs support that exercise is a powerful tool to reduce the migraine experience in terms of frequency, intensity, and duration.

Summary

Acute pain has been experienced by almost everyone but is important because it provides a critical signal for people to change their behaviors to limit tissue damage. By contrast, chronic pain can be debilitating and can limit a person's ability to participate in normal activities of daily living. Evidence supports that both acute and chronic exercise can reduce the perception of pain in both acute and chronic pain situations. A single session of exercise has been shown to increase a healthy person's pain threshold and pain tolerance in response to laboratory-based pain stimuli. Meta-analytic evidence supports that these benefits can be observed in response to aerobic, isometric, and resistance forms of exercise. Some evidence also supports that higher-intensity exercise has bigger effects than does low-intensity exercise. Cross-sectional studies comparing athletes and nonathletes and quasiexperimental studies comparing exercisers to nonexercisers also suggest that chronic exercise can increase pain tolerance relative to laboratory-based pain stimuli. However, this study design limits the extent to which we can say that exercise *causes* changes in pain perception. RCTs in which sedentary adults are randomly assigned to begin an exercise program or to maintain their normal lifestyle have been reviewed meta-analytically and show that small benefits can be achieved with more limited evidence suggesting that these effects are larger for women, for moderate-intensity exercise, and for strength training. When exploring the benefits of chronic exercise for persons experiencing chronic pain conditions, a reasonable body of evidence exists for lower back pain, FMS, knee osteoarthritis, and migraines. In all cases, meta-analytic reviews show that small to large positive effects are evident. Relative to lower back pain, evidence is strongest for Pilates, aerobic exercise, and stabilization exercises. For FMS, the largest effects have been reported for yoga and tai chi, but positive effects are observed across many forms of land- and water-based aerobic exercise. For knee osteoarthritis, reductions in perceptions of pain are evident for aerobic exercise and for weight-bearing strength exercise but are dramatically larger for nonweight-bearing strength exercise. Lastly, for migraines, aerobic exercise reduces the intensity, duration, and frequency of migraines. Overall, evidence clearly supports the role of exercise as a way to mitigate pain experiences relative to both acute and chronic pain.

Discussion Questions

1. Schmitt and colleagues (2020) conducted a study exploring the effects of exercise intensity on pain threshold and tolerance. Describe the methods of the study and explain what the results regarding heat pain threshold from table 8.1 convey relative to the study.

2. Choose from lower back pain or fibromyalgia syndrome. Describe the meta-analyses that have been conducted on exercise and pain in one of these conditions, and based on those findings, provide specifics regarding the types of exercise that should be conducted.

3. Summarize what we know regarding the effects of a single session of exercise on the perception of pain. What are the implications of these findings?

4. Explain the series of physiological events that results in the experience of a dull, aching, diffuse pain.

Exercise and Cognitive Performance

CHAPTER OBJECTIVES

After studying this chapter, you should be able to do the following:

- Recognize that cognition can be considered both globally and as subdomains of specific types of cognitive performance
- Describe the hypotheses and mechanisms proposed to explain the benefits of both acute and chronic exercise for cognitive performance
- Understand the findings for cognitive performance during acute exercise and following acute exercise and recognize the critical importance of exercise intensity
- Describe the potential of chronic physical activity as a way to improve cognitive performance for healthy and cognitively impaired individuals and to prevent clinical cognitive impairment

KEY TERMS

cognitive performance

age-related decline

clinical cognitive decline

dementia

Alzheimer's disease

cognitive reserves

neurogenesis

synaptogenesis

angiogenesis

general cognition

cognitive domain

executive function

> Julio and Hector are identical twins who grew up playing numerous sports including basketball, soccer, and baseball. In high school they both lettered in all three sports for their varsity team. In college they went their separate ways for the first time in their lives.
>
> Julio went to a university, where he continued to play sports in intramurals, majored in kinesiology, and developed an interest in fitness training and strength and conditioning. During his university years, he began to compete in triathlon and smaller running events. He continued this active lifestyle throughout adulthood, playing pickup basketball and soccer with friends, training for weekend recreational races, and walking and jogging with his wife. Although he eventually gave up basketball and soccer, he continued to stay active into middle and older age.
>
> Hector also went to a big university and began his course of study in engineering. Hector initially joined the ultimate Frisbee club and remained active his freshman and sophomore years. Due to his solid academic performance, he got the opportunity to do an internship the summer after his sophomore year, and this quickly transitioned into a part-time job that he maintained for the remainder of his university years. Although this part-time job did wonders for his professional career, the time demands of work and school meant that Hector could no longer participate in ultimate Frisbee. Hector's first job took him to Atlanta, where he worked downtown and lived three subway stops away from his office. Because of the job demands and his loss of the habit of physical activity, Hector became sedentary and did not regularly incorporate physical activity into his lifestyle.
>
> When Julio and Hector were 55 years old, Julio was still active, was accumulating approximately 300 minutes of physical activity per week, and had extremely good cardiovascular health. By contrast, Hector was almost completely sedentary and was showing some signs of poor cardiovascular health (e.g., high total cholesterol, high blood pressure, high BMI). When the twins took part in a research study specifically comparing cognitive performance relative to physical activity status, researchers observed that Julio performed significantly better than Hector on measures of processing speed, immediate and delayed measures of story recall (measures of memory), and a task that required the participant to respond quickly to a green light displayed on a computer screen but to not respond at all if the green light had a red outline around it. Given that Julio and Hector are identical twins and that both are well educated and have cognitively demanding jobs, these results suggest that the one big lifestyle difference between them (level of physical activity) might play a role in the differences in physical health and in cognitive performance.

This story gives a good example of the cognitive benefits that are associated with a lifelong commitment to exercise. In fact, substantial empirical evidence supports that the adoption of a physically active lifestyle results in either cognitive performance gains or at least maintenance of cognitive skills in the face of advancing age. Another body of evidence tells us that even a single session of exercise can have benefits for cognitive performance. In this chapter, we will learn more about the measurement of cognition, explore theories and mechanisms purported to explain why exercise might benefit cognitive performance, and review some of the empirical and meta-analytic evidence relative to this relationship.

What Is Cognitive Performance?

When we speak of cognitive performance we are talking about performance on tasks that require mental processing (or cognition). The word *cognitive*

---

cognitive performance—Performance on tasks that require mental processing (or cognition) is called cognitive performance.

(or *cognition*) comes from the Latin word *cognitio*, which means "examining" or "learning." When you think of cognitive performance, you might think of taking a test for a class where you demonstrate your knowledge within a particular content area. Or you might remember taking the ACT or SAT, which almost certainly taxed your thinking abilities because of these tests were designed to assess your cognitive abilities in quantitative and verbal areas. These types of measures clearly assess cognitive performance and knowledge, but they aren't typical of the types of cognitive tasks used in research.

From a research perspective, we are often interested in understanding cognition through the use of methods that allow us to reduce cognition to a very basic level, and we are committed to assessments that do not display any kind of cultural bias. In lab-based studies, cognition is typically measured using paper-and-pencil or computerized tasks designed to assess one particular aspect of cognition within a given domain of cognition. Common cognition domains assessed in the exercise psychology literature include memory, attention, and executive function. Each of these will be described in more detail later in this chapter. In addition to assessing cognitive performance in particular domains of cognition, researchers also use more general measures that are designed to assess cognition more broadly (and hence often include numerous specific cognitive measures). These general measures are most commonly used with older adults in whom age-related or clinical cognitive decline is of interest. **Age-related decline** describes normal changes in cognitive performance that are seen in association with advanced age—for example, the expected decline in memory as a person gets older. **Clinical cognitive decline** describes the situation where the declines that are observed are greater than would be expected based on age alone and where those declines begin to impede a person's ability to perform normal daily activities.

Prevalence and Costs

It makes the most sense to consider prevalence and cost relative to Alzheimer's disease because the benefits of exercise for this clinical form of cognitive impairment are the most widely studied. **Dementia** is a general term used to describe a variety of diseases that result in a decline in cognitive abilities that is dramatic enough to interfere with daily life. Alzheimer's disease is the most common form of dementia, accounting for 60% to 80% of dementia cases. **Alzheimer's disease** is distinguished from other forms of dementia in that it is a progressive illness that involves the buildup of amyloid plaques and neurofibrillary tangles in the brain that block nerve signals or destroy nerve cells. In adults over 65, more than 11% have Alzheimer's disease, with the prevalence increasing with increasing age such that 5.3% of those aged 65 to 74 years, 13.8% of those aged 75 to 84, and 34.6% of those over aged 85 have Alzheimer's disease. The risk of Alzheimer's disease is also linked to race and ethnicity, with greater risk for Blacks and Hispanics than for Whites. In total, it affects approximately 6 million Americans and 50 million people worldwide, with predictions that this total will be over 12 million in the United States and 152 million worldwide by 2050. The total costs of health care, long-term care, and end-of-life care related to Alzheimer's disease is estimated at $350 billion in 2021 and is expected to rise to $1.1 trillion in 2050 (Alzheimer's Association, 2021a). Given that there is currently no cure for Alzheimer's disease, exercise could be particularly important if it is shown to delay the onset of Alzheimer's. Evidence suggests that delaying the onset of Alzheimer's disease by 5 years would decrease costs by 33% in 2050 (Alzheimer's Association, 2021b). As such, numerous studies have been completed and many are ongoing to understand better the potential role of physical activity as a preventative tool against Alzheimer's disease.

Theories, Mechanisms, and Mediators

When considering cognition, the exercise psychology literature has approached this outcome from several points of view. One point of view is to consider the potential role of exercise in terms of an acute benefit to cognitive performance. That is, researchers are interested in identifying the cognitive benefit of performing a single session of

---

age-related decline—Normal changes in cognitive performance that are seen in association with advanced age are described as age-related declines.

clinical cognitive decline—Clinical cognitive decline is when observed cognitive declines are greater than would be expected based on age alone and when those declines begin to impede a person's ability to perform normal daily activities.

dementia—Dementia is a general term used to describe a variety of diseases that result in a decline in cognitive abilities that is dramatic enough to interfere with daily life.

Alzheimer's disease—Alzheimer's disease is a neurodegenerative disease that is caused by an increase in amyloid plaques and neurofibrillary tangles in the brain that disrupt neurological functioning.

exercise. Another approach is to consider the benefits of chronic exercise as a way to benefit cognitive performance by those who are cognitively normal. This approach has been taken with all age groups, from children through adulthood to advancing age. Finally, scientific studies have been published that consider the use of exercise as a way to prevent cognitive decline in those at risk for decline (e.g., due to advancing age or early signs of clinical impairment) or to protect or improve cognition for those already experiencing cognitive decline or cognitive impairment.

Given that acute exercise benefits are expected to be relatively transient and chronic exercise benefits are expected to be relatively enduring, it is logical that different theories have been proposed based on the exercise paradigm. Thus, in considering the causal links between exercise and cognitive performance, we must discern between those that have been proposed for acute exercise and those relevant to chronic exercise.

Theories for Acute Exercise

Explanations for the benefits of acute exercise include the inverted-U hypothesis, cognitive-energetic theories, the reticular-activating hypothesis (RAH), the catecholamine hypothesis, and the brain-derived neurotrophic factor (BDNF) hypothesis.

Inverted-U Hypothesis and Cognitive-Energetic Theories

The inverted-U hypothesis initially was applied to cognitive performance by Davey (1973). He predicted that exercise would increase arousal and that the relationship between arousal and cognitive performance would be in the shape of an inverted-U such that with arousal plotted on the *x*-axis and cognitive performance plotted on the *y*-axis, the plotted data would take on the shape of an upside-down letter U. In other words, Davey expected that exercise at low intensity and at high intensity would not benefit cognitive performance but that exercise at moderate intensity would benefit cognitive performance (figure 9.1). This hypothesis forms the basis for many other cognitive-energetic theories of the link between a single session of exercise and cognitive performance. These other cognitive-energetic theories incorporate additional complexities in terms of considering the demand of the cognitive task and the notion that arousal is multidimensional (see McMorris, 2016, for additional information).

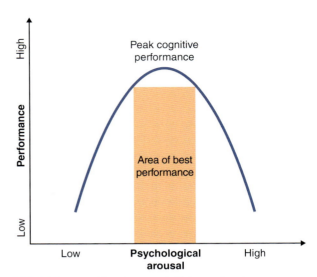

FIGURE 9.1 The inverted-U hypothesis suggests that the relationship between physiological arousal and cognitive performance assumes the shaped of an upside-down U.

Briefly, they suggest that a person can perform a simple well-learned task even with high levels of arousal but that performance of a more complex or novel task will be more readily disrupted by high levels of arousal but will be improved at low levels of arousal.

Reticular-Activating Hypofrontality Hypothesis

The reticular-activating hypofrontality hypothesis (RAH) (Dietrich, 2003; Dietrich & Audiffren, 2011) is only relevant to cognitive performance performed during exercise. This theory posits that moderate-intensity exercise benefits the performance of well-learned and nonfrontal tasks because of increases in catecholamines but that high-intensity exercise is so demanding in terms of cerebral resources that performance of novel tasks or of frontal lobe tasks necessarily suffer. In other words, when the exercise intensity is high enough, the RAH predicts that cerebral resources are prioritized for completion of the exercise bout itself. Because cerebral resources are finite, this results in a reduction of resources available to the prefrontal cortex, and this effect is observable through measurable declines in cognitive performance for tasks that rely on the prefrontal cortex (i.e., frontal tasks). Results from a meta-analytic review testing this hypothesis found support for the expectation that high-intensity exercise has a negative effect on frontal tasks that is not observed in nonfrontal tasks (Jung et al., 2022).

Catecholamine Hypothesis

The catecholamines hypothesis was initially described by Cooper (1973) and proposes that exercise results in the release of catecholamines (norepinephrine, epinephrine, dopamine) both centrally and peripherally and that those that are released centrally have a beneficial impact on cognitive performance. During exercise (and even immediately before exercise in an anticipatory response), catecholamines are released in the periphery. Although catecholamines do not cross the blood-brain barrier, evidence suggests that higher levels in the periphery indirectly result in higher levels in the brain (McMorris & Hale, 2012). The largest changes in catecholamine levels occur when exercise is performed at a relatively high intensity, but even less intense exercise can affect catecholamine levels if performed for a sufficient duration. Although evidence supports this hypothesis in the animal literature, evidence provided through human studies is less clear largely because of the inability to measure central (e.g., levels in the brain) catecholamine levels.

Brain-Derived Neurotrophic Factor (BDNF)

Researchers are also interested in the role of BDNF in explaining the benefits of acute exercise on cognitive performance. BDNF is a neurotrophic factor that is important for neuron synthesis and pruning and that also plays a role in memory. BDNF is to neurons as a gardener is to a shrub: The gardener encourages healthy growth through the provision of nutrients while also pruning away unwanted growth. Because BDNF crosses the blood-brain barrier, the increases in BDNF that have been demonstrated consistently in the periphery in response to exercise are thought to be indicative of higher levels of BDNF in the brain. Importantly, although the increases in BDNF are relatively transient, the effects on other downstream variables that are important for cognition are thought to be the key, which might explain why acute exercise benefits can be observed following the cessation of activity (McMorris & Hale, 2012).

Theories for Chronic Exercise

Explanations for the benefits of chronic exercise include the cardiovascular fitness hypothesis, the selective improvement hypothesis, the cognitive reserves hypothesis, the neurovisceral integration hypothesis, and a specific focus on changes in brain structure.

Cardiovascular Fitness Hypothesis

The cardiovascular fitness hypothesis predicts that exercise that results in gains in cardiovascular fitness (e.g., aerobic exercise) will result in improvements in cognitive performance. Although studies show a relationship between fitness and cognitive performance, the evidence does not support that this is a causal relationship. In fact, in a large meta-

---

The Secret Sauce

Using an animal model, Horowitz and colleagues (2020) identified another potential mechanism to explain the cognitive benefits of exercise. They randomly assigned younger and older mice to have access to a running wheel (active) or to have access to nesting material (sedentary). After 6 weeks, they found that the active mice had increases in BDNF and increased neurogenesis and performed better on learning and memory tasks. Next, they took blood plasma from the active mice and injected that plasma into another group of older sedentary mice. After receiving blood plasma from active mice, the older sedentary mice demonstrated increases in neuronal growth in the hippocampus and performed better on tests that specifically measured hippocampal-dependent learning and memory. Because they found higher levels of glycosylphosphatidylinositol-specific phospholipase D1 (Gpld1) in the blood plasma, they hypothesized that this was the critical mechanism ("the secret sauce"). They conducted another study in which they increased the levels of Gpld1 produced by the livers of older mice. They found that these mice also had enhanced neuronal growth and did better on the same types of cognitive tests. Finally, they have begun to translate these findings to studies with humans and have discovered that older adults (66-78 yr) who are physically active have higher levels of Gpld1 in their plasma than do sedentary older adults. This series of studies provides a great example of how animal research can pave the way for important discoveries in humans and suggests that Gpld1 may be "the secret sauce" that is critical for explaining the link between physical activity and cognitive performance.

regression analysis, Etnier and colleagues (2006) reported that the change in fitness in response to an exercise intervention did not predict the change in cognitive performance. In other words, across RCTs in which exercise was manipulated with a goal of improving fitness, the actual amount of improvement in fitness was not critical in predicting the amount of gain in cognitive performance. Instead, the results showed that for groups that exercised, cognitive gains were experienced irrespective of the actual fitness improvements. This finding likely tells us that it's not aerobic fitness that matters, but rather other changes that are happening in the body in response to the exercise that are important for predicting cognitive gains.

Selective Improvement Hypothesis

Another hypothesis that has been proposed is the selective improvement hypothesis (Kramer et al., 1999). This hypothesis is closely linked to the frontal lobe hypothesis of aging. The frontal lobe hypothesis tells us that changes in brain function and brain structure with advancing age are most evident in the frontal lobe. Based on this hypothesis, Kramer and associates predicted that exercise would have its greatest benefits for tasks that were dependent on frontal lobe activity. Specifically, they posited that exercise would result in selective improvements in cognitive performance, with the most robust gains seen in executive function tasks, which are known to be frontal lobe dependent. In fact, they demonstrated exactly this in an RCT (Kramer et al., 1999) and in the findings of a meta-analytic review (Colcombe & Kramer, 2003), which yielded larger effects for executive function tasks than for other types of cognitive tasks. Although evidence supports this hypothesis, it is important to recognize that exercise has been shown to benefit other cognitive domains as well, so the effects are not limited to frontal lobe–dependent tasks.

Cognitive Reserves Hypothesis

The cognitive reserves hypothesis proposes that cognitive reserves develop through childhood and young adulthood. These reserves are thought to reach a peak when a person is in their early 20s and are typically maintained through adulthood, and then the reserves start to decline in middle and older age. These *cognitive reserves* are the resources that are used to perform cognitive tasks in the face of challenge. Hence, a person's cognitive performance is expected to be better when they have more cognitive reserves available. This is particularly true if they are performing a very difficult task or performing under stress when cognitive reserves might be truly challenged. Cognitive reserves are also critically important for the maintenance of cognitive ability following the onset of brain pathology. Cognitive reserves can be functional (i.e., functional redundancies and flexibility that can help the individual cope with challenges) or structural (i.e., greater brain volume, number and size of neurons, and cortical thickness that serves a protective function in the face of challenges). As applied to exercise, the expectation is that participation in physical activity increases cognitive reserves. In particular, regular exercise is expected to increase cognitive reserves, which would then allow for better cognitive performance in the face of a challenge and provide a higher level of cognitive reserves to start with such that declines due to advancing age or brain pathology might not affect cognitive performance.

Neurovisceral Integration Hypothesis

Thayer and Lane (2000) laid out the premise of the neurovisceral integration hypothesis, which focuses on the integration between the central nervous system and the autonomic nervous system as a means of understanding the complex experiences of emotion and self-regulation. In 2009 Thayer and colleagues provided an explanation of how this hypothesis is also important for understanding executive functions such as working memory and inhibitory control. The important link underlying this hypothesis is between a network of functional units within the central nervous system that are critical for goal-directed behavior and for adapting to changing environmental demands. This network is called the *central autonomic network* (CAN), and it has been shown to be linked to both heart rate variability (HRV) and performance on cognitive tasks that are considered to assess executive function (and hence are linked to prefrontal cortex function). Importantly, evidence suggests that being physically active is associated with higher HRV (DeMeersman, 1993), that a decrease in fitness is associated with a decline in HRV (Hansen et al., 2004), and that an exercise intervention improved HRV variables (Phoemsapthawee et al., 2019). Thus, this hypothesis predicts that the benefits of exercise for HRV are suggestive of benefits for the CAN, which is impor-

---

cognitive reserves—Cognitive reserves are the resources used to perform cognitive tasks in the face of a challenge, and they can be functional (i.e., functional redundancies and flexibility that can help the individual cope with challenges) or structural (i.e., greater brain volume, number and size of neurons, and cortical thickness that serves a protective function in the face of challenges).

tant for executive function. A meta-analytic review (Zou et al., 2018) of 17 studies exploring the effects of tai chi and yoga found significant improvements in HRV variables (ES = 0.37-0.58), thus supporting that aspect of the hypothesis. Researchers are actively engaging in studies to advance our understanding of the viability of this hypothesis as it links exercise to cognition.

Brain Structure and Function

Finally, many researchers are beginning to suggest that a regular program of exercise positively affects the structure and function of the brain (see chapter 10 for more details). This hypothesis is not necessarily unique from either the selective improvement hypothesis or the cognitive reserves hypothesis because these changes to structure and function might explain the observation of selective improvements or of an increase in cognitive reserves. That said, evidence from the animal literature shows that participating in exercise increases **neurogenesis** (the creation of new neurons), **synaptogenesis** (the creation of new synapses), and **angiogenesis** (the creation of new capillaries). Evidence from studies with humans also shows increases in white matter density and in hippocampal volume in response to exercise. Studies using event-related potentials support that differences in brain function occur during task performance in association with fitness, and research with functional magnetic resonance imaging (fMRI) shows that aerobic fitness changes brain connectivity at rest. These effects will be explored in detail in chapter 10.

> Thinking about your own opportunities for cognitive performance, what do you think about the potential role of exercise? If you have a test tomorrow, do you think exercising before the test will help? It is interesting to think about this possibility and the implications. If exercising before a test will help your performance but studying also will help your performance, and if you have to make a choice between the two, which should you pick? Perhaps that's a silly question because you should choose to spend your time studying. But if you have time to do both, the question becomes more interesting. If you were to exercise before you study, while you're studying, or after you've studied, would that exercise benefit your performance?

The Measurement of Cognition

The measurement of cognition has evolved over time in response to our increased understanding of the complexities of this construct. Research in the late 1800s initially focused on the development of measures of general intelligence predominantly as a basis for exploring nature-and-nurture questions related to a person's career success and talent development. Galton (in London) and Cattell (in New York City) independently developed a compilation of measures of sensory abilities such as the ability to discern between two similar weights or two similar smells. They proposed that the ability to make fine-tuned distinctions between stimuli was indicative of general intelligence. In the early 1900s the development of the first acceptable measure of intelligence was led by Binet and Simon (in Paris), who were motivated by the need to identify school-aged children who would benefit from special education. This resulted in the Binet-Simon intelligence scale (Binet & Simon, 1916). The measurement approach used in this test was considered to reflect performance on multiple independent factors; the test consisted of 30 cognitive tests measuring skills such as language, memory, reasoning, and digit span. In 1916 Terman, a psychologist at Stanford University, added additional tests to the Binet-Simon intelligence scale, resulting in the Stanford-Binet Intelligence Scale, which became the predominant measure of intelligence used in the United States. Terman also promoted a new composite score called an *intelligence quotient* (IQ), which was based on a ratio of the age level of tests that could be accomplished (mental age) relative to the child's chronological age. This is the standard IQ test that you have likely heard of and that is purported to indicate a person's cognitive capacity. The score is a ratio of the person's mental age (as determined by the test) relative to their chronological age and then multiplied by 100, so, for example, a child who has a mental age of 13 and a chronological age of 10 would have an IQ of 130. The efficacy of this measure was supported by subsequent longitudinal work that established that a large portion of children under 14 years of age who were identified as having high IQs went on to great accomplishments (Sternberg, 2019).

In terms of administration, tasks that have been developed to assess cognition were initially administered in paper-and-pencil format or by using a spe-

---

neurogenesis—The creation of new neurons is referred to as neurogenesis.

synaptogenesis—The creation of new synapses is called synaptogenesis.

angiogenesis—Angiogenesis is the creation of new capillaries.

cifically developed measurement tool such as a reaction time task or the Tower of London task (figure 9.2). In recent years, most cognitive tasks have been translated into versions that can be administered by computer or delivered via the Internet or a phone-based app. Most cognitive tasks that are used in the exercise psychology literature have long-established psychometrics with reliability and validity further established when new administration methods have been developed. Regardless of the format of test administration, cognitive performance tasks yield measures such as accuracy (e.g., the percent of trials with a correct response), a score to reflect the number of items recalled (e.g., in a memory task), errors, and reaction time (typically just for trials in which a correct response was given).

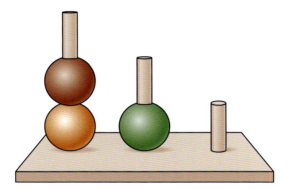

FIGURE 9.2 The equipment referred to as the *Tower of London*, which provides an assessment of planning.

General Cognition and Cognitive Domains

As previously mentioned, in the exercise psychology literature scholars have shown interest both in studying general cognition and in examining more specific aspects of cognition. General cognition can be assessed using the measures of intelligence just discussed and is an overarching factor that represents general mental ability. Research focused on general cognition typically has been conducted with children in academic settings or with older adults looking at general cognitive ability. With children, these measures of general cognition include alternative measures of intelligence (e.g., Wechsler Intelligence Scale for Children), standardized state tests of achievement (e.g., California Standardized Tests for Math and English, Illinois Standards Achievement Test, Texas Assessment of Knowledge and Skills),

and measures developed specifically for research (e.g., d2 Test of Attention, Woodcock-Johnson Test of Achievement). With older adults, general measures of cognition that are typically used in research were often designed from a deficit perspective with the intention of identifying individuals with or at risk for clinical forms of cognitive impairment. These measures (e.g., Mini-Mental Status Exam, Montreal Cognitive Assessment, Alzheimer's Disease Assessment Scale) are most typically used as outcomes in large-scale epidemiological studies in which physical activity is examined as a protective behavior relative to scores indicative of a risk of dementia.

In addition to measures of general cognition (or general intelligence), measurements also have been developed to assess specific cognitive domains. A cognitive domain is a higher-order level of cognitive performance that has been proposed to include orientation and attention, perception, memory, verbal functions and language skills, construction, concept formation and reasoning, and executive function. When turning our attention to tasks that measure performance in specific cognitive domains, a huge number have been used in the scientific literature, so much so that entire volumes have been written to describe these various measures. For example, Lezak and colleagues (2004) described over 400 cognitive tests that fall into the previously identified seven domains of cognitive function (see figure 9.3). Although general measures of cognition have been used in exercise psychology research, these are typically only used in prospective studies with large samples sizes. It is more common for domain-specific measures to be used as outcomes in studies in which the efficacy of exercise interventions is being assessed. This is because these measures have a much greater sensitivity than do the general measures of cognition. In some studies, multiple cognitive tasks are used to assess the same cognitive domain, and in these cases a composite score for the domain can provide both enhanced sensitivity and reliability.

Measurement in Three Cognitive Domains

Memory is a cognitive domain that has received substantial attention in the exercise literature. In particular, in the area of acute exercise, the number of studies focused on memory has increased dra-

---

general cognition—General cognition is assessed using measures of intelligence and is an overarching factor that represents general mental ability.

cognitive domain—A cognitive domain is defined as a higher-order level of cognitive performance that has been proposed to include orientation and attention, perception, memory, verbal functions and language skills, construction, concept formation and reasoning, and executive function.

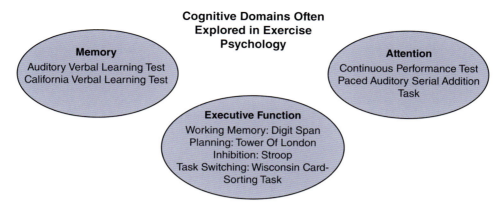

FIGURE 9.3 Cognitive domains often explored in exercise psychology.

matically in recent years. One common measure of memory is a word-learning task, either the Auditory Verbal Learning Test or the California Verbal Learning Test. In these word-learning tasks, participants are asked to remember and recall a list of unrelated words. The participant is exposed to the list of words (typically through having the list read to them). They are then asked to recall as many of the words as they can remember. The first recollection provides a measure of short-term memory. The list is then repeated and recalled for additional trials, providing a measure of learning with repeated exposure. In some administrations, the participants are exposed to a different word list with the purpose of creating interference and challenging the long-term recall of the first list. After hearing and recalling this different list, the participant is asked to recall the initial list again without hearing it, providing a measure of long-term memory in the face of interference. In some studies, participants also are asked to recall the list one last time after an extended (e.g., 24 hr) delay without hearing it again. This provides an indicant of the durability of the effects for long-term memory.

Measures of attention also are commonly used as outcomes in the exercise psychology literature. A common sustained attention task is the continuous performance task (CPT) in which the participant is asked to watch a series of letters presented one at a time on a screen. The participant is instructed to press the space bar anytime they see an X but not to do anything when other letters are presented. This task is commonly used to assess attention, particularly in participants who have attention deficit hyperactivity disorder (ADHD). The Paced Auditory Serial Addition Task (PASAT) is another commonly used measure of attention. In this task, participants are asked to listen to a series of 60 single digits that are presented verbally. Participants are to verbally respond after hearing every number (except the first number) by telling the sum of the previous two numbers. This task is challenging when presented at a slow speed but is also presented at a fast speed, which is particularly challenging.

Executive function is a cognitive domain that is extremely important in the exercise psychology literature. Early interest in executive function likely was reflective of an interest in understanding the potential of exercise to affect higher-order cognitive tasks (e.g., executive function). Interest also was piqued because executive functions have been shown to be important for numerous valued outcomes. Executive function is thought to be critically important because this higher-order cognitive ability can affect our ability to be successful today and in the future. In fact, evidence supports that executive functioning at 54 months is important for academic achievement during adolescence (Ahmed et al., 2019) and adulthood (Ahmed et al., 2021). Furthermore, in longitudinal studies, executive function prior to the age of 10 was found to predict financial well-being and physical health (Moffitt et al., 2011), and executive functioning assessed in older adults was predictive of mortality 10 years later (Hall et al., 2009). Executive function is critical for the performance of goal-oriented behaviors, and in the exercise psychology literature, it has typically been defined to include the four subdomains of working memory, inhibitory control, planning, and task switching (Etnier & Chang, 2009). Tasks that require executive function result in activation of the frontal lobe and are reliant on precortical development such that these tasks are sometimes also called

---

executive function—Executive function is a higher-order cognitive domain that is critical for the performance of goal-oriented behaviors; it includes the four subdomains of working memory, inhibitory control, planning, and task switching.

frontal lobe tasks or *prefrontal lobe tasks*. Typical measures of executive function that have been used in the exercise psychology literature include the Digit Span Test, which measures working memory; the Stroop Test, which measures inhibitory control; the various towers tests (e.g., Tower of Hanoi, Tower of London), which measure planning; and the Wisconsin Card-Sorting Test, which measures task switching.

> ### Executive Function Subdomains
>
> The various cognitive domains sometimes include subdomains. Within executive function are four subdomains that are often specifically explored in research.
>
> - *Working memory:* A type of memory that allows a person to use recalled information in the execution of cognitive tasks. It is critical to the conductance of planned behaviors because it allows for the storage of an end goal and of the subgoals that help us to reach the end goal.
> - *Inhibitory control:* The cognitive ability to inhibit acting on our impulses or pursuing goal-irrelevant stimuli so that we can focus on goal-directed behaviors.
> - *Planning:* The ability to generate a series of steps that can be organized and prioritized in a way that will allow a person to reach a specific goal.
> - *Task switching:* An ability to move between various sets of rules governing our behavior and the ability to switch our focus to different aspects of a stimulus.

The Stroop Test (Stroop, 1935) is a measure of inhibitory control, which is a subdomain of executive function. The Stroop Test consists of different forms or conditions with varying levels of challenge. In the neutral condition, participants see a stimulus ("XXX" or a colored box) printed in colored ink and are asked to identify the color of ink as quickly as possible. In the congruent condition, participants see the name of a color printed in colored ink that matches (e.g., "RED" printed in red ink). In the incongruent condition, participants see the name of a color printed in colored ink that does not match (e.g., "BLUE" printed in red ink). In both the congruent and incongruent tasks, the participant identifies the color of the ink and ignores what the word itself says (e.g., in all examples provided here, the answer would be red). Performance on the neutral and congruent tasks provide simple measures of speed of processing because these are simple tasks and identifying a color generally is automatic for most people. But performance on the incongruent task provides a measure of inhibitory control (an aspect of executive function) because the person has to ignore the color word that the letters spell out (i.e., they have to inhibit this automatic response of reading the word) so that they can instead identify the ink color. This measure provides an indicant of inhibitory control when speed of processing is controlled (often by simply subtracting the average reaction time for incongruent trials minus the average reaction time for congruent or neutral trials).

The Wisconsin Card-Sorting Test (WCST) is a commonly used measure of task switching (figure 9.4). This task originally was administered using a deck of cards with printed symbols on them. Each card displayed some number (1-4) of symbols (plus sign, circle, triangle, square) in one of four colors (red, green, blue, yellow). Cards are placed one at a time in front of the participant, who has to identify the sorting rule that is currently in place (that only the researcher knows). Based on the feedback provided to their response, they are expected to correctly identify the sorting rule and then to maintain that correct knowledge for 10 cards in a row, at which point the sorting rule changes.

Evidence Relative to the Effects of Exercise on Cognitive Performance

Early research on exercise and cognition was largely focused on relatively simple types of cognitive performance, with a substantial body of literature examining effects on simple or choice reaction time tasks. In fact, some of the earliest work in this area emerged from the sport psychology interests, with researchers focusing on differences in cognitive ability between athletes and nonathletes. (Remember back to chapter 1 when you learned about the studies comparing reaction time between fencers and nonfencers).

The first meta-analytic review of the literature on exercise and cognitive performance was published by Etnier and colleagues (1997). We were able to find almost 200 studies that had been conducted on

The answer key is shown the entire time the participant is doing the task. The participant says the number of the card that represents a match to the stimulus card based upon the sorting rule.

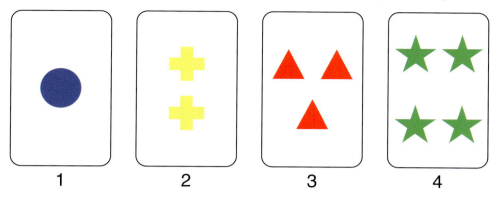

Stimuli shown to the participants one card at a time. For example, the participant is shown a card with three green circles.

The participant guesses the sorting rule. If they guess:

Shape, they'd say card 1 because the circles match

Number, they'd say card because the number of items match

Color, they'd say card 4 because the colors match

Based on the feedback they're given, they have to figure out if they've guessed the right sorting rule or if they need to try a different sorting rule. Then, they'll apply this sorting rule to the next stimulus card.

FIGURE 9.4 In the Wisconsin Card-Sorting Test, a participant is shown one card at a time. The participant looks at the card, provides a response meant to demonstrate the sorting rule and so identifies some relevant characteristic of the card (initially this is just a guess), uses the feedback to determine if the sorting rule is correct or not, and works to ultimately discover the correct sorting rule.

exercise and cognition, which allowed us to include over 800 effect sizes in the analysis. The studies were examined separately based on their design, and results showed that cross-sectional studies yielded an effect size of 0.53, chronic studies an effect size of 0.33, and acute studies an effect size of 0.16. This initial review was important in part because of showing the hints of a dose–response relationship between exercise and cognition such that small effects were found after a single session of exercise (i.e., after physical activity participa-

tion for minutes), small to moderate effects were observed in response to a chronic exercise program (i.e., after physical activity participation for weeks or months), and moderate effects were evident with a lifelong commitment to exercise (i.e., the results from cross-sectional studies representing physical activity performed over years). In other words, while they are somewhat speculative, the results suggest that increasing the dose of exercise participation increases the cognitive benefits that are observed such that small effects are evident after a single session, but moderate effects can be obtained with a more long-term commitment to being physically active. This meta-analytic review was also important because it presaged an increase in interest in this topic; for example, a search conducted June 20, 2021, at https://pubmed.gov using the terms *exercise* and *cognition* showed that 25,631 studies are relevant to those keywords and one conducted on April 18, 2023 (approximately 2 years later), yielded 28,076 studies. Clearly, a lot of research is being done on this topic to advance our understanding in terms of both acute and chronic exercise.

Acute Exercise

As mentioned, the potential cognitive benefits of a single session of exercise have been examined in numerous scientific studies and, in fact, have been reviewed in several meta-analyses as well. Importantly, in this literature we have to consider whether the cognitive task performance takes place during the exercise or once the exercise has been completed. We'll consider the question of whether cognitive performance during exercise is improved or hampered and whether exercising before a cognitive task benefits or impairs cognitive performance performed after the exercise. The former is interesting relative to situations such as athletic performances, military operations, jobs with high vigilance demands (e.g., air traffic controller), and job and academic performance, with the latter having clear implications for when classes occur after physical education or recess or when people choose to exercise before they start their school or work day.

Cognitive Performance During Exercise

When considering studies in which the cognitive performance occurs during exercise, meta-analytic results are not consistent. Chang and associates (2012) reported a small positive overall benefit (ES = 0.10), Lambourne and Tomporowski (2010) reported a small overall decrement (ES = −0.14), McMorris and Hale (2012) reported a negligible (ES = −0.08) effect for accuracy and a moderate benefit (ES = 0.48) for speed of performance when exercise was at moderate intensity, and Loprinzi and colleagues (2019) reported a small negative effect for memory encoding (ES = −0.12). Considering these effect sizes (see figure 9.5; 0.10, −0.14, −0.08, 0.48, −0.12), it is clear that cognitive performance during exercise might not change much at all, might get a little worse, or might get better. Given

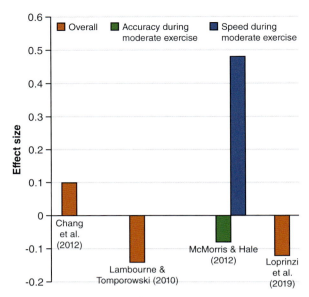

FIGURE 9.5 A range of effect sizes have been calculated in meta-analytic reviews of the effects of acute exercise on cognition when the task is performed during the exercise bout. The only positive effects during exercise are evident for speed of processing when the exercise is at moderate intensity.

that the theories proposed to explain the potential effects on cognitive performance during exercise (dual mode theory, reticular-activating hypothesis) explain that exercise intensity and the specific type of cognitive task play critical roles in the observed effect, these results might not be surprising. That's because when averaged across studies (as is done in a meta-analysis), the unique contributions of exercise intensity and the specific cognitive task are hard to distinguish. In this case, it might be helpful to consider the findings of a specific study that was designed to advance understanding of how exercise intensity influences the extent to which exercise can improve cognitive performance when the two are performed simultaneously.

To understand dose–response questions relative to exercise intensity, let's consider a study performed by Wang and colleagues (2013) who specifically examined the dose–response effects of aerobic exercise intensity on executive function performance during exercise. Using a between-subjects design, they randomly assigned 80 young adults to a no-exercise condition or to a low-, moderate-, or high-intensity exercise condition. Participants in the exercise conditions warmed up and then completed 30 minutes of exercise at their assigned intensity level. During exercise, they performed the WCST to measure the executive function of task switching. The control participants performed the WCST while sitting on the exercise bike. Results showed that those in the high-intensity condition performed significantly worse than any of the other conditions, with no differences between the control, low-intensity, and moderate-intensity conditions. These results provide a clear demonstration of the importance of exercise intensity in terms of the expected effects of exercise on cognitive performance during exercise. In particular, theory and evidence suggest that cognitive performance suffers when the task is performed during high-intensity exercise particularly if the task is frontal lobe dependent, complex, or novel. However, in this study the other intensity levels of exercise were not found to be beneficial. This might suggest that future studies should look at other types of cognitive performance to see if particular exercise intensities might benefit performance when performed concurrently with exercise.

Cognitive Performance After Exercise

When considering studies in which cognitive performance is assessed after the cessation of exercise, meta-analytic reviews consistently support small to moderate benefits (figure 9.6). Chang and associates (2012) reported an overall effect size of 0.10 for all studies conducted on the topic. This is consistent with findings from meta-analyses that have adopted inclusion criteria limiting their review to smaller subsets of the literature. For example, Lambourne and Tomporowski (2010) found an overall small effect size (ES = 0.20) for studies testing the effects in healthy adults using within-subjects designs. Loprinzi and colleagues (2019) and Roig and associates (2013) reported small to moderate effects (ES = 0.11-0.52) for studies looking at acute exercise and memory. These meta-analyses support the existence of a relatively small but robust effect of a single session of exercise across various types of cognitive performance following the cessation of exercise. To apply this to a topic relevant to college students, this tells us that if you exercise before taking a test, you might be expected to perform slightly better on that test than if you had not exercised.

Given the relatively small observed benefits of exercise on cognition following the exercise bout, researchers in this area are encouraged to look closely at the moderators that have been tested meta-analytically so that they can use this knowledge to design their studies to maximize expected results. For example, in their meta-analysis, Chang and colleagues (2012) found that very light-, light-, and moderate-intensity exercise benefited cognition performed immediately after exercise, but that light, moderate, hard, and very hard exercise benefited cognition performed after a delay following exercise. They interpreted this finding as providing support for mechanisms that are affected differently based on exercise intensity and that are relatively transient

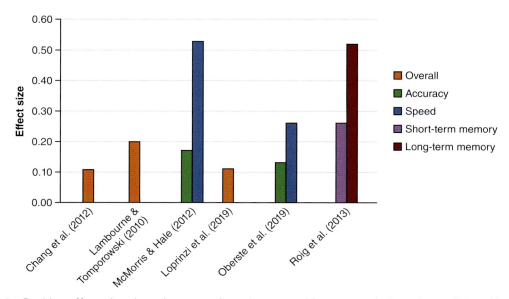

FIGURE 9.6 Positive effect sizes have been consistently reported in meta-analytic reviews of the effects of acute exercise on cognition when the task is performed after the exercise bout. The most robust effects are observed for measures of speed of processing and short- and long-term memory.

(i.e., the benefits dissipate relatively quickly). They bolstered this argument with additional evidence in their review, showing that small effects are evident when assessed within 15 minutes of exercise cessation but that effects become negligible after longer delays. Again, this suggests that the effects of a single session of exercise are relatively transient and might reflect the physiological changes in response to exercise, which would be expected to be higher immediately following exercise and to dissipate as the body returns to homeostasis. If the goal is for these relatively transient effects to have a more lasting effect, a higher intensity of exercise might need to be performed. Again, applying this finding to life as a college student, this would suggest that exercising before the test has to be done in close proximity to the test-taking time, that the benefits might only be observed during the initial part of the test, and that only higher-intensity exercise would be expected to have somewhat enduring effects.

As mentioned, when it comes to looking at specific moderators (e.g., exercise intensity) one of the limitations of a meta-analysis is that the effects have been averaged across the whole group of studies. To understand more clearly the effects of a moderator, it is actually better to test those effects within a single study. Chang and Etnier (2009) conducted a study with resistance exercise to test the hypothesis that exercise intensity would influence the observed benefits of exercise. Using a between-subjects design, they randomly assigned 68 men and women to one of 4 exercise intensity conditions (0% [control], 40%, 70%, and 90%) relative to each participant's 10-repetition max for 6 different strength-training exercises. Cognitive performance was assessed before and following the treatment using the Stroop Test and the PASAT. Scores were calculated for posttest minus pretest, with a larger negative value indicating faster performance (a smaller reaction time) at the posttest than the pretest. Results of the study suggested that higher intensities of exercise were beneficial for the simple, information-processing aspects of the Stroop Test and for the slower administration of the PASAT. But with increasing task difficulty as evidenced by the color–word condition of the Stroop Test and the faster administration of the PASAT, the relationship between intensity and performance became curvilinear such that performance suffered at the highest intensity of exercise (figure 9.7). This provides evidence that the question of the ideal exercise intensity might be dependent on the particular task being performed. To apply this to a college student's life, if you were taking a test on well-mastered material and you felt pretty confident, performing high-intensity exercise before the test should be most beneficial. But if you are taking a test on material that you're less confident in and that will require more problem-solving, lower intensities of exercise are likely to help you the most.

Interestingly, researchers exploring the potential benefits of a single session of exercise for memory have observed that effects can be relatively long-lasting. That is, rather than the effects dissipating within 15 minutes as reported by Chang and associates (2012) for averages from studies testing cognitive performance after a delay following exercise, benefits have been observed as long as 24 hours following the exercise. This is likely unique to this particular form of cognition because the exercise is benefiting the encoding and consolidation of the memory stimuli (in the short term), which then can be assessed through recall performed at a later time. Etnier and colleagues have been exploring questions related to the specific timing of the exercise bout relative to the encoding of stimuli for short- and long-term memory. Their results consistently show that exercise performed prior to exposure to a to-be-remembered list of words results in the greatest benefits for long-term memory. However, with older adults, results also have shown that exercise performed after exposure provides benefits to long-term memory. In addition, numerous studies have shown that the benefits of exercise for long-term memory can be observed for up to 24 hours after the exposure (Etnier et al., 2021; Labban & Etnier, 2018; Slutsky-Ganesh et al., 2020), and this is supported by the Roig and colleagues (2013) meta-analysis, which showed larger effects for long-term memory (ES = 0.52) than for short-term memory (ES = 0.26). To put this effect size into perspective and into academic terms, if college students are taking a test that is fully reliant on memory (e.g., an anatomy test), exercising prior to studying would be expected to benefit recall on the test. That is, imagine that the grades on a test are normally distributed, and the average is an 80% with a standard deviation of 10%. In this case, the average student who exercised prior to studying for the test and took the test within the next 24 hours would be predicted to earn an 85% rather than an 80% simply because of the exercise. If the standard deviation were 20%, the exerciser would be expected to score 10% higher (0.52 effect size × 20% standard deviation = 10%). Clearly, the implication is that performing 20 to 30 minutes

CHAPTER 9 • Exercise and Cognitive Performance | 149

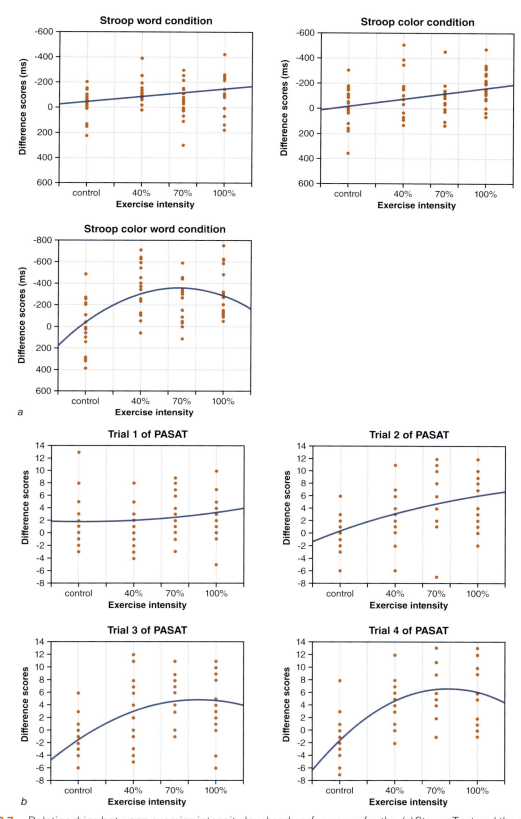

FIGURE 9.7 Relationships between exercise intensity level and performance for the (a) Stroop Test and the (b) PASAT.

Reprinted by permission from Y.K. Chang and J.L. Etnier, "Exploring the Dose-Response Relationship Between Resistance Exercise Intensity and Cognitive Function," *Journal of Exercise Psychology* 30, no. 5 (2009): 640-656.

of moderate-intensity exercise prior to your study time might result in benefits when you take a memory-based exam administered up to 24 hours later.

Chronic Exercise

As described earlier, chronic exercise has been tested as a means of improving cognition, protecting against cognitive decline, and treating cognitive decline. The research in this area has been focused largely on children or older adults. In fact, Sanders and associates (2019) conducted a search of the literature in preparation for conducting a meta-analytic review and only found one RCT with young adults; all others were with adults >50 years of age. The focus on children and older adults likely reflects the cognitive reserves hypothesis, which predicts that exercise might be most beneficial for those experiencing cognitive development (children) or those experiencing cognitive decline (older adults). Here we discuss meta-analytic and empirical evidence relative to children, epidemiological (prospective) studies with adults, and meta-analyses for both the general population of older adults and cognitively impaired older adults.

The Benefits of Chronic Exercise for Children

Several recent meta-analytic reviews of studies have been conducted, focused on chronic exercise in children. The results are consistent in showing a beneficial effect of chronic physical activity on cognitive performance with effects ranging from small to moderate. Among recent meta-analytic reviews, Fedewa and Ahn (2011) found a small benefit (ES = 0.32) across all cognitive tasks and study designs, Alvarez-Bueno and colleagues (2017) reported a small effect for both nonexecutive cognitive functions (ES = 0.23) and executive functions (ES = 0.20) across all studies, and Vazou and associates (2019) found a moderate overall effect size (0.46). In these meta-analyses, the authors included cross-sectional and quasiexperimental designs in addition to RCTs, thus perhaps inflating the effect size by including studies of lower quality. Importantly, however, even though Xue and colleagues (2019) limited their inclusion criteria to RCTs, they still reported a small overall benefit (ES = 0.20) for executive function tasks. This tells us that even when the studies are conducted using the highest quality design, a beneficial effect of chronic exercise on executive function is evident. In the beginning of this chapter, we discussed how important executive function during childhood is for academic performance and for physical health and success in later life. Although the evidence doesn't exist yet to confirm this link, the implication is that physically active children will experience gains in executive function that might translate into more positive outcomes across the life span.

Because all of these studies were focused on typically developing children, it is interesting to point out that some researchers have focused on the potential benefits for children with conditions that make school-based learning more challenging. Cerrillo-Urbina and associates (2015) limited their review to RCTS with children with ADHD to further our understanding of the potential benefits for children facing cognitive challenges. Their results showed moderate effects for physical activity on attention (ES = 0.84) and executive function (ES = 0.58). Tan and colleagues (2016) included studies with a broader age range of participants from children to young adults (3-25 yr) with ADHD or who were on the autism spectrum disorder. They reported benefits for both those with ADHD (ES = 0.18) and those with autism (ES = 0.47). Given that the effect sizes from these meta-analytic reviews with children with special needs tend to be larger than we see in the general population, this might suggest that exercise is particularly beneficial for children with ADHD or autism. Although these findings are encouraging, this body of evidence is not yet well developed, and additional research is needed to enhance our understanding of the potential role of exercise for these individuals.

Overall, when considering this literature with children, it is important to recognize that only a very small number of RCTs with large sample sizes have been conducted. This reflects the challenges in gaining access to children for this kind of long-term, invasive research, but this lack of RCTs is problematic in terms of our ability to pursue important research questions relative to children. Most of the RCTs that have been conducted have implemented their programs as after-school activities and have recruited younger (elementary school–aged) children. No doubt, this indicates the obstacles in place that make it incredibly challenging to manipulate physical activity exposure during the school day in a randomized trial, and the focus on younger children likely reflects that older children become unavailable due to their own extracurricular activities or homework.

An example of how these studies have typically been conducted is the FITKids trial, in which 221 children (7-9 yr of age) were randomly assigned to participate in physical activity after school (2 hr/day for 5 days/wk) or a wait-list control for 9 months (Hillman et al., 2014). The physical activity program was 2 hours in length, consisting of at least 70 minutes of moderate to vigorous physical activity achieved through age-appropriate physical activities. Following a healthy snack and a rest period, participants then played aerobically active games for 45 to 55 minutes. Measures of executive function were taken at the pretest (prior to the intervention) and at the posttest (at the conclusion of the 9-month intervention). Results of the FITKids trial showed that children in the physical activity group improved significantly more than did those in the wait-list control group for behavioral measures of executive function. Intriguingly, the results also showed that improvements in brain function (as assessed with EEG measures) and the improvement in performance on the cognitive flexibility task were correlated with the number of days participants attended the intervention. This lends credence to the hypothesis that the exercise was responsible for the observed changes in cognitive performance. This is an example of the important work being done to further our understanding of the value of physical activity for cognitive performance by school-aged children.

Research exploring the effects of exercise on cognition for children consistently shows that there are benefits. This is true when examined cross-sectionally and in the more limited body of evidence using RCTs. Given the relative deemphasis on the provision of physical education and physical activity during the school day for children, it will be critically important for additional RCTs to be conducted to better understand the potential role of physical activity for helping children reach their academic potential during their school-aged years. Furthermore, additional well-controlled studies are needed to enhance our understanding of specifically how we might achieve cognitive benefits in response to exercise. Interesting questions that have not yet been satisfactorily examined include the benefits of movement during classroom instruction, the benefits of recess and physical education during the day for cognitive performance, and the influence of the time of day of exercise on school-day cognitive performance.

The Benefits of Chronic Exercise for Adults

In the 21st century, over 20 meta-analytic reviews of the evidence for chronic exercise on cognitive performance by older adults have been conducted. Some have looked at the general population using epidemiological designs (Daviglus et al., 2011; Hamer & Chida, 2009; Sofi et al., 2011), some have tested the efficacy of physical activity programs conducting RCTs in the general population (e.g., Colcombe & Kramer, 2003; Falck et al., 2019; Northey et al., 2018), and others have focused on RCTs conducted with people with dementia (e.g., Farina, Rusted, & Tabet, 2014; Jia et al., 2019).

Epidemiological Designs in the General Population As a reminder, epidemiological studies are those in which researchers measure the independent variable (e.g., physical activity) at baseline and then measure the dependent variable (e.g., cognitive performance or clinical indicants of cognitive impairment) at a date that is typically several years in the future. In terms of the epidemiological evidence for exercise and cognition, the meta-analyses consistently find that participation in physical activity is protective against the risk of cognitive impairment (Blondell et al., 2014; Sofi et al., 2011), Alzheimer's disease (Daviglus et al., 2011; Hamer & Chida, 2009), and dementia (Blondell et al., 2014; Hamer & Chida, 2009). In particular, the risk of clinical impairment is 14% to 45% lower for those in the highest physical activity group compared to those in the lowest physical activity group. That means that older adults who play pickleball, walk, cycle, or swim are 14% to 45% less likely to become cognitively impaired in the future relative to the older adults who are not engaged in any form of physical activity. Importantly, the findings from the review by Sofi and associates (2011) further indicate that both the moderate physical activity group and the highest physical activity group achieved almost the same reduction of risk compared to the lowest physical activity group. This suggests that benefits can accrue even for those who are not participating in the highest levels of physical activity for their age group. The implication of these results is that you should encourage your middle-aged and older friends and family to initiate or maintain a lifestyle of physical activity because it will protect them against cognitive decline and perhaps clinical cognitive impairment as they get older. Even just walking has been shown to be effective in reducing the risk of subsequent cognitive impairment in older adults, with longer distances (Yaffe, Barnes, Nevitt, Lui, & Covinsky, 2001) and faster pace (Quan et al., 2017) being associated with less risk. So tell your mom, your dad, your aunt, your uncle, and even your grandparents that they need to get off the couch and start walking if they want to increase their likelihood of staying cognitively astute into older age.

RCTs Exploring the Benefits of Chronic Exercise for the General Population Colcombe and Kramer (2003) published a meta-analytic review that was extremely important in terms of promoting subsequent research on exercise and cognition. In their review, they focused exclusively on older adults (55-80 yr) and on randomized chronic exercise interventions. Their results showed an overall positive effect of exercise on cognitive performance (ES = 0.48). This was an important finding because of our knowledge that older adults often experience age-related cognitive decline and the implication that exercise might serve to slow down that decline. In other words, we know that as people age, we often see observable declines in their ability to do well on mental tasks. For example, you might notice that your grandmother isn't problem-solving as well or your grandfather is having a harder time remembering the groceries he was supposed to pick up on the way home. However, the great news from this review is that studies in which the physical activity levels of older adults were increased caused small improvements in cognitive performance. Colcombe and Kramer (2003) also reported that results were larger for studies focused on executive function tasks (ES = 0.68). This was important because these higher-order tasks are thought to be important for independent living and quality of life for older adults. Although results of the meta-analysis were also robust for controlled tasks (ES = 0.46) and spatial tasks (ES = 0.43), other scientists increasingly began to conduct research focused on executive function outcomes, and the literature in this area increased exponentially beginning a short time later (see figure 9.8).

In more recent meta-analytic reviews that limited the inclusion criteria to cognitively normal older adults, Northey and colleagues (2018) and Falck and associates (2019) reported small benefits for exercise on cognitive performance (ES = 0.29 and 0.24, respectively). Both of these overall effects are quite a bit smaller than was reported in the earlier review by Colcombe and Kramer (2003). Falck and associates attributed this to the importance of considering whether cognitive outcomes serve as primary or secondary outcomes in the original studies. That is, they made the important point that authors sometimes include numerous cognitive outcomes to test the specificity of the effects of the exercise intervention but don't actually expect exercise to benefit all of the outcomes assessed. For example, in the Physical Activity and Alzheimer's Disease-2 (PAAD-2) study, Park and colleagues (2020) assessed cognitive performance on 25 tasks from 5 different cognitive domains so that they could understand the specificity of the benefits of a 1-year exercise program for middle-aged and older adults with a family history of Alzheimer's disease. That is, they wanted to understand if the effects of exercise are greater for particular types of cognitive outcomes. They did not actually anticipate finding benefits on all 25 measures; they had primary and secondary outcomes and only expected to find changes in the primary outcomes. However, when they publish their results, they will likely report the findings for all measures. This would then mean that a reviewer conducting a meta-analysis might include all of their effect sizes in a review. In other words, in meta-analytic reviews, these effect sizes would all be averaged together, which would result

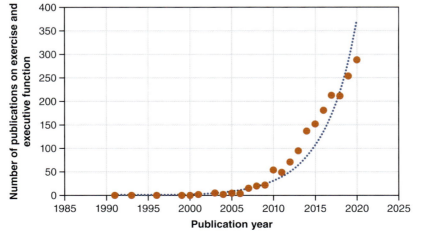

FIGURE 9.8 Graph of studies on exercise and executive function from 1990 to present.

in the secondary outcomes (which aren't expected to receive much benefit from exercise), biasing the overall effect size toward a smaller effect. In fact, Falck and associates examined this as a moderator and found that smaller effects were reported for secondary outcomes (ES = 0.15) compared to primary outcomes (ES = 0.36). Thus, we should expect to see an effect size of approximately one-third of a standard deviation for those cognitive outcomes expected to be most sensitive to the effects of chronic exercise.

Although this probably does not sound as powerful as a 14% to 45% reduced risk of cognitive impairment, these results are important because they tell us that older adults who have been sedentary for decades but who change their lifestyle to become more active can experience observable cognitive benefits after several months of physical activity participation. Results from a systematic review of this literature provide us with some initial guidance regarding the total amount of exercise necessary to observe benefits. Gomes-Osman and colleagues (2018) found that studies in which participants exercised for a total of 52 hours or more (typically administered as 1 hr/day, 3 days/wk for 20 wk) consistently experienced cognitive benefits, while those exercising for a total of <32 hours did not realize improvements. So even if your parents or grandparents have been sitting for years, they can start being active—even walking—to improve their cognitive performance with a 5-month commitment of 1 hour per day for 3 days per week being enough to see measurable cognitive gains. This is critically important from a public health perspective and when considering our aging society, but this is also important for all of us who have older adults in our lives about whom we care.

RCTs Exploring the Benefits of Chronic Exercise for Cognitively Impaired Individuals

A final body of evidence on this topic has developed around the beneficial effects of exercise for individuals who are already beginning to experience clinical forms of cognitive impairment (e.g., mild cognitive impairment [MCI], dementia, or Alzheimer's disease). Again, numerous meta-analytic reviews have been conducted to summarize the findings of these studies, and they consistently report beneficial effects. In fact, large effect sizes (>1.0) have been reported by Farina, Rusted, and Tabet (2014) and Jia et al. (2019), suggesting that exercise is particularly important for the maintenance of cognitive function in those who are already experiencing clinical measurable declines. This is perhaps startling given that these individuals are already experiencing significant, measurable declines, but it provides evidence that the brain remains plastic even in the face of serious challenges. This is important because it suggests that older adults with clinical impairment can experience substantive gains in cognitive performance that might dramatically enhance their quality of life. Although this evidence is very promising, future larger-scale RCTs are needed in this area because the existing research is typified by small sample sizes and less than ideal study designs.

Alternative Exercises to Benefit Cognitive Performance

Some researchers have been interested in examining specific modes of exercise such as resistance exercise, multimodal exercise (a combination of aerobic activities, resistance exercises, and balance training), tai chi, and cognitively engaging forms of physical activity. Results for these forms of exercise tend to be promising compared to the effects of aerobic exercise, which is the most commonly tested mode of exercise. For example, Northey and associates (2018) reported that aerobic exercise (ES = 0.24), resistance training (ES = 0.29), multimodal training (ES = 0.33), and tai chi (ES = 0.52) all significantly benefited cognitive performance.

Summary

Researchers have long been interested in the potential benefit of exercise for cognitive performance. Cognitive performance includes all kinds of thinking abilities from responding quickly to a green light to solving math problems and is important for academic success; job performance; and the ability to prioritize, organize, and plan in daily life. The intriguing aspect of this body of literature is that implications can be found for both acute and chronic exercise performed across the life span and by individuals who are both cognitively normal and cognitively impaired. In summary, the existing research suggests that a single session of exercise can have small but inconsistent benefits for cognitive performance during exercise and that these effects are likely to be intensity dependent and might be task specific. If performed in advance of the cognitive task, exercise has small, consistent benefits for cognitive performance in general and moderate benefits for measures of both short- and long-term memory. These benefits have been observed across the life span. Chronic exercise also has been shown to benefit cognitive performance, with the strongest empirical evidence available for older adults and weaker yet promising results for children and older adults with cognitive impairments. Perhaps most importantly, results strongly suggest that regular physical activity in older age can protect against the experience of clinical cognitive impairment and that even low-intensity physical activity, such as walking, can be beneficial. Overall, both single sessions of exercise and chronic participation in exercise have been shown to benefit cognitive performance.

Discussion Questions

1. Explain how inhibition is typically measured in laboratory settings. How is the time needed for inhibitory control isolated from the time needed for speed of processing?

2. Figure 9.7a shows part of the results from the Chang and Etnier (2009) study. Provide a brief explanation of the purpose of the study and the design. Explain what the results shown in this graph convey.

3. Looking at the chronic exercise literature, compare the findings from meta-analyses conducted on the general population of children compared to children with learning challenges. Explain how the cognitive reserves hypothesis might explain the findings observed.

4. Describe evidence showing that cognitive performance during exercise does not demonstrate consistent benefits, and discuss an empirical study that suggests that exercise intensity might determine the effects.

Exercise and Brain Health

OBJECTIVES

After studying this chapter, you should be able to do the following:

- Recognize the potential benefits of exercise for brain health in general and following a brain injury
- Understand the prevalence and implications of brain insults
- Characterize the different information provided by electroencephalography (EEG), magnetic resonance imaging (MRI), and functional MRI (fMRI)
- Describe parameters associated with brain health that are affected by exercise

KEY TERMS

traumatic brain injury (TBI)

concussion

sport-related concussions

stroke

neuroplasticity, brain plasticity, plastic

neurons

gray matter

white matter

invasive measure

electroencephalography (EEG)

spectral data

event-related potentials (ERPs)

functional magnetic resonance imaging (fMRI)

magnetic resonance imaging (MRI)

counterbalanced

"cocooning" model of care

Buffalo Concussion Treadmill Test (BCTT)

> Abigail was 9 years old when she suffered her first concussion during a soccer practice. She and her teammates were playing a game that resulted in her colliding head to head with another child on the team. She maintained consciousness but had a headache after the concussion. Fortunately, this initial concussion had only limited symptoms that cleared up within a couple weeks. In an effort to keep Abigail safe, her parents took her off her soccer team and enrolled her in crew to maintain her physical activity. About 4 months later, Abigail was playing soccer with her family in their backyard and was struck in the head with a soccer ball kicked by her dad. This second concussion was dramatically worse in terms of the severity and duration of the symptoms. Abigail had light and sound sensitivity, had difficulty concentrating, and had increasingly frequent migraine headaches. Her parents took her to the doctor for testing, and he recommended an MRI to make sure all was okay. This kicked off a series of visits to doctors' offices to seek help for Abigail. Although the light and sound sensitivity has abated over time, even years after the concussions, Abigail still experiences migraines that have limited her activities for years beyond the initial events.

After reading about Abigail and how she clearly experienced a concussion that occurred during physical activity participation, it might seem counterintuitive that this chapter is focused on how exercise might benefit brain health. These are two separate things because a collision or fall that occurs during physical activity participation and causes a concussion doesn't have any implications for how physical activity might generally affect brain health. The questions we should ask are how exercise might help with limiting the damage caused by an initial insult to the head, if exercise could play a role in helping alleviate symptoms and in facilitating a return to preconcussion behaviors, and more broadly if physical activity contributes to overall brain health.

Given the pervasiveness of the psychological benefits of exercise that we have discussed in previous chapters, it makes sense that exercise must be having an effect on the brain itself. In fact, for psychological outcomes such as depression, cognition, stress, and sleep, we have already considered some of the changes in the brain that might be mechanisms of the effects. In this chapter, we describe the existing evidence for effects of both acute exercise and chronic exercise on brain health. We'll talk about exercise and brain health in a presumably healthy organism and in an organism that has experienced a brain injury. As you'd expect, the effects in response to acute exercise are more transient in nature, while those in response to chronic exercise are more enduring. Different from previous chapters, in this chapter we discuss results from nonhuman animal studies because these provide a unique glimpse into the mechanisms and changes that cannot be directly observed in human studies. Neuroimaging studies also are presented because these provide an indirect view of changes in the human brain in response to exercise. Lastly, we will explore the literature that has considered how exercise might be protective against and used as a treatment for traumatic brain injuries (TBIs) including concussion and stroke.

What Is Brain Health?

When we speak of brain health, we are talking about the notion that a healthy brain allows for functioning across a variety of areas (e.g., cognitive, motor, behavioral, emotional) that allows the person to reach their potential. Brain health has been defined as "the preservation of optimal brain integrity and mental and cognitive function at a given age in the absence of overt brain diseases that affect normal brain function" (Wang et al., 2020, p. 1). Brain health also can be considered resiliency to injury and attributes that contribute to recovery from injury. Brain injuries consist of traumatic brain injuries and strokes. A **traumatic brain injury (TBI)** is defined by the Centers for Disease Control as a "disruption in the normal function of the brain that

---

traumatic brain injury (TBI)—TBI is defined by the Centers for Disease Control and Prevention as a "disruption in the normal function of the brain that can be caused by a bump, blow, or jolt to the head or a penetrating head injury" (Centers for Disease Control and Prevention, 2015, p. 15).

can be caused by a bump, blow, or jolt to the head or a penetrating head injury" (Centers for Disease Control and Prevention, 2015, p. 15). Symptoms of a TBI include a loss of consciousness, a loss of memory, neurologic deficits, and a state of altered thinking (e.g., disorientation, confusion, difficulty concentrating). Concussions are a subset of TBIs. A concussion results when the head moves rapidly in response to an impact, causing the brain to bounce against the skull or to twist such that brain cells are damaged. Sport-related concussions are a common form of a mild TBI experienced by adolescents and young adults and acquired during sport participation. Stroke is another form of brain injury that has a wide range of recovery outcomes ranging from complete recovery to years of lingering disability and even death. Stroke occurs when a blood vessel in the brain is either blocked (ischemic stroke) or ruptures (hemorrhagic stroke), resulting in a lack of oxygen supply to brain cells, which begin to die within minutes.

In addition to these brain injuries, other challenges to brain health can result from various diseases. Alzheimer's disease is a neurodegenerative disease that is caused by an increase in amyloid plaques and neurofibrillary tangles in the brain that disrupt neurological functioning. All dementias result in memory loss and declines in other cognitive abilities that ultimately affect daily living. Alzheimer's disease is the most common cause of dementia, accounting for approximately three-fourths of cases. Given that there is currently no cure for Alzheimer's disease, researchers are exploring the potential of physical activity to delay the onset of this disease and to slow its progression.

Risk of Repeat Concussion

The story about Abigail probably makes you think that this is a girl with bad luck. In fact, evidence suggests that having one concussion might increase your likelihood of having a subsequent concussion. Guskiewicz and colleagues (2003) reported on data from the NCAA Concussion Study, which reflected findings from 2,905 college football players across all three divisions. Results showed that athletes who self-reported previous concussions were more likely to have a concussion during the study. In fact, a dose–response relationship was observed such that compared to athletes who had not experienced a concussion within the previous 7 years, athletes with 1 previous concussion were 1.5 times more likely, those with 2 concussions were 2.8 times more likely, and those with 3 or more previous concussions were 3.4 times more likely to be concussed during the study period. Results also showed that those with three or more previous concussions had a longer recovery period compared to others. These findings suggest that those who have experienced multiple concussions might be more susceptible to future concussions, which the authors attribute to a possible increase in neuronal vulnerability.

Alzheimer's Treatments

Although there is currently no cure for Alzheimer's disease, the U.S. Food and Drug Administration approved the use of two drugs (aducanumab and lecanemab) for persons with early signs of Alzheimer's and with elevated levels of beta-amyloid (amyloid plaques) in the brain. Both of these drugs are considered monoclonal antibodies, and they work by targeting beta-amyloid plaque formation. Although the early findings for these drugs are incredibly promising because they reduce plaques and offer some hope regarding cognitive performance, they both come with concerning side effects. In trials with both of these drugs, adverse side effects were more common in the treatment group than in the placebo control group (Piller, 2022; Woloshin & Kesselheim, 2022), and some patients died when in the lecanemab condition (Piller, 2022). Although these serious side effects are of concern, it is hoped that through proper monitoring of patients and a recognition that blood thinners are contraindicated, the drug can effectively delay Alzheimer's disease while doctors also manage the risks from side effects.

---

concussion—A concussion can result when the head moves rapidly in response to an impact, causing the brain to bounce against the skull or to twist such that brain cells are damaged.

sport-related concussions—A common form of a mild TBI typically experienced by adolescents and young adults and acquired during sport participation is a sport-related concussion.

stroke—Stroke occurs when a blood vessel in the brain is either blocked (ischemic stroke) or ruptures (hemorrhagic stroke), resulting in a lack of oxygen supply to brain cells, which begin to die within minutes.

Remarkably, evidence suggests that the brain is much more plastic than once thought. **Neuroplasticity, brain plasticity,** or **plastic** are all terms used to describe the concept that the brain can be altered in terms of structure, function, or connections. Between 1890 and 1894, Cajal is credited with suggesting that brain capacity could be increased through the development of additional neural connections, and in 1894 he used the term *plasticity* to describe the brain's potential to show positive adaptations in response to environmental demands (DeFelipe, 2006). Plasticity is particularly relevant to this chapter because it describes the phenomenon by which the brain is able to recover after damage caused by TBI or strokes. It is intriguing to consider the potential of exercise to increase brain plasticity in healthy individuals and in those who have experienced brain injury. Continued advances in neuroimaging techniques will allow us to better understand the mechanisms underlying these effects, with a goal of being able to prescribe exercise as a preventative measure and a treatment.

Prevalence and Costs

As we know from previous chapters, exercise is important in terms of fostering a healthier brain to allow for better cognitive performance, mood, and stress management. Given that we have already reviewed prevalence data relative to these psychological outcomes, in this chapter we focus more on TBIs and stroke in terms of prevalence and costs. Exercise might be important in terms of providing a level of protection in the face of a trauma to the brain (e.g., concussion, traumatic brain injury, stroke), against the experience of clinical cognitive impairments due to diseases such as Alzheimer's and Parkinson's, and in terms of providing a treatment option for brain trauma and these chronic diseases.

In 2010 it was estimated that approximately 2.5 million individuals experienced TBIs that resulted in some form of hospital care (Centers for Disease Control and Prevention, 2015). Of these, 87% were treated and then released from emergency departments, 11% were hospitalized for some period of time and then released, and approximately 2% (52,844) died. In 2020 it's estimated that approximately 64,000 deaths occurred related to TBIs in the United States (Centers for Disease Control and Prevention, 2022). TBIs present a particular challenge to health care systems because they can cause both lingering and delayed deficits and often result in irreversible, permanent health effects. As a result, medical practitioners are beginning to consider TBIs to be a disease rather than a discrete event. In fact, estimates suggest that as many as 3.17 to 3.32 million people in the United States might have a compromised quality of life because of a TBI-related disability (Zaloshnja et al., 2008). Even more disturbing, when you consider people who have experienced a TBI that results in the need for acute inpatient rehabilitation, approximately 40% report that symptoms worsen over time and 20% become deceased within 5 years of the injury (Corrigan et al., 2014).

Survey data collected from high school students indicated that 20.8% of athletes and 11.2% of nonathletes had been diagnosed with at least one concussion in their lifetime (Veliz et al., 2019). Symptoms from sport-related concussions typically decline rapidly over the first 2 weeks after the incident; however, 10% or more of adolescents and adults may experience symptoms beyond this time period (Haider et al., 2021). TBIs obviously have significant negative effects on individuals, but they are also very costly injuries from an economic point of view. It is estimated that TBI-related medical costs are $37.6 billion annually and that the total costs of TBI are $93.0 billion per year (Lo et al., 2021).

It is estimated that 7 million adults have had a stroke and that 600,000 to 800,000 new or recurrent strokes occur in a given year. The incidence of stroke is essentially the same in men (192/100,000) and women (198/100,000) and increases with age. Stroke-related medical costs are estimated at $28.0 billion, with the annual total costs of stroke being estimated at $45.5 billion (Lo et al., 2021).

Mechanisms Explaining the Potential Effects of Exercise on Brain Health

Brain health can be improved by enhancements in brain structure and by increases in levels of neurochemicals and neurotransmitters in the brain. In thinking of brain structure (figure 10.1),

---

neuroplasticity, brain plasticity, plastic—Neuroplasticity, brain plasticity, and plastic are terms used to describe the concept that the brain can be altered in terms of structure, function, or connections.

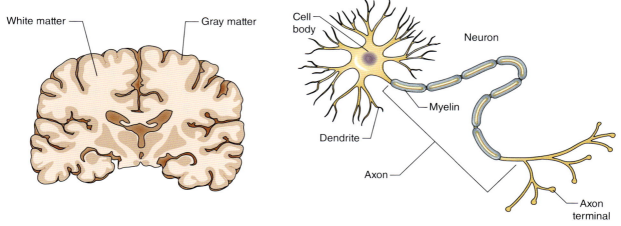

FIGURE 10.1 The brain is made up of neurons, which transmit messages in the nervous system.

it's important to consider neurons and the brain itself. Neurons are the cells that are responsible for transmitting messages within the brain and from the brain to the rest of the nervous system. They use a combination of electrical and chemical signals to relay these messages. **Neurons** consist of a cell body, an axon (which delivers messages away from the neuron), and a dendrite (which delivers messages to the neuron). The brain itself is made up of neurons, and we can identify two different kinds of tissue: gray matter and white matter. **Gray matter** consists of the cell bodies, dendrites, and axon terminal, which is where all of the synapses (connections between neurons) are. **White matter** consists of the axons and works to connect the gray matter areas with one another and with the brain's emotion system (the limbic system). White matter is organized into tracts, which are bundles of axons connecting various areas of the nervous system. These two tissues got their names because of how they look when examining tissue samples. Gray matter appears gray because of the gray nuclei contained in the cells, while white matter appears white due to the white fatty myelin tissue that surrounds the axons. Myelin is responsible for increasing the speed of transmission of messages along the axons.

In terms of the influence of exercise on healthy brain structure, changes that have been shown to be associated with better brain health include greater total brain volume, greater volume of specific structures with the brain (e.g., the hippocampus), better white matter tract integrity (Zarnani et al., 2019), and greater gray and white matter density (Franke & Gaser, 2019). With respect to neurochemicals and neurotransmitters, those that have been suggested as possible mechanisms in the relationship between exercise and brain health include brain-derived neurotrophic factor (BDNF), serotonin, dopamine, insulin-like growth factor (IGF-1), and vascular-endothelial growth factor (VEGF). To date, the vast majority of research has focused on BDNF.

Another proposition to explain the benefits of exercise for brain health is the cognitive reserves hypothesis. As it applies to brain health, the cognitive reserves hypothesis proposes that in the face of challenges to the brain (e.g., aging, depression, TBIs), participation in exercise enhances brain health. The cognitive reserves hypothesis suggests that brain health is improved through increases in cognitive reserves that are either functional (the idea that the brain develops functional redundancies and flexibility that can help the individual cope with challenges) or structural (greater brain volume, number and size of neurons, and cortical thickness that serves a protective function in the face of challenges). The cognitive reserves hypothesis proposes that exercise increases reserves in ways that are protective in the face of injury or other challenges to brain health (e.g., mental illness, normal aging) and that can improve functioning following a brain injury or relative to normal- or disease-related declines in functioning.

---

neurons—Neurons are cells in the nervous system that transmit information using electrical and chemical signals. They consist of a cell body (including the nuclei), dendrites (which receive information from other neurons), and axons (which transmit information to other neurons).

gray matter—Gray matter is tissue in the brain that consists of the cell bodies, dendrites, and axon terminals (where all of the connections between neurons are). When tissue samples are examined, gray matter looks gray because the cell nuclei of neurons are gray.

white matter—White matter is tissue in the brain that consists of the axons, which are organized into tracts or bundles, and provides the connections for the gray matter areas with one another and with the brain's emotion system (the limbic system). When tissue samples are examined, white matter looks white because of the white myelin sheath coating the axons.

Measurement

When considering the impact of exercise on the brain, the approach taken is dependent on whether nonhuman animal studies (referred to simply as *animal studies* going forward) or human studies are being conducted. One major benefit of animal studies is that measurements of brain health can be more invasive, making these studies valuable in terms of allowing a direct assessment of underlying mechanisms. An **invasive measure** is one that provides direct access to the interior of the body through an existing orifice or the creation of access through an incision. With animal models, researchers can assess changes in the brain through methods that are simply too invasive to be used with humans. In these studies, the animals sometimes are subjected to surgeries to allow for direct assessment or even manipulation of variables relevant to brain function. In other cases, animals are sacrificed at the end of the study so that surgical methods can allow direct assessment of brain neurochemicals or structure. This ability to gain direct access to the brain is a strength of animal research. Other advantages of using animal models are that the researcher can directly control the TBI event in terms of the cause, location, and intensity. This allows for the study on TBIs to be the same across animals. With humans who have experienced a TBI through natural causes, the cause, location, and intensity will vary significantly, which makes it harder to study TBI using human subjects. Finally, the use of animal models allows a direct and precise assessment of physical activity behaviors that is not possible to obtain in

Commotio Cordis and Animal Research

You might be familiar with an incident that occurred in an NFL football game on January 2, 2023. In that game, Damar Hamlin was struck in the chest during a tackle. He completed the tackle, got to his feet, and then just a few seconds later collapsed and lay motionless for an extended period of time. Emergency personnel got to him quickly to administer CPR and after spending approximately 1 week in the hospital, thankfully Damar has made a full recovery. In fact, on April 18, 2023, he was cleared by his physicians to return to football. Despite being only 25 years old, Damar actually went into cardiac arrest as a result of the blow to his chest. This is a good example of where research with animals has really informed our medical understanding of this event, which is called *commotio cordis* and occurs most commonly in young people.

Commotio cordis was first reported in the medical literature in the mid-1700s. It was first reported in sporting events in the 1905-1910 Reach Official American League Baseball Guide over which time frame 18 cases were reported (Boren, 2010). Commotio cordis is defined as "ventricular fibrillation and sudden death triggered by a blunt, nonpenetrating, ... blow to the chest without damage to the ribs, sternum, or heart and in the absence of underlying cardiovascular disease" (Maron & Estes, 2010, p. 917). Although Damar Hamlin survived this event, the vast majority of individuals who experience commotio cordis do not survive. For commotio cordis to occur, the blow must occur directly over the heart. Knowledge regarding the precise location of the blow comes partially from clinical evidence of bruises in that location. The timing of the blow is the other critical factor, and this knowledge comes directly from animal studies, which have been really important for allowing us to understand the critical timing for commotio cordis. Using anesthesized young pigs, researchers determined that the blow to the sternum has to occur within a specific 10-20 msec period within the cardiac cycle. This 10-20 msec window accounts for only 1% of the cardiac cycle, and a blow that occurs outside of that window will not cause the heart to go into arrythmia. Clearly, research with animals is the only way we could learn about the precise timing requirements of the blow, and this information may be important for helping to consider preventative measures and educational materials that can limit the incidence of commotio cordis.

---

invasive measure—An invasive measure provides direct access to the interior of the body through an existing orifice or the creation of access through an incision.

studies of humans in real-world environments. However, using animals to study the benefits of exercise for brain health also presents challenges. The primary challenge is that humans and animals are not equivalent, so responses observed with animals might not reflect what would be observed in humans. A second challenge is that the exercise being conducted by animals in research studies is not normal exercise for them. When forced to exercise, animals might have increased corticosterone responses that are different than they would have with voluntary exercise. But even with voluntary access provided through access to a running wheel, the living conditions of the animal cannot be considered normal because they are housed in a laboratory, regularly handled by humans, fed human-made processed foods, and often do not have access to litter mates or other animals. These limitations mean that we need to be cautious in how we interpret the results from animal studies with respect to generalizing to humans.

Studies looking at exercise in humans are obviously forced to rely on methods that are less invasive and hence less direct. One approach is to study changes in brain function using either electroencephalography (EEG) or functional magnetic resonance imaging (fMRI) or to look at brain structure using MRI. **EEG** is the measurement of brain activity by assessing electrical activity collected at the scalp. To assess EEG activity, an electrode cap or individual electrodes are affixed to the surface of the head with sites defined according to the International 10-20 system. Electrode gel is used to help transmit the small electrical current that is detected at the scalp and that is indicative of neural firing in the vicinity of the electrode. EEG recordings have relatively poor spatial sensitivity but have good temporal sensitivity. EEG data can be collected as **spectral data**, which can be decomposed to provide an indicant of the relative amount of activity of various frequencies (i.e., delta, theta, alpha, beta) (figure 10.2). This type of data is used primarily in sleep studies to ascertain the stage of sleep a person is in. In terms of brain health, measures of **event-related potentials (ERPs)** are more commonly used to look at brain function. ERPs are generated from extremely small electrical impulses (potentials) produced by the brain in response to a stimulus (the event). When assessed using EEG to measure electrical activity at the scalp, ERPs are the summation of these small electrical responses across the large number of neurons that are activated in response to a stimulus. Thus, ERPs are time-locked to the exposure to a stimulus and represent an average of neural activity in response to that stimulus. They are typically interpreted by identifying the peaks of the averaged electrical response in a predetermined window of time relative to the stimulus and then by calculating the amplitude and latency (time delay) of those peaks (see figure 10.2). For example, P300 is a positive-going peak activation that occurs at approximately 300 milliseconds after the stimulus exposure. This ERP component is interpreted as reflecting attentional focus. Functional MRI also provides an indication of brain function either at rest or in response to the performance of some task. **Functional MRI** provides data reflecting the level of oxygenated blood in various areas of the brain, and this provides an indirect indication of neural activity. FMRI has exceptional spatial sensitivity, allowing us to explore the effects of exercise on brain function locations with a high degree of accuracy. It does not have good temporal sensitivity, however. **MRI** uses a magnetic field and radio waves to provide three-dimensional anatomical images of soft tissues in the body. This provides structural data with a high level of precision that allows for the calculation of white and gray matter density and volumes of specific regions of the brain (e.g., hippocampus).

Another indirect approach that is used to assess brain health is to take blood samples from the periphery (often from venipuncture to draw blood from the median cubital vein in the arm) and to assess blood-based biomarkers of interest. These peripheral measures are then used to make inferences about what is happening centrally (i.e., in the brain). This approach has been commonly used with BDNF and other blood-based markers (e.g., IGF-1), with higher levels in the periphery being used to infer higher levels centrally.

---

electroencephalography (EEG)—EEG is the measurement of electrical current at the scalp, which is used to infer brain activity.

spectral data—Data obtained from EEG, which indicates the relative amount of activity of various frequencies (i.e., delta, theta, alpha, beta) are known as spectral data.

event-related potentials (ERPs)—Data generated from the summation of extremely small electrical impulses (potentials) produced by the brain in response to a stimulus (the event) are called ERPs.

functional magnetic resonance imaging (fMRI)—fMRI data reflects the level of oxygenated blood in various areas of the brain and provides an indirect indication of neural activity.

magnetic resonance imaging (MRI)—An MRI generates a magnetic field and radio waves to provide three-dimensional anatomical images of soft tissues in the body.

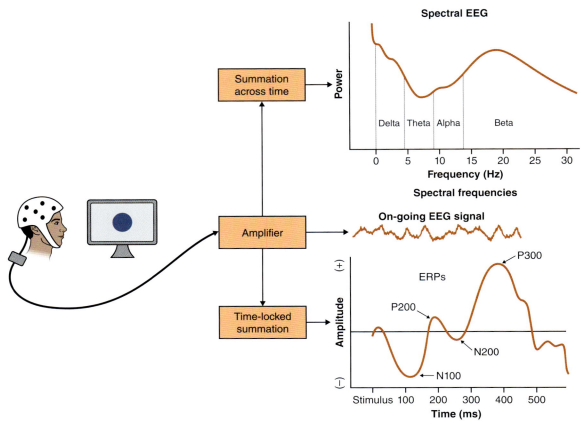

FIGURE 10.2 How electrical activity at the scalp in response to a stimulus can be analyzed to derive spectral frequency measures or event-related potential (ERP) measures.

Evidence Relative to the Effects of Exercise on Brain Health

As we move our attention to empirical and meta-analytic evidence relative to the effects of exercise on brain health, studies exploring the effects of both acute exercise and chronic exercise on brain health will be considered. This is because the relevant mechanisms and the nature of the effects are likely to be different for these two paradigms.

Acute Exercise

Given that the effects of acute exercise on brain health are thought to be relatively transient, it is perhaps not surprising that this body of literature is small. Researchers focused on the benefits of acute exercise typically have looked at effects on BDNF or effects as observed using measures of brain function. Thus, meta-analytic reviews of the literature on acute exercise on the brain have focused on studies examining changes in BDNF or that have used EEG measures to explore brain function.

BDNF

Szuhany and colleagues (2015) summarized the results of 14 studies and reported that a single session of exercise resulted in a moderate increase in BDNF (ES = 0.46). The authors interpreted these findings as showing that an individual session of exercise reliably increases BDNF. Dinoff and associates (2017) summarized results from 55 studies looking at acute exercise and BDNF in healthy adults. They found similar results to Szuhany and colleagues (2015) in that BDNF increased by approximately 60% following exercise. Dinoff and associates also looked at a dose–response question with their moderators and reported that longer duration and higher intensity exercise resulted in a greater increase in BDNF. With respect to duration, they found that sessions that were longer than 30 minutes resulted in a larger effect size (ES = 0.81) than did sessions shorter than 30 minutes (ES = 0.47).

In summary, evidence with healthy adults supports that a single session of exercise results in a significant increase in peripheral levels of BDNF. The expectation is that because BDNF crosses the blood-brain barrier, these increases peripherally reflect increases that are also occurring centrally and that are expected to benefit brain health and performance.

EEG

Studies that have examined EEG following an acute bout of exercise have focused primarily on children or young adults. Chu and colleagues (2017) conducted a study that provides a good example of the typical design of these studies. They recruited 40 healthy preadolescents and young adults. Fitness was tested on the first day using a standardized submaximal method, and then participants returned to the laboratory for 2 additional testing days. Using a within-subjects design, participants were asked to exercise for 30 minutes on one day and to read for 30 minutes on the other day with the order of conditions counterbalanced across participants. Counterbalanced means that one-half of the sample performed the treatment (exercise) on day one and the control condition on day two, while the other one-half of the sample performed the conditions in the reverse order. The use of this protocol is important because it ensures that any effects due to the order of presentation of the conditions are controlled. During the exercise condition, participants did a 5-minute warm-up, 20 minutes of exercise at 65% to 75% heart rate reserve, and a 5-minute cool-down. During the control condition, participants read educational documents for 30 minutes. Immediately following the treatment or control condition, participants performed the Stroop Test while having EEG recorded to capture ERPs. Results showed that P300 amplitudes were higher after exercise than after the control condition. In addition, reaction time was faster after exercise as compared to after control. (This effect was significant for the young adults and close to significant for the children.) Given the behavioral and ERP findings, the authors interpreted their results as showing that exercise results in a greater allocation of attentional resources during task performance that then benefited performance on an inhibitory control task. These benefits to ERP and concomitant improvements in cognitive performance are interpreted as supporting brain health benefits in response to acute exercise.

The literature examining the effects of physical activity on brain structure and EEG outcomes in children was meta-analytically reviewed by Meijer and associates (2020). Across nine studies, Meijer and associates reported that acute exercise resulted in small improvements in EEG (ES = 0.32). The studies used EEG to assess various aspects of brain functioning including neurophysiological functioning during rest and goal-directed behavior, the allocation of attentional resources, and conflict processing. Overall, a small body of evidence supports that a single session of exercise has a positive impact on brain function as observed using ERPs in studies with children.

Chronic Exercise

With chronic exercise, effects are expected to take longer to be observed but also to be more durable in nature. In looking at chronic exercise, some attention has been focused on BDNF because it is thought to be critically important as a mechanism of the benefits for brain structure. Changes in brain structure in response to exercise have also been explored using animal models and MRI.

BDNF

Szuhany and colleagues (2015) summarized the findings of 13 studies that explored the effects of chronic exercise lasting from 3 weeks to 2 years on resting levels of BDNF, and they reported a significant small increase in BDNF (ES = 0.27). They also considered the potential for a chronic training program to increase the BDNF response to a single session of exercise. Reviewing findings from eight studies, they reported that the pre- to postexercise increase in BDNF was significantly larger following chronic (3-24 wk) exercise programs (ES = 0.59). This suggests that the responsiveness or sensitivity of the BDNF system is increased through training, resulting in enhanced benefits from even an acute bout of exercise. This finding is intriguing because if the benefits of a single session of exercise are meaningful, given that they can be enhanced by regular exercise, that suggests that benefits are actually cumulative.

Brain Structure

More long-lasting benefits to brain health are expected to occur in response to chronic exercise. In fact, in response to chronic exercise that lasts for several months, scientists expect to see changes to actual brain structure. Both animal models (which allow for direct assessments of brain structure) and human models (which allow for indirect assess-

---

counterbalanced—A counterbalanced method of assigning participants means that one-half of the sample performs the treatment on day one and the control condition on day two, while the other half of the sample performs the conditions in the reverse order. This design ensures that any effects due to the order of presentation of the conditions will be controlled.

ments of brain structure using MRI scans) have been used to advance our understanding of the plasticity of the brain in response to exercise.

A seminal study on chronic exercise and brain health was conducted by Black and associates (1990) with female rats. Thirty-eight rats were raised in small groups until they were 10 months of age. At that time, they were randomly assigned to one of four treatment conditions for 30 days. The treatment conditions were a voluntary exercise condition (VX), a forced exercise condition (FX), an acrobatic condition (AC), and an inactive condition (IC). Rats in the VX group were given free access to a running wheel and learned quickly how to use the wheel to exercise. Rats in the FX group were placed on a treadmill designed specifically for rats and were trained to walk on the treadmill until they were exercising for 60 minutes per day. Rats in the AC group were trained to traverse a veritable obstacle course including balance beams, seesaws, and bridges (figure 10.3). Eventually, they were able to complete five trials of seven obstacles per day with the level of difficulty also increasing over time. These rats were encouraged and trained through the use of treats and gentle nudging. Rats in the IC group were in a sterile laboratory cage with limited opportunities for exercising or exploring. The researchers included some important controls to help them be able to attribute the changes they saw to the independent variables of the experiment (exercise and learning). For example, rodents in the VX and IC conditions were handled by the experimenters for 1 minute each day to help control for the handling necessary for those in the FX and AC groups, and those in the VX, IC, and FX groups were given small treats to control for the treats given for training in the AC condition. At the end of the study, the groups differed in terms of how much physical activity they had gotten as follows: IC—0 km; AC—0.6 miles (0.9 km); FX—6.7 miles (10.8 km); VX—11.8 miles (19 km). The design also meant that they differed in how much motor learning they accomplished, with the AC group being exposed to new learning across the entire 30 days while the FX and VX groups learned how to be active in a short period of time and the IC group had essentially no opportunity for learning. In terms of brain health, the results were truly remarkable. The FX and VX groups had an increase in the density of the capillaries in the motor areas of the cerebellum, which are important for movement, while the AC group had a 25% increase in the number of synapses without any measurable changes in capillary density. These results are incredible because they have important implications with respect to brain plasticity and health. If these results apply to humans, they suggest that brain health in terms of vascularization (the presence of capillaries, which provide nutrients and for the removal of waste products) is improved through repetitive, well-learned physical activity at a level that is not excessive for an animal. They further suggest that lower levels of physical activity when combined with learning of novel movements improves brain health by enhancing the communication system (i.e., the synapses). These findings suggest that the specific mode and intensity level of chronic physical activity are important for determining the changes in brain structure that occur. Future research with animals might show that combining higher levels of physical activity with motor learning promotes both types of benefits.

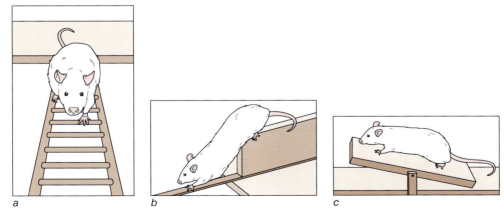

FIGURE 10.3 In Black and associates' (1990) study, animals in the acrobatic condition had *(a)* a rope ladder, *(b)* a high step, and *(c)* a seesaw to traverse.

Adapted from Black et al. (1990).

> Consider the findings from Black and associates' (1990) study. What types of activities for humans might achieve the same outcomes as were observed for the voluntary exercise (VX) and the acrobatic (AC) groups? What do you think about the forced exercise (FX) group as it might relate to humans? If future research with animals showed that combined physical activity with motor learning yielded the largest benefits, what types of activities might make sense for humans to replicate this?

Colcombe and colleagues (2006) presented results from the first randomized clinical trial (RCT) to explore the effects of a 6-month physical activity program on brain structure in older (60-79 yr) adults using MRI. In this study, 59 healthy older adults were randomly assigned to either an aerobic exercise group (AX) or a stretching and toning control group for 6 months. The key difference between the groups was the performance of aerobic exercise at 60% to 70% heart rate reserve (moderate intensity) for the AX group, while the control group met for the same amount of time (3 times/wk for 1 hr) but only did a stretching program. The researchers hypothesized that the participants in the AX group would realize benefits to brain health that could be measured using MRI and that would not be observed in the control group. Their results supported the hypothesis in that participants in the AX group had increases in brain volume, particularly in the frontal lobes, that were not evident for the control group. Results of this study are astounding because they showed for the first time that participation in an exercise program that meets the current physical activity recommendations (USDHHS, 2018) is sufficient in older adults to improve brain health by changing the structure of the brain to increase the resources available for performance.

Most of the research on chronic exercise and brain structure has been conducted with older, healthy adults. This is likely a reflection of interest in the cognitive reserves hypothesis, which posits that older adults are probably experiencing declines in their cognitive reserves that are measurable using MRI and that are amenable to change in response to exercise. Systematic and meta-analytic reviews of this literature are fairly consistent in showing significant changes in brain structure in response to chronic exercise (Firth et al., 2018; Sexton et al., 2016; Zheng et al., 2015).

Zheng and associates (2015) reviewed findings from nine studies exploring the effects of RCTs on brain structure in adults over 55 years of age. Results showed significant increases in the volume of several regions of the brain. In particular, they found significant benefits of exercise in terms of increases in volume in the frontal cortex (important for higher-order cognitive processing), temporal cortex (important for the perception of emotions of others), and cingulate gyri (a part of the limbic system important for the experience of emotions). In their conclusions, Zheng and associates pointed out that the number of studies is relatively small given the heterogeneity of the intervention length (12 wk to 14 mo), the type of exercise used (including walking, dancing, tai chi), the duration of sessions (ranging from 10 to 90 min per session and from 1 to 5 sessions per wk). Although this heterogeneity is viewed by the authors as a limitation, it might also be considered a strength because significant effects were found on average, suggesting a relatively robust relationship that can be observed across a variety of exercise programs.

Sexton and colleagues (2016) reviewed five cross-sectional studies that looked at total white matter volume and nine cross-sectional studies that looked at white matter lesions relative to groups participating in different levels of physical activity. With age, white matter volume is known to decrease, and the volume and severity of white matter lesions are known to increase. White matter lesions are areas where the myelin sheath has been disrupted, resulting in communication disruptions. Results from this review indicated that exercise was associated with greater white matter volume (ES = 0.22) and fewer white matter lesions (ES = 0.17) for healthy older (>60 years) adults. The authors of this review drew cautiously optimistic conclusions from their data, suggesting that physical activity has the potential to benefit white matter brain health in older adults.

Firth and associates (2018) summarized the results from 14 studies (N = 737 participants) examining the effects of chronic exercise specifically on hippocampal volume. They found no effect for total hippocampal volume when examined across all studies. However, when they excluded studies of adults with clinical psychiatric disorders and older adults with clinical cognitive impairment and limited the analyses to studies that focused on healthy older adults (6 studies; N = 390 participants), they did find significant increases in the volume of both the left (ES = 0.36) and right (ES = 0.24) hippocampus. These findings for exercise benefiting hippocampal volume are important because

> ### Exercise and Chromosomes
>
> One interesting line of research has focused on the relationship between exercise and telomere length. Telomeres are protein structures that occur at the ends of chromosomes and that are important for preserving genome information during cell division. Telomeres are shortened as a side effect of cell division, and this shortening is a biomarker of cell aging. It has been suggested that a healthy lifestyle including physical activity can preserve telomere length and hence provide a level of protection against dementia and cognitive impairment. Mundstock and colleagues (2015) meta-analytically reviewed 11 studies testing correlations between physical activity behavior and telomere length and 15 studies testing differences in telomere length between active and inactive participants. Results for the correlational analysis were not significant. But results for the cross-sectional comparisons showed a large benefit of activity level on telomere length (ES = 0.91). This finding has since been replicated in a large RCT. Sindi and associates (2021) reported on a subsample of participants from the Finnish Geriatric Intervention Study to Prevent Cognitive Impairment and Disability (FINGER). Older adults (60-77 yr) who were cognitively normal (or experiencing only slight impairment) were randomly assigned to a 2-year multidomain intervention (nutrition, exercise, cognitive training, management of metabolic and vascular risk factors) or a control condition (regular health advice). Although overall significant differences were observed in the change in telomere length between control and experimental groups, important differences occurred in particular subgroups. That is, participants in the experimental group who were APOE e4 carriers (those at greatest genetic risk for Alzheimer's disease) (M = 0.049), younger (<70 yr) (M = 0.035), and who made the largest healthy lifestyle changes (M = 0.022) all showed slight increases in telomere length (i.e., the means are positive) in response to the multidomain intervention, while participants who were noncarriers, older, and made the least amount of healthy lifestyle change showed negligible changes in telomere length. These findings have important implications because they suggest that exercise might affect telomere length in a way that would lessen cell death and therefore might protect against age-related and clinical declines in cognitive performance.

we know that hippocampal volume decreases with increasing age (even during healthy aging) and that this decrease is associated with cognitive decline. Hence, these results suggest that exercise might play a role in protecting the hippocampus against normal age-related declines.

Although this body of evidence is fairly small, the results of these reviews provide evidence to support that physical activity is beneficial for brain structure. This is clearly important because it is only recently that we've even understood that brain health can be improved in the face of advancing age. The implications of these improvements in brain health for cognitive performance and for the long-term protection against cognitive decline will be important directions for future research.

Exercise, TBI, and Stroke

In addition to exercise having benefits for healthy brains, exercise also might be important as a way of mitigating the effects of a TBI, treating a patient after a TBI, preventing a stroke, and treating a patient following a stroke. These bodies of evidence are just emerging, so this will be an intriguing area of research to follow in upcoming years.

Exercise and the Mitigation of the Effects of TBI

An emerging area of research is to explore the potential for the benefits of exercise for overall brain health to then mitigate the effects of a TBI. Animal studies provide a way to explore the effects of preinjury exercise on the actual damage caused by a TBI. This idea has been termed *exercise preconditioning*, and it's been noted that it's inherent in many situations with a high risk for TBI (e.g., American football, boxing, military). Researchers studying this notion typically have exercised rodents and then exposed them to a carefully controlled traumatic brain event such as a decrease in blood supply. Results show that exercise provides a kind of neuroprotection such that the damage caused by the TBI is less and recovery is faster for exercised rodents as compared to unexercised rodents. Mechanisms that have been proposed include increases in neurotrophin availability, strengthening of the blood-brain barrier, enhanced vascularization in the brain, decreased inflammation and cell death, and enhanced cerebral metabolism (Yokobori et al., 2013).

Exercise in the Treatment of TBI

Early research in this area focused on the use of animal models as a way to safely explore the potential benefits of exercise for humans following a concussive event. However, the body of evidence from animal studies is relatively challenging to interpret given the wide variety of protocols that have been used. In animal studies, rodent models are most common, but various models of TBI have been used to mimic direct blows, noncontact concussive events, and stroke, and exercise has been implemented as either voluntary or forced with different starting dates of the exercise relative to the injury and highly variable doses of exercise. The distinction between voluntary and forced exercise in animal models is clearly an important one because forced exercise can result in elevations in corticosterone indicative of a stress response, and corticosterone is likely to exacerbate the effects of a TBI. In general, results from these animal studies show that exercise increases cerebral growth factors, neurogenesis, neuronal survival, neuronal regeneration, and cerebral blood flow, and it decreases apoptosis (cell death) and lesion sizes (Wogensen, Mala, & Mogensen, 2015). Additionally, it increases the integrity of the blood-brain barrier (Archer, Svensson, & Alricsson, 2012). Hence it is expected to have a positive impact on cognitive performance after a TBI. When considered in whole, results generally show that for either voluntary or forced exercise, studies that use early starting points for the exercise see negative effects, but studies using later starting points for the exercise (e.g., 14 days after injury) tend to show consistent benefits to cognitive recovery (Wogensen et al., 2015).

For years, the standard of care for concussions for humans used the "cocooning" model of care, which prescribed complete rest and the avoidance of all physical and cognitive activity until the symptoms had fully abated. This recommendation was made even to people who were experiencing persistent postconcussive symptoms (i.e., lasting more than 2 wk for adults or more than 1 mo for adolescents). More recently, the Concussion in Sport Group recommended that this rest period be limited to 24 to 48 hours, followed by a gradual increase in physical activity that does not exacerbate symptoms (McCrory et al., 2017). This gradual increase in exercise intensity and duration allows the body time to recover from the concussion in terms of being able to tolerate the exercise bout. Leddy and colleagues (2018) explained that metabolic and physiologic changes in the aftermath of a concussion result in individuals initially experiencing hypoventilation during exercise, which exacerbates the concussion symptoms. The hypoventilation results in increased partial pressure of CO_2, which increases cerebral blood flow in a way that is disproportionate to the exercise intensity and is associated with the increased reports of symptoms. By contrast, when exercise is performed at a low enough intensity, the exercise ventilation and the partial pressure of CO_2 become normalized, and symptoms are not experienced.

Leddy and associates (2019) conducted an RCT to compare the efficacy of subsymptom threshold aerobic exercise (exercise) with a stretching exercise (control) program. Adolescents (*n* = 103) were enrolled within 10 days of sustaining a sport-related concussion and were randomly assigned to the exercise or control groups. Participation in the study was not initiated until participants were at least 48 hours after the concussive event. All participants performed the Buffalo Concussion Treadmill Test (BCTT) to identify their heart rate at the point of symptom exacerbation (BCTT HR). In this treadmill protocol, participants begin at a speed that results in a brisk walk on a level grade. At 1-minute intervals, the grade is increased by 1 degree until the treadmill is at 15 degrees. At this point, speed is increased every minute. The test is stopped when participants have an increase in symptoms, reach 90% of age-predicted heart rate max, ask to stop, or report a rating of perceived exertion (RPE) >17. Participants in the exercise group were asked to exercise daily at an intensity of 80% of BCTT HR until one of two things occurred: Symptoms increased by 2 or more points on a 10-point scale or they had completed 20 minutes of exercise. Control participants were asked to perform low-intensity, whole-body stretching exercise for 20 minutes per day. All participants performed the BCTT weekly to identify full recovery (the ability to exercise to exhaustion without exacerbating symptoms) and to adjust the BCTT HR for those in the exercise group. Results showed that exercisers recovered significantly more quickly (median = 13 days) than did controls (*M* = 17 days), were less likely to experience delayed (>30 days) recovery (*n* = 2/52 participants; *M* = 50 days) than controls (*n* = 7/51 participants; *M* = 58 days), and

---

"cocooning" model of care—The cocooning model of care was the standard of care for individuals who had experienced a concussion, and it recommended complete rest from physical and cognitive activities until symptoms completely abated.

Buffalo Concussion Treadmill Test (BCTT)—The BCTT is an exercise test performed on a treadmill by a person who has sustained a concussion to identify the heart rate at the point of symptom exacerbation (BCTT HR). This heart rate is then used to guide recommendations of intensity for daily subsymptom threshold exercise intended to hasten recovery.

showed a tendency to report lower daily symptom scores than did the controls across time. The authors concluded that subsymptom threshold aerobic exercise safely improved recovery for adolescents who had experienced a sport-related concussion. These results are fascinating because they suggest that the performance of exercise can actually speed recovery from a concussion.

Exercise and the Prevention of Stroke

Physical activity has been shown to reduce the risk of stroke in older adults in numerous prospective studies. For example, Lee and Blair (2002) measured aerobic fitness using a maximal exercise test (the gold standard or best measure of aerobic fitness) in 16,878 men ages 40 to 87 years. They followed these men for an average of 10 years to identify deaths from stroke. Results showed that high-fit men had a 72% reduction in risk and moderately fit men had a 65% reduction in risk compared to low-fit men. It is important to point out that aerobic fitness has both a genetic and a behavioral component, so the results of this study cannot be distinguished as being due to physical activity because physical activity was not manipulated to increase aerobic fitness.

Meta-analytic reviews summarize the findings from prospective studies that have focused on physical activity as a predictor of the subsequent risk of stroke. The findings of individual prospective studies have been meta-analytically reviewed on several occasions, with results confirming a reduction in risk for those individuals who are the most physically active (see figure 10.4). Lee and colleagues (2003) summarized the findings of 23 studies and found that very active individuals had a 27% reduction in risk and moderately active individuals had a 20% reduction in risk compared to those with low levels of physical activity. Interestingly, Wendel-Vos and associates (2004) reported on the effects of physical activity when considered as leisure activity versus occupational activity. The results from the 33 studies they reviewed showed that both leisure and occupational physical activity offered protection against the risk of stroke with reductions in risk ranging from 15% to 43%. More recently, Reimers and associates (2009) conducted a meta-analytic review of 33 studies and found that people who were the most physically active had a 20% to 30% reduction in the risk of fatal or nonfatal stroke compared to those who were the least active. Although the precise amount of reduction in risk differs between these meta-analytic reviews, it is

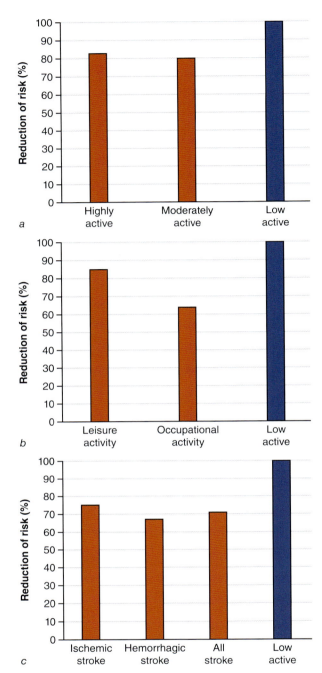

FIGURE 10.4 Results of three meta-analytic reviews summarizing the effects of prospective studies looking at the potential benefits of physical activity for stroke prevention: (a) Lee et al. (2003), (b) Wendel-Vos et al. (2004), and (c) Reimers et al. (2009).

(a) Adapted from Lee et al. (2003). (b) Adapted from Wendel-Vos et al. (2004). (c) Adapted from Reimers et al. (2009).

clear that the summary statistics support that those with higher levels of physical activity have a reduced risk of stroke in their future, and some evidence supports that this is a dose–response relationship such that higher levels of physical activity are more protective than moderate levels of physical activity.

Exercise in the Treatment of Stroke

Treatment of stroke has only relatively recently begun to include physical exercise. The outcomes that are typically reported in these studies are traditional cardiovascular risk factors rather than reporting on the effects on the symptoms of the stroke or the experience of a subsequent stroke. D'Isabella and colleagues (2017) summarized findings from 14 RCTs examining the effects of a chronic exercise intervention on cardiovascular outcomes for stroke survivors. Results showed that exercise significantly reduced resting systolic blood pressure, fasting glucose, and fasting insulin and significantly increased high-density cholesterol. All of these are positive responses to the exercise that would be expected to lead to a decreased risk of a subsequent stroke. In fact, resting systolic blood pressure was found to decrease by 5.3 mm Hg, which might have clinical meaningfulness because evidence suggests that a 10 to 12 mm Hg reduction reduces the risk of stroke by 30% and the risk of cardiovascular mortality by 25%.

Vanderbeken and Kerckhofs (2017) reviewed studies looking at the effects of exercise for participants who had previously experienced a stroke. In their review, they focused on cognitive outcomes and reported that in chronic exercise studies lasting longer than 8 weeks, gains in global neurocognitive functioning were consistently observed. Interestingly, this was only true when the exercise intervention took place after a delay following the stroke. When the exercise intervention was implemented in the early stages of recovery from the stroke (i.e., within the first year), benefits of exercise beyond what was observed in the usual care comparison group were not observed. The authors hypothesized that the benefits obtained from physical therapy and other rehabilitation techniques in the first year made it difficult to see additional benefits from physical activity. However, studies that looked at the effects when exercise was initiated more than a year after the stroke consistently showed positive effects. Most studies looked at aerobic training with exercise performed from 3 times per week to daily and lasting 30 to 90 minutes per session.

Exercise and the Recurrence of Stroke

Exercise has also been directly explored as a behavior that might reduce the risk of having a second stroke after experiencing a first stroke (i.e., recurrence). The rate of recurrence in the United States is estimated at 16% to 29%, and in China it's comparable at 29.43%. In a study conducted in China, Hou and associates (2021) conducted a 6-year prospective study with 760 participants who had survived their first ischemic stroke and were capable of exercising. They were interviewed at baseline and at 3-month intervals to capture their physical activity behaviors and numerous covariates that were controlled for in their statistical modeling. Results showed that compared to nonexercisers (the reference group), the risk of a second stroke was significantly reduced for those who exercised, with a dose–response relationship evident for the number of exercise sessions per week and the number of hours per week (see figure 10.5).

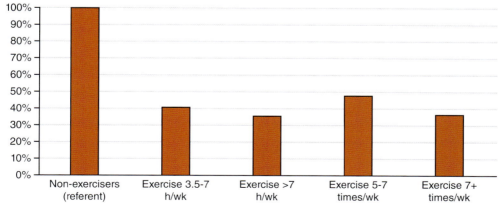

FIGURE 10.5 Odds ratios of having a second stroke after an initial ischemic stroke (Hou et al., 2021). This suggests a dose–response effect such that increasingly more exercise (h/wk or times/wk) provides added risk reduction.
Adapted from Hou et al. (2021).

Summary

Given the many psychological benefits of exercise that have been discussed, it is probably not surprising to learn that exercise has an effect on brain health in terms of brain structure and function. Acute exercise has observable benefits for BDNF availability, and evidence shows that the BDNF increase in response to a single session of exercise is enhanced by participation in regular physical activity. EEG evidence also supports that a single session of exercise can enhance brain function through increasing our ability to allocate attentional resources. Chronic exercise is expected to have more enduring benefits than does acute exercise. Evidence for benefits to structure are observed in response to regular exercise, with animal studies showing increases in capillary density and synapses depending on the particular type of activity performed. Human studies also have shown that participation in 6 months of regular physical activity increases brain volumes, with the largest benefits observed in frontal areas. When meta-analytically reviewed, the body of evidence with chronic exercise in humans consistently shows increases in white matter volume, decreases in white matter lesions, increases in left and right hippocampal volume in healthy older adults, and increases in volume in frontal cortex and temporal cortex.

These benefits of exercise in terms of improving brain health have implications for situations where the brain is exposed to injury. In animal studies, regular exercise has been shown to mitigate the effects of a TBI. In human studies, exercise has been shown to reduce the risk of an initial stroke and of a second stroke. Furthermore, exercise initiated between 3 and 10 days after the concussive event and performed at subsymptom threshold levels for 20 minutes per day hastens the recovery period. Regular exercise also has been shown to improve cardiovascular risk factors in stroke survivors and to benefit global cognitive functioning when performed 1 year after the stroke. Thus, overall, exercise has clear benefits to brain structure and function (brain health) and has been shown to mitigate the negative consequences of TBIs when performed before exposure and to facilitate the recovery process when appropriately administered following exposure.

Discussion Questions

1. What did Black and colleagues (1990) do, and what did they find? What are the implications of their findings for exercise by humans?
2. When we talk about the cognitive reserves hypothesis, what are the two types of reserves and how are they defined?
3. What is the implication that the effects of a single session of exercise on BDNF are increased for regular exercisers?
4. What are some of the challenges of studying TBI in humans?
5. What is a major pro and some cons of conducting research using nonhuman animals?
6. Describe how exercise should be used to reduce symptoms after a concussion, and explain the key factors in these recommendations.

Exercise and Self-Esteem

CHAPTER OBJECTIVES

After studying this chapter, you should be able to do the following:

- Understand what self-esteem is and that it is a multidimensional, hierarchical construct
- Recognize that the adoption of a multidimensional, hierarchical model for self-esteem guides the measurement instruments that will be used and the research questions that can be answered
- Discuss the psychological mediators of the effects of exercise on self-esteem
- Describe research evidence relative to the effects of exercise on self-esteem in children and older adults

KEY TERMS

self-concept

global self-esteem

multidimensional

hierarchical

self-confidence

self-efficacy

> In high school Naomi was an athlete and a strong student who had a lot of good friends and seemed to be happy and confident. Her self-esteem was high; she saw herself as an accomplished student-athlete with good interpersonal skills and a strong network of social support. Naomi decided to take a gap year to give herself the chance to learn more about the best college and career path for her. Now, Naomi is 19 years old and living at home while taking some online classes and working a part-time job. Her closest friends from high school have all gone away to college, and she hasn't made any new friends at her job. Naomi's self-esteem is low because she feels embarrassed to be living at home, disappointed not to be in a new town meeting new friends, and sad to not have her closest friends around to hang out with. When a coworker invites Naomi to join a group of people going to a nightclub, she declines because she is intimidated by the thought of dressing up to go to a social place where people will be checking each other out. Naomi's parents are concerned because their daughter doesn't seem to be brimming with the same level of confidence and happiness as she had been in high school. They consider asking Naomi to seek therapy but also wonder if joining a local running club might give Naomi a chance to engage in an activity she previously had enjoyed and provide another avenue to meet new people. In the end, they suggest the running club and are pleasantly surprised when Naomi agrees to attend a daily group run. Naomi returns from the run feeling tired but also seems more positive and self-assured than she has in recent weeks. Her parents hope that continued participation will help Naomi regain her previously high self-esteem and will start her on a path toward being happier.

This story demonstrates a potential link between physical activity and self-esteem. Self-esteem is an important construct both because it defines how we feel about ourselves and because it is so closely linked to other psychological constructs such as well-being, overall happiness, emotional stability, and resilience to stress. In fact, as we will learn in this chapter, self-esteem is considered a basic psychological need that we are driven to satisfy. The question we consider in this chapter is whether physical activity participation influences self-esteem and whether this is specific to aspects of self-esteem that are tied to physical performance or athleticism or if they extend to more global (whole-person) self-esteem.

Defining Self-Esteem and Self-Concept

Before considering research on the topic of exercise and self-esteem, we need to define several constructs to help us refine our focus on this topic. **Self-concept** is a broad term that describes the way we see or define ourselves. When we ask ourselves the question "Who am I?" our answers describe our self-concept or how we view ourselves. When I ask myself this question, my answer includes that I am a mother, a spouse, a scientist, a teacher, and an athlete. These aspects of my identity have an impact on my view of the world and how I make sense of the world. Because I consider myself to be a mother, I have a difficult time seeing children in distress even in commercials or movies, and I feel myself wanting to provide support for people in need. Because I am a scientist, I listen critically to news stories about exciting new findings, and I consider ways to scientifically address challenging problems. Because I see myself as an athlete, I make exercising a part of my daily life and seek opportunities to engage in recreationally competitive sport activities. These are examples of how self-concept affects the way we interact with others and the world.

Closely tied to self-concept is the construct of self-esteem. **Global self-esteem** brings in the idea of worth or value. It is the evaluative or affective consequence of my judgments of success relative to my self-concept. It is how we answer questions such as "How do I feel about who I am?" If my self-

---

self-concept—Self-concept is a broad term that describes the way we see or define ourselves.

global self-esteem—The evaluative or affective consequence of judgments of success relative to self-concept is called global self-esteem.

Self-concept is how we see ourselves. If we have high self-esteem, we evaluate our self-concept in a positive way.

esteem is high, I tend to evaluate myself positively in most aspects of my self-concept. However, if my self-esteem is low, that means that I evaluate myself negatively in most aspects. Interestingly, we also must consider how important the various aspects of our self-concept are to us at a given point in our lives. When I participated in sport in college, this was a top priority for me, and I cared very much about how I was judged and how I evaluated myself as an athlete. But, at this point in my life, while being an athlete remains something I am proud of and that I know affects my choices and behaviors, it is not something in which I am very invested. Therefore, when I judge myself as being slower, weaker, and less agile than I once was, it does not have a big impact on my overall self-esteem. By contrast, because I place great emphasis on my role as a teacher, being a good teacher is important for my overall self-esteem. A conceptual formula for self-esteem that reflects these ideas was proposed by William James (1883). He said:

> So our self-feeling in the world depends entirely on what we *back* ourselves to be and do. It is determined by the ratio of our actualities to our supposed potentialities; a fraction of which our pretensions are the denominator and the numerator our success; thus,
>
> self-esteem = Successes/Pretensions

Such a fraction might be increased as well by diminishing the denominator as by increasing the numerator.

This language from 1883 is a little hard to follow. James is using *pretensions* and *supposed potentialities* equivalently, both terms referring to our expectations for ourselves, and this is in the denominator of the formula. The numerator is our evaluation of areas of our self-esteem where we have been successful. If our successes match with our expectations, self-esteem will be high (i.e., 100%). If our successes do not match up to our expectations, self-esteem will be relatively lower (e.g., 80%). If you apply this formula to the relevant domains of your life, this should make sense. If you care a lot about your academic performance, your successes in academics have the potential to contribute to higher levels of self-esteem (and vice versa). But if you don't care much about, for example, your ability to play a musical instrument, then being unable to play an instrument is not likely to have a negative impact on your self-esteem.

> On a piece of paper, write down descriptors that explain who you are. Consider the many roles that you fill in your life. Once you have written these down, now draw a large circle. Divide the circle into "pie pieces" with each descriptor being placed into a pie piece. The size of the pie piece should represent how important that aspect of your identity is to you. Outside of each pie piece, write down some characteristics or positive words that describe your successes relative to each descriptor. After you have finished, look over your work and notice if there is anything that surprises you about your self-concept circle or about the evaluations on the outside. What does this tell you about the factors that contribute to your self-esteem?

Self-esteem is deemed so important that Maslow's psychological needs theory (Maslow, 1943) includes self-esteem as a psychological need that is linked to happiness and that serves as an important motivator (figure 11.1). The illustration of the needs hierarchy demonstrates how psychological needs are viewed. That is, according to Maslow, our primary need that will be our greatest motivator is to satisfy our immediate physiological requirements (the bottom of the hierarchy). This includes things such as hunger and warmth, suggesting that we will be very motivated to act if we experience either of these needs (i.e., if we are hungry or cold). Once these needs have been satisfied, our attention turns to safety, which can be thought of broadly in modern society to include feeling physically safe but also having financial stability, safety to express our feelings, and safety to be ourselves. Once this need is satisfied, the next priority is to experience a sense of belongingness and affection. We will seek this from our immediate family members, from our significant others, and from our friends. Next comes the need to have positive feelings of esteem, which Maslow also describes as self-respect. When other needs have been satisfied, the need for self-esteem—that is, the need to feel valued, capable, and accomplished—becomes a priority. Last in Maslow's hierarchy is self-actualization, which suggests that we all have a need to perceive that we have reached our full potential.

It is an indicant of the enduring accuracy of Maslow's needs hierarchy that the model remained essentially unchanged for more than 70 years. Kenrick and colleagues (2010) proposed a modification of the hierarchy that was meant to more clearly describe the idea of self-actualization. In Maslow's hierarchy, self-actualization was at the pinnacle of the hierarchy, but Kenrick and colleagues replaced self-actualization with needs related to procreation. Importantly, even this reenvisioned hierarchy retains the prioritization of self-esteem before these other primary needs. You might notice that constructs that we sometimes believe should be associated with happiness are not included in either model. That is, even people who are popular, rich, or powerful are not necessarily happy if they have not met the needs described in these models.

As currently considered, self-esteem is important for psychological health and identity and is viewed as both a resource and an asset. As such, it is important for a person's well-being. It is also

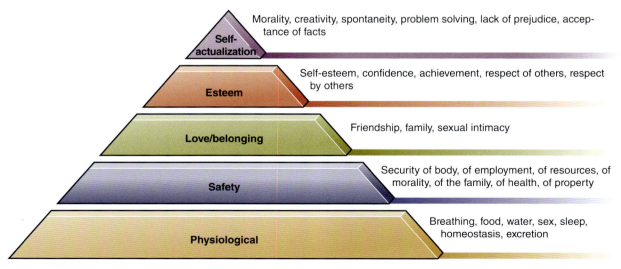

FIGURE 11.1 Maslow's original hierarchy of needs.

important to point out that self-esteem is in many ways a reflection of our expectation for evaluation by others. In other words, self-esteem is at least in part a reflection of ourselves as viewed in a social mirror, with the reflection itself strongly influenced by our social group (Hill, 2017).

> ### Social Media and Self-Esteem
>
> You are probably well aware that the use of social media has been increasing over time. For Americans, only 5% reported using social media in 2005, but this number has risen to 72% in 2019. On average across the world, people spend over 2 hours per day on social media. Social media provides some benefits such as increased access to information, facilitation of communication, and opportunities for creative expression. But it also comes with some downsides, particularly with regards to the impact on self-esteem. Midgley and associates (2021) conducted a series of four studies that they packaged under the title "When Every Day Is a High School Reunion: Social Media Comparisons and Self-Esteem." Across their four studies, they consistently found that college students with lower self-esteem tend to respond to social media posts on Facebook and Instagram by comparing themselves to others whom they judge to be "better" than they are and that these comparisons then further negatively affect their self-esteem. These findings suggest that individuals with relatively low self-esteem should be cautious in their use of social media platforms that might negatively influence their already low self-esteem.

From an exercise psychology perspective, the importance of self-esteem to overall happiness might suggest its role as a potential mediator of the effects of exercise on other psychological outcomes such as depression and anxiety. That is, given that self-esteem is believed to be a critical need for human beings, it makes sense that a lack of self-esteem might be a precursor to feelings of anxiety or depression. As such, it further makes sense that increases in self-esteem, which might result from increases in physical activity behavior, could be a causal mechanism explaining an observed decrease in anxiety or depression in response to physical activity. Self-esteem also might be important in exercise psychology because of its potential impact on exercise participation. In other words, because the need to maintain high levels of self-esteem is a basic psychological need and a powerful motivator, evidence supporting positive effects of exercise on self-esteem could be influential in the adoption and maintenance of physical activity behaviors, and increases in self-esteem in response to physical activity participation might create a positive cycle of reinforcement for continued physical activity.

Another key point about the construct of self-esteem is that modern viewpoints of self-esteem recognize that it is both multidimensional and hierarchical. **Multidimensional** means that we have an overall judgment of self-esteem, but we also have judgments of self-esteem in specific areas such as academics, social relationships, emotional resilience, and physical competencies. **Hierarchical** means that global self-esteem is informed by self-esteem in specific areas, and each of these specific areas is affected by a variety of lower-level contributors to self-esteem. So, for example, physical self-esteem is influenced by factors including physical self-competence, strength, endurance, and appearance. However, the idea is that each of these factors supports an area and each of the areas contributes to our overall sense of self-esteem. For example, if I have a positive evaluation of my physical self-competence, strength, and appearance, even if my evaluation of my endurance is not high, my overall physical self-esteem is likely to be pretty high (unless, of course, endurance is something I care about a lot, which might then pull my overall physical self-esteem down). If my physical self-esteem is high and positive, this will contribute to an overall positive self-esteem, particularly if my physical self-esteem is important to me and I also have generally positive evaluations of myself in other areas (e.g., academics, social relationships, emotional resilience). The hierarchical nature of this construct also means that self-construct and self-esteem are expected to be more stable over time, while self-esteem in specific areas is expected to show more fluctuations across time and experiences. For example, your judgments of your academic abilities might change slightly in response to your performance in a particular semester, but your overall sense of self-esteem is not likely to be affected as readily.

---

multidimensional—As it relates to self-esteem, multidimensional means that self-esteem can be specific to areas such as academics, social relationships, emotional resilience, and physical competencies.

hierarchical—As it relates to self-esteem, hierarchical means that global self-esteem is informed by self-esteem in specific areas, each of which is affected by a variety of lower-level contributors to self-esteem.

Before describing models relevant to the potential effects of exercise on self-esteem, we also need to consider the constructs of self-confidence and self-efficacy. Self-confidence is a broad term that describes one's overall judgment of one's ability to be successful in a variety of activities. Self-confident individuals believe that they perform well in many different situations. Self-efficacy is a more specific aspect of self-confidence because it describes one's feelings of being capable to perform a certain activity in a certain situation. For example, you might have overall high self-confidence in your athletic abilities but low self-efficacy for downhill skiing on a double black diamond slope (the most difficult level) in Colorado. Or you might have overall low self-confidence in your social abilities but have high self-efficacy for your ability to interact well with old friends from high school.

Prevalence and Self-Esteem

Self-esteem is a slightly different construct than others we've considered thus far, which makes the discussion of prevalence different. For instance, no clinical disorder is focused specifically on self-esteem. Rather, low self-esteem is thought to be important for understanding mental health disorders such as disordered eating, generalized anxiety disorder, or body image concerns, and high self-esteem is evident in individuals with narcissistic personality disorder. Although we are not able to discuss prevalence with regards to self-esteem, we do have information about how self-esteem changes across the life span and about other variables that are related to self-esteem.

From longitudinal studies, we know that self-esteem starts out low and is relatively unstable in childhood; increases and becomes more stable through adolescence, young adulthood, and middle age; peaks in level and stability between the ages of 50 and 60 years; and is followed by a decrease in level and stability during older age (Orth et al., 2018; Trzesniewski et al., 2003). Intriguingly, a person's rank order in terms of their self-esteem relative to others remains relatively the same across time so that people who are relatively low in self-esteem compared to others as children will typically still have relatively low self-esteem compared to others as adults (Trzesniewski et al., 2003). Scientists studying self-esteem also provide evidence that self-esteem has a genetic component such that self-esteem tends to be more alike for people within the same family than for people between different families (Mruk, 2006).

In addition to variability as a function of age, evidence also supports that various demographic factors are related to self-esteem. Griffiths and colleagues (2010) systematically reviewed the literature on self-esteem in obese children and adolescents. They reported that six of nine cross-sectional studies demonstrated lower global self-esteem for obese children and adolescents as compared to healthy-weight children and adolescents. All studies testing for differences on athletic or physical competence ($n = 5$) and physical appearance ($n = 6$) showed lower scores for obese children and adolescents.

Self-esteem is also related to other psychological constructs that help us understand why self-esteem is so important. For instance, high levels of self-esteem are correlated with emotional stability, extraversion, conscientiousness (Robins et al., 2001), happiness, and resilience to stress (Baumeister, Campbell, Krueger, & Vohs, 2003). In adolescents who have sought treatment for anxiety or depression, high levels of self-esteem are associated with a reduction in anxiety, depression, and attention problems 3 years later (Henriksen et al., 2017). Importantly, evidence also suggests that self-esteem is predictive of generally positive life outcomes at a broad level including success and well-being (Orth & Robins, 2014). This has been shown in well-designed prospective studies that look at self-esteem at one point in time as a predictor of success and well-being at a future time.

Models, Theories, and Mediators of Self-Esteem

The theoretical model that is adopted for self-esteem for a research study is important because it guides the manner in which the construct is assessed. In research conducted in the 1960s and early 1970s self-esteem was thought of as a unidimensional construct (see figure 11.2a). This resulted in the development of survey instruments that produced a single global measure of self-esteem. In the 1980s scientists began to conceive of self-esteem as being multidimensional (see figure 11.2b). At this same time, other researchers began to conceive of self-esteem as being both multidimensional and hierarchical (see figure 11.2c). Shavelson and associates (1976) proposed a model for education-related self-esteem

---

self-confidence—Self-confidence is a broad term that describes a person's overall judgment of their ability to be successful in a variety of activities.

self-efficacy—Self-efficacy is a more specific aspect of self-confidence that describes the feeling of being capable of performing a certain activity in a certain situation.

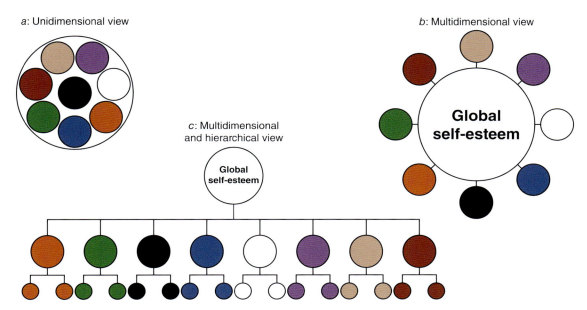

FIGURE 11.2 Conceptualizations of self-esteem including (a) a unidimensional view, (b) a multidimensional view, and (c) a multidimensional and hierarchical view.

Adapted by permission from K.R. Fox and C.B. Corbin, "The Physical Self-Perception Profile: Development and Preliminary Validation," *Journal of Sport and Exercise Psychology* 11, no. 4 (1989): 409.

that included a general measure at the top that was predicated on academic, social, emotional, and physical domains, which were themselves reliant on subdomains of perceived ability. This multidimensional and hierarchical view of self-esteem guides research conducted today.

Self-Esteem Models Specific to Exercise

When adapted for the exercise science literature, researchers began with the concept that self-esteem was both multidimensional and hierarchical. Sonstroem and Morgan (1989) proposed the Exercise and Self-Esteem Model (EXSEM) that explains how performance outcomes affect physical self-efficacy to then influence the physical subdomains of physical competence and physical acceptance and ultimately to affect global self-esteem. The idea is that increases in self-efficacy in response to successful exercise experiences or skillful motor performance are the most proximal impact on the behavior. Over time, a regular increase in self-efficacy in response to successful outcomes is expected to feed forward to influence subdomains of self-esteem and, ultimately, to influence self-esteem itself. As shown in figure 11.3, one example of the relationships between the constructs is to recognize that the ability to run a mile in 8 minutes would be viewed as an

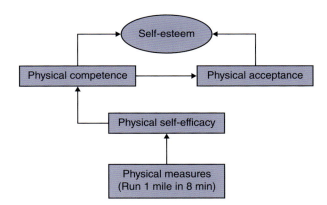

FIGURE 11.3 Sonstroem & Morgan's (1989) self-esteem model.

Adapted from Sonstroem and Morgan (1989).

accomplishment by most college students. As such, this outcome would increase physical self-efficacy, which would increase a person's sense of physical competence, which would lead to increased physical acceptance. Both physical competence and physical acceptance are then predicted to lead to heightened self-esteem.

Another self-esteem model that has been important in the exercise psychology literature is the Physical Self-Perception Profile (PSPP) (Fox, 1990; Fox & Corbin, 1989). This model provides a clear depiction of the various types of physical activity behaviors or of fitness attributes (called *subfacets* in this model) that contribute to facets that are broader activity or body image characteristics. These facets then contribute to subdomains of physical self-esteem. Looking at figure 11.4, it is important to recognize that the subfacets and facets could have an almost infinite number of exemplars, but the subdomains are limited by the model to the ones you see here: competence, strength, endurance, and appearance. Research that is conducted based on this model relies on the PSPP to measure physical self-esteem subdomains and hence produces these same four subdomains.

Psychological Mediators

For self-esteem, the potential mediators that might explain the benefits of exercise are themselves psychological constructs. Therefore, they are variables that also are measured by self-report. The primary variables that have been considered include self-awareness, self-efficacy, and body image.

Self-Awareness

One explanation for the effects of exercise on self-esteem is provided by the theory of objective self-awareness. This theory posits that activities that focus attention inwardly or toward the self will have a negative effect on self-esteem. An example is asking participants to complete a self-esteem survey while listening to a recording of their own voice, which has been demonstrated to reduce self-esteem scores (Ickes et al., 1973). Interestingly, it is possible that the effects of exercise on self-esteem are influenced by self-awareness. For example, if the exercise intensity is low to moderate, this might facilitate a person's ability to dissociate (i.e., focus their attention outwardly), which might then reduce self-awareness and result in a benefit for self-esteem. But if the exercise intensity is high, the person likely would not be able to dissociate, so one might expect self-awareness to increase and self-esteem to be hindered. This hypothesis was proposed in early research in this area (Sonstroem & Morgan, 1989) but has not been systematically tested.

Self-Efficacy

Given the hierarchical nature of self-esteem, it makes sense that the benefits of exercise for self-efficacy regarding the performance of physical tasks would have an effect on the higher-order factor of self-esteem. In fact, self-efficacy is explicitly identified in Sonstroem and Morgan's (1989) model as a requisite first step toward affecting the more global measure of self-esteem (see figure 11.3). By completing an exercise test or performing well on a physical skill, self-efficacy for that behavior increases. With repeated exposure, it is expected that these increases in self-efficacy will affect relevant subdomains of self-esteem and ultimately have an impact on the broader construct of self-esteem.

Body Image

Another factor that is likely to be relevant to the relationship between exercise and self-esteem is

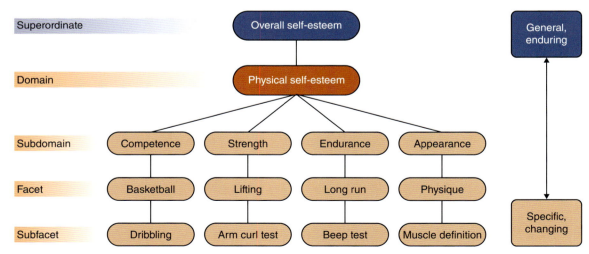

FIGURE 11.4 Hierarchical model depicting the relationship between subfacets, facets, subdomains, physical self-esteem, and overall self-esteem.

Adapted from Sonstroem et al. (1994). Adapted from Berger and Eklund (2015).

body image. Given that physical appearance is a subdomain of self-esteem and is included in numerous self-esteem models, it is logical to expect that changes in body image in response to exercise might contribute to changes in self-esteem. This is a complicated mediator to explore because it is likely to be a bidirectional relationship, such that exercise might lead to more positive body image, resulting in more positive self-esteem, but it is also possible that increases in self-esteem in response to exercise might contribute to more positive body image. The effects of exercise on body image are explored in chapter 12.

Measurement

Self-report is by far the most frequently used method to assess self-esteem (Butler & Gasson, 2005), and the Rosenberg Self-Esteem Scale (SES) (Rosenberg, 1965) is the most commonly used measure. The Rosenberg SES consists of 10 statements describing general feelings about the self, and respondents are asked to indicate the extent to which they agree with the statement from "strongly disagree" to "strongly agree." These responses are converted to numbers from 1 to 4 and then summed to provide an assessment of global self-esteem, with a higher score indicating a higher level of self-esteem. Some example items include "On the whole, I am satisfied with myself" and "At times I think I am no good at all." With children and adolescents, in addition to the SES, two other commonly used self-report measures are the Piers-Harris Children's Self-Concept Scale (SCS) (Piers & Herzberg, 2002) and the Tennessee Self-Concept Scale (TSCS) (Fitts, 1965). The SCS and the TSCS assess both global self-esteem and self-esteem in specific domains (e.g., physical appearance). All of these measures have acceptable psychometrics that have been established for ages 7 to 18 for the SCS, 11 and older for the SES, and 13 to 68 for the TSCS. Although the psychometrics of these scales are acceptable, it is important to recognize that self-report measures have some inherent limitations including the reliance on self-awareness and verbal abilities, susceptibility to bias or a desire to put forth a positive image, and cultural differences in the emphasis on the self as opposed to an emphasis on the collective whole. Furthermore, these measures of self-esteem are not specific to exercise and physical activity and hence might not be as sensitive as measures specifically developed to include questions relevant to perceptions of the physical self.

In examining the literature on exercise and self-esteem, the SES is commonly used, but you will also see measures that are specific to physical aspects of self-esteem. These include the Physical Self-Perception Profile (PSPP) and the Physical Self-Description Questionnaire (PSDQ).

The PSPP consists of 30 questions and results in 4 subscale scores (perceived sport competence, perceived bodily attractiveness, perceived physical strength and muscular development, and perceived physical conditioning) and a general physical self-worth score. This survey also has been dramatically adapted for use with children in the Children and Youth PSPP (CY-PSPP). One of the challenging aspects of the CY-PSPP and the PSPP is that the question formats are different from normal. That is, each question gives two options for response. The participant has to identify which response is most true for them and then to rate if that option is "sort of true" or "really true" of them. Despite this challenge, both have been shown to have sound psychometrics and to be appropriate for use across age groups. Table 11.1 shows some sample items from the PSPP.

The PSDQ consists of 70 items assessing self-concept in each of 9 areas (strength, body fat, endurance and fitness, sport competence, physical activity, coordination, appearance, health, and flexibility) and provides a measure of global physical self-esteem and of global self-esteem. Each of these areas is assessed by six to eight items that are presented in a way that requires a true-or-false response. This instrument has been shown to be reliable and valid when administered to participants over 12 years of age. Examples of items from this survey include "I am a physically strong person" and "I am attractive for my age."

The questionnaires that have been developed specifically for exercise provide a way of assessing self-efficacy and self-esteem constructs that are directly relevant to exercise-based experiences. Hence, they have helped to advance our understanding of the link between physical activity and global self-esteem. Importantly, these measures share the same limitations as all self-report measures in that they are reliant on honesty and self-awareness on the part of the participant.

TABLE 11.1 Sample Items From the Physical Self-Perception Profile (PSPP)

Sports competence	Really true for me	Sort of true for me	Some people feel that they are not very good when it comes to playing sport	BUT	Others feel that they are really good at just about every sport	Sort of true for me	Really true for me
Physical condition	Really true for me	Sort of true for me	Some people do not usually have a high level of stamina and fitness	BUT	Others always maintain a high level of stamina and fitness	Sort of true for me	Really true for me
Body attractiveness	Really true for me	Sort of true for me	Some people are extremely confident about the appearance of their bodies	BUT	Others are a little self-conscious about the appearance of their bodies	Sort of true for me	Really true for me
Physical strength	Really true for me	Sort of true for me	Some people feel that they are physically stronger than most people of their sex	BUT	Others feel that they lack physical strength compared to most others of their sex	Sort of true for me	Really true for me
Physical self-worth	Really true for me	Sort of true for me	Some people feel extremely satisfied with the kind of person they are physically	BUT	Others sometimes feel a little dissatisfied with their physical selves	Sort of true for me	Really true for me

Adapted from Fox and Corbin (1989).

Evidence for Exercise and Self-Esteem

A substantial portion of the literature on exercise and self-esteem has focused on children. This is undoubtedly because we know that self-esteem tends to be lower in children than in other age groups and also because self-esteem during childhood has important implications for self-esteem in adulthood. The body of evidence in this population is limited, but declines in self-esteem have been observed in older age.

Empirical Evidence

One study that provides a nice example of a randomized clinical trial (RCT) designed to test the effects of different modes of exercise on self-esteem was conducted by Goldfield and colleagues (2015). The study was called the Healthy Eating, Aerobic and Resistance Training in Youth (HEARTY) study, and it was designed to compare the additive benefits of aerobic exercise, resistance exercise, or a combined program on body composition, body image, and self-esteem following a dietary intervention implemented with obese (BMI >95% for age and sex) adolescents (14-18 yr, 70% females). All participants received dietary counseling to produce a daily energy deficit of 250 kcal, and all initially performed aerobic and resistance exercises 4 times per week for 4 weeks to ensure appropriate adherence for the remainder of the program (i.e., only those who attended 80% or more of the sessions were invited to remain in the study). At that point, 304 participants were assigned randomly to aerobic training, resistance training, both, or neither (control) for 22 weeks. Training programs were implemented 4 days per week and progressed from 20 minutes per day to 45 minutes per day for the individual training groups. Participants in the combined training group also met 4 days per week but performed both the aerobic and the resistance training and so exercised for twice as long (i.e., 40 to 90 minutes per day). Findings showed differences in the change in self-esteem from pretest to posttest based on group assignment. For perceived physical conditioning, the combined group improved significantly more than the control group. For perceived strength, both the resistance group and the combined group improved significantly more than the control group. For global self-esteem, the resistance group improved significantly more than the control group. Reductions in body fat (assessed objectively) were predictive of increased body satisfaction, physical self-worth, and global self-esteem, and increases in strength (measured objectively) were related to increases in perceived physical condition, perceived strength, and physical self-worth.

Two important limitations of this study should be mentioned. First, the sample was predominantly female (70%), so results might not generalize to samples with a larger percentage of male participants. However, that being said, the authors suggest that given the emphasis on strength training for men, larger benefits might be expected for male participants. The second limitation is that the researchers only included participants who demonstrated 80% adherence during the first month of the trial. Thus, these results might not be attainable in a population for whom adherence is not so high. Despite these limitations, this study is important because it provides evidence for a causal relationship between resistance training and various aspects of physical self-esteem and even global self-esteem. Given that this issue is particularly relevant to obese adolescents, these findings hold promise for future interventions that combine dieting with resistance training. Interestingly, the largest effects in this trial were observed for the resistance training group, which differs from findings with other psychological outcomes that have tended to be larger for aerobic exercise.

Awick and associates (2017) provide an example of a study examining the potential benefits of exercise on self-esteem in older adults. They conducted an RCT to test the effects of a 6-month DVD-administered, home-based exercise program on the self-esteem of older adults. They provide a strong rationale for the importance of this work by pointing out that the maintenance of self-esteem is associated with lower levels of cortisol, reduced anxiety, decreased depression, and improved quality of life in the face of advancing age. Older ($M = 71.01$ years) low-active adults were assigned randomly to the DVD-based exercise group or the attentional control DVD group. Those in the exercise group were instructed to perform the exercises 3 days per week. The attentional control group was asked to watch a single 85-minute DVD focused on healthy aging. From the beginning to the end of the trial, the exercise group experienced improvements in physical self-worth and perceptions of physical condition that were significantly larger than observed in the control group. Additionally, evidence showed that improvements in self-efficacy were associated with improvements in self-worth and perceptions of physical condition, which is supportive of the EXSEM model. Because both groups improved equally in self-esteem, the authors concluded that this home-based exercise program provided benefits for domain (physical self-worth) and subdomain (perceptions of physical condition) levels of self-esteem but that effects were not strong enough to affect global self-esteem. Given the study's primary limitation of not providing any description of the exercise behaviors performed by those in the exercise group, it is impossible to know if the exercise intervention was performed as intended. Thus, while it is possible that a stronger dose of physical activity or a longer intervention would be necessary to affect the more stable construct of global self-esteem, it is also possible that a high level of adherence to the intervention as prescribed would have been suffi-

Alternative Form of Exercise and Self-Esteem

Most of the research in exercise psychology has focused on traditional forms of aerobic activity such as walking and jogging or on resistance training using weights or a person's own body weight. In studying the outcome of self-esteem, it is worthwhile to consider forms of physical activity that might provide additional benefits. In particular, Woodman and colleagues (2020) were interested in the potential of high-risk sports (those where serious injury or death are inherent risks) to benefit self-esteem. These sports include rock climbing, white-water kayaking, and skydiving. They hypothesized that because high-risk sports require athletes to experience and control their emotions regularly to successfully perform in these activities, they would then experience better emotion regulation, a greater sense of agency (i.e., a greater sense of control), and higher self-esteem. They recruited 194 participants identified as high-risk athletes (rock climbers), low-risk athletes (badminton players, runners), and nonathletes (photographers, musicians). Their results showed that high-risk athletes had greater emotion regulation and greater agency than the other two groups, that emotional regulation and agency were predictive of self-esteem, and that high-risk athletes had greater self-esteem even when controlling for emotional regulation and agency. The authors suggest that these benefits might make high-risk sports an attractive alternative to other risky behaviors (e.g., substance use) and have clear benefits for self-esteem.

cient. The use of home-based exercise is wonderful for generalizability, but in the absence of measures of adherence, it is challenging to know if the intervention was actually performed.

Meta-Analytic Reviews

The empirical evidence on exercise and self-esteem has been reviewed meta-analytically on numerous occasions. The most recent meta-analyses that have been conducted with children present summary data from intervention studies using RCT and non-experimental designs (Collins et al., 2019; King et al., 2020; Park et al., 2014). Across all reviews, data consistently support a small to moderate positive effect of exercise on self-esteem.

Collins and associates (2019) conducted a meta-analysis restricted to studies looking at resistance exercise in children and adolescents (5-18 yr). Summary statistics from four studies supported that resistance training improves resistance training self-efficacy (ES = 0.54), perceived physical strength (ES = 0.29), physical self-worth (ES = 0.32), and global self-esteem (ES = 0.41). These findings support the EXSEM model in that they indicate that resistance exercise most strongly benefits self-efficacy, but that this then has implications for subdomains of self-esteem (e.g., perceived physical strength and physical self-worth) and ultimately also shows benefits at a global level (i.e., global self-esteem). The resistance training programs implemented in the studies ranged in length from 8 to 24 weeks with exercise performed 100 to 225 minutes per week across 2 to 4 sessions per week.

King and colleagues (2020) included all types of physical activity but limited their review to studies testing the effects of exercise interventions on self-esteem in overweight or obese children and adolescents (≤18 yr old). Results from 21 studies testing the effects of physical activity in isolation or in combination with a dietary intervention showed an increase in self-esteem (ES = 0.34) in response to structured physical activity interventions. They did not find a significant difference in the effect size for studies looking at physical activity in isolation compared to those looking at physical activity and diet in combination. This is interesting because the combined physical activity and diet interventions resulted in significantly larger weight loss (ES = 0.56) than did the physical activity only interventions (ES = 0.16). This suggests that physical activity might be the key component of the intervention and that, counter to the findings reported by Goldfield and associates (2015), benefits to self-esteem are evident irrespective of weight loss. In studies that included a follow-up assessment of self-esteem obtained between 14 weeks and 2.4 years from baseline, results supported that the effects of the physical activity intervention were relatively enduring (ES = 0.30). The researchers reported that the duration of the interventions ranged from 7 weeks to 1 year, and the summary results indicated that longer interventions resulted in significantly bigger effects. Overall, the results of this meta-analysis support the use of physical activity interventions as a way of improving self-esteem in overweight and obese children and adolescents.

Park and colleagues (2014) limited their review to studies focused on older adults. They only found two studies that met their inclusion criteria, which demonstrates the relative lack of research interest in exploring this question with older adults. One of the studies explored the effects of functional exercise performed for 30 minutes, 2 times per week, for 16 weeks, and the other looked at qigong performed for 30 to 45 minutes per week for 16 weeks. Across these two studies, results supported a moderate effect size (ES = 0.49). Given the aforementioned decreases in self-esteem observed in older age, this positive and moderate effect suggests the value of future research exploring the potential of physical activity to mitigate these age-related declines.

Summary

Exercise has the potential to influence self-efficacy, subdomains of self-esteem, and even global levels of self-esteem. Given that self-esteem is an important predictor of positive mental health outcomes, happiness, resilience to stress, and positive life outcomes at a broad level, understanding the potential benefits of exercise for self-esteem is important. Knowing that children and adolescents tend to have lower and less stable self-esteem than young adults and adults, much of the research has focused on the potential of physical activity in younger populations. This evidence consistently shows that participation in a chronic exercise program (aerobic or resistance) has small to moderate benefits for self-esteem. These results are observed in the general population of children and adolescents and specifically in children and adolescents who are overweight or obese. In overweight and obese samples, physical activity has been shown to improve self-esteem when administered by itself and when administered in conjunction with a dietary intervention, and there is some evidence that resistance exercise may be particularly beneficial. The results of Goldfield and associates' (2015) empirical study indicated that decreases in body fat during their trial were predictive of increases in self-esteem, while King and colleagues (2020) reported no relationship between weight loss and the average effects across studies. This might suggest a need to understand better whether weight, body fat, body image, or body image dissatisfaction are important for predicting the potential benefits of a physical activity intervention. Research has been conducted with other age groups and supports the benefits of physical activity; however, this body of evidence is relatively limited, and additional research is warranted.

Discussion Questions

1. If a researcher only used the Rosenberg measure of self-esteem, why might that researcher fail to observe benefits in response to an exercise intervention? What should they do?

2. Name and describe a psychological mediator that has been proposed to explain the effects of exercise on self-esteem.

3. Goldfield and associates (2015) conducted the HEARTY study to explore the effects of different modes of exercise on self-esteem in overweight and obese adolescents. Review the design of the study, discuss what they found, think about the limitations of the study, and consider their conclusions. How does this study contribute to the literature?

4. In China, if you have a tan, this is considered evidence that you are from the working class. In the United States, having a tan is considered evidence that you have leisure time that allows you to be outside. Use this example as a springboard to consider how cultural differences might affect hierarchical, multidimensional models of self-esteem relative to physical activity participation.

Exercise and Body Image

OBJECTIVES

After studying this chapter, you should be able to do the following:

- Define body image and understand the components that contribute to body image
- Explain why body concerns are important
- Describe the evidence supporting the benefits of exercise for body image
- Recognize the possibility that sports that emphasize leanness might be a more difficult setting in which to improve the body image of athletes

KEY TERMS

body concerns

body image

body-related behaviors

body perception

body evaluation

body satisfaction

body dissatisfaction

affective component

social physique anxiety (SPA)

muscle dysmorphia

clinical eating disorders

anorexia

bulimia

disordered eating

single-group studies

aesthetic sports

endurance sports

weight class sports

> Adelaide is a sophomore in college who is not satisfied with her physical appearance. She was a volleyball player in high school and had always been thin and fit. But in her first year of college she experienced the Freshman 15; she has gained 17 pounds relative to her weight as a senior in high school. She now perceives that she is fat relative to her peers and in particular thinks that her legs and stomach are too big. Adelaide is experiencing depression and anxiety in response to her negative body image. She has started wearing baggy clothes and dresses in sweatpants whenever possible. She considers going to the student recreation center to start exercising, but the thought of walking into that space with the other college students wearing spandex, tank tops, and tight-fitting, revealing attire is intimidating. At her parents' urging, she has signed up for a strength and conditioning class offered by the department of kinesiology at her university. When she attends class the first day, she is nervous but is pleased to see that most of her classmates are also somewhat overweight and are dressed in body-concealing clothing. The instructor explains that the class is going to be self-paced so that each person can begin at a level of activity that is right for them and then advance as appropriate for them. The instructor further discusses the benefits of light- to moderate-intensity exercise and the value of a strength-training program that is largely based on moving one's own body weight, and she expresses confidence and pride in the students for joining the class. Adelaide feels supported and proud of herself for being a part of the class. She introduces herself to a woman sitting near her whose name is Gia, and they make a pact to attend class every day to make sure they get the most benefit possible. As the semester progresses, Adelaide begins to perceive benefits in terms of her weight, body image, and depression and anxiety.

This scenario provides an example of how body concerns can affect behavior in a way that can become a vicious cycle. That is, if someone is overweight and has body concerns, they may be too self-conscious to go to a gym or to be physically active, which might contribute to further weight gain. This can also work for people who have body concerns related to being small, thin, or frail, which also might lead them to restrict their activities because of concerns of being judged. The irony is that physical activity participation has the potential to improve a person's body image in ways that can minimize body concerns.

Terms and Definitions

Body concerns describe a broad construct and include a variety of relevant outcomes that have been examined in the exercise psychology literature. **Body concerns** include the outcomes of body image, body satisfaction or dissatisfaction, body attractiveness, and social physique anxiety. **Body image** is itself a multidimensional construct consisting of a person's body-related behaviors, their perception of their body, their evaluation of their body relative to their ideal standard, their satisfaction or dissatisfaction with that evaluation (body satisfaction), and the affective component of that evaluation. A person's **body-related behaviors** are behaviors that give an indication of how the person perceives, feels about, and thinks about their body. Examples of body-related behaviors include practices such as looking in a mirror and choosing to wear revealing or concealing clothing. A person's **body perception** is their own sense of what their body looks like, which might be accurate or inaccurate relative to

---

body concerns—Body concerns include the outcomes of body image, body satisfaction or dissatisfaction, body attractiveness, and social physique anxiety.

body image—Body image is a multidimensional construct consisting of a person's body-related behaviors, their perception of their body, their evaluation of their body relative to their ideal standard, their satisfaction or dissatisfaction with that evaluation (body satisfaction), and the affective component of that evaluation.

body-related behaviors—Body-related behaviors are those that give an indication of how the person perceives, feels about, and thinks about their body.

body perception—A person's sense of what their body looks like, which might be accurate or inaccurate relative to their actual body shape and size, is their body perception.

their actual body shape and size. It is how the person sees themselves when they look in a mirror or when they simply imagine how they look to others. A person's body evaluation typically is made relative to some ideal standard, which is where the role of the media and societal pressures are realized. That is, a person's evaluation of their body is informed by the ways in which body shape has been judged and promoted in their particular environment and broader community. Based on an evaluation of perceived body shape and size relative to perceived ideals, a person might experience either satisfaction or dissatisfaction with that evaluation. Body satisfaction describes a situation where a person is content with their evaluation of their body or specific body parts, while body dissatisfaction describes when they are not content with their evaluations. Lastly, the affective component of the evaluation is how a person feels about that evaluation and could include feelings of shame and distress or pride and happiness. To summarize, body image describes our cognitive appraisal of our perception of our body relative to perceived norms or goals and might include affective components based on the extent to which we are satisfied or dissatisfied with our bodies relative to those norms or goals. Our body image can be focused on our overall shape or weight or on specific aspects of our body such as our hips or waist, and we might be motivated to behave in certain ways based on our body image.

Social Physique Anxiety

Social physique anxiety (SPA) is a type of body concern that describes the experience of anxiety due to perceptions that others are negatively evaluating a person's physique. SPA is likely to be particularly salient when a person is interested in making a good impression. SPA is important in its own right because of the influence it can have on a person's willingness to, for example, participate in group exercise. SPA is also important because it has been tied to eating disorders.

The Importance of Body Image

The importance of body image is due partially to the value of a person's physical appearance in our society. That is, our physical appearance has a social currency because perceptions of constructs such as beauty, fitness, and healthiness that are associated with particular bodies are a form of capital in the social interactions that take place in families, schools, businesses, and social groups. In other words, value can be found in having a body that is perceived to be beautiful, fit, and healthy. The value of the body is that it is a symbol of health, success, and even wealth. This has several implications. First, because a person's physical shape and looks are social currency, this might motivate people to present themselves in a particular way. That is, they might choose a style of dress that is intended to relay to others that they are an exerciser or an athlete, serious or laid-back, or effeminate or masculine.

The Value of Attractiveness

Researchers in a variety of venues have looked at the influence of physical attractiveness on outcomes that are perceived to be of value. In a review of this literature, Frevert and Walker (2014) shared that being more physically attractive has been shown to be predictive of the following:

- More positive judgments of intelligence, academic potential, and social skills; better performance evaluations and grades for students in academic settings
- Higher ratings of quality and expertise for professors as evaluated by their students
- A greater likelihood of being hired for a job (but note that attractive women are less likely to be hired for a managerial job or other positions considered to be men's jobs)
- A shorter length of a penal sentence
- More willingness to be cooperated with

---

body evaluation—An assessment of the body that is typically made relative to some ideal standard is considered a body evaluation.
body satisfaction—Body satisfaction is when a person is content with their evaluation of their body or specific body parts.
body dissatisfaction—Body dissatisfaction is when a person is not content with their evaluation of their body or specific body parts.
affective component—The affective component of body image is how a person feels about their evaluation (satisfaction or dissatisfaction) and could include feelings of shame and distress or pride and happiness.
social physique anxiety (SPA)—SPA is a type of body concern that describes the experience of anxiety due to perceptions that others might be negatively evaluating a person's physique.

A second reason that body image is important is because body dissatisfaction has been shown to be related to negative psychological outcomes. For example, body dissatisfaction can be predictive of symptoms of disordered eating in females across the life span (Attie & Brooks-Gunn, 1989; Cattarin & Thompson, 1994; Gardner et al., 2002; Neumark-Sztainer et al., 2006; Polivy & Herman, 2002) and in male adolescents and adults (Keel et al., 1997; Leon et al., 1995). In addition, body dissatisfaction has been shown to be predictive of other negative mental health outcomes such as depression and reductions in self-esteem (Sarwer et al., 2005). In participants enrolled in a longitudinal study of parents and children conducted in Avon, United Kingdom, body dissatisfaction at 14 years of age was found to be predictive of risky health behaviors at 21 years of age. In particular, greater body dissatisfaction at age 14 predicted increased rates of smoking for both males and females and of cannabis use, drug use, self-harm, and high-risk drinking for females (Bornioli et al., 2019).

An additional reason that body image is important is because it can serve as a mediator of beneficial effects of exercise on a host of other psychological outcomes. For example, Wilson and colleagues (2013) showed that body image dissatisfaction mediates the relationship between body mass index (BMI) and physical health–related quality of life partially for women and completely for men. In other words, their results suggest that BMI doesn't directly influence quality of life, but rather the effects of BMI on quality of life are at least partially explained by a person's satisfaction or dissatisfaction with their BMI. This further emphasizes the importance of identifying ways to improve body image satisfaction through exercise because it can modulate the relationship between BMI and quality of life.

Prevalence

Data regarding the prevalence of body image dissatisfaction indicate that it is fairly widespread. Based on a review of studies on this topic, Fiske and associates (2014) estimated that between 46% and 66% of women and 35% and 52% of men report weight dissatisfaction, with 23% to 56% of women and 15% to 43% of men reporting dissatisfaction with overall appearance (figure 12.1). In a survey of 8,925 U.S. residents and 1,900 non-U.S. residents, 89% of women indicated that they wanted to be a different size than they perceived that they were (84.1% wanted to be thinner, 4.9% wanted to be larger) (Swami et al., 2015). Clearly, these numbers suggest a disturbingly high prevalence of body image dissatisfaction among both women and men but suggest that prevalence is higher in women than in men. These differences in body image dissatisfaction as a function of gender have been reported in several countries including Canada, New Zealand,

---

Social Media and Body Concerns

The relationship between the consumption of traditional media (e.g., television and magazines) and body image concerns has been well documented for decades. Recent research has explored the influence of social media use on body image. Correlational studies have shown that more time spent on Facebook is predictive of greater body dissatisfaction for females from preadolescence through the freshman year at a university (Fardouly & Vartanian, 2015; Tiggemann & Miller, 2010; Tiggemann & Slater, 2013, 2014) and greater self-objectification (i.e., seeing oneself as an object to be evaluated based on appearance) for men (Fox & Rooney, 2015). In an intriguing experimental study, Hogue and Mills (2019) instructed 118 young adult women (17-27 yr) to spend one time period of 5 minutes engaging with Facebook content and 5 minutes engaging with Instagram content for a particular person. Participants were randomly assigned to do this either for a peer (within 5 yr of their age) whom they thought was more attractive than themselves or with a nonpeer, family member (more than 5 yr age difference) whom they did not think was more attractive than themselves. Body dissatisfaction was measured before and following the intervention. Results showed that women in the peer condition experienced a decrease in their body image (ES = 0.25), while those in the family condition did not experience a change (ES = 0.03). Although this effect size is small, this might have larger implications given that this effect occurred after only 10 minutes of exposure and the average daily time spent on social media by young adults is 145 minutes (Dixon, 2022). This example lends credence to the argument that understanding ways to improve body image is an important topic for research.

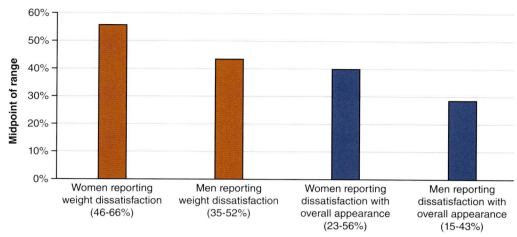

FIGURE 12.1 Data from the Fiske, Fallon, Blissmer, and Redding (2014) review displayed as the midpoint of the ranges reported in a review of the literature.
Adapted from Fiske et al. (2014).

Australia, and the United States, with researchers consistently reporting that girls and women are more dissatisfied with their bodies than are boys and men in studies conducted with children, adolescents, and midlife adults (Frederick et al., 2006; Kostanski et al., 2004; MacNeill et al., 2017; McGuinness & Taylor, 2016).

Body image dissatisfaction is reported even by individuals at normal weight. Perrin and colleagues (2010) reported on approximately 13,000 adolescents and young adults (11-21 yr) and found that among normal-weight participants, approximately 25% of girls and approximately 8% of boys perceived themselves to be overweight. In this study, normal weight was defined as having a BMI <85% of the population norms based on age and sex. This emphasizes that body image dissatisfaction can be experienced even when someone is at a healthy or normal weight. These researchers also looked at the relationship between global self-esteem assessed with the Self-Esteem Scale and perceptions of overweight in normal weight and overweight (>85% of the population norms based on age and sex). Based on these analyses, they found that among normal-weight girls and among boys with weights between 60% and 85% of population norms, those with lower self-esteem were more likely to report misperceived overweight, while higher self-esteem was associated with a more accurate body image. Self-esteem also had psychological benefits among overweight boys and girls, such that those with higher self-esteem were more likely to have a positive body image because of their perception (albeit inaccurate) that they were of normal weight.

Additional evidence shows that BMI is related to body concerns. This might be important relative to a potential role of exercise as a way of improving body image. In nonclinical samples, higher BMI has been shown to be predictive of greater body image dissatisfaction (Sarwer et al., 2005; Wilson et al., 2013). This is not surprising, but because of the link between BMI and body image dissatisfaction, this suggests that interventions (e.g., diet and exercise) that lead to weight reductions might then be expected to positively affect body image dissatisfaction. Importantly, the precise nature of the relationship between BMI and body image dissatisfaction differs for men and women. In particular, girls experience a linear relationship between BMI and body image dissatisfaction such that women with a low BMI are satisfied with their body image and increasing BMI is always associated with greater dissatisfaction (less satisfaction). However, in boys this relationship is curvilinear, so those with the lowest or highest BMI are most dissatisfied. However, the nature of the dissatisfaction differs. Those with low BMI want to be larger (i.e., they are experiencing the drive for muscularity), while those with high BMI want to be smaller (Frederick et al., 2006; Kostanski et al., 2004).

Relevant differences are observed between males' and females' body image and must be considered. For females, body image dissatisfaction typically arises from a desire to be thinner. While this can also be the case for males, some men might experience a drive for muscularity that can be reflected in a desire to gain leanness and increase muscle mass. As a result, measurement of body image dissatisfaction for men needs to include assessments of dissatisfaction with body fat, height, and muscularity because these all have been shown to contribute uniquely to relationships with psychological outcomes such as self-esteem, psychological distress, and depressive symptomology (Bergeron & Tylka, 2007).

Links Between Body Image and Clinical Disorders

Some evidence shows that body image concerns are related to the experience of clinical disorders. Although this evidence is correlational in nature, the findings might have important implications relative to the treatment of these clinical disorders.

Muscle Dysmorphia

Muscle dysmorphia is defined as a pathological preoccupation with muscularity, and it tends to be experienced by men. Pope and associates (2000) asked college-aged men from Austria, France, and the United States to identify the body shape that was ideal for them and that they thought would be most attractive to women. Across all three countries, men consistently chose an ideal body that was approximately 28 pounds (13 kg) more muscular than they perceived themselves to be. They also found that men thought that women preferred a body that was 27 to 32 pounds (12-15 kg) bigger than they themselves were. Ironically, when given the opportunity to select the body size they found most attractive, the women in the study chose normal-weight men.

Clinical Eating Disorders and Disordered Eating

Because of the expected link between body image dissatisfaction, disordered eating, and eating disorders, prevalence data for disordered eating and for eating disorders is relevant for further understanding the importance of a potential positive link between exercise and body image. To clarify, **clinical eating disorders** are diagnosed by psychologists or physicians based on persistent abnormal eating habits that impair physical and mental health and that limit an individual's ability to function. Two well-known and relatively common clinical eating disorders are anorexia nervosa (anorexia) and bulimia nervosa (bulimia). **Anorexia** is characterized by lower weight than normal for height, a fear of gaining weight, and a distorted perception of body weight or shape. It is potentially life-threatening because of the enduring efforts to lose weight when a person is already underweight. **Bulimia** is characterized by bingeing and purging and a sense of a lack of control over eating. It is also life-threatening because the resultant electrolyte imbalances from repeated purging can lead to cardiac or respiratory arrest. **Disordered eating** is defined as behaviors that fall short of a clinical diagnosis of an eating disorder but that demonstrate that the individual has an unhealthy relationship with food and weight. Examples of disordered eating include restrictive eating, compulsive eating, and irregular or inflexible eating patterns. Disordered eating is a risk factor for the development of an eating disorder.

Among high school students in the United States, 16% reported practicing disordered eating behaviors in the past 30 days, with a larger percentage of girls reporting these behaviors than boys (Beccia et al., 2019). When asked about these behaviors within the past year, 50% of girls and 38% of boys reported practicing unhealthy weight-control behaviors (e.g., fasting, skipping meals, taking diet pills), and 46% of girls and 31% of boys dieted (Neumark-Sztainer et al., 2012). These findings are consistent with a more recent survey that also looked at the influence of race or ethnicity on the findings. Simone and colleagues (2022) assessed unhealthy weight-control behaviors and binge eating in the past year among men and women aged 11 to 33 years. Results generally showed that girls reported performing these behaviors more frequently than did men (figure 12.2). In terms of diagnosis, in the United States it is estimated that 8.4% of women and 2.2% of men will be diagnosed with a clinical eating disorder over their lifetime, with the concerning finding that the prevalence has more than doubled from 2000-2006 to 2013-2018 (Galmiche et al., 2019).

---

muscle dysmorphia—A pathological preoccupation with muscularity that tends to be experienced by men is called muscle dysmorphia.

clinical eating disorders—Clinical eating disorders are diagnosed by psychologists or physicians based on persistent abnormal eating habits that impair physical and mental health and that limit an individual's ability to function.

anorexia—Anorexia is an eating disorder characterized by lower weight than normal for height, a fear of gaining weight, and a distorted perception of body weight or shape.

bulimia—Bulimia is an eating disorder characterized by bingeing and purging and a sense of a lack of control over eating.

disordered eating—Behaviors that fall short of a clinical diagnosis of an eating disorder but that demonstrate an unhealthy relationship with food and weight are referred to as disordered eating.

CHAPTER 12 • Exercise and Body Image | 191

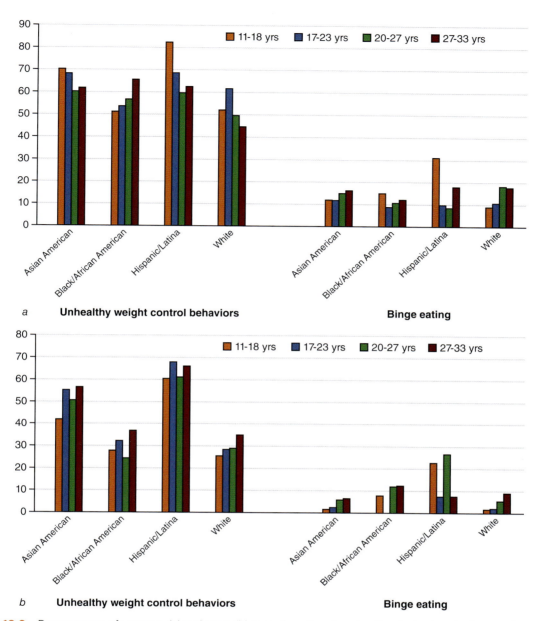

FIGURE 12.2 Percentages of women *(a)* and men *(b)* reporting disordered eating behaviors in the previous year as a function of race or ethnicity and age group.
Adapted from Simone et al. (2022).

> If you believe you have an eating disorder and are ready to seek help, please contact your university counseling department or a mental health care professional. If you are concerned about a friend or relative whom you believe might have an eating disorder, educate yourself about appropriate ways to intervene and remember to lead with compassion and care rather than phrases that might convey a judgment or evaluation relative to body size, appearance, or eating behaviors. Visit sites maintained by these organizations to learn more or use the hotlines (available on weekdays) to speak with trained volunteers.
>
> National Eating Disorders Hotline: 1-800-931-2237
> National Association of Anorexia Nervosa and Associated Disorders: 1-630-577-1330

Mechanisms and Mediators

As mentioned, it is likely that changes in body image in response to exercise can mediate the effects of exercise on other psychological outcomes such as depression and anxiety. However, we also must consider the mechanisms and mediators that explain any observed benefits of exercise on body image. The mechanisms that have been proposed include real or perceived changes in various measures of fitness (aerobic fitness, strength, body composition, flexibility) and increases in self-efficacy (situation-specific self-confidence).

Martin Ginis and associates (2012) proposed that there are three categories of variables that can act as mechanisms or mediators of the link between exercise and body image. These are objective changes in physical fitness (mechanism), perceived changes in physical fitness (mediator), and changes in self-efficacy (mediator). Martin Ginis and associates reviewed the literature to examine the evidence relative to each of these potential variables. They found 13 studies that had conducted appropriate statistical tests to consider the effects of an exercise intervention on body image and one or more of the hypothesized mechanisms or mediators and that also had looked at correlations between body image and the purported mechanisms or mediators. Only three of the studies looked at self-efficacy as a mechanism, but all three found positive results. That is, even after controlling for objective change in physical fitness, changes in self-efficacy were found to predict changes in body image. All of the studies included an objective measure of fitness as a potential mechanism. However, results were not consistent across the studies, and even in those where a significant association was observed, it only accounted for approximately 15% of the variance in body image. Overall, Martin Ginis and associates concluded that not much support has been shown for the role of objective fitness measures in terms of explaining the benefits for body image. They suggested that this is most likely because the actual amount of change in fitness is not important to a person's evaluation of their body relative to their perceived ideal. In other words, if a person were to begin an exercise program and improve their ability to run a mile, that change would only be important if they perceived that the fitness gain was moving them closer to their perceived ideal in terms of body shape. One study in their review included a measure of perceived change in fitness rather than absolute change. Martin Ginis and associates (2005) implemented a 12-week strength-training program and found that for both men and women, changes in perceptions of muscularity and strength were associated with changes in body satisfaction and SPA. Thus, overall, Martin Ginis and associates concluded that support was consistent for self-efficacy as a mechanism, and the one study that looked at perceived changes in measures of fitness found positive results. However, findings for objective measures of fitness are mixed, and Martin Ginis and associates concluded that these changes did not seem critical for improvements in body image.

Measurement

Given that body image includes perceptions, thoughts, and feelings and that body image can influence behavior, measures of body image concerns exist that reflect each of these aspects of the construct. One of the challenges in this body of research is that numerous measures have been developed (over 50 were reported in Thompson, 2004), so a researcher should be sure to choose a measure that addresses the specific aspect of body image that is of interest and that has been shown to be valid and reliable with the population of interest (Thompson, 2004).

Body Perception and Dissatisfaction

The Body Cathexis Scale (Secord & Jourard, 1953) was one of the first to be developed to assess body satisfaction. This scale includes assessment of satisfaction with various body parts (including many that are not weight-related such as eyes, ears, and nose) and measures of satisfaction with bodily functions related to physical activity participation (e.g., energy level and coordination). It consists of 46 items that are rated on a 5-point scale with the anchors of "Have strong feelings and wish change could somehow be made" and "Consider myself fortunate." This survey is commonly used in the exercise literature.

Measures of discrepancies between a person's ideal body image and their perceived body image (body perception) provide another way of assessing a body dissatisfaction score. In these measures, participants see silhouettes of generic body shapes, computer-generated images of various body shapes, or their own body shown in its actual proportions and then in computer-generated proportions below and above actual body weight. Existing measures include silhouettes developed by Stunkard, Sorenson, and Schulsingser (1983), modifications of these in the Body Silhouette Scale modified for children and preadolescents (Vernon-Guidry & Williamson, 1996), and photographs in the Children's Body Image Scale (CBIS) (Truby & Paxton, 2002). The CBIS includes images of boys and girls between 7 and 12 with seven levels of adiposity ranging from the 3rd to the 97th percentile for BMI. Children are asked to identify the image that most closely approximates their body size (body perception) and then to identify the image showing the body size they would like to be. The difference between these two reflects their satisfaction (if they choose the same number to answer both questions) or dissatisfaction (the difference between the two numbers given to answer the questions) with their body size.

Affective Component

Measures that assess thoughts and feelings about body image (the affective component) include the Tennessee Self-Concept Scale (TSCS) (Fitts, 1965) and the body attractiveness subscale of the Physical Self-Perception Profile (PSPP, described in more detail in chapter 11). The TSCS consists of 76 items when used with children (7-14 yr) and 82 items when used with older children and adults (>13 yr). Participants respond on a scale of 1 to 5, from "Always false" to "Always true," and example items include "I am an attractive person" and "I feel happy most of the time." It includes a subscale that is focused on physical self-concept, and normative data is available for ages 7 to 90 years.

Body-Related Behaviors

Body-related behaviors are often assessed using self-report. The most commonly used measure is the Body Checking Questionnaire (BCQ), a 23-item scale that was designed to assess these behaviors using stereotypically female behaviors (Reas et al., 2002). The Male Body Checking Questionnaire (MBCQ) is a 19-item scale that was created to allow for the assessment of behaviors that more likely would be observed in men. In demonstrating the validity and reliability of this scale, the developers confirmed that the scale had good psychometrics for use with men but was not appropriate to be used with women (Hildebrandt et al., 2010).

Related Measures

To assess drive for muscularity, researchers have used a variety of self-report measures including the Male Body Attitudes Scale (MBAS) (Tylka et al., 2005), the Drive for Muscularity Scale (DMS) (McCreary & Sasse, 2000), the Drive for Muscularity Attitudes Questionnaire (DMAQ) (Morrison et al., 2004), and the Muscle Dysmorphic Disorder Inventory (MDDI) (Hildebrandt et al., 2004). The MBAS is the most comprehensive of these scales because it is the only one that provides measures of dissatisfaction relative to muscularity, height, and weight, and it includes questions about six different body areas. The DMS and the DMAQ are also commonly used, but they are limited in that the DMS only provides measures of muscularity-oriented body image and behaviors to increase muscularity, while the DMAQ provides a single score of attitudes toward muscularity. Further, neither of these provides a measure of dissatisfaction, and both only assess attitudes toward three body areas. The MDDI assesses three aspects of muscle dysmorphia by calculating scores for desire for size, appearance anxiety and avoidance, and functional impairment. Desire for size questions focus on respondents' desire to be bigger, more muscular, or stronger. Appearance anxiety and avoidance questions ask respondents about behaviors that are designed to hide body size (e.g., wearing loose clothing) and anxiety about body exposure. The functional impairment questions revolve around behaviors and emotions relative to exercise. This questionnaire also provides a total score.

Evidence Relative to Exercise and Body Image

The literature on exercise and body concerns is relatively small compared to other outcomes in exercise psychology. In empirical studies, researchers have tested relationships using correlational or cross-sectional designs and intervention studies as is similar to previous bodies of evidence we have reviewed. But single-group studies also have been commonly conducted to explore the potential of physical activity relative to body image. In **single-group studies** physical activity is manipulated for a single group so that changes in the outcome variable (e.g., body image concerns) can be observed from pretest to posttest. Because no control group exists, conclu-

---

single-group studies—When physical activity is manipulated for a single group so that changes in the outcome variable (e.g., body image concerns) can be observed from pretest to posttest, this is called a single-group study.

sions are limited to those of association and cannot be used to draw conclusions about cause and effect. Despite the relatively smaller body of empirical evidence, several meta-analytic reviews have been conducted to summarize the results of correlational, single-group, and experimental studies. These are reviewed first, and then we turn our attention to a consideration of the effects of exercise (or sport participation) on body image and the impact on disordered eating.

Meta-Analytic Findings

Hausenblas and Fallon (2006) meta-analytically reviewed findings from 121 studies identified as interventions with an exercise group and a control group, single-group studies that included only pre- and post-measures for an exercise group, or correlational and cross-sectional studies in which a relationship between physical activity behavior and body image was reported or body image was compared between an exercise group and a nonexercise group. Although the largest effect size was observed for correlational studies (ES = 0.41), a positive effect also was observed for the single-group (ES = 0.24) and intervention (ES = 0.27) studies (figure 12.3). Because larger effects were observed when looking at long-term physical activity behavior, as is the case with the correlational studies, compared to shorter-term intervention studies, this difference in effect sizes might suggest that longer interventions are necessary to observe greater benefits. However, the small positive effect for intervention studies is promising in suggesting that a causal relationship might exist between exercise participation and improvements in body image and that this can be observed after relatively short-term exercise participation. With respect to exercise mode, Hausenblas and Fallon reported larger effects for interventions in which both aerobic and anaerobic exercise were used (ES = 0.45) compared to either aerobic exercise alone (ES = 0.25) or anaerobic exercise alone (ES = 0.27) (figure 12.3). This suggests the value of incorporating both aerobic and anaerobic activities when the goal is to improve body image. In their review, they included studies looking at female-only samples (48%), male and female samples (39%), and male-only samples (10%). Given that they had heterogeneity in the sex makeup of the samples, they also looked at sex as a moderator. Larger effects were evident for women compared to men for both the intervention studies (women: ES = 0.43; men: ES = 0.39) and the single-group studies (women: ES = 0.45; men: ES = 0.26). Because evidence generally shows that women have worse body image than

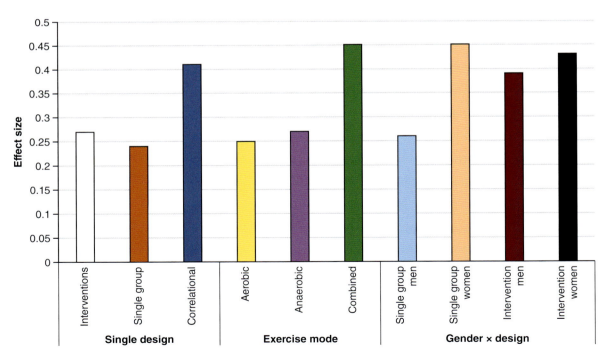

FIGURE 12.3 Data from the review by Hausenblas et al. (2006) revealed some interesting differences in effect sizes as a function of the moderator analyses.

Based on data from Hausenblas and Fallon (2006).

men, this might indicate that women have more room to demonstrate improvement.

In 2017, Bassett-Gunter and colleagues (2017) conducted a meta-analysis focused on the effects of exercise for body image concerns expressed by boys and men and used a similar approach to that taken by Hausenblas and Fallon (2006). This allows for direct comparisons of the findings between the previous review focused on men and women. The overall effect size across the 36 studies reviewed was moderate to large (ES = 0.57), with the largest effects observed for correlational studies (ES = 0.66) and controlled trials (ES = 0.65) and much smaller effects for single-group studies (ES = 0.28). These large effects for correlational studies are consistent with the findings of Hausenblas and Fallon (2006), but the effect sizes for the intervention studies are dramatically larger in this review. This overall effect size suggests that larger effects are possible for boys and men than previously reported. This provides an important addition to our understanding by showing the value of physical activity interventions for improving body image in boys and men. In this review, the moderator of exercise mode also was examined, with results showing the largest benefits for aerobic exercise (ES = 0.61) followed by anaerobic exercise (ES = 0.45) and then the combined programs (ES = 0.11). This finding for the combined programs should be considered tenuous because this level of the moderator variable had only two effect sizes. Nonetheless, these findings suggest that for male-only samples, single exercise mode programs yield moderate to large benefits.

Reel and associates (2007) included 35 studies using a variety of experimental designs and reported a moderate beneficial effect of exercise on body image (ES = 0.45) with no difference in effect size based on study design. An interesting finding from this review is that larger benefits were observed in studies that used single-sex samples (ES = 0.50) compared to mixed-sex samples (ES = 0.17). This might relate to issues of SPA that arise when exercising in groups that allow for men and women to perceive that they might be evaluated by members of the opposite sex.

Alleva and colleagues (2015) conducted a meta-analytic review in which they tested the effects of various forms of interventions on body image. They included cognitive behavioral techniques, fitness training programs, media literacy interventions, self-esteem enhancement approaches, and psychoeducation aimed at teaching about the causes and consequences of negative body image. Relevant to our interest in whether exercise is effective in enhancing body image, these authors reported that across all of these interventions, the average effect size across 62 interventions was 0.38. Unfortunately, the authors did not test the particular intervention category as a moderator, so we don't know how effects compare between these various approaches.

Evidence Specific to the Anticipated Effects of Exercise on Disordered Eating

As previously explained, some evidence supports a link between body image and disordered eating such that better body image is associated with less disordered eating. Additionally, evidence shows that participation in exercise improves body image. The implication, then, is that exercise might have the potential to reduce disordered eating through its positive effect on body image.

That said, concern has been expressed over the possibility that when performed excessively, exercise might lead to disordered eating or even eating disorders. This concern is particularly relevant when one considers the sports for which the pressure for leanness is likely to contribute to unhealthy eating practices. Three primary groups of sports emphasize leanness. **Aesthetic sports** are those in which performance is evaluated by judges and appearance is a factor in their judgments. These sports include figure skating, dance, gymnastics, and diving. **Endurance sports** are ones that have an expectation that a leaner build is necessary to be competitive. These sports include cross country running, track, rowing, cycling, and swimming. Finally, a group of sports use weight classes (**weight class sports**) to ensure that groups of athletes are competitive with size essentially controlled. These sports include wrestling, judo, and weightlifting. For athletes in these sports, exercise sometimes might be used as a way to control weight in an inappropriate way. Mancine, Gusfa, Moshrefi, and Kennedy (2020) conducted a systematic review of this literature and found that six of seven studies observed statistically significant differences between disordered eating

---

aesthetic sports—Aesthetic sports are those in which performance is evaluated by judges and appearance is a factor in their judgments (e.g., figure skating, dance, gymnastics, diving, ballet).

endurance sports—Endurance sports are those with an expectation that a leaner build is necessary to be competitive (e.g., cross-country running, track, rowing, cycling, swimming).

weight class sports—Weight class sports categorize athletes into groups based upon their weight to ensure that groups of athletes are competitive with size controlled (e.g., wrestling, judo, weightlifting).

rates in lean sports and nonlean sports. The authors concluded that health care professionals should be aware of this risk to allow for early intervention for patients with disordered eating to help prevent the progression to an eating disorder.

The question then becomes if participation in these sports has an impact on body image that manifests in the form of disordered eating or if this behavior is more related to the pressures previously identified (i.e., the pressures associated with sport performance) than to body image. Although no study has looked at this directly, Hausenblas and Downs (2001) conducted a meta-analysis specifically comparing body image between athletes and nonathletes. Clearly, this is not a perfect way to address this question because of the cross-sectional design of the studies, but the findings from this review do indirectly address the question of whether exercise participation conveys a positive effect on body image or if the pressures of sport participation result in the athlete's exercise failing to protect them from those influences. Given the nature of the research question, it is not surprising that the vast majority of the 74 studies in the review were correlational (95%). Overall, their results showed that athletes had a more positive body image than did nonathletes (ES = 0.27). Their results showed no difference between effects observed for aesthetic sports, endurance sports, or ball sports. However, the level of significance was very close ($p < 0.07$ instead of the required $p < 0.05$), and the trend in these findings showed that differences were smaller between athletes and nonathletes for aesthetic sports (ES = 0.23) than for endurance sports (ES = 0.43) or ball sports (ES = 0.40). This might suggest that the benefits of exercise for body image are reduced in the aesthetic sports that emphasize leanness. Further research will be needed to see if this is a reliable difference and to understand better the implications for using exercise as a means of improving body image.

The Risks of Rapid Weight Loss

In 1997 University of Michigan wrestler Jeff Reese died while attempting to make a weight class for an upcoming wrestling competition. To lose 17 pounds (8 kg) as quickly as possible, he was exercising in a rubber suit in a room that was 92 °F (33 °C). He died of kidney failure and heart malfunction, which occurred in response to severe dehydration. That year in a 6-week period, two other collegiate wrestlers, who were trying to make weight for a competition over a short period of time, also died. With Jeff Reese's father and others advocating for change, the NCAA Wrestling Committee quickly made significant rule changes in an attempt to keep athletes safe. In particular, the use of rubber suits, diuretics, and hot rooms (over 79 °F [26 °C]) was forbidden. Weigh-ins were conducted 2 hours before a match rather than the night before. This rule was expected to be effective because rapid weight-loss techniques are known to reduce strength, so athletes would not subject their body to this with weigh-ins so close to the time of competition. Weight classes were established at the beginning of the season, and athletes were limited in how much weight they could lose per week. Finally, a hydration status test became required before the start of the season. Although these changes had a positive effect on athletes' behaviors, 28 deaths of high school wrestlers and 7 deaths of collegiate wrestlers occurred between 1983 and 2018 that could be linked to dehydration. More recently, before the start of the 2017-2018 season, the NCAA implemented stiffer penalties for violations of these rules, which are hoped to further decrease the number of tragic deaths (Zuke, 2018).

Summary

Body image is a complex term that includes the constructs of body perception, body satisfaction or dissatisfaction, an affective response, and body-related behaviors. Poor body image has been shown to be related to negative psychological outcomes including anxiety, depression, disordered eating, and clinical eating disorders. Results of meta-analytic reviews support that regular participation in exercise is associated with better body image. Exercise might improve body image due to its positive impact on objective measures of fitness, perceived measures of fitness, or self-efficacy. Results support that perceived fitness and self-efficacy explain most of the variance in body image improvements. Results from meta-analytic reviews show that exercise results in moderate benefits (ES = 0.45-0.57) to body image, with larger benefits typically observed for women compared to men. The results of moderator analyses also suggest that when interventions are implemented with men and women, benefits are larger for programs that combine aerobic and anaerobic training. However, when implemented with just men, the benefits are largest for aerobic exercise alone and for anaerobic exercise alone compared to combined training programs. Importantly, benefits appear to be largest overall when exercise is performed by single-sex groups rather than co-ed groups. These findings suggest that interventions to improve body image should be conducted with single-sex groups and that the specifics of whether to recommend aerobic exercise, anaerobic exercise, or a combination is dependent on the person's gender. Although there is some concern that participation in sports that emphasize leanness has a negative impact on body image, which then might contribute to disordered eating, the evidence actually supports that exercise benefits athletes in both lean and nonlean sports. In other words, the benefits of exercise for body image appear to be consistent across aesthetic, endurance, and ball sports.

Discussion Questions

1. Imagine that you have a friend who has body dissatisfaction. Based on the evidence in this chapter, what advice could you give them relative to exercise?

2. What do we know about negative body image and its relationship with BMI? How is this different or the same for men and women?

3. Hausenblas and Fallon (2006) and Bassett-Gunter and colleagues (2017) conducted meta-analytic reviews of the literature on exercise and body image. Describe these two meta-analyses including where their inclusion criteria and findings were similar and where they differed.

4. Exercise has the potential to reduce disordered eating through its positive effect on body image. However, it is possible that participation in sports that emphasize leanness might actually cause poor body image and lead to the development of eating disorders. Explain the distinction between sports that emphasize leanness and those that don't, and describe evidence relevant to this consideration.

13

Exercise and Sleep

CHAPTER OBJECTIVES

After studying this chapter, you should be able to do the following:

- Identify the negative implications of chronic sleep deprivation for individuals and for society
- Summarize both subjective and objective measures of sleep quantity and quality
- Recognize the limitations of research on sleep
- Describe theories explaining the purpose of sleep
- Understand meta-analytic findings with respect to acute and chronic exercise benefits for good sleepers, people with insomnia, and cancer patients and survivors

KEY TERMS

sleep

sleep quantity (sleep duration, total sleep time)

sleep quality

sleep disturbances

sleep latency

sleep efficiency

waking after sleep onset

insomnia

sleep-related breathing disorders

circadian rhythm sleep–wake disorders

parasomnia

sleep-related movement disorders

restless legs syndrome

hypersomnia

obstructive sleep apnea

ghrelin

leptin

REM (rapid-eye movement) sleep

non-REM sleep

sleep hygiene

polysomnography

sleep architecture

T'Shawn is 27 years old and has been working for 3 years as a reservation manager at a well-known hotel chain. She has been experiencing increasing stress at her job and lately has been having trouble sleeping. It is hard to wake up in the morning even with an alarm, and she feels exhausted for much of the day. She's increased her coffee consumption and regularly goes out with friends after work for dinner and drinks. She's starting to feel stressed even about the idea of sleep because it's been so difficult to come by. She turns her alarm clock to the wall so she can't see the time, has taken her television out of her bedroom, and makes sure to leave her phone in the kitchen and set to "do not disturb" when she goes to bed. Her friend Dante recently suggested that she should start an exercise program with him so they could both get some much-needed physical activity. They join a gym and start attending exercise classes 3 days a week at 6:30 p.m. After working out, T'Shawn heads home for a hot shower and dinner and skips those nights in terms of socializing with her friends. After the first month of working out together, T'Shawn and Dante begin to go on bicycle rides on the weekends and to play tennis with another couple of friends on some afternoons. Remarkably, T'Shawn notices that her sleep is starting to improve. She falls asleep more quickly and doesn't wake up as many times during the night. She feels more refreshed and energized during the day and is starting to feel healthier overall. She wonders aloud to Dante, "Do you think exercise is what's helping me sleep better?" Dante replies, "No way, hon. It's not the exercise, it's that you're falling in love!" Although love and a reduction in stress could have much to do with it, exercise also might be playing a role in improving T'Shawn's sleep quality and quantity.

This story demonstrates a possible link between regular exercise and sleep. It certainly makes sense that if you have a more physically active day than normal, like on a day when you rake leaves for 4 hours or go on a 6-hour hike, your body would be more fatigued, resulting in better sleep quality. However, the question we're interested in is really about regular exercise that is typically performed in shorter bouts (30-60 min) and that wouldn't be expected to affect fatigue.

Sleep is such an important determinant of our ability to manage our emotions, efforts, and interests over the course of the day. When we get sufficient and good-quality sleep, we are able to focus, be emotionally stable, and give high effort. By contrast, when our sleep is of poor quality or insufficient quantity, we might have trouble paying attention, be short-tempered, and be unable to sustain effort for cognitive or physical tasks. Exercise can play an important role in helping us to get better quality sleep and, in situations where we are able to choose our own sleeping and waking times, also might contribute to greater quantity of sleep. In this chapter, we will learn why we need to sleep, how sleep patterns have evolved throughout the centuries, and ways to measure sleep, and we will consider the evidence to see if exercise has been shown to be effective in improving sleep quality or quantity.

Definitions of Sleep and Its Attributes

We begin with some definitions. Sleep is defined as a temporary state that affects the body and mind; that typically occurs for several hours every night; and that is characterized by a relatively inactive nervous system, closed eyes, relaxed muscles, and reversible unconsciousness. Sleep is an important contributor to physical and mental health in part because the purpose of sleep is to allow the brain and body to rest and recover from the activities of the day. Although most people get some sleep every night, in this current era, the quality and quantity of sleep that people get tends to be insufficient to meet their needs, resulting in a negative impact on both physical and mental health. Sleep quantity is also called sleep duration and total sleep time and is the total amount of time a person is asleep minus any time they are awake across a 24-hour

---

sleep—Sleep is a temporary state that affects the body and mind, that typically occurs for several hours every night, and that is characterized by a relatively inactive nervous system, closed eyes, relaxed muscles, and reversible unconsciousness.

sleep quantity (sleep duration, total sleep time)—The total amount of time a person is asleep minus any time they are awake across a 24-hour period is known as sleep quantity, sleep duration, or total sleep time.

period. **Sleep quality** is a complex construct that includes both objective and subjective attributes. Subjectively, sleep quality is determined by the person's assessment of how they feel upon waking up and their general sleepiness and so is defined as the overall satisfaction with the sleep experience (Nelson et al., 2022). Objectively, sleep quality is affected by four factors: sleep disturbances, sleep latency, sleep efficiency, and waking after sleep onset. **Sleep disturbances** can occur as a person is falling asleep or while they are asleep and include characteristics of sleep disorders such as periodic limb movements, nightmares, and sudden awakenings and can also relate to environmental triggers such as noises or medications. **Sleep latency** is the time that elapses between when a person turns the light off until they fall asleep, with a shorter sleep latency indicating better sleep quality. **Sleep efficiency** is defined as the proportion of the total time in bed that is spent asleep; this is presented as a percentage, with a higher percentage indicating better sleep efficiency. **Waking after sleep onset** is described as the total time a person is awake between initial sleep onset and final wakening, with a shorter time associated with better quality sleep. When considering variables that influence sleep and those that are associated with sleep quality, these terms will help us understand the specific aspects of the sleep experience.

A Brief History of Sleep

The patterns and amount of sleep that people get changed dramatically with the advent of technology. In the 20th century, the widespread availability of electricity resulted in equally widespread access to artificial lighting (figure 13.1). The provision of artificial light created a dramatic increase in people's opportunities to stay up late into the night. In the modern age, with the introduction of restaurants, bars, movie theaters, and night clubs that stay open well past midnight, as well as the availability of television, social media, and the Internet 24 hours a day, people have lots of reasons to stay up late, and the number of people experiencing sleep deprivation is particularly high. In addition to leisure pursuits, numerous industries require shift workers (26% of workers), some of whom might work through the night (17% of workers), and various professions such as physicians and nurses working in hospitals, firefighters, police, and EMTs often require 24-hour or late-night shifts (Lieberman et al., 2020). All of this has contributed to what has been described as an epidemic in sleep deprivation (Watson et al., 2010). In fact, evidence suggests that approximately 35% of U.S. adults and almost 80% of high school students are chronically sleep deprived (National Center for Chronic Disease Prevention and Health Promotion, 2022). In other words, over one-third of adults and four out of five teenagers are functioning in a state of chronically failing to get enough rest for their physical and mental health. This is important because of the negative consequences of sleep deprivation, which are both acute and chronic. In particular, chronic sleep deprivation has a negative impact on the waking state (i.e., people have trouble staying awake) and on cognition and behavior (e.g., people can't focus or pay attention and might make poor decisions as a result), increases risk for disease (e.g., has serious health consequences), and has numerous economic costs (e.g., financial or social).

> If you get into bed at 11:20 p.m. and fall asleep at 11:30 p.m., your sleep onset latency would be 10 minutes. If you wake up at 1:30 a.m., are restless until 2:30 a.m., and then ultimately wake up for good at 9:30 a.m., your total sleep time would be the time between 11:30 p.m. and 9:30 a.m., less the 1 hour of wake after sleep onset, so 9 hours. One hour of wake after sleep onset is an indicant of the quality of your sleep as is your sleep efficiency, which is approximated as follows:
>
> $$9\ hrs\ total\ sleep\ /\ 10\ hrs\ total\ time\ in\ bed = 90\%$$

---

sleep quality—Sleep quality is subjectively determined by the person's assessment of how they feel upon waking up and their general sleepiness; the overall satisfaction with the sleep experience.

sleep disturbances—Sleep disturbances can occur as a person is falling asleep or while they are asleep and include characteristics of sleep disorders such as periodic limb movements, nightmares, and sudden awakenings and can also relate to environmental triggers such as noises or medications.

sleep latency—The time that elapses between when a person turns the light off until they fall asleep is known as sleep latency, with a shorter sleep latency indicating better sleep quality.

sleep efficiency—The proportion of the total time in bed that is spent asleep is called sleep efficiency, with a higher percentage being better.

waking after sleep onset—The total time a person is awake between initial sleep onset and final wakening is referred to as waking after sleep onset, with a shorter time being associated with better quality sleep.

FIGURE 13.1 The widespread availability of electricity has resulted in increased exposure to artificial light, which can affect sleep patterns.

Life Without Electricity

An interesting study was conducted in 2019 to test the question of whether electric light has an impact on sleep deprivation (Smit et al., 2019). Researchers compared sleep between two villages of Indigenous Melanesians on Tanna Island, Vanuatu (Fiji Islands). The primary difference between the villages was that one village had access to electricity, while the other did not. None of the villagers tracked time during the day with a watch or clock, and because the villagers were living as horticultural farmers, they did not have regular working hours. Villagers participating in the study wore an accelerometer on their wrist for 7 days. Although the total sleep was greater than 7 hours in both groups, those in the electric community slept significantly less (7.42 hours) than those in the nonelectric community (7.88 hours). Researchers learned that the electric village had delayed sleep onset of approximately 23 minutes and more fragmented sleep (30% vs. 20%) relative to the nonelectric village. In this study, fragmented sleep was defined as sleep that was interrupted by an awakening period that was shorter than the shortest sleep period (e.g., a person was asleep for 2 hr, then awake for 30 min, and then asleep again for 6 hr). Interestingly, this difference was particularly evident in breastfeeding females: Those in the electric village got 65 minutes less sleep than their counterparts in the nonelectric village. Because villagers in the electric community took significantly more naps than those in the nonelectric community, researchers concluded that ready access to electric light causes sleep deficits even in this nonindustrialized nation. Consider the difference in sleep quantity and quality that might be observed between these Fijians and you.

How Much Sleep Do We Need?

How much sleep is enough? In a consensus statement, the American Academy of Sleep Medicine and the Sleep Research Society advocated for 7 hours of sleep per night for adults aged 18 to 60 years (Consensus Conference Panel, 2015). This is based on a substantial evidence base demonstrating that this amount of sleep is necessary for good health, performance, and psychological and physical functions. Based on data reviewed by the Centers for Disease Control, children and teenagers need substantially more sleep, with recommendations for 9 to 12 hours for school-age children and 8 to 10 hours for teenagers, to satisfy the needs of their growing bodies and to allow for sufficient rest after busy days (see table 13.1). Older adults tend to sleep more lightly and in a more interrupted fashion but still need 7 to 8 hours of sleep per night. Reflective of evidence that most Americans do not get enough sleep, the U.S. Department of Health and Human Services included a Sleep Health Objective in its Healthy People 2030 report to encourage adults to get sufficient sleep (U.S. Department of Health and Human Services, n.d.). Included in this objective are goals for reducing vehicular crashes due to drowsiness and increasing the percent of high school students and adults who get sufficient sleep.

The question of how we define good sleep quality is one that only recently has been addressed from a data-based perspective. The National Sleep Foundation established a panel of 18 experts who agreed that for young adults, sleep latency of ≤30 minutes, awakening fewer than 2 times during the night, and napping 0 days per week were all characteristics of good sleep quality. By contrast, sleep latency of >45 minutes, 4 or more awakenings, and napping for >100 minutes were consistently identified as indicative of poor sleep quality. Those with sleep parameters in between these extremes (i.e., sleep latency of 30-45 min, 2-3 awakenings per night, napping ≤100 min) are in the middle with regards to sleep quality.

School Day Start Time

Researchers have demonstrated that middle school and high school students would benefit from the school day starting later. This is because adolescents experience a delay in the release of melatonin and have a slower increase in desire to sleep during waking hours than do other age groups. Carvalho-Mendes and colleagues (2020) conducted a study using actimetry measures to measure sleep parameters in adolescents attending morning and afternoon shifts at school. Both groups went to sleep at similar times, but those attending the morning shift got 105 minutes less sleep than did the students attending the afternoon shift. The authors recommended that school start times be adjusted dramatically to better match the circadian rhythms of adolescents.

Prevalence and Costs of Sleep Disorders and Sleep Deprivation

You might find it surprising to learn that 90 different kinds of sleep disorders chronically affect between 50 and 70 million Americans (Institute of

TABLE 13.1 Recommended Amount of Sleep Based on a Person's Age

Age	Average amount of sleep per 24-hr period (including naps)
Newborn (0-3 mo)	14-17 hr
4-11 mo	12-15 hr
1-2 yr	11-14 hr
3-5 yr	10-13 hr
6-13 yr	9-11 hr
14-17 yr	8-10 hr
18-60 yr	>7 hr

From Hirschkowitz et al. (2015).

Medicine [US] Committee on Sleep Medicine and Research, 2006). The International Classification of Sleep Disorders has identified and described these various sleep disorders and categorized them into one of seven broad types: **insomnia** (difficulty falling or staying asleep), **sleep-related breathing disorders** (abnormal and difficult breathing during sleep), hypersomnia (excessive sleepiness), **circadian rhythm sleep–wake disorders** (difficulty falling asleep, waking up during sleep, or waking up too early due to the body's internal clock being poorly aligned with the social clock), **parasomnia** (abnormal sleep such as night terrors, sleepwalking, and sleep talking), **sleep-related movement disorders** (rhythmic movements that disrupt sleep), and other sleep disorders. Although we all experience troubled sleep on occasion, these sleep disorders are chronic experiences that affect a person's ability to perform daily activities. For example, insomnia is considered a sleep disorder when it occurs for 3 or more nights within a week for at least 3 months and is causing serious challenges with respect to daily functioning. Insomnia is the most frequently experienced sleep disorder with up to 33% of adults reporting insomnia symptoms and 6-10% of Americans reaching criteria for diagnosis as a disorder, but sleep-related movement disorders (particularly restless legs syndrome), hypersomnia, and obstructive sleep apnea are also relatively common sleep disorders (see table 13.2) (American Psychiatric Association, 2023). **Restless legs syndrome** is the experience of uncomfortable sensations in the legs during sleep. These sensations make it difficult for the person to fall asleep and may even wake them up during the night. In contrast to these two disorders that result in too little sleep, **hypersomnia** is defined as excessive sleepiness even when getting at least 7 hours of sleep per night, taking unintentional naps, not feeling rested when sleeping more than 9 hours within a day, and difficulty with waking up fully. Again, although all of us might experience these types of challenges to our sleep from time to time, they are diagnosed as sleep disorders when they are chronic and have a demonstrable negative effect on the performance of normal daily activities.

One particular sleep disorder, obstructive sleep apnea, is a severe disorder that affects approximately 2% to 15% of the population (American Psychiatric Association, 2023). If a person has **obstructive sleep apnea**, that means that during their sleep, they occasionally will stop breathing for at least 10 seconds during the night. This typically occurs because the throat muscles relax during sleep, thus blocking the airway. If you've ever heard a person snoring heavily, reach a crescendo, stop and be silent for a period of time, and then gasp or snort, this can be scary and is a sign of obstructive sleep apnea. Not many treatment options exist for people experiencing obstructive sleep apnea. The use of a machine that provides continuous positive airway pressure

TABLE 13.2 Prevalence of Various Sleep Disorders in Americans

Category	Definition	% of Americans
Insomnia	Difficulty falling or staying asleep	6-10%
Restless legs syndrome	Uncomfortable sensations in the legs during sleep	2-7.2%
Hypersomnia	Excessive sleepiness	5-10% of patients seeking help for sleep disorders
Obstructive sleep apnea	Brief cessation of breathing during sleep	2-15% of middle-aged adults; >20% of older adults

Adapted from American Psychiatric Association (2023).

insomnia—Insomnia is defined as difficulty falling or staying asleep that occurs for 3 or more nights within a week for at least 3 months and causes serious challenges with respect to daily functioning.

sleep-related breathing disorders—Sleep-related breathing disorders are characterized by abnormal and difficult breathing during sleep.

circadian rhythm sleep–wake disorders—Difficulty falling asleep, waking up during sleep, or waking up too early due to the body's internal clock being poorly aligned with the social clock are all indicative of circadian rhythm sleep–wake disorders.

parasomnia—Parasomnia is abnormal sleep due to night terrors, sleepwalking, and sleep talking.

sleep-related movement disorders—Rhythmic movements that disrupt sleep are known as sleep-related movement disorders.

restless legs syndrome—Restless legs syndrome is the experience of uncomfortable sensations in the legs during sleep.

hypersomnia—Excessive sleepiness even when getting at least 7 hours of sleep per night, unintentional naps, not feeling rested when sleeping more than 9 hours within a day, and difficulty with waking up fully are all characteristics of hypersomnia.

obstructive sleep apnea—Obstructive sleep apnea is a sleep disorder characterized by a person repeatedly stopping breathing for at least 10 seconds and restarting breathing while sleeping.

(CPAP) can be effective, but patients typically show low adherence rates because of the discomfort and invasiveness of the equipment (see figure 13.2). This poor adherence is part of the reason that researchers have been interested in exploring the effects of exercise in the treatment of obstructive sleep apnea.

Many sleep disorders result in sleep deprivation due to low quality or quantity of sleep, and even in the absence of a diagnosed sleep disorder, we know that many individuals are not getting sufficient sleep relative to the recommendations of the National Sleep Foundation. Meta-analytic results from studies conducted in the United States, the United Kingdom, and the Netherlands indicate that 24.5% of people sleep less than recommended, with people in the United States reporting an even greater frequency of sleep deprivation (30.3%) (Kocevska et al., 2021). The economic costs of sleep deprivation are staggering. Sleep deprivation is associated with an increase in human error–related accidents and motor vehicle accidents, costing an estimated $43 to $56 billion per year. Medical costs in 2021 were estimated at $94.9 billion per year and include visits to health care professionals, tests, treatments, hospital services, and medicines (Huyett et al., 2021). Estimates of the associated indirect costs such as losses in productivity and increased comorbidities have been estimated using economic modeling techniques and suggest that the overall cost of sleep deprivation in terms of its impact on the economy is between $280 billion and $411 billion (Hafner et al., 2017).

Another cost of sleep deprivation is that poor sleep quality is tied to overweight and obesity, which has important health implications. Body mass index (BMI) and sleep duration are significantly negatively correlated: Those who get less sleep have higher BMI. Furthermore, studies have shown that compared to individuals who get sufficient sleep (7-8 hr/night), those who sleep 6 hours or less per night have a greater risk of obesity. The link between exercise and overweight is likely tied to the impact of sleep on hunger hormones (ghrelin and leptin). **Ghrelin** is a hunger hormone that increases your appetite, and **leptin** is a hunger hormone that increases feelings of being full after eating. When you get good-quality

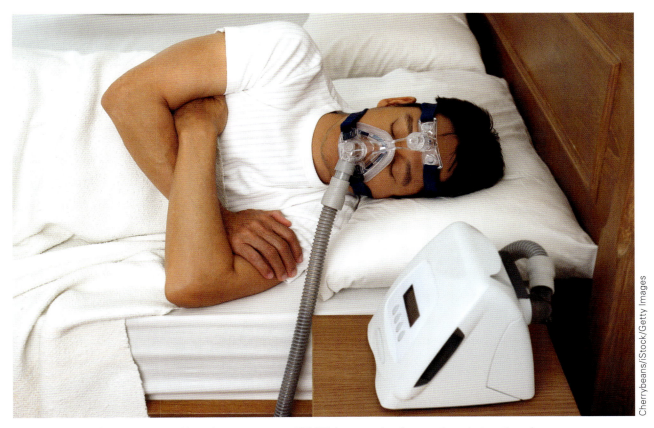

FIGURE 13.2 Continuous positive airway pressure (CPAP) is an option for treating obstructive sleep apnea.

---

ghrelin—Ghrelin is a hunger hormone that increases appetite.
leptin—Leptin is a hunger hormone that increases feelings of being full after eating.

sleep, ghrelin decreases (decreasing your appetite) and leptin increases (increasing your feelings of satiation or fullness). When you get poor-quality sleep, the converse is true: Ghrelin rises (making you experience more hunger) and leptin decreases (so that you don't feel as full after eating). This link between sleep quality, appetite, and BMI has clear relevance to exercise psychology since acute and chronic exercise are expected to improve sleep quality and chronic exercise is expected to also decrease BMI.

Finally, evidence supports that a relationship exists between the experience of sleep disorders and the risk of mortality. In a study reporting on data from 2009-2010, researchers followed participants for 5 years (Huyett et al., 2021). After 5 years, 9.3% of those who initially had reported a diagnosed sleep disorder were deceased compared to 5.2% of individuals without a diagnosed sleep disorder. This represents an almost twofold increase in the risk of death for those with a diagnosed sleep disorder, and this increased risk remained even after controlling for age, sex, BMI, and various chronic health conditions. Furthermore, for individuals with severe obstructive sleep apnea, the risk of all-cause mortality was 50% to almost 100% higher than for individuals without obstructive sleep apnea (Wang et al., 2013; Xie et al., 2017). These are staggering increases in the risk of mortality that are tied to sleep quality.

Theories and Mechanisms of Sleep

Numerous hypotheses have been proposed to explain why we sleep, but scientists acknowledge that we don't really know the answer to this question. In fact, Dr. Michael Halassa, a neuroscientist, said, "It's kind of embarrassing. . . . It's obvious why we need to eat, for example, and reproduce . . . but it's not clear why we need to sleep at all" (Pappas, 2017). Chokroverty described the reason for sleep as "the greatest biologic mystery of all times" (Chokroverty, 2017, p. 19). To put this question another way, why aren't our bodies designed to function at a high level all day every day? This seems like it would benefit us in terms of the amount of work (e.g., hunting and gathering) we could accomplish. However, evidence clearly shows that going without sleep for extended periods of time is not even possible. In an animal study conducted with rats, complete sleep deprivation resulted in the death of 10 out of 10 rats within 11 to 32 days (Everson et al., 1989). This isn't research that would ever be conducted with humans, but we infer from these animal findings that sleep is required for life in all mammals.

Popular theories to explain why we need to sleep include the energy conservation theory, the restorative theory, and several theories that focus on specific restorative processes in the brain (e.g., the synaptic and neural integrity theory, the memory consolidation and reinforcement theory, and the metabolic homeostasis theory) (Chokroverty, 2017). Knowing why we need sleep and the function of sleep might help with understanding whether exercise would be expected to contribute to sleep quality or quantity.

Energy Conservation Theory

The energy conservation theory suggests that we sleep simply to save energy. This hypothesis is supported by the fact that our circadian rhythm is tied to dark–light cycles such that we tend to sleep during the night when energy expenditure would be less effectively used because the darkness impedes our ability to hunt for food. It is also supported by the fact that our metabolic rate decreases dramatically when we sleep, resulting in an overall savings in the amount of energy expended. That said, the fact that only 120 calories are saved by sleeping for 8 hours provides an argument against energy conservation being a primary need for sleep. In addition, given that being asleep puts animals in a vulnerable state, the risk doesn't seem worth the conservation of a mere 120 calories. Thus, this theory probably is not a great explanation of why we need to sleep, and it has fallen into disfavor.

Restorative Hypothesis

The restorative hypothesis focuses more on the idea that sleep is a necessary time for repair. This is supported by evidence that many repair processes do take place during sleep, including muscle repair, protein synthesis, and tissue growth. These repair processes are responsive to anabolic hormones and occur through protein synthesis, which takes place predominantly at night.

Specific Restorative Processes in the Brain

The theories that focus on the restorative processes for the brain all suggest that sleep provides a time period necessary for critical activities in the brain. Support for these theories comes from evidence that REM sleep increases following sleep deprivation and strenuous physical activity and from studies showing that sleep deprivation negatively affects cognitive performance (Lim & Dinges, 2010). These theories include the memory consolidation and reinforcement theory and the metabolic homeostasis theory.

Memory Consolidation and Reinforcement Theory

The memory consolidation and reinforcement theory is based on empirical evidence showing that memory consolidation and reconsolidation are reliant on both REM and non-REM sleep. **REM sleep** (or rapid-eye movement sleep) occurs periodically throughout the night and is the time during which dreams occur. It is characterized by rapid eye movements, some bodily movement, faster heart rate, and faster breathing. **Non-REM sleep** makes up the remainder of our sleep and is characterized by quiet or restful sleep. During non-REM sleep, brain activity, breathing, and heart rate slow down, muscles relax, and eye movements are minimal. According to this theory, sleep is necessary so that we can process information from the previous day and to prepare ourselves to take in new information in the coming day. In particular, learning-associated synapses grow and are reinforced during sleep, while seldom-used synapses are pruned. The analogy to think of here is a gardener shaping a bush to a particular shape. The gardener who is shaping the plant might provide fertilizer and water to support growth in a particular direction but also will prune the unwanted growth to create the desired look. Support for this theory is provided by studies showing that sleep deprivation negatively affects our ability to remember and recall information (Born & Wilhelm, 2012).

An analogy to express the memory consolidation and reinforcement theory is to think of a gardener who provides fertilizer and water to encourage growth in some directions while also pruning to get the desired outcome.

REM (rapid-eye movement) sleep—REM sleep is a phase of sleep that occurs periodically throughout the night; is the time during which dreams occur; and is characterized by rapid eye movements, some bodily movement, faster heart rate, and faster breathing.

non-REM sleep—Non-REM sleep is a phase of sleep that is characterized by quiet or restful sleep such that brain activity, breathing, and heart rate slow down; muscles relax; and eye movements are minimal.

Metabolic Homeostasis Theory

The metabolic homeostasis theory has been proposed relatively recently and is based on evidence that neural metabolic waste products, which accumulate during waking hours, are cleared from the brain during sleep. This theory is based on evidence from animal studies showing a significant increase (60%) in the space between brain blood vessels during sleep, which results in a larger space being available to clean out toxic waste (Xie et al., 2013). Think of the movie *Harry Potter and the Prisoner of Azkaban*, and picture a magic bus called the Knight Bus racing through the streets of London. Because it was a magic bus, other cars, buildings, and even people were magically moved out of the way so it could move through the city unimpeded. Now, imagine wizards cleaning the streets by first casting a spell that makes the buildings shrink back so that the streets are wider and the sanitation trucks and personnel can more quickly and efficiently clean the city. This analogy illustrates the notion proposed in the metabolic homeostasis theory that spaces in the brain are expanded during sleep to make cleanup more efficient.

Two-Process Model of Sleep Regulation

Conceptually, the two-process model of sleep regulation explains that a person's urge to sleep is controlled by two processes. The first process is the body's need to return to homeostasis through the restorative properties of sleep. The second process manifests through the person's circadian rhythm (Goel et al., 2009). The homeostatic process describes the drive for sleep experienced as the body senses a need to return to homeostasis when we move away from that balance. The homeostatic process demonstrates an expected increase in the demand for sleep during waking hours, decreases during sleep, and has a threshold above which sleep is initiated. This drive for sleep appears to be linked to adenosine, which is produced in the brain. During the day, adenosine levels increase as tiredness increases. During sleep, adenosine is broken down.

The homeostatic process works in conjunction with the body's circadian rhythm. A circadian rhythm (or daily rhythm) describes the fact that many functions in the body (e.g., temperature, metabolism, hormone release) exhibit a regularity in their fluctuations throughout the day and thus affect a person's daily behavior. The biological clock that regulates sleeping and waking is located in the suprachiasmatic nuclei (SCN) of the hypothalamus in the brain. The SCN receives light exposure information and controls the sleep–wake cycle. The SCN is responsible for the release of melatonin, which makes us feel sleepy. When exposed to light in the evening and early night, the circadian clock is delayed so that sleep comes on later in the evening. You can see evidence of this when a person is exposed to light later in the evening during longer days in the summer and thus their eating and sleep schedules adjust to be later than in the winter when light exposure is decreased. The best example of how strong the circadian rhythm is occurs when you have experienced significant time changes during travel. If you've crossed three or more times zones, you've likely experienced this when your body tells you one thing while the time of day in your current time zone suggests something different. For example, if you were to fly from the east coast of the United States to the United Kingdom, the time on the clock might say 11:00 a.m., but your body would feel like it was 6:00 a.m. You'd be handed a lunch menu in a restaurant, but your body would be making you think about breakfast. This demonstrates the strength of your circadian rhythm, and it is likely to take a few days to adjust to the new time zone.

The Risks of Daylight Saving Time

Zhang and associates (2020) compiled data from insurance claims to explore the effects of daylight savings time (DST) on health. In states that observe DST, the clock "springs" forward by one hour in the spring and "falls back" by one hour in the fall. Their findings are startling in that they report significant increases in cardiovascular disease (e.g., heart attacks), physical injuries, mental health disorders, and immune-related diseases (e.g., colitis) in association with this shift of the clock. With regards to injuries, one estimate indicated that children, teenagers, and young adults (younger than 21 yr of age) experience a 30% increase in the risk of injuries to the head, wrists, and hands in association with DST. The implication is that this increase in injuries reflects the disruption of sleep and of the circadian rhythm that occurs in response to the changing of the clock.

Mechanisms for Exercise Affecting Sleep

Although the mechanisms for why exercise might benefit sleep are not yet well understood, there are several possibilities that might explain this relationship. One link is through the potential psychological mediators of depression and anxiety. As previously discussed, exercise leads to reductions in anxiety and depression, both of which are linked to poor sleep quality. Hence, exercise might exert its benefits through these mediators. Exercise also can affect sleep through its effect on biochemicals that are known to be associated with sleep. Both adenosine and prostaglandins are known to promote sleep. In studies in which these biochemicals are blocked, results show that the beneficial effects of exercise on sleep are not observed. Although this is an indirect approach, it suggests that these biochemicals are critically engaged in the effects of exercise on sleep.

Treatment for Sleep Disorders

Treatments for sleep disorders include making minor adjustments that affect sleep hygiene, cognitive behavioral therapy to identify and cope with stressors that are affecting sleep, supplements, and prescription medicines. Currently, approximately 7,500 physicians are board-certified in sleep medicine, and >2,500 accredited sleep centers exist (American Academy of Sleep Medicine, 2022). **Sleep hygiene** refers to the environment and routines that a person uses to increase the likelihood of having consistent, uninterrupted sleep. Minor adjustments to improve sleep hygiene typically include things such as keeping a regular sleep schedule, minimizing noise, minimizing light, managing the temperature for comfort, and stopping screen time at least 2 hours before going to bed. Supplements that are commonly used and for which some evidence of effectiveness exists include melatonin (Chan & Lo, 2022), lavender (Luo & Jiang, 2022), and valerian (Shinjyo et al., 2020). Pharmacological treatment for sleep disorders is dependent on the specific sleep disorder. Evidence clearly supports the use of benzodiazepines for insomnia (Holbrook et al., 2000), and other medications have been shown to be effective for specific sleep disorders, such as modafinil and armodafinil for narcolepsy (Bhattarai & Sumerall, 2017), a form of hypersomnia, and dopaminergic drugs for restless legs syndrome (Lv et al., 2021).

Measurement

Measuring sleep can be challenging. The measurement of quantity is perhaps not that hard, but the assessment of quality requires more sophisticated assessment tools. Both objective measures (using devices to assess movement, brain activity, heart rate, and muscular activity) and subjective (self-report measures using surveys or questionnaires) can provide insights into sleep quantity and quality. When used in combination, they provide the best measures because they allow the participant to confirm the impact of various sleep parameters on their perceived sleep quality.

Polysomnography

The gold standard for the measurement of sleep is provided by **polysomnography**. Polysomnography is recorded using electrodes that allow for the simultaneous collection of brain (electroencephalographic, EEG), muscular (electromyographic, EMG), and heart (electrocardiographic, ECG) activity. When polysomnography is used in a laboratory setting, 16 electrodes typically are used. When a portable polysomnography system is used in a home setting, substantially fewer electrodes are likely to be worn, but this might allow for more natural sleep due to the lessened invasiveness, and, of course, sleep is also more likely to be typical because the participant is sleeping in their own home. Ideally, polysomnography is assessed for at least two nights, with the first night serving as a familiarization night. Importantly, participants should be instructed to follow their normal routine with regards to when they turn out the lights to go to bed if data are to represent what they experience on a typical night.

Numerous outcomes can be captured using polysomnography. EEG activity is used to help discern a person's sleep architecture. **Sleep architecture** is the manner in which a person cycles through the various stages of sleep. The term *architecture* reflects the way that sleep cycles are depicted, which looks

---

sleep hygiene—The environment and routines that a person uses to increase the likelihood of having consistent, uninterrupted sleep is known as sleep hygiene.

polysomnography—Polysomnography is an objective measure of sleep architecture that is recorded using electrodes that allow for the simultaneous collection of brain (electroencephalographic, EEG), muscular (electromyographic, EMG), and heart (electrocardiographic, ECG) activity.

sleep architecture—The manner in which you cycle through the various stages of sleep is known as sleep architecture, with the term *architecture* reflecting the way that sleep cycles are depicted, which looks like a skyline in a big city.

like a skyline in a big city (see figure 13.3). Early depictions of sleep architecture identified five stages of sleep, but more recent models consider only four stages of sleep. In addition to assessing stage of sleep as an aspect of sleep architecture, polysomnography also allows for the identification of numerous other variables including sleep onset latency, total sleep time, wake after sleep onset, and sleep efficiency.

As previously mentioned, recent models define sleep as consisting of four stages including one with REM that accounts for approximately 20% to 25% of sleep and three without REM (stages 1-3 of non-REM sleep) that account for the remaining 75% to 80% of sleep (see table 13.3). During a typical night of sleep, you cycle through these various stages more than once (typically 4-6 cycles) with increasingly more REM sleep as the night progresses (see figure 13.3). Stage 1 sleep is the phase when you are moving from wakefulness to drowsiness to being asleep. It is a light stage of sleep characterized by the slowing of heart rate, breathing rate, and eye movements and muscle relaxation. During stage 1, EEG data shows how brain activity transitions from alpha (8-13 Hz) to theta (4-7 Hz) activity. Stage 2 sleep is a slightly deeper stage of sleep during which heart rate and breathing continue to slow, eye movements stop, and your muscles relax even further. During stage 2 sleep, brief sporadic periods of brain activity called *sleep spindles* (12-14 Hz) are evident in the EEG signal. Stage 2 sleep makes up approximately half of total sleep time. Stage 3 sleep is a very deep sleep that is critical to how you feel the next morning. It occurs in longer periods of time in the second half of the night and is the period of time when a person is hard to wake up. Brain activity consists primarily of delta activity (0.5-2 Hz), so this stage is also sometimes called *delta sleep* or *slow-wave sleep*. Although the link between the various stages of sleep and sleep quality isn't perfect, it is clear that stage 3 is critical for the experience of good quality sleep. REM sleep is first experienced approximately 90 minutes after sleep onset and is typically experienced three to five times during the night. REM sleep is characterized by rapid eye movements but is also accompanied by faster heart rate and breathing. Most, but not all, dreaming occurs during REM sleep. Interestingly, EEG activity during REM sleep looks similar to when a person is awake. Because a person who is not allowed to get into REM sleep one night will then have more REM sleep than usual on a subsequent night, it is thought that REM sleep is also critical to sleep quality.

TABLE 13.3 Typical Time in Each Sleep Stage

Sleep stage	Sleep time (%)
Non-REM sleep	75-80%
Stage 1	3-8%
Stage 2	45-55%
Stage 3	15-23%
REM	20-25%

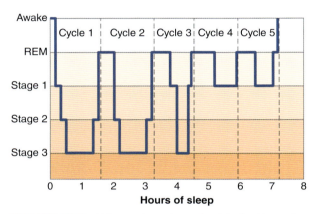

FIGURE 13.3 When plotted out in this fashion, the sleep cycles, indicated by the heavy blue lines, make the shape of a city skyline and hence this is referred to as *sleep architecture*.

Wearable Devices

Measures of sleep quality are now readily available through wearable devices that provide acceptable measures of sleep patterns including wake time and sleep time. The wearable devices that are most appropriate for research are those that can measure both movement and cardiac activity. The benefit of these devices is that they can be used to obtain data from naturalistic settings (i.e., from a participant sleeping at home in their own bed with only the wearable device). By comparing data from wearable devices to that obtained using polysomnography (the gold standard), scientists have demonstrated that some commercially available wearable devices are acceptable for the provision of research-grade data. In particular, the Apple Watch, Fitbit Charge 2, and Oura Ring have been demonstrated to provide accurate measures of sleep onset, wake times, sleep efficiency, and total sleep time; however, because of their limitations, these commercial devices are not useful for understanding stages of sleep, REM sleep, or specific types of sleep disorders (Liang & Chapa Martell, 2018; Roberts et al., 2020).

Behavioral Measures

Some behavioral measures have been used to assess various aspects of sleep. Sleep latency has been used as a measure of sleepiness (Multiple Sleep Latency Test, MSLT) and as a measure of the ability to resist sleep (Maintenance of Wakefulness Test, MWT). For the MSLT, the time until participants fall asleep naturally is assessed, while the MWT requires that participants try to stay awake as long as possible. Both of these latencies are decreased when a person is sleep deprived, and these measures can be used in the absence of polysomnography, making them amenable for use in studies with larger sample sizes.

Self-Report Measures

Many sleep measures also can be self-reported. The Pittsburgh Sleep Quality Index (PSQI) (Buysse et al., 1989) was developed for clinical populations but has been commonly used in exercise and sleep research. This survey consists of questions that ask about typical sleep patterns and the frequency of having challenges related to sleep. It also includes questions about challenges to a person's sleep that emanate from another person sleeping in the same room (e.g., a snoring roommate). Recently, Knutson and colleagues (2017) of the National Sleep Foundation developed a brief survey instrument designed to assess sleep health. Sleep health is described as being more than simply the absence of sleep disorders, but rather also to include the duration, quality, and impact of sleep. The survey includes 12 questions that provide a total sleep health index composed of sleep health subindices for sleep duration, sleep quality, and sleep disorders. Questionnaires like these can be used to measure sleep in relatively large samples, making them useful for studies designed to explore the effects of behaviors (e.g., exercise) on sleep.

Measurement Limitations

The measurement tools currently available to assess sleep make this a challenging area for research. Self-report measures can be inaccurate because people might not have a good sense of the variables they are being asked to report (e.g., they might not know when they fell asleep or they might not be aware of restless sleep). Objective measures provide valid and reliable data but present their own challenges. When someone sleeps in a lab environment, this clearly is not similar to when they are sleeping in their home environment. In addition, lab-based study can be particularly challenging for people with sleep disturbances. If you were a person troubled with insomnia, imagine how off-putting it would be to consider taking part in a research study where you would be asked to wear electrodes for collection of polysomnography data and to sleep in a laboratory while being observed by researchers. It would take a lot of motivation to want to do this because of the anxiety that typically surrounds having difficulty with sleeping. As a result of this, most studies have been conducted with good sleepers who are not intimidated by the thoughts of participating in lab-based sleep studies. In addition, because lab-based sleep studies are expensive to conduct, small sample sizes are always a challenge in this research. As technology continues to advance, small wearable devices that provide objective measures and can be worn while sleeping at home are likely to dramatically improve the ability to conduct research in general and particularly research with poor sleepers.

Sleep Hygiene Advice

Here is some advice for how to get enough sleep:

- Go to sleep 15 minutes earlier every night until you wake up refreshed.
- Use a regular sleeping and waking schedule.
- Identify and remove stimuli in your nighttime routine that might be keeping you up.
- Stop using all devices (including telephone, television, gaming) at least 2 hours before your normal bedtime.
- Make your bedroom dark and cool.
- Learn your caffeine tolerance and avoid caffeine too late in the day. Wine also might keep you up.
- Exercise within 3 to 4 hours of your normal bedtime.
- Don't nap for more than 20 minutes, and don't sleep more than 2 hours past your normal wake-up time.
- Don't lie in bed awake. Read a book, listen to music, or write down your stressors, and then try again.

Evidence on the Benefits of Exercise for Sleep

The exercise and sleep literature presents numerous challenges and considerations for researchers. One important consideration is if the researchers are interested in understanding the potential benefits of exercise for normal or good sleepers, or if they are interested in using exercise as a form of treatment for individuals with sleep challenges. To date, most studies have been conducted with normal or good sleepers due to the previously described challenges of recruiting individuals with sleep issues. Another challenge relates to the measurement of sleep in laboratory settings. Because researchers need to include familiarization nights and to have someone present to monitor the participant, this is a very costly type of study to conduct. This is reflected in the small numbers of participants typical for studies including objective measures of sleep (e.g., that require sleeping in the laboratory). This also explains why many studies have relied on the use of self-report measures of sleep, which allow for the inclusion of larger sample sizes but don't provide the fine-grained analysis of sleep quality that objective measures offer. A final challenge is the question of how you disentangle the acute effects of exercise from the chronic. If a regular exerciser participates in physical activity 3 to 5 days per week, which days do you use to measure sleep? If you choose the days when they are exercising, you might be capturing the effects of both regular exercise and the most recent single session of exercise. If you choose the days when they are not exercising, you might not be observing the true benefits of exercise because now you've withheld exercise on that day. These are but a few of the challenges of conducting research on this topic. See the sidebar for an example of a unique challenge for a sleep study that could not have been anticipated but that illustrates a real example of how difficult sleep research can be to conduct.

An Empirical Study With Poor Sleepers

Kline and associates (2011) conducted a study that provides a great example of a study focused on people with a sleep disorder, using a reasonable sample size, and including both objective and subjective measures of sleep (figure 13.4). They recruited 43 adults (18-55 yr) who had moderate to severe obstructive sleep apnea, were overweight or obese, and were currently sedentary. They collected baseline data consisting of a polysomnography recording during an overnight visit, sleep data from a wrist-worn device, measures of fitness, and subjective assessments of sleep through completion of the PSQI. At that point, participants were randomly assigned to a 12-week supervised exercise program or a 12-week supervised stretching program, which served as the control condition. Those in the exercise condition performed aerobic exercise 4 days per week at increasing durations up to a total of 150 minutes per week. On 2 days per week, they also performed resistance exercises. Those in the

An Unexpected Challenge

Several years ago graduate students in a kinesiology department were conducting a study focused on the impact of sleep deprivation on the body's physiological response to exercise performed in the morning. This flipped the question being addressed in this chapter by asking not if exercise benefits sleep but rather if sleep deprivation negatively affects exercise. Volunteers were invited to the laboratory for a shortened night of sleep. In the morning, they were woken up early to have an IV inserted to draw blood during a 30-minute bout of aerobic exercise. Most nights, this study was just burdensome. At least one graduate student had to be present and awake throughout the entire night in the lab with the participants. The researchers used a shift pattern whereby one graduate student would stay until 3:00 a.m. and then be replaced by another graduate student. Clearly, the graduate students were themselves experiencing sleep deprivation to work on this study. The additional complication that illustrates the particular challenges of this type of research is that one Friday night when a volunteer was sleeping in the lab, it turned out that local area students had scheduled a rave to take place in the gym right next door to the lab. The scheduling of this event wasn't shared with the researchers, so you can imagine their surprise when loud music started playing at 10:00 p.m. and a huge party was happening right outside their doors. Needless to say, the volunteer had to be rescheduled and the graduate students actually got a good night's sleep that evening.

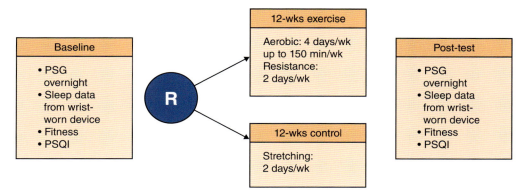

FIGURE 13.4 The experimental design for Kline and associates' study (R = randomly assigned).

stretching condition met two times per week to perform a series of stretching exercises. At the end of 12 weeks, researchers collected the same data as at baseline. Results showed that as compared to the controls, the exercisers experienced significant reductions in apnea symptoms and in the number of apneas per hour of sleep. They also experienced significant improvements in sleep onset latency, sleep efficiency, and sleep fragmentation (defined in this study as a measure of movement and restlessness). The authors made several important points relative to their findings and the potential of exercise as a treatment. First, 63% of exercisers experienced a >20% reduction in apnea symptoms, which is comparable to that observed in response to surgical treatments and to studies in which a 10% reduction in body weight is achieved. Second, the effects on sleep were observed on a nonexercise day to ensure that the researchers were keeping the chronic effects distinct from any potential acute effects. Thus, the fact that benefits were observed is important because it suggests that these effects in response to chronic exercise are enduring in that they are experienced even on days without exercise. This is in contrast to the transient benefits of sleeping with a CPAP, which are only evident on the same day as the CPAP is used and have no lasting effects. Thus, this study provides important support for regular exercise as a way to improve sleep in persons suffering from sleep apnea.

Benefits of Exercise for Good Sleepers

Although good sleepers are easier to recruit for sleep studies, the challenges related to the cost of these studies and the experimenter burden still exist. Thus, the primary limitation of this body of evidence is that studies tend to have small sample sizes. This makes meta-analytic techniques particularly valuable in this area because they allow researchers to combine results across individual studies to statistically increase sample size, allowing for stronger tests of the hypotheses. The first meta-analysis of this research was conducted by Kubitz and colleagues (1996). In this early review, the authors confirmed this challenge of small sample sizes when they pointed out that most studies at that time used sample sizes of $n = 9$. With only nine participants on average, the results of a single study likely would be nonsignificant, suggesting that exercise doesn't have a significant effect on sleep. But with such a small sample size, this nonsignificant finding shouldn't be considered the final answer, and an exploration of effect sizes using meta-analytic techniques becomes important. In their review, Kubitz and colleagues included studies using all designs, and they summarized results from 32 acute exercise studies and 12 chronic exercise studies. They found significant increases in stage 3, stage 4, slow-wave sleep, total sleep time, and REM latency and decreases in REM sleep and sleep onset latency in response to acute exercise (ES = 0.14-0.75) (see figure 13.5a). Among the chronic exercise studies, they reported increases in slow-wave sleep and total sleep time and decreases in REM sleep, sleep onset latency, and awake time (ES = 0.40-0.94) (see figure 13.5b). This early meta-analytic review suggests that both single sessions of exercise and regular exercise participation can increase the quantity of sleep (i.e., total sleep time) and can have an impact on aspects of sleep that might be associated with the perceived quality of sleep.

More recently, Kredlow and associates (2015) conducted a comprehensive meta-analytic review of this literature and included studies using ran-

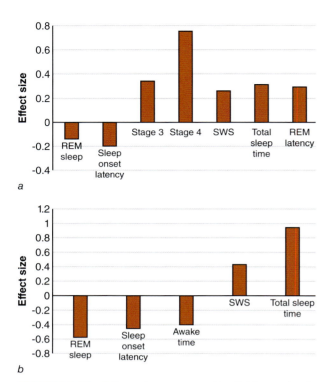

FIGURE 13.5 Effect sizes reported in Kubitz and colleagues (1996) for the significant effects of *(a)* acute exercise and *(b)* chronic exercise on sleep outcomes.
Adapted from Kubitz et al. (1996).

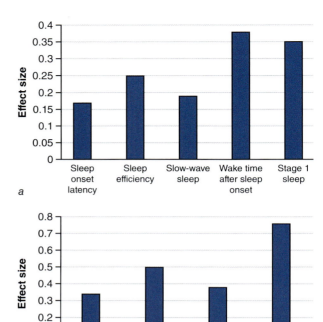

FIGURE 13.6 Effect sizes reported in Kredlow and associates (2015) for the significant effects of *(a)* acute exercise and *(b)* chronic exercise on sleep outcomes.
Adapted from Kredlow et al. (2015).

domized clinical trials (RCTs) or within-subjects designs. They statistically summarized findings from 25 studies on chronic exercise and 41 studies on the effects of acute exercise, with most (89%) of the studies looking at good sleepers. This review included more than twice as many studies on chronic exercise and half again as many studies on acute exercise as were included in Kubitz and colleagues (1996). For chronic exercise, Kredlow and colleagues reported benefits to various sleep parameters, with effect sizes ranging from small for objective measures (total sleep time: ES = 0.25; sleep efficiency: ES = 0.30; sleep onset latency: ES = 0.35) to large for subjective measures (self-reported sleep quality: ES = 0.74) (see figure 13.6a). For a frame of reference, normative sleep data for college students indicates that the average total sleep time per night is 6.85 hours, with a standard deviation of 1.04 hours (Hicks et al., 2001). The meta-analytic results tell us that exercise increases total sleep time by 0.25 standard deviations, so this would mean that a college student who exercises would sleep approximately 16 minutes longer per night than a student who doesn't exercise. Although this might

seem like a relatively small amount, given that this benefit was observed in good sleepers, this is an impressive increase and might have implications for overall health across a semester or a year.

> ### Converting Effect Size to Actual Sleep Impact
>
> Hicks and colleagues' (2001) data lets us know that the average total sleep time is 6.85 hours with a standard deviation of 1.04 hours (SD = 62.4 min).
>
> Kredlow and associates' (2015) meta-analysis showed that the average effect size for the impact of acute exercise on total sleep time is 0.25 (ES = 0.25).
>
> The formula that allows us to convert from effect size to how many minutes would be added to a person's total sleep in response to acute exercise is as follows:
>
> Total Sleep Time Minutes With Acute
> Exercise = ES × SD
> = 0.25 × 62.4 min = 15.6 min

> A person who has not done any exercise would be expected to sleep for the average amount of time (6.85 hr), but a person who has done acute exercise would be expected to sleep for an additional 15.6 minutes (15.6 min / 60 min per hr = 0.26 hr), which means they would get more than 7 hours of total sleep (6.85 hr + 0.26 hr = 7.11 hr).

In this review, they also were able to look at the benefits of acute exercise. Across studies, data supported beneficial effects, with small effect sizes for a variety of objective measures (sleep onset latency: ES = 0.17; slow-wave sleep: ES = 0.19; sleep efficiency: ES = 0.25; wake time after sleep onset: ES = 0.38; stage 1 sleep: ES = 0.35) (see figure 13.6b). In examining moderators of the effects, one interesting finding reported by Kredlow and associates was that acute exercise performed within 3 hours of bedtime was associated with less disturbed sleep. This is a fascinating finding because we might offer guidance to exercise in the evenings within 3 hours of an intended bedtime. This is consistent with findings from a meta-analysis focused exclusively on acute exercise performed in the evening. Stutz, Eiholzer, and Spengler (2019) found that evening exercise has a positive effect on sleep parameters and concluded that acute exercise should be performed within 4 hours of bedtime for the biggest effects. What we don't know is if some time frame of exercise closer to bedtime does not have beneficial effects. It might be that exercise should not be performed within, say, 30 minutes of normal bedtime. Future research will be necessary to inform the nuances of this recommendation.

Lang and associates (2016) limited their review to chronic exercise studies focused on children, adolescents, and young adults (14-24 yr old). They particularly targeted young people for many reasons including because sleep is so important to their development and ability to perform well, because a lack of sleep is linked to psychiatric illness in this age group, and because so many young people are not getting sufficient sleep. They reported a large effect when averaged across subjective and objective measures (ES = 0.74). Importantly, they reported the largest benefits from studies that used objective measures of physical activity and objective measures of sleep quality (ES = 1.02), suggesting that this effect is robust in these age groups when using the strongest measures of the independent and dependent variables.

Benefits of Exercise for Insomnia

Given that the previous reviews focused on good sleepers, it also is important to consider the findings of a meta-analysis by Banno and colleagues (2018) that only included RCTs focused on participants with diagnosed insomnia. Across 10 studies (9 chronic, 1 acute), Banno and colleagues found significant benefits of exercise when measured using subjective measures such as scores on the PSQI and self-reports of insomnia severity. However, they did not find benefits when sleep was assessed using objective measures (e.g., sleep onset latency, total sleep time, and sleep efficiency). It is a limitation of this review that the results from the single acute exercise study were included with the results from the chronic exercise studies. However, these findings are important because they suggest the existence of perceived benefits to regular exercise for individuals with insomnia. The 9 chronic exercise studies ranged in length from 4 weeks to 6 months, with the number of sessions per week ranging from 1 to 7 and with most using walking as the exercise. Based on this review, we would recommend that individuals suffering from insomnia begin walking for exercise and would expect that they might experience subjective improvements in sleep quality after only 4 weeks.

Benefits of Exercise for Cancer Patients

Numerous studies have looked specifically at the potential benefits of chronic exercise for sleep quality by cancer patients. This is important because 30% to 60% of cancer patients experience sleep disturbances during treatment, approximately 20% of cancer patients are diagnosed with insomnia disorder, and sleep problems can persist for years after treatment. Among studies looking at the potential of exercise to benefit sleep in cancer patients, two meta-analyses have been conducted yielding consistent results. Kreutz and associates (2019) reviewed 22 RCTs focused on women with breast cancer who participated in exercise during or after treatment, and they found small benefits for studies testing mind–body exercises (ES = 0.27) or looking at physical exercise programs (ES = 0.32). In this review, mind–body exercises included yoga, tai chi, or qigong, and physical exercise included aerobic exercise, resistance exercise, both, or walking. The effect sizes were roughly equivalent for both subjective measures of sleep quality (ES = 0.28) and objective measures of sleep disturbances (ES = 0.26). Fang and colleagues (2019) also reviewed RCTs looking at any type of cancer in men and women who were either in treatment or had completed treatment, but they excluded studies looking at mind–body exercises. Across 22 studies, they reported an average positive effect of exercise for total subjective sleep quality (ES = 0.38), for the PSQI measure of sleep quality (ES = 0.26), and for subjective reports of sleep onset latency (ES = 0.27). They also found significant benefits for sleep onset latency when assessed using objective measures (ES = 0.21). In both these meta-analyses, interventions were 4 to 24 weeks in duration, with exercise performed 1 to 5 times per week with a typical goal of 150 minutes per week. Thus, results of these two reviews show that cancer patients who are in the midst of treatment or have completed treatment can expect to achieve small improvements in subjective and objective measures of sleep in response to a regular program of exercise.

Summary

Sleep is a necessary bodily function that provides an opportunity for the body to rest, recover, and restore itself for the next day. In the modern world, sleep deprivation and poor sleep quality are common and have associated costs in terms of lost productivity, increased risk of accidents, and increased risk of all-cause mortality. Evidence suggests that exercise can result in improvements in sleep quality in good sleepers, in people suffering from sleep disorders, and in people having sleep disturbances in conjunction with cancer treatment.

The literature on exercise and sleep has been reviewed meta-analytically on numerous occasions. With good sleepers, results consistently support that acute exercise has a small positive effect on objective measures of sleep. With regards to chronic exercise, meta-analyses also consistently support the effects on objective measures of sleep, with slightly larger effects than observed for acute exercise. For subjective measures of sleep quality, chronic exercise demonstrates moderate to large benefits. When children, adolescents, and young adults are considered, benefits of exercise are large, suggesting the importance of regular physical activity for positive sleep patterns for young people. For individuals with insomnia, improvements in sleep quality are reported, but these effects are most apparent with self-report measures of sleep quality, and the effects for objective measures of sleep are inconsistent. For cancer patients and survivors, a relatively robust body of evidence supports small benefits of regular physical activity in terms of improving sleep quantity and quality.

Overall, this is a promising body of evidence, suggesting that regular exercise and even single sessions of exercise can contribute to more positive sleep patterns across a wide variety of populations. The magnitude of the effect ranges from small to large but consistently demonstrates beneficial effects of exercise. Future research in this area could lead us to understanding how best to prescribe exercise to achieve benefits that are consistent and robust for both good sleepers and those with sleep disorders or for people experiencing challenges to their sleep due to chronic illness.

Discussion Questions

1. What variables related to acute exercise might influence the effects it has on sleep? Relative to this, what questions should be addressed?
2. Is it possible that beneficial effects of exercise on sleep could mediate the effects of exercise on other outcomes? Which outcomes discussed in this book are most likely and why?
3. What do you think about the meaningfulness of the slight changes in sleep parameters? That is, would you expect 15 to 16 minutes of additional total sleep to make a difference?
4. Provide a summary of what the results of the Kredlow and colleagues (2015) meta-analysis tell us about the potential benefits of chronic exercise for sleep for good sleepers. What are the implications?

Exercise and Quality of Life

OBJECTIVES

After studying this chapter, you should be able to do the following:

- Define quality of life and describe the domains that contribute to global quality of life
- Recognize why quality of life is an important construct
- Present evidence relative to mediators of the effects of exercise on quality of life
- Describe empirical and meta-analytic studies that have tested the effects of exercise on quality of life

KEY TERMS

quality of life

World Health Organization (WHO) definition of quality of life

health-related quality of life (HRQL)

activities of daily living (ADLs)

basic ADLs

instrumental ADLs (IADLs)

wait-list control group

> Sarah is a 45-year-old single woman who has been living with multiple sclerosis (MS), a chronic neurodegenerative disease with no cure, since she was 18 years old. Regular physical activity reduces symptoms, slows the progression of MS, and is considered critical to overall disease management. Partially because of this knowledge, Sarah leads an active lifestyle. She used to run, but now, due to some loss in coordination that limits running, she rides her bicycle, travels to cycling events, and even speaks to others who recently have been diagnosed with MS about how regular exercise has given her the ability to live an active and normal life. She has an entire community of friends with whom she rides and exercises, and she considers these people her "bike family." On some days she has to alter or even skip her planned exercise because of her MS symptoms, but this is just part of what she has to do to navigate life and it does not change her overall activity level. Sarah lives what she would describe as a happy, full life despite having MS, and she attributes this to her regular exercise routine.
>
> Sarah's friend Anthony was diagnosed with MS 3 years ago. Anthony was an avid cyclist, but since diagnosis he has stopped cycling and doing other types of exercise. He changed his exercise behavior because when he was initially diagnosed with MS, he had some numbness and coordination problems in his left leg that made it difficult to ride. These problems have subsided, but Anthony still does not want to exercise. He feels that MS controls his life and exercise is not worth his time. He is always tired and does not see why Sarah is constantly telling him to get out and move. He describes his life in terms of before and after MS and is incredibly negative about his future.
>
> These two contrasting examples illustrate the role exercise can play in enhancing overall quality of life for people living with chronic disease. Sarah has created a life where she is living with an incurable disease but is still thriving, and this is reflected in everything she does. Exercise is part of what makes her life full and rewarding, in addition to helping her stay healthy. Conversely, Anthony is consumed by the negative factors in his life and sees exercise as one more thing to add stress to his already busy life.
>
> Contributed by Dr. Kym Facszewski, Associate Professor, Appalachian State University

At its simplest, **quality of life** describes a person's perception of their well-being across a variety of dimensions including physical, social, emotional, and spiritual. The relative importance of quality of life as an outcome for research and for medical consideration has increased dramatically in recent years. This is in response to the facts that people are living longer so might spend many years in advanced older age and that more individuals are living with chronic illness due to advances in medicine and health care. In other words, with such a large number of people surviving with chronic illness and living into advanced older age, the focus of treatments and interventions now includes a consideration of quality-of-life outcomes. Although exercise might not be able to prevent aging or lead to full remission from a chronic illness, it may contribute to a better quality of life for individuals who are moving into older age or living with a chronic disease. We all aspire to have a high quality of life, and as young people who are presumably healthy, you hopefully do have a high quality of life at this time. But you might be dealing with a chronic illness or you might have family members or friends whose quality of life has declined either in association with advancing age or as a reflection of chronic illness, disease, or disability. In fact, as a result of the increased attention being paid to quality of life, Healthy People 2010 includes increasing quality and years of life as the first goal in the list; Healthy People 2020 includes a goal to "promote quality of life, healthy development, and healthy behaviors

---

quality of life—A person's perception of their well-being across a variety of dimensions including physical, social, emotional, and spiritual is referred to as quality of life.

across all life stages"; and Healthy People 2030 lists overall well-being as a top-tier outcome where well-being "reflects the cumulative contributions of health and non-health factors" (U.S. Department of Health and Human Services, n.d.). In this chapter, we will consider how quality of life is defined, why it is important, the putative mechanisms supporting a possible link between exercise and quality of life, and the evidence relative to this link.

Defining Quality of Life

The term *quality of life* has proven difficult to define because it has the potential to be a broad construct but also might be specific in terms of aspects that are particularly relevant to a certain group of people at a certain time. In a simple sense, quality of life is meant to provide a measure of perceived health that goes beyond the negative impacts of health concerns (e.g., morbidities or the negative impact of disease) and instead attempts to capture positive aspects of life that are important even in the face of disease. In fact, the focus on quality of life is in some ways a result of the recognition that a healthy life is not defined merely by the absence of disease. The **World Health Organization's definition of quality of life** captures these issues well: "An individual's perception of their position in life in the context of the culture and value systems in which they live and in relation to their goals, expectations, standards and concerns" (World Health Organization, 2022). Clearly, this definition conveys that quality of life is judged relevant to a person's own unique life experience and their personal standards. In some contexts, a distinction is made between quality of life and **health-related quality of life (HRQL)**. Quality of life is considered to be broader and might include domains such as a person's occupation, housing, schools, and neighborhood. HRQL refers to the specific aspects of overall quality of life that are directly relevant to a person's physical or mental health. In this chapter, unless it is clearly specified in a source that we are discussing, we will use the term *quality of life* to reflect the possible breadth of the construct while also being inclusive of HRQL.

As an example of how judgments of quality of life can differ relative to an individual's perspective, imagine two individuals who have been diagnosed with cancer, have undergone surgery to remove the tumor, are undergoing radiation and chemotherapy treatments, and have been advised to limit social activities during treatment because of a suppressed immune system. Now imagine that one of these individuals is a 20-year-old who has no other serious health concerns and the other is an 80-year-old who has already survived a heart attack 5 years earlier. In this example, the 20-year-old who is unable to participate fully in social activities after recovering from surgery and during treatment might have a very low judgment of their quality of life because participation in social activities is so important. By contrast, the 80-year-old who has had to limit social activities due to increasing frailty might view this as typical for their age and a lower priority compared to being able to continue to live independently. Hence, the impact on quality of life made by a limitation on social activities is judged by an individual relative to their own life experiences. Quality of life is kind of like beauty in that it is in the eye of the beholder, or based purely on the perception of the person.

Quality of life is important to decisions that people make in their lives. Imagine the same scenario just described, but now add the fact that the patient has a choice about which treatment options to pursue. Imagine that the surgical procedure offered is a highly invasive surgical procedure to remove a slow-growing cancerous tumor from the brain. The surgery is necessary if the person hopes to live cancer free but is likely to require an extended recovery period and comes with some risks. You can imagine how concerns about quality of life relative to remaining years of life might become important in the decision-making of the individual. The 20-year-old might willingly accept a significant short-term decline in quality of life to have the surgery because they recognize that they have approximately 60 years remaining in terms of life expectancy, so the short-term negatives are worth the long-term gain. However, the 80-year-old might consider that their other health concerns and advanced age make quality of life the priority, so they might decide not to have the surgery to ensure that their remaining years are not hampered by the effects of the surgery itself. The 80-year-old still might choose to have the radiation and chemotherapy because of a view that these treatments are less risky in their advanced age and because of a willingness to endure the treatment side effects for a matter of weeks knowing that tumor growth will be slowed and their life will be prolonged.

World Health Organization (WHO) definition of quality of life—Quality of life is defined by WHO as "An individual's perception of their position in life in the context of the culture and value systems in which they live and in relation to their goals, expectations, standards and concerns" (World Health Organization, 2022).

health-related quality of life (HRQL)—HRQL refers to the specific aspects of overall quality of life that are directly relevant to a person's physical or mental health.

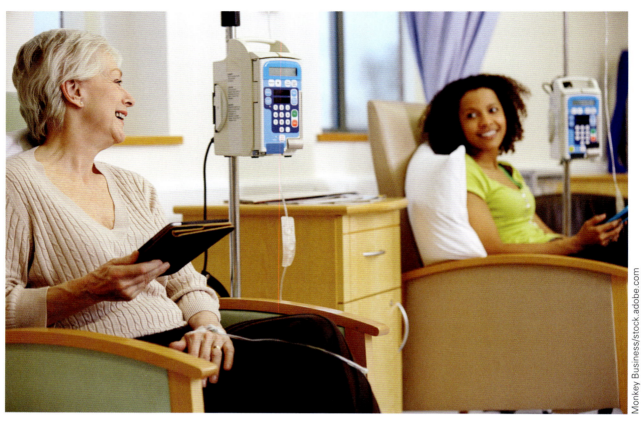

The impact of chemotherapy treatment on quality of life might depend upon a person's stage of life.

In addition to recognizing that quality of life must be judged from the perspective of the individual, it is also important to understand that quality of life is not a unitary construct. The World Health Organization explains that quality of life is multidimensional and suggests that it includes judgments of physical health, psychological health, independence, social relationships, environment, and spirituality. The World Health Organization further acknowledges that a person might judge the various domains of quality of life differently and that quality of life might change across time in any or all of these dimensions. This is consistent with the views of quality of life that have been described in the exercise psychology literature. For example, Rejeski and associates (1996) identified that the quality-of-life outcomes most evident in the physical activity literature include global indices of quality of life, physical symptoms, and the perception of function in four areas: physical, emotional, social, and cognitive. More recently, Gill and colleagues (2011) defined quality of life as "a subjective, multidimensional, integrative construct that reflects optimal well-being and positive health" (p. 184), and Gill and associates (2013) added spiritual well-being to the list of four function areas previously described.

> Think about what quality of life means to you. What are the most important aspects of your life when you consider physical health, psychological health, independence, social relationships, environment, and spirituality? How do you judge the quality of these aspects of your life? If they are positive and good, your overall satisfaction with your life is probably high. But if you judge the quality to be low in areas that are important to you, you might have a more negative view of your life. Think about someone you know who objectively has more challenges than you do—maybe they have physical or cognitive impairments, a job they hate, or are in a relationship that is not good. How do you think they judge their quality of life? What are your thoughts about how exercise might help you and this person you've identified?

Prevalence and Costs

Advances in medicine have resulted in an increasing population of adults who are living with chronic diseases such as heart disease, stroke, cancer, chronic lung disease, arthritis, diabetes, Alzheimer's disease, and chronic kidney disease. When one considers all chronic diseases, in the United States it is estimated that 60% of adults have a chronic disease, and 40% of adults have two or more chronic diseases (Centers for Disease Control and Prevention, 2022). The impact of this high prevalence of chronic disease on quality of life is apparent in that many chronic diseases have an enduring impact on a person's ability to function in daily life and to participate in enjoyable activities.

Costs of Various Chronic Diseases in the United States

Following are some facts about chronic disease in the United States (Centers for Disease Control and Prevention, 2023):

- *Heart disease and stroke:* First leading cause of death; direct medical costs of $216 billion per year and $147 billion in lost productivity
- *Cancer:* Second leading cause of death; direct medical costs expected to reach $240 billion by 2030
- *Arthritis:* 58.5 million people affected in the United States; direct medical costs of $303.5 billion in 2013
- *Diabetes:* 37 million people with diabetes and 96 million with prediabetes in the United States; leading cause of blindness, kidney failure, and nonemergency lower-leg amputations; direct medical costs and lost productivity total $327 billion in 2017

As evidence of the impact of chronic disease on perceived health, Zhao and colleagues (2018) reported that in working-aged adults, 14.8% reported that their health was poor or fair, and 12.5% reported frequent mental distress. Similarly, Chen and associates (2011) found that among 430,912 Americans who completed the Behavioral Risk Factor Surveillance Survey, the likelihood of reporting negative health outcomes increased in a dose–response fashion relative to the number of chronic health conditions a person had. This was true for the outcomes of perceiving health as poor or fair, reporting physical distress, reporting mental distress, and experiencing activity limitations (figure 14.1). Although the outcome measures reported in these studies are not precisely the same construct as quality of life, these findings do give an indication of the large number of people who are likely to perceive that their quality of life is not as high as they would like it to be due to chronic health conditions.

As previously illustrated, patients who are undergoing cancer treatment might be faced with particularly difficult decisions regarding quality of life versus length of life. Some cancer treatments that are particularly aggressive (e.g., radiation and chemotherapy) can prolong life but be accompanied by a dramatic loss of quality of life. In a recent review of studies examining this tradeoff, Shrestha and colleagues (2019) found that older individuals prioritize quality of life, while younger individuals were more willing to pursue aggressive treatment plans to increase their length of life. This is consistent with the example given earlier in this chapter. An additional consideration with respect to cancer treatments is the relationship between financial burden and quality of life, with evidence showing that the rising costs of treatment (which can exceed $5,000) can cause patients to ration their care or stop their treatments altogether (Tran & Zafar, 2018). This decision is related to the impact of the financial burden on their family's financial quality of life. Although physical activity can be beneficial in improving HRQL, these impacts of treatments on financial well-being are less likely to be affected by exercise.

Interestingly, evidence suggests that HRQL differs relative to variables associated with socioeconomic status (SES). Studies conducted in countries including the United States, the United Kingdom, and Sweden consistently show that HRQL increases as SES goes up and that this relationship holds even after controlling for chronic diseases and risk factors such as smoking and obesity. In a study conducted in Germany, Mielck and associates (2014) collected survey data from a representative sample of 11,177 adults. They examined both education level and per capita income and found that both were predictive of various quality-of-life outcomes even after controlling for age and sex. In particular, those with lower education or with lower per capita income

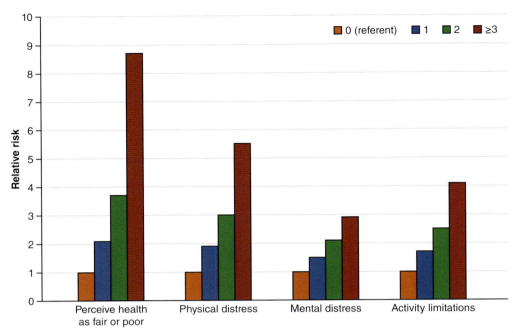

FIGURE 14.1 The dose–response relationship between the number of chronic health conditions a person has (0, 1, 2, or ≥ 3) and their perception that their health is poor or fair, reports of physical and mental distress, and the experience of activity limitations.
Adapted from Chen et al. (2011).

reported more "moderate or severe problems" and had generally lower scores on the quality-of-life outcomes of mobility, self-care, usual activities, pain and discomfort, and anxiety and depression.

Mechanisms and Mediators

If evidence supports a beneficial effect of exercise on quality of life, we must consider the potential mechanisms or mediators of this effect. Mechanisms that have been proposed include improvements in physical fitness and in functional fitness (an enhanced ability to perform activities of daily living) and psychological mediators including self-efficacy, mastery, and perceived pain. Studies exploring these variables as a way to explain the effects of exercise on quality of life are relatively limited but do provide some promising results. Research focused specifically on cancer patients also has considered other biological factors such as proinflammatory cytokines and inflammatory proteins and other psychological variables such as fatigue. These variables are likely to be affected by exercise and might play a role in the judgments of quality of life during and following cancer treatment (Buffart et al., 2014).

Physical Fitness

Participation in exercise at a sufficient level and for a long enough period of time will result in improvements in fitness. In particular, the FITT principle describes that the frequency (how many days per week), intensity (percent of age-predicted heart rate for aerobic exercise, amount of weight for resistance exercise), time (number of minutes per session or repetitions and sets for resistance exercise), and type (the mode of exercise; e.g., aerobic or resistance) of exercise will determine the fitness benefits achieved. If a person is participating in aerobic exercise at a sufficient load, they will experience gains in aerobic fitness. Participation in resistance training at a sufficient load will provide gains in terms of strength and possibly power. Some evidence supports that gains in fitness help explain observed benefits to quality of life. Perez-Sousa and colleagues (2020) tested measures of fitness as mechanisms in a quasi-experimental study designed to test the effects of a 6-month exercise program on quality of life in obese and overweight children (see figure 14.2). Overweight and obese children (*n* = 121) who lived in a community that was offering a supervised

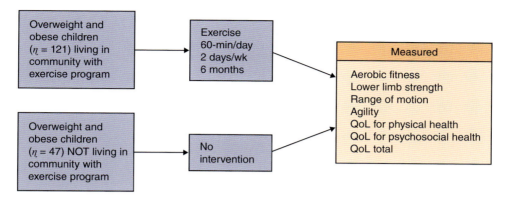

FIGURE 14.2 Perez-Souza and colleagues (2020) measured fitness and quality-of-life outcomes in overweight and obese children and compared between those in an exercise program and those not in an exercise program.

physical exercise program participated in two 60-minute sessions of supervised exercise per week for 6 months. Overweight and obese children (n = 47) who did not live in a community where the program was being offered served as the control group. The exercise program consisted of physically active games and physical fitness activities. Participants in the exercise group achieved greater improvements in aerobic fitness, lower limb strength, range of motion, and agility than observed in the control group. They also experienced greater improvements in quality of life relative to physical health, psychosocial health, and in total. Results of the statistical analysis to test the role of fitness supported that fitness gains were significant in explaining the benefits observed for the quality-of-life measures. These findings support the potential role of fitness as a mechanism that can explain improvements in quality of life in response to exercise by overweight and obese children.

Functional Fitness

Functional fitness is a construct that is most relevant when considering older adults or people with physical impairments. It is often considered in terms of its relationship with the ability to perform activities of daily living. Activities of daily living (ADLs) are fundamental activities that allow a person to care for themselves independently. They include both basic and instrumental ADLs. Basic ADLs are those activities needed to manage one's basic physical needs and include maintaining personal hygiene, dressing, continence, toileting, transferring or ambulating, and eating. Instrumental ADLs (IADLs) are more complex activities that include the ability to live completely independently in the community. These activities include transportation, shopping, handling finances, meal preparation, housecleaning, laundry, managing communications, and taking responsibility for one's own medications. If you are young and do not have any physical impairments, these ADLs and IADLs likely are rudimentary for you. However, for individuals who have disabilities, the ability to perform these types of activities might be a key component of their judgments of quality of life. That is, if exercise improves a person's ability to meet their own basic physical needs, one might imagine that their perception of their quality of life would improve.

Buffart and associates (2015) conducted a study to assess the role of functional fitness on observed benefits of exercise for quality of life in prostate cancer survivors. Using a randomized clinical trial (RCT) design (see figure 14.3), 100 physically inactive men who had completed treatment for prostate cancer were assigned randomly to a supervised aerobic and resistance exercise program for 6 months or to a control group that received printed educational materials regularly for 6 months. Participants in the exercise group performed resistance exercises and 20 to 30 minutes of aerobic exercise at a moderate intensity twice a week with a trainer, and were asked to accumulate an additional 90 minutes of aerobic activity on their own every week. After the intervention, the exercise group reported significantly

---

activities of daily living (ADLs)—Fundamental activities that allow a person to care for themselves independently are called ADLs and include both basic and instrumental ADLs.

basic ADLs—Activities that are needed to manage one's basic physical needs including maintaining personal hygiene, dressing, continence, toileting, transferring or ambulating, and eating are known as basic ADLs.

instrumental ADLs (IADLs)—IADLs are more complex activities that render the ability to live completely independently in the community, including transportation, shopping, handling finances, meal preparation, housecleaning, laundry, managing communications, and taking responsibility for one's own medications.

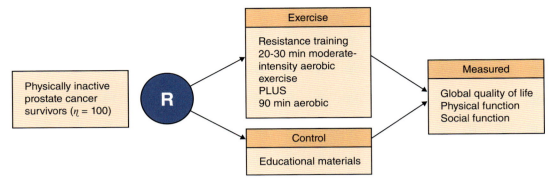

FIGURE 14.3 Buffart and associates (2015) randomly assigned participants to one of two treatment conditions and tested for differences in quality of life, physical function, and social function.

higher global quality of life, physical function, and social function. Results of the mediation analysis showed that changes in chair rise time (a measure of lower-body physical function) was significant in explaining the effects for global quality of life, physical function, and social function. These results suggest that changes in physical function might be important mechanisms to explain why exercise improves quality of life for older male cancer survivors.

Psychological Mediators

Changes in psychological mediators also have been proposed as a way to explain why physical activity participation benefits quality of life. In particular, in studies of participants who have knee osteoarthritis, self-efficacy for mobility (Rejeski et al., 1998) and satisfaction with physical function and pain ratings (Rejeski et al., 2002) were shown to mediate the effects of an exercise intervention on quality of life. The role of self-efficacy also has been demonstrated in samples of community-dwelling older adults (Elavsky et al., 2005; McAuley et al., 2006) and in individuals with MS (Motl & McAuley, 2009). Hence, psychological mediators can be important to explain benefits for quality of life.

Buffart and colleagues (2014) conducted another study in which they tested several psychological mediators. They enrolled 209 cancer survivors (3 months or more after treatment) in a physical exercise intervention for 12 weeks ($n = 147$) or assigned them to a wait-list control condition ($n = 62$) (see figure 14.4). A **wait-list control** condition is one in which participants are asked to maintain their normal lifestyle and then receive the intervention at the conclusion of the control period. The exercise intervention group met 2 times per week for 2 hours and performed 30 minutes of stationary cycling, 30 minutes of strength training, and 60 minutes of group sports and games designed to promote enjoyment and self-efficacy. The researchers assessed changes in physical activity participation and perceptions of fatigue, self-efficacy, mastery, distress, and global quality of life at the pretest and posttest. The intervention group experienced significant improvements in several aspects of quality of life that were not experienced by those in the wait-list control group (Korstjens et al., 2008). Using path analysis statistical techniques, the researchers showed that the exercise intervention improved quality of life through its effects on increasing physical activity levels, improving self-efficacy and mastery, and decreasing perceptions of fatigue and distress. Remarkably, these effects on the mediators accounted for 53% of the variance in quality of life, suggesting a robust impact of the physical activity intervention on this outcome through these mediators. In other words, these findings provided strong support for the importance of these psychological mediators as explaining the quality-of-life benefits in response to exercise. This study is valuable because it suggests that several different psychological mediators might be sensitive to an exercise intervention and contribute to the observed benefits in quality of life.

Measurement

A plethora of self-report measures of quality of life have been developed, with some being global in nature (e.g., life satisfaction or overall quality of

---

wait-list control group—A control group in which participants are asked to maintain their normal lifestyle and then receive the intervention at the conclusion of the control period is called a wait-list control group.

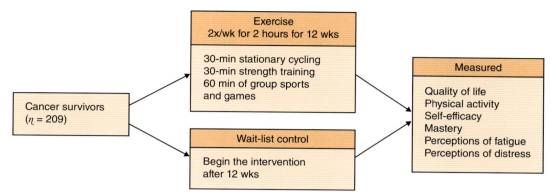

FIGURE 14.4 Buffart and colleagues (2014) assigned participants to one of two treatment conditions for 12 weeks and tested for differences in quality of life, physical function, and social function.

life) and others being specific to a particular disease state (e.g., cancer).

Global Measures

The 36-item Short Form Health Survey (SF-36) was developed as a part of the Medical Outcomes Study, which was focused on variations in patient outcomes. The SF-36 was designed to be a generic and easy-to-administer survey to assess quality of life broadly. This survey is commonly used in the exercise psychology literature; however, two limitations of this measure are that the focus is exclusively on health attributes and the questions are worded in a negative way so it is not possible to capture positive aspects of quality of life. For example, the survey includes a series of questions about physical health problems, emotional health problems, and pain, with all questions asking how these have interfered with various kinds of activities.

Gill and associates (2013) criticized the fact that the most commonly used quality-of-life measure in the exercise psychology literature is the SF-36. Their concern was that the SF-36 was developed specifically for clinical studies and therefore does not provide a good assessment of positive health outcomes. Gill and colleagues (2011) developed and assessed the psychometric properties for a 32-item questionnaire (the Quality of Life Survey) to assess quality of life as specific to the exercise experience. In their instrument, Gill and colleagues (2011) focused on capturing positive experiences, defining quality of life as "a subjective multidimensional, integrative construct that reflects optimal well-being and positive health" (p. 184). In their conceptual model, they suggested that physical health symptoms, physical fitness, and physical functioning all contribute to physical well-being, and that well-being in the domains of physical, social, cognitive, emotional, and spiritual all then contribute to an integrative quality of life.

The Centers for Disease Control have been tracking quality of life for decades using a measure they developed called the Healthy Days Measure. This measure has been administered to a nationally representative sample of adults since 1993 as a part of the Behavioral Risk Factor Surveillance System (BRFSS) and to a nationally representative sample of persons 12 and older since 2000 as a part of the National Health and Nutrition Examination Survey (NHANES). This measure is designed to capture perceptions of health status and activity limitations broadly through responses to four questions (Centers for Disease Control and Prevention, 2018). A participant is asked to report overall how they judge their health, to report on how many days out of 30 they would describe their physical health and mental health as "not good," and to identify how many days out of 30 their poor health kept them from doing their normal activities. Although this measure is useful for understanding population-level changes in quality of life in the United States, it has not been used much in the exercise literature.

The World Health Organization (WHO) developed a comprehensive quality-of-life (QOL) measure consisting of 100 questions (WHOQOL-100) and a shorter instrument consisting of 26 questions (the WHOQOL-BREF) to be used across cultures and languages, with versions in 29 different languages. The WHOQOL-100 assesses quality of life in six domains (physical, psychological, level of independence, social relationships, environment, and spirituality or religious beliefs) that were found to all contribute to overall quality of life (as an integrative construct).

Given the definition of quality of life, it is not surprising that this construct requires the use of self-report measures for assessment. All of the global measures described here have acceptable validity and reliability and therefore are appropriately used in research. In addition to these global measures, disease-specific measures of quality of life also have been developed to specifically address issues relevant to each particular disease.

Specific Disease States

Two important surveys were developed specifically for use in cancer patients and survivors. The Functional Assessment of Cancer Therapy - General (FACT-G) and the European Organization for Research and Treatment of Cancer Quality of Life Questionnaire-Core 30 (EORTC QLQ-C30) are widely used in studies focused on these patient groups. The FACT-G is a 28-item survey that provides scores for physical, functional, social, and emotional well-being as well as an overall total score. Responses to descriptions of experiences relevant to cancer (e.g., "I have pain"; "I get emotional support from my family") are rated on a scale of 1 to 5, from "Not at all" to "Very much," with higher scores indicative of better quality of life. The FACT-G has been shown to be useful in discriminating between cancer patients at various stages of disease and relative to hospitalization status and therefore is thought to be a sensitive instrument appropriate for use relative to interventions. The EORTC QLQ-C30 is a 30-item questionnaire designed to assess quality of life in five functional areas (physical, role, cognitive, emotional, social function), to measure three symptoms of cancer treatment (pain, fatigue, and vomiting and nausea), and to provide global measures of quality of life and HRQL. Participants are asked to indicate the extent to which they experience various limitations related to their health over the past week (e.g., Were you short of breath? Did you worry?) on a four-point scale from "Not at all" to "Very much." Scores on this questionnaire are converted to a 0-to-100 scale such that higher scores for the functional areas indicate worse function, whereas for the symptom and global scales, higher scores represent better quality of life. This questionnaire is available in 100 different languages, making it ideal for studies focused on cross-country comparisons.

The choice of which instrument to use is dependent on the goals for its assessment. If one is interested in global quality of life, one of those measures is most appropriate. However, if one is interested in examining quality of life within a specific population, it makes the most sense to choose a measure that was developed specifically for that population. That's because the questions will be the ones most relevant to that group given the unique aspects of their condition. If one is interested in quality-of-life outcomes relative to exercise, it would be important to consider the use of the Quality of Life Survey because this was developed specifically to assess the expected positive effects of exercise on domains that are relevant to physical activity participation.

Quality of Life in Alzheimer's Disease

Manson and associates (2020) collected interview data from individuals living with the early stages of Alzheimer's disease with support from their caregivers. The goal was to understand the nature of change in quality of life associated with disease progression (albeit in the early stages). The data supported three major themes. First, the memory problems and diagnosis led to an experience of loss as participants adjusted their activities to match their current capabilities. The sense of loss was both in the short-term and for the long-term. Second, to cope with the disease, participants made efforts to focus on what they were capable of doing rather than what they could not do. Finally, because the maintenance of social interconnectedness was important, they and their caregiver recognized the need to accept limitations while also facilitating continued engagement with others. Overall, the authors concluded that in these early stages of Alzheimer's disease, the participants were able to maintain a generally positive quality of life by working to maintain meaningful engagement in their lives.

Evidence Relative to the Effects of Exercise on Quality of Life

The literature on exercise and quality of life is quite expansive, but early research in this area was lacking in quality. In fact, in 1998 in the American College of Sports Medicine's position stand on exercise for older adults the authors concluded that "although physical activity seems to be positively associated with some aspects of QOL [quality of life], the precise nature of the relationship is poorly understood" (American College of Sports Medicine

Position Stand, 1998, p. 1522) and pointed out that most of the evidence was at the lowest quality level. However, since that time, numerous RCTs have been conducted, improving our understanding of the role of exercise in quality of life. In this area of research, several systematic and meta-analytic reviews provide us with insightful summaries of the published evidence.

Empirical Evidence

A study conducted in Germany provides an example of an RCT in healthy adults. Brand and colleagues (2006) recruited participants from three places of business that employed both white- and blue-collar workers (see figure 14.5). Volunteers were assigned randomly to an exercise intervention or a wait-list control for 13 weeks. The exercise intervention consisted of one supervised and one unsupervised exercise session per week with a focus on calisthenics, muscle relaxation, and back-strengthening exercises. Participants in the wait-list control group were asked to maintain their normal lifestyle and then received the intervention at the conclusion of the control period. Quality of life was measured using the WHOQOL-BREF. Results of this study showed that the exercise group experienced moderate to large improvements in quality of life that were not realized by the control participants. Follow-up analyses indicated that these improvements were evident for both physical and psychological domains of quality of life but were not observed for the domains of social relationships or environment. Although this study provides evidence that this particular intervention was linked to changes in quality of life, it is important to note that the specific types of exercise are not what is typically used. That is, most studies focus on aerobic exercise or resistance training. Thus, this study suggests that a broader range of types of activities can be beneficial for improving quality of life.

Kampshoff and associates (2015) conducted an RCT designed to explore dose–response effects between exercise intensity and quality-of-life outcomes in a group expected to be experiencing challenges to their quality of life (see figure 14.6). They recruited 277 cancer survivors who were 4 to 6 weeks past chemotherapy treatment and randomly assigned them to high-intensity exercise, low-intensity exercise, or a wait-list control for 12 weeks. Both exercise groups performed resistance exercise, interval exercise, and endurance interval exercise twice per week with supervision. Those in the high-intensity group exercised at ≥80% heart rate reserve, and those in the low-intensity group exercised at 40% to 50% heart rate reserve. At the conclusion of the intervention, participants in the high-intensity group had significant improvements in quality of life relative to the wait-list control group. The magnitude of these effects was determined to be clinically meaningful. Those in the low-intensity group showed benefits that were lower than observed for the high-intensity group but higher than the wait-list control group. The observed benefits for the participants in the high-intensity group were larger for participants who were younger, had breast cancer, and were female. Thus, results suggest a dose–response relationship between exercise intensity and quality-of-life outcomes among cancer survivors, with higher-intensity exercise yielding the greatest benefits. These results are important for showing that exercise can benefit quality of life when a person has been challenged by dealing with cancer, but also because they support the existence of a dose–response relationship between exercise and quality-of-life outcomes such that higher intensity might be required to observe the greatest benefits.

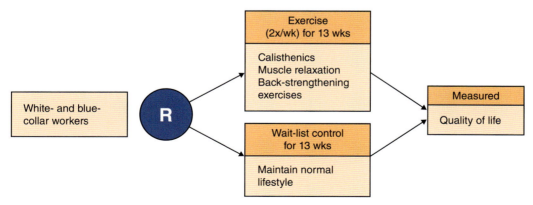

FIGURE 14.5 Brand and colleagues (2006) randomly assigned white- and blue-collar workers to one of two treatment conditions for 13 weeks and tested for differences in quality of life.

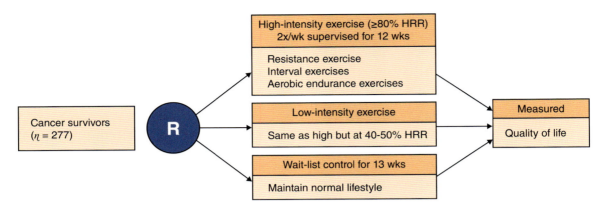

FIGURE 14.6 Kampshoff and associates (2015) randomly assigned cancer survivors to one of three treatment conditions for 12 weeks and tested for differences in quality of life.

Although numerous studies have been conducted to test the effects of exercise on quality of life, the early research was limited because of the use of relatively weak experimental designs. Here we considered two studies that used RCTs to allow for the establishment of a causal link between exercise and quality of life. Brand and colleagues (2006) and Kampshoff and associates (2015) provided evidence that individuals who participate in a 12- to 13-week exercise program will experience significant improvements in quality of life that can be attributed to the exercise. These studies suggest that the exercise can include a wide variety of types of exercise including resistance exercise, interval exercise, calisthenics, muscle relaxation, and back-strengthening exercise. Furthermore, the results indicate that higher-intensity exercise yields the largest benefits over a 12-week intervention with cancer survivors.

Meta-Analytic and Systematic Reviews

In recent years, substantially more RCTs have been conducted, so it is not surprising that several meta-analytic reviews of this literature have been published. Perhaps surprising is that only one meta-analysis has focused on healthy adults, while the others looked at specific disease states such as cancer, stroke, MS, chronic brain disorders, and depression.

Gillison and colleagues (2009) reviewed findings from RCTs that had tested the effects of exercise in well people ($n = 11$ studies) and in those in rehabilitation ($n = 12$ studies) and disease management ($n = 24$ studies) phases for seven disease categories (cancer, cardiovascular disease, musculoskeletal, neurological, pulmonary, renal disease, autoimmune). They looked separately at results for those studies using exercise as a preventative (for well individuals), for rehabilitation following treatment when full recovery was expected, or for disease management when symptom management or the prevention of further deterioration was the goal. To allow for comparisons across studies, they only looked at findings reported between 3 and 6 months. Their results showed that the largest benefits of exercise for overall quality of life were realized in the studies looking at rehabilitation interventions (ES = 0.55). In other words, exercise had its greatest benefits for those who were in the process of recovering and rehabilitating immediately after treatment for their condition. However, when limited to studies looking at preventative interventions, positive (albeit small) effects still were observed for both psychological and physical aspects of quality of life (ES = 0.21). The overall effect size for studies looking at patients during disease management studies showed no effect (ES = 0.00). This was because findings were opposite for subdomains of quality of life, with a small negative effect of exercise reported for psychological quality of life (ES = –0.26) and a small nonsignificant benefit (ES = 0.19) for physical quality of life.

Let's unpack the findings for the disease management studies and also consider findings relative to intensity. The identification of one positive and one negative finding for disease management is perplexing because it suggests that exercise might have mixed effects depending on the specific aspect of quality of life that is of interest during the disease management phase. This might be logical, however, when one considers that for patients in disease management the goal is symptom management or the prevention of further deterioration. Hence, one might expect that significant gains would not be observed for psychological outcomes (because exercise isn't affecting the disease state and so their overall prognosis has not changed) but that it does help with physical outcomes that are responsive to physical activity programming and still important to the individual. Overall, the authors concluded that even a relatively short exercise intervention of 3 to 6 months results in small to moderate positive benefits for quality of life for those in rehabilitation following treatment or who are currently well. Interestingly, looking at the influence of exercise intensity, rehabilitation studies found the largest effects of light-intensity exercise (ES = 1.30), while disease management studies reported the largest effects for physical aspects of quality of life with moderate-intensity exercise (ES = 0.57). These findings suggest that health professionals should use only light-intensity exercise with patients who are rehabilitating following a treatment, but can progress their patients to moderate-intensity exercise if they are living with a disease. Perhaps this makes intuitive sense because the person in the rehabilitation setting might be adjusting to a new normal, which might make light-intensity exercise the appropriate level of challenge, while those living with a disease likely have a stable baseline, allowing them to progress to higher intensities of exercise.

Two meta-analyses focused specifically on cancer have generally supported small beneficial effects of physical activity on quality of life. Sweegers and associates (2018) summarized results from 66 studies testing the effects of physical activity on quality of life for cancer patients during and following treatment. They reported a significant small benefit of supervised exercise (ES = 0.20) but found a nonsignificant benefit when the exercise was not supervised (ES = 0.04). This review found no significant differences in the effect size based on the exercise program parameters (e.g., frequency, intensity, type, time), suggesting that any amount of physical activity was better than none as long as it was supervised. Although the authors were not able to further explore the reason for this difference, it is possible that the supervised exercise resulted in better adherence and compliance than did the unsupervised exercise. Soares Falcetta and colleagues (2018) focused exclusively on breast cancer and summarized results from 54 studies testing the effects of exercise interventions within 5 years of diagnosis for breast cancer patients who had completed their treatment (with the exception of hormone therapy treatment). They reported a small to moderate benefit to quality of life overall (ES = 0.45), with larger benefits for physical quality of life (ES = 0.51) than for mental quality of life (ES = 0.28). The results of these two meta-analyses are important because they argue for quality-of-life benefits in response to exercise specifically for cancer survivors.

Dauwan and associates (2021) focused on studies using exercise as an additional treatment for participants being treated for chronic brain disorders (e.g., Alzheimer's disease, Huntington's disease, Parkinson's disease). This meta-analytic review was fairly large, including 64 RCTs. Findings supported a beneficial effect of exercise on quality of life (ES = 0.40). This small to moderate effect size supports the value of physical activity for chronic brain disorders in terms of a person's overall quality of life. Meta-analyses focused on other diseases have much smaller bodies of evidence to review but also report small to moderate benefits as follows (see figure 14.7): stroke survivors (n = 9; ES = 0.32) (Chen &

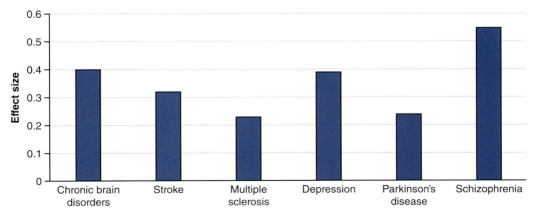

FIGURE 14.7 Meta-analytic reviews of a variety of chronic illnesses generally support that exercise benefits quality of life, with effect sizes ranging from 0.23 to 0.55.

Rimmer, 2011), adults with MS (*n* = 13; ES = 0.23) (Motl & Gosney, 2008), depression (*n* = 6; ES = 0.39) (Schuch et al., 2016), Parkinson's disease (*n* = 20; ES = 0.24) (Chen et al., 2020), and schizophrenia (*n* = 11; ES = 0.55) (Dauwan et al., 2016).

Overall, the findings of these meta-analytic reviews are remarkably consistent and suggest that physical activity participation results in small to moderate benefits in terms of quality of life for healthy populations and for populations with clinical cognitive impairments, mental health disorders, or physical disabilities and disease. This is important because modern medicine enables people to live longer despite these medical challenges. However, the value of those extra days, months, or years of life to the individual and their families is largely dependent on the quality of life during that time period. Hence, understanding that physical activity contributes to quality of life is valuable for individuals, families, and health care providers.

Summary

Quality of life is a perceptual outcome that has become increasingly important as the population of older adults continues to grow and as modern medicine enables more individuals to live with chronic disease. Given that many older adults are living with various health conditions and that numerous diseases affect people over a long time with no current cure (e.g., Parkinson's disease, MS, Alzheimer's disease), quality of life is an important outcome to consider. In fact, quality of life might be the ultimate consideration when patients are considering various treatment options. For example, we consider decisions a person might make with respect to treatment for cancer. When given the option of chemotherapy for months and the concomitant lower quality of life versus allowing a cancer to run its course, some individuals choose the latter to maintain a higher quality of life in the months or years they have remaining.

Exercise has been shown to be effective in improving quality of life in well individuals, suggesting it can positively affect quality of life even for individuals who should already have relatively high levels of HRQL or whose quality of life is affected by nonhealth-related variables. There is also substantial evidence supporting benefits for those who are recovering and rehabilitating following a medical treatment for their chronic health condition. Evidence suggests that with cancer patients, effects are larger with supervised exercise sessions and for physical quality of life relative to mental quality of life. Positive benefits for exercise on quality of life are also observed in individuals with other chronic health conditions including stroke survivors and people with MS, depression, Parkinson's disease, or schizophrenia. Although early evidence supporting these effects was of relatively low quality, more recent studies have used RCT designs and provide support for a causal relationship such that participation in exercise improves quality of life and effects tend to be small to moderate in size across populations.

Discussion Questions

1. Discuss the findings that were presented that consider the potential influence of exercise intensity on quality-of-life outcomes. Talk about empirical findings with cancer survivors and meta-analytic findings relative to participants in rehabilitation and maintenance phases. What are the implications in terms of recommendations?

2. Provide a summary of what the results of two meta-analyses tell us about the potential benefits of chronic exercise for quality of life for cancer survivors.

3. Provide an explanation of why it is important to examine quality of life as an outcome that is potentially influenced by physical activity participation. Explain which aspects of quality of life are most relevant when considering the potential benefits of physical activity, and explain why this is the case.

4. Buffart and colleagues (2014) conducted a study in which they examined numerous psychological mechanisms of the effects of exercise on quality of life for cancer survivors. Describe the study, what they found, and why this work was important.

References

Chapter 1

American Kinesiology Association. (2023, May 6). *American Kinesiology Association: About AKA.* https://americankinesiology.org/about-us/#:~:text=Definition%20of%20Kinesiology,society%2C%20and%20quality%20of%20life.

Barrow, H.M., & Brown, J.P. (1988). *Man and movement: Principles of education* (4th ed.). Lea & Febiger.

Bennett, B.L. (1978). Dudley A. Sargent—A man for all seasons. *Quest, 29*(1), 33-45. https://doi.org/10.1080/00336297.1978.10519909

Bunn, G.C. (2017). Wilhelm Wundt and the emergence of scientific psychology. *Psychology Review, 22*(3), 10-12.

Camilleri, M. (2019). Leaky gut: Mechanisms, measurement and clinical implications in humans. *Gut, 68*(8), 1516-1526. https://doi.org/10.1136/gutjnl-2019-318427

Coakley, J. (2021). Connecting with kinesiology: Observations of an outsider. *Kinesiology Review, 10*(2), 133-139.

Cordain, L., Gotshall, R.W., Eaton, S.B., & Eaton, S.B., III. (1998). Physical activity, energy expenditure and fitness: An evolutionary perspective. *International Journal of Sports Medicine, 19*(5), 328-335. https://doi.org/10.1055/s-2007-971926

Crews, D.J., & Landers, D.M. (1987). A meta-analytic review of aerobic fitness and reactivity to psychosocial stressors. *Medicine & Science in Sports & Exercise, 19*(5 Suppl), S114-120. www.ncbi.nlm.nih.gov/pubmed/3316910

Department of the Interior. (1918). *Cardinal principles of secondary education.* Bureau of Education, Department of the Interior. https://eric.ed.gov/?id=ED541063

Etnier, J.L., Nowell, P.M., Landers, D.M., & Sibley, B.A. (2006). A meta-regression to examine the relationship between aerobic fitness and cognitive performance. *Brain Research Reviews, 52*(1), 119-130. https://doi.org/10.1016/j.brainresrev.2006.01.002

Fasano, A. (2020). All disease begins in the (leaky) gut: Role of zonulin-mediated gut permeability in the pathogenesis of some chronic inflammatory diseases. *F1000Research, 9.* https://doi.org/10.12688/f1000research.20510.1

Feltz, D.L., & Landers, D.M. (1983). The effects of mental practice on motor skill learning and performance: A meta-analysis. *Journal of Sport Psychology, 5*(1), 25-57.

Fitz, G.W. (1895). A location reaction apparatus. *Psychological Review, 2*(1), 37-42.

Franz, S.I., & Hamilton, G.V. (1905). The effects of exercise upon the retardation in conditions of depression. *American Journal of Psychiatry, 62*(2), 239-256.

Georgoulis, A.D., Kiapidou, I.S., Velogianni, L., Stergiou, N., & Boland, A. (2007). Herodicus, the father of sports medicine. *Knee Surgery, Sports Traumatology, Arthroscopy, 15*(3), 315-318. https://doi.org/10.1007/s00167-006-0149-z

Gill, D.L. (1986). *Psychological dynamics of sport.* Human Kinetics.

Gould, D., & Pick, S. (1995). Sport psychology: The Griffith era, 1920-1940. *The Sport Psychologist, 9,* 391-405.

Green, C.D. (2012). America's first sport psychologist. *Monitor on Psychology, 43*(4). www.apa.org/monitor/2012/04/sport

Griffith, C.R. (1926). *Psychology of coaching: A study of coaching methods from the point of view of psychology.* C. Scribner's Sons.

Griffith, C.R. (1928). *Psychology and athletics: A general survey for athletes and coaches.* New C. Scribner's sons.

Harlow, H.F. (1932). Social facilitation of feeding in the albino rat. *The Pedagogical Seminary and Journal of Genetic Psychology, 41*(1), 211-221.

Harris, D.V., & Harris, B.L. (1984). *The athlete's guide to sports psychology: Mental skills for physical people.* Leisure Press.

James, W. (1907). The energies of men. *Science, 25*(635), 321-332. https://doi.org/10.1126/science.25.635.321

Kennedy, J.F. (1960, December 26). The soft American. *Sports Illustrated,* 15-17.

King, D.B., Raymond, B.L., & Simon-Thomas, J.A. (1995). History of sport psychology in cultural magazines of the Victorian Era. *The Sport Psychologist, 9,* 376-390.

Kornspan, A.S. (2007a). E.W. Scripture and the Yale Psychology Laboratory: Studies related to athletes and physical activity. *The Sport Psychologist, 21,* 152-169.

Kornspan, A.S. (2007b). The early years of sport psychology: The work and influence of Pierre de Coubertin. *Journal of Sport Behavior, 30,* 77-93.

Krane, V., & Whaley, D.E. (2010). Quiet competence: Writing women into the history of U.S. sport and exercise psychology. *The Sport Psychologist, 18,* 349-372.

Kraus, H., & Hirschland, R.P. (1954). Minimum muscular fitness tests in school children. *Research Quarterly. American Association for Health, Physical Education, and Recreation, 25*(2), 178-188.

Kroll, W., & Lewis, G. (1970). America's first sport psychologist. *Quest, 13,* 1-4.

Kubitz, K.A., Landers, D.M., Petruzzello, S.J., & Han, M. (1996). The effects of acute and chronic exercise on sleep. A meta-analytic review. *Sports Medicine, 21*(4), 277-291. https://doi.org/10.2165/00007256-199621040-00004

Landers, D.M. (1995). Sport psychology: The formative years, 1950-1980. *The Sport Psychologist, 9,* 406-417.

Lawson, H.A. (2018). Physical education in the industrial age: An institutional perspective. In *Redesigning physical education: An equity agenda in which every child matters* (pp. 23-40). Routledge.

Layman, E.M. (1955). *Mental health through physical education and recreation.* Burgess.

Layman, E.M. (1974). Psychological effects of physical activity. *Exercise and Sport Sciences Reviews, 2,* 33-70. www.ncbi.nlm.nih.gov/pubmed/4619369

Liberti, R. (2017). "Gendering the gym": A history of women in physical education. *Kinesiology Review, 6,* 153-166. https://doi.org/10.1123/kr.2017-0005

McCullick, B.A., & Lomax, M. (2000). The Boston Normal School of Gymnastics: An unheralded legacy. *Quest, 52,* 49-59.

McEvoy, E., Heikinaro-Johansson, P., & MacPhail, A. (2017). Physical education teacher educators' views regarding the purpose(s) of school physical education. *Sport, Education, and Society, 22*(7), 812-824. http://dx.doi.org/10.1080/13573322.2015.1075971

Newell, K.M. (1990a). Kinesiology: The label for the study of physical activity in higher education. *Quest, 42*(3), 269-278.

Newell, K.M. (1990b). Physical education in higher education: Chaos out of order. *Quest, 42*(3), 227-242.

O'Keefe, J.H., Vogel, R., Lavie, C.J., & Cordain, L. (2010). Achieving hunter-gatherer fitness in the 21(st) century: Back to the future. *The American Journal of Medicine, 123*(12), 1082-1086. https://doi.org/10.1016/j.amjmed.2010.04.026

Petruzzello, S.J., Landers, D.M., Hatfield, B.D., Kubitz, K.A., & Salazar, W. (1991). A meta-analysis on the anxiety-reducing effects of acute and chronic exercise. Outcomes and mechanisms. *Sports Medicine, 11*(3), 143-182. https://doi.org/10.2165/00007256-199111030-00002

Raichlen, D.A., Pontzer, H., Harris, J.A., Mabulla, A.Z., Marlowe, F.W., Snodgrass, J., Eick, G., Berbesque, C., Sancilio, A., & Wood, B.M. (2017). Physical activity patterns and biomarkers of cardiovascular disease risk in hunter-gatherers. *American Journal of Human Biology, 29*(2). https://doi.org/10.1002/ajhb.22919

Ralphs, M.H., Graham, D., & James, L.F. (1994). Social facilitation influences cattle to graze locoweed. *Rangeland Ecology & Management/Journal of Range Management Archives, 47*(2), 123-126.

Ransdell, L.B. (2014). Women as leaders in kinesiology and beyond: Smashing through the glass obstacles. *Quest, 66*(2), 150-168. https://doi.org/10.1080/00336297.2014.895953

Rejeski, W.J., & Brawley, L.R. (1988). Defining the boundaries of sport psychology. *The Sport Psychologist, 2,* 231-242.

Rethorst, C.D., Wipfli, B.M., & Landers, D.M. (2009). The antidepressive effects of exercise: A meta-analysis of randomized trials. *Sports Medicine, 39*(6), 491-511. https://doi.org/10.2165/00007256-200939060-00004

Sage, G.H. (2013). Resurrecting thirty years of historical insight about kinesiology: A supplement to "What is kinesiology? Historical and philosophical insights." *Quest, 65*(2), 133-138. https://doi.org/10.1080/00336297.2013.773534

Triplett, N.L. (1898). Dynamogenic factors in pacemaking and competition. *The American Journal of Psychology, 9,* 507-533.

Twietmeyer, G. (2012). What is kinesiology? Historical and philosophical insights. *Quest, 64*(1), 4-23.

Urban, E. (2018). On matters of mind and body: Regarding Descartes. *Journal of Analytical Psychology, 63*(2), 228-240. https://doi.org/10.1111/1468-5922.12395

U.S. Department of Health and Human Services. (2018). *Physical Activity Guidelines for Americans* (2nd ed.). U.S. Department of Health and Human Services.

Vealey, R.S. (2006). Smocks and jocks outside the box: The paradigmatic evolution of sport and exercise psychology. *Quest, 58*(1), 128-159. https://doi.org/10.1080/00336297.2006.10491876

Vertinsky, P. (2017). A question of the head and the heart: From physical education to kinesiology in the gymnasium and the laboratory. *Kinesiology Review, 6,* 140-152.

Weiss, M.M., & Jamieson, K.J. (2017). The way we never were: Postracial kinesiology and America. *Kinesiology Review, 6,* 167-177.

Weiss, M.R. (2004). *Developmental sport and exercise psychology: A lifespan perspective.* Fitness Information Technology.

Wiggins, D.K. (1984). The history of sport psychology in North America. In J.M.I. Silva & R.S. Weinberg (Eds.), *Psychological foundations of sport* (pp. 9-22). Human Kinetics.

Williams, J.M. (1986). *Applied sport psychology: Personal growth to peak performance.* Mayfield.

Wipfli, B.M., Rethorst, C.D., & Landers, D.M. (2008). The anxiolytic effects of exercise: A meta-analysis of randomized trials and dose-response analysis. *Journal of Sport and Exercise Psychology, 30*(4), 392-410. https://doi.org/10.1123/jsep.30.4.392

Yang, L., Cao, C., Kantor, E.D., Nguyen, L.H., Zheng, X., Park, Y., Giovannucci, E.L., Matthews, C.E., Colditz, G.A., & Cao, Y. (2019). Trends in sedentary behavior among the US population, 2001-2016. *Journal of the American Medical Association, 321*(16), 1587-1597. https://doi.org/10.1001/jama.2019.3636

Zajonc, R.B., Heingartner, A., & Herman, E.M. (1969). Social enhancement and impairment of performance in the cockroach. *Journal of Personality and Social Psychology, 13*(2), 83-92.

Chapter 2

Alderman, B.L., & Olson, R.L. (2014). The relation of aerobic fitness to cognitive control and heart rate variability: A neurovisceral integration study. *Biological Psychology, 99,* 26-33. https://doi.org/10.1016/j.biopsycho.2014.02.007

Baranowski, T., Anderson, C., & Carmack, C. (1998). Mediating variable framework in physical activity interventions. How are we doing? How might we do better? *American Journal of Preventive Medicine, 15*(4), 266-297. https://doi.org/10.1016/s0749-3797(98)00080-4

Bloodgood, B.L., & Sabatini, B.L. (2009). NMDA receptor-mediated calcium transients in dendritic spines. In A.M. Van Dongen (Ed.), *Biology of the NMDA Receptor* (pp 201-211). CRC Press.

Ekkekakis, P. (2009). The dual-mode theory of affective responses to exercise in metatheoretical context: I. Initial impetus, basic postulates, and philosophical framework. *International Review of Sport and Exercise Psychology, 2*(1), 73-94.

Lee, S. (2020). Perceived neighborhood environment associated with older adults' walking and positive affect: Results from the health and retirement study. *Journal of Aging and Physical Activity, 29*(3), 536-543.

Lesnewich, L.M., Conway, F.N., Buckman, J.F., Brush, C.J., Ehmann, P.J., Eddie, D., Olson, R.L., Alderman, B.L., Bates, M.E. (2019). Associations of depression severity with heart rate and heart rate variability in young adults across normative and clinical populations. *International Journal of Psychophysiology, 142,* 57-65. https://doi.org/10.1016/j.ijpsycho.2019.06.005

Ludyga, S., Gerber, M., Mucke, M., Brand, S., Weber, P., Brotzmann, M., & Puhse, U. (2020). The acute effects of aerobic exercise on cognitive flexibility and task-related heart rate variability in children with ADHD and healthy controls. *Journal of Attention Disorders, 24*(5), 693-703. https://doi.org/10.1177/1087054718757647

Nahm, E.S., Resnick, B., Bellantoni, M., Zhu, S., Brown, C., Brennan, P.F., Charters, K., Brown, J., Rietschel, M., Pinna, J., An, M., Park, B.K., & Plummer, L. (2015). Dissemination of a theory-based online bone health program: Two intervention approaches. *Health Informatics Journal, 21*(2), 120-136. https://doi.org/10.1177/1460458213505573

Sylvester, B.D., Curran, T., Standage, M., Sabiston, C.M., & Beauchamp, M.R. (2018). Predicting exercise motivation and exercise behavior: A moderated mediation model testing the interaction between perceived exercise variety and basic psychological needs satisfaction. *Psychology of Sport & Exercise, 36*, 50-56.

Thayer, J.F., & Lane, R.D. (2000). A model of neurovisceral integration in emotion regulation and dysregulation. *Journal of Affective Disorders, 61*(3), 201-216. https://doi.org/10.1016/s0165-0327(00)00338-4

Yaffe, J., Montgomery, P., Hopewell, S., & Shepard, L.D. (2012). Empty reviews: A description and consideration of Cochrane systematic reviews with no included studies. *PLoS One, 7*(5), e36626. https://doi.org/10.1371/journal.pone.0036626

Yerkes, R.M., & Dodson, J.D. (1908). The relation of strength of stimulus to rapidity of habit-formation. *Journal of Comparative Neurology and Psychology, 18*, 459-482.

Zhu, S., Nahm, E.S., Resnick, B., Friedmann, E., Brown, C., Park, J., Cheon, J., & Park, D. (2017). The moderated mediating effect of self-efficacy on exercise among older adults in an online bone health intervention study: A parallel process latent growth curve model. *Journal of Aging and Physical Activity, 25*(3), 378-386. https://doi.org10.1123/japa.2016-0216

Zou, L., Sasaki, J.E., Wei, G.X., Huang, T., Yeung, A.S., Neto, O.B., Chen, K.W., & Hui, S.S. (2018). Effects of mind(-)body exercises (tai chi/yoga) on heart rate variability parameters and perceived stress: A systematic review with meta-analysis of randomized controlled Trials. *Journal of Clinical Medicine, 7*(11). https://doi.org/10.3390/jcm7110404

Chapter 3

Ainsworth, B.E., Haskell, W.L., Herrmann, S.D., Meckes, N., Bassett, D.R., Jr., Tudor-Locke, C., Greer, J.L., Vezina, J., Whitt-Glover, M.C., & Leon, A.S. (2011). 2011 Compendium of Physical Activities: A second update of codes and MET values. *Medecine & Science in Sports & Exercise, 43*(8), 1575-1581. https://doi.org/10.1249/MSS.0b013e31821ece12

American College of Sports Medicine. (2022). *ACSM's guidelines for exercise testing and prescription* (11th ed.). Wolters Kluwer.

Buckley, J.P., Hedge, A., Yates, T., Copeland, R.J., Loosemore, M., Hamer, M., Bradley, G., & Dunstan, D.W. (2015). The sedentary office: An expert statement on the growing case for change towards better health and productivity. *British Journal of Sports Medicine, 49*(21), 1357-1362. https://doi.org/10.1136/bjsports-2015-094618

Butte, N.F., Watson, K.B., Ridley, K., Zakeri, I.F., McMurray, R.G., Pfeiffer, K.A., Crouter, S.E., Herrmann, S.D., Bassett, D.R., Long, A., Berhane, Z., Trost, S.G., Ainsworth, B.E., Berrigan, D., & Fulton, J.E. (2018). A Youth Compendium of Physical Activities: Activity codes and metabolic intensities. *Medicine & Science in Sports & Exercise, 50*(2), 246-256. https://doi.org/10.1249/MSS.0000000000001430

Camhi, S.M., Bray, G.A., Bouchard, C., Greenway, F.L., Johnson, W.D., Newton, R.L., Ravussin, E., Ryan, D.H., Smith, S.R., & Katzmarzyk, P.T. (2011). The relationship of waist circumference and BMI to visceral, subcutaneous, and total body fat: Sex and race differences. *Obesity, 19*(2), 402-408.

Centers for Disease Control and Prevention. (2019). *Nutrition, physical activity, and obesity: Data, trend and maps.* Centers for Disease Control and Prevention. https://nccd.cdc.gov/dnpao_dtm/rdPage.aspx?rdReport=DNPAO_DTM.ExploreByTopic&islClass=PA&islTopic=PA1&go=GO

Eitzen, D.S., & Sage, G.H. (1997). *Sociology of North American sport* (6th ed.). Brown & Benchmark.

Haskell, W.L. (2012). Physical activity by self-report: A brief history and future issues. *Journal of Physical Activity and Health, 9* Suppl 1, S5-10. https://doi.org/10.1123/jpah.9.s1.s5

Mama, S.K., Bhuiyan, N., Lee, R.E., Basen-Engquist, K., Wetter, D.W., Thompson, D., & McNeill, L.H. (2019). Comparing multiple measures of physical activity in African-American adults. *Americal Journal of Health Behavior, 43*(5), 877-886. https://doi.org/10.5993/AJHB.43.5.1

McKenzie, T.L. (2002). The use of direct observation to assess physical activity. In G. Welk (Ed.). *Physical activity assessments for health-related research.* Human Kinetics.

McKenzie, T.L., Sallis, J.F., & Nader, P.R. (1992). SOFIT: System for Observing Fitness Instruction Time. *Journal of Teaching in Physical Education, 11*(2), 195-205.

Mitchell, L.A., MacDonald, R.A., & Brodie, E.E. (2004). Temperature and the cold pressor test. *Journal of Pain, 5*(4), 233-237. https://doi.org/10.1016/j.jpain.2004.03.004

National Center for Health Statistics. (2020). *Physical activity among adults aged 18 and over: United States, 2020.* National Center for Health Statistics. www.cdc.gov/nchs/products/databriefs/db443.htm#:~:text=Among%20all%20adults%2C%2046.9%25%20met,the%20muscle%2Dstrengthening%20activity%20guidelines

Park, J.H., Moon, J.H., Kim, H.J., Kong, M.H., & Oh, Y.H. (2020). Sedentary lifestyle: Overview of updated evidence of potential health risks. *Korean Journal of Family Medicine, 41*, 365-373. https://doi.org/https://doi.org/10.4082/kjfm.20.0165

Prentice, A.M., & Jebb, S.A. (2001). Beyond body mass index. *Obesity Reviews, 2*(3), 141-147.

Prince, S.A., Adamo, K.B., Hamel, M.E., Hardt, J., Connor Gorber, S., & Tremblay, M. (2008). A comparison of direct versus self-report measures for assessing physical activity in adults: A systematic review. *International Journal of Behavioral Nutrition and Physical Activity, 5*, 56. https://doi.org/10.1186/1479-5868-5-56

Rowe, P.J., Schuldheisz, J.M., & van der Mars, H. (1997). Validation of SOFIT for measuring physical activity of first- to eighth-grade students. *Pediatric Exercise Science, 9*, 136-149.

Rowe, P.J., Van der Mars, H., Schuldheisz, J., & Fox, S. (2004). Measuring students' physical activity levels: Validating SOFIT for use with high-school students. *Journal of Teaching in Physical Education, 23*, 235-251.

Sharma, S., Chuang, R.J., Skala, K., & Atteberry, H. (2011). Measuring physical activity in preschoolers: Reliability and validity of The System for Observing Fitness Instruction Time for Preschoolers (SOFIT-P). *Measurement in Physical Education and Exercise Science, 15*(4), 257-273. https://doi.org/10.1080/1091367X.2011.594361

Shiroma, E.J., Freedson, P.S., Trost, S.G., & Lee, I.M. (2013). Patterns of accelerometer-assessed sedentary behavior in older women. *Journal of the American Medical Association, 310*(23), 2562-2563. https://doi.org/10.1001/jama.2013.278896

Steene-Johannessen, J., Anderssen, S.A., van der Ploeg, H.P., Hendriksen, I.J., Donnelly, A.E., Brage, S., & Ekelund, U. (2016). Are self-report measures able to define individuals as physically active or inactive? *Medicine & Science in*

Sports & Exercise, 48(2), 235-244. https://doi.org/10.1249/MSS.0000000000000760

U.S. Department of Health and Human Services. (2022). *Physical Activity Guidelines for Americans*. U.S. Department of Health and Human Services. https://health.gov/our-work/physical-activity/current-guidelines/top-10-things-know

World Health Organization. (2020). *Physical activity*. World Health Organization. www.who.int/news-room/fact-sheets/detail/physical-activity

Chapter 4

American Psychological Association (APA). (2019). *Stress in America: Stress and current events*. www.apa.org/news/press/releases/stress/2019/stress-america-2019.pdf

American Psychological Association (APA). (2020). *Stress in America 2020: A national mental health crisis*. www.apa.org/news/press/releases/stress/2020/sia-mental-health-crisis.pdf

Brummett, B.H., Babyak, M.A., Siegler, I.C., Vitaliano, P.P., Ballard, E.L., Gwyther, L.P., & Williams, R.B. (2006). Associations among perceptions of social support, negative affect, and quality of sleep in caregivers and noncaregivers. *Health Psychology, 25*(2), 220-225. https://doi.org/10.1037/0278-6133.25.2.220

Chovanec, L., & Gropel, P. (2020). Effects of 8-week endurance and resistance training programmes on cardiovascular stress responses, life stress and coping. *Journal of Sports Sciences, 38*(15), 1699-1707. https://doi.org/10.1080/02640414.2020.1756672

Crews, D.J., & Landers, D.M. (1987). A meta-analytic review of aerobic fitness and reactivity to psychosocial stressors. *Medicine & Science in Sports & Exercise, 19*(5), S114-S120.

Dienstbier, R.A. (1989). Arousal and physiological toughness: Implications for mental and physical health. *Psychological Review, 96*(1), 84-100. https://doi.org/10.1037/0033-295x.96.1.84

Fredrikson, M., & Matthews, K.A. (1990). Cardiovascular responses to behavioral stress and hypertension: A meta-analytic review. *Annals of Behavioral Medicine, 12*(1), 30-39.

Hamer, M., Taylor, A., & Steptoe, A. (2006). The effect of acute aerobic exercise on stress-related blood pressure responses: A systematic review and meta-analysis. *Biological Psychology, 71*(2), 183-190. https://doi.org/10.1016/j.biopsycho.2005.04.004

Kamarck, T.W., Everson, S.A., Kaplan, G.A., Manuck, S.B., Jennings, J.R., Salonen, R., & Salonen, J.T. (1997). Exaggerated blood pressure responses during mental stress are associated with enhanced carotid atherosclerosis in middle-aged Finnish men: Findings from the Kuopio Ischemic Heart Disease Study. *Circulation, 96*(11), 3842-3848. https://doi.org/10.1161/01.cir.96.11.3842

Karlamangla, A.S., Singer, B.H., & Seeman, T.E. (2006). Reduction in allostatic load in older adults is associated with lower all-cause mortality risk: MacArthur studies of successful aging. *Psychosomatic Medicine, 68*(3), 500-507. https://doi.org/10.1097/01.psy.0000221270.93985.82

Kim, H.G., Cheon, E.J., Bai, D.S., Lee, Y.H., & Koo, B.H. (2018). Stress and heart rate variability: A meta-analysis and review of the literature. *Psychiatry Investigation, 15*(3), 235-245. https://doi.org/10.30773/pi.2017.08.17

Lazarus, R.S., & Folkman, S. (1984). *Stress, appraisal, and coping*. Spring Publishing Company.

McEwen, B.S. (1998). Stress, adaptation, and disease: Allostasis and allostatic load. *Annals of the New York Academy of Sciences, 840*(1), 33-44.

McEwen, B.S., & Stellar, E. (1993). Stress and the individual. Mechanisms leading to disease. *Archives of Internal Medicine, 153*(18), 2093-2101. www.ncbi.nlm.nih.gov/pubmed/8379800

Miller, G.E., Chen, E., & Zhou, E.S. (2007). If it goes up, must it come down? Chronic stress and the hypothalamic-pituitary-adrenocortical axis in humans. *Psychological Bulletin, 133*(1), 25-45. https://doi.org/10.1037/0033-2909.133.1.25

Mohney, G. (2018). *Stress costs U.S. 4300 billion every year*. Healthline. www.healthline.com/health-news/stress-health-costs#How-stress-impacts-certain-groups-

Moreira, S.R., Lima, R.M., Silva, K.E., & Simoes, H.G. (2014). Combined exercise circuit session acutely attenuates stress-induced blood pressure reactivity in healthy adults. *Brazilian Journal of Physical Therapy, 18*(1), 38-46. https://doi.org/10.1590/s1413-35552012005000135

Patterson, E. (2022). *Stress facts and statistics*. The Recovery Village. www.therecoveryvillage.com/mental-health/stress/stress-statistics/

Perales, F., Pozo-Cruz, J.D., & Pozo-Cruz, B.D. (2014). Impact of physical activity on psychological distress: A prospective analysis of an Australian national sample. *American Journal of Public Health, 104*(12), e91-97. https://doi.org/10.2105/AJPH.2014.302169

Salonen, J.T., & Salonen, R. (1993). Ultrasound B-mode imaging in observational studies of atherosclerotic progression. *Circulation, 87*(3 Suppl), II56-65. www.ncbi.nlm.nih.gov/pubmed/8443925

Schilling, O.K., & Diehl, M. (2014). Reactivity to stressor pile-up in adulthood: Effects on daily negative and positive affect. *Psychology and Aging, 29*(1), 72-83. https://doi.org/10.1037/a0035500

Seeman, M., Stein Merkin, S., Karlamangla, A., Koretz, B., & Seeman, T. (2014). Social status and biological dysregulation: The "status syndrome" and allostatic load. *Social Science & Medicine, 118*, 143-151. https://doi.org/10.1016/j.socscimed.2014.08.002

Segerstrom, S.C., & Miller, G.E. (2004). Psychological stress and the human immune system: A meta-analytic study of 30 years of inquiry. *Psychological Bulletin, 130*(4), 601-630. https://doi.org/10.1037/0033-2909.130.4.601

Selye, H. (1950). *The physiology and pathology of exposure to stress: A treatise based on the concepts of the general-adaptation-syndrome and the diseases of adaptation*. Acta.

Smyth, J.M., Sliwinski, M.J., Zawadzki, M.J., Scott, S.B., Conroy, D.E., Lanza, S.T., Marcusson-Clavertz, Kim, J., Stawski, R.S., Stoney, C.M., Buxton, O.M., Sciamanna, C.N., Green, P.M., & Almeida, D.M. (2018). Everyday stress response targets in the science of behavior change. *Behaviour Research and Therapy, 101*, 20-29. https://doi.org/10.1016/j.brat.2017.09.009

Sterling, P., & Eyer, J. (1988). Allostasis: A new paradigm to explain arousal pathology. In S. Fisher & J. Reason (Eds.), *Handbook of life stress, cognition and health*. John Wiley & Sons.

Strehli, I., Burns, R.D., Bai, Y., Ziegenfuss, D.H., Block, M.E., & Brusseau, T.A. (2021). Mind-body physical activity interventions and stress-related physiological markers in educational settings: A systematic review and meta-analysis. *International Journal of Environmental Research and Public Health, 18*(1), 224. https://doi.org/10.3390/ijerph18010224

Stubbs, B., Vancampfort, D., Rosenbaum, S., Firth, J., Cosco, T., Veronese, N., Salum, G.A., Schuch, F.B. (2017). An examination of the anxiolytic effects of exercise for people with anxiety and stress-related disorders: A meta-analysis. *Psychiatry Research, 249,* 102-108. https://doi.org/10.1016/j.psychres.2016.12.020

Wang, C., Bannuru, R., Ramel, J., Kupelnick, B., Scott, T., & Schmid, C.H. (2010). Tai chi on psychological well-being: Systematic review and meta-analysis. *BMC Complementary and Alternative Medicine, 10,* 23. https://doi.org/10.1186/1472-6882-10-23

Chapter 5

American Psychological Association. (2022). *Anxiety.* American Psychological Association. www.apa.org/topics/anxiety#:~:text=Anxiety%20is%20an%20emotion%20characterized,certain%20situations%20out%20of%20worry

Anderson, E., & Shivakumar, G. (2013). Effects of exercise and physical activity on anxiety. *Front Psychiatry, 4,* 27. https://doi.org/10.3389/fpsyt.2013.00027

Anxiety & Depression Assocation of America. (2022). *Anxiety disorders - facts & statistics.* Anxiety & Depression Assocation of America. https://adaa.org/understanding-anxiety/facts-statistics

Aylett, E., Small, N., & Bower, P. (2018). Exercise in the treatment of clinical anxiety in general practice - a systematic review and meta-analysis. *BMC Health Services Research, 18*(1), 559. https://doi.org/10.1186/s12913-018-3313-5

Balsamo, M., Cataldi, F., Carlucci, L., & Fairfield, B. (2018). Assessment of anxiety in older adults: A review of self-report measures. *Clinical Interventions in Aging, 13,* 573-593.

Bandelow, B., Baldwin, D., Abelli, M., Bolea-Alamanac, B., Bourin, M., Chamberlain, S.R., Cinosi, E., Davies, S., Domschke, K., Fineberg, N., Grünblatt, E., Jarema, M., Kim, Y.-K., Maron, E., Masdrakis, V., Mikova, O., Nutt, D., Pallanti, S., Pini, S., . . . Riederer, P. (2017). Biological markers for anxiety disorders, OCD and PTSD: A consensus statement. Part II: Neurochemistry, neurophysiology and neurocognition. *World Journal of Biological Psychiatry, 18*(3), 162-214. https://doi.org/10.1080/15622975.2016.1190867

Brooks, S.J., & Kutcher, S. (2003). Diagnosis and measurement of anxiety disorder in adolescents: A review of commonly used instruments. *Journal of Child and Adolescent Psychopharmacology, 13*(3), 351-400.

Chisholm, D., Sweeny, K., Sheehan, P., Rasmussen, B., Smit, F., Cuijpers, P., & Saxena, S. (2016). Scaling-up treatment of depression and anxiety: A global return on investment analysis. *Lancet Psychiatry, 3*(5), 415-424. https://doi.org/10.1016/S2215-0366(16)30024-4

Elwood, L.S., Wolitzky-Taylor, K., & Olatunji, B.O. (2012). Measurement of anxious traits: A contemporary review and synthesis. *Anxiety, Stress & Coping, 25*(6), 647-666. https://doi.org/10.1080/10615806.2011.582949

Ensari, I., Greenlee, T.A., Motl, R.W., & Petruzzello, S.J. (2015). Meta-analysis of acute exercise effects on state anxiety: An update of randomized controlled trials over the past 25 years. *Depression and Anxiety, 32*(8), 624-634. https://doi.org/10.1002/da.22370

Faravelli, C., Lo Sauro, C., Lelli, L., Pietrini, F., Lazzeretti, L., Godini, L., Benni, L., Fioravanti, G., Talamba, G.A., Castellini, G., & Ricca, V. (2012). The role of life events and HPA axis in anxiety disorders: A review. *Current Pharmaceutical Design, 18*(35), 5663-5674.

Gottschalk, M.G., & Domschke, K. (2017). Genetics of generalized anxiety disorder and related traits. *Dialogues in Clinical Neuroscience, 19*(2), 159-168. www.ncbi.nlm.nih.gov/pubmed/28867940

Grosz, H.J., & Farmer, B.B. (1972). Pitts' and McClure's lactate-anxiety study revisited. *British Journal of Psychiatry, 120,* 415-418.

Harvard Medical School. (2007a). *National Comorbidity Survey (NCS) table 1.* Harvard Medical School. www.hcp.med.harvard.edu/ncs/ftpdir/table_ncsr_LTprevgenderxage.pdf

Harvard Medical School. (2007b). *National Comorbidity Survey (NCS) table 2.* Harvard Medical School. www.hcp.med.harvard.edu/ncs/ftpdir/table_ncsr_12monthprevgenderxage.pdf

Hegberg, N.J., Hayes, J.P., & Hayes, S.M. (2019). Exercise intervention in PTSD: A narrative review and rationale for implementation. *Frontiers in Psychiatry, 10,* 133. https://doi.org/10.3389/fpsyt.2019.00133

Lang, P.J., & Cuthbert, B.N. (1984). Affective information processing and the assessment of anxiety. *Journal of Psychopathology and Behavioral Assessment, 6*(4), 369-395. https://doi.org/10.1007/BF01321326

Marciniak, M.D., Lage, M.J., Dunayevich, E., Russell, J.M., Bowman, L., Landbloom, R.P., & Levine, L.R. (2005). The cost of treating anxiety: The medical and demographic correlates that impact total medical costs. *Depression and Anxiety, 21*(4), 178-184. https://doi.org/10.1002/da.20074

Mental Health America. (2021). *COVID-19 and mental health: A growing crisis.* Mental Health America. www.mhanational.org/research-reports/2021-state-mental-health-america

Mikkelsen, K., Stojanovska, L., Polenakovic, M., Bosevski, M., & Apostolopoulos, V. (2017). Exercise and mental health. *Maturitas, 106,* 48-56.

Petruzzello, S.J., & Landers, D.M. (1983). Exercise and anxiety reduction: Examination of temperature as an explanation for affective change. *Journal of Sport and Exercise Psychology, 15*(1), 63-76.

Petruzzello, S.J., Landers, D.M., Hatfield, B.D., Kubitz, K.A., & Salazar, W. (1991). A meta-analysis on the anxiety-reducing effects of acute and chronic exercise. Outcomes and mechanisms. *Sports Medicine, 11*(3), 143-182. https://doi.org/10.2165/00007256-199111030-00002

Pitts, F.N., Jr. (1971). Biochemical factors in anxiety neurosis. Behavioral Science. *Behavioral Science, 16*(1), 82-91.

Pitts, F.N., Jr., & McClure, J.N., Jr. (1967). Lactate metabolism in anxiety neurosis. *New England Journal of Medicine, 277*(25), 1329-1336.

Rebar, A. L., Stanton, R., Geard, D., Short, C., Duncan, M. J., & Vandelanotte, C. (2015). A meta-meta-analysis of the effect of physical activity on depression and anxiety in non-clinical adult populations. *Health Psychology Review, 9*(3), 366-378.

Reynolds, K., Pietrzak, R.H., El-Gabalawy, R., Mackenzie, C.S., & Sareen, J. (2015). Prevalence of psychiatric disorders in U.S. older adults: Findings from a nationally representative survey. *World Psychiatry, 14*(1), 74-81. https://doi.org/10.1002/wps.20193

Rice, D.P., & Miller, L.S. (1998). Health economics and cost implications of anxiety and other mental disorders in the United States. *British Journal of Psychiatry, Suppl*(34), 4-9. www.ncbi.nlm.nih.gov/pubmed/9829010

Rosenbaum, S., Sherrington, C., & Tiedemann, A. (2015). Exercise augmentation compared with usual care for post-traumatic stress disorder: A randomized controlled trial. *Acta Psychiatrica Scandinavica, 131*(5), 350-359. https://doi.org/10.1111/acps.12371

Rosenbaum, S., Vancampfort, D., Steel, Z., Newby, J., Ward, P.B., & Stubbs, B. (2015). Physical activity in the treatment of post-traumatic stress disorder: A systematic review and meta-analysis. *Psychiatry Research, 230*(2), 130-136. https://doi.org/10.1016/j.psychres.2015.10.017

Salcedo, B. (2018). *The comorbidity of anxiety and depression.* National Alliance on Mental Illness. www.nami.org/Blogs/NAMI-Blog/January-2018/The-Comorbidity-of-Anxiety-and-Depression

Shechner, T., & Bar-Haim, Y. (2016). Threat monitoring and attention-bias modification in anxiety and stress-related disorders. *Current Directions in Psychological Science, 25*(6), 431-437.

Shri, R. (2010). Anxiety: Causes and management. *The Journal of Behavioral Science, 5*(1), 100-118.

Smith, J.C. (2013). Effects of emotional exposure on state anxiety after acute exercise. *Medicine & Science in Sports & Exercise, 45*(2), 372-378. https://doi.org/10.1249/MSS.0b013e31826d5ce5

Stubbs, B., Vancampfort, D., Rosenbaum, S., Firth, J., Cosco, T., Veronese, N., Salum, G.A., & Schuch, F.B. (2017). An examination of the anxiolytic effects of exercise for people with anxiety and stress-related disorders: A meta-analysis. *Psychiatry Research, 249,* 102-108. https://doi.org/10.1016/j.psychres.2016.12.020

The Recovery Village. (2022). *Anxiety disorders facts and statistics.* The Recovery Village. www.therecoveryvillage.com/mental-health/anxiety/related/anxiety-disorder-statistics/

Therrien, Z., & Hunsley, J. (2012). Assessment of anxiety in older adults: A systematic review of commonly used measures. *Aging & Mental Health, 16*(1), 1-16. https://doi.org/10.1080/13607863.2011.602960

Twenge, J.M., & Joiner, T.E. (2020). U.S. Census Bureau-assessed prevalence of anxiety and depressive symptoms in 2019 and during the 2020 COVID-19 pandemic. *Depression and Anxiety, 37*(10), 954-956. https://doi.org/10.1002/da.23077

Van Bockstaele, B., Verschuere, B., Tibboel, H., De Houwer, J., Crombez, G., & Koster, E.H. (2014). A review of current evidence for the causal impact of attentional bias on fear and anxiety. *Psychological Bulletin, 140*(3), 682-721. https://doi.org/10.1037/a0034834

Wegner, M., Helmich, I., Machado, S., Nardi, A.E., Arias-Carrion, O., & Budde, H. (2014). Effects of exercise on anxiety and depression disorders: Review of meta-analyses and neurobiological mechanisms. *CNS & Neurological Disorders - Drug Targets, 13*(6), 1002-1014. https://doi.org/10.2174/1871527313666140612102841

Wipfli, B.M., Rethorst, C.D., & Landers, D.M. (2008). The anxiolytic effects of exercise: A meta-analysis of randomized trials and dose-response analysis. *Journal of Sport & Exercise Psychology, 30*(4), 392-410. https://doi.org/10.1123/jsep.30.4.392

Chapter 6

American Psychological Association. (2022). *Depression.* American Psychological Association. www.apa.org/topics/depression#:~:text=Depression%20is%20a%20real%20illness,%2Dbehavioral%20techniques%2C%20and%20medication

Ashdown-Franks, G., Firth, J., Carney, R., Carvalho, A.F., Hallgren, M., Koyanagi, A., Rosenbaum, S., Schuch, F.B., Smith, L., Solmi, M., Vancampfort, D., & Stubbs, B. (2020). Exercise as medicine for mental and substance use disorders: A meta-review of the benefits for neuropsychiatric and cognitive outcomes. *Sports Medicine, 50*(1), 151-170. https://doi.org/10.1007/s40279-019-01187-6

Berrocoso, E., Sanchez-Blazquez, P., Garzon, J., & Mico, J.A. (2009). Opiates as antidepressants. *Current Pharmaceutical Design, 15*(14), 1612-1622. https://doi.org/10.2174/138161209788168100

Beserra, A.H.N., Kameda, P., Deslandes, A.C., Schuch, F.B., Laks, J., & Moraes, H.S. (2018). Can physical exercise modulate cortisol level in subjects with depression? A systematic review and meta-analysis. *Trends in Psychiatry and Psychotherapy, 40*(4), 360-368. https://doi.org/10.1590/2237-6089-2017-0155

Brody, D.J., Pratt, L.A., & Hughes, J.P. (2018). Prevalence of depression among adults aged 20 and over: United States, 2013-2016. *NCHS Data Brief* (303), 1-8. www.ncbi.nlm.nih.gov/pubmed/29638213

Brooks, S.J., & Kutcher, S. (2003). Diagnosis and measurement of anxiety disorder in adolescents: A review of commonly used instruments. *Journal of Child and Adolescent Psychopharmacology, 13*(3), 351-400.

Chang, S.C., Pan, A., Kawachi, I., & Okereke, O.I. (2016). Risk factors for late-life depression: A prospective cohort study among older women. *Preventive Medicine, 91,* 144-151. https://doi.org/10.1016/j.ypmed.2016.08.014

Cohen, Z.D., & DeRubeis, R.J. (2018). Treatment selection in depression. *Annual Review of Clinical Psychology, 14,* 209-236. https://doi.org/10.1146/annurev-clinpsy-050817-084746

Collins, F.S., & Varmus, H. (2015). A new initiative on precision medicine. *New England Journal of Medicine, 372*(9), 793-795. https://doi.org/10.1056/NEJMp1500523

Cuijpers, P., Karyotaki, E., de Wit, L., & Ebert, D.D. (2020). The effects of fifteen evidence-supported therapies for adult depression: A meta-analytic review. *Psychotherapy Research, 30*(3), 279-293. https://doi.org/10.1080/10503307.2019.1649732

Daley, A., Jolly, K., & MacArthur, C. (2009). The effectiveness of exercise in the management of post-natal depression: Systematic review and meta-analysis. *Family Practice, 26*(2), 154-162. https://doi.org/10.1093/fampra/cmn101

Dauwan, M., Begemann, M.J., Heringa, S.M., & Sommer, I.E. (2016). Exercise improves clinical symptoms, quality of life, global functioning, and depression in schizophrenia: A systematic review and meta-analysis. *Schizophrenia Bulletin, 42*(3), 588-599. https://doi.org/10.1093/schbul/sbv164

Dishman, R.K. (1997). Brain monoamines, exercise, and behavioral stress: Animal models. *Medicine & Science in Sports & Exercise, 29*(1), 63-74. https://doi.org/10.1097/00005768-199701000-00010

Dishman, R.K., Hales, D.P., Pfeiffer, K.A., Felton, G.A., Saunders, R., Ward, D.S., Dowda, M., & Pate, R.R. (2006). Physical self-concept and self-esteem mediate cross-sectional relations of physical activity and sport participation with depression symptoms among adolescent girls. *Health Psychology, 25*(3), 396-407. https://doi.org/10.1037/0278-6133.25.3.396

Duan, L., Xu, Y., & Li, M. (2020). Effects of mind-body exercise in cancer survivors: A systematic review and meta-analysis. *Evidence-Based Complementary and Alternative Medicine, 2020,* 7607161. doi:10.1155/2020/7607161

Duman, R.S., & Monteggia, L.M. (2006). A neurotrophic model for stress-related mood disorders. *Biological Psychiatry, 59*(12), 1116-1127. https://doi.org/10.1016/j.biopsych.2006.02.013

Dunn, A.L., Trivedi, M.H., Kampert, J.B., Clark, C.G., & Chambliss, H.O. (2002). The DOSE study: A clinical trial to examine efficacy and dose response of exercise as treatment for depression. *Controlled Clinical Trials, 23*(5), 584-603. https://doi.org/10.1016/s0197-2456(02)00226-x

Dunn, A.L., Trivedi, M.H., Kampert, J.B., Clark, C.G., & Chambliss, H.O. (2005). Exercise treatment for depression: Efficacy and dose response. *American Journal of Preventive Medicine, 28*(1), 1-8. https://doi.org/10.1016/j.amepre.2004.09.003

Elkin, I., Shea, M.T., Watkins, J.T., Imber, S.D., Sotsky, S.M., Collins, J.F., Glass, D.R., Pilkonis, P.A., Leber, W.R., Docherty, J.P., & Fiester, S.J. (1989). National Institute of Mental Health treatment of depression collaborative research program: General effectiveness of treatments. *Archives of General Psychiatry, 46*(11), 971-982.

Erickson, K.I., Raji, C.A., Lopez, O.L., Becker, J.T., Rosano, C., Newman, A.B., Gach, H.M., Thompson, P.M., Ho, A.J., & Kuller, L.H. (2010). Physical activity predicts gray matter volume in late adulthood: The Cardiovascular Health Study. *Neurology, 75*(16), 1415-1422. https://doi.org/10.1212/WNL.0b013e3181f88359

Erickson, K.I., Voss, M.W., Prakash, R.S., Basak, C., Szabo, A., Chaddock, L., Kim, J.S., Heo, S., Alves, H., White, S.M., Wojcicki, T.R., Mailey, E., Vieira, V.J., Martin, S.A., Pence, B.D., Woods, J.A., McAuley, E., & Kramer, A.F. (2011). Exercise training increases size of hippocampus and improves memory. *Proceedings of the National Academy of Sciences of the United States of Aerica, 108*(7), 3017-3022. https://doi.org/10.1073/pnas.1015950108

Ernst, C., Olson, A.K., Pinel, J.P., Lam, R.W., & Christie, B.R. (2006). Antidepressant effects of exercise: Evidence for an adult-neurogenesis hypothesis? *Journal of Psychiatry & Neuroscience, 31*(2), 84-92. www.ncbi.nlm.nih.gov/pubmed/16575423

Gbyl, K., & Videbech, P. (2018). Electroconvulsive therapy increases brain volume in major depression: A systematic review and meta-analysis. *Acta Psychiatrica Scandinavica, 138*(3), 180-195. https://doi.org/10.1111/acps.12884

Geerlings, M.I., & Gerritsen, L. (2017). Late-life depression, hippocampal volumes, and hypothalamic-pituitary-adrenal axis regulation: A systematic review and meta-analysis. *Biological Psychiatry, 82*(5), 339-350. https://doi.org/10.1016/j.biopsych.2016.12.032

Greenberg, P.E., Fournier, A.A., Sisitsky, T., Pike, C.T., & Kessler, R.C. (2015). The economic burden of adults with major depressive disorder in the United States (2005 and 2010). *Journal of Clinical Psychiatry, 76*(2), 155-162. https://doi.org/10.4088/JCP.14m09298

Gujral, S., Aizenstein, H., Reynolds, C.F., III, Butters, M.A., & Erickson, K.I. (2017). Exercise effects on depression: Possible neural mechanisms. *General Hospital Psychiatry, 49,* 2-10. https://doi.org/10.1016/j.genhosppsych.2017.04.012

Gustafsson, G., Lira, C.M., Johansson, J., Wisén, A., Wohlfart, B., Ekman, R., & Westrin, Å. (2009). The acute response of plasma brain-derived neurotrophic factor as a result of exercise in major depressive disorder. *Psychiatry Research, 169*(3), 244-248.

Heissel, A., Zech, P., Rapp, M.A., Schuch, F.B., Lawrence, J.B., Kangas, M., & Heinzel, S. (2019). Effects of exercise on depression and anxiety in persons living with HIV: A meta-analysis. *Journal of Psychosomatic Research, 126,* 109823. https://doi.org/10.1016/j.jpsychores.2019.109823

Heron, M. (2021). Deaths: Leading causes. National Vital Statistics Reports, 70(9), Hyattsville, MD: National Center for Health Statistics. DOI: https://dx.doi.org/10.15620/cdc:107021.

Hu, M.X., Turner, D., Generaal, E., Bos, D., Ikram, M.K., Ikram, M.A., Cuijpers, P., & Penninx, B. (2020). Exercise interventions for the prevention of depression: A systematic review of meta-analyses. *BMC Public Health, 20*(1), 1255. https://doi.org/10.1186/s12889-020-09323-y

Humphreys, K.L., LeMoult, J., Wear, J.G., Piersiak, H.A., Lee, A., & Gotlib, I.H. (2020). Child maltreatment and depression: A meta-analysis of studies using the Childhood Trauma Questionnaire. *Child Abuse & Neglect, 102,* 104361. https://doi.org/10.1016/j.chiabu.2020.104361

Jesulola, E., Micalos, P., & Baguley, I.J. (2018). Understanding the pathophysiology of depression: From monoamines to the neurogenesis hypothesis model - are we there yet? *Behavioural Brain Research, 341,* 79-90. https://doi.org/10.1016/j.bbr.2017.12.025

Kessler, R.C., Petukhova, M., Sampson, N.A., Zaslavsky, A.M., & Wittchen, H.U. (2012). Twelve-month and lifetime prevalence and lifetime morbid risk of anxiety and mood disorders in the United States. *International Journal of Methods in Psychiatric Research, 21*(3), 169-184.

Kiive, E., Maaroos, J., Shlik, J., Toru, I., & Harro, J. (2004). Growth hormone, cortisol and prolactin responses to physical exercise: Higher prolactin response in depressed patients. *Progress in Neuro-Psychopharmacology & Biological Psychiatry, 28*(6), 1007-1013. https://doi.org/10.1016/j.pnpbp.2004.05.035

Kim, Y.K., Lee, H.P., Won, S.D., Park, E.Y., Lee, H.Y., Lee, B.H., Lee, S.W., Yoon, D., Han, C., Kim, D.J., & Choi, S.H. (2007). Low plasma BDNF is associated with suicidal behavior in major depression. *Progress in Neuro-Psychopharmacology & Biological Psychiatry, 31*(1), 78-85. https://doi.org/10.1016/j.pnpbp.2006.06.024

Laske, C., Banschbach, S., Stransky, E., Bosch, S., Straten, G., Machann, J., Fritsche, A., Hipp, A., Niess, A., & Eschweiler, G.W. (2010). Exercise-induced normalization of decreased BDNF serum concentration in elderly women with remitted major depression. *International Journal of Neuropsychopharmacology, 13*(5), 595-602. https://doi.org/10.1017/S1461145709991234

Lee, B.H., Kim, H., Park, S.H., & Kim, Y.K. (2007). Decreased plasma BDNF level in depressive patients. *Journal of Affective Disorders, 101*(1-3), 239-244. https://doi.org/10.1016/j.jad.2006.11.005

Lima, N.N., Nascimento, V.B., Peixoto, J.A., Moreira, M.M., Neto, M.L., Almeida, J.C., Vasconcelos, C., Teixeira, S.A., Júnior, J.G., Junior, F., Guimãeres, D., Brasil, A.Q., Cartaxo, J.S., Akerman, M., & Reis, A.O. (2013). Electroconvulsive therapy use in adolescents: A systematic review. *Annals of General Psychiatry, 12*(1), 17. https://doi.org/10.1186/1744-859X-12-17

Lin, T.W., & Kuo, Y.M. (2013). Exercise benefits brain function: The monoamine connection. *Brain Sciences, 3*(1), 39-53. https://doi.org/10.3390/brainsci3010039

Lubans, D., Richards, J., Hillman, C., Faulkner, G., Beauchamp, M., Nilsson, M., Kelly, P., Smith, J., Raine, L., & Biddle, S. (2016). Physical activity for cognitive and mental health in youth: A systematic review of mechanisms. *Pediatrics, 138*(3). https://doi.org/10.1542/peds.2016-1642

Mammen, G., & Faulkner, G. (2013). Physical activity and the prevention of depression: A systematic review of prospective studies. *American Journal of Preventive Medicine, 45*(5), 649-657. https://doi.org/10.1016/j.amepre.2013.08.001

McPhie, M.L., & Rawana, J.S. (2012). Unravelling the relation between physical activity, self-esteem and depressive symptoms among early and late adolescents: A mediation analysis. *Mental Health and Physical Activity, 5,* 43-49. https://doi.org/10.1016/j.mhpa.2012.03.003

Menke, A. (2019). Is the HPA axis as target for depression outdated, or is there a new hope? *Frontiers in Psychiatry, 10,* 101. https://doi.org/10.3389/fpsyt.2019.00101

Molendijk, M.L., Spinhoven, P., Polak, M., Bus, B.A., Penninx, B.W., & Elzinga, B.M. (2014). Serum BDNF concentrations as peripheral manifestations of depression: Evidence from a systematic review and meta-analyses on 179 associations (N=9484). *Molecular Psychiatry, 19*(7), 791-800. https://doi.org/10.1038/mp.2013.105

Moreno-Agostino, D., Wu, Y. T., Daskalopoulou, C., Hasan, M. T., Huisman, M., & Prina, M. (2021). Global trends in the prevalence and incidence of depression: A systematic review and meta-analysis. *Journal of Affective Disorders, 281,* 235-243.

National Institute of Mental Health. (2022a). *Major depression.* National Institute of Mental Health. www.nimh.nih.gov/health/statistics/major-depression#part_155031

National Institute of Mental Health. (2022b). *Suicide.* National Institute of Mental Health. https://www.nimh.nih.gov/health/statistics/suicide

Phillips, C. (2017). Brain-derived neurotrophic factor, depression, and physical activity: Making the neuroplastic connection. *Neural Plasticity, 2017,* 7260130. https://doi.org/10.1155/2017/7260130

Polanczyk, G.V., Salum, G.A., Sugaya, L.S., Caye, A., & Rohde, L.A. (2015). Annual research review: A meta-analysis of the worldwide prevalence of mental disorders in children and adolescents. *Journal of Child Psychology and Psychiatry, 56*(3), 345-365. https://doi.org/10.1111/jcpp.12381

Resnick, B., Luisi, D., & Vogel, A. (2008). Testing the Senior Exercise Self-Efficacy Project (SESEP) for use with urban dwelling minority older adults. *Public Health Nursing, 25*(3), 221-234. https://doi.org/10.1111/j.1525-1446.2008.00699.x

Rosenbaum, S., Hobson-Powell, A., Davison, K., Stanton, R., Craft, L.L., Duncan, M., Elliot, C., & Ward, P.B. (2018). The role of sport, exercise, and physical activity in closing the life expectancy gap for people with mental illness: An international consensus statement by Exercise and Sports Science Australia, American College of Sports Medicine, British Association of Sport and Exercise Medicine, and Sport and Exercise Science New Zealand. *Translational Journal of the American College of Sports Medicine, 3*(10), 72-73.

Ruhe, H.G., Huyser, J., Swinkels, J.A., & Schene, A.H. (2006). Dose escalation for insufficient response to standard-dose selective serotonin reuptake inhibitors in major depressive disorder: Systematic review. *British Journal of Psychiatry, 189,* 309-316. https://doi.org/10.1192/bjp.bp.105.018325

Rush, A.J., Trivedi, M.H., Wisniewski, S.R., Nierenberg, A.A., Stewart, J.W., Warden, D., Niederehe, G., Thase, M.E., Lavori, P.W., Lebowitz, B.D., McGrath, P.J., Rosenbaum, J.F., Sackeim, H.A., Kupfer, D.J., Luther, J., & Fava, M. (2006). Acute and longer-term outcomes in depressed outpatients requiring one or several treatment steps: A STAR*D report. *American Journal of Psychiatry, 163*(11), 1905-1917. https://doi.org/10.1176/ajp.2006.163.11.1905

Santomauro, D.F., Herrera, A.M.M., Shadid, J., Zheng, P., Ashbaugh, C., Pigott, D.M., Abbafati, C., Adolph, C., Amlag, J.O., Aravkin, A.Y. & Bang-Jensen, B.L. (2021). Global prevalence and burden of depressive and anxiety disorders in 204 countries and territories in 2020 due to the COVID-19 pandemic. *The Lancet, 398*(10312), 1700-1712.

Schmaal, L., Veltman, D.J., van Erp, T.G., Samann, P.G., Frodl, T., Jahanshad, N., Loehrer, E., Tiemeier, H., Hofman, A., Niessen, W.J., Vernooij, M.W., Ikram, M.A., Wittfeld, K., Grabe, H.J., Block, A., Hegenscheid, K., Völzke, H., Hoehn, D., Czisch, M., . . . Hibar, D.P. (2016). Subcortical brain alterations in major depressive disorder: Findings from the ENIGMA Major Depressive Disorder working group. *Molecular Psychiatry, 21*(6), 806-812. https://doi.org/10.1038/mp.2015.69

Schuch, F.B., Vancampfort, D., Firth, J., Rosenbaum, S., Ward, P.B., Silva, E.S., Hallgren, M., Ponce De Leon, A., Dunn, A.L., Deslandes, A.C., Fleck, M.P., Carvalho, A.F., & Stubbs, B. (2018). Physical activity and incident depression: A meta-analysis of prospective cohort studies. *American Journal of Psychiatry, 175*(7), 631-648. https://doi.org/10.1176/appi.ajp.2018.17111194

Sharp, L. K., & Lipsky, M. S. (2002). Screening for depression across the lifespan: A review of measures for use in primary care settings. *American Family Physician, 66*(6), 1001-1008.

Stubbs, B., Vancampfort, D., Hallgren, M., Firth, J., Veronese, N., Solmi, M., Brand, S., Cordes, J., Malchow, B., Gerber, M., Schmitt, A., Correll, C.U., De Hert, M., Gaughran, F., Schneider, F., Kinnafick, F., Falkai, P., Möller, H.J., & Kahl, K.G. (2018). EPA guidance on physical activity as a treatment for severe mental illness: A meta-review of the evidence and Position Statement from the European Psychiatric Association (EPA), supported by the International Organization of Physical Therapists in Mental Health (IOPTMH). *European Psychiatry, 54,* 124-144. https://doi.org/10.1016/j.eurpsy.2018.07.004

Sullivan, P.F., Neale, M.C., & Kendler, K.S. (2000). Genetic epidemiology of major depression: Review and meta-analysis. *American Journal of Psychiatry, 157*(10), 1552-1562. https://doi.org/10.1176/appi.ajp.157.10.1552

Twenge, J.M., Joiner, T.E., Rogers, M.L., & Martin, G.N. (2018). Increases in depressive symptoms, suicide-related outcomes, and suicide rates among U.S. adolescents after 2010 and links to increased new media screen time. *Clinical Psychological Science, 6,* 3-17. https://doi.org/10.1177/2167702617723376

Vella, S.A., Swann, C., Allen, M.S., Schweickle, M.J., & Magee, C.A. (2017). Bidirectional associations between sport involvement and mental health in adolescence. *Medicine & Science in Sports & Exercise, 49*(4), 687-694. https://doi.org/10.1249/MSS.0000000000001142

Videbech, P., & Ravnkilde, B. (2004). Hippocampal volume and depression: A meta-analysis of MRI studies. *American Journal of Psychiatry, 161*(11), 1957-1966. https://doi.org/10.1176/appi.ajp.161.11.1957

Watt, J.A., Goodarzi, Z., Veroniki, A.A., Nincic, V., Khan, P.A., Ghassemi, M., Lai, Y., Treister, V., Thompson, Y., Schneider, R., Tricco, A.C., & Straus, S.E. (2021). Comparative efficacy of interventions for reducing symptoms of depression in people with dementia: Systematic review and network meta-analysis. *BMJ, 372,* n532. https://doi.org/10.1136/bmj.n532

Wegner, M., Amatriain-Fernandez, S., Kaulitzky, A., Murillo-Rodriguez, E., Machado, S., & Budde, H. (2020). Systematic review of meta-analyses: Exercise effects on depression in children and adolescents. *Frontiers in Psychiatry, 11*, 81. https://doi.org/10.3389/fpsyt.2020.00081

Wegner, M., Helmich, I., Machado, S., Nardi, A.E., Arias-Carrion, O., & Budde, H. (2014). Effects of exercise on anxiety and depression disorders: Review of meta-analyses and neurobiological mechanisms. *CNS & Neurological Disorders - Drug Targets, 13*(6), 1002-1014. https://doi.org/10.2174/18715273 13666140612102841

Weinberger, A.H., Gbedemah, M., Martinez, A.M., Nash, D., Galea, S., & Goodwin, R.D. (2018). Trends in depression prevalence in the USA from 2005 to 2015: Widening disparities in vulnerable groups. *Psychological Medicine, 48*(8), 1308-1315. https://doi.org/10.1017/S0033291717002781

World Health Organization. (2017). *Depression and other common mental disorders: Global health estimates*. World Health Organization. https://apps.who.int/iris/bitstream/handle/10665/254610/WHO-MSD-MER-2017.2-eng.pdf

Yoshida, T., Ishikawa, M., Niitsu, T., Nakazato, M., Watanabe, H., Shiraishi, T., Shiina, A., Hashimoto, T., Kanahara, N., Hasegawa, T., Enohara, M., Kimura, A., Iyo, M., & Hashimoto, K. (2012). Decreased serum levels of mature brain-derived neurotrophic factor (BDNF), but not its precursor proBDNF, in patients with major depressive disorder. *PLoS One, 7*(8), e42676. https://doi.org/10.1371/journal.pone.0042676

Chapter 7

American Psychiatric Association. (2022). *Diagnostics and statistical manual of mental disorders* (5th ed.). American Psychiatric Publishing.

Arent, S.M., Landers, D.M., & Etnier, J.L. (2000). The effects of exercise on mood in older adults: A meta-analytic review. *Journal of Aging and Physical Activity, 8*(4), 407-430.

Belitardo de Oliveira, A., de Mello, M.T., Tufik, S., & Peres, M.F.P. (2019). Weight loss and improved mood after aerobic exercise training are linked to lower plasma anandamide in healthy people. *Physiology & Behavior, 201*, 191-197. https://doi.org/10.1016/j.physbeh.2018.12.018

Boecker, H., Sprenger, T., Spilker, M.E., Henriksen, G., Koppenhoefer, M., Wagner, K.J., Valet, M., Berthele, A., & Tolle, T.R. (2008). The runner's high: Opioidergic mechanisms in the human brain. *Cerebral Cortex, 18*(11), 2523-2531. https://doi.org/10.1093/cercor/bhn013

Egorov, A.Y., & Szabo, A. (2013). The exercise paradox: An interactional model for a clearer conceptualization of exercise addiction. *Journal of Behavioral Addictictions, 2*(4), 199-208. https://doi.org/10.1556/JBA.2.2013.4.2

Ekkekakis, P. (2003). Pleasure and displeasure from the body: Perspectives from exercise. *Cognition and Emotion, 17*(2), 213-239.

Ekkekakis, P. (2005). The Dual Mode model of affective responses to exercise of varying intensities: A new perspective on the dose response relationship. In T. Morris (Ed.), *Proceedings of the 11th World Congress of Sport Psychology*. International Society of Sport Psychology. International Society of Sport Psychology.

Ekkekakis, P. (2009a). The Dual-Mode Theory of affective responses to exercise in metatheoretical context: I. Initial impetus, basic postulates, and philosophical framework. *International Review of Sport and Exercise Psychology, 2*(1), 73-94. https://doi.org/10.1080/17509840802705920

Ekkekakis, P. (2009b). The Dual-Mode Theory of affective responses to exercise in metatheoretical context: II. Bodiless heads, ethereal cognitive schemata, and other improbable dualistic creatures, exercising. *International Review of Sport and Exercise Psychology, 2*(2), 139-160.

Ekkekakis, P., & Zenko, Z. (2016). Measurement of affective responses to exercise: From "affectless arousal" to "the most well-characterized" relationship between the body and affect. In H.L. Meiselman (Ed.), *Emotion measurement* (pp. 299-321). Elsevier.

Ekkekakis, P., Hall, E.E., & Petruzzello, S.J. (2008). The relationship between exercise intensity and affective responses demystified: To crack the 40-year-old nut, replace the 40-year-old nutcracker! *Annals of Behavioral Medicine, 35*(2), 136-149. https://doi.org/10.1007/s12160-008-9025-z

Gauvin, L., & Rejeski, W.J. (1993). The exercise-induced feeling inventory: Development and initial validation. *Journal of Sport and Exercise Psychology, 15*(4), 403-423.

Gendron, M., Crivelli, C., & Barrett, L.F. (2018). Universality reconsidered: Diversity in making meaning of facial expressions. *Current Directions in Psychological Science, 27*(4), 211-219. https://doi.org/10.1177/0963721417746794

Hardy, C.J., & Rejeski, W.J. (1989). Not what, but how one feels: The measurement of affect during exercise. *Journal of Sport and Exercise Psychology, 11*, 304-317.

McAuley, E., & Courneya, K.S. (1994). The subjective exercise experiences scale (SEES): Development and preliminary validation. *Journal of Sport and Exercise Psychology, 16*, 163-177.

McNair, D.M., Lorr, M., & Droppleman, L.F. (1971). *Profile of moods states*. Educational and Industrial Testing Service.

Puetz, T.W., O'Connor, P.J., & Dishman, R.K. (2006). Effects of chronic exercise on feelings of energy and fatigue: A quantitative synthesis. *Psychological Bulletin, 132*(6), 866-876. https://doi.org/10.1037/0033-2909.132.6.866

Reed, J., & Buck, S. (2009). The effect of regular aerobic exercise on positive-activated affect: A meta-analysis. *Psychology of Sport and Exercise, 10*(6), 581-594.

Reed, J., & Ones, D.S. (2006). The effect of acute aerobic exercise on positive activated affect: A meta-analysis. *Psychology of Sport and Exercise, 7*(5), 477-514.

Rejeski, W.J., Hardy, C.J., & Shaw, J. (1991). Psychometric confounds of assessing state anxiety in conjunction with acute bouts of vigorous exercise. *Journal of Sport and Exercise Psychology, 13*, 65-74.

Russell, J.A. (1980). A circumplex model of affect. *Journal of Personality and Social Psychology, 39*(6), 1161-1178.

Siebers, M., Biedermann, S.V., & Fuss, J. (2022). Do endocannabinoids cause the runner's high? Evidence and open questions. *Neuroscientist*, 10738584211069981. https://doi.org/10.1177/10738584211069981

Spielberger, C.D., Gorsuch, R.L., & Lushene, P. (1970). *State-Trait Anxiety Inventory manual*. Consulting Psychologists Press.

Thayer, J.F., & Lane, R.D. (2000). A model of neurovisceral integration in emotion regulation and dysregulation. *Journal of Affective Disorders, 61*(3), 201-216. https://doi.org/10.1016/s0165-0327(00)00338-4

Trott, M., Jackson, S.E., Firth, J., Fisher, A., Johnstone, J., Mistry, A., Stubbs, B., & Smith, L. (2020). Exercise addiction prevalence and correlates in the absence of eating disorder symptomology: A systematic review and meta-analysis. *Journal of*

Addiction Medicine, 14(6), e321-e329. https://doi.org/10.1097/ADM.0000000000000664

Velasco, P.F., & Loev, S. (2020). Affective experience in the predictive mind: A review and new integrative account. *Synthese, 198,* 10847-10882. https://doi.org/10.1007/s11229-020-02755-4

Vytal, K., & Hamann, S. (2010). Neuroimaging support for discrete neural correlates of basic emotions: A voxel-based meta-analysis. *Journal of Cognitive Neuroscience, 22*(12), 2864-2885. https://doi.org/10.1162/jocn.2009.21366

Watson, D., Clark, L.A., & Tellegen, A. (1988). Development and validation of brief measures of positive and negative affect: The PANAS scales. *Journal of Personality and Social Psychology, 54*(6), 1063-1070. https://doi.org/10.1037//0022-3514.54.6.1063

Williams, D.M., Dunsiger, S., Jennings, E.G., & Marcus, B.H. (2011). Does affective valence during and immediately following a 10-min walk predict concurrent and future physical activity? *Annals of Behavioral Medicine, 44,* 43-51.

Williams, D.M., Dunsiger, S., Ciccolo, J.T., Lewis, B.A., Albrecht, A.E., & Marcus, B.H. (2008). Acute affective response to a moderate-intensity exercise stimulus predicts physical activity participation 6 and 12 months later. *Psychology of Sport and Exercise, 9*(3), 231-245. https://doi.org/10.1016/j.psychsport.2007.04.002

Chapter 8

Brosseau, L., Milne, S., Robinson, V., Marchand, S., Shea, B., Wells, G., & Tugwell, P. (2002). Efficacy of the transcutaneous electrical nerve stimulation for the treatment of chronic low back pain: A meta-analysis. *Spine (Phila Pa 1976), 27*(6), 596-603. https://doi.org/10.1097/00007632-200203150-00007

Burch, R., Rizzoli, P., & Loder, E. (2018). The prevalence and impact of migraine and severe headache in the United States: Figures and trends from government health studies. *Headache, 58*(4), 496-505. https://doi.org/10.1111/head.13281

Coutaux, A. (2017). Non-pharmacological treatments for pain relief: TENS and acupuncture. *Joint Bone Spine, 84*(6), 657-661. https://doi.org/10.1016/j.jbspin.2017.02.005

Dahlhamer, J.L., J., Zelaya, C., Nahin, R., Mackey, S., DeBar, L., Kerns, R., Von Korff, M., Porter, L., & Helmick, C. (2018). Prevalence of chronic pain and high-impact chronic pain among adults—United States, 2016. *Morbidity and Mortality Weekly Report, 67,* 1001-1006. www.cdc.gov/mmwr/volumes/67/wr/mm6736a2.htm?s_cid=mm6736a2_w

Elzahaf, R.A., Tashani, O.A., Unsworth, B.A., & Johnson, M.I. (2012). The prevalence of chronic pain with an analysis of countries with a Human Development Index less than 0.9: A systematic review without meta-analysis. *Current Medical Research and Opinion, 28*(7), 1221-1229. https://doi.org/10.1185/03007995.2012.703132

Flood, A., Waddington, G., Thompson, K., & Cathcart, S. (2017). Increased conditioned pain modulation in athletes. *Journal of Sports Science, 35*(11), 1066-1072. https://doi.org/10.1080/02640414.2016.1210196

Gaskin, D.J., & Richard, P. (2012). The economic costs of pain in the United States. *Journal of Pain, 13*(8), 715-724. https://doi.org/10.1016/j.jpain.2012.03.009

Hagen, K., Wisloff, U., Ellingsen, O., Stovner, L.J., & Linde, M. (2016). Headache and peak oxygen uptake: The HUNT3 study. *Cephalalgia, 36*(5), 437-444. https://doi.org/10.1177/0333102415597528

Hauser, W., Klose, P., Langhorst, J., Moradi, B., Steinbach, M., Schiltenwolf, M., & Busch, A. (2010). Efficacy of different types of aerobic exercise in fibromyalgia syndrome: A systematic review and meta-analysis of randomised controlled trials. *Arthritis Research & Therapy, 12*(3), R79. https://doi.org/10.1186/ar3002

Hoffman, M.D., Shepanski, M.A., Ruble, S.B., Valic, Z., Buckwalter, J.B., & Clifford, P.S. (2004). Intensity and duration threshold for aerobic exercise-induced analgesia to pressure pain. *Archives of Physical Medicine and Rehabilitation, 85*(7), 1183-1187. https://doi.org/10.1016/j.apmr.2003.09.010

Jones, M.D., Booth, J., Taylor, J.L., & Barry, B.K. (2014). Aerobic training increases pain tolerance in healthy individuals. *Medicine & Science in Sports & Exercise, 46*(8), 1640-1647. https://doi.org/10.1249/MSS.0000000000000273

Kelman, L. (2007). The triggers or precipitants of the acute migraine attack. *Cephalalgia, 27*(5), 394-402. https://doi.org/10.1111/j.1468-2982.2007.01303.x

Kosek, E., & Lundberg, L. (2003). Segmental and plurisegmental modulation of pressure pain thresholds during static muscle contractions in healthy individuals. *European Journal of Pain, 7*(3), 251-258.

La Touche, R., Fernandez Perez, J.J., Proy Acosta. A., Gonzalez Campodonico, L., Martinez Garcia, S., Adraos Juarez, D., Serrano Garcia, B., Angulo-Díaz-Parreño, S., Cuenca-Martínez, F., Suso-Martí, L., & Paris-Alemany, A. (2020). Is aerobic exercise helpful in patients with migraine? A systematic review and meta-analysis. *Scandinavian Journal of Medicine & Science in Sports, 30*(6), 965-982.

Lemmens, J., De Pauw, J., Van Soom, T., Michiels, S., Versijpt, J., van Breda, E., Castien, R., & De Hertogh, W. (2019). The effect of aerobic exercise on the number of migraine days, duration and pain intensity in migraine: A systematic literature review and meta-analysis. *Journal of Headache and Pain, 20*(1), 16. https://doi.org/10.1186/s10194-019-0961-8

Lima, L.V., Abner, T.S.S., & Sluka, K.A. (2017). Does exercise increase or decrease pain? Central mechanisms underlying these two phenomena. *Journal of Physiology, 595*(13), 4141-4150. https://doi.org/10.1113/JP273355

Lo, J., Chan, L., & Flynn, S. (2021). A systematic review of the incidence, prevalence, costs, and activity and work limitations of amputation, osteoarthritis, rheumatoid arthritis, back pain, multiple sclerosis, spinal cord injury, stroke, and traumatic brain injury in the United States: A 2019 update. *Archives of Physical Medicine and Rehabilitation, 102*(1), 115-131. https://doi.org/10.1016/j.apmr.2020.04.001

Melzack, R., & Wall, P.D. (1965). Pain mechanisms: A new theory. *Science, 150*(3699), 971-979. https://doi.org/10.1126/science.150.3699.971

Merskey, H., Albe-Fessard, D.G., & Bonica, J.J. (1979). International association for the study of pain: Pain terms: A list with definitions and notes on usage. *Pain, 6,* 249-252.

Mist, S.D., Firestone, K.A., & Jones, K.D. (2013). Complementary and alternative exercise for fibromyalgia: A meta-analysis. *Journal of Pain Research, 6,* 247-260. https://doi.org/10.2147/JPR.S32297

Molarius, A., Tegelberg, A., & Ohrvik, J. (2008). Socio-economic factors, lifestyle, and headache disorders — A population-based study in Sweden. *Headache, 48*(10), 1426-1437. https://doi.org/10.1111/j.1526-4610.2008.01178.x

Naugle, K.M., Fillingim, R.B., & Riley, J.L., III. (2012). A meta-analytic review of the hypoalgesic effects of exercise. *Journal of Pain, 13*(12), 1139-1150. https://doi.org/10.1016/j.jpain.2012.09.006

Osypiuk, K., Ligibel, J., Giobbie-Hurder, A., Vergara-Diaz, G., Bonato, P., Quinn, R., Ng, W., & Wayne, P.M. (2020). Qigong mind-body exercise as a biopsychosocial therapy for persistent post-surgical pain in breast cancer: A pilot study. *Integrative Cancer Therapies, 19*, 1534735419893766. https://doi.org/10.1177/1534735419893766

Owen, P.J., Miller, C.T., Mundell, N.L., Verswijveren, S., Tagliaferri, S.D., Brisby, H., Bowe, S.J., & Belavy, D.L. (2020). Which specific modes of exercise training are most effective for treating low back pain? Network meta-analysis. *British Journal of Sports Medicine, 54*(21), 1279-1287. https://doi.org/10.1136/bjsports-2019-100886

Pacheco-Barrios, K., Carolyna Gianlorenco, A., Machado, R., Queiroga, M., Zeng, H., Shaikh, E., Yang, Y., Nogueira, B., Castelo-Branco, L., & Fregni, F. (2020). Exercise-induced pain threshold modulation in healthy subjects: A systematic review and meta-analysis. *Principles and Practice of Clinical Research, 6*(3), 11-28. https://doi.org/10.21801/ppcrj.2020.63.2

Park, J.W., Chu, M.K., Kim, J.M., Park, S.G., & Cho, S.J. (2016). Analysis of trigger factors in episodic migraineurs using a smartphone headache diary applications. *PLoS One, 11*(2), e0149577. https://doi.org/10.1371/journal.pone.0149577

Queiroz, L.P., Peres, M.F., Piovesan, E.J., Kowacs, F., Ciciarelli, M.C., Souza, J.A., & Zukerman, E. (2009). A nationwide population-based study of migraine in Brazil. *Cephalalgia, 29*(6), 642-649. https://doi.org/10.1111/j.1468-2982.2008.01782.x

Raja, S.N., Carr, D.B., Cohen, M., Finnerup, N.B., Flor, H., Gibson, S., Keefe, F.J., Mogil, J.S., Ringkamp, M., Sluka, K.A., Song, X.J., Stevens, B., Sullivan, M.D., Tutelman, P.R., Ushida, T., & Vader, K. (2020). The revised International Association for the Study of Pain definition of pain: Concepts, challenges, and compromises. *Pain, 161*(9), 1976-1982. https://doi.org/10.1097/j.pain.0000000000001939

Schmitt, A., Wallat, D., Stangier, C., Martin, J.A., Schlesinger-Irsch, U., & Boecker, H. (2020). Effects of fitness level and exercise intensity on pain and mood responses. *European Journal of Pain, 24*(3), 568-579. https://doi.org/10.1002/ejp.1508

Searle, A., Spink, M., Ho, A., & Chuter, V. (2015). Exercise interventions for the treatment of chronic low back pain: A systematic review and meta-analysis of randomised controlled trials. *Clinical Rehabilitation, 29*(12), 1155-1167. https://doi.org/10.1177/0269215515570379

Simpson, P.M., Fouche, P.F., Thomas, R.E., & Bendall, J.C. (2014). Transcutaneous electrical nerve stimulation for relieving acute pain in the prehospital setting: A systematic review and meta-analysis of randomized-controlled trials. *European Journal of Emergency Medicine, 21*(1), 10-17. https://doi.org/10.1097/MEJ.0b013e328363c9c1

Song, T.J., & Chu, M.K. (2021). Exercise in treatment of migraine including chronic migraine. *Current Pain and Headache Reports, 25*(3), 14. https://doi.org/10.1007/s11916-020-00929-w

Sosa-Reina, M.D., Nunez-Nagy, S., Gallego-Izquierdo, T., Pecos-Martin, D., Monserrat, J., & Alvarez-Mon, M. (2017). Effectiveness of therapeutic exercise in fibromyalgia syndrome: A systematic review and meta-analysis of randomized clinical trials. *BioMed Research International, 2017*, 2356346. https://doi.org/10.1155/2017/2356346

Tanaka, R., Ozawa, J., Kito, N., & Moriyama, H. (2013). Efficacy of strengthening or aerobic exercise on pain relief in people with knee osteoarthritis: A systematic review and meta-analysis of randomized controlled trials. *Clinical Rehabilitation, 27*(12), 1059-1071.

Tesarz, J., Schuster, A.K., Hartmann, M., Gerhardt, A., & Eich, W. (2012). Pain perception in athletes compared to normally active controls: A systematic review with meta-analysis. *Pain, 153*(6), 1253-1262. https://doi.org/10.1016/j.pain.2012.03.005

van Dijk, A., McGrath, P., Pickett, W., & VanDenKerkhof, E.G. (2006). Pain prevalence in nine- to 13-year-old schoolchildren. *Pain Research & Management, 11*(4), 234-240. https://doi.org/10.1155/2006/835327

Vickers, A.J., Vertosick, E.A., Lewith, G., MacPherson, H., Foster, N.E., Sherman, K.J., Irnich, D., Witt, C.M., Linde, K., & Acupuncture Trialists, C. (2018). Acupuncture for chronic pain: Update of an individual patient data meta-analysis. *Journal of Pain, 19*(5), 455-474. https://doi.org/10.1016/j.jpain.2017.11.00

Wewege, M.A., & Jones, M.D. (2021). Exercise-induced hypoalgesia in healthy individuals and people with chronic musculoskeletal pain: A systematic review and meta-analysis. *Journal of Pain, 22*(1), 21-31. https://doi.org/10.1016/j.jpain.2020.04.003

Chapter 9

Ahmed, S.F., Tang, S., Waters, N.E., & Davis-Kean, P. (2019). Executive function and academic achievement: Longitudinal relations from early childhood to adolescence. *Journal of Educational Psychology, 111*(3), 446-458.

Ahmed, S.F., Kuhfeld, M., Watts, T.W., Davis-Kean, P.E., & Vandell, D.L. (2021). Preschool executive function and adult outcomes: A developmental cascade model. *Developmental Psychology Journal, 57*(12), 2234-2249. https://doi.org/10.1037/dev0001270

Alvarez-Bueno, C., Pesce, C., Cavero-Redondo, I., Sanchez-Lopez, M., Martinez-Hortelano, J.A., & Martinez-Vizcaino, V. (2017). The effect of physical activity interventions on children's cognition and metacognition: A systematic review and meta-analysis. *Journal of the American Academy of Child and Adolescent Psychiatry, 56*(9), 729-738. https://doi.org/10.1016/j.jaac.2017.06.012

Alzheimer's Association. (2021a). Alzheimer's disease facts and figures. *Alzheimer's and Dementia, 17*(3), 1-104.

Alzheimer's Association. (2021b). *Changing the trajectory of Alzheimer's disease: How a treatment by 2025 saves lives and dollars*. Alzheimer's Association. www.alz.org/media/documents/changing-the-trajectory-r.pdf

Binet, A., & Simon, T. (1916). New methods for the diagnosis of the intellectual level of subnormals. In H.H. Goddard (Ed.), *Development of intelligence in children (the Binet-Simon Scale)* (pp. 9-36). Williams & Wilkins.

Blondell, S.J., Hammersley-Mather, R., & Veerman, J.L. (2014). Does physical activity prevent cognitive decline and dementia?: A systematic review and meta-analysis of longitudinal studies. *BMC Public Health, 14*, 510. https://doi.org/10.1186/1471-2458-14-510

Cerrillo-Urbina, A.J., Garcia-Hermoso, A., Sanchez-Lopez, M., Pardo-Guijarro, M.J., Santos Gomez, J.L., & Martinez-Vizcaino, V. (2015). The effects of physical exercise in children with attention deficit hyperactivity disorder: A systematic review and meta-analysis of randomized control trials. *Child: Care, Health* and *Development, 41*(6), 779-788. https://doi.org/10.1111/cch.12255

Chang, Y.K., & Etnier, J.L. (2009). Exploring the dose-response relationship between resistance exercise intensity and cognitive function. *Journal of Sport and Exercise Psychology, 31*(5), 640-656. https://doi.org/10.1123/jsep.31.5.640

Chang, Y.K., Labban, J.D., Gapin, J.I., & Etnier, J.L. (2012). The effects of acute exercise on cognitive performance: A meta-analysis. *Brain Research, 1453,* 87-101. https://doi.org/10.1016/j.brainres.2012.02.068

Colcombe, S., & Kramer, A.F. (2003). Fitness effects on the cognitive function of older adults: A meta-analytic study. *Psychological Science, 14*(2), 125-130. https://doi.org/10.1111/1467-9280.t01-1-01430

Cooper, C.J. (1973). Anatomical and physiological mechanisms of arousal, with special reference to the effects of exercise. *Ergonomics, 16*(5), 601-609.

Davey, C.P. (1973). Physical exertion and mental performance. *Ergonomics, 16*(5), 595-599.

Daviglus, M.L., Plassman, B.L., Pirzada, A., Bell, C.C., Bowen, P.E., Burke, J.R., Connolly, E.S., Dunbar-Jacob, J.M., Granieri, E.C., McGarry, K., Patel, D., Trevisan, M., & Williams, J.W., Jr. (2011). Risk factors and preventive interventions for Alzheimer disease: State of the science. *Archives of Neurology, 68*(9), 1185-1190. https://doi.org/10.1001/archneurol.2011.100

DeMeersman, R.E. (1993). Heart rate variability and aerobic fitness. *American Heart Journal, 125*(3), 726-731.

Dietrich, A. (2003). Functional neuroanatomy of altered states of consciousness: The transient hypofrontality hypothesis. *Consciousness and Cognition, 12*(2), 231-256. https://doi.org10.1016/s1053-8100(02)00046-6

Dietrich, A., & Audiffren, M. (2011). The reticular-activating hypofrontality (RAH) model of acute exercise. *Neuroscience & Biobehavioral Reviews, 35*(6), 1305-1325. https://doi.org/10.1016/j.neubiorev.2011.02.001

Du, Z., Li, Y., Li, J., Zhou, C., Li, F., & Yang, X. (2018). Physical activity can improve cognition in patients with Alzheimer's disease: A systematic review and meta-analysis of randomized controlled trials. *Clinical Interventions in Aging, 13,* 1593-1603.

Etnier, J.L., & Chang, Y.K. (2009). The effect of physical activity on executive function: A brief commentary on definitions, measurement issues, and the current state of the literature. *Journal of Sport and Exercise Psychology, 31,* 469-483.

Etnier, J.L., Nowell, P.M., Landers, D.M., & Sibley, B.A. (2006). A meta-regression to examine the relationship between aerobic fitness and cognitive performance. *Brain Research Reviews, 52*(1), 119-130. https://doi.org/10.1016/j.brainresrev.2006.01.002

Etnier, J.L., Salazar, W., Landers, D.M., Petruzzello, S.J., Han, M., & Nowell, P. (1997). The influence of physical fitness and exercise upon cognitive functioning: A meta-analysis. *Journal of Sport and Exercise Psychology, 19*(3), 249-277.

Etnier, J.L., Vance, J.C., & Ueno, A. (2021). Effects of acute exercise on memory performance in middle-aged and older adults. *Journal of Aging and Physical Activity, 29*(5), 753-760.

Falck, R.S., Davis, J.C., Best, J.R., Crockett, R.A., & Liu-Ambrose, T. (2019). Impact of exercise training on physical and cognitive function among older adults: A systematic review and meta-analysis. *Neurobiology of Aging, 79,* 119-130. https://doi.org/10.1016/j.neurobiolaging.2019.03.007

Farina, N., Rusted, J., & Tabet, N. (2014). The effect of exercise interventions on cognitive outcome in Alzheimer's disease: A systematic review. *International Psychogeriatrics, 26*(1), 9-18. https://doi.org/10.1017/S1041610213001385

Fedewa, A.L., & Ahn, S. (2011). The effects of physical activity and physical fitness on children's achievement and cognitive outcomes: A meta-analysis. *Research Quarterly for Exercise and Sport, 82*(3), 521-535. https://doi.org/10.1080/02701367.2011.10599785

Gomes-Osman, J., Cabral, D.F., Morris, T.P., McInerney, K., Cahalin, L.P., Rundek, T., Oliveira, A., & Pascual-Leone, A. (2018). Exercise for cognitive brain health in aging: A systematic review for an evaluation of dose. *Neurology Clinical Practice, 8*(3), 257-265. https://doi.org/10.1212/CPJ.0000000000000460

Hall, P.A., Dubin, J.A., Crossley, M., Holmqvist, M.E., & D'Arcy, C. (2009). Does executive function explain the IQ-mortality association? Evidence from the Canadian study on health and aging. *Psychosomatic Medicine, 71*(2), 196-204. https://doi.org/10.1097/PSY.0b013e318190d7f0

Hamer, M., & Chida, Y. (2009). Physical activity and risk of neurodegenerative disease: A systematic review of prospective evidence. *Psychological Medicine, 39*(1), 3-11. https://doi.org/10.1017/S0033291708003681

Hansen, A.L., Johnsen, B.H., Sollers, J.J., III, Stenvik, K., & Thayer, J.F. (2004). Heart rate variability and its relation to prefrontal cognitive function: The effects of training and detraining. *European Journal of Applied Physiology, 93*(3), 263-272. https://doi.org/10.1007/s00421-004-1208-0

Hillman, C.H., Pontifex, M.B., Castelli, D.M., Khan, N.A., Raine, L.B., Scudder, M.R., Drollette, E.S., Moore, R.D., Wu, C.T., & Kamijo, K. (2014). Effects of the FITKids randomized controlled trial on executive control and brain function. *Pediatrics, 134*(4), e1063-1071. https://doi.org/10.1542/peds.2013-3219

Horowitz, A.M., Fan, X., Bieri, G., Smith, L.K., Sanchez-Diaz, C.I., Schroer, A.B., Gontier, G., Casaletto, K.B., Kramer, J.H., Williams, K.E., & Villeda, S.A. (2020). Blood factors transfer beneficial effects of exercise on neurogenesis and cognition to the aged brain. *Science, 369*(6500), 167-173. https://doi.org/10.1126/science.aaw2622

Jia, R., Lian, J., Xu, Y., & Wang, Y. (2019). Effects of physical activity and exercise on the cognitive function of patients with Alzheimer disease: A meta-analysis. *BMC Geriatrics, 19,* 181-195. https://doi.org/10.1186/s12877-019-1175-2

Jung, M., Ryu, S., Kang, M., Javadi, A.H., & Loprinzi, P.D. (2022). Evaluation of the transient hypofrontality theory in the context of exercise: A systematic review with meta-analysis. *Quarterly Journal of Experimental Psychology, 75*(7), 1193-1214. https://doi.org/10.1177/17470218211048807

Kramer, A.F., Hahn, S., Cohen, N.J., Banich, M.T., McAuley, E., Harrison, C.R., Chason, J., Vakil, E., Bardell, L., Boileau, R.A., & Colcombe, A. (1999). Ageing, fitness and neurocognitive function. *Nature, 400*(6743), 418-419. https://doi.org/10.1038/22682

Labban, J.D., & Etnier, J.L. (2018). The effect of acute exercise on encoding and consolidation of long-term memory. *Journal of Sport and Exercise Psychology, 40*(6), 336-342 https://doi.org/10.1123/jsep.2018-0072

Lambourne, K., & Tomporowski, P. (2010). The effect of exercise-induced arousal on cognitive task performance: A meta-regression analysis. *Brain Research, 1341,* 12-24. https://doi.org/10.1016/j.brainres.2010.03.091

Lezak, M.D., Howieson, D.B., Loring, D.W., & Fischer, J.S. (2004). *Neuropsychological assessment*. Oxford University Press.

Loprinzi, P.D., Blough, J., Crawford, L., Ryu, S., Zou, L., & Li, H. (2019). The temporal effects of acute exercise on episodic memory function: Systematic review with meta-analysis. *Brain Sciences, 9*(4). https://doi.org/10.3390/brainsci9040087

McMorris, T. (2016). History of research into the acute exercise–cognition interaction: A cognitive psychology approach. In T. McMorris (Ed.), *Exercise-cognition interaction: Neuroscience perspectives* (pp. 1-28): Elsevier Academic Press.

McMorris, T., & Hale, B.J. (2012). Differential effects of differing intensities of acute exercise on speed and accuracy of cognition: A meta-analytical investigation. *Brain and Cognition, 80*(3), 338-351. https://doi.org/10.1016/j.bandc.2012.09.001

Moffitt, T.E., Arseneault, L., Belsky, D., Dickson, N., Hancox, R.J., Harrington, H., Houts, R., Poulton, R., Roberts, B.W., Ross, S., Sears, M.R., Thomson, W.M., & Caspi, A. (2011). A gradient of childhood self-control predicts health, wealth, and public safety. *Proceedings of the National Academy of Sciences of the United States of America, 108*(7), 2693-2698. https://doi.org/10.1073/pnas.1010076108

Northey, J.M., Cherbuin, N., Pumpa, K.L., Smee, D.J., & Rattray, B. (2018). Exercise interventions for cognitive function in adults older than 50: A systematic review with meta-analysis. *British Journal of Sports Medicine, 52*(3), 154-160. https://doi.org/10.1136/bjsports-2016-096587

Park, K.S., Ganesh, A.B., Berry, N.T., Mobley, Y.P., Karper, W.B., Labban, J.D., Wahlheim, C.N., Williams, T.M., Wideman, L., & Etnier, J.L. (2020). The effect of physical activity on cognition relative to APOE genotype (PAAD-2): Study protocol for a phase II randomized control trial. *BMC Neurology, 20*(1), 231. https://doi.org/10.1186/s12883-020-01732-1

Phoemsapthawee, J., Prasertsri, P., & Leelayuwat, N. (2019). Heart rate variability responses to a combined exercise training program: Correlation with adiposity and cardiorespiratory fitness changes in obese young men. *Journal of Exercise Rehabilitation, 15*(1), 114-122. https://doi.org/10.12965/jer.1836486.243

Quan, M., Xun, P., Chen, C., Wen, J., Wang, Y., Wang, R., Chen, P., & He, K. (2017). Walking pace and the risk of cognitive decline and dementia in elderly populations: A meta-analysis of prospective cohort studies. *Journal of Gerontology, 72*(2), 266-270. https://doi.org/10.1093/gerona/glw121

Roig, M., Nordbrandt, S., Geertsen, S.S., & Nielsen, J.B. (2013). The effects of cardiovascular exercise on human memory: A review with meta-analysis. *Neuroscience & Biobehavioral Reviews, 37*(8), 1645-1666. https://doi.org/10.1016/j.neubiorev.2013.06.012

Sanders, L.M.J., Hortobagyi, T., la Bastide-van Gemert, S., van der Zee, E.A., & van Heuvelen, M.J.G. (2019). Dose-response relationship between exercise and cognitive function in older adults with and without cognitive impairment: A systematic review and meta-analysis. *PLoS One, 14*(1), e0210036. https://doi.org/10.1371/journal.pone.0210036

Slutsky-Ganesh, A.B., Etnier, J.L., & Labban, J.D. (2020). Acute exercise, memory, and neural activation in young adults. *International Journal of Psychophysiology, 158*, 299-309. https://doi.org/10.1016/j.ijpsycho.2020.09.018

Sofi, F., Valecchi, D., Bacci, D., Abbate, R., Gensini, G.F., Casini, A., & Macchi, C. (2011). Physical activity and risk of cognitive decline: A meta-analysis of prospective studies. *Journal of Internal Medicine, 269*(1), 107-117. https://doi.org/10.1111/j.1365-2796.2010.02281.x

Sternberg, R.J. (2019). *A history of research on intelligence*. Cambridge University Press.

Stroop, J.R. (1935). Studies of interference in serial verbal reactions. *Journal of Experimental Psychology, 18*(6), 643-662.

Tan, B.W., Pooley, J.A., & Speelman, C.P. (2016). A meta-analytic review of the efficacy of physical exercise interventions on cognition in individuals with autism spectrum disorder and ADHD. *Journal of Autism and Developmental Disorders, 46*(9), 3126-3143. https://doi.org/10.1007/s10803-016-2854-x

Terman, L.M. (1916). *The measurement of intelligence: An explanation of and a complete guide for the use of the Stanford Revision and Extension of the Binet-Simon Intelligence Scale*. Houghton Miffin.

Thayer, J. F., Hansen, A. L., Saus-Rose, E., & Johnsen, B. H. (2009). Heart rate variability, prefrontal neural function, and cognitive performance: The neurovisceral integration perspective on self-regulation, adaptation, and health. *Annals of Behavioral Medicine, 37*(2), 141-153.

Thayer, J.F., & Lane, R.D. (2000). A model of neurovisceral integration in emotion regulation and dysregulation. *Journal of Affective Disorders, 61*(3), 201-216. https://doi.org/10.1016/s0165-0327(00)00338-4

Vazou, S., Pesce, C., Lakes, K., & Smiley-Oyen, A. (2019). More than one road leads to Rome: A narrative review and meta-analysis of physical activity intervention effects on cognition in youth. *International Journal of Sport and Exercise Psychology, 17*(2), 153-178. https://doi.org/10.1080/1612197X.2016.1223423

Wang, C.C., Chu, C.H., Chu, I.H., Chan, K.H., & Chang, Y.K. (2013). Executive function during acute exercise: The role of exercise intensity. *Journal of Sport and Exercise Psychology, 35*(4), 358-367. https://doi.org/10.1123/jsep.35.4.358

Xue, Y., Yang, Y., & Huang, T. (2019). Effects of chronic exercise interventions on executive function among children and adolescents: A systematic review with meta-analysis. *British Journal of Sports Medicine, 53*(22), 1397-1404. https://doi.org/10.1136/bjsports-2018-099825

Yaffe, K., Barnes, D., Nevitt, M., Lui, L.Y., & Covinsky, K. (2001). A prospective study of physical activity and cognitive decline in elderly women: Women who walk. *Archives of Internal Medicine, 161*(14), 1703-1708. https://doi.org/10.1001/archinte.161.14.1703

Zou, L., Sasaki, J.E., Wei, G.X., Huang, T., Yeung, A.S., Neto, O.B., Chen, K.W., & Hui, S.S. (2018). Effects of mind(-)body exercises (tai chi/yoga) on heart rate variability parameters and perceived stress: A systematic review with meta-analysis of randomized controlled trials. *Journal of Clinical Medicine, 7*(11). https://doi.org/10.3390/jcm7110404

Chapter 10

Archer, T., Svensson, K., & Alricsson, M. (2012). Physical exercise ameliorates deficits induced by traumatic brain injury. *Acta Neurologica Scandinavica, 125*(5), 293-302. https://doi.org/10.1111/j.1600-0404.2011.01638.x

Black, J.E., Isaacs, K.R., Anderson, B.J., Alcantara, A.A., & Greenough, W.T. (1990). Learning causes synaptogenesis, whereas motor activity causes angiogenesis, in cerebellar cortex of adult rats. *Proceedings of the National Academy of Sciences of the United States of America, 87*(14), 5568-5572. https://doi.org/10.1073/pnas.87.14.5568

Boren, S. D. (2010). To the Editor. *New England Journal of Medicine, 362*(23): 2229-2230.

Centers for Disease Control and Prevention. (2015). *Report to Congress on Traumatic Brain Injury in the United States: Epidemiology and Rehabilitation.* Centers for Disease Control and Prevention. www.cdc.gov/traumaticbraininjury/pdf/TBI_Report_to_Congress_Epi_and_Rehab-a.pdf

Centers for Disease Control and Prevention. (2022). *Get the facts about TBI.* Centers for Disease Control and Prevention. www.cdc.gov/traumaticbraininjury/get_the_facts.html

Chu, C.H., Kramer, A.F., Song, T.F., Wu, C.H., Hung, T.M., & Chang, Y.K. (2017). Acute exercise and neurocognitive development in preadolescents and young adults: An ERP study. *Neural Plasticity, 2017,* 2631909. https://doi.org/10.1155/2017/2631909

Colcombe, S.J., Erickson, K.I., Scalf, P.E., Kim, J.S., Prakash, R., McAuley, E., Elavksy, S., Marquez, D.X., Hu, L., & Kramer, A.F. (2006). Aerobic exercise training increases brain volume in aging humans. *Journals of Gerontology, Series A, 61*(11), 1166-1170. https://doi.org/10.1093/gerona/61.11.1166

Corrigan, J.D., Cuthbert, J.P., Harrison-Felix, C., Whiteneck, G.G., Bell, J.M., Miller, A.C., Coronado, V.G., & Pretz, C.R. (2014). US population estimates of health and social outcomes 5 years after rehabilitation for traumatic brain injury. *Journal of Head Trauma Rehabilitation, 29*(6), E1-9. https://doi.org/10.1097/HTR.0000000000000020

D'Isabella, N.T., Shkredova, D.A., Richardson, J.A., & Tang, A. (2017). Effects of exercise on cardiovascular risk factors following stroke or transient ischemic attack: A systematic review and meta-analysis. *Clinical Rehabilitation, 31*(12), 1561-1572. https://doi.org/10.1177/0269215517709051

DeFelipe, J. (2006). Brain plasticity and mental processes: Cajal again. *Nature Reviews Neuroscience, 7*(10), 811-817. https://doi.org/10.1038/nrn2005

Dinoff, A., Herrmann, N., Swardfager, W., & Lanctot, K.L. (2017). The effect of acute exercise on blood concentrations of brain-derived neurotrophic factor in healthy adults: A meta-analysis. *European Journal of Neuroscience, 46*(1), 1635-1646. https://doi.org/10.1111/ejn.13603

Firth, J., Stubbs, B., Vancampfort, D., Schuch, F., Lagopoulos, J., Rosenbaum, S., & Ward, P.B. (2018). Effect of aerobic exercise on hippocampal volume in humans: A systematic review and meta-analysis. *NeuroImage, 166,* 230-238. https://doi.org/10.1016/j.neuroimage.2017.11.007

Franke, K., & Gaser, C. (2019). Ten years of BrainAGE as a neuroimaging biomarker of brain aging: What insights have we gained? *Frontiers in Neurology, 10,* 789. https://doi.org/10.3389/fneur.2019.00789

Guskiewicz, K.M., McCrea, M., Marshall, S.W., Cantu, R.C., Randolph, C., Barr, W., Onate, J.A., & Kelly, J.P. (2003). Cumulative effects associated with recurrent concussion in collegiate football players: The NCAA Concussion Study. *Journal of the American Medical Association, 290*(19), 2549-2555.

Haider, M.N., Bezherano, I., Wertheimer, A., Siddiqui, A.H., Horn, E.C., Willer, B.S., & Leddy, J.J. (2021). Exercise for sport-related concussion and persistent postconcussive symptoms. *Sports Health, 13*(2), 154-160. https://doi.org/10.1177/1941738120946015

Hou, L., Li, M., Wang, J., Li, Y., Zheng, Q., Zhang, L., Yao, Q., Zhang, J., Dong, S., Zhou, M., & Zhu, C. (2021). Association between physical exercise and stroke recurrence among first-ever ischemic stroke survivors. *Scientific Reports, 11*(1), 13372. https://doi.org/10.1038/s41598-021-92736-5

Leddy, J.J., Haider, M.N., Ellis, M., & Willer, B.S. (2018). Exercise is medicine for concussion. *Current Sports Med Reports, 17*(8), 262-270. https://doi.org/10.1249/JSR.0000000000000505

Leddy, J.J., Haider, M.N., Ellis, M.J., Mannix, R., Darling, S.R., Freitas, M.S., Suffoletto, H.N., Leiter, J., Cordingley, D.M., & Willer, B. (2019). Early subthreshold aerobic exercise for sport-related concussion: A randomized clinical trial. *JAMA Pediatrics, 173*(4), 319-325. https://doi.org/10.1001/jamapediatrics.2018.4397

Lee, C.D., & Blair, S.N. (2002). Cardiorespiratory fitness and stroke mortality in men. *Medicine & Science in Sports & Exercise, 34*(4), 592-595. https://doi.org/10.1097/00005768-200204000-00005

Lee, C.D., Folsom, A.R., & Blair, S.N. (2003). Physical activity and stroke risk: A meta-analysis. *Stroke, 34*(10), 2475-2481. https://doi.org/10.1161/01.STR.0000091843.02517.9D

Lo, J., Chan, L., & Flynn, S. (2021). A systematic review of the incidence, prevalence, costs, and activity and work limitations of amputation, osteoarthritis, rheumatoid arthritis, back pain, multiple sclerosis, spinal cord injury, stroke, and traumatic brain injury in the United States: A 2019 update. *Archives of Physical Medicine and Rehabilitation, 102*(1), 115-131. https://doi.org/10.1016/j.apmr.2020.04.001

Maron, B. J., & Estes III, N. M. (2010). Commotio cordis. *New England Journal of Medicine, 362*(10), 917-927.

McCrory, P., Meeuwisse, W., Dvorak, J., Aubry, M., Bailes, J., Broglio, S., Cantu, R.C., Cassidy, D., Echemendia, R.J., Castellani, R.J., Davis, G.A., Ellenbogen, R., Emery, C., Engebretsen, L., Feddermann-Demont, N., Giza, C.C., Guskiewicz, K.M., Herring, S., . . . Vos, P.E. (2017). Consensus statement on concussion in sport—the 5th international conference on concussion in sport held in Berlin. *British Journal of Sports Medicine, 51*(11), 838-847.

Meijer, A., Konigs, M., Vermeulen, G.T., Visscher, C., Bosker, R.J., Hartman, E., & Oosterlaan, J. (2020). The effects of physical activity on brain structure and neurophysiological functioning in children: A systematic review and meta-analysis. *Developmental Cognitive Neuroscience, 45,* 100828. https://doi.org/10.1016/j.dcn.2020.100828

Mundstock, E., Zatti, H., Louzada, F.M., Oliveira, S.G., Guma, F.T., Paris, M.M., Rueda, A.B., Machado, D.G., Stein, R.T., Jones, M.H., Sarria, E.E., Barbé-Tuana, F.M., & Mattiello, R. (2015). Effects of physical activity in telomere length: Systematic review and meta-analysis. *Ageing Research Reviews, 22,* 72-80. https://doi.org/10.1016/j.arr.2015.02.004

Piller, C. (2022). Revised clinical trial form for Alzheimer's antibody warned of fatal brain bleeds. *Science Insider.* Science. www.science.org/content/article/revised-clinical-trial-form-alzheimer-s-antibody-warned-fatal-brain-bleeds?cookieSet=1

Reimers, C.D., Knapp, G., & Reimers, A.K. (2009). Exercise as stroke prophylaxis. *Deutsch Arzteblatt International, 106*(44), 715-721. https://doi.org/10.3238/arztbl.2009.0715

Sexton, C.E., Betts, J.F., Demnitz, N., Dawes, H., Ebmeier, K.P., & Johansen-Berg, H. (2016). A systematic review of MRI studies examining the relationship between physical fitness and activity and the white matter of the ageing brain. *NeuroImage, 131,* 81-90. https://doi.org/10.1016/j.neuroimage.2015.09.071

Sindi, S., Solomon, A., Kåreholt, I., Hovatta, I., Antikainen, R., Hänninen, T., Levaalahti, E., Laatikainen, T., Lehtisalo, J., Lindström, J., Paajanen, T., Peltonen, M., Khalsa, D.S., Wolozin, B., Strandberg, T., Tuomilehto, J., Soininen, H., Ngandu, T., Kivipelto, M., & Group, F.S. (2021). Telomere length change in a multidomain lifestyle intervention to prevent cognitive decline: A randomized clinical trial. *Journal of Gerontology, Series A, 76*(3), 491-498. https://doi.org/10.1093/gerona/glaa279

Szuhany, K.L., Bugatti, M., & Otto, M.W. (2015). A meta-analytic review of the effects of exercise on brain-derived neurotrophic factor. *Journal of Psychiatric Research, 60,* 56-64. https://doi.org/10.1016/j.jpsychires.2014.10.003

USDHHS. (2018). *Physical Activity Guidelines for Americans.* 2nd edition. U.S. Department of Health and Human Services.

Vanderbeken, I., & Kerckhofs, E. (2017). A systematic review of the effect of physical exercise on cognition in stroke and traumatic brain injury patients. *NeuroRehabilitation, 40*(1), 33-48. https://doi.org/10.3233/NRE-161388

Veliz, P., Eckner, J.T., Zdroik, J., & Schulenberg, J.E. (2019). Lifetime prevalence of self-reported concussion among adolescents involved in competitive sports: A national U.S. study. *Journal of Adolescent Health, 64*(2), 272-275. https://doi.org/10.1016/j.jadohealth.2018.08.023

Wang, Y., Pan, Y., & Li, H. (2020). What is brain health and why is it important? *BMJ, 371,* m3683. https://doi.org/10.1136/bmj.m3683

Wendel-Vos, G.C., Schuit, A.J., Feskens, E.J., Boshuizen, H.C., Verschuren, W.M., Saris, W.H., & Kromhout, D. (2004). Physical activity and stroke. A meta-analysis of observational data. *International Journal of Epidemiology, 33*(4), 787-798. https://doi.org/10.1093/ije/dyh168

Wogensen, E., Mala, H., & Mogensen, J. (2015). The effects of exercise on cognitive recovery after acquired brain injury in animal models: A systematic review. *Neural Plasticity, 2015,* 830871. https://doi.org/10.1155/2015/830871

Woloshin, S., & Kesselheim, A.S. (2022). What to know about the Alzheimer drug aducanumab (Aduhelm). *JAMA Internal Medicine, 182*(8), 892. https://doi.org/10.1001/jamainternmed.2022.1039

Yokobori, S., Mazzeo, A.T., Hosein, K., Gajavelli, S., Dietrich, W.D., & Bullock, M.R. (2013). Preconditioning for traumatic brain injury. *Translational Stroke Research, 4*(1), 25-39. https://doi.org/10.1007/s12975-012-0226-1

Zaloshnja, E., Miller, T., Langlois, J.A., & Selassie, A.W. (2008). Prevalence of long-term disability from traumatic brain injury in the civilian population of the United States, 2005. *Journal of Head Trauma Rehabilitation, 23*(6), 394-400. https://doi.org/10.1097/01.HTR.0000341435.52004.ac

Zarnani, K., Nichols, T.E., Alfaro-Almagro, F., Fagerlund, B., Lauritzen, M., Rostrup, E., & Smith, S.M. (2019). Discovering markers of healthy aging: A prospective study in a Danish male birth cohort. *Aging (Albany NY), 11*(16), 5943-5974. https://doi.org/10.18632/aging.102151

Zheng, G., Huang, M., Liu, F., Li, S., Tao, J., & Chen, L. (2015). Tai chi chuan for the primary prevention of stroke in middle-aged and elderly adults: A systematic review. *Evidence-Based Complementary and Alternative Medicine, 2015,* 742152. https://doi.org/10.1155/2015/742152

Chapter 11

Awick, E.A., Ehlers, D., Fanning, J., Phillips, S.M., Wojcicki, T., Mackenzie, M.J., Motl, R., & McAuley, E. (2017). Effects of a home-based DVD-delivered physical activity program on self-esteem in older adults: Results from a randomized controlled trial. *Psychosomatic Medicine, 79*(1), 71-80. https://doi.org/10.1097/PSY.0000000000000358

Baumeister, R.F., Campbell, J.D., Krueger, J.I., & Vohs, K.D. (2003). Does high self-esteem cause better performance, interpersonal success, happiness, or healthier lifestyles? *Psychological Science in the Public Interest, 4*(1), 1-44. https://doi.org/10.1111/1529-1006.01431

Butler, R.J., & Gasson, S.L. (2005). Self esteem/self concept scales for children and adolescents: A review. *Child and Adolescent Mental Health, 10*(4), 190-201. https://doi.org/10.1111/j.1475-3588.2005.00368.x

Collins, H., Booth, J.N., Duncan, A., Fawkner, S., & Niven, A. (2019). The effect of resistance training interventions on "the self" in youth: A systematic review and meta-analysis. *Sports Medicine - Open, 5*(1), 29. https://doi.org/10.1186/s40798-019-0205-0

Fitts, W.H. (1965). *Tennessee self concept scale manual* (2nd ed.). Western Psychological Services.

Fox, K.R. (1990). *The physical self-perception profile manual.* North Illinois University Office of Health Promotion.

Fox, K.R., & Corbin, C.B. (1989). The physical self-perception profile: Devlopment and preliminary validation. *Journal of Sport and Exercise Psychology, 11*(4), 408-430.

Goldfield, G.S., Kenny, G.P., Alberga, A.S., Prud'homme, D., Hadjiyannakis, S., Gougeon, R., Phillips, P., Tulloch, H., Malcolm, J., Doucette, S., Wells, G.A., Ma, J., Cameron, J.D., & Sigal, R.J. (2015). Effects of aerobic training, resistance training, or both on psychological health in adolescents with obesity: The HEARTY randomized controlled trial. *Journal of Consulting and Clinical Psychology, 83*(6), 1123-1135. https://doi.org/10.1037/ccp0000038

Griffiths, L.J., Parsons, T.J., & Hill, A.J. (2010). Self-esteem and quality of life in obese children and adolescents: A systematic review. *International Journal of Pediatric Obesity, 5*(4), 282-304. https://doi.org/10.3109/17477160903473697

Henriksen, I. O., Ranøyen, I., Indredavik, M. S., & Stenseng, F. (2017). The role of self-esteem in the development of psychiatric problems: A three-year prospective study in a clinical sample of adolescents. *Child and Adolescent Psychiatry and Mental Health, 11,* 1-9.

Hill, A.J. (2017). Obesity in children and the "myth of psychological maladjustment": Self-esteem in the spotlight. *Current Obesity Reports, 6*(1), 63-70. https://doi.org/10.1007/s13679-017-0246-y

Ickes, W.J., Wicklund, R.A., & Ferris, C.B. (1973). Objective self awareness and self esteem. *Journal of Experimental Social Psychology, 9,* 202-219.

James, W. (1883). *The principles of psychology.* Harvard University Press.

Kenrick, D.T., Griskevicius, V., Neuberg, S.L., & Schaller, M. (2010). Renovating the pyramid of eeeds: Contemporary extensions built upon ancient foundations. *Perspectives on Psychological Science, 5*(3), 292-314. https://doi.org/10.1177/1745691610369469

King, J.E., Jebeile, H., Garnett, S.P., Baur, L.A., Paxton, S.J., & Gow, M.L. (2020). Physical activity based pediatric obesity treatment, depression, self-esteem and body image: A systematic review with meta-analysis. *Mental Health and Physical Activity, 19,* 1-11. https://doi.org/10.1016/j.mhpa.2020.100342

Maslow, A.H. (1943). A theory of human motivation. *Psychological Review, 50*(4), 370-396.

Midgley, C., Thai, S., Lockwood, P., Kovacheff, C., & Page-Gould, E. (2021). When every day is a high school reunion: Social media comparisons and self-esteem. *Journal of Personal and Social Psychology, 121*(2), 285-307. https://doi.org/10.1037/pspi0000336

Mruk, C.J. (2006). *Self-esteem research, theory and practice: Toward a positive psychology of self-esteem* (3rd ed.). Springer.

Orth, U., & Robins, R.W. (2014). The development of self-esteem. *Current Directions in Psychological Science, 23*(5), 381-387.

Orth, U., Erol, R.Y., & Luciano, E.C. (2018). Development of self-esteem from age 4 to 94 years: A meta-analysis of longitudinal studies. *Psychological Bulletin, 144*(10), 1045-1080. https://doi.org/10.1037/bul0000161

Park, S.H., Han, K.S., & Kang, C.B. (2014). Effects of exercise programs on depressive symptoms, quality of life, and self-esteem in older people: A systematic review of randomized controlled trials. *Applied Nursing Research, 27*(4), 219-226. https://doi.org/10.1016/j.apnr.2014.01.004

Piers, E.V., & Herzberg, D.S. (2002). *Piers-Harris 2; Children's self concept scale*. Western Psychological Services.

Robins, R.W., Tracy, J.L., Trzesniewski, K., Potter, J., & Gosling, S.D. (2001). Personality correlates of self-esteem. *Journal of Research in Personality, 35*(4), 463-482.

Rosenberg, M. (1965). *Society and the adolescent self image*. Princeton University Press.

Shavelson, R.J., Hubner, J.J., & Stanton, G.C. (1976). Self-concept: Validation of construct interpretations. *Review of Educational Research, 46*(3), 407-441.

Sonstroem, R.J., & Morgan, W.P. (1989). Exercise and self-esteem: Rationale and model. *Medicine & Science in Sports & Exercise, 21*(3), 329-337. www.ncbi.nlm.nih.gov/pubmed/2659918

Trzesniewski, K.H., Donnellan, M.B., & Robins, R.W. (2003). Stability of self-esteem across the life span. *Journal of Personal and Social Psychology, 84*(1), 205-220. www.ncbi.nlm.nih.gov/pubmed/12518980

Woodman, T., MacGregor, A.L., & Hardy, L. (2020). Risk can be good for self-esteem: Beyond self-determination theory. *Journal of Risk Research, 23*(4), 411-423.

Chapter 12

Alleva, J.M., Sheeran, P., Webb, T.L., Martijn, C., & Miles, E. (2015). A meta-analytic review of stand-alone interventions to improve body image. *PLoS One, 10*(9), e0139177. https://doi.org/10.1371/journal.pone.0139177

Attie, I., & Brooks-Gunn, J. (1989). Development of eating problems in adolescent girls: A longitudinal study. *Developmental Psychology, 25*(1), 70-79.

Bassett-Gunter, R., McEwan, D., & Kamarhie, A. (2017). Physical activity and body image among men and boys: A meta-analysis. *Body Image, 22*, 114-128. https://doi.org/10.1016/j.bodyim.2017.06.007

Beccia, A.L., Baek, J., Jesdale, W.M., Austin, S.B., Forrester, S., Curtin, C., & Lapane, K.L. (2019). Risk of disordered eating at the intersection of gender and racial/ethnic identity among U.S. high school students. *Eating Behaviors, 34*, 101299. https://doi.org/10.1016/j.eatbeh.2019.05.002

Bergeron, D., & Tylka, T.L. (2007). Support for the uniqueness of body dissatisfaction from drive for muscularity among men. *Body Image, 4*(3), 288-295. https://doi.org/10.1016/j.bodyim.2007.05.002

Bornioli, A., Lewis-Smith, H., Smith, A., Slater, A., & Bray, I. (2019). Adolescent body dissatisfaction and disordered eating: Predictors of later risky health behaviours. *Social Science & Medicine, 238* (112458), 1-8.

Cattarin, J.A., & Thompson, J.K. (1994). A three-year longitudinal study of body image, eating disturbance, and general psychological functioning in adolescent females. *Eating Disorders, 2*(2), 114-125.

Dixon, S. (2022). *Average daily time spent on social media worldwide 2012-2022*. Statista. www.statista.com/statistics/433871/daily-social-media-usage-worldwide/#:~:text=As%20of%202019%2C%20the%20average,minutes%20in%20the%20previous%20year.?ref=DigitalMarketing.org).%5C

Fardouly, J., & Vartanian, L.R. (2015). Negative comparisons about one's appearance mediate the relationship between Facebook usage and body image concerns. *Body Image, 12*, 82-88. https://doi.org/10.1016/j.bodyim.2014.10.004

Fiske, L., Fallon, E.A., Blissmer, B., & Redding, C.A. (2014). Prevalence of body dissatisfaction among United States adults: Review and recommendations for future research. *Eating Behaviors, 15*(3), 357-365. https://doi.org/10.1016/j.eatbeh.2014.04.010

Fitts, W.H. (1965). *Tennessee self concept scale manual* (2nd ed.). Western Psychological Services.

Fox, J., & Rooney, M.C. (2015). The Dark Triad and trait self-objectification as predictors of men's use and self-presentation behaviors on social networking sites. *Personality and Individual Differences, 76*, 161-165.

Frederick, D.A., Peplau, L.A., & Lever, J. (2006). The swimsuit issue: Correlates of body image in a sample of 52,677 heterosexual adults. *Body Image, 3*(4), 413-419. https://doi.org/10.1016/j.bodyim.2006.08.002

Frevert, T.K., & Walker, L.S. (2014). Physical attractiveness and social status. *Sociology Compass, 8*(3), 313-323.

Galmiche, M., Dechelotte, P., Lambert, G., & Tavolacci, M.P. (2019). Prevalence of eating disorders over the 2000-2018 period: A systematic literature review. *American Journal of Clinical Nutrition, 109*(5), 1402-1413. https://doi.org/10.1093/ajcn/nqy342

Gardner, R.M., Stark, K., Friedman, B.N., & Jackson, N.A. (2000). Predictors of eating disorder scores in children ages 6 through 14: A longitudinal study. *Journal of Psychosomatic Research, 49*(3), 199-205. https://doi.org/10.1016/s0022-3999(00)00172-0

Hausenblas, H.A., & Downs, D.S. (2001). Comparison of body image between athletes and nonathletes: A meta-analytic review. *Journal of Applied Sport Psychology, 13*(3), 323-339.

Hausenblas, H.A., & Fallon, E.A. (2006). Exercise and body image: A meta-analysis. *Psychology and Health, 21*(1), 33-47.

Hildebrandt, T., Langenbucher, J., & Schlundt, D. G. (2004). Muscularity concerns among men: Development of attitudinal and perceptual measures. *Body Image, 1*(2), 169-181. https://doi.org/10.1016/j.bodyim.2004.01.001

Hildebrandt, T., Walker, D. C., Alfano, L., Delinsky, S., & Bannon, K. (2010). Development and validation of a male specific body checking questionnaire. *International journal of Eating Disorders, 43*(1), 77-87.

Hogue, J.V., & Mills, J.S. (2019). The effects of active social media engagement with peers on body image in young women. *Body Image, 28,* 1-5. https://doi.org/10.1016/j.bodyim.2018.11.002

Keel, P.K., Fulkerson, J.A., & Leon, G.R. (1997). Disordered eating precursors in pre-and early adolescent girls and boys. *Journal of Youth and Adolescence, 26*(2), 203-216.

Kostanski, M., Fisher, A., & Gullone, E. (2004). Current conceptualisation of body image dissatisfaction: Have we got it wrong? *Journal of Child Psychology and Psychiatry, 45*(7), 1317-1325. https://doi.org/10.1111/j.1469-7610.2004.00315.x

Leon, G.R., Fulkerson, J.A., Perry, C.L., & Early-Zald, M.B. (1995). Prospective analysis of personality and behavioral vulnerabilities and gender influences in the later development of disordered eating. *Journal of Abnormal Psychology, 104*(1), 140-149. https://doi.org/10.1037//0021-843x.104.1.140

MacNeill, L.P., Best, L.A., & Davis, L.L. (2017). The role of personality in body image dissatisfaction and disordered eating: Discrepancies between men and women. *Journal of Eating Disorders, 5,* 44. https://doi.org/10.1186/s40337-017-0177-8

Mancine, R.P., Gusfa, D.W., Moshrefi, A., & Kennedy, S.F. (2020). Prevalence of disordered eating in athletes categorized by emphasis on leanness and activity type — a systematic review. *Journal of Eating Disorders, 8,* 47. https://doi.org/10.1186/s40337-020-00323-2

Martin Ginis, K.A., Bassett-Gunter, R.L., & Conlin, C. (2012). Body image and exercise. In E. O. Acevedo (Ed.), *The Oxford Handbook of Exercise Psychology*. Oxford University Press.

Martin Ginis, K. A., Eng, J. J., Arbour, K. P., Hartman, J. W., & Phillips, S. M. (2005). Mind over muscle?: Sex differences in the relationship between body image change and subjective and objective physical changes following a 12-week strength-training program. *Body Image, 2*(4), 363-372.

McCreary, D.R., & Sasse, D.K. (2000). An exploration of the drive for muscularity in adolescent boys and girls. *Journal of American College Health, 48*(6), 297-304. https://doi.org/10.1080/07448480009596271

McGuinness, S., & Taylor, J.E. (2016). Understanding body image dissatisfaction and disordered eating in midlife adults. *New Zealand Journal of Psychology, 45*(1), 4-12.

Morrison, T.G., Morrison, M.A., Hopkins, C., & Rowan, E.T. (2004). Muscle mania: Development of a new scale examining the drive for muscularity in Canadian males. *Psychology of Men & Masculinity, 51,* 30-39.

Neumark-Sztainer, D., Paxton, S. J., Hannan, P. J., Haines, J., & Story, M. (2006). Does body satisfaction matter? Five-year longitudinal associations between body satisfaction and health behaviors in adolescent females and males. *Journal of Adolescent Health, 39*(2), 244-251.

Neumark-Sztainer, D., Wall, M.M., Larson, N., Story, M., Fulkerson, J.A., Eisenberg, M.E., & Hannan, P.J. (2012). Secular trends in weight status and weight-related attitudes and behaviors in adolescents from 1999 to 2010. *Preventive Medicine, 54*(1), 77-81. https://doi.org/10.1016/j.ypmed.2011.10.003

Perrin, E.M., Boone-Heinonen, J., Field, A.E., Coyne-Beasley, T., & Gordon-Larsen, P. (2010). Perception of overweight and self-esteem during adolescence. *International Journal of Eating Disorders, 43*(5), 447-454. https://doi.org/10.1002/eat.20710

Polivy, J., & Herman, C.P. (2002). Causes of eating disorders. *Annual Review of Psychology, 53,* 187-213. https://doi.org/10.1146/annurev.psych.53.100901.135103

Pope, H.G., Jr., Gruber, A.J., Mangweth, B., Bureau, B., deCol, C., Jouvent, R., & Hudson, J.I. (2000). Body image perception among men in three countries. *American Journal of Psychiatry, 157*(8), 1297-1301. https://doi.org/10.1176/appi.ajp.157.8.1297

Reas, D.L., Whisenhunt, B.L., Netemeyer, R., & Williamson, D.A. (2002). Development of the body checking questionnaire: A self-report measure of body checking behaviors. *International Journal of Eating Disorders, 31*(3), 324-333. https://doi.org/10.1002/eat.10012

Reel, J.J., Greenleaf, C., Baker, W.K., Aragon, S., Bishop, D., Cachaper, C., Handwerk, P., Locicero, J., Rathburn, L., Reid, W.K., & Hattie, J. (2007). Relations of body concerns and exercise behavior: A meta-analysis. *Psychological Reports, 101*(3), 927-942. https://doi.org/10.2466/pr0.101.3.927-942

Sarwer, D.B., Thompson, J.K., & Cash, T.F. (2005). Body image and obesity in adulthood. *Psychiatric Clinics of North America, 28*(1), 69-87. https://doi.org/10.1016/j.psc.2004.09.002

Secord, P.F., & Jourard, S.M. (1953). The appraisal of body-cathexis: Body-cathexis and the self. *Journal of Consulting and Clinical Psychology, 17*(5), 343-347. https://doi.org/10.1037/h0060689

Simone, M., Telke, S., Anderson, L.M., Eisenberg, M., & Neumark-Sztainer, D. (2022). Ethnic/racial and gender differences in disordered eating behavior prevalence trajectories among women and men from adolescence into adulthood. *Social Science & Medicine, 294,* 114720. https://doi.org/10.1016/j.socscimed.2022.114720

Stunkard, A., Sorenson, T., & Schulsinger, F. (1983). Use of the Danish adoption register for the study of obesity and thinness. In S. Kety, L. Rowland, R. Sidman, & S. Matthysse (Eds.), *The genetics of neurological and psychiatric disorders* (pp. 115-120). Raven Press.

Swami, V., Tran, U.S., Stieger, S., & Voracek, M. (2015). Associations between women's body image and happiness: Results of the YouBeauty.com Body Image Survey (YBIS). *Journal of Happiness Studies, 16,* 705-718.

Thompson, J.K. (2004). The (mis)measurement of body image: Ten strategies to improve assessment for applied and research purposes. *Body Image, 1*(1), 7-14. https://doi.org/10.1016/S1740-1445(03)00004-4

Tiggemann, M., & Miller, J. (2010). The Internet and adolescent girls' weight satisfaction and drive for thinness. *Sex Roles, 63,* 79-90.

Tiggemann, M., & Slater, A. (2013). NetGirls: The Internet, Facebook, and body image concern in adolescent girls. *International Journal of Eating Disorders, 46*(6), 630-633. https://doi.org/10.1002/eat.22141

Tiggemann, M., & Slater, A. (2014). NetTweens: The Internet and body image concerns in preteenage girls. *Journal of Early Adolescence, 34,* 606-620.

Truby, H., & Paxton, S.J. (2002). Development of the Children's Body Image Scale. *British Journal of Clinical Psychology, 41*(2), 185-203. https://doi.org/10.1348/014466502163967

Tylka, T.L., Bergeron, D., & Schwartz, J.P. (2005). Development and psychometric evaluation of the Male Body Attitudes Scale (MBAS). *Body Image, 2*(2), 161-175. https://doi.org/10.1016/j.bodyim.2005.03.001

Vernon-Guidry, S., & Williamson, D. (1996). Development of a Body Image Assessment procedure for children and pre-adolescents. *International Journal of Eating Disorders, 20*(3), 287-293.

Wilson, R.E., Latner, J.D., & Hayashi, K. (2013). More than just body weight: The role of body image in psychological and physical functioning. *Body Image, 10*(4), 644-647. https://doi.org/10.1016/j.bodyim.2013.04.007

Zuke, R. (2018). *Wrestling has come a long way since 3 weight-loss related deaths in 1997*. MLive. www.mlive.com/sports/2018/03/wrestling_has_come_a_long_way.html

Chapter 13

American Academy of Sleep Medicine. (2022). *Sleep medicine in America: Infographic*. American Academy of Sleep Medicine. https://sleepeducation.org/sleep-medicine-america-infographic/

American Psychiatric Association. (2023). *What are sleep disorders?*. American Psychiatric Association. https://www.psychiatry.org/patients-families/sleep-disorders/what-are-sleep-disorders.

Banno, M., Harada, Y., Taniguchi, M., Tobita, R., Tsujimoto, H., Tsujimoto, Y., Kataoka, Y., & Noda, A. (2018). Exercise can improve sleep quality: A systematic review and meta-analysis. *PeerJ, 6*, e5172. https://doi.org/10.7717/peerj.5172

Bhattarai, J., & Sumerall, S. (2017). Current and future treatment options for narcolepsy: A review. *Sleep Science, 10*(1), 19-27. https://doi.org/10.5935/1984-0063.20170004

Born, J., & Wilhelm, I. (2012). System consolidation of memory during sleep. *Psychological Research, 76*(2), 192-203. https://doi.org10.1007/s00426-011-0335-6

Buysse, D.J., Reynolds, C.F. III, Monk, T.H., Berman, S.R., & Kupfer, D.J. (1989). The Pittsburgh Sleep Quality Index: A new instrument for psychiatric practice and research. *Psychiatry Research, 28*, 193-213.

Carvalho-Mendes, R.P., Dunster, G.P., de la Iglesia, H.O., & Menna-Barreto, L. (2020). Afternoon school start times are associated with a lack of both social jetlag and sleep deprivation in adolescents. *Journal of Biological Rhythms, 35*(4), 377-390. https://doi.org/10.1177/0748730420927603

Chan, V., & Lo, K. (2022). Efficacy of dietary supplements on improving sleep quality: A systematic review and meta-analysis. *Postgraduate Medical Journal, 98*(1158), 285-293. https://doi.org/10.1136/postgradmedj-2020-139319

Chokroverty, S. (2017). Overview of normal sleep. In S. Chokroverty (Ed.), *Sleep disorders medicine* (4th ed., pp. 19-22). Springer.

Consensus Conference Panel. (2015). Recommended amount of sleep for a healthy adult: A joint consensus statement of the American Academy of Sleep Medicine and Sleep Research Society. *Sleep, 38*(6), 843-844. https://doi.org/10.5665/sleep.4716

Everson, C.A., Bergmann, B.M., & Rechtschaffen, A. (1989). Sleep deprivation in the rat: III. Total sleep deprivation. *Sleep, 12*(1), 13-21. https://doi.org/10.1093/sleep/12.1.13

Fang, Y. Y., Hung, C. T., Chan, J. C., Huang, S. M., & Lee, Y. H. (2019). Meta-analysis: Exercise intervention for sleep problems in cancer patients. *European Journal of Cancer Care, 28*(5), 1-18.

Goel, N., Rao, H., Durmer, J.S., & Dinges, D.F. (2009). Neurocognitive consequences of sleep deprivation. *Seminars in Neurology, 29*(4), 320-339. https://doi.org/10.1055/s-0029-1237117

Hafner, M., Stepanek, M., Taylor, J., Troxel, W.M., & van Stolk, C. (2017). Why sleep matters—the economic costs of insufficient sleep: A cross-country comparative analysis. *Rand Health Quarterly, 6*(4), 11. www.ncbi.nlm.nih.gov/pubmed/28983434

Hicks, R.A., Fernandez, C., & Pellegrini, R.J. (2001). The changing sleep habits of university students: An update. *Perceptual and Motor Skills, 93*(3), 648. https://doi.org/10.2466/pms.2001.93.3.648

Hirshkowitz, M., Whiton, K., Albert, S.M., Alessi, C., Bruni, O., DonCarlos, L., Hazen, N., Herman, J., Adam Hillard, P.J., Katz, E.S., Kheirandish-Gozal, L., Neubauer, D.N., O'Donnell, A.E., Ohayon, M., Peever, J., Rawding, R., Sachdeva, R.C., Setters, B., Vitiello, M.V., & Ware, J.C. (2015). National Sleep Foundation's updated sleep duration recommendations: Final report. *Sleep Health, 1*(4), 233-243. https://doi.org/10.1016/j.sleh.2015.10.004

Holbrook, A.M., Crowther, R., Lotter, A., Cheng, C., & King, D. (2000). Meta-analysis of benzodiazepine use in the treatment of insomnia. *Canadian Medical Association Journal, 162*(2), 225-233. www.ncbi.nlm.nih.gov/pubmed/10674059

Huyett, P., Siegel, N., & Bhattacharyya, N. (2021). Prevalence of sleep disorders and association with mortality: Results from the NHANES 2009-2010. *Laryngoscope, 131*(3), 686-689. https://doi.org/10.1002/lary.28900

Institute of Medicine (US) Committee on Sleep Medicine and Research. (2006). Extent and health consequences of chronic sleep loss and sleep disorders. In H.R. Colten & B.M. Altevogt (Eds.), *Sleep disorders and sleep deprivation: An unmet public health problem*. National Academies Press.

Kline, C.E., Crowley, E.P., Ewing, G.B., Burch, J.B., Blair, S.N., Durstine, J.L., Davis, J.M., & Youngstedt, S.D. (2011). The effect of exercise training on obstructive sleep apnea and sleep quality: A randomized controlled trial. *Sleep, 34*(12), 1631-1640. https://doi.org/10.5665/sleep.1422

Knutson, K.L., Phelan, J., Paskow, M.J., Roach, A., Whiton, K., Langer, G., Hillygus, D.S., Mokrzycki, M., Broughton, W.A., Chokroverty, S., Lichstein, K.L., Weaver, T.E., & Hirshkowitz, M. (2017). The National Sleep Foundation's Sleep Health Index. *Sleep Health, 3*(4), 234-240. https://doi.org/10.1016/j.sleh.2017.05.011

Kocevska, D., Lysen, T.S., Dotinga, A., Koopman-Verhoeff, M.E., Luijk, M., Antypa, N., Biermasz, N.R., Blokstra, A., Brug, J., Burk, W.J., Comijs, H.C., Corpeleijn, E., Dashti, H.S., de Bruin, E.J., de Graaf, R., Derks, I.P.M., Dewald-Kaufmann, J.F., Elders, P.J.M., Gemke, R.J.B.J., . . . Tiemeier, H. (2021). Sleep characteristics across the lifespan in 1.1 million people from the Netherlands, United Kingdom and United States: A systematic review and meta-analysis. *Nature Human Behavior, 5*(1), 113-122. https://doi.org/10.1038/s41562-020-00965-x

Kredlow, M.A., Capozzoli, M.C., Hearon, B.A., Calkins, A.W., & Otto, M.W. (2015). The effects of physical activity on sleep: A meta-analytic review. *Journal of Behavioral Medicine, 38*(3), 427-449. https://doi.org/10.1007/s10865-015-9617-6

Kreutz, C., Schmidt, M.E., & Steindorf, K. (2019). Effects of physical and mind-body exercise on sleep problems during and after breast cancer treatment: A systematic review and meta-analysis. *Breast Cancer Research and Treatment, 176*(1), 1-15. https://doi.org/10.1007/s10549-019-05217-9

Kubitz, K.A., Landers, D.M., Petruzzello, S.J., & Han, M. (1996). The effects of acute and chronic exercise on sleep. *Sports Medicine, 21*, 277-291.

Lang, C., Kalak, N., Brand, S., Holsboer-Trachsler, E., Puhse, U., & Gerber, M. (2016). The relationship between physical activity and sleep from mid adolescence to early adulthood. A systematic review of methodological approaches and meta-analysis. *Sleep Medicine Reviews, 28*, 32-45. https://doi.org/10.1016/j.smrv.2015.07.004

Liang, Z., & Chapa Martell, M.A. (2018). Validity of consumer activity wristbands and wearable EEG for measuring overall sleep parameters and sleep structure in free-living conditions. *Journal of Healthcare Informatics Research, 2*(1), 152-178. https://doi.org/10.1007/s41666-018-0013-1

Lieberman, H.R., Agarwal, S., Caldwell, J.A., & Fulgoni, V.L. (2020). Demographics, sleep, and daily patterns of caffeine intake of shift workers in a nationally representative sample of the US adult population. *Sleep, 43*(3). https://doi.org/10.1093/sleep/zsz240

Lim, J., & Dinges, D.F. (2010). A meta-analysis of the impact of short-term sleep deprivation on cognitive variables. *Psychological Bulletin, 136*(3), 375-389. https://doi.org/10.1037/a0018883

Luo, J., & Jiang, W. (2022). A critical review on clinical evidence of the efficacy of lavender in sleep disorders. *Phytotherapy Research, 36*(6), 2342-2351. https://doi.org/10.1002/ptr.7448

Lv, Q., Wang, X., Asakawa, T., & Wang, X.P. (2021). Pharmacologic treatment of restless legs syndrome. *Current Neuropharmacology, 19*(3), 372-382. https://doi.org/10.2174/1570159X19666201230150127

National Center for Chronic Disease Prevention and Health Promotion. (2022). *Sleep and sleep disorders.* Centers for Disease Control and Prevention. www.cdc.gov/sleep/index.html

Nelson, K.L., Davis, J.E., & Corbett, C.F. (2022). Sleep quality: An evolutionary concept analysis. *Nursing Forum, 57*(1), 144-151. https://doi.org/10.1111/nuf.12659

Pappas, S. (2017). *Why do we sleep?* Live Science. www.livescience.com/32469-why-do-we-sleep.html

Roberts, D.M., Schade, M.M., Mathew, G.M., Gartenberg, D., & Buxton, O.M. (2020). Detecting sleep using heart rate and motion data from multisensor consumer-grade wearables, relative to wrist actigraphy and polysomnography. *Sleep, 43*(7). https://doi.org/10.1093/sleep/zsaa045

Shinjyo, N., Waddell, G., & Green, J. (2020). Valerian root in treating sleep problems and associated disorders—a systematic review and meta-analysis. *Journal of Evidence-Based Integrative Medicine, 25.* https://doi.org/10.1177/2515690X20967323

Smit, A.N., Broesch, T., Siegel, J.M., & Mistlberger, R.E. (2019). Sleep timing and duration in indigenous villages with and without electric lighting on Tanna Island, Vanuatu. *Scientific Reports, 9*(1), 17278. https://doi.org/10.1038/s41598-019-53635-y

Stutz, J., Eiholzer, R., & Spengler, C.M. (2019). Effects of evening exercise on sleep in healthy participants: A systematic review and meta-analysis. *Sports Medicine, 49*(2), 269-287. https://doi.org/10.1007/s40279-018-1015-0

U.S. Department of Health and Human Services. (n.d.). *Healthy People 2030.* U.S. Department of Health and Human Services. https://health.gov/healthypeople

Wang, X., Ouyang, Y., Wang, Z., Zhao, G., Liu, L., & Bi, Y. (2013). Obstructive sleep apnea and risk of cardiovascular disease and all-cause mortality: A meta-analysis of prospective cohort studies. *International Journal of Cardiology, 169*(3), 207-214. https://doi.org/10.1016/j.ijcard.2013.08.088

Watson, N.F., Buchwald, D., Vitiello, M.V., Noonan, C., & Goldberg, J. (2010). A twin study of sleep duration and body mass index. *Journal of Clinical Sleep Medicine, 6*(1), 11-17. www.ncbi.nlm.nih.gov/pubmed/20191932

Xie, C., Zhu, R., Tian, Y., & Wang, K. (2017). Association of obstructive sleep apnoea with the risk of vascular outcomes and all-cause mortality: A meta-analysis. *BMJ Open, 7*(12), e013983. https://doi.org/10.1136/bmjopen-2016-013983

Xie, L., Kang, H., Xu, Q., Chen, M.J., Liao, Y., Thiyagarajan, M., O'Donnell, J., Christensen, D.J., Nicholson, C., Iliff, J.J., Takano, T., Deane, R., & Nedergaard, M. (2013). Sleep drives metabolite clearance from the adult brain. *Science, 342*(6156), 373-377.

Zhang, H., Dahlen, T., Khan, A., Edgren, G., & Rzhetsky, A. (2020). Measurable health effects associated with the daylight saving time shift. *PLoS Computational Biology, 16*(6), e1007927. https://doi.org/10.1371/journal.pcbi.1007927

Chapter 14

American College of Sports Medicine Position Stand. (1998). Exercise and physical activity for older adults. *Medicine & Science in Sports & Exercise, 30*(6), 992-1008.

Brand, R., Schlicht, W., Grossmann, K., & Duhnsen, R. (2006). Effects of a physical exercise intervention on employees' perceptions of quality of life: A randomized controlled trial. *Sozial-und Präventivmedizin, 51*(1), 14-23.

Buffart, L.M., Newton, R.U., Chinapaw, M.J., Taaffe, D.R., Spry, N.A., Denham, J.W., Joseph, D.J., Lamb, D.S., Brug, J., & Galvão, D.A. (2015). The effect, moderators, and mediators of resistance and aerobic exercise on health-related quality of life in older long-term survivors of prostate cancer. *Cancer, 121*(16), 2821-2830. https://doi.org/10.1002/cncr.29406

Buffart, L.M., Ros, W.J., Chinapaw, M.J., Brug, J., Knol, D.L., Korstjens, I., van Weert, E., Mesters, I., van den Borne, B., Hoekstra-Weebers, J.E.H.M., & May, A.M. (2014). Mediators of physical exercise for improvement in cancer survivors' quality of life. *Psychooncology, 23*(3), 330-338. https://doi.org/10.1002/pon.3428

Centers for Disease Control and Prevention. (2018). *Health-related quality of life (HRQOL).* Centers for Disease Control and Prevention. www.cdc.gov/hrqol/methods.htm

Centers for Disease Control and Prevention. (2022). *Chronic diseases in America.* Centers for Disease Control and Prevention. www.cdc.gov/chronicdisease/resources/infographic/chronic-diseases.htm

Centers for Disease Control and Prevention. (2023). *Health and economic costs of chronic diseases.* Centers for Disease Control and Prevention. https://www.cdc.gov/chronicdisease/about/costs/index.htm#print

Chen, H.Y., Baumgardner, D.J., & Rice, J.P. (2011). Health-related quality of life among adults with multiple chronic conditions in the United States, Behavioral Risk Factor Surveillance System, 2007. *Preventing Chronic Disease, 8*(1), A09. www.ncbi.nlm.nih.gov/pubmed/21159221

Chen, K., Tan, Y., Lu, Y., Wu, J., Liu, X., & Zhao, Y. (2020). Effect of exercise on quality of life in Parkinson's disease: A systematic review and meta-analysis. *Parkinson's Disease, 2020,* 3257623. https://doi.org/10.1155/2020/3257623

Chen, M.D., & Rimmer, J.H. (2011). Effects of exercise on quality of life in stroke survivors: A meta-analysis. *Stroke, 42*(3), 832-837. https://doi.org/10.1161/STROKEAHA.110.607747

Dauwan, M., Begemann, M.J., Heringa, S.M., & Sommer, I.E. (2016). Exercise improves clinical symptoms, quality of life, global functioning, and depression in schizophrenia: A systematic review and meta-analysis. *Schizophrenia Bulletin, 42*(3), 588-599. https://doi.org/10.1093/schbul/sbv164

Dauwan, M., Begemann, M.J.H., Slot, M.I.E., Lee, E.H.M., Scheltens, P., & Sommer, I.E.C. (2021). Physical exercise improves quality of life, depressive symptoms, and cognition across chronic brain disorders: A transdiagnostic systematic review and meta-analysis of randomized controlled trials. *Journal of Neurology, 268*(4), 1222-1246. https://doi.org/10.1007/s00415-019-09493-9

Elavsky, S., McAuley, E., Motl, R.W., Konopack, J.F., Marquez, D.X., Hu, L., Jerome, G.J., & Diener, E. (2005). Physical activity enhances long-term quality of life in older adults: Efficacy, esteem, and affective influences. *Annals of Behavioral Medicine, 30*(2), 138-145. https://doi.org/10.1207/s15324796abm3002_6

Gill, D.L., Chang, Y.K., Murphy, K.M., Speed, K.M., Hammond, C.C., Rodriguez, E.A., Lyu, M., & Shang, Y.T. (2011). Quality of life assessment for physical activity and health promotion. *Applied Research Quality Life, 6,* 181-200. https://doi.org/10.1007/s11482-010-9126-2

Gill, D.L., Hammond, C.C., Reifsteck, E.J., Jehu, C.M., Williams, R.A., Adams, M.M., Lange, E.H., Becofsky, K., Rodriguez, E., & Shang, Y.T. (2013). Physical activity and quality of life. *Journal of Preventive Medicine and Public Health, 46 Suppl 1,* S28-34. https://doi.org/10.3961/jpmph.2013.46.S.S28

Gillison, F.B., Skevington, S.M., Sato, A., Standage, M., & Evangelidou, S. (2009). The effects of exercise interventions on quality of life in clinical and healthy populations; a meta-analysis. *Social Science and Medicine, 68*(9), 1700-1710. https://doi.org/10.1016/j.socscimed.2009.02.028

Kampshoff, C.S., Chinapaw, M.J., Brug, J., Twisk, J.W., Schep, G., Nijziel, M.R., van Mechelen, W., & Buffart, L.M. (2015). Randomized controlled trial of the effects of high intensity and low-to-moderate intensity exercise on physical fitness and fatigue in cancer survivors: Results of the Resistance and Endurance exercise After ChemoTherapy (REACT) study. *BMC Medicine, 13,* 275. https://doi.org/10.1186/s12916-015-0513-2

Korstjens, I., May, A.M., van Weert, E., Mesters, I., Tan, F., Ros, W.J., Hoekstra-Weebers, J.E.H.M., van der Schans, C.P., & van den Borne, B. (2008). Quality of life after self-management cancer rehabilitation: A randomized controlled trial comparing physical and cognitive-behavioral training versus physical training. *Psychosomatic Medicine, 70*(4), 422-429. https://doi.org/10.1097/PSY.0b013e31816e038f

Manson, A., Ciro, C., Williams, K.N., & Maliski, S.L. (2020). Identity and perceptions of quality of life in Alzheimer's disease. *Applied Nursing Research, 52,* 151225. https://doi.org/10.1016/j.apnr.2019.151225

McAuley, E., Konopack, J.F., Motl, R.W., Morris, K.S., Doerksen, S.E., & Rosengren, K.R. (2006). Physical activity and quality of life in older adults: Influence of health status and self-efficacy. *Annals of Behavioral Medicine, 31*(1), 99-103. https://doi.org/10.1207/s15324796abm3101_14

Mielck, A., Vogelmann, M., & Leidl, R. (2014). Health-related quality of life and socioeconomic status: Inequalities among adults with a chronic disease. *Health and Quality of Life Outcomes, 12,* 58. https://doi.org/10.1186/1477-7525-12-58

Motl, R.W., & Gosney, J.L. (2008). Effect of exercise training on quality of life in multiple sclerosis: A meta-analysis. *Multiple Sclerosis Journal, 14*(1), 129-135. https://doi.org/10.1177/1352458507080464

Motl, R.W., & McAuley, E. (2009). Pathways between physical activity and quality of life in adults with multiple sclerosis. *Health Psychology, 28*(6), 682-689. https://doi.org/10.1037/a0015985

Perez-Sousa, M.A., Olivares, P.R., Garcia-Hermoso, A., & Gusi, N. (2020). Fitness as a mediator of the enhancement of quality of life after a 6-months exercise program. *Research Quarterly for Exercise and Sport, 91*(1), 24-33. https://doi.org/10.1080/02701367.2019.1645939

Rejeski, W.J., Brawley, L.R., & Shumaker, S.A. (1996). Physical activity and health-related quality of life. *Exercise and Sport Sciences Reviews, 24,* 71-108. www.ncbi.nlm.nih.gov/pubmed/8744247

Rejeski, W.J., Ettinger, W.H., Jr., Martin, K., & Morgan, T. (1998). Treating disability in knee osteoarthritis with exercise therapy: A central role for self-efficacy and pain. *Arthritis Care & Research, 11*(2), 94-101. https://doi.org/10.1002/art.1790110205

Rejeski, W.J., Focht, B.C., Messier, S.P., Morgan, T., Pahor, M., & Penninx, B. (2002). Obese, older adults with knee osteoarthritis: Weight loss, exercise, and quality of life. *Health Psychology, 21*(5), 419-426. https://doi.org/10.1037//0278-6133.21.5.419

Schuch, F.B., Vancampfort, D., Rosenbaum, S., Richards, J., Ward, P.B., & Stubbs, B. (2016). Exercise improves physical and psychological quality of life in people with depression: A meta-analysis including the evaluation of control group response. *Psychiatry Research, 241,* 47-54. https://doi.org/10.1016/j.psychres.2016.04.054

Shrestha, A., Martin, C., Burton, M., Walters, S., Collins, K., & Wyld, L. (2019). Quality of life versus length of life considerations in cancer patients: A systematic literature review. *Psychooncology, 28*(7), 1367-1380. https://doi.org/10.1002/pon.5054

Soares Falcetta, F., de Araujo Vianna Trasel, H., de Almeida, F.K., Rangel Ribeiro Falcetta, M., Falavigna, M., & Dornelles Rosa, D. (2018). Effects of physical exercise after treatment of early breast cancer: Systematic review and meta-analysis. *Breast Cancer Research and Treatment, 170*(3), 455-476. https://doi.org/10.1007/s10549-018-4786-y

Sweegers, M.G., Altenburg, T.M., Chinapaw, M.J., Kalter, J., Verdonck-de Leeuw, I.M., Courneya, K.S., Newton, R.U., Aaronson, N.K., Jacobsen, P.B., Brug, J., & Buffart, L.M. (2018). Which exercise prescriptions improve quality of life and physical function in patients with cancer during and following treatment? A systematic review and meta-analysis of randomised controlled trials. *British Journal of Sports Medicine, 52*(8), 505-513. https://doi.org/10.1136/bjsports-2017-097891

Tran, G., & Zafar, S. Y. (2018). Price of cancer care and its tax on quality of life. *JCO Oncology Practice, 14*(2), 69-71. https://doi.org/10.1200/JOP.2017.028498

U.S. Department of Health and Human Services. (n.d.). *Healthy People 2030*. U.S. Department of Health and Human Services. https://health.gov/healthypeople

World Health Organization. (2022). *WHOQOL: Measuring Quality of Life*. World Health Organization. www.who.int/tools/whoqol

Zhao, G., Okoro, C.A., Hsia, J., & Town, M. (2018). Self-perceived poor/fair health, frequent mental distress, and health insurance status among working-aged US adults. *Preventing Chronic Disease, 15,* E95. https://doi.org/10.5888/pcd15.170523

Index

Note: The italicized *f* and *t* following page numbers refer to figures and tables, respectively.

A
AAPE (Association for the Advancement of Physical Education) 10
AASP (Association for Applied Sport Psychology) 14
accelerometers 6, 45
acetaminophen 126
acrophobia 74
ACSM (American College of Sports Medicine) 8, 37, 226-227
ACTH (adrenocorticotropic hormone) 59
activities of daily living (ADLs) 223
acupuncture 125-126
acute (state) anxiety 72
acute exercise
    acute pain and 127-128, 128*t*
    brain health and 162-163
    cognitive performance and 145-148, 146*f*, 147*f*
    mood or affect and 114-115, 114*t*
    paradigm of 42
    sleep outcomes and 213, 214*f*, 215
    stress and 67-68
    theories of benefits 138-139
acute pain. *See also* pain
    acute exercise and 127-128, 128*t*
    versus chronic 121-122
    chronic exercise and 128-130
    defined 121
Addison's disease 59
A-delta fibers 123, 123*f*
adenosine 208, 209
ADIS-C/P (Anxiety Disorders Interview Schedule for Children/Parents) 81
ADLs (activities of daily living) 223
adolescents. *See* children and adolescents
adrenal cortex 59
adrenal glands 58, 59
adrenaline 59
adrenocorticotropic hormone (ACTH) 59
Adult Manifest Anxiety Scale 82
aerobic activities 38, 41
aerobic exercise
    anxiety and 84
    brain health and 165
    cognitive performance and 146, 153
    pain and 128, 130-132
    stress and 62, 67
aerobic fitness 40, 131. *See also* cardiovascular fitness hypothesis
aesthetic sports 195-196
affect 105, 111-113. *See also* mood
affective component of body image 187, 193
affective information processing theory 80
affective response, as predictive factor 105-106, 109
age. *See* children and adolescents; older adults

age-related decline 137
Alaska, suicide rates in 91
Alleva, J.M. 195
allostasis 60
allostatic load 60, 61-62
Alzheimer's disease
    described 137, 157
    exercise effects on 151, 152, 153
    neuroimaging in studies of 50, 51
    quality of life and 226
American College of Sports Medicine (ACSM) 8, 37, 226-227
American Journal of Psychology 9
American Psychological Association (APA) 9, 73
anaerobic activities 38
analgesia, exercise-induced 127
analgesics (medications) 126
Anderson, William G. 7, 10
anesthetics 126
angiogenesis 141
animal studies
    benefits and limitations 160-161
    brain health and exercise 164, 164*f*
    brain injury and exercise 166-167
    cognitive performance and exercise 139
anorexia 190
ANS (autonomic nervous system) 58, 59
antidepressants 77, 77*t*, 92, 94-95, 95*t*, 99
anxiety
    definition and types 72
    exercise effects on 68, 82-84
    measurement of 80-82, 81*f*
    physiological mechanisms of exercise and 78-79
    psychological mediators of exercise and 79
    self-esteem and 175, 176
anxiety disorders
    causes of 77
    comorbidities 76, 80
    costs of 76
    prevalence 72, 75-76, 75*t*
    treatment of 77, 77*t*
    types and symptoms 73-75, 73*f*
Anxiety Disorders Interview Schedule for Children/Parents (ADIS-C/P) 81
anxiety-related behaviors 80, 81*f*
anxiety sensitivity hypothesis 79
APA (American Psychological Association) 9, 73
Apple Watch 210
approach response 106
arachnophobia 74
Arent, S.M. 116
arthritis 221
Ashdown-Franks, G. 100-101

Association for Applied Sport Psychology (AASP) 14
Association for the Advancement of Physical Education (AAPE) 10
attention, measurement of 143
Auditory Verbal Learning Test 143
author citations 18-19
autonomic nervous system (ANS) 58, 59
avoidance response 106
Awick, E.A. 181
Aylett, E. 84

B
back pain 122, 130-131
Banno, M. 215
Bard, Philip 108
baseline measurement 22
basic ADLs 223
Bassett-Gunter, R. 195
BCQ (Body Checking Questionnaire) 193
BCTT (Buffalo Concussion Treadmill Test) 167
BDNF. *See* brain-derived neurotrophic factor (BDNF)
Beck Depression Inventory (BDI) 96
Beecher, Catharine 6
behavioral measures
    described 49
    of executive function 150-151
    of pain 126-127
    of sleep 211
Behavioral Risk Factor Surveillance System (BRFSS) 225
Belitardo de Oliveira, A. 115
benzodiazepines 77, 77*t*
beta-blockers 77, 77*t*
beta-endorphins 124
between-subjects design 23-24
Binet-Simon intelligence scale 141
biofeedback 125
biologically based theories 31-32
biological measures 49
biological mechanisms. *See* mechanisms
Black, J.E. 164, 164*f*
blood samples, for brain health assessment 161
BMI. *See* body mass index (BMI)
Body Cathexis Scale 192
Body Checking Questionnaire (BCQ) 193
body concerns 186-187, 188. *See also specific concerns*
body dissatisfaction
    described 187
    measurement of 192-193
    negative associations 188
    prevalence 188-189, 189*f*
body evaluation 187
body fat percentage 40

251

body image
 defined 186
 dimensions of 186-187
 dissatisfaction prevalence 188-189, 189f
 exercise effects on 193-196
 importance of 187-188
 link to clinical disorders 190
 measurement of 192-193
 mechanisms and mediators of exercise and 192
 self-esteem and 178-179, 189
body mass index (BMI)
 body image and 188, 189
 defined 40
 sleep duration and 205-206
body perception 186-187, 192-193
body-related behaviors 186
body satisfaction 187
Boecker, H. 110-111
Borg's Rating of Perceived Exertion 41
brain activity and function
 assessment of 49-51, 50f
 during sleep 206-208
brain-derived neurotrophic factor (BDNF)
 as biological mechanism 33
 brain health and 159, 163-164
 cognitive performance and 139
 depression and 93
brain disorders, and exercise effects 229, 229f
brain health
 acute exercise effects on 162-163
 chronic exercise effects on 163-166
 defined 156
 measurement of 160-161
 mechanisms of exercise effects on 158-159
brain injuries
 exercise effects on 166-169, 168f, 169f
 prevalence and costs 158
 types of 156-157
brain plasticity 153, 158
brain structure
 in affect, mood and emotion 109-110
 assessments of 49-51, 50f
 components of 159, 159f
 exercise effects on 163-166
 as mechanism of exercise effects 33, 141
 neurogenesis and 33, 92-93, 141
Brand, R. 227, 227f
breast cancer survivors. See cancer patients and survivors
BRFSS (Behavioral Risk Factor Surveillance System) 225
Buck, S. 115-116
Buffalo Concussion Treadmill Test (BCTT) 167
Buffart, L.M. 223-224, 224f, 225f
bulimia 190

C
California Verbal Learning Test 143
CAN (central autonomic network) 140-141
Canadian Society for Psychomotor Learning and Sport Psychology (CLPLSP) 13
cancer costs 221
cancer patients and survivors
 exercise and pain reduction in 130
 quality of life and exercise in 227, 229

quality of life decisions in 219, 221
quality of life surveys for 226
sleep quality in 215-216
Cannon, Walter 108
Cannon-Bard theory of mood 108, 113f
cardiorespiratory fitness 40, 131
cardiovascular fitness hypothesis 32, 139-140
catecholamine hypothesis 139
CAT (computed tomography) scans 50
causation, and research design 22
CBIS (Children's Body Image Scale) 193
CBT (cognitive behavioral therapy) 77, 99
CDC (Centers for Disease Control) 225
CDRS (Children's Depression Rating Scale-Revised) 96
Center for Epidemiological Studies Depression scale (CESD) 96
Centers for Disease Control (CDC) 225
central autonomic network (CAN) 140-141
centrally acting analgesics 126
central nervous system 58, 59
CESD (Center for Epidemiological Studies Depression scale) 96
C fibers 123, 123f
Chang, S.C. 97-98
Chang, Y.K. 148
childhood obesity. See obesity and overweight
childhood trauma 91
children and adolescents
 circadian rhythms and school start time 203
 cognition and exercise in 149-151
 depression in 90, 100-101
 executive function in 143
 pain experienced in 122
 perceived exertion scale for 41, 41f
 physical activity recommendations for 46
 quality of life and exercise in 222-223, 223f
 self-esteem and exercise in 180-182
 self-esteem levels in 176
 self-esteem measurement tools for 179
 sleep and exercise studies on 215
 sleep needs in 203, 203t
Children and Youth PSPP (CY-PSPP) 179
Children's Body Image Scale (CBIS) 193
Children's Depression Rating Scale-Revised (CDRS) 96
Chovanec, L. 67
chromosomes, and exercise 166
chronic (trait) anxiety 72, 79, 80
chronic brain disorders 229, 229f
chronic disease
 exercise effects on quality of life in 228-230, 229f
 perceived health and 221-222, 222f
 prevalence and costs 221
 quality of life surveys for 226
chronic exercise
 acute pain and 128-130
 brain health and 163-166
 brain injuries and 166-169, 168f, 169f
 chronic pain and 130-132
 cognitive performance and 148-153
 mood or affect and 115-116
 paradigm of 42

sleep outcomes and 212-214, 213f, 214f, 215
stress and 67
theories of benefits 139-141
chronic pain. See also pain
 versus acute 121-122
 chronic exercise and 130-132
 high-impact 122
 prevalence and costs 122
 types defined 121
chronic sleep deprivation 201. See also sleep deprivation
Chu, C.H. 163
CIPA (congenital insensitivity to pain and anhidrosis) 121
circadian rhythm
 daylight savings time effects on 208
 in energy conservation theory 206
 school start time and 203
 in two-process model of sleep regulation 208
circadian rhythm sleep–wake disorders 204
circumplex model of affect 112, 113f
claustrophobia 74
clinical cognitive decline 137, 151, 153
clinical depression. See depression, clinical
clinical eating disorders 190. See also eating disorders and disordered eating
CLPLSP (Canadian Society for Psychomotor Learning and Sport Psychology) 13
"cocooning" model of care 167
cognitive behavioral therapy (CBT) 77, 99
cognitive decline or impairment 137, 151, 153
cognitive domains 142-144, 143f
cognitive-energetic theories 138
cognitive pain treatments 126
cognitive performance
 acute exercise effects on 145-148, 146f, 147f
 animal research on 139
 assessment tests and tasks 141-142, 142f
 chronic exercise effects on 148-153, 152f
 costs of 137
 defined 136-137
 dose-response of exercise and 145, 146-147
 measurement of 137, 141-144
 prevalence of 137
 theories of exercise effects on 138-141
cognitive reserves, defined 140
cognitive reserves hypothesis 32, 140, 148, 159, 165
cognitive theories 31
Colcombe, S.J. 165
cold pressor task 49, 65, 66-67, 66f, 127
Collins, H. 182
commotio cordis 160
computed tomography (CAT) scans 50
concussions 157, 158, 167-168
confounding variables 19, 27
congenital insensitivity to pain and anhidrosis (CIPA) 121
continuous performance task (CPT) 143
continuous positive airway pressure (CPAP) 204-205, 205f, 213
control
 inhibitory 144
 perceived 60, 62, 181

correlational studies 21, 22
corticotropin-releasing hormone (CRH) 59
cortisol
    chronic exercise and 32-33
    in exercise and depression 92
    for stress assessment 65, 65f
    in stress reaction 59
Coubertin, Pierre de 12
counterbalanced, defined 163
counter-balanced design 23
Courneya, K.S. 113
covariates 19
COVID-19 pandemic
    anxiety and 75-76
    depression and 89
    stress and 58
CPAP (continuous positive airway pressure) 204-205, 205f, 213
CPT (continuous performance task) 143
Crews, D.J. 67
CRH (corticotropin-releasing hormone) 59
criterion (dependent) variables 19, 27
cross-sectional studies 21-22, 42
cross-stressor adaptation hypothesis 62
cupping 125
Cushing syndrome 59
Cybex training system 7
cynophobia 74
CY-PSPP (Children and Youth PSPP) 179

D

daily hassles 64
daylight savings time (DST) 208
Delsarte System of Physical Culture 6
delta sleep 210
dementia 137, 151, 153, 157
dependent (criterion) variables 19, 27
depression, clinical
    anxiety and 76
    bidirectional relationship with exercise 101
    body dissatisfaction and 188
    brain function measures and 51
    causes of 91
    costs of 91
    defined 89
    exercise benefits for 96-101, 98t, 99f, 229f, 230
    versus grief 89
    help for 89
    hippocampus link 33
    measurement of 96
    physiological mechanisms of exercise and 91-94
    prevalence 89-91
    preventing with exercise 97-98, 98f, 100
    psychological mediators of exercise and 94
    self-esteem and 175, 176
    specific population studies 101
    treatment of 94-96, 98-99, 98t, 100-101
Depression Outcomes Study of Exercise (DOSE) 98-99, 98t, 99f
depressive symptoms
    defined 88-89
    reducing with exercise 97, 99-100
Descartes, René 9
diabetes 221
Dienstbier, R.A. 61-62

diffusion tensor imaging 50
Digit Span Test 144
direct measures 44-45, 49-51, 50f
discipline, defined 2
disordered eating 190, 191f. *See also* eating disorders and disordered eating
distraction (time-out) hypothesis 31, 62
distressors 60-61
DLW (doubly labeled water techniques) 44-45
DMAQ (Drive for Muscularity Attitudes Questionnaire) 193
DMS (Drive for Muscularity Scale) 193
Dodson, J.D. 31
dopamine 139, 159
DOSE (Depression Outcomes Study of Exercise) 98-99, 98t, 99f
dose-response 42-43
doubly labeled water techniques (DLW) 44-45
dreams, during REM sleep 207, 210
Drive for Muscularity Attitudes Questionnaire (DMAQ) 193
Drive for Muscularity Scale (DMS) 193
DST (daylight savings time) 208
dualism 9
dual mode theory 31, 109, 114-115, 146
Duda, Joan 14, 15t
Dunn, A.L. 98-99
duration of exercise 41, 42
duration of measurement 44

E

eating disorders and disordered eating
    body concerns link 187, 188
    definitions and types 190
    help for 196
    lean sports and 195-196
    prevalence by race and age 191f
eCB (endocannabinoid) system 111, 115, 124
ECG (electrocardiography) 209
ECT (electroconvulsive therapy) 95
education, and physical activity 47, 47f
EEG. *See* electroencephalography (EEG)
effect size (ES) 25, 214, 214f. *See also* meta-analytic reviews
Eisenhower, Dwight D. 8
Ekkekakis, P. 31, 108-109, 114
electric light, and sleep deprivation 201, 202, 202f
electrocardiography (ECG) 209
electroconvulsive therapy (ECT) 95
electroencephalography (EEG)
    brain activity studies 161, 163
    described 49-50
    sleep studies 209, 210
electromyography (EMG) 209
emotion
    defined 106
    facial expressions of 107
    measurement of 111-113
    regulation of, and high-risk sports 181
empirical (term), defined 18
empirical studies
    anxiety and exercise 75, 83
    brain health and exercise 164-165, 164f
    brain injury and exercise 167-168, 169, 169f

cognitive performance and exercise 148
depression and exercise 97-99, 98f, 98t, 99f
mood or affect and exercise 114-115, 114t
pain and exercise 127-128, 129
quality of life and exercise 227-228, 228f
review methods for 24-26
self-esteem and exercise 180-182
sleep and exercise 212-213, 213f
stress and exercise 66-67
endocannabinoid hypothesis 33, 111, 124
endocannabinoid (eCB) system 111, 115, 124
endocrine system
    depression and 93-94
    stress response and 58, 59
endogenous opiates 93-94
endorphin hypothesis
    described 33
    exercise effect on anxiety 79
    exercise effect on depression 93-94
    exercise effect on mood 110-111
endorphins, defined 110
endurance sports 195-196
energy conservation theory 206
Ensari, I. 83
environment, and depression 91
EORTC QLQ-C30 (European Organization for Research and Treatment of Cancer Quality of Life Questionnaire-Core 30) 226
epidemiological studies 151
epinephrine 58-59, 139
ERPs (event-related potentials) 161, 162f
ES (effect size) 25, 214, 214f. *See also* meta-analytic reviews
Etnier, J.L. 145, 148
European Organization for Research and Treatment of Cancer Quality of Life Questionnaire-Core 30 (EORTC QLQ-C30) 226
eustressors 60
event-related potentials (ERPs) 161, 162f
evolutionary theory 109
executive function
    exercise effects on 146, 150, 151, 152f
    measurement of 143-144
    in neurovisceral integration hypothesis 140-141
    subdomains of 144
exercise. *See also* physical activity
    acute versus chronic 42
    anxiety and 68, 78-79, 82-84
    body image and 193-196
    brain health and 158-159, 162-166
    brain injury and 166-169, 168f, 169f
    cognitive performance and 138-141, 144-153, 146f, 147f, 152f
    defined 37
    depression and 96-101, 98f, 98t, 99f
    mood or affect and 114-116, 114t
    pain and 124, 127-132, 128t
    quality of life and 226-230, 227f, 228f
    self-esteem and 180-182
    sleep outcomes and 212-216, 213f, 214f
    stress and 61-62, 66-68
exercise addiction 105

Exercise and Self-Esteem Model (EXSEM) 177, 177f
exercise bouts 42
exercise-induced analgesia 127
Exercise-Induced Feeling Inventory 113
exercise participation
    affect as predictor of 105-106, 109
    self-esteem and 175
exercise preconditioning 166
exercise prescription 39-40, 41
exercise psychology
    contemporary 14-15
    defined 14-15
    history of 9-14
    mediators and mechanisms in 30-31, 32-33
    physical activity measurement in 43-46
    psychological outcomes measurement in 48-51
    theories and hypotheses in 31-33
exercise science 3
exercise-specific measures 112
expectations, in self-esteem formula 173
experiment, defined 11
experimental pain paradigms 126-127
experimenter burden 44
EXSEM (Exercise and Self-Esteem Model) 177, 177f

F
facial expressions 107
FACT-G (Functional Assessment of Cancer Therapy-General) 226
Fallon, E.A. 194-195, 194f
Fang, Y.Y. 216
fatigue, and exercise 116
Faulkner, G. 100
feel-good phenomenon 12, 33, 94, 104-105
Feeling Scale 112
Felt Arousal Scale 112
Feltz, Deb 14, 15t
fibromyalgia syndrome (FMS) 131
fight-or-flight response 56, 57, 59
Finnish Geriatric Intervention Study to Prevent cognitive Impairment and Disability (FINGER) 166
Firth, J. 165
Fiske, L. 188, 189f
Fitbit Charge 2 model 210
FITKids trial 150
FITT principle 41, 222
Fitz, George Wells 11
Flood, A. 129
fMRI (functional magnetic resonance imaging) 50, 161
FMS (fibromyalgia syndrome) 131
frequency, in FITT 41
Frevert, T.K. 187
frontal lobe hypothesis 140
frontal lobe tasks 144
Functional Assessment of Cancer Therapy-General (FACT-G) 226
functional fitness 223-224, 224f
functional magnetic resonance imaging (fMRI) 50, 161

G
GAS (general adaptation syndrome) 56-57, 56f
gate-control theory of pain 123-124
Gauvin, L. 113
gender, and body dissatisfaction 188-190
general adaptation syndrome (GAS) 56-57, 56f
general cognition 142
generalizability 19
generalized anxiety disorder 73, 73f, 75t
genetics
    anxiety and 77
    depression and 91
    self-esteem and 176
Geriatric Mental State Examination 82
ghrelin 205-206
Gill, Diane 14, 15t
Gill, D.L. 225
Gillison, F.B. 228
Global Burdens of Diseases, Injuries, and Risk Factors Study 122
global self-esteem 172-173. See also self-esteem
glutamate 123
glycosylphosphatidylinositol-specific phospholipase D1 (Gpld1) 139
Goldfield, G.S. 180-181
gray matter 159
grief, versus depression 89
Griffith, Coleman R. 12
Gropel, P. 67
group assignments, in research studies 22-24
growth hormone 93, 94
Gulick, Luther 8
gymnastic training 6

H
Hall, G. Stanley 9
Hamer, M. 67-68
Hamilton Depression Rating Scale (HDRS) 96
Hamlin, Damar 160
Harris, Dorothy 14, 15t
Hausenblas, H.A. 194-195, 194f
HDRS (Hamilton Depression Rating Scale) 96
headaches 122, 124, 125, 131-132
health impacts of stress 61, 62
health-related quality of life (HRQL) 219
Healthy Days Measure 225
Healthy Eating, Aerobic and Resistance Training in Youth (HEARTY) study 180-181
Healthy People 2010 218
Healthy People 2020 218-219
Healthy People 2030 122, 203, 219
heart disease 221
heart rate variability (HRV) 32, 64-65, 140-141
HEARTY (Healthy Eating, Aerobic and Resistance Training in Youth) study 180-181
Henry, Franklin 8-9
Herodicus 9
Hewlett, Aaron Molyneaux 6
hierarchical, defined 175
high-impact chronic pain 122
high-intensity interval exercise (HIIE) 38. See also intensity of activity
high-intensity interval training (HIIT) 38
high-risk sports, and self-esteem 181
HILDA (Household Income and Labour Dynamics in Australia) Survey 66
hippocampus 33, 165-166
Hitchcock, Edward Jr. 7
Homans, Amy Morris 7
homeostasis 59, 208
Horn, Thelma 14, 15t
Horowitz, A.M. 139
Hou, L. 169
Household Income and Labour Dynamics in Australia (HILDA) Survey 66
HPA (hypothalamic-pituitary-adrenal) axis
    in exercise effect on anxiety 78, 79f
    in exercise effect on depression 92
    in stress reaction 59, 59f
HRQL (health-related quality of life) 219
HRV (heart rate variability) 32, 64-65, 140-141
Hu, M.X. 100
human movement. See kinesiology
hunger hormones 205-206
hunter-gatherers, physical activity in 6, 109
hypersomnia 204, 204t
hypothalamic-pituitary-adrenal axis. See HPA (hypothalamic-pituitary-adrenal) axis
hypothalamus 59, 78
hypotheses, in exercise psychology 31-33. See also specific hypotheses

I
IADLs (instrumental ADLs) 223
IASP (International Association for the Study of Pain) 121
IGF (insulin-like growth factor) 33, 159
immigrants, and physical education 6, 8
independent (predictor) variables 19, 27
indirect (self-report) measures
    affect, mood and emotion 111-113
    anxiety 81-82
    depression 96
    physical activity 45-46
    psychological outcomes 48
    quality of life 224-226
    self-esteem 179
    sleep 211
industrialization, and physical activity 5-6
inequality, and allostatic load 60
inhibitory control 144
insomnia 204, 204t, 215
instrumental ADLs (IADLs) 223
insulin-like growth factor (IGF) 33, 159
intelligence quotient (IQ) 141
intensity of activity
    cognitive performance and 138, 146-148, 149f
    in dual mode theory 31, 109, 114-115
    in FITT principle 41
    levels of 37
    mood or affect and 114-115, 114t
    quality of life and 227, 228-229
internal consistency 20-21
International Association for the Study of Pain (IASP) 121
International Physical Activity Questionnaire (IPAQ) 46
International Society of Sport Psychology (ISSP) 13

interviews
    depression measurement 96
    psychological outcome measurement 48
    semi- versus fully structured 96
    stress measurement 64
invasive measures 160
inverted-U hypothesis 31-32, 31f, 138, 138f
IPAQ (International Physical Activity Questionnaire) 46
IQ test 141
isometric exercise 128
ISSP (International Society of Sport Psychology) 13

J

James, William 9-10, 11-12, 107, 173
James-Lange theory of mood 106-107, 113f
Jones, M.D. 128
journals, in history of sport and exercise psychology 13, 14

K

Kampshoff, C.S. 227, 228f
Kennedy, John F. 8
kenophobia 74
Kenrick, D.T. 174, 174f
Kerckhofs, E. 169
kinesiology
    defined 2
    history of 2-3
    reasons to study 3-4
    subdisciplines of 3f, 4
King, J.E. 182
Kline, C.E. 212-213, 213f
knee osteoarthritis 131
Kramer, A.F. 140
Kredlow, M.A. 213-215
Kreutz, C. 215-216
KSADS (Schedule for Affective Disorders and Schizophrenia for School-Age Children) 81
Kubitz, K.A. 213

L

lactate threshold 127-128
Landers, Dan 14
Landers, D.M. 67, 78
Lane, R.D. 32
Lang, C. 215
Lange, Carl 107
Layman, Emma McCloy 12
lean sports 195-196
Leddy, J.J. 167
leptin 205-206
Lewis, Diocletian (Dio) 7
light-intensity physical activity 37. *See also* intensity of activity
"Like the Weather" (10,000 Maniacs) 89
local anesthetics 126
lower back pain 122, 130-131

M

magnetic resonance imaging (MRI) 50, 50f, 161
Maintenance of Wakefulness Test (MWT) 211
major depressive disorder. *See* depression, clinical
major life stressors 63-64
Male Body Attitudes Scale (MBAS) 193
Male Body Checking Questionnaire (MBCQ) 193
Mammen, G. 100
Manson, A. 226
MAOI (monoamine oxidase inhibitors) 92, 94
Martens, Rainer 13
Martin Ginis, K.A. 192
Maslow's hierarchy of needs 174, 174f
mastery, and quality of life 224
mastery hypothesis 94
maximal graded exercise test 40
MBAS (Male Body Attitudes Scale) 193
MBCQ (Male Body Checking Questionnaire) 193
McAuley, E. 113
McClure, J.N., Jr. 82
McCullagh, Penny 14, 15t
McGill Pain Questionnaire 126
MCI (mild cognitive impairment) 153
MDDI (Muscle Dysmorphic Disorder Inventory) 193
measurement, in exercise psychology 43-46. *See also* indirect (self-report) measures
mechanisms
    defined 27-28, 27f
    in exercise psychology 30-31, 32-33
    versus mediators 27
    in stress response 58-60
    study limitations 29-31, 30f
mechanisms of exercise effects
    on anxiety 78-79
    on body image 192
    on brain health 158-159
    on depression 91-94
    on mood 109-111
    on quality of life 222-224, 223f, 224f
    on sleep 209
mediators
    defined 27-28
    in exercise psychology 29, 29f
    versus mechanisms 27
    study limitations 29-30
mediators of exercise effects
    on anxiety 79
    on body image 192
    on depression 94
    on quality of life 224, 225f
    on self-esteem 178-179
medications. *See* pharmacological treatments
Melzack, R. 123-124
memory, measurement of 142-143, 148
memory consolidation and reinforcement theory 207
meta-analytic reviews
    anxiety and exercise 83, 84
    body image and exercise 194-195, 194f
    brain health and exercise 162-163, 165-166
    brain injury and exercise 168-169, 168f
    cognitive performance and exercise 144-153, 146f, 147f
    depression and exercise 99-101
    method described 25-26
    mood or affect and exercise 115-116
    pain and exercise 128, 129-132
    quality of life and exercise 228-230, 229f
    self-esteem and exercise 182
    sleep and exercise 213-216, 214f
    stress and exercise 67-68
metabolic homeostasis theory 208
migraine headaches 122, 124, 131-132
mild cognitive impairment (MCI) 153
mind-body connection 9
mind-body physical activity, effect on stress 68
mixed design 24
modality of exercise 41
moderated mediation models 29, 29f
moderate-intensity physical activity 37. *See also* intensity of activity
moderators 28-29, 28f, 29f
monoamine deficiency hypothesis 92
monoamine neurotransmitters 92
monoamine oxidase inhibitors (MAOI) 92, 94
mood
    biological mechanisms in 109-111
    defined 106
    exercise effects on 110-111, 114-116, 114t
    measurement of 111-113
    theories of 106-109, 107f
Moreira, S.R. 66-67
Morgan, Bill 14
Morgan, W.P. 177, 177f
mortality
    allostatic load and 60
    sleep disorders and 206
MRI (magnetic resonance imaging) 50, 50f, 161
MSLT (Multiple Sleep Latency Test) 211
multidimensional, defined 175
multimodal training 153
multiple sclerosis 229f, 230
Multiple Sleep Latency Test (MSLT) 211
muscle dysmorphia 190
Muscle Dysmorphic Disorder Inventory (MDDI) 193
MWT (Maintenance of Wakefulness Test) 211

N

nanotechnology 49
narrative reviews 24-25, 26
NASPSPA (North American Society for the Psychology of Sport and Physical Activity) 13
National Academy of Kinesiology 8
National Association of Anorexia Nervosa and Associated Disorders 191
National Eating Disorders Hotline 191
National Health and Nutrition Examination Survey (NHANES) 225
National Suicide Prevention Lifeline 91
Naugle, K.M. 128
NCAA Concussion Study 157
NDRIs (norepinephrine and dopamine reuptake inhibitors) 94-95, 95t
negative affective response 107
negative feedback loop 59, 59f
neurochemicals 159
neurogenesis 33, 92-93, 141
neuroimaging measures 49-50
neurons 159, 159f
neuroplasticity 153, 158
neurotransmitter hypothesis 77, 78-79

neurotransmitters 159
neurotrophic factors 33
neurovisceral integration hypothesis 140-141
neurovisceral integration model 32
New Gymnastics for Men, Women, and Children (Lewis) 7
NHANES (National Health and Nutrition Examination Survey) 225
nociceptors 123, 123f
non-REM sleep 207, 210
nonsteroidal anti-inflammatories (NSAIDs) 126
noradrenaline 59
norepinephrine 58-59, 139
norepinephrine and dopamine reuptake inhibitors (NDRIs) 94-95, 95t
North American Society for the Psychology of Sport and Physical Activity (NASPSPA) 13
noxious dental pulp stimulation technique 127
NSAIDs (nonsteroidal anti-inflammatories) 126
Nurses' Health Study 97-98

O
obesity and overweight
    in quality of life study 222-223, 223f
    self-esteem and 176, 182
    sleep quality and 205-206
objective self-awareness theory 178
observation 44
obsessive-compulsive disorder (OCD) 73f, 74, 75t
obstructive sleep apnea. *See* sleep apnea
OCD (obsessive-compulsive disorder) 73f, 74, 75t
office environments 39
Oglesby, Carole 14, 15t
older adults
    anxiety in 76, 76f, 81-82
    cognition measurement in 142
    cognitive performance and exercise in 148, 151-153, 152f
    executive function in 143, 151
    knee osteoarthritis in 131
    mood or affect and exercise in 116
    self-esteem and exercise in 180, 181, 182
    self-esteem decrease in 176
    Senior Exercise Self-Efficacy Project 97
    sleep needs in 203, 203t
OMNI scale 41, 41f
1 metabolic equivalent (1 MET) 37
Ones, D.S. 115
ophidiophobia 74
Osypiuk, K. 130
Oura Ring 210
overweight. *See* obesity and overweight

P
PAAD-2 (Physical Activity and Alzheimer's Disease-2) study 152
Paced Auditory Serial Addition Task (PASAT) 143, 148
Pacheco-Barrios, K. 129-130
pain
    acute versus chronic 121-122
    costs of 122
    definition and types 121
    descriptors for 120-121
    exercise effects on 124, 127-132, 128t
    insensitivity to 121
    measurement of 126-127, 127f
    physiological mechanisms of 122-123, 123f
    prevalence 121-122
    quality of life and 224
    theories of 123-124
    treatment of 124-125
pain relievers 126
pain threshold 127, 128t
pain tolerance 127, 128t
PANAS (Positive and Negative Affect Schedule) 111
panic disorder 73f, 74, 75t
parasomnia 204
parasympathetic nervous system (PSNS) 58, 59, 64-65
Park, S.H. 182
Parkinson's disease 229f, 230
participant burden 44
PASAT (Paced Auditory Serial Addition Task) 143, 148
pedometers 45
pendulum chronometer 10, 10f
Perales, F. 66
perceived control
    allostatic load and 60
    self-esteem and 181
    sense of control hypothesis 62
perceived pain, and quality of life 224
Perez-Sousa, M.A. 222-223, 223f
peripherally acting analgesics 126
peripheral nervous system 58
Petruzzello, S.J. 78
PET (positron emission tomography) scans 50
pharmacological treatments
    for Alzheimer's disease 157
    for anxiety 77, 77t
    for depression 92, 94-95, 99
    for pain 124, 126
phobias 73f, 74, 75, 75t
physical activity. *See also* exercise
    affective response as predictor of 105-106, 109
    changes in response to 39-40
    defined 36-37
    effect on stress 67-68
    history of 4-6
    in hunter-gatherers 6
    measurement of 43-46
    recommendations and compliance 46-47, 47f
Physical Activity and Alzheimer's Disease-2 (PAAD-2) study 152
physical appearance 187
physical attractiveness 187
physical education
    history of 6-9
    in history of kinesiology 2-3
    psychology connection 10-11
"Physical Education-An American Discipline" (Henry) 8-9
physical fitness
    body image and 192
    defined 40
    quality of life and 222-223, 223f
Physical Self-Description Questionnaire (PSDQ) 179
Physical Self-Perception Profile (PSPP) 177-178, 178f, 179, 180t, 193
physiological measures of stress 64-65
physiological mechanisms. *See* mechanisms
physiological toughness hypothesis 61-62
pickleball 4
Piers-Harris Children's Self-Concept Scale (SCS) 179
Pilates 130-131
Pitts, F.N., Jr. 82
Pittsburgh Sleep Quality Index (PSQI) 211
pituitary 59
planning (executive function subdomain) 144
plastic (brain plasticity) 153, 158
polysomnography 209-210
POMS (Profile of Mood States) 96, 111
Pope, H.G., Jr. 190
positive affective response 105-106, 109
Positive and Negative Affect Schedule (PANAS) 111
positron emission tomography (PET) scans 50
postpartum depression 101
post-traumatic stress disorder (PTSD) 73f, 74-75, 75t, 76, 83, 84
potentialities, in self-esteem formula 173
Pozo-Cruz, B.D. 66
Pozo-Cruz, J.D. 66
Precision Medicine Initiative 95-96
predictor (independent) variables 19, 27
prefrontal lobe tasks 144
President's Council on Sports, Fitness, and Nutrition 8
pressure stimulus, as pain measure 127, 127f
pretensions, in self-esteem formula 173
pretest measurement 22
Principles of Psychology (James) 10
Profile of Mood States (POMS) 96, 111
prospective studies 22, 42
prostaglandins 209
PSDQ (Physical Self-Description Questionnaire) 179
PSNS (parasympathetic nervous system) 58, 59, 64-65
PSPP (Physical Self-Perception Profile) 177-178, 178f, 179, 180t, 193
PSQI (Pittsburgh Sleep Quality Index) 211
psychological measures of stress 63-64
psychological mediators. *See* mediators
psychological outcome measurement methods 48-51
psychology
    historical figures in 9-10
    physical education connection 10-11
Psychology of Athletics, The (Griffith) 12
Psychology of Coaching, The (Griffith) 12
psychometric properties, defined 19-20
psychotherapy 95
PTSD (post-traumatic stress disorder) 73f, 74-75, 75t, 76, 83, 84
Puetz, T.W. 116

Q
qigong 68, 130, 131
quality of life
    chronic disease and 221-222, 222f

defined 218, 219
exercise effects on 226-230, 227f, 228f
individual perspective on 219
measurement of 224-226
mechanisms of exercise and 222-224, 223f, 224f
as multidimensional 220
psychological mediators of exercise and 224, 225f
term use 219
Quality of Life Survey 225, 226
quasi-experimental study 24
questionnaires 45-46, 48. *See also* indirect (self-report) measures

R
race and ethnicity
Alzheimer's disease risk and 137
anxiety and 76
BMI and 40
depression and 89
disordered eating and 191f
physical activity and 46
RAH (reticular activating hypofrontality hypothesis) 138, 146
randomized clinical trials (RCTs) 22
rapid eye movement (REM) sleep) 207, 210
ratings of perceived exertion (RPE) 41
RCMAS (Revised Children's Manifest Anxiety Scale) 81
RCTs (randomized clinical trials) 22
Reed, J. 115-116
Reel, J.J. 195
Reese, Jeff 196
regional anesthetics 126
Rejeski, W.J. 113
relaxation, as pain treatment 125
reliability 20
REM (rapid eye movement) sleep 207, 210
research studies. *See also* empirical studies; meta-analytic reviews
author citations for 18-19
experiment designs 21-22
participant assignment to groups 22-24
review methods for 24-26
term definitions 18-21
variables in 19, 26-31
resistance activities and exercise
cognitive performance and 153
defined 39
depression and 100
pain and 128, 130
self-esteem and 180-181, 182
stress and 67
Resnick, B. 97
resting metabolic rate 36-37
restless legs syndrome 204, 204t
restorative hypothesis 206
reticular activating hypofrontality hypothesis (RAH) 138, 146
Revised Children's Manifest Anxiety Scale (RCMAS) 81
risky health behaviors, and body dissatisfaction 188
robot programming 4
Rosenbaum, S. 83, 84
Rosenberg Self-Esteem Scale (SES) 179
RPE (ratings of perceived exertion) 41
runner's high 104-105

RUSHS (University Student Hassles Scale) 64
Russell, J.A. 112

S
SAMHSA (Substance Abuse and Mental Health Services Administration) 89
sample sizes
measurement tools and 44, 46
underpowered 21, 25
Sargent, Dudley 7
Scanlan, Tara 14, 15t
Schachter, Stanley 108
Schedule for Affective Disorders and Schizophrenia for School-Age Children (KSADS) 81
Schedule of Recent Experience (SRE) 63-64, 63t
schizophrenia 229f, 230
Schmitt, A. 127-128
Schuch, F.B. 100
scientific literature reviews 24-26. *See also* meta-analytic reviews
Scripture, Edward 10
SCS (Piers-Harris Children's Self-Concept Scale) 179
sedentary behavior 5, 39-40
SEES (Subjective Exercise Experiences Scale) 113
selective improvement hypothesis 140
selective serotonin reuptake inhibitors (SSRIs) 77, 77t, 92, 94-95, 95t
self-actualization 174, 174f
self-awareness 178
self-concept, defined 172
self-confidence 176
self-efficacy
body image and 192
defined 176
depression and 94
quality of life and 224
self-esteem and 177, 177f, 178
self-efficacy hypothesis 79
self-esteem
body dissatisfaction and 188
body image and 189
conceptual formula for 173
conceptual views of 175, 176-177, 177f
exercise effects on 180-182
in exercise psychology 175
factors affecting 176
global, defined 172-173
in Maslow's hierarchy of needs 174, 174f
measurement of 179
models of 176-178, 177f
psychological mediators of 178-179
social media and 175
self-esteem hypothesis 94
self-report measures. *See* indirect (self-report) measures
Selye, Hans 56
Senior Exercise Self-Efficacy Project (SESEP) 97
seniors. *See* older adults
sensation threshold 127
sense of control hypothesis 62
separation anxiety disorder 75
serotonin 124, 159
serotonin and norepinephrine reuptake

inhibitors (SNRIs) 77, 77t, 92, 94-95, 95t
SES (Rosenberg Self-Esteem Scale) 179
SESEP (Senior Exercise Self-Efficacy Project) 97
Sexton, C.E. 165
SHAPE America 7
Short Form Health Survey (SF-36) 225
Singer, Jerome E. 108
single-group studies 193-194
sit-to-stand desks 39
sleep
advice for good sleep 211
amount needed 203, 203t
cycles and stages of 209-210, 210f
defined 200
exercise effects on 212-216, 213f, 214f
measurement of 209-211
mechanisms of exercise and 209
research challenges 212
theories of 206-208
sleep apnea
described 204, 204t
exercise effects on 212-213, 213f
mortality and 206
treatment of 204-205, 205f
sleep architecture 209-210, 210f
sleep cycles 209-210, 210f
sleep deprivation
electric light and 201, 202, 202f
prevalence and costs 201, 205-206
sleep disorders
costs of 205-206
exercise effects on 212-213, 213f, 215
mortality and 206
treatment of 209
types and prevalence 203-205, 204t
sleep disturbances 201
sleep duration 200
sleep efficiency 201
sleep health 211
sleep hygiene 211
sleep latency 201, 203, 211
sleep quality
defined 201, 203
measurement of 210-211
negative affect and 66
REM sleep and 210
sleep quantity (duration, total sleep time) 200
sleep-related breathing disorders 204. *See also* sleep apnea
sleep-related movement disorders 204, 204t
sleep spindles 210
sleep stages 210
slow-wave sleep 210
smartphones 45
smart watches 45, 49
Smith, J.C. 82
snapshots, in research 22
SNRIs (serotonin and norepinephrine reuptake inhibitors) 77, 77t, 92, 94-95, 95t
SNS (sympathetic nervous system) 58-59
social anxiety disorder 73f
social facilitation 11
social media 175, 188
social physique anxiety (SPA) 187

social status, and allostatic load 60
Society for Sport, Exercise, and Performance Psychology 73
socioeconomic status
    depression and 89
    physical activity and 47, 47f
    quality of life and 221-222
SOFIT (System for Observing Fitness Instruction Time) 44
"Soft American, The" (Kennedy) 8
somatic activation 80
Sonstroem, R.J. 177, 177f
SPA (social physique anxiety) 187
spectral data 161
sport
    defined 37-38
    high-risk sports and self-esteem 181
    lean sports and eating disorders 195-196
sport and exercise psychology. *See* exercise psychology
sport-related concussions 157, 158
SRE (Schedule of Recent Experience) 63-64, 63t
SSRIs (selective serotonin reuptake inhibitors) 77, 77t, 92, 94-95, 95t
Stanford-Binet Intelligence Scale 141
state (acute) anxiety 72
State-Trait Anxiety Inventory (STAI) 81, 82, 111-112
State-Trait Anxiety Inventory version for children (S-TAIC) 81
statistical power 23
statistical significance 21
Strehli, I. 68
strength-training. *See* resistance activities and exercise
stress
    aspects of 61
    biological response to 58-59, 59f
    costs of 58
    defined 55
    effective, ineffective responses to 60
    eustressors and distressors 60-61
    exercise effects on 66-68
    general adaptation syndrome 56-57, 56f
    health impacts of 61, 62
    inducing for research 65
    measurement of 62-66, 65f
    prevalence 57-58, 58f
    stress-reduction theories 61-62
    symptoms of 55-56, 56f
stress hormone. *See* cortisol
stressors
    defined 54
    nature of and stress impact 61
    physical versus psychological 57
stress pileup 62, 63f, 66
stress reactivity 62, 63f, 66
stress recovery 62, 63f, 66
strokes
    defined 157
    exercise effects on 168-169, 168f, 169f, 229, 229f
    prevalence and costs 158, 221
Stroop Test 144, 149f
Stubbs, B. 68, 84

subdisciplines 3, 3f, 4
subfacets, in PSPP model 178
Subjective Exercise Experiences Scale (SEES) 113
Substance Abuse and Mental Health Services Administration (SAMHSA) 89
substance P 123, 124
substance use disorder, and anxiety 76
successes, in self-esteem formula 173
suicide 90-91, 90f
suicide belt 90-91, 90f
Suicide Prevention Lifeline 91
surgery, as pain treatment 126
Swedish Movement Cure 6
sympathetic nervous system (SNS) 58-58
synapses, during sleep 207
synaptogenesis 141, 207
systematic reviews 25, 26
System for Observing Fitness Instruction Time (SOFIT) 44
Szuhany, K.L. 162, 163

T
tai-chi
    cognitive performance and 153
    HRV variables and 141
    pain and 131
    stress and 68
task switching 144
TBI. *See* traumatic brain injury (TBI)
telomere length 166
Tennessee Self-Concept Scale (TSCS) 179, 193
TENS (transcutaneous electrical nerve stimulation) 124-125
10,000 Maniacs 89
Tesarz, J. 129
Thayer, J.F. 32
theories, in exercise psychology 31-32. *See also specific theories*
therapy (psychotherapy) 95
thermogenic hypothesis 32, 78
thyroid hormones 93
time, in FITT 41
time-out (distraction) hypothesis 31, 62
total sleep time 200
Tower of London task 142, 142f, 144
trait (chronic) anxiety 72, 79, 80
transcutaneous electrical nerve stimulation (TENS) 124-125
traumatic brain injury (TBI)
    defined 156-157
    exercise effects on 166-168
    prevalence and costs 158
Triplett, Norman 11
true experimental studies 22
TSCS (Tennessee Self-Concept Scale) 179, 193
Turnen 6
Turner, Anita Julurness 7-8
two-factor theory of emotion 108, 113f
two-process model of sleep regulation 208
type, in FITT 41

U
umbrella reviews 84, 100
underpowered samples 21, 25

universality hypothesis of facial expressions 107
University Student Hassles Scale (RUSHS) 64
U.S. Department of Health and Human Services (USDHHS) 46

V
validity 20
Vanderbeken, I. 169
variables, in research studies 19, 26-31
vascular-endothelial growth factor (VEGF) 33, 159
ventilatory threshold (VT) 109
very light or light-intensity physical activity 37. *See also* intensity of activity
vigorous-intensity physical activity 37. *See also* intensity of activity
visual analog pain scale 126, 127f
visualization 126
$\dot{V}O_2$max 40
$\dot{V}O_2$peak 40
VT (ventilatory threshold) 109

W
wait-list control group 224
waking after sleep onset 201
Walker, L.S. 187
Wall, P.D. 123-124
Wang, C. 68
Wang, C.C. 146
WCST (Wisconsin Card-Sorting Test) 144, 145f
wearable technology 45, 49, 210-211
Wegner, M. 99-100
weight class sports 195-196
weight loss, rapid 196
Weiss, Maureen 14, 15t
Wewege, M.A. 128
white matter 159, 165
WHO (World Health Organization) 219, 220, 225
WHOQOL-100 225
WHOQOL-BREF 225
Williams, Jean 14, 15t
Wisconsin Card-Sorting Test (WCST) 144, 145f
withdrawal response 106
within-subjects design 23
women
    anxiety in 76, 76f
    depression in 89, 90
    exercise effects on pain in 130
    in history of physical education 7-8
    in sport psychology 14, 15t
Woodman, T. 181
word-learning tasks 143
working memory 144
World Health Organization (WHO) 219, 220, 225
Wundt, Wilhelm 9

Y
Yerkes, R.M. 31
yoga 68, 141

Z
Zheng, G. 165

About the Author

Jennifer L. Etnier, PhD, is a Julia Taylor Morton Distinguished Professor and chair in the department of kinesiology in the School of Health and Human Sciences at the University of North Carolina at Greensboro, where she has received the Health and Human Performance Teaching Award, UNCG Alumni Teaching Excellence Award, and Senior Research Excellence Award. She is an accomplished scholar, with nearly 100 publications and over 150 presentations, and has received over $3.8 million in external funding to support her research. In addition to her data-based scholarship, Etnier has written two books for youth sport participants (*Bring Your 'A' Game* and *Coaching for the Love of the Game*), has given over 20 podcast and radio interviews touching on youth sport issues, and is the author of a *New York Times* op-ed titled "Your Kids' Coach Is Probably Doing It Wrong."

Etnier is a fellow of the American College of Sports Medicine (ACSM) and the National Academy of Kinesiology (NAK). She previously served as president of the North American Society for the Psychology of Sport and Physical Activity (NASPSPA) and as editor of the *Journal of Aging and Physical Activity*, associate editor for the *Journal of Sport and Exercise Psychology*, and section editor for *Research Quarterly for Exercise and Sport*. She is currently an editorial board member for five peer-reviewed journals. In her free time, Etnier is an exercise enthusiast who loves to play soccer and pickleball, downhill ski, hike, bike, and paddle.